P9-EMP-653

*Major Problems in
American Urban History*

MAJOR PROBLEMS IN AMERICAN HISTORY SERIES

GENERAL EDITOR
THOMAS G. PATERSON

Major Problems in American Urban History

DOCUMENTS AND ESSAYS

EDITED BY
HOWARD P. CHUDACOFF
BROWN UNIVERSITY

D. C. HEATH AND COMPANY
Lexington, Massachusetts   Toronto

Address editorial correspondence to:

D. C. Heath and Company
125 Spring Street
Lexington, MA 02173

Acquisitions Editor: James Miller
Developmental Editor: Sylvia Mallory
Production Editor: Lyri Merrill
Designer: Sally Steele
Photo Researcher: Martha Shethar
Production Coordinator: Charles Dutton
Permissions Editor: Margaret Roll

Illustration Credits
Front Cover: *Midtown Sunset 1981* by Romare Beardon. Estate of Romare Beardon.
Page 35: The Library of Congress; page 66: I.N. Phelps Stokes Collection, Miriam and Ira
D. Wallach Division of Art, Prints, and Photographs, New York Public Library, Astor,
Lenox and Tilden Foundations; page 123: Courtesy of Rhode Island Historical Society; page
145: International Museum of Photography at George Eastman House; page 179: Historical
Pictures Collection; page 199: Photograph by Adolph Wittemann, Museum of the City of
New York; page 227: The Jacob A. Riis Collection, Museum of the City of New York; page
278: Chicago Commons Collection, Chicago Historical Society; page 319: Seaver Center for
Western History Research, Natural History Museum of Los Angeles County; page 335: The
Library of Congress; pages 357, 391: U.S. Department of Housing and Urban Development.

Copyright © 1994 by D. C. Heath and Company.

All rights reserved. No part of this publication may be reproduced or transmitted in any
form or by any means, electronic or mechanical, including photocopy, recording, or any
information storage or retrieval system, without permission in writing from the publisher.

Published simultaneously in Canada.

Printed in the United States of America.

International Standard Book Number: 0–669–24376–0

Library of Congress Catalog Number: 92–75663

10   9   8   7   6   5   4   3   2   1

Preface

In 1790, when the first United States census was taken, 5 percent of the nation's population lived in places defined as cities; in 1990 about 80 percent did so. In 200 years a profound change had occurred. Why? Historians have been providing answers in the last few decades, but until the mid-twentieth century, most scholars viewed cities as incidental to American history. They considered urbanization a phenomenon that arose at the end of the process of settlement—after pioneer exploration, the establishment of small farms, the growth of large farms, and the rise of villages and towns. In these scholars' minds, cities were also linked to industrialization—it too, a relatively recent phenomenon in U.S. history.

During the 1950s and 1960s, however, historians began to understand that the United States had become an urban nation and that many of its social, economic, and political problems stemmed from urbanization and from the basic conditions of life in the expanding cities. They also realized that cities had existed since the beginning of American history and had played a greater role in national development than the numbers of their inhabitants might have warranted. Moreover, a growing interest in the history of ordinary people—social history "from the bottom up"—focused attention on the complex social mosaics of cities, with their assortments of racial, ethnic, and socioeconomic groups and their diverging gender cultures. This new direction also provoked inquiry about the relationship between the urban environment and the ways in which people lived, worked, and played in that milieu.

A fascinating, sometimes confusing field of urban historical research has developed, one lacking the kind of uniform focus that characterizes, for example, diplomatic and economic history. Yet perhaps *because of* its multifaceted quality, American urban history has attracted scholars, students, and the general public. The field has its own periodical, the *Journal of Urban History,* and its own organization, the Urban History Association; and it has become a basic component of urban studies programs in universities across the country. With so many Americans living in cities, the urban environment exerts a powerful force on the popular imagination, and urban history has played a central role in fostering that keen interest. This book draws upon the rich scholarship of its field and attempts to explore many facets of the city's widespread allure. In this, it hopes to reflect the view of reformer Lyman Abbott, who wrote in 1891, "The city is not all bad nor all good. It is humanity compressed, the best and the worst combined, in a strongly composite community."

Major Problems in American Urban History combines primary documents and excerpts from scholarship to approach key questions in the field from a range of perspectives. The book is organized along roughly chronological lines from colonial times to the present, although the chapter topics occasionally overlap the same chronological period. After an introductory chapter on the different approaches to studying urban history, the second and third chapters examine the social and economic environments of early American cities. The fourth and fifth chapters also consider the early nineteenth century, with special attention to the provision of such services as police protection and public health and to the effects of incipient industrialization. Chapter 6 then examines issues relating to urban newcomers, including African-American migrants and European and Asian immigrants. The seventh and eighth chapters explore the ways in which various individuals and groups tried to control the dynamic and perplexing urban environment of the late nineteenth and early twentieth century through politics and reform. The documents and essays in these chapters also speak to questions of gender in urban problems. The next two chapters address changes in urban culture between 1900 and 1930, first considering popular culture in the era's dance halls and sports arenas and then examining the automobile and its impact on suburbanization. Chapter eleven highlights the growing relationship between cities and the federal government in response to the crisis of the Great Depression and the needs of various groups, including Mexican-Americans. The twelfth chapter extends the analysis of federal intervention into urban affairs in the mid-twentieth century. The final two chapters turn their lens on the recent, postindustrial city—first analyzing political, economic, and geographical developments and then probing the ongoing problems of poverty and race relations.

As in other volumes in D. C. Heath's Major Problems in American History Series, each chapter begins with a brief introduction that sets the historical stage and identifies the central themes of the documents and scholarly essays that follow. In some instances, I have chosen primary sources and essays that offer different perspectives on the same issue; in other cases, the documents and essays illustrate different problems related to the same general topic. In the hope that some of the topics might provoke further interest, I have included a list of related scholarly works at the end of each chapter.

Several people assisted and advised me as I prepared this volume. First and foremost, I wish to thank Judith E. Smith, coauthor and friend, whose suggestions have stimulated me for two decades. I also am grateful for the insights of my Brown University colleagues Mari Jo Buhle, Naomi Lamoreaux, William G. McLoughlin, James T. Patterson, John L. Thomas, and Gordon S. Wood, whose influence, direct and indirect, has helped to shape this book. For general comments on various aspects of American urban history, I thank Howard N. Rabinowitz, Kenneth T. Jackson, Zane L. Miller, and Raymond A. Mohl. Another friend and colleague, Thomas G. Paterson, the general editor of this series, offered countless valuable insights and recommendations. The reviewers who read the draft tables of contents for D. C. Heath provided constructive criticism and wise counsel; they include Kathleen C. Berkeley, University of North Carolina, Wilmington; Albert S. Broussard, Texas A & M University; Kathleen Neils Conzen, University of Chicago; Duncan R. Jamieson, Ashland University; Kenneth L. Kusmer, Temple University; Peter Rachleff, Macalester College; Neil Larry Shumsky, Virginia Polytechnic Institute and State University; and Judith Ann Trolander, University of Minnesota, Duluth. In addition, I am grateful to all the scholars and publishers represented in this volume, who graciously agreed to let me include their work. Finally, I thank the professionals at D. C. Heath—managing editor Sylvia Mallory, production editor Lyri Merrill, history editor James Miller, and permissions editor Margaret Roll—for their support and assistance. My wife, Nancy Fisher Chudacoff, did not participate directly in this project, but her inspiration marks everything I do. I alone am responsible for errors of judgment in the selection of materials.

H. P. C.

Contents

CHAPTER 7
Bosses and Reformers at the Turn of the Century
Page 189

CHAPTER 8
Urban Professionals in the Progressive Era
Page 225

Major Problems in
American Urban History

CHAPTER

1

The Making of

American Urban History

※

In 1790, when the United States was in its infancy, just 5 percent of its population lived in cities, then defined as places with 2,500 or more people. Today, some 80 percent of Americans reside in communities categorized as urban. To the historian, whose major task is to analyze change over time, the growth of the urban population marks one of the most remarkable transformations in the nation's existence. Yet the field of urban history has existed for a relatively short time. Except for a few scholarly studies, serious historical research on American urbanization began just over a generation ago. Cultural biases against cities; preoccupations with other topics, whether national politics, wars, or the frontier; and disregard for the historical role of ordinary people such as immigrants, laborers, and racial minorities, all combined to deflect historians from urban-related topics. But recent recognition that the experiences and problems of American society are those of an urban society, as well as acknowledgment that urban dwellers have exerted an influence on national development in greater proportion than their numbers have warranted, has prompted an outpouring of scholarship on cities, their growth, and their inhabitants.

※ *E S S A Y S*

The following three essays and one interview illustrate both the flowering of the field of urban history and the variation in approaches to the topics included in the field. Arthur M. Schlesinger, Sr., an eminent historian at Harvard University, was one of the first to suggest that cities needed more attention from historians. The essay reprinted here, first published in 1940, challenged the prevailing interpretation of American history, which saw the frontier as the determining factor in national development, and instead presented the city as a significant influencing element. Schlesinger's ideas inspired a number of graduate students working after World War II to follow up on the urban topics suggested in his essay. Richard C. Wade, first at the University of Chicago and then at the City University of New York, was one of those students, and he pioneered in establishing the

1

legitimacy of the field of urban history. His interview with urban historian Bruce M. Stave of the University of Connecticut sheds light on how he became an urban historian and conceived the field.

As social problems focused attention on cities during the 1960s, Stephan Thernstrom of Harvard University and other young historians formed the vanguard of what was called the new urban history, an attempt to analyze social processes of urbanization and to consider the historical contributions of nonelites in such processes. Thernstrom's essay provides a retrospective view of the new urban history. Finally, Raymond Mohl's essay offers an overview of a recent branching-out of the field to include a wide variety of topics and methodologies. In his essay Mohl, who teaches at Florida Atlantic University, also previews several issues and topics that succeeding chapters of this volume will examine.

The City in American History

ARTHUR M. SCHLESINGER

"The true point of view in the history of this nation is not the Atlantic Coast," declared Frederick Jackson Turner in his famous paper of 1893, "it is the Great West." Professor Turner had formed his ideas in an atmosphere of profound agrarian unrest; and an announcement of the superintendent of the census in 1890 that the frontier line could no longer be traced impelled him to the conclusion that "the first period of American history" had closed. His brilliant essay necessitated a fundamental reappraisal of the springs of national development. Today, however, it seems clear that in his zeal to correct older views he overlooked the antithetical form of social organization which, coeval with the earliest frontier, has played a significant and ever-enlarging part in American life. Turner himself wrote in a private letter in 1925, though with evident misgiving, "There seems likely to be an urban reinterpretation of our history."

A reconsideration of American history from the urban point of view need not lead to the distortion which Professor Turner feared. It should direct attention to a much neglected influence and, by so doing, help to illumine the historian's central problem: the persistent interplay of town and country in the evolution of American civilization. . . .

Though agriculture occupied the vast bulk of the colonists, many of them, through personal liking or for economic reasons, preferred town life. Usually the first object upon reaching the Atlantic shore was to found an urban community which might serve as a means of companionship and mutual protection and as a base from which to colonize the neighboring country. In time these towns did duty as business centers, assembling the agricultural products of the adjacent regions for export and paying for them with imported wares. . . .

Small as these places seem by modern standards, they compared favorably in size and wealth with English provincial cities before the Industrial Revolution began to pile up their populations. As the larger American towns gained in corpo-

Arthur M. Schlesinger, "The City in American History," from *Mississippi Valley Historical Review,* 27 (June 1940), excerpts from pp. 43–66. Reprinted by permission of the Organization of American Historians.

rate consciousness, they reached out for dependent territories and engaged in contests with one another for economic dominion. Much of colonial history might be rewritten in terms of these activities. Boston, the first to enter the race, possessed special trading advantages which enabled her for nearly a century to maintain a position of primacy, with New York, Philadelphia, and lesser centers hardly more than commercial satellites. These other towns, however, strove for their share of ocean-borne traffic and briskly cultivated their own local trading areas. . . .

As the eighteenth century progressed, Boston's rivals, helped by the occupation of their back-country districts, securely established their independent right to existence. New York completed her sway over western Connecticut and eastern New Jersey as well as over her own hinterland, while Philadelphia held in thrall Maryland. It is evident of the energy and enterprise of urban business that the chambers of commerce of New York and Charleston, formed respectively in 1768 and 1774, antedated all others in English-speaking lands. Beneficial as were the relations of these towns to their dependent areas, urban dominance bred jealousies and resentments which were to reach critical intensity in the later history of the nation. The ascendant city of a given district became a symbol of deception and greed. "A Connecticut Farmer," venting his spleen against New York in the *New London Gazette*, August 17, 1770, expressed the fervent hope that "the plumes of that domineering city may yet feather the nests of those whom they have long plucked."

From the outset the inhabitants of the towns were confronted with what would today be called "urban problems." The conditions of living in a circumscribed community forced attention to matters of common concern which could not be ignored even by a people individualistically inclined. Lighting, fire protection, the care of streets, crime prevention, sewage disposal, water, community health, marketing facilities—such needs as these evoked remedial efforts which, if primitive in modern eyes, matched those of English cities of comparable size. In some places public-spirited citizens for a time maintained night watches out of their own purses, or else the towns required persons to serve their turns on penalty of fines. Sooner or later, however, policing after dark was accepted as a regular charge on the taxpayers. The removal of garbage generally devolved on roving swine and goats, while drainage remained pretty much an unsolved problem, though in a few communities householders laid private sewers. The fire hazard early stirred the municipal authorities to impose regulations as to the construction of chimneys and the keeping of water buckets. Civic spirit in the eighteenth century supplemented official efforts with the formation of volunteer fire companies which, long after the colonial period, continued to be the principal agency of fire fighting. The pressure of urban needs also fostered American inventiveness, producing Franklin's lightning rod and the fireplace stove.

As these illustrations suggest, the people of the cities evolved a pattern of life increasingly unlike that of the countryside or the frontier. The necessary concern with the general welfare contravened the doctrine of individualism and nourished a sense of social responsibility. This training in collective action, constantly reenforced by the everyday contact of the citizens in less formal undertakings, assumed a commanding importance as the Revolution approached. Happily for the future independence of America, the new policy of the British government, begun in 1763–1764, struck deeply at the roots of urban prosperity. The business classes rallied promptly to the defense of their interests and, heedless of the possible political consequences, enlisted the support of the artisan and mechanic groups. Throughout the decade of controversy the seaport towns set the pace of colonial resistance, furnishing most of the high-pressure leaders, staging turbulent demonstrations at every crisis, and laboring to mobilize rural support for the cause. . . . Boston's preeminence in such exertions may well have been due to the fact that, having recently fallen behind Philadelphia and New York as an emporium, she was resolved at any cost to stay the throttling hand of the British government. With the assembling of the first Continental Congress the direction of the patriot movement shifted to Philadelphia, where presently the first capital of the new republic was established.

It would be a misconception, however, to consider the colonial town merely as an expression of political or economic energies. The city, then as now, was a place where men found a variety of outlets for their special talents, an opportunity to cultivate the art as well as the business of living. Ports of entry for European settlers and goods, the larger places were also ports of entry for European ideas and standards of taste. In nearly every respect city life had a transforming effect on all who came within its orbit. A knowledge of the "three R's" was more widely diffused there than among rural inhabitants. The urban monopoly of the printing presses, newspapers, and bookstores insured both the preservation and the extension of knowledge at many levels. . . . It was city folk who took the lead in founding schools and colleges. The protracted battle to establish inoculation as a preventive against smallpox was fought out in the towns. The first great victory for freedom of the press greeted the efforts of a Philadelphia lawyer defending a New York editor. . . .

It would be folly to deny that the city, both in its internal life and its external relations, played a role of critical importance in colonial society. Just as the biologist learns about complex organisms from studying the simpler forms, so the historical student may enrich his understanding of the later implications of urbanism by a better knowledge of colonial conditions. Though only Philadelphia contained as many as 30,000 people on the eve of Independence, and though less than one out of every twenty-five Americans lived in places of eight thousand or more, these towns revealed in embryo the shape of things to come. . . .

The spectacular size of the westward movement beginning shortly after the Revolution has obscured the fact that the city not only soon regained its relative position in the total population, but after 1820 grew very much faster than the rural regions. In 1790 one out of every thirty Americans lived in places of eight thousand or more; in 1820 one out of twenty; in 1840 one out of twelve; and in 1860 nearly one in every six. The explanation of this apparent paradox is to be found in a number of factors, not the least of which is the sources of the trans-Appalachian country in breeding its own urban communities. These raw western towns at first served as distributing points for commodities between the seaboard and the interior; but they soon became marts where the local manufacturer and the country dweller plied a trade to mutual advantage. Pittsburgh early began to branch out into manufacturing; already by 1807 her atmosphere was described as choked with soot. Two years later Cincinnati possessed two cotton mills. Up and down the Ohio Valley many a rude settlement sought to emulate their example;

the ambition to become a city dazzled nearly every cluster of log huts. The Indiana pioneers, for instance, hopefully named their tiny hamlets Columbia City, Fountain City, Saline City, Oakland City, and Union City or, flaunting their ambitions more daringly, called them New Philadelphia, New Paris, and even New Pekin.

Meanwhile, in the East, scores of new cities sprang into being, generally at the fall line of the rivers, where water power was available for utilizing the industrial secrets which sharp-witted Americans had recently filched from Britain. It has often been remarked of the early days of New England manufacturing that the farmers' daughters went to the mill towns while their brothers sought the fertile West. But it is clear that, in this section as well as in the Middle Atlantic states, many a farm lad also joined the urban procession; for, long before the great foreign immigration of the forties, the leading cities began to increase rapidly in size. To such places went young men gregarious in temperament, or of a mechanical bent, or ambitious of gain, or fond of book learning. . . .

With the settlement of the trans-Appalachian hinterland, New York, Philadelphia, and Baltimore engaged in a mighty struggle with one another for the conquest of western trade. Content no longer with near-by tributary districts, they sought to carve out economic dependencies and spheres of influence in the more distant country. This conflict of urban imperialism was most strikingly evidenced in the rivalry for transportation routes connecting with the West. It is unnecessary here to do more than recall the main weapons with which this prolonged contest was waged—first with turnpikes, then with canals, and, finally, with the all-conquering steam railroads. Meanwhile middle-western cities, inspired by the eastern example, entered upon a somewhat similar struggle for power, each seeking to enlarge its orbit of trading operations at the expense of rivals and to benefit from the new ties with the seaboard. With a view to the commercial possibilities of the farther West, Chicago, St. Louis, Memphis, and New Orleans pushed competing plans for the construction of a Pacific railroad, a maneuvering for position which had important national political repercussions, notably in the Kansas-Nebraska Act.

This protracted strife for transportation facilities in the pre–Civil War era determined the trend of future urban growth in all parts of the North. The Erie Canal, reenforced by the later railroad construction, established conclusively the preeminence of New York on the seaboard and in the nation. As the new lines of communication penetrated Middle America, they expedited settlement and energized cities into being; oftentimes the railroad ran through the main street. The rise of populous centers increased the market for foodstuffs, accelerated the invention of labor-saving implements such as the steel plow and the reaper, and thus furthered commercial agriculture, which in turn contributed to city growth. Chicago, though still far behind New Orleans, St. Louis, and Cincinnati in size and wealth, had by 1860 already acquired the economic sinews which would make her New York's chief rival before the century closed.

If the urban advance can be measured in terms of the size of cities abroad, it is instructive to recall that in 1800 London, the largest European city, possessed around 800,000 people, Paris somewhat more than a half million. Philadelphia, then America's chief center, had less than 70,000, New York only 60,000.

Though both London and Paris trebled in size by 1860, New York with 800,000 inhabitants (not counting Brooklyn) ranked as the third city of the Occidental world, while Philadelphia with nearly 565,000 surpassed Berlin. Six other American cities contained more than 100,000, four of them west of the Appalachians.

To master the new intricacies of metropolitan living called for something more than the easy-going ways of colonial times. Yet the municipal authorities, loath to increase taxes, usually shouldered new responsibilities only at the prod of grim necessity. It required the lethal yellow-fever epidemics of the 1790s to induce Philadelphia to set the example of installing a public water system. But with the speeding up of urban concentration after 1820 improvements came thick and fast. Over a hundred municipal water works were introduced before the Civil War, though in every case ignorance of the germ theory of disease necessarily centered attention on clear water rather than pure water. In 1822 Boston inaugurated gas lighting, and the following year she installed the first public-owned sewerage system. About the same time, regular stagecoach service was begun on the streets of New York, to be followed in the next decade by the introduction of horse-car lines. The primitive system of fire fighting by voluntary companies, however, continued everywhere until Boston in 1837 established a paid municipal department.

These civic advances were, of course, unevenly distributed. The smaller cities felt less keenly the pressure for change, while even the larger ones tended to subordinate community need to ulterior considerations. Thus, New York and Philadelphia, daunted by the political power of the volunteer companies, delayed the creation of fire departments until 1865 and 1870. Nor did any city try to combat the evil of slums which began to flourish along the seaboard in the 1840s as a result of the enlarging influx of immigrants. Recruiting their strength from the slum dwellers, the criminal classes, and the fire companies, political machines came into being, trafficking in franchises for the new municipal services and preparing the way for the notorious misrule of cities after the Civil War. The use of municipal offices for partisan purposes long antedated the introduction of the spoils system into state and national politics.

Despite such deterrent influences, it was from the cities that issued most of the humanitarian impulses of the pre–Civil War period. The compactness of living dramatized all inequalities of condition, facilitated the banding together of the tender-hearted, and sometimes enlisted the support of wealthy philanthropists. . . . From the cities came the effective energies behind the establishment of free public education, the more humane treatment of the insane, penal reform, the beginning of free public libraries, and the women's rights' movement. Such places also exerted an important influence on the struggle for universal manhood suffrage, the effort to abolish war, and the antislavery cause.

In the cities, too, were felt the first stirrings of the labor movement. For the increasing numbers of urban wage-earners the so-called safety valve of the frontier failed to work. "The wilderness has receded," declared an eastern observer in 1840, "and already the new lands are beyond the reach of the mere laborer, and the employer has him at his mercy." In self-protection the workingmen early in the 1830s organized trade unions, first along the seaboard and then in such inland cities as Buffalo, Pittsburgh, Cincinnati, and St. Louis; and for a time the principal centers combined in a national federation of labor. . . .

The determined purpose of the city reformers to employ the power of government to remove social inequalities heightened the contrast between urban and frontier conceptions of democracy; the lag of the rural sections in cultural achievements marked an even wider gap between the two ways of life. The enlargement and multiplication of urban centers not only insured a greater appreciation and patronage of arts and letters, but immensely broadened the field for the recruitment of talent. . . .

A varied and vital intellectual life resulted, of which any nation might be proud. Magazines proliferated until every taste and interest was regaled; newspapers became legion; publishing houses sprang up to supply the unprecedented demand for books. The story of this richly creative period in American letters can be told almost wholly in terms of Boston and its environs and of New York. Imaginative literature, however, also had its devotees in Cincinnati, St. Louis, and other inland cities. In the related arts the urban record showed less distinction; yet, apart from architecture, American civilization made fresh advances. . . . Progress in music consisted chiefly in the broadening of musical appreciation, though in Stephen C. Foster Pittsburgh supplied a composer of genius. The theater became firmly established as an urban institution, and players like Charlotte Cushman and Edwin Booth won repute in England as well as at home. Painters no longer felt the urgent need of seeking inspiration and support abroad. Their prestige was high, the products of their brush found a ready market, and, with the formation of the National Academy of Design in 1826, New York became the nation's art center.

Whatever the benefits accruing to the higher life, the waxing importance of the city occasioned increasing fear and resentment among country dwellers. This was especially true of the years from 1820 to 1860, which saw the urban population grow elevenfold. Country ministers denounced big cities, "cursed with immense accumulations of ignorance and error, vice and crime"; farm journals exhorted young men not to sacrifice their independence in order to "cringe and flatter, and . . . attend upon the wishes of every painted and padded form of humanity." The printing press poured forth books, such as Clement Bobbins' *Vampires of New York* and the anonymous paper-back series published by C. H. Brainard on the *Tricks and Traps* of New York, New Orleans, St. Louis, and Chicago. Writers of popular fiction, sensing the sales possibilities, eagerly embroidered upon the theme. George Lippard's melodramatic novel, *The Quaker City . . . A Romance of Philadelphia Life, Mystery and Crime* (1844), ran through twenty-seven editions in five years. . . .

Politics also reflected the deepening rural distrust of city domination. The western opposition to the second United States Bank sprang largely from alarm at the control of credit facilities by the branch banks at Boston, New York, Philadelphia, and Baltimore. Likewise, the widening breach between South and North rested in considerable part on differences between rural and urban ways of life. The South, possessing few sizable towns and believing itself yoked to agriculture by slavery, became increasingly isolated from the currents of civilization flowing through the northern cities. It did not join in establishing free public schools; it feared and misunderstood the social experimentation rampant in the urban North; and, lacking the necessary nerve centers for creative cultural achievement, it fell far behind in arts, science, and letters. Moreover, southern economic life lay under constant tribute to northern urban enterprise. . . . For twenty years before the war southern commercial conventions sought ways and means to escape this subordination, but their hope of building their own trading centers had no chance for success so long as land and Negroes held a superior attraction for capital.

Historians might well give greater attention to the question of the extent to which southern secession was a revolt against the urban imperialism of Yankeedom. The grievance of the planting elements seems clear; and the bitter comment of the *Charleston Mercury,* May 20, 1858, that "Norfolk, Charleston, Savannah, Mobile, are only suburbs of New York, suggests the rankling resentment of the population centers. . . . It is significant that one of the early acts of the Confederate and state authorities was to outlaw the accumulated indebtedness of many millions owing to northern merchants, bankers, and manufacturers.

The years following the Civil War ushered in the modern era of cities. In the East and the Middle West urbanization proceeded apace. By 1890 New York–Brooklyn with nearly two and a half million people rivaled Paris, and Chicago and Philadelphia with more than a million each ranked as the sixth and seventh cities of the Occident. Hardly less significant was the rise of cities in the Far West and the New South. If most of them seemed small by the new yardstick of urban magnitude, their rate of growth was spectacular, and even their size would earlier have gained them respect. Thus, Los Angeles jumped from less than 5000 in 1860 to more than 100,000 in 1900, and Denver from nothing at all to 134,000, while Memphis with 23,000 in the earlier year exceeded 100,000 in the later. In the nation as a whole, the proportion of people living in towns of eight thousand or more grew from one out of every six persons in 1860 to about one out of four in 1880 and by 1900 to one in every three. Moreover, of this increasing horde of urban dwellers, considerably more than half resided in places of twenty-five thousand or more.

The city had at last become a national rather than a sectional institution. This development rested on the occupation of the Great West and the economic rehabilitation of the post-war South and, in all sections, on an application of business enterprise to the exploitation of natural resources such as the world had never known. To recount this material transformation at length would be to recite an oft-told tale. The urban dynamic, grotesquely magnified, was the governing force. Railroads, industrial combinations, financial power, legislative favors formed the instruments of conquest. A complex of city imperialisms arose, each scheming for dominion, each battling with its rivals for advantage, and each perforce yielding eventual tribute to the lord of them all. . . .

As urban centers grew in size and wealth, they cast an ever-stronger enchantment over the mind of the nation. Walt Whitman, returning after a short absence to New York and Brooklyn in September 1870, hymned the "splendor, picturesqueness, and oceanic amplitude and rush of these great cities." . . . Little wonder that young men and women yielded to the potent allure. "We cannot all live in cities," wrote Horace Greeley in the *New York Tribune,* February 5, 1867, "yet nearly all seem determined to do so. Millions of acres . . . solicit cultivation . . . yet hundreds of thousands reject this and rush into the cities."

Historians in their preoccupation with the dispersion of settlers over the wide expanse of the public domain have given little attention to this countermovement which even more profoundly altered the tissue of American life. In many parts the pull of the city depopulated the countryside. Over two-fifths of the townships of Pennsylvania, three-fifths of those of New England, and more than two-thirds of New York's suffered depletion between 1880 and 1890, while the cities in these states grew by leaps and bounds. Similar rural losses occurred in the Middle West, though there the attraction of free homesteads doubtless played a larger part. The rapid dwindling of the open frontier during this decade came with little shock to a people who for many years had shown an increasing preference for city life and an eagerness to avail themselves of its social amenities and expanding economic opportunities. From 1790 to 1890 the whole population of the republic had grown 16-fold, the urban population 139-fold. The historic announcement of the superintendent of the census in 1890 was significant less as marking the end of an old America than as a long-overdue admission of the arrival of a new one.

If, as Walt Whitman thought, the city was the most comprehensive of the works of man, its lusty growth created problems which tried to the utmost the resourcefulness of the inhabitants. In some measure European experience furnished a guide, but to an increasing extent, notably in rapid transit, lighting, and communication, America pointed the way for the Old World. The record is extraordinary. Hardly had New York undertaken the first elevated railway in 1868 than San Francisco contrived the cable car, and hardly had this new means of conveyance begun to spread than Richmond demonstrated the superiority of the electric trolley system, and presently Boston added the subway. The need for better lighting led to the invention of Brush's outdoor arc-light and of Edison's incandescent bulb for indoors. Still another application of electric power, the telephone, laced the urban population into the texture of a neighborhood. By means of the multicelled department store, cities simplified the problem of shopping; and by means of the steel-framed skyscraper, they economized ground space by building their business districts upward.

This civic advance, however, entailed a shocking degradation of political standards. Americans had gained their experience in self-government under rural conditions; they had yet to learn how to govern concentrated populations. Preyed upon by self-interested men eager to exploit the expanding public utilities, municipal politics became a saturnalia of corruption. . . .

Against the entrenched forces of greed and graft the reformers fought undismayed. Defeated at many points, they at least awakened the nation to the growing problems of social maladjustment and human misery which the teeming cities exhibited. Through a concerted attack on the slum evil they induced the New York legislature to adopt a series of laws for better housing, though the results proved disappointing. They replaced the indiscriminate alms-giving of early times with scientific principles of charity, and established social settlements and playgrounds. Organized religion, harking to the need, responded with slum missions, institutional churches, and the preaching of the social gospel. In the cities, too, the modern labor movement was born, wresting concessions from the employing class through sheer bulk of numbers, joining with the humanitarians in securing factory legislation, and organizing labor's strength on an intercity, nationwide basis. . . .

Urban communities, however, made their greatest contribution as a cultural force. The larger cities now rounded out their cultural equipment. The establishment of art museums, the multiplication of public libraries, the increase of publishing houses, the founding of art schools, conservatories of music, and new universities—these were signs of urban maturity which deeply affected all who came in contact with them. Statistical studies, concerned in considerable part with men who won note during these years, merely confirm what has already been evident as to the relation of urban birth to leadership in fields of achievement. Based on analyses of *Who's Who in America, American Men of Science,* and similar compilations, these investigations show conclusively the advantages resulting from concentrated wealth, superior educational and cultural opportunities, the friction of mind on mind, and the encouragement given to arts and letters. One student found that towns of eight thousand or more produced nearly twice as many persons of distinction as their proportionate share. In particular fields, such as science, literature, art, and engineering, the urban differential was far greater. Such findings, however, understate the significance of the city, for they leave out of consideration the countless gifted individuals who, born in rural districts or in other nations, found in the urban world their Promised Land. . . .

As the city forged ahead, imposing its economic fiat on the rest of the nation, developing ever more sharply its special way of life and opening new vistas of civilization, the rift between town and country reached threatening proportions. This antagonism had generally been conceived by historians in broad geographic terms. An accredited scholar, writing in the 1890s, saw the issue with clearer eyes. The "new sectionalism," he affirmed, is geographic only "in so far as the East is the section of the cities, while the South and West are the sections containing the bulk of the farmers." The decisive difference everywhere, he asserted, lay between urban and rural communities. "The people on the farms and in the villages in the East have shared no more in the advancing wealth of the past quarter of a century than the people on the farms and in the villages of the South and West." He estimated the average wealth of urban families at nearly three times that of rural families.

If the typical country dweller had little conception of these larger economic factors, the passage of years brought him a growing sense of deprivation in his daily round of living. Contrasted with the rewards of urban life, he felt cheated of his due share of opportunities, comforts, and pleasures. . . .

To this rural feeling of inferiority, this deepening sense of frustration, the historian must look for the basic explanation of the recurrent agrarian uprisings. Tangible economic grievances, particularly in times of agricultural depression, merely stirred the smoldering embers into blaze. Such grievances assumed a variety of forms, but all of them represented extensions of urban imperialism at the cost of rural welfare. Farm leaders likened the big cities to giant cuttlefish running out their suckers into the blood stream of the countryside. . . .

Few persons in 1900 could have foreseen the trends of urban development which the twentieth century has brought forth. These attest the vast recuperative powers of American society. One of the most notable advances has been the concerted effort to bridle the predatory forces which, in James Bryce's phrase, had made municipal government "the one conspicuous failure of the United States." To this end, four hundred and fifty cities have adopted the commission-manager plan. A radical departure from the clumsy nineteenth-century form which had been based on the analogy of state governments, the new system seeks to apply to complex urban communities the principles of expert management rendered familiar by business corporations. . . .

The new municipal ideals, operating with varying intensity in different parts of the nation, made progress in face of the continued headlong rush into the cities both from the countryside and from foreign lands. With a third of the people living in places of eight thousand and upward in 1900, approximately half did so by 1930. In the latter year nearly a third of the population resided in centers of one hundred thousand or more. During the three decades the country population gained less than eleven and a half million while the city population leaped more than thirty-five million. In reality, urban preponderance was bigger than these figures indicate, thanks to the rise of great metropolitan districts in all parts of the nation. These supercommunities had begun to form in the nineteenth century as swifter means of transportation and communication flung the population outward into the suburbs. But it was the coming of the automobile and the motor truck that raised them to their paramount position in the national economy. The census of 1930 disclosed ninety-six metropolitan districts, composed of one or more central cities with peripheral towns and rural communities, each district comprising a territory united by common social, industrial, and financial interests. The metropolitan areas of New York City lay in three states, embracing a region twice the size of Rhode Island and containing 272 incorporated communities. Greater Chicago in 1930 included 115 incorporated places, and greater San Francisco, 38. . . .

Of all the new trends in urban development, however, none has had such profound effects on American civilization as the altered relationship between country and city. Historians usually ascribe the subsidence of the agrarian revolt of the nineties to the discovery of fresh sources of gold supply. But perhaps a more fundamental explanation lies in the amelioration of many of the social and psychological drawbacks of farm life. The last decade of the century beheld an ampler provision of rural educational facilities, a rapid extension of the good-roads movement due to the bicycle craze, the penetration of the countryside by an increasing network of interurban trolley lines, the introduction of rural free delivery, and the spread of farm telephones following the expiration of the basic Bell patents. All these events helped to break down the ancient isolation and loneliness, and lent a new attraction to country existence.

Yet these mitigations seem small, compared with the marvels which the present century has wrought. The automobile has shortened all distances, while the radio and the movies have brought urbanizing influences to nearly every rural home. At the same time the tractor and other labor-saving devices have lightened the drudgery of the day's task. . . .

While the farmers have shared more richly in advantages once confined to townfolk, urban life in turn has become increasingly ruralized. Parks, playgrounds, and tree-lined boulevards have multiplied far out of proportion to the growth of population, while enlarging numbers of city workers have used the new means of transit to go farther and farther into the rustic suburbs. Retail trade has also felt the centrifugal pull, and even factories have shown a tendency to move outward into villages where taxes are low, and food and rent cheap. The extension of giant power will doubtless accelerate this diffusion and afford an increasing number of wage-earners a chance to work and live in semi-rural surroundings.

When the city encroaches sufficiently on the country and the country on the city, there will come an opportunity for the development of a type of civilization such as the world has never known. The old hard-and-fast distinction between urban and rural will tend to disappear, and a form of society take its place which, if America is to realize her promise, will blend the best features of the two traditional modes of life.

From humble beginnings in the early days of settlement the city has thus traced a varied course. In Europe the urban community emerged by imperceptible stages out of the town economy and culture of the Middle Ages; by comparison the American city leaped into being with breath-taking suddenness. At first servant to an agricultural economy, then a jealous contestant, then an oppressor, it now gives evidence of becoming a comrade and cooperator in a new national synthesis. Its economic function has been hardly more important than its cultural mission or its transforming influence on frontier conceptions of democracy. A force both for weal and woe, the city challenges the attention of scholars who will find in its ramifying history innumerable opportunities for rewarding research.

The Making of an Urban Historian: An Interview

BRUCE M. STAVE AND RICHARD C. WADE

STAVE: I'd like to start off with a discussion of your background, youth, and family. I've noticed that you were born in Iowa.

WADE: Yes, that's true, but I was taken, when I was three years old, to Chicago. The family stayed very briefly in the north side of Chicago, an area which was largely Irish at the time, and then moved up to Evanston. Later we moved out to Winnetka. My days in grade school were at a Catholic school, St. Francis Xavier. So my early life was suburban. . . .

STAVE: Now when did you develop your interest in studying history?

WADE: Well, I went to a Catholic grammar school, and I never much went for history there, but geography interested me. I learned the state capitals—you learned things by rote in those days—I learned them faster than anybody else in my class. We used to have big geography books on China and India and Africa—Catholicism was the universal church and therefore they taught us about those areas. . . . The second thing was that my father had an intense interest in current affairs. There were four newspapers in Chicago at the time and he'd get them the night before—the morning papers—and he'd bring home at 6:00 the evening papers. So I grew up reading the newspapers and it had a profound influence on me. . . .

By Richard C. Wade from Bruce M. Stave, ed., *The Making of Urban History: Historiography Through Oral History,* excerpts from pp. 159–88. Copyright © 1977 Sage Publications, Inc. Reprinted by permission of the publisher.

. . . When I was a Senior at New Trier High School (I had done very poorly in Freshman and Sophomore years), I took a course in American history with the person who ran my homeroom. I just dared not do well because he was my homeroom leader. And so I memorized history. Looking back, it was a dreadful course in American history, but somehow it all stuck. I always had great regard for him. Everybody else in the class was bored. But I memorized and suddenly when I was all through I had some sense of the factual structure of American history. That one thing. And the second thing is that when I got to be a Senior, we had a fellow who taught sociology. And the first day he said: "Anyone who will work down at the Northwestern University settlement house will get an *A* in the course." And so I started going down to the settlement house. It was on Milwaukee Avenue on the North Side of Chicago. There I discovered a world I had never known before. This was real poverty. This was in the late (19)30s, heavily Polish immigrants. . . . I only spent one day a week there, a Saturday afternoon, but that made a big difference in my perspective.

STAVE: Now, to get to the choice of college situation.

WADE: You'll never know how I got into the University of Rochester [laughs]. I was a tennis player and I thought I was going to the University of Chicago because they were hiring tennis players. But my father said, "What would happen if you broke your wrist?" And so I got worried about this and . . .

STAVE: You mean what would happen in terms of a scholarship?

WADE: Yes. . . . When I got to Rochester I did very poorly in my Freshman year. I didn't know if I could keep my scholarship at all . . . but then I had a person named Arthur May in an introductory course in Western Civilization and he interested me a lot. I think I only got a *B,* but that was pretty good compared with the other grades I was getting in those days. And so I sort of came to the conclusion that I wanted to be in History, but it was no burning passion. . . .

STAVE: Now, in terms of interest in the city as such, . . . was there much about the city that you got involved in?

WADE: No. I got an M.A. at Rochester because I knew so little I said I better stick around and get a basic background. And when I went to Harvard [for a Ph.D.], I remember the first seminar with Arthur Schlesinger, Sr. I didn't know anything about American history, much less that the city was an important factor. . . . But in the seminar [Schlesinger] handed around ten or twelve names which we were supposed to write a little biography about—they were social figures—and I got Charles Loring Brace . . . [who] founded the Children's Aid Society [in 1853] and wrote *The Dangerous Classes.* He introduced me to urban history. I got so interested that I took my spring vacation in New York and went around to the Children's Aid Societies and looked back at the old records. I was going well beyond what was normally done for a seminar paper. But I went around and saw a lot of the early statistics and manuscript censuses and things of that sort. It was at that time I decided what I was going to do for my thesis. I knew I wanted something on cities. Then I began to read various things written on the history of cities. . . .

STAVE: Once you came back from New York and decided that you were going to write a dissertation on an urban topic, how did you decide on the final dissertation?

WADE: Well, I didn't know yet whether I wanted to be a historian; also, I didn't know whether I could be. I was determined not to take a small topic. I would undertake a big topic and if I could do it I would know I was an historian. If I couldn't do it I'd find something else. I had in mind already that American history could be interpreted from an urban viewpoint. Very early I had the notion that there are three things which distinguish American history. . . . There were three things that seemed to be uniquely American. One was the frontier; the other was the institution of slavery; and the third was the party machine. . . .

STAVE: You say you taught urban history in 1956 for the first time [while on the faculty of the University of Rochester]. I find this interesting. . . .

WADE: . . . My own framework was uncertain, hence I had trouble with my reading lists. I thought it would be hard to get students in urban history so I sugared the pill a bit by putting in a lot of novels that students would like. My introduction of urban history at Rochester was so popular that I could drop off Latin American history [from my teaching]. From the beginning I could see that the generation of students coming up were interested in urban history . . . especially at Rochester where most of the students came from cities or suburbs. . . .

. . . My own theory about the whole question of urban history is that you don't want to define it. . . . I don't know what the new urban history is and I don't know what the old urban history is. The only thing I can see that is new is the interest in quantification which is, after all, not history but methodology. To that extent it is new. But when you look at the writings of the "new" urban historians they are not dealing with topics which are different from a more traditional interest. I don't see any subject that wasn't in Arthur Schlesinger's seminars in the 1940s.

STAVE: If you had to choose a half a dozen books in urban history that you most admire, that most influenced you, what would you choose?

WADE: Oh, boy. Well, I would say Schlesinger's *Rise of the City,* Handlin's *The Uprooted,* Handlin's *Boston's Immigrants* (I would say that this book had a very great influence). Homer Hoyt's book on land values. This will sound corny—Lincoln Steffens' *Shame of the Cities.* The census of 1880.

STAVE: The census of 1880?

WADE: Yes, I read that like it was a novel. There are a lot of good books recently, but they're not the kind of books that are formative. You're talking about the formative books.

STAVE: Right. Do you have any concluding words for the younger people in the profession interested in urban history?

WADE: Write on [laughs]. One thing I do think is important—and not confined to urban history—is to get rid of this fascination with historiography. History is much richer than anything we think about it. Increasingly, I go to meetings and the papers tell us what so-and-so said and how that was different from what someone else said. You never get what the author thinks. To be sure, it's possible to build a reputation by climbing up some established historian's back. Perhaps it's a fine corrective for the book he's handling, but it doesn't create an alternative way to look at things. When you ask on an oral exam about the origins of the Civil War, for example, the student will give a good review of the literature. Then you ask, "Well, what do you think?" It's often at that time that you discover they thought history was historiography.

STAVE: And not synthesis.

WADE: History is a good deal richer than anything any of us will ever say about it, and I think that's what people ought to know.

What Was the "New Urban History" All About?

STEPHAN THERNSTROM

The boundaries of the modern metropolis are elastic. Once the city could be described as "a tightly settled and organized unit in which people, activities, and riches are crowded into a very small area clearly separated from its nonurban surroundings," but no more. Instead there is mixture, coalescence, "urban sprawl," which has blurred or erased delineations which earlier seemed meaningful.

The boundaries of the field of urban history today seem equally elusive. The label "urban" is now coming into fashion in history, as in some other disciplines. Courses in the subject have multiplied, texts and readers are being rushed into print; there are urban history newsletters published in both the United States and Britain, and an enormous, monographic literature that professes to be urban history or at least is so considered by some observers. What unites this large and disparate body of work, however, is unclear. Urban history apparently deals with cities, or with city-dwellers, or with events that transpired in cities, or with attitudes toward cities—which makes one wonder what is *not* urban history.

Nearly a decade ago Eric Lampard attempted to bring some order into the chaos by offering a penetrating critique of the existing literature and a series of suggestions for the systematic historical study not of "the city" but of "urbanization as a societal process." . . . Urban history in this view was not a distinct field but a part of social history; Lampard at one point declared that his aim was to provide "a more certain and systematic foundation for the writing of American social history." . . .

Lampard's insistence on the relevance of demographic and ecological perspectives . . . prefigured a development that took place in the United States in the 1960s—the emergence of an intellectual tendency that I have called, for want of a better term, "the new urban history."

The label "the new urban history" may have been somewhat misleading in three respects. First, the image it conveyed of a monolithic "old" history was obviously oversimplified. Earlier work by a number of well-established scholars pointed in the direction in which the new urban historians were to move. . . .

It did, however, seem that most historical writing about cities and city-dwellers was deficient not only because it lacked the breadth and analytical rigor which Lampard called for but because it dealt with only a small segment of the population—the visible, articulate elements of the community rather than the masses of ordinary people. The existing literature was based largely upon traditional literary sources, sources which were socially skewed. They revealed

"Reflections on the New Urban History," reprinted by permission of *Daedalus,* Journal of the American Academy of Arts and Sciences, from the issue entitled, "The Historian and the World of the Twentieth Century," pp. 359–372, Spring 1971, vol. 100, no. 2.

relatively little of the social experience of ordinary people, and when they did treat ordinary people they spoke with the accent of a particular class, and too often indicated more about the perceptions of that class than about life at the lower rungs of the social ladder.

This complaint, and consequent appeals for a new "grassroots" history, a history "from the bottom up," had often been heard before. What was somewhat new in this instance was the awareness of readily available and largely unexploited historical sources which could be used for these purposes. . . . [T]he discovery of surviving manuscript schedules of the United States Census, and then of a host of similar materials—city directories, local tax lists, and so forth—provided the base for the new urban history in the United States.

. . . The problem was how to use them to full advantage. The sheer quantity and complexity of the information they contained was bewildering; simply reading the material and turning it over in one's mind would not do at all. It was this pressing need, I think, more than any prior conviction about the desirability of importing the methods of other social sciences into history that made us look to other disciplines for useful concepts, analytical techniques, and data-processing methods. . . .

A second possibly misleading feature of the phrase, "the new urban history," lies with the term "urban," which seems to imply that this is a distinctive specialized field of historical inquiry. I am doubtful about that. The city is a distinctive legal entity, and there are certain phenomena peculiar to it. But the decisive features of urban life in modern times are not spatially distributed in a way that justifies urban history, or for that matter urban sociology, as a special field. . . . It is important . . . to recognize that most of the subjects that have preoccupied the new urban historians—the flow of population from country to city, patterns of social stratification and social mobility, the social consequences of technological change, the distribution of property and power, the position of ethnic and racial groups, and so on—are not confined to the city, and should not be approached as if they were. They involve the workings of the society as a whole, though of course they have different manifestations in communities of varying size and types. . . . The modern city is so intimately linked to the society around it, and is so important a part of the entire social order that few of its aspects can safely be examined in isolation. The term "urban" in the label "the new urban history" is thus not to be taken as a disavowal of interest in what happens outside cities, nor as a claim that here is a new historical field with a turf of its own from which trespassers should be warned. The ultimate aim of the new urban historian, in my view at least, is to understand how and why the complex of changes suggested by the concept "urbanization" reshaped society. Urban history, in this formulation, lies squarely within the domain of social history, and for the student of modern society it is indeed nearly conterminous with social history.

A final comment on the label "the new urban history" is that although it consciously echoes "the new economic history," the analogy should not be pressed too far. Quantitative evidence plays a greater role in both types of literature than in their traditional counterparts. In both there is less sheer description, and more use of theory. But the differences are important.

The new economic historians are equipped with a theory that purports to represent the workings of a total system and which can be employed to resolve questions about the past as well as the present. The relationship of the new urban historians to theory is quite different. There can be debate over the applicability of modern economic theory to particular historical problems, but there is little question that it is a very powerful tool for dealing with certain kinds of issues. A comparably powerful general social theory which bears upon the matters of prime concern to the urban historian simply does not exist as yet.

. . . The historian, I think, should generalize as widely as he can, and should strive to "make his conceptualizations more explicitly, his use of theory more deliberate, his effort to derive further hypotheses for testing bolder and more systematic." But when the desire to abstract, schematize, and universalize leads to the neglect of *essential* features of the historical context, as can be said about a number of efforts to apply imported social science theories to historical problems, we have not advanced knowledge. One principal function of historical research informed by social science concerns is precisely to edit, refine, and enrich theory by identifying and exploring important historical developments which cannot be neatly explained by existing theory.

The relationship of the new urban historian to social science theory, therefore, is critical and eclectic. Instead of applying a theory, like the new economic historian, he must draw upon a variety of social sciences, as well as his own historical sense, to identify elements of the historical situation that may have been important and to gain clues as to how these might be measured and analyzed. . . .

For the present, high priority must go to the careful description and analysis of particular communities and the processes which formed them, for little is known about even some of the most elementary aspects of these matters. As J. A. Banks sensibly observes, "no useful purpose is served by putting forward plausible hypotheses to explain the 'facts' when we do not know what the facts are." There are, of course, facts in abundance in the massive existing literature of American urban history, but they are of little value for two reasons. For the most part, as previously noted, these works focused upon formal institutions and the articulate elements of the community, to the neglect of underlying social processes and mass behavior. Second, earlier investigations typically assumed the uniqueness of the community with which they dealt, and arranged their evidence in categories that precluded systematic comparison with other cities. . . . As the following examples illustrate, a number of studies already done have corrected significant distortions in our understanding of the past and have shed new light on important issues.

1. Urban Population Fluidity.   Nineteenth-century Americans assumed that the supply of free land in the West assured free movement, and that the city was a closed, confining, static environment. . . . Recent research, however, places the matter in a very different perspective, for it appears that the urban population was if anything more volatile than the rural population. The burgeoning cities drew into them many more newcomers than rural areas long before the closing of the frontier at the end of the century. What is more, migration to the city was a more complex and dynamic process than has been understood, for only a minority of newcomers permanently settled in the community they first entered. Cities grew rapidly from the heavy volume of net in-migration, but gross in-migration was several times higher than that, for there was massive out-migration at the same time. Boston, for example, then a city of less than half a million, gained some 65,000 new residents from net migration between 1880 and 1890, but more than a million people moved through the city in those years to produce that net gain! The typical urban migrant moved through three or more communities before he settled down around middle age. We have long been aware that cities grew by attracting outsiders into them, but the magnitude of the incessant flow of people into and out of them has never been suspected. . . . Despite the automobile, improved national communications, and other developments which have generally been thought to have facilitated the flow of people from place to place, the fragmentary data on the period since 1890 suggest the opposite trend—toward a less volatile population.

2. Class and Ethnic Differentials in Spatial Mobility.   Poor people, immigrants, and blacks were trapped in "slums" and "ghettos," while the middle class was free to move on when opportunity beckoned: such is the prevailing stereotype of the American city of the past. Today there is some grain of truth to this view, for well-educated professionals and managers do indeed move from place to place more often than other occupational groups, and it appears that spatial mobility and economic success are positively correlated. In the nineteenth- and early-twentieth-century city, however, the situation was radically different. Groups low on the social scale were spatially much more volatile than their social betters. There were indeed certain ecological clusterings of poor people in particular neighborhoods, though the prevalence of ghettos in even this sense has long been exaggerated. More important, though, is the recent discovery that few of these individuals lived in any one neighborhood for very long. If there was anything like "a culture of poverty" in the American city, it lacked deep local roots, for most of the people exposed to it were incessantly on the move from place to place. . . .

Two implications follow from this. One is that, while contemporary migration differentials may plausibly be interpreted in terms of an economic model in which labor mobility yields higher return, the older pattern hints at the existence of a quite different phenomenon—a permanent floating proletariat, ever on the move physically but rarely winning economic gains as a result of movement. . . .

A second conclusion of importance may be drawn from the finding: the extreme volatility of the urban masses severely limited the possibilities of mobilizing them politically and socially, and facilitated control by other more stable elements of the population. It is suggestive, for example, that less than a quarter of the working-class residents of Los Angeles in 1900 were still to be found there two decades later, but more than 80 percent of the members of the six middle-class Protestant sects that dominated the city politically and economically. In these sharp class differentials in out-migration rates lies a clue, perhaps, to the neglect of ordinary working people in the newspapers, local histories, and so on. The bulk of the citizens who had lived for long in one place and had a wide circle of acquaintances were in fact part of the middle class; they were "the community," while the masses of ordinary workers were transients who could easily be ignored.

3. Rates and Trends in Social Mobility.   No aspect of urban life in the past is more important than the class structure, and none has received so little attention. Implicit assumptions about the functioning of the class system abound in conventional historical accounts, but empirical research into the dynamics of social stratification is rare. Particularly lacking are careful accounts of class as it shapes the life cycle of individuals and their children. The meaning of one's class position depends not only on the advantages or disadvantages it entails today but upon how it affects one's prospects in the future. The study of social mobility, therefore, occupies a central role in the work of the new urban historians.

It is difficult as yet to generalize broadly on the basis of the scattered findings available, for local and temporal variation in opportunity levels were considerable, but it does seem clear that . . . [c]areer mobility a notch or two up the occupational ladder was common, and intergenerational mobility more common still. Four in ten of the sons of the unskilled and semi-skilled workers of Boston attained a middle-class job (though only a minor clerical or sales position in most cases), and another 15 or 20 percent became skilled craftsmen. Analysis by category more refined than "skilled," "low white collar," "unskilled," and so on discloses that a great deal of this occupational movement involved only slight changes in status, but the over-all impression of fluidity and openness remains. . . .

4. Immigration and Differential Opportunity.   Though the social system was impressively fluid, there was enormous variation in the opportunities open to particular ethnic groups. Native Americans of native parentage were generally in a much more advantageous situation than second-generation immigrants of similar class origins, who were in turn better able to advance themselves than their immigrant fathers. As important as these broad differences were variations within these general categories. Poor white rural migrants to Birmingham and Atlanta remained more heavily proletarian than migrants to Boston from rural New England. Particular European groups—the British, the Germans, the Jews— rose quickly, while others like the Irish and the Italians found the environment far more constricted. It may have been the extreme diversity of the experience of particular groups more than general satisfaction with the social system that accounted for the relative absence of militant working-class protest aimed at fundamental social change. With all of the major immigrant groups, however, there was general upward movement with increased length of residence in America.

5. Negro Migrants and European Immigrants.   In recent years the clustering of black city-dwellers on the lowest rungs of the social ladder has often been attributed to the continuing influx of uneducated, unskilled migrants from backward rural areas. Earlier European immigrant groups entered American society at the bottom too, the argument runs, because they were unfamiliar with and ill-adapted to urban industrial ways. It took generations for them to rise. Negroes in general have not yet done so because so many are still first-generation newcomers from the southern countryside. A test of the "last of the immigrants" theory in late-nineteenth-century Boston, however, suggests that few of the economic disabilities of black people were attributable to their lack of acquaintance with urban culture. . . . Even in what was widely regarded as the most advanced and progressive northern city with respect to race relations, and even by comparison with the European immigrant group which was slowest to rise, the situation of blacks was *sui generis.*

This brief review of some of the findings of recent research in the new urban history is meant to be illustrative, not exhaustive. Fascinating work is now under way on black family structure in nineteenth- and early-twentieth-century cities, work which promises to shatter the conventional wisdom on that subject and to force the rewriting of a major portion of American social history. The family structure of other groups and its relationship to other phenomena is just beginning to receive the scrutiny it so clearly deserves. The texture of neighborhood life, and the flow of people between socially distinct sections of the city, is coming into focus as another major area for investigation. Institutions like schools, churches, and voluntary associations are coming to be approached in terms of functions as well as formal arrangements. The interaction between urban environments and the social organization of work too is beginning to receive serious study.

All this is heartening, but it would be well to conclude on a cautionary note. The emphasis of research in the new urban history thus far has been heavily quantitative. The sources which had been most neglected by previous investigators were peculiarly well-suited to quantitative treatment and seemed to offer a quick pay-off to those willing to attempt it. This was salutary on the whole, I think, because there was a great deal to be learned from even the most simple-minded efforts to measure phenomena which in the past had been discussed on the basis of colorful examples and casual impressions. . . . Some of this work has been superficial, to be sure, or positively misleading. An inadequate formulation of the research problem, the use of categories which blur significant distinctions, employing mathematical techniques ill-suited to the problem at hand: any of these can lead the investigator badly astray. But there are comparable pitfalls for the unwary in every branch of history, and an abundant supply of researchers who will stumble upon them. And it seems to me that the blunders of quantifiers are at least a little more open to exposure and future correction, since the procedure itself forces an investigator to make explicit assumptions which are left implicit in other kinds of work.

There are, however, abuses that eager quantifiers are especially likely to commit, and a word of warning about these is in order. Some enthusiasts appear to assume that the hard evidence that can be gleaned from census schedules, city directories, and the like is the only reliable source of knowledge about past social behavior, and that more traditional sources—newspapers, sermons, manuscripts, novels, and so forth—are so socially skewed as to be quite worthless. What can be counted is real; what cannot is to be left to the storytellers and mythmakers.

This is dangerously obtuse. The descriptive material available in such sources serves several indispensable functions. First, it can provide information essential to arranging harder data in meaningful categories, for instance, instead of imposing an occupational classification scheme derived from research by contemporary sociologists, one may gain clues as to the extent to which division of labor and skill dilution had taken place in particular trades in a given community and develop a scheme more appropriate to the context. Second, such evidence may yield hints of patterns whose existence can be confirmed and explored through statistical analysis, the complaint of a social worker that Irish laborers withdrew their children from school and sacrificed their education in order to accumulate funds to purchase homes suggests a hypothesis worth careful testing. . . .

Most important, it is only through such evidence that the investigator may begin to understand the perceptions and emotions of the people he is dealing with. The austerely objective facts uncovered by empirical social research influence the course of history as they are filtered through the consciousness of obstinately subjective human beings. Religion, ideology, cultural tradition—these affected human behavior in the past and shaped the meaning of the demographic and ecological patterns which can be neatly plotted on a map or graph. If we fail to grapple with these dimensions of the past and make no effort to examine them in the light of what we know from harder data, we will have shirked the most difficult but also the most rewarding of challenges.

New Perspectives on American Urban History

RAYMOND A. MOHL

The writing of American history has been transformed dramatically over the past two decades. In particular, a new interest in social history has energized the field and substantially altered the way historians research, understand, and interpret the past. In the field of urban history, a subdivision of the larger province of social history, scholars have brought exciting new perspectives to the study of the American city. New methods, new approaches, and new interpretations have enlightened dim corners of the urban past and pushed back the frontiers of historical understanding.

The rise of the American industrial city came to be one of the dominant characteristics of the late nineteenth century. Since the turn of the twentieth century, the city in its various permutations has continued to reflect or to shape modern American social, economic, and political life. Yet American historians, Richard C. Wade has suggested, "arrived at the study of the city by slow freight." . . . Indeed, American urban history as a distinctive field of scholarly inquiry does not date much earlier than 1940, when Arthur M. Schlesinger published his landmark article, "The City in American History." But interest in the field grew rather slowly, and by the mid-1950s only a few universities offered courses on the subject. Progress in urban history research was also less than dynamic, the chief accomplishments being several fine urban biographies and a handful of

"New Perspectives on American Urban History," Raymond Mohl, from *International Journal of Social Education,* vol. 1, no. 1 (Spring 1986), excerpts from pp. 69–97. Reprinted by permission of the publisher.

monographs. Among the best were the works of Carl Bridenbaugh on the colonial seaport towns, Oscar Handlin's study of Boston's immigrants, and Richard C. Wade's *The Urban Frontier.*

The decade of the 1960s, however, brought powerful changes to the historical profession, changes that affected research and writing in urban history in significant ways. The mainstream consensus history that grew out of the conditions of the Great Depression, the Second World War, and the Cold War peaked in the Eisenhower era of the 1950s but began to crack amidst the social strains and political conflicts of the 1960s. The ghetto riots of the 1960s and the social-crusading spirit of the Kennedy-Johnson years riveted attention on the American city and its discontents. The writing of history generally reflects the climate of opinion at any particular moment in time, and certainly this was the case in the 1960s. Traditional interest in political and diplomatic history—a sort of elitist history concerned with the ideas and activities of decision makers, opinion-shapers, and power-wielders—gave way to a new and invigorated commitment to social history broadly considered. American historians began to examine with new interest such subjects as race, ethnicity, and class, and the ways in which people ordered their lives in the family, at work, and in various group and community settings; they began to look into the social values, behaviors, and processes that shaped the lives of people; and they began to pay attention to the local level as well as the national, and to the people at the bottom of the social hierarchy as well as at the top. . . .

These shifts in historiographical tradition coincided with two other powerful changes in the America of the 1960s. First, the computer revolution made possible a more careful and exact social science history based on analysis of massive amounts of information collected, stored, and manipulated by computer. Second, the arrival of the baby-boom generation at the college gate spurred an explosion of graduate education, generating in turn a substantial amount of new research as young historians wrote dissertations, articles, and books. . . .

Urban history, in particular, was energized by the convergence of these changing social patterns and historiographical trends. The ferment of scholarly innovation and shifting interests pushed urban history in at least two new directions in the early 1960s. Each new path was illuminated by an important and innovative book—one path by Sam Bass Warner's *Streetcar Suburbs: The Process of Growth in Boston, 1870–1900* (1962), and the other by Stephan Thernstrom's *Poverty and Progress: Social Mobility in a Nineteenth-Century City* (1964).

Warner's work had an ecological slant, focusing on the spatial redistribution of population in the Boston metropolitan area in response both to technological innovation in urban transit and to the rural appeal of suburbia. He also used an inventive methodology. The examination of some 23,000 building permits for three Boston suburbs enabled him to make certain judgments about construction patterns, architectural and building styles, and the class structure underlying neighborhood formation. The result was a book that leaped beyond the established parameters of urban history and provided powerful insights into the growth of the American industrial city.

In *Streetcar Suburbs* and in some of his other work, Warner essentially dealt with the process of urbanization. In rejecting more traditional approaches to urban history, such as urban biography or the study of social problems or political movements within an urban context, he demonstrated the ways in which fresh thinking can be historiographically liberating. . . .

The work of Stephan Thernstrom staked out a second new path in American urban history in the 1960s. In *Poverty and Progress,* he tested the widely asserted conception of nineteenth-century America as a land of opportunity for the urban working class. Drawing samples from manuscript census schedules for Newburyport, Massachusetts, between 1850 and 1880, Thernstrom pioneered in the use of new kinds of sources and in quantitative analysis, although he did not ignore more traditional literary sources. His chief concern was the relatively narrow question of social mobility rather than the larger process of urbanization or city building. Nevertheless, Thernstrom's approach was widely imitated and came to be associated with a "new urban history."

Younger historians began pumping out a stream of books and articles replicating Thernstrom's work for other cities. By the early 1970s the new urban history had been taken over by the quantifiers in the Thernstrom tradition who were mostly studying mobility and related issues. . . .

Thernstrom's approach rather than Warner's came to dominate among practitioners of the new urban history by the early 1970s. Michael Frisch has suggested that the popularity and influence of Thernstrom's *Poverty and Progress* "stemmed less from the book's substance than from the way it brought together a number of diverse concerns central to the historiographical moment." These included a methodology conducive to quantification at the beginning of the computer age, a model that could be applied easily to other communities, and, finally, a concern for nonelitist history, or history from the bottom up. . . .

Thus, the new urban history came to be perceived as a special sort of quantitative history. Yet, ironically, at about the same time that he was carrying his quantitative methodology to a new level of sophistication in his prize-winning book, *The Other Bostonians* (1973), Thernstrom had begun having second thoughts about the term "new" urban history. Indeed, as he confessed . . . in 1975, he had not only given up the term, but he also had even stopped labeling himself as an urban historian at all. Rather, Thernstrom contended that urban historians were really engaged in social history, and that "the modern city [was] so intimately linked to the society around it, and [was] so important a part of the entire social order that few of its aspects [could] safely be examined in isolation."

Always difficult to categorize, Warner, too, rejected the emerging notion of a new urban history. In a 1977 article he labeled the narrow mobility studies "a bare-boned empiricism" and "a quantitative antiquarianism," the purpose behind such studies "lost in technique." . . . Building on his earlier emphasis on the process of urbanization, Warner asserted that the central focus of urban history should be the spatial distribution of population, institutions, activities, and artifacts—the basic elements in all human communities that are continuously evolving in relation to each other over time. By the mid-1970s, therefore, the two chief pioneers of new ways of doing urban history had abandoned or rejected the notion altogether.

The new urban history made one last gasp, however. Theodore Hershberg and others associated with the Philadelphia Social History Project promoted the continued viability of a new, quantified urban history. In an important article in 1978 and in the introduction to a collection of essays on Philadelphia, Hershberg provided yet another prescriptive statement about urban history. For him, the essential distinction between the old and the new urban history was one between the city as site and the city as process. By site, he meant "the conceptual treatment of the city as a passive backdrop to whatever else [was] the subject of central concern." By contrast, he wrote, "urban as process should be thought of as the dynamic modelling of the interrelationships among environment, behavior, and group experience—three basic components in the larger urban system." Such an approach, Hershberg contended, would explain what was distinctively different about life and change in the city. By Hershberg's account, neither Warner nor Thernstrom had been pursuing a new urban history; they were simply working with the older tradition of urban as site rather than urban as process. . . .

The now perceived weaknesses of an exclusively quantitative approach to urban history research have liberated urban historians to pursue many other diverse paths of the urban experience, to follow their instincts and their interests. The results have been fruitful and stimulating. Historians of the American city have begun to carve out a variety of new and exciting areas of urban research. . . . The remainder of this article will survey briefly a dozen or so of these new perspectives on American urban history.

Urban Politics and Government.   Studies of urban politics traditionally focused on the urban political machines that emerged in the late nineteenth century and on the reformers and reform organizations that challenged the city bosses. The traditional view was highly moralistic; the bosses and machines were corrupt and venal, while the reformers upheld the democratic ideal. In the 1950s and 1960s sociologists and historians reversed these widely accepted stereotypes, suggesting instead that the bosses extended democratic politics down to the neighborhood level, provided needed services, supported urban growth and development, and centralized power and decision making at a time of rapid urbanization and social change. . . . More recent studies of the urban political machine and its origins have made fewer expansive claims for the city boss, seeking instead to locate the machine within the broader pattern of American political and social processes.

Meanwhile, the historians of the 1960s and 1970s were revising the traditional picture of the urban reformer. Increasingly, urban reform was perceived as badly splintered, a congeries of separate little movements devoted to single issues like the saloon or playgrounds or civil service reform. The general thrust of recent research suggests that urban reform was a complex, constantly shifting, multidimensional movement. Reformers, it seems, came from all social and economic classes, and they supported a diversity of often conflicting reform legislation, programs, and causes. Some reformers, it now appears, took extremely elitist and undemocratic positions in their attack on the electoral base of the machine. At the same time, other reformers supported social causes dear to the hearts of the bosses; indeed, some reformers were bosses and vice versa. As a result of this research, the traditional practice of portraying urban politics as a sharply defined struggle between bosses and reformers seems less useful now than it did a decade or so ago.

The now acknowledged weaknesses of the boss-reformer interpretive model have forced urban historians to pose new questions and view the evidence in alternative ways. In the past decade, for instance, some historians have begun to challenge the functional view of the boss as a provider of positive government. More research is needed, Jon C. Teaford has written, to determine "to what degree the boss actually bossed." Teaford's important book, *The Unheralded Triumph: City Government in America* (1984), demonstrated the powerful and decisive role of urban professionals and experts in running the industrial city. More important than bosses or reformers, Teaford contended, the growing army of city bureaucrats and technicians may have been the real shapers of the city. Public policymaking depended on what was technically or financially feasible. Thus, the politicians came to rely on the experts, who by the twentieth century staffed the administrative departments in city government. They were municipal engineers, landscape architects, city planners, public health officials, accountants, attorneys, educators, even librarians. . . .

Political Power. Other historians have begun addressing the issue of urban political power, particularly its distribution and uses. Established political science models advocate either elitist or pluralist positions regarding the distribution of power: political power is either concentrated among the wealthy or widely dispersed among competing social groups. Recent historical research offers some alternatives to these political science models, while illuminating new dimensions of the American urban experience.

In his book, *Political Power in Birmingham, 1871–1921* (1971), for instance, Carl V. Harris focused on two interrelated aspects of political power, office holding and governmental decision making. He concluded that the elitist model did fit electoral patterns in Birmingham, where office holding was concentrated heavily among the richest 20 percent of the city's population. But these office-holding patterns did not always dictate public policy outcomes. Indeed, decision-making power in Birmingham was distributed in complex ways. Depending on the policy issue involved, the city's politics were complicated by shifting alliances among and within economic groups, and by religious, ethnic, and racial influences. Neither the power-elite thesis nor the pluralist interpretation matched perfectly the political reality in this growing industrial city of the New South. . . . The chief interpretive thrust of these new studies [of urban political power] is that political decision making reflected the economic, ethnic, and cultural complexity of the cities. The new city of the industrial era, it now appears, was shaped by the continual political interaction of competing elites, pluralistic interest groups, and urban technicians.

Suburbanization. Recent historians of the American city have demonstrated great interest in suburbs. Census statistics have revealed that more Americans now live in the suburban rings surrounding big cities than in the central cities themselves. Thus, it is appropriate that the historical process that created this demographic reality has been brought under scholarly examination. . . .

The most important of these studies is Kenneth T. Jackson's *Crabgrass Frontier: The Suburbanization of the United States* (1985). His masterful and literate book provides a synthesis of two centuries of the suburbanization process in the United States. It begins with the preindustrial "walking city" of the eighteenth and early nineteenth century, a residential pattern gradually altered by new transit provisions and the romantic lure of suburbia. By the 1850s and after, revolutionary transit technology—first the horsecar, later the electric trolley—encouraged the deconcentration of population to the urban periphery. There was a political dimension to the process as well, as cities sought to recapture lost population through the annexation of the suburbs. Much of the municipal political history of the late nineteenth century reflected the conflict between the center and the periphery. For the twentieth century, Jackson focuses on the impact of the automobile and on the role of the federal government. Since the 1930s, especially, the suburbanization process has been shaped by federal policymaking; government highway construction, federal housing programs, and federal mortgage and tax policies have all propelled the suburban drift of population and economic activities. Jackson's study is the most sophisticated and thorough account of these subjects. . . .

The New Regionalism.   Increasingly, some urban historians have sought to link the American city to its hinterland, to the surrounding region of which it is a part. As historian David R. Goldfield has suggested, by the 1970s historians in the United States and elsewhere had begun to pursue urban research within a regional framework. . . . For urban historians, the regional approach promised to broaden the study of the city to the wider region to which it was linked geographically, economically, and culturally. By this method, it has been argued, the city and the character of its development might be more precisely examined and defined.

Goldfield himself has provided the best example of how the regionalist approach can invigorate the writing of urban history. His book, *Cotton Fields and Skyscrapers: Southern City and Region, 1607–1890* (1982), analyzed southern urbanization within the context of southern history and culture. Goldfield challenged earlier views that the pattern of southern urban development was similar to the national urban experience, a position that he himself had once taken. . . . More specifically, he argued that three distinctive aspects of southern regional history and culture have shaped southern urbanization. These are, first, a rural life-style in which the cities maintained a symbiotic relationship with staple agriculture, cotton especially; second, the importance of race and the reality of a biracial society; and third, a colonial economy in which southern cities remained "in economic servitude to the North not only for manufactured products but for all of the financial, credit, legal, accounting, and factoring services that attend a national economy." . . .

Sunbelt Cities.   One of the most dramatic demographic and structural shifts in American history has occurred in the years since 1940 with the growth of the so-called sunbelt cities. Carl Abbott's *The New Urban America* (1981) presented the first full-scale historical analysis of sunbelt city growth. Abbott identified two distinct growth regions—a seven-state sunbelt Southeast, and a ten-state sunbelt West. Since 1950 these regions experienced population increases, urban and metropolitan growth, and expansion in government employment and per capita income. These growth patterns, Abbott suggested, began during World War II, when the federal government built military bases and training facilities in the South and Southwest. . . . Wartime migration and new federal contracts made boomtowns of Atlantic, Gulf, and Pacific coastal cities. By 1980 five of the nation's ten largest cities—Houston, Dallas, Phoenix, San Diego, and Los Angeles—were located in the Southwest.

The post–World War II sunbelt boom was characterized by sustained economic growth, particularly in defense and high-technology industries, as well as in tourism, recreation, and retirement activities. In the automobile era, speedy population dispersal from the central city was commonplace, often following new highway construction and the decentralization of economic activities. Suburban growth accompanied the rise of the sunbelt cities, as the social ecology of the central cities was reproduced at the metropolitan periphery. Population growth and dispersal eventually led the sunbelt cities to active programs of annexation, often on a massive scale. . . .

In an innovative section on sunbelt politics, Abbott identified three successive stages in postwar political development. In the immediate postwar era, the urban boosters and chamber-of-commerce reformers who controlled city governments sought to manage physical and economic growth so as to benefit central city business interests. A new political pattern began to emerge by the 1950s, as vigorous suburban politicians and interest groups fought central city establishments on various issues. More recently, urban politics in the sunbelt has been characterized by neighborhood and ethnic conflict in which local communities within the urban region have become "focal points for political action." Metropolitan politics in the sunbelt, Abbott has argued, reflected urban spatial and territorial realities. Indeed, the crucial issues of local politics—growth policies, annexation, consolidation, school integration, urban renewal, public housing location, highway planning, environmental protection, taxes, and service—are at least partly spatial issues, and local political actors perceive them in terms of their spatial consequences. These are only some of the conclusions drawn in this pioneering study of the sunbelt cities. . . .

Technology and the City.   From the mid-nineteenth century, technological innovation has provided one of the chief stimulants to urban growth and development. New transit technology encouraged the outward movement of population, new or improved municipal services made urban life safer and more pleasant, new building technology permitted the rise of the skyscraper. A number of studies have elaborated on these aspects of urban history. For example, Charles W. Cheape's *Moving the Masses: Urban Public Transit in New York, Boston, and Philadelphia, 1880–1912* (1980) provides an excellent analysis of the financial, political, and technological context of the building of city transit systems, particularly subways. . . .

Moving into the twentieth century, an especially useful book is Mark S.

Foster's *From Streetcar to Superhighway* (1981), a study of city planners and urban transportation between 1900 and 1940. The chief innovation of these years was the automobile and the consequent decline of city streetcar systems. Foster attributes the decline of mass transit to the perceived flexibility and economy of the automobile, an interesting conclusion in light of an extensive recent literature advancing a conspiracy theory by which automobile, highway, and related interest groups set out to dismantle and destroy fixed-rail mass transit. . . . The central achievement of these varied recent works on technology has been to demonstrate the important link between technological change and urban development.

Planning and Housing.   Technology is related closely to the ways in which Americans planned and built their cities. Technological innovation established the parameters of what was possible and feasible in the built environment. Studies of planning history published in the 1960s and 1970s focused inordinately on the nineteenth-century roots of city planning. These works emphasized the landscape architecture tradition, in which Frederick Law Olmsted played such a major role, and the emergence of the "city beautiful" movement under the leadership of such Chicago figures as architect and planner Daniel Burnham and architect Louis Sullivan. These traditions, and Olmsted especially, continue to attract scholarly interest. However, planning history in recent years has moved solidly into the twentieth century and has concentrated on the practical and utilitarian side of planning: the efficient implementation of zoning policies, urban transit, highway building, public utilities, and central-city development and redevelopment. Moreover, current writing in planning history tends strongly toward placing planning decisions into a wider political and social context. . . .

Twentieth-century planning has been centrally related to the expansion of modern government. Governmental decision making in this area often stems from motives other than those originally conceived by planners—making cities more rational, more pleasant, and more livable. The recent planning histories emphasize the governmental role in urban planning, and they demonstrate the often negative consequences of governmental action such as highway construction that helped destroy central city areas, or urban renewal programs that leveled vibrant inner-city neighborhoods. . . .

The Urban Working Class.   Building on the insights of the British historian E. P. Thompson, students of the American working class have been revamping our understanding of workers and of class relations in the American city. Herbert Gutman's important study, *Work, Culture, and Society in Industrializing America* (1976), led the way. His research on the first generation of industrial workers in America demonstrated the surprising strength and persistence of the communal, preindustrial work patterns, even in the midst of the drive toward industrialization. The chief thrust of Gutman's work has been that workers had some control over their lives and over the workplace. . . .

During the industrialization process, urban artisans became factory workers, skilled craftsmen suffered loss of status and economic position as the production process was mechanized and skill became less important. A number of studies have focused on the ways in which the urban working class resisted, protested, and adapted to the changes brought about by industrialization. . . . As Daniel T. Rodgers suggested in *The Work Ethic in Industrial America, 1850–1920* (1976), "There is ample evidence that large numbers of industrial workers failed to internalize the faith of the factory masters. Closely allied to this position is David Montgomery's argument in *Workers' Control in America* (1979) that trade unions ultimately became the mechanism for maintaining craft-worker autonomy and for enforcing traditional work rules.

Race and Ethnicity.   Recent historians have altered dramatically the portrait of immigration and ethnic groups in the American city. The traditional view had been summarized ably in Oscar Handlin's *The Uprooted* (1951). Handlin depicted the immigrants as a displaced peasantry wrenched from the communal past and thrust into the industrial city in a harsh, foreign land. In the urban ghettos of industrial America, the newcomers suffered the destruction of their traditional cultures, social breakdown and disorganization, and eventual assimilation. Virtually every aspect of Handlin's "ghetto hypothesis" of immigrant adjustment has been rewritten by recent historians.

The historical scholarship of the past decade has provided new perspectives on the migration process, the creation of the ethnic village in the American city, and the development of immigrant institutional life. Historians have discovered the importance of "chain migration"—the family- and community-based process which brought most immigrants to America. Once in the new land, the immigrant family structure remained a powerful determinant of life and culture. . . .

Rather than weakening under the strains of migration and urban life, historians have concluded, the ties of family, kinship, and community remained strong in the American industrial city. Ethnic churches, parochial schools, and a bewildering variety of cultural and fraternal groups kept ethnicity alive despite the powerful forces of assimilation. . . .

Moreover, as historian Rudolph J. Vecoli has argued, the immigrants demonstrated "a powerful tendency to reconstitute community in accordance with Old World origins." Thus, Chicago's "Little Italies" were, in reality, dozens of old-country village groups reorganized and reconstituted in the new land. . . .

Such research has uncovered important dimensions of the immigrant experience. Portraying dynamic and vibrant ethnic communities in the industrial city, this new work effectively demolished the traditional ghetto hypothesis of Handlin and others. The most sophisticated summary of recent interpretations may be found in John Bodnar's *The Transplanted: A History of Immigrants in Urban America* (1985), which pulls together in a seamless account the many and varied strands of immigrant history research.

Immigrants were not the only newcomers to the industrial city who sought to keep alive the communal traditions of the premodern past. Among black migrants from the rural South to the Urban and industrial North, the old folkways and family patterns persisted into the twentieth century. Buffeted first by slavery and then by modernization, nineteenth-century urban blacks found it difficult to enjoy the full measure of freedom in the city, as Leonard P. Curry has suggested in *The Free Black in Urban America, 1800–1850* (1981). Nevertheless, the black family remained a strong and vital institution, as Herbert Gutman demonstrated in *The*

Black Family in Slavery and Freedom, 1750–1925 (1976). Similarly, more recent studies of blacks in Boston and Cleveland revealed that southern blacks in northern cities maintained stable, two-parent families supported by extended kin networks. . . . As in the case of white immigrants, the new historical research depicts a group of urban Americans who rejected passivity before powerful forces of change and who sought to shape their own lives despite pressures of the city, the factory, and the reality of white racism.

Urban Culture.   Some historians of the city have turned their attention to aspects of urban culture, to the popular institutions and ideas that shaped the way people thought and behaved. The best example of this genre of writing can be found in Gunther Barth's *City People: The Rise of Modern City Culture in Nineteenth-Century America* (1980). In this somewhat eclectic book, Barth contends that out of diversity and heterogeneity American urbanites created a modern city culture oriented around common institutions and forms. These common cultural patterns, he argues, helped Americans of vastly different backgrounds "cope with the complex demands of a strange cityscape." . . .

Other aspects of urban culture have been addressed, as well, by historians of the city. In an influential earlier study, *The Intellectual versus the City* (1962), Morton and Lucia White traced deep-seated patterns of antiurbanism among the American intelligentsia from the colonial era to mid-twentieth century. By contrast, Adrienne Siegel, in *The Image of the American City in Popular Literature, 1820–1870* (1981), demonstrated that widely read popular books, although perhaps not great literature, presented a positive, upbeat, even exciting picture of urban life. . . .

Research on the history of urban sports also has begun to fill in gaps in our knowledge of urban culture and the uses of leisure time. Baseball, in particular, was extremely popular in the city from the late nineteenth century, but other sporting and recreational activities also caught on. As sports historian Stephen Hardy has suggested in *How Boston Played* (1982), "The athletic germ that infected the country after the Civil War found its most fertile ground in cities." . . .

Another urban leisure institution—the saloon—has been investigated by recent urban historians. Serving many functions (social, political, and economic), the saloon became a ubiquitous urban institution. The most detailed recent study is Perry L. Duis's *The Saloon: Public Drinking in Chicago and Boston, 1880–1920* (1983), which details the multifaceted roles of these city watering holes, while contrasting their place in two very different cities. . . .

Federal-City Relations/Urban Public Policy.   As urban history has begun to focus on the twentieth century, the increasingly powerful role of the federal government in urban policymaking has come under study. Two books in the mid-1970s initiated research on this subject. Mark I. Gelfand's *A Nation of Cities: The Federal Government and Urban America, 1933–1965* (1975) and Philip Funigiello's *The Challenge to Urban Liberalism: Federal-City Relations during World War II* (1978). Both volumes demonstrated the hesitant effort of the federal government to grapple with urban issues during the economic disaster of the 1930s and the wartime emergency of the early 1940s. While government did embark on a range of new programs for relief, employment, and wartime planning—programs particularly welcomed in America's big cities—what is remarkable is the lack of any really national political commitment to the city. Indeed, governmental initiatives were usually undermined by the enduring strength of a localist tradition, the power of entrepreneurialism and privatism, and destructive competition among various interest groups for governmental favoritism.

Several more recent books have developed some of these themes. Roger W. Lotchin's edited collection, *The Martial Metropolis: U.S. Cities in War and Peace* (1984), explores the connection between federal military spending and urban development. In what is now referred to as the Lotchin thesis, the city and the sword are seen as inseparably linked in such cities as Norfolk, San Francisco, San Antonio, Los Angeles, Seattle, and Portland. . . .

Comparative Urban History. In the past decade, American urban historians have become much more aware of the international dimensions of urban history research. Some efforts at comparative urban research have proven fruitful, particularly geographer Brian J. L. Berry's *Comparative Urbanization: Divergent Paths in the Twentieth Century* (1981). Berry placed American urban patterns in the perspective of the larger forces reshaping the city in postwar Europe and Japan, and more recently the Third World. . . . [A]n enormous secondary literature has emerged on the history of cities throughout the world, making it possible for American urbanists to draw their own parallels with the urban experience of Canada, Australia, Great Britain, Europe, India, Latin America, Africa, and the Middle East. . . .

The Search for Synthesis. The foregoing general topics all represent important new thrusts of urban history research in the United States. With sufficient space, attention might have been given as well to new studies on women and gender relations in the city, to work on the visual dimension of the city, to biographical studies of urban movers and shakers like Robert Moses, to work on the city in American thought, to studies of urban architecture, crime, violence, and a dozen or more other subjects. This essay has concentrated on books and monographs, but the reader also should be aware of an enormous article literature on all of these subjects. The field, in short, has been livened and invigorated with a monumental amount of new research. . . .

※ *FURTHER READING*

Howard P. Chudacoff and Judith E. Smith, *The Evolution of American Urban Society,* 4th ed. (1993)

Kathleen N. Conzen, "Community Studies, Urban History, and American Local History," in Michael Kammen, ed., *The Past Before Us: Contemporary Historical Writings in the United States* (1980)

Michael H. Ebner, "Urban History: Retrospect and Prospect," *Journal of American History* 68 (June 1981), 69–84

Michael Frisch, "American Urban History as an Example of Recent Historiography," *History and Theory* 18 (1979), 350–377

Charles Glaab and A. Theodore Brown, *A History of Urban America,* 3d ed. (1983)

David R. Goldfield and Blaine A. Brownell, *Urban America: A History,* 2d ed. (1990)

Oscar Handlin and John Burchard, eds., *The Historian and the City* (1963)

Theodore Hershberg, ed., *Philadelphia: Work, Space, Family and Group Experience in the Nineteenth Century* (1984)

Eric Monkkonen, *America Becomes Urban: The Development of U.S. Cities and Towns, 1780–1980* (1988)

Arthur M. Schlesinger, *The Rise of the City, 1878–1898* (1933)

Leo F. Schnore, ed., *The New Urban History: Quantitative Explorations by American Historians* (1975)

Stephan Thernstrom and Richard Sennett, eds., *Nineteenth Century Cities: Essays in the New Urban History* (1969)

Richard Wade, "Urbanization," in C. Vann Woodward, ed., *The Comparative Approach to American History* (1968)

Sam Bass Warner, Jr., *The Urban Wilderness: A History of the American City* (1972)

CHAPTER 2

Urban Life
in Colonial America

✼

Although the native peoples who inhabited North America before the seventeenth century built important urban communities that exerted considerable influence over broad hinterlands, the various cities founded by European colonists on the Atlantic coast in the seventeenth and eighteenth centuries contained the most fertile seeds of American urban development. The European settlers were urban-minded people to whom civilization and city were equivalent. It was no accident, then, that they tried to transfer urban forms and urban culture from the Old World as soon as they reached the New. With their eye on profits from commerce and land speculation, the early settlers gave prime importance to their cities as places where goods and commu- nications were accumulated and distributed. The five largest colonial settlements— Boston, New York, Philadelphia, Newport, and Charleston—were "cities in the wil- derness," places that contained societies and an economic organization different from those of rural communities. Further, they spawned several secondary cities—Albany, Providence, Baltimore, and New Haven—that adopted similar characteristics. Just what those characteristics were and how they were reflected in urban organization form the themes of this chapter.

✼ *D O C U M E N T S*

These documents present several perspectives on city growth during the colonial era. The first selection, from an admirer of William Penn, the founder of Philadel- phia, was meant to advertise Philadelphia to Europeans in the 1690s; it therefore contains many exaggerations, including a vast overestimation of the city's popu- lation. Yet the account provides a telling glimpse of colonial Americans' expec- tations of their cities. The second document is a treatise in defense of slavery, but it also shows how some colonials viewed their society as organized according to rigid and unchangeable social ranks. The third document features entries from the diary of James Allen, a prominent Philadelphia attorney. Although much of the diary pertains to Allen's cautiously pro-American stance during the American

Revolution, the excerpts here illustrate the importance of face-to-face relationships in the colonial urban world. The fourth document, a statement from William
Penn, shows that the promise of profits from real-estate investment already was a
driving force behind American urbanization. The fifth document presents travel
notes of the Swedish observer Peter Kalm, who emphasizes here the commercial
ascendancy of New York City in the 1740s, a predominance that would help it
become the leading American port in the early nineteenth century. The final document shows the inner workings of a colonial urban government, that of Albany,
New York, in the 1750s. These excerpts from the town-council meetings provoke
questions about what exactly were the responsibilities of government in a
city's—and the nation's—formative stages.

Gabriel Thomas Promotes Early Philadelphia, 1698

[The region of Pennsylvania] remain'd with very little improvement till the year
1681, in which William Penn Esq; had the Country given him by King Charles
the Second, in lieu of Money that was due to (and signed Service done by) his
Father, Sir William Penn, and from him bore the Name of Pensilvania.

Since that time, the Industrious (nay Indefatigable) Inhabitants have built a
Noble and Beautiful City, and called it Philadelphia, which contains above two
thousand Homes, all Inhabited, and most of them Stately, and of Brick, generally
three Stories high, after the Mode in London, and as many several Families in
each. There are very many Lanes and Alleys, as first, Huttons-Lane, Morris-
Lane, Jones's-Lane, wherein are very good Buildings, Shorters-Alley, and
Flowers-Alley. All these Alleys and Lanes extend from the Front Street to the
Second Street. There is another Alley in the Second Street, called Carters-Alley.
There are also besides these Alleys and Lanes, several fine Squares and Courts
within this Magnificent City, (for so I may justly call it). As for the particular
Names of the several Streets contained therein, the Principal are as follows, *viz,*
Walnut-Street, Vine-Street, Mulberry-Street, Chestnut-Street, Sassafras-Street,
taking their Names from the abundance of those Trees that formerly grew there,
High-Street, Broad-Street, Delaware-Street, Front-Street, with several of less
Note, too tedious to insert here.

It hath in it Three Fairs every Year, and Two Markets every Week. They kill
above Twenty Fat Bullocks every Week, in the hottest time in Summer, for their
present spending in that City, besides many Sheep, Calves, and Hogs.

This City is Situated between Schoolkill-River and the great River Delaware,
which derives its Name from Captain Delaware, who came there pretty early:
Ships of Two or Three Hundred Tuns may come up to this City, by either of these
two Rivers. Moreover, in this Province are Four Great Market-Towns, *viz,* Chester, the German Town, New-Castle, and Lewis-Town, which are mightily Enlarged in this latter Improvement. Between these Towns, the Water-Men constantly Ply their Wherries [light boats]; likewise all those Towns have Fairs kept
in them, besides there are several Country Villages, *viz,* Dublin, Harford,
Merioneth, and Radnor in Cambry; all which Towns, Villages and Rivers took
their Names from the several Countries whence the present Inhabitants came.

The Air here is very delicate, pleasant, and wholesome; the Heavens serene,

Philadelphia, 1702

In 1862 William Penn planned this city to be laid out with a grid design between the Delaware and Schuylkill rivers. He originally intended that four small squares and one large square of open space be preserved for civic and religious purposes, but as this drawing shows, the need for buildings quickly upset Penn's scheme.

rarely overcast, bearing mighty resemblance to the better part of France; after Rain they have commonly a very clear Sky, the Climate is something Colder in the depth of Winter and Hotter in the height of Summer; (the cause of which is its being a Main Land or Continent; the Days also are two Hours longer in the shortest Day in Winter, and shorter by two Hours in the long Day of Summer) than here in England, which makes the Fruit so good, and the Earth so fertil. . . .

It is now time to return to the City of Brotherly-Love (for so much the Greek Word or Name Philadelphia imports) which though at present so obscure, that neither the Map-Makers nor Geographers have taken the least notice of her, tho she far exceeds her Namesake of Lydia [a town named Philadelphia was located in Lydia in Asia Minor] . . . yet in a very short space of time she will, in all probability, make a fine Figure in the World, and be a most Celebrated Emporium. Here is lately built a Noble Town-House or Guild-Hall, also a Handsom Market-House, and a convenient Prison. The Number of Christians both Old and Young Inhabiting in that Countrey, are by a Modest Computation, adjudged to amount to above Twenty Thousand.

The Laws of this Countrey, are the same with those in England; our Constitution being on the same Foot: Many Disputes or Differences are determined and composed by Arbitration; and all Causes are decided with great Care and Expedition, being concluded (generally) at furthest at the Second Court, unless they happen to be very Nice and Difficult Cases; under Forty Shillings any one Justice of the Peace has Power to Try the Cause. Thieves of all sorts, are oblig'd to restore four fold after they have been Whipt and Imprison'd, according to the Nature of their Crime; and if they be not of Ability to restore four fold, they must be in Servitude till 'tis satisfied. They have Curious Wharfs as also several large and fine Timber-Yards, both at Philadelphia, and New-Castle, especially at the Metropolis, before Robert Turner's Great and Famous House, where are built Ships of considerable Burthen; they Cart their Goods from that Wharf into the City of Philadelphia, under an Arch, over which part of the Street is built, which is called Chestnut-Street-Wharf, besides other Wharfs, as High-Street Wharf, Mulberry-Street Wharf, and Vine-Street Wharf, and all those are Common Wharfs; and likewise there are very pleasant Stairs, as Trus and Carpenter-Stairs, besides several others. There are above Thirty Carts belonging to that City, Four or Five Horses to each. There is likewise a very convenient Wharf called Carpenter's Wharf, which hath a fine necessary Crain belonging to it, with suitable Granaries, and Store-Houses. A Ship of Two Hundred Tun may load and unload by the side of it, and there are other Wharfs (with Magazines and Ware-houses) which front the City all along the River. . . . They have very Stately Oaks to build Ships with, some of which are between Fifty and Sixty Foot long, and clear from Knots, being very straight and well Grain'd. In this famous City of Philadelphia there are several Rope-Makers, who have large and curious Rope-Walks, especially one Joseph Wilcox. Also Three or Four Spacious Malt-Houses, as many large Brew-Houses, and many handsom Bake-Houses for Publick Use.

In the said City are several good Schools of Learning for Youth, in order to the Attainment of Arts and Sciences, as also Reading, Writing, etc. Here is to be had on any Day in the Week, Tarts, Pies, Cakes, etc. We have also several Cooks-Shops, both Roasting and Boyling, as in the City of London; Bread, Beer, Beef, and Pork are sold at any time much cheaper than in England (which arises from their Plenty) our Wheat is very white and clear from Tares, making as good and white Bread as any in Europe. Happy Blessings, for which we owe the highest Gratitude to our Plentiful Provider, the great Creator of Heaven and Earth. The Water-Mills far exceed those in England, both for quickness and grinding good Meal, their being great choice of good Timber, and earlier Corn than in the aforesaid Place, they are made by one Peter Deal, a Famous and Ingenious Workman, especially for inventing such like Machines.

All sorts of very good Paper are made in the German-Town; as also very fine German Linen, such as no Person of Quality need be asham'd to wear; and in several places they make very good Druggests, Crapes, Camblets, and Serges, besides other Woollen Cloathes, the Manufacture of all which daily improves: And in most parts of the Countey, there are many Curious and Spacious Buildings, which several of the Gentry have erected for their Country-Houses. As for the Fruit-Trees they Plant, they arrive at such Perfection, that they bear in a little more than half the time that they commonly do in England. . . .

What I have deliver'd concerning this Province, is indisputably true, I was an Eye-Witness to it all, for I went in the first Ship that was bound from England for that Country, since it received the Name of Pensilvania, which was in the Year 1681. The Ship's Name was the *John and Sarah* of London, Henry Smith Commander. I have declin'd giving any Account of several things which I have only heard others speak of, because I did not see them my self, for I never held that way infallible, to make Reports from Hear-say. I saw the first Cellar when I was digging it for the use of our Governor Will. Penn.

Observations on the Social Structure in Colonial Boston, 1701

That Honourable and Learned Gentleman, the Author of a Sheet, Entitled, *The Selling of Joseph, A Memorial,* seems from thence to draw this conclusion, that because the Sons of *Jacob* did very ill in Selling their Brother *Joseph* to the *Ishmaelites,* who were Heathen, therefore it is utterly unlawful to Buy and Sell Negroes, though among Christians; which conclusion I presume is not well drawn from the Premise, nor is the case parallel; for it was unlawful for the *Israelites* to Sell their Brethren upon any account, or pretence whatsoever during life. But it was not unlawful for the Seed of *Abraham* to have Bond men, and Bond women, either born in their House, or bought with their Money, as it is written of *Abraham, Gen.* 14.14. & 21.10. & *Exod.* 21.16. & *Levit.* 25.44, 45, 46 *v.* After the giving of the Law: And in *Josh.* 9.29. That famous Example of the *Gideonite* is a sufficient proof were there no other.

To speak a little to the Gentleman's first Assertion: *That none ought to part with their Liberty themselves, or deprive others of it but upon mature consideration;* a prudent exception, in which he grants, that upon some consideration a man may be deprived of his Liberty. And then presently in his next Position or Assertion he denies it, *viz. It is most certain, that all men as they are the Sons of Adam are brothers, and have equal right to Liberty, and all other Comforts of Life,* which he would prove out of *Psal.* 115.16. *The Earth hath he given to the Children of men.* True, but what is this to the purpose, to prove that all men have equal right to Liberty, and all outward comforts of this life; which Position seems to invert the Order that God hath set in the World, who hath Ordained different degrees and orders of men, some to be High and Honourable, some to be Low and Despicable; some to be Monarchs, Kings, Princes and Governors, Masters and Commanders, others to be Subjects, and to be Commanded; Servants of sundry sorts and degrees, bound to obey; yes some to be born Slaves, and so to remain during their lives, as hath been proved. Otherwise there would be a near parity among men, contrary to that of the Apostles, 1 *Cor.* 12. from the 13. to the 24 *verse,* where he sets forth (by way of comparison) the different sorts and offices of the Members of the Body, indicating that they are all of use, but not equal, and of like dignity. So God hath set different Orders and Degrees of men in the World, both in Church and Common weal. Now if this Position of parity should be true, it would then follow that the ordinary Course of Divine Providence of God in the World should be wrong, and unjust (which we must not dare to think, much less to affirm) and all the sacred Rules, Precepts and Commands of the Almighty which he hath given the Sons of men to observe and keep in their respective Places, Orders and Degrees, would be to no purpose; which unaccountably derogate from this Divine Wisdom of the most High, who hath made nothing in vain, but hath Holy Ends in all his Dispensations to the Children of men.

. . . We grant it for a certain and undeniable verity, That all Mankind are the

Sons and Daughters of *Adam,* and the Creatures of God; But it doth not therefore follow that we are bound to love and respect all men alike; this under favor we must take leave to deny; we ought in charity, if we see our Neighbour in want, to relieve them in a regular way, but we are not bound to give them so much of our Estates, as to make them equal with ourselves, because they are our Brethren, the Sons of *Adam,* no not our own natural Kinsmen: We are Exhorted *to do good unto all, but especially to them who are of the Household of Faith, Gal.* 6.10. And we are to love, honor and respect all men according to the gift of God that is in them: I may love my Servant well, but my Son better; Charity begins at home, it would be a violation of common prudence, and a breach of good manners, to treat a Prince like a Peasant. And this worthy Gentleman would deem himself much neglected, if we should show him no more Deference than to an ordinary Porter: And therefore these florid expressions, the Sons and Daughters of the First *Adam,* the Brothers and Sisters of the Second *Adam,* and the Offspring of God, seem to be misapplied to import and insinuate, that we ought to tender Pagan Negroes with all love, kindness, and equal respect as to the best of men. . . .

Attorney James Allen Views Life in Eighteenth-Century Philadelphia (1770–1775), 1885

November 6th, 1770.   I have often thought that committing to writing little occurrences in private matters might in some future period of life afford amusement in the perusal, & have frequently regretted, my inability of recalling to mind many past scenes of my earlier days. To run over the employments of times past with the catalogue of former acquaintance, thro' all their changes, must be an high gratification. These reflections have led me into the design of keeping a Diary, in which I do not propose to admit any occurrences of a publick nature; I shall leave those to Gazettes & Magazines, and only preserve the remembrance of such private interesting scenes & conversations as will be entertaining in a review. And I will take special care, not to make my Diary a register of such things as ought to be forgotten, or can possibly do an injury to any one; & on this principle neither the follies or vices of any one shall find admission here. . . .

Sept. 13th, 1771.   Lord Dunmore passed thro' this town on his way to Virginia; I dined & supped with him. This day I set off for Trent hall with my Wife and child and Mrs Lawrence; they have not been there since I finished my house.

   Tho' I have advanced so little ways in my diary I find the fatigue and trouble of keeping it regularly too great & makes too great a waste of time; & am apprehensive it will fall thro', or at least grow irregular.

May 29th, 1772.   I am now convinced that I shall not be able to continue this journal; finding my business will not admit of so much leisure as a journalist should have. This day I moved into my house in Chestnut Street, where I hope to end my days. I am at present much engaged in prosecutions for breaches of the laws of Trade & have libelled four of five Vessels & Cargoes for Capt Talbot of the Lively Man of War. I am doing, as a Lawyer what I would not do as a politician; being fully persuaded of the oppressive nature of those laws. I have however refused to prosecute two or 3 persons on the penal clauses, as thinking it invidious & rigid.

May 19th, 1773. ... Governor Eden & Coll. Washington are in Town come to the races. Waters's horse Herod won the £100 yesterday & Mr Delancey's Sultan £50 today. The town is very gay & invitations frequent. I asked Gov. Eden & Coll. Washington to dinner but they are engaged during their stay. ...

Oct. 19th, 1773. Yesterday morning about 5 o'clock as I lay in Bed I felt a severe pain in my instep & on getting up found that the sinew was strained. As I had received no injury to my foot from any external cause & was not sensible of having a fit of the Cramp my friends pronounced it a gouty symptom. I continued in great pain for 4 to 5 hours but towards evening the sinew recovered its Tone. This morning I am lame with a pain under the Instep in the bottom of the foot resembling a strain also. I make this Memorandum, that if I should ever be afflicted with the Gout, I may date it from this Period. NB I eat no supper & have been very sparing in that Article for a long time.

Octob. 30th, 1773. ... I often reflect how happy it was for me that I took to the practice of the law. Added to the uneasiness that it gave my father & all my friends to find that after having served a regular clerkship & been three years at the temple, I should continue an Idel man I say added to this consideration I have now made myself easy in my circumstances. I compute my business this year 1773 will be between £3(00) & 400, which added to my estate will fall but little short of £:8(00)–1000 (per) annum. For these last two or three years, which is the time that I resumed the practice of the Law, I have read pretty diligently & have overcome the difficulty of speaking in publick. In short both the study & practice are become agreeable to me. ...

Jany. 19th, 1775. ... The variance subsisting between Mr Masters's family & mine is like to be healed, as the Ladies, (who have on all sides been uneasy, lent from a fatality attending female differences, can never make mutual advances) have by consent met together at Mr Lawrences & when my wife returns from New-York she will visit them. I have ever had an abhorrence of family quarrells & am convinced that good Temper & civility will make friends & carry a man peaceably thro' the world without any unworthy condescension.

Mrs Allen has now been absent 3 weeks on a Journey to New York with the Governor & Mrs Penn, & is expected home this Evening. It is the first excursion she has made since her marriage. ...

October 11th, 1775. Johnny Mifflin came this day to study law with me.

About 2 Months ago I heard Mr Hamilton say that he formerly knew every person white & black men women, & children, in the City of Philadelphia, by name.

Oct. 14th, 1775. Yesterday the Gridiron Grove Club gave an entertainment in their usual frugal style to 23 Ladies; we dined till 10 o'clock & were very chearful; I was in remarkable good spirits; Miss Sally Robinson bore the belle; she is a very fine woman both in person and understanding. . . .

William Penn on the Promise of Real-Estate Investment, c. 1687

II.   Philadelphia, and our intended Metropolis, as I formerly Writ, is two Miles long, and a Mile broad, and at each end it lies that mile upon a Navigable River. The situation high and dry, yet replenished with running streams. Besides the High Street, that runs in the middle from River to River, and is an hundred foot broad, it has Eight streets more that run the same course, the least of which is fifty foot in breadth. And besides Broad Street, wich crosseth the Town in the middle, and is also an hundred foot wide, there are twenty streets more, that run the same course, and are also fifty foot broad. The names of those Streets are mostly taken from the things that Spontaneously grow in the Country, As Vine Street, Mulberry Street, Chestnut Street, Wallnut Street, Strawberry Street, Cranberry Street, Plumb Street, Oake Street, Beach Street, Ash Street, Poplar Street, Sassafras Street, and the like.

III.   I mentioned in my last Account that from my Arrival, in Eighty-Two, to the Date thereof, being ten Moneths, we had got up Fourscore Houses at our Town, and that some Villages were settled about it. From that time to my coming away, which was a Year within a few Weeks, the Town advanced to Three hundred and fifty-seven Houses; divers of them large, well built, with good Cellars, three stories, and some with Balconies.

IV.   There is also a fair key [wharf] of about three hundred foot square, Built by Samuel Carpenter, to which a ship of five hundred Tuns may lay her broadside, and others intend to follow his example. We have also a Ropewalk made by B. Wilcox, and cordage for shipping already spun at it.

V.   There inhabits most sorts of useful Tradesmen, As Carpenters, Joyners, Bricklayers, Masons, Plasterers, Plumers, Smiths, Glasiers, Taylers, Shoemakers, Butchers, Bakers, Brewers, Glovers, Tanners, Felmongers, Wheelrights, Millrights, Shiprights, Boatrights, Ropemakers, Saylmakers, Blockmakers, Turners, etc.

VI.   There are Two Markets every Week, and Two Fairs every year. . . .

IX.   After nine at Night the Officers go the Rounds, and no Person, without very good cause, suffered to be at any Publick House that is not a Lodger. . . .

XIV.   The Improvement of the place is best measur'd by the advance of Value upon every man's Lot. I will venture to say that the worst Lot in the Town, without any Improvement upon it, is worth four times more than it was when it was lay'd out, and the best forty. . . .

Swedish Traveler Peter Kalm Considers New York in the 1740s

New York probably carries on a more extensive commerce than any town in the English North American provinces, at least it may be said to equal them. Boston and Philadelphia however come very close to it. The trade of New York extends to many places, and it is said they send more ships from there to London than they do from Philadelphia. They export to that capital all the various sorts of skins which they buy of the Indians, sugar, logwood, and other dyeing woods, rum, mahogany, and many other goods which are the produce of the West Indies, together with all the specie which they get in the course of trade. Every year several ships are built here, which are sent to London and there sold; and of late years a quantity of iron has been shipped to England. In return for all these, cloth is imported from London and so is every article of English growth or manufacture, together with all sorts of foreign goods. England, and especially London, profits immensely by its trade with the American colonies; for not only New York but likewise all the other English towns on the continent import so many articles from England that all their specie, together with the goods which they get in other countries must all go to Old England to pay their accounts there, for which they are, however, insufficient. Hence it appears how much a well regulated colony contributes to the increase and welfare of its mother country.

New York sends many ships to the West Indies with flour, grain, biscuit, timber, tuns, boards, meat and pork, butter, and other provisions, together with some of the few fruits that grow here. Many ships go to Boston in New England with grain and flour, and take in exchange, meat, butter, timber, different sorts of fish, and other articles, which they carry further to the West Indies. They now and then carry rum from Boston, which is distilled there in great quantities, and sell it here at a considerable advantage. Sometimes they send vessels with goods from New York to Philadelphia; and at other times they are sent from Philadelphia to New York, which is only done, as appears from the gazettes, because certain articles are cheaper at one place than at the other. They send ships to Ireland every year, laden with all kinds of West India goods, but especially with linseed, which is collected in this country. . . .

For the goods which are sold in the West Indies either ready money is accepted or West India goods, which are either first brought to New York or immediately sent to England or Holland. If a ship does not choose to take West India goods on its return to New York, or if nobody will freight it, it often goes to Newcastle in England to take on coal for ballast, which when brought home sells for a pretty good price. In many parts of the town coal is used both for kitchen fires and in other rooms, because it is considered cheaper than wood, which at present costs thirty shillings of New York currency per fathom, of which measure I have before made mention. New York has likewise some trade with South

Carolina, to which it sends grain, flour, sugar, rum, and other goods, and takes rice in return, which is almost the only commodity exported from South Carolina. . . .

The country people come to market in New York twice a week, much in the same manner as they do at Philadelphia, with this difference, that the markets are here kept in several places, and one has to go from one to another sometimes to get what one needs. . . .

The Albany City Council at Work, c. 1701–1702

Nov. 11 (1701). Ms. Johannis Lydius minister, Anthony van Schaick and Hendk. van Rensselaer elders, in the behalfe of the Church Wardens of the Reformed Netherdutch Congregation of Albany, doo appear and verbally actt forth how that in Collecting of money for the Minsters Sallary severall of said Congregation do refuse to contribute any more thereto, alleadgeing that they have no settled place in the Church to sett on and hear the word of God.

Doe therefore Request that the Mayor, Aldermen and Commonality will be pleased to permit them to appoint persones to goe round by the Inhabitants of this Citty and others in the County belonging to said Congregation, to see what money can be voluntarily procured for the enlargeing of said Church for the more accommodation. . . .

The Mayor, Aldermen and Commonality have appointed the following persones as fyre masters of the Citty for the ensueing year, viz: Ryer Gerritse, Thomas Williams, Abraham Kip, Elbert Gerritse, Thomas Harmense, and Gerrit Ryckse, who are once in each three weeks till the 14th of October next ensueing, to goe rounde with the assistance of one or more Constables, and vew each house or room where fyre is held, and wherever a Chimney shall be founde too foul or fyre keep in unconvenient places, to cause the same to be removed the owner paying as a fyne, 3s. for the behoofe of the fyre masters. . . .

It is concluded that a proclamation be made that no person shall sell strong Liquor by Retaile without Lycence, upon paine and penalty of forfeiting the summe of £5, according to act of assembly.

As also, that the fyre ladders and hooks be laid by the Church, and whosoever as shall presume to use the same, unless in distress of fyre, shall forfeit the summe of 3s. as often as they shall be used, for the Behoofe of the Sheriffe, who is to take care of the same. . . .

Att a Common Councill held in the Citty Hall of Albany the 15th December, 1701.

Mr. Mayor proposes desyring the opinion of the Commonality if it is not requisite to issue a warrant to the assessors to make an assessment for as many stockades as will require to fortifye the Citty with the new stockades sett up this summer. The Commonality are of opinion that it may be referred till the post arrives from New Yorke, which will be about new years day, alleadgeing that perhaps wee may receive assured news of the continuation of peace, when it will not so necessarily require so great a reparation in one winter. . . .

Albany, the 21st of Feb. 1702.

A Proclamation proclaimed that all persons within this Citty and County doe cause there weights and measures be adjusted by Coenraet ten Eyck, in the space of six months, upon pain of forfeiting the sum of sixty shillings; and whoever as shall send bags to the mill with Corn without the owners mark forfeits the bags for the behoofe of the . . . sheriffe; . . .

Att a Meeting of the Mayor, Aldermen and Common Council in Albany, the 31st of March, 1702.

It is Resolved that a Proclamation be made to Ring the hogs belonging to this Citty, in there noses, in the space of thrice 24 hours, upon penalty of forfeiting the same, as also that each Inhabitant doe remove there fyre wood from the streets, and to lay the timber wood together, before the first of May next ensueing, upon penalty of forfeiting for each day after primo May not so removed, the summe of three shillings, and that the Constables be not neglecting by turns to goe round and see that the Sabbath day be not Broak, which proclamation is accordingly proclaimed. . . .

Att a Mayor's Court held in the Citty Hall of Albany, the 18th of August, 1702.

Upon the request of Coll. Peter Schuyler in the behalfe of his Mother, Mrs. Margaret Schuyler, on the 16th instant a warrant was issued to the Sheriffe to fetch the negroe Tam, belonging to Claes van Bockhorne, who is accused to have received severall goods and money from the two negroe women of said Mrs. Schuyler, who have taken the same from her, whereupon the said negroe Tam appears here, and being examined confesses to have received money from the said negroe woman, but hath sometime thereafter delivered the same to the negro of Johannis Beckman, the Court are thereof of opinion, since he hath returned said money that he or his master shall be pay the Charges fallen thereon, in the meantime the said negroe shall remain the custody of the Sheriffe till such time he hath received satisfaction. . . .

Sept. 2 (1702). Ordered that the Following Proclamation be Proclaimed, viz: By Authority Aforesaid, and Justices of the County.

Whereas wee are sencible of the dayly visitations of Almighty God to our neighbours of New Yorke, with great sicknesse and sudden death, altho lesse punishment than they or wee have deserved, yet not to withstand the hand of Almighty, but as much as in us lyes to shun any ill distemper, wee, the Mayor, Recorder, Aldermen, and Commonality, and Justices, doe hereby Publish and Prohibite that no Person or Personnes, either with Sloop, Boat, Canoe or other Vessell, shall from hence depart to New Yorke, except it be an Expresse, and that no person or persons shall in like manner, on any other way, come from New Yorke to this Citty, nearer than the Island called Bearen Island, twelve miles to the south of this Citty, and there to remain till further order from us, and also that no (woolen) goods be landed from the sloop or vessell of Peter Bogardus late arrived, or any other vessells that arrives, as they will answer to the contrary on there outmost peril. . . .

✳ E S S A Y S

These essays present different perspectives on colonial-era urban communities. The first, by Gary B. Nash of the University of California, Los Angeles, is taken from *The Urban Crucible* (1979), an important book on how cities developed and eventually contributed to the American Revolution. This excerpt includes an especially comprehensive analysis of the commercial foci of the cities, their complex social composition, and the importance of the social hierarchy that influenced social relations. The second essay, by Ira Berlin of the University of Maryland, offers a unique vantage on the black communities in colonial cities in terms of social and economic issues, particularly the "Africanization" of such communities.

The Web of Seaport Life, 1600–1700*

GARY B. NASH

Water dominated the life of America's northern seaport towns in the seventeenth century, dictating their physical arrangement, providing them with their links to the outer world, yielding up much of their sustenance, and subtly affecting the relationships among the different groups who made up these budding commercial capitals. Boston was almost entirely surrounded by water. Built on a tadpole-shaped peninsula that jutted into island-dotted Massachusetts Bay, the town was connected to the mainland only by the mile-long causeway called the Neck. New York was literally an island, set in perhaps the finest natural harbor on the continent and separated from its hinterland by the East and Hudson rivers. At a time when steel bridge construction was still more than a century away, it was accessible only by ferry, barge, or small wind-propelled craft. Philadelphia was almost one hundred miles from the sea, but it was planted on a broad strip of land between the Schuylkill and Delaware rivers—the latter providing its access to the ocean.

The colonial seaports existed primarily as crossroads of maritime transport and commercial interchange. European cities had often grown up as centers of civil and ecclesiastical administration and by the early nineteenth century they would expand greatly as centers of industrial production. But Boston, New York, and Philadelphia served primarily as points of entry for immigrating Europeans and Africans and as commercial marts serving hinterland populations. The ocean was the highway connecting the Old World and the New, and the seaport towns were the vital link between the two. They gathered in the timber, fish, and agricultural produce that came from the rural settlers who made up the vast majority of the colonial population, sending it off to West Indian and European markets and distributing finished European goods throughout the regions they served.

At the end of the seventeenth century the seaport towns were really only

---

*For permission to photocopy this selection, please contact Harvard University Press. Reprinted by permission of the publishers from *The Urban Crucible: Social Change, Political Consciousness, and the Origins of the American Revolution* by Gary B. Nash, excerpts from pp. 3–25, Cambridge, Mass.: Harvard University Press. Copyright © 1979 by the President and Fellows of Harvard College.

overgrown villages. Boston was the largest. Growing slowly for six decades after the Great Migration of English Puritans in 1630, it reached a population of about 6,000 by 1690. New York, founded five years before Boston by the Dutch West India Company and known as New Amsterdam until conquered by the English in 1664, increased only to 3,500 by 1674 and to about 4,500 by 1690. Philadelphia, not planted until 1681, when William Penn received an immense grant from Charles II and promoted a movement of English and Irish Quakers across the Atlantic, was still in its infancy at the turn of the century, counting only about 2,200 inhabitants. None of the American port towns could compare with even the secondary commercial centers of western Europe such as Lyon, which had reached 45,000 in the 1530s, or Norwich, which had grown to 19,000 by the 1570s. Nor could they claim equal status with the cities of the Spanish and Portuguese colonies to the south, where Bahia, Cartagena, Potosi, and Mexico City, built on the ruins of ancient Indian urban centers, numbered 50,000 or more by the end of the seventeenth century.

The insignificant size of these seaports in British North America did not indicate English backwardness or a preference for the pastoral, agricultural life. The port towns were small because they served regional populations that themselves were still very limited. The population of Massachusetts had not yet reached 50,000 in 1690, so it is not surprising that Boston counted only 6,000 souls. Similarly, New York and Philadelphia served agricultural populations that had grown to no more than 14,000 and 12,000 respectively.

The reduced scale of life in these late seventeenth-century ports made face-to-face relationships important. Craftsmen did not produce for anonymous customers or distant markets but labored almost entirely at turning out "bespoke goods"—articles made to order for individual customers. Nor would anybody long be a stranger in a town whose boundaries could be traversed on foot in a brisk thirty-minute walk. Bostonians did not spread out across their peninsula but crowded together between Beacon Hill, Copp's Hill, and Fort Hill along the southeastern shore that faced the harbor. New Yorkers did not range across the island of Manhattan but squeezed together at its southern tip, in the area known today as Wall Street. Philadelphia, where as late as 1750 the skyline was unbroken by a single building of more than three stories, covered a tract of about 1,200 acres. But its inhabitants chose their building sites along a one-mile stretch of Delaware River frontage, penetrating inland from the rivers no more than three blocks in the first quarter-century of settlement. Proximity to the harbor and wharves was on everyone's mind. A byproduct of this mode of settlement, in what urban historians call "walking cities," was a mixing of classes, occupations, religious beliefs, and ethnic backgrounds in the early years. . . .

In probing the social dynamics of the early towns, it is essential to recognize that these were preindustrial societies in which tradition held sway. Little about the late seventeenth-century towns would be recognizable to the twentieth-century urbanite. Cows were commonly tethered behind the crudely built wooden houses, for milk was a commodity that most householders could not afford to purchase. Hogs roamed the streets because, as scavengers of refuse, they were the chief sanitary engineers in an age when most household wastes were emptied into ditches running down the middle of the streets. Indian shell beads, called wampum, were still in use as a medium of exchange in New York at the end of the seventeenth century, and paper money was as yet unknown except in Boston where it made its first appearance in 1690. There were no newspapers printed in the colonies before 1704, when the *Boston News-Letter* was first published. Philadelphians would wait until 1719 to see a newspaper in their city and New Yorkers until 1725. Lawyers, another fixture of the modern city, were everywhere regarded with suspicion, and the few who practiced in the late seventeenth century were largely untrained, unorganized, and little respected. . . .

We must consider the values that lay behind human behavior in the context of these premodern aspects of urban life. Superstition and belief in the supernatural were widespread, for though urban dwellers might be more worldly than their country cousins, they were still bound within an inherited mental framework that had been formed by the precariousness of life and the incomprehensibility of nature. The seaport towns were not traumatized in 1690 by the witchcraft hysteria that shook Salem, Boston's neighbor, but most town dwellers believed that witches were truly abroad in Salem. Witches were as real as the devil, and witchcraft was a crime "as definite and tangible as is treason today." As late as 1727 an earthquake that shook most of New England was interpreted by the lettered and unlettered alike as evidence of God's displeasure with his people in this corner of the earth. . . .

Another part of the value system was the prevailing orientation toward the proper arrangement and functioning of society. . . . Virtually everyone of wealth or position in the port towns adhered to the axiom that rank and status must be carefully preserved and social roles clearly differentiated if society was to retain its equilibrium. This was a cast of thought inherited from the Old World, although some colonizers recognized that a new environment might call for alterations. Social stability was uppermost in the minds of most of these leaders, and they believed that nothing counted for more in its achievement than a careful demarcation of status and privilege. John Winthrop, the leader of the Puritan occupation of Massachusetts Bay, echoed ancient thinking that social unity and political stability were the products of a hierarchical social system that preserved distances between occupational groups and limited movement between them. "In all times," he wrote, "some must be rich, some poor, some highe and eminent in power and dignitie, others meane and in subjecion." Winthrop's conception of the carefully layered society where mobility was limited was perpetuated in Boston by a long line of Puritan clergymen who exhorted their auditors in this vein for many decades to come. . . .

In New York and Philadelphia it was much the same. The religious impulse that reverberated so powerfully in Boston was more subdued in the Manhattan port, the least utopian of the northern capitals, but it was widely believed by those at the apex of the social pyramid that all men, by God's design, were created unequal. In Pennsylvania, also, the "holy experiment" was thought by its founder to depend for success on orderly patterns of taking up land, economic regulation, and firm lines of authority. . . .

This perpetuation of social hierarchy can be seen in many of the conventions of urban life at the end of the seventeenth century. Puritans did not file into church on Sunday morning and occupy the pews in random fashion. Each was assigned a seat according to his or her rank in the community. "Dooming the seats" was the responsibility of a church committee that used every available yardstick of social status—age, parentage, social position, service to the community, and wealth—in drawing up a seating plan for the congregation. In New York, whipping, the most common punishment meted out by the courts for minor offenses, was not permitted for men of rank, though the stripping away of the right to use "Mister" before one's name, or "Gentleman" after it, may have been more painful than the lash. In their dress, speech, manners, and even the food on their tables, urban dwellers proclaimed their place in the social order.

While this replication of traditional European social attitudes regarding the structuring of society was widespread, and even regarded by many as God-ordained, it was not universally accepted; nor was it unaffected by the environment of the New World. Those already in positions of authority or possessed of economic advantage were the principal proponents of a paternalistic system that steadfastly advocated social gradations and subordination, for they, after all, were the chief beneficiaries of such an arrangement. Those below them in the social order were often less eager merely to recreate the past in the new land. As early as 1651 in Massachusetts the magistrates of the General Court expressed their "utter detestation and dislike that men and women of meane Condition should take upon themselves the garb of Gentlemen by wearing gold or silver, lace or buttons, or points at their knees or to walk in bootes or women of the same rancke to weare silk or tiffany horlles or scarfes, which though allowable to persons of greater estate, or more liberal education, yet we cannot but judge it intollerable in persons of like condition." Here was a signal that many early Bostonians not only were able to improve their condition but also intended to use their newfound prosperity to enhance their wardrobes, thereby upgrading their class identification, of which clothes were a primary badge. Such upward striving might have been expected, for the immigrants who settled the early towns were generally recruited from the middling ranks of English society and had been drawn to the western edge of the Atlantic because they were motivated, among other things, by a desire to better themselves economically. The impressive quantity of late seventeenth-century jeremiads concerning the need for order and discipline in Massachusetts is one more indication that many colonists, especially those not at the top of the social pyramid, found the old hierarchical code out of place and out of time.

To what extent hierarchical thinking pervaded the upper ranks of seaport society and to what degree it was resisted from below cannot be measured quantitatively. It is safe to say, however, that although almost every urban dweller knew instinctively his or her relation to those below and above, there was much crossing of lines between social layers and, even by the 1690s, a long history of un-deferential behavior among plebeian sorts. We employ the term deference to describe the unquestioning acceptance of the superior wisdom of an elite by the broad mass of people. It is easy, however, to overstate the operation of a well-oiled set of relationships between superiors and inferiors, and the unresentful acceptance of them as natural. Many urban people deferred because their economic security was bound up with a landlord, employer, or creditor. This was economic clientage, and it doubtlessly produced social deference. But the obliging comment and passive demeanor of a journeyman carpenter or merchant seaman could melt away in moments of passion or collective action and often did not extend at all to other powerful figures whose control was less direct. Many vertical links bound urban society together and inhibited the formation of solidarities that were horizontal in nature. But these interrank bonds forged by vertical loyalty and obligations were by no means all-encompassing or unchanging. Time and circumstances altered social consciousness, wore away at deferential behavior, and gave rise to feelings of solidarity that were based on occupation, economic position, and class standing.

Closely tied to attitudes about the structural arrangement of society was the urban dweller's sense of whether his or her community functioned equitably. The important gap to measure is the one between aspiration and achievement. We must tread carefully in approaching this question, for twentieth-century concepts of mobility and contemporary expectations of success will help us little in studying preindustrial people. The rise from rags to riches cannot be taken as a universal expectation.

In the late seventeenth century the limits of possibility had not yet been raised very high in the minds of most urban dwellers. Few Scots-Irish or German immigrants in Philadelphia, Dutch residents of New York, or English inhabitants of Boston dreamed of becoming wealthy merchants or country gentlemen. Nor did they regard themselves as "blocked" if they, or even their sons, could not make it to the top. They were coming from a society where intergenerational movement was almost imperceptible, where sons unquestioningly followed their father's trades, where the Protestant work ethic did not beat resoundingly in every breast, and where security from want, rather than the acquisition of riches, was the primary goal. It was modest opportunity (access to sufficient capital, land, and labor to produce material well-being) rather than rapid mobility (social ascendancy at the expense of others) that was most important in their calculations of whether equity prevailed in their society.

Much of the urban laboring man's sense of what was possible was shaped by the distinctly premodern nature of economic life in the port towns. Routinized, repetitive labor and the standardized work day, regulated by the clock, were unknown in this preindustrial era. Even the Protestant work ethic could not change irregular work patterns, for they were dictated by weather, hours of daylight, and the erratic delivery of raw materials. When the cost of fuel for artificial light was greater than the extra income that could be derived from laboring before or after sunlight hours, who would not shorten his day during winter? Similarly, when winter descended, business often ground to a halt. Even in the southernmost of the northern ports, ice frequently blocked maritime traffic. In the winter of 1728–29, 36 ships lay frozen at dockside in Philadelphia; several decades later a visitor counted 117 ships icebound in the Delaware. This meant slack time for mariners and dockworkers, just as laborers engaged in well digging, road building, and cellar excavating for house construction were idled by frozen ground. The hurricane season in the West Indies forced another slowdown because few shipowners were willing to place their ships and cargoes before the killer winds that prevailed in the Caribbean from August to October. If prolonged rain delayed the slaughter of cows in the country or made impassable the rutted roads into the city, then the tanner laid his tools aside and for lack of his deliveries the cordwainer was also idle. The hatter was dependent upon the supply of beaver skins, which could stop abruptly if disease struck an Indian tribe or war disrupted the fur trade. Weather, disease, and equinoxial cycles all contributed to the fitful pace of urban labor—

and therefore to the difficulties of producing a steady income. Food and housing cost money every day of the year, but in calculating his income the urban dweller had to count on many "broken days," slack spells, and dull seasons. . . .

From attitudes and aspirations we must turn to the actual structure of the late seventeenth-century port towns and reach some understanding of how they differed from the European commercial centers that the urban colonists had left behind.

At the bottom of the social hierarchy were black slaves. The common view that slavery in colonial America was overwhelmingly a southern plantation phenomenon must be modified, for slavery took root early in the northern port towns and persisted there throughout the colonial period. By 1690, in fact, slaves represented as large a proportion of the northern urban populations as they did in tobacco-growing Maryland and Virginia. Boston was only eighty years old, a town with fewer than 1,500 inhabitants, when it began its connection with the "peculiar institution." Victorious in a war of extermination against the Pequot Indians, Massachusetts shipped several hundred captive Pequot women and children to the West Indies, where they were exchanged for African slaves. A few years later, in 1645, the brother-in-law of John Winthrop counseled war against another Indian tribe, the Narragansetts, and argued "if upon a Just warre the Lord should deliver them [the Narragansetts] into our hands, wee might easily have men, women, and children enough to exchange for Moores, which wilbe more gaynefull pilladge for us than wee conceive, for I doe not see how wee can thrive untill wee gett into a stock of slaves sufficient to doe all our business, . . . [for] I suppose you know verie well how wee shall mainteyne 20 Moores cheaper than one Englishe servant." . . .

While the roots of slavery slowly penetrated the soil of Boston, they sank faster and deeper into that of New York. Boston's initiation to black slavery had been indirect, coming as a result of the enslavement of Indians; New York's introduction stemmed directly from the extensive early Dutch participation in the international slave trade to West Africa. Dutch New Netherlands traded extensively with Dutch Curaçao, a sugar island off the coast of South America that produced a steady stream of "unworkable" slaves who were consequently transported for nonplantation labor to the mainland colony. In the last five years before the English takeover of New Netherlands, more than 400 slaves entered its capital city. The English, in capturing New Amsterdam in 1664, were seizing a city whose population was 20 percent black, about four times the incidence of blacks in Virginia and Maryland at this time. The English imported fewer Africans than the Dutch but they made no attempt to phase out slave labor. By 1698, when the first English census was conducted in the city, Negroes represented more than 14 percent of the population. Even more indicative of the extent to which the master-slave relationship was incorporated into the social structure was the number of slaveholding families in the society. In 1698, almost 35 percent of the heads of household owned slaves and five years later the percentage had increased to 41. . . .

In Philadelphia slavery also found its place from the beginning, although most historical accounts leave the impression that the institution was incidental to the city's development. The spirit of Quaker abolitionism was still a half century away when the earliest settlers gladly received a shipload of African slaves, who arrived only three years after the Delaware River capital had been established. Quaker settlers, engaged in the difficult work of clearing trees and brush and erecting crude houses eagerly exhausted most of the specie brought from England to purchase Africans. Extant inventories of estate indicate that about one of every fifteen families owned slaves in the last decade of the seventeenth century—a rate understandably below that of New York and Boston since Philadelphia was in its infancy and had not yet generated sufficient capital for the importation of large numbers of involuntary servants.

Above slaves in the urban social structure were indentured servants. Trading four to seven years of their labor for passage across the Atlantic and sold at dockside to the highest bidder, they were circumscribed so thoroughly by the law that most rights regarded as basic to the English heritage were held in abeyance until their terms of service were up. They formed an important part of the labor force in New York and Philadelphia but not in Boston. Urban indentured servitude was never so debilitating and exploitative as in the early Chesapeake tobacco colonies, where most servants did not survive to breathe the air of freedom they sought, and only a few of those who completed their indentures matched legal freedom with freedom from want. Yet it is evident from the considerable number of suicides and the great number of runaways that the life of the servant-immigrant, who was typically between thirteen and twenty years old, was frequently miserable and often unbearable. . . .

Above slaves and indentured servants—bound laborers who occupied a kind of subbasement of society from which ascent into the main house was difficult or impossible—stood apprentices and hired servants. Apprentices were servants too, but they differed from indentured servants in serving in the locale where they were born, usually in a family known to their parents, and contracting out to another familial setting by consent of their parents or guardians. They were rarely bought and sold, as were indentured servants. Especially in Boston the apprentice system bolstered familial forms by training up the young in the families of friends and acquaintances who were usually coreligionists. In all the port towns the principal purpose of apprenticing was the same as it had been for generations in England—to educate the youth in the "arts and mysteries" of the various crafts, thus providing an adequate pool of skilled labor.

Free unskilled laborers occupied the next rank of society. In the preindustrial era they performed the essential raw labor associated with construction and shipping. Along the waterfront, they loaded and unloaded the ships and manned the vessels that provided the lifelines between the seaports of North America and the world beyond. Each of the northern port towns, even in the early stages of development, had hundreds of such laborers. They are perhaps the most elusive social group in early American history because they moved from port to port with far greater frequency than other urban dwellers, shifted occupations, died young, and, as the poorest members of the free white community, least often left behind traces of their lives on the tax lists or in land and probate records. Grouped with them in social status were common laborers who stayed on land. In the port towns, where house, wharf, road, and bridge construction was a major enterprise throughout the colonial years, they were the diggers of basement and wells, the pavers of streets, the cutters and haulers of wood, and the carters of everything that needed moving. It is difficult to assess how large a proportion of the working force they represented, but of the 304 estates inventoried in Boston between 1685 and 1699, they constitute nearly one-fifth of the decedents. Together with apprentices, indentured servants, and slaves, these free laborers probably constituted as much as half the labor force at the end of the seventeenth century.

Artisans—known also as "tradesmen," "mechanics," "artificers," and "leather apron men"—filled the wide social space between laborers and an upper-class elite. This is a group so large and diverse that historians have never quite been able to agree on how to define it in occupational or class terms. Most of them were self-employed, proudly so, and they included everyone from silversmiths and hatters to shoemakers, tailors, and mast and sailmakers. Within most of the occupational subdivisions a wide range of wealth and status existed. In part this reflected the age-old hierarchy within each craft, composed of apprentices, journeymen, and master craftsmen. At each step along the way the economic security and material rewards could normally be expected to rise, so that the range of wealth that can be observed in the tax lists for carpenters in Boston or clockmakers in New York reflects to some degree the age of the particular artisan and the acquisition of skills associated with his work. Age was by no means the only or even the most important factor, however. Stephen Coleman, a Philadelphia glover, died in 1699 with an estate valued at £580, including two houses, while John Simons, also a glover of about the same age, died in the same year with an estate of only £51. . . .

The opportunities of the late seventeenth-century urban artisan varied considerably within crafts but no more so than variations between occupational groups. A hierarchy of trades existed in all of the towns—after the Revolution this was sometimes symbolized by the marching order of the various crafts at public celebrations— and to some degree the success of individual mechanics can be predicted by the trade they followed. Everyone knew that artisans working with precious metals got ahead faster than those who worked at the cobbler's bench and that house carpenters were far more likely to become property owners than tailors and weavers. Nonetheless, young men chose their careers far more with reference to that of their fathers—or their uncles, older brothers, or cousins—than to a rational calculation of future material rewards. . . . Such intergenerational artisan continuity was one more proof that urban dwellers who worked with their hands retained part of the traditional mentality which held that a decent subsistence or a slow inching forward was more the norm than the rapid aggrandizement of wealth.

Standing at the top of the urban pyramid were two groups, one distinguished by its high social status and the other by its wealth. The first of these was composed of the professionals— government officials, doctors, clergymen, schoolteachers, and, eventually, lawyers. Often they were rewarded more by the community's respect than by material benefits. Boston, for example, paid its public school teachers only about £25 sterling per year in the 1690s and forty years later New York had only £30 sterling to spare for a teacher's wages. . . . But nobody denied that these educated men performed vital functions in the community, and the fact that their wealth rarely proximated their prestige serves as a reminder that parallel hierarchies of wealth, power, and prestige existed and did not precisely overlap.

Held in lower regard but dominating economic life were the seaport merchants, and, to a lesser degree, the shopkeepers, who often aspired to merchant status. These were the urban dwellers who controlled the lifelines between the seaports and the hinterland and between the ports and the outside world. Without these importers and exporters, wholesalers and retailers, builders of ships, wharves, and warehouses there could have been no commercial centers. It should come as no surprise that those who controlled mercantile endeavors quickly gained a disproportionate share of economic leverage in the urban centers of colonial life, not only in dominating the flow of marketable goods but also in their control of shipbuilding, credit facilities, and urban real estate. Political power to match their economic influence was established early in all the northern ports; how this power was used would become one of the most enduring issues of the eighteenth century. . . .

Within the upper-middle tier of urban society stood the prospering merchants and shopkeepers, a sprinkling of master craftsmen, and the widows of men who had left their wives securely situated at death. In Boston almost three-quarters of these persons passed on to their heirs substantial amounts of real estate, including wharves, shops, and warehouses, as well as land and houses. . . . Men who had achieved material success of this kind had mahogany furniture in the parlor instead of oak, slept in canopied beds with fine linen, ate from silver rather than wood or pewter, and owned imported clocks, books, and other accoutrements of the moderately affluent life. . . . In all of the port towns this group claimed hold of about 40 percent of the collective assets in their communities.

The top 10 percent of the wealthholders, who can loosely be designated as the economic elite, were almost all officeholders, merchants, and others closely associated with mercantile pursuits or the widows of such men. Among the thirty Boston decedents between 1685 and 1699 who occupied this uppermost rank, for example, there were nineteen merchants, four sea captains, who also usually acted as importers on their own, two officeholders, a distiller, house carpenter, brazier, butcher, miller, and minister. All but two of these men owned real estate, and most could boast of property worth £500 sterling or more. . . . Their Philadelphia counterparts were also mostly men involved in commerce. . . . In both towns, and also in New York, about 40 percent of the total taxable assets or inventoried wealth fell under the control of this wealthiest tenth—about the same percentage possessed by the next richest three-tenths of society.

We need not be surprised that the top tenth of society controlled 40 percent of the community's wealth and the bottom half possessed only about 10 percent. So it had been throughout history, especially in urban centers, where the division of material goods and property was almost always less even than in the countryside. It is likely, in fact, that the wealth of European towns in this period was maldistributed to a far greater degree. So long as the unequal division of wealth had proceeded only this far, it was of far less concern than the actual conditions of life and how they compared to what the previous generation had known. Laboring people had never controlled more than a tiny fraction of the community's total wealth and did not imagine that social relationships were deranged because assets were disproportionately concentrated at the top of society. What mattered to them was that in some places in the world the laboring poor lived in abject misery while in others they knew a spare but decent existence.

In the American port towns of the 1690s life at the bottom compared favorably with conditions in any of the English, Irish, and Scottish towns from which urban dwellers or their parents had come. Mariners, laborers, and many of those at the lower levels of the artisanry labored long hours under unpleasant and often unhealthy conditions; and at the end of their lives they had little to show for their efforts by modern standards. But they did not starve or go unclothed and unhoused. They were far better off than their counterparts in the late seventeenth-century English towns, where unemployment and acute poverty were major problems and political economists were busily planning workhouses to sponge up the jobless poor and set them to hard labor that would relieve taxpayers of supporting them through the poor rates. The incidence of poverty, in fact, was extremely low and was confined for the most part to the widowed, disabled, and orphaned, who were decently cared for. Thoroughly Elizabethan in their attitudes to the poor, townspeople regarded the small number of indigents as wards of the community, whose members should collectively assume responsibility for those in distress. Little stigma was attached to being poor, for it was generally due to circumstances beyond the individual's control. If Widow Chambers in Boston was old, infirm, and without children to care for her, the selectmen saw to it that wood was delivered to her door during the winter months. . . . In Philadelphia the law until 1700 required the justices of the peace to see to the needs of the indigent. Within a social system fundamentally based on family and kinship, remedies for dealing with the community's unfortunates were familial in form. Most often, persons in need remained in their homes or in the homes of others and were given "out-relief" there—clothes, firewood, bread, and often small weekly cash payments. In all of the port towns poverty was not regarded as a social defect and a sense of social responsibility pervaded poor relief measures. . . .

If life at the bottom of northern seaport society put laboring people ahead of their European relatives, life at the top left the colonial economic elite far behind. Just as a subbasement for slaves and indentured servants had been added, the colonial structure lacked a tower full of glittering diamonds and gold. Even the richest merchants of Boston, New York, and Philadelphia cut a poor figure compared to the overseas traders of Bristol, Hull, Cork, Dublin, and Edinburgh. The point is important because the gap between rich and poor was one of those measures by which ordinary town dwellers and even upper-class leaders judged equity and virtue in their society. Nobody, at least at this time, questioned the right of the rich to their worldly goods. But too much wealth was suspect, especially in Boston and Philadelphia, where the Puritan notion that making money was legitimate only when profits were put to public uses and the Quaker emphasis on "plain living" subtly curbed the aggrandizement of large fortunes. Religious restraints on the aggressive accumulations of riches were strengthened by a pervasive secular feeling that transplanted Europeans were building a better kind of society in the New World, one where neither jewel-bedecked lords nor impoverished vassals would be known. There was no inconsistency between adherence to social hierarchy and disdain for too great a gap between rich and poor.

Hierarchy was best preserved from challenges, in fact, when the social spectrum did not include degrading indigency at the lower end and sumptuous wealth at the upper. . . .

All three port towns by the end of the seventeenth century had evolved into bustling entrepôts through which the lifeblood of their colonies flowed. As everywhere, the benefits of a commercial way of life were shared unequally among their members. But by European standards, which, after all, provided the American urban dwellers with their frame of reference, the relationships among the constituent parts of society functioned in a generally equitable fashion. Lower-class artisans and laborers might regard upper-class leaders as too inflexibly committed to the concept of an ordered and immobile society; and upper-class merchants and professionals might see dangerous leveling tendencies in lower-class pretensions to a more genteel manner of living. But most people took satisfaction in the fact that William Phips, a sheep farmer and ship's carpenter from Maine, could rise to the governorship of Massachusetts in 1692 and that Griffith Jones, a glover from County Surrey in England, could become mayor of Philadelphia in 1704. If the expectations of not every inhabitant of the port towns were fully met, there was at least a general sense that life was fulfilling in the northern English colonies and that the future was bright.

Colonial Black Communities and the Evolution of African-American Society

IRA BERLIN

Generally the importance of . . . slaves to the growth of northern cities increased during the eighteenth century. Urban slavery moved steadily away from the household to the docks, warehouses, and shops, as demonstrated by the growing disproportion of slave men in the urban North. Aside from those skills associated with the maritime trades, however, few slaves entered artisan work. Only a handful could be found in the carriage trades that enjoyed higher status and that offered greater opportunity for an independent livelihood and perhaps the chance to buy freedom.

In the cities as in the countryside, blacks tended to live and work in close proximity to whites. Northern slaves not only gained first-hand knowledge of their masters' world, but they also rubbed elbows with lower-class whites in taverns, cock fights, and fairs where poor people of varying status mingled. If urban life allowed slaves to meet more frequently and enjoy a larger degree of social autonomy than did slavery in the countryside, the cosmopolitan nature of cities speeded the transformation of Africans to Afro-Americans. Acculturation in the cities of the North was a matter of years, not generations.

For many blacks, the process of cultural transformation was well under way before they stepped off the boat. During the first century of American settlement, few blacks arrived in the North directly from Africa. Although American slavers

From "Time, Space, and the Evolution of Afro-American Society on Mainland British North America" by Ira Berlin, *American Historical Review* 85 (February, 1980), excerpted from pp. 44–64. Reprinted by permission of the author.

generally originated in the North, few gave priority to Northern ports. The markets to the south were simply too large and too lucrative. Slaves dribbled into the Northern colonies from the West Indies or the mainland South singly, in twos and threes, or by the score but rarely by the boatload. Some came on special order from merchants or farmers with connections to the West Indian trade. Others arrived on consignment, since few Northern merchants specialized in selling slaves. Many of these were the unsalable "refuse" (as traders contemptuously called them) of larger shipments. Northern slaveholders generally disliked these scourings of the transatlantic trade who, the governor of Massachusetts observed, were "usually the worst servants they have"; they feared that the West Indian re-exports had records of recalcitrance and criminality as well as physical defects. In time, some masters may have come to prefer seasoned slaves because of their knowledge of English, familiarity with work routines, or resistance to New World diseases. But, whatever their preference, Northern colonies could not compete with the wealthier staple-producing colonies for prime African field hands. Before the 1740s, Africans appear to have arrived in the north only when a temporary glut made sale impossible in the West Indies and the mainland South. Even then they did not always remain in the North. When conditions in the plantation colonies changed, merchants re-exported them for a quick profit. The absence of direct importation during the early years and the slow, random, haphazard entry to West Indian creoles shaped the development of black culture in the Northern colonies. While the nature of the slave trade prevented the survival of tribal or even shipboard ties that figured so prominently in Afro-American life in the West Indies and the Lower South, it better prepared blacks to take advantage of the special circumstances of their captivity.

Newly arrived blacks, most already experienced in the New World and familiar with their proscribed status, turned Northern bondage to their advantage where they could. They quickly established a stable family life and, unlike newly imported Africans elsewhere on the continent, increased their numbers by natural means during the first generation. . . . The transplanted creoles also seized the opportunities provided by the complex Northern economy, the relatively close ties of master and slave, and, for many, the independence afforded by urban life. In New Amsterdam, for example, the diverse needs of the Dutch mercantile economy induced the West India Company, the largest slaveholder in the colony, to allow its slaves to live out and work on their own in return for a stipulated amount of labor and an annual tribute. "Half-freedom," as this system came to be called, enlarged black opportunities and allowed for the development of a strong black community. When the West India Company refused to make these privileges hereditary, "half-free" slaves organized and protested, demanding that they be allowed to pass their rights to their children. Failing that, New Amsterdam slaves pressed their masters in other ways to elevate their children's status. Some, hearing rumors that baptism meant freedom, tried to gain church membership. . . . Even after the conquering English abolished "half-freedom" and instituted a more rigorous system of racial servitude, blacks continued to use the leverage gained by their prominent role in the city's economy to set standards of treatment well above those in the plantation colonies. Into the eighteenth century, New York slaves informally enjoyed the rights of an earlier era, including the right to hold property of their own. "The Custome of this Country," bristled a frustrated New

York master to a West Indian friend, "will not allow us to use our Negroes as you doe in Barbados." . . .

During the middle decades of the eighteenth century, the nature of Northern slavery changed dramatically. Growing demand for labor, especially when Europeans wars limited the supply of white indentured servants and when depression sent free workers west in search of new opportunities, increased the importance of slaves in the work force. Between 1732 and 1754, blacks composed fully a third of the immigrants (forced and voluntary) arriving in New York. The new importance of slave labor changed the nature of the slave trade. Merchants who previously took black slaves only on consignment now began to import them directly from Africa, often in large numbers. Before 1741, for example, 79 percent of the slaves arriving in New York originated in the West Indies and other mainland sources and only 30 percent came directly from Africa. After that date, the proportions were reversed. Specializing in the slave trade, African slavers carried many times more slaves than did West Indian traders. Whereas slaves had earlier arrived in small parcels rarely numbering more than a half-dozen, direct shipments from Africa at times now totaled over a hundred and, occasionally, several times that. Slaves increasingly replaced white indentured servants as the chief source of unfree labor not only in the areas that had produced for the provisioning trade, where their pre-eminence had been established earlier in the century, but in the cities as well. In the 1760s, when slave importation into Pennsylvania peaked, blacks composed more than three-quarters of Philadelphia's servant population.

Northern whites generally viewed this new wave of slaves as substitutes for indentured labor. White indentured servants had come as young men without families, and slaves were now imported in much the same way. . . . As a result, the sex ratio of the black population, which earlier in the century had been roughly balanced, suddenly swung heavily in favor of men. In Massachusetts, black men outnumbered black women nearly two to one. Elsewhere sex ratios of 130 or more became commonplace. Such sexual imbalance and the proscription of interracial marriage made it increasingly difficult for blacks to enjoy normal family lives. As the birth rate slipped, mortality rates soared, especially in the cities where newly arrived blacks appeared to be concentrated. Since most slaves came without any previous exposure to New World diseases, the harsh Northern winters took an even higher toll. Blacks died by the score; the crude death rate of Philadelphia and Boston blacks in the 1750s and 1760s was well over sixty per thousand, almost double that of whites. In its demographic outline, Northern slavery at midcentury often bore a closer resemblance to the horrors of the West Indies during the height of a sugar boom than to the relatively benign bondage of the earlier years.

Whites easily recovered from this demographic disaster by again switching to European indentured servants and then to free labor as supplies became available, and, as the influx of slaves subsided, black life also regained its balance. But the transformation of Northern slavery had a lasting influence on the development of Afro-American culture. Although the Northern black population remained predominantly Afro-American after nearly a century of slow importation from the West Indies and steady natural increase, the direct entry of Africans into Northern society reoriented black culture.

Even before the redirection of the Northern slave trade, those few Africans in the Northern colonies often stood apart from the creole majority. While Afro-American slaves established precedents and customs, which they then drew upon to improve their condition, Africans tended to stake all to recapture the world they had lost. Significantly, Africans, many of whom did not yet speak English and still carried tribal names, composed the majority of the participants in the New York slave insurrection of 1712, even though most of the city's blacks were creoles. The division between Africans and Afro-Americans became more visible as the number of Africans increased after midcentury. Not only did creoles and Africans evince different aspirations, but their life-chances—as reflected in their resistance to disease and their likelihood of establishing a family—also diverged sharply. Greater visibility may have sharpened differences between creoles and Africans, but Africans were too few in number to stand apart for long. Whatever conflicts different life-chances and beliefs created, whites paid such distinctions little heed in incorporating the African minority into their slaveholdings. The propensity of Northern whites to lump blacks together mitigated intraracial differences. Rather than permanently dividing blacks, the entry of Africans into Northern society gave a new dimension to Afro-American culture.

Newly arrived Africans reawakened Afro-Americans to their African past by providing direct knowledge of West African society. Creole blacks began to combine their African inheritance into their own evolving culture. In some measure, the easy confidence of Northern whites in their own dominance speeded the syncretization of African and creole culture by allowing blacks to act far more openly than slaves in the plantation colonies. Northern blacks incorporated African culture into their own Afro-American culture not only in the common-place and unconscious way that generally characterizes the transit of culture but also with a high degree of consciousness and deliberateness. They designated their churches "African," and they called themselves "Sons of Africa." They adopted African forms to maximize their freedom, to choose their leaders, and, in general, to give shape to their lives. This new African influence was manifested most fully in Negro election day, a ritual festival of role reversal common throughout West Africa and celebrated openly by blacks in New England and a scattering of places in the Middle Colonies.

The celebration of Negro election day took a variety of forms, but everywhere it was a day of great merrymaking that drew blacks from all over the countryside. "All the various languages of Africa, mixed with broken and ludicrous English, filled the air, accompanied with the music of the fiddle, tambourine, the banjo, [and] drum," recalled an observer of the festival in Newport. Negro election day culminated with the selection of black kings, governors, and judges. These officials sometimes held symbolic power over the whole community and real power over the black community. While the black governors held court, adjudicating minor disputes, the blacks paraded and partied, dressed in their masters' clothes and mounted on their masters' horses. Such role reversal, like similar status inversions in Africa and elsewhere, confirmed rather than challenged the existing order, but it also gave blacks an opportunity to express themselves more fully than the narrow boundaries of slavery ordinarily allowed. Negro election day permitted a seeming release from bondage, and it also provided a mechanism for blacks to recognize and honor their own notables. Most important, it established a framework for the development of black politics. In the places where Negro election day survived into the nineteenth century, its politics shaped the politics within the black community and merged with partisan divisions of American society. Slaves elsewhere in the New World also celebrated this holiday, but whites in the plantation colonies found the implications of role reversal too frightening to allow even symbolically. Northern whites, on the other hand, not only aided election day materially but sometimes joined in themselves. Still, white cooperation was an important but not the crucial element in the rise of Negro election day. Its origins in the 1740s and 1750s suggests how the entry of Africans reoriented Afro-American culture at a formative point in its development.

African acculturation in the Northern colonies at once incorporated blacks into American society and sharpened the memory of their African past and their desire to preserve it. While small numbers and close proximity to whites forced blacks to conform to the forms of the dominant Euro-American culture, the confidence of whites in their own hegemony allowed black slaves a good measure of autonomy. . . .

Unlike African acculturation in the Northern colonies, the transformation of Africans into Afro-Americans in the Carolina and Georgia lowcountry was a slow, halting process whose effects resonated differently within black society. While creolization created a unified Afro-American population in the North, it left lowcountry blacks deeply divided. . . .

One branch of black society took shape within the bounds of the region's cities and towns. If planters lived removed from most slaves, they maintained close, intimate relations with some. The masters' great wealth, transient life, and seasonal urban residence placed them in close contact with house servants who kept their estates, boatmen who carried messages and supplies back and forth to their plantations, and urban artisans who made city life not only possible but comfortable. In addition, coastal cities needed large numbers of workers to transport and process the plantation staples, to serve the hundreds of ships that annually visited the lowcountry, and to satisfy the planters' newly acquired taste for luxury goods. Blacks did most of this work. Throughout the eighteenth century they composed more than half the population of Charles Town and other lowcountry ports. Probably nothing arrived or left these cities without some black handling it. Black artisans also played a large role in urban life. Master craftsmen employed them in every variety of work. . . . Although most black artisans labored along the waterfront as shipwrights, ropemakers, and coopers, lowcountry blacks—unlike blacks in Northern cities—also entered the higher trades, working as gold beaters, silversmiths, and cabinetmakers. In addition, black women gained control over much of the marketing in the lowcountry ports, mediating between slave-grown produce in the countryside and urban consumption. White tradesmen and journeymen periodically protested against slave competition, but planters, master craftsmen, and urban consumers who benefited from black labor and services easily brushed aside these objections.

Mobile, often skilled, and occasionally literate, urban slaves understood the white world. They used their knowledge to improve their position within lowcountry society even while the condition of the mass of black people deteriorated. . . . Many urban creoles not only retained the independence of the earlier years but enlarged upon it. They hired their own time, earned wages from "overwork," kept market stalls, and sometimes even opened shops. Some lived apart from their masters and rented houses of their own, paying their owners a portion of their earnings in return for *de facto* freedom. Such liberty enabled a few black people to keep their families intact and perhaps even accumulate property for themselves. The small black communities that developed below the Bluff in Savannah and in Charles Town's Neck confirm the growing independence of urban creoles.

The incongruous prosperity of urban bondsmen jarred whites. By hiring their own time, living apart from their masters, and controlling their own family life, these blacks forcibly and visibly claimed the white man's privileges. Perhaps no aspect of their behavior was as obvious and, hence, as galling as their elaborate dress. While plantation slaves—men and women—worked stripped to the waist wearing no more than loin cloths (thereby confirming the white man's image of savagery), urban slaves appropriated their masters' taste for fine clothes and often the clothes themselves. Lowcountry legislators enacted various sumptuary regulations to restrain the slaves' penchant for dressing above their station. The South Carolina Assembly once even considered prohibiting masters from giving their old clothes to their slaves. But hand-me-downs were clearly not the problem as long as slaves earned wages and had easy access to the urban marketplace. Frustrated by the realities of urban slavery, lawmakers passed and repassed the old regulations to little effect. On the eve of the Revolution, a Charles Town Grand Jury continued to bemoan the fact that the "Law for preventing the excessive and costly Apparel of Negroes and other Slaves in this province (especially in *Charles Town*) [was] not being put into Force."

Most of these privileged bondsmen appear to have been creoles with long experience in the New World. Although some Africans entered urban society, the language skills and the mastery of the complex interpersonal relations needed in the cities gave creoles a clear advantage over Africans in securing elevated positions within the growing urban enclaves. To be sure, their special status was far from "equal." No matter how essential their function or intimate their interaction, their relations with whites no longer smacked of the earlier "sawbuck equality." Instead, these relations might better be characterized as paternal, sometimes, literally so.

Increasingly during the eighteenth century, blacks gained privileged positions within lowcountry society as a result of intimate, usually sexual, relations with white slave masters. Like slaveholders everywhere, lowland planters assumed that sexual access to slave women was simply another of the master's prerogatives. Perhaps because their origin was West Indian or perhaps because their dual residence separated them from their white wives part of the year, white men established sexual liaisons with black women frequently and openly. Some white men and black women formed stable, long-lasting unions, legitimate in everything but law. More often than other slaveholders in continental British North America, lowcountry planters recognized and provided for their mulatto offspring, and, occasionally, extended legal freedom. South Carolina's small free Negro population, almost totally confined to Charles Town, was largely the product of such relations. Light-skinned people of color enjoyed special standing in the lowcountry ports, as they did in the West Indies, and whites occasionally looked the other way when such creoles passed into the dominant caste. But even when the planters did not grant legal freedom, they usually assured the elevated standing of their mulatto scions by training them for artisan trades or placing them in household positions. If the countryside was "blackened" by African imports, Charles Town and the other lowcountry ports exhibited a melange of "colored" peoples.

✳ *F U R T H E R   R E A D I N G*

Thomas J. Archdeacon, *New York City, 1664–1710: Conquest and Change* (1976)

E. Digby Baltzell, *Puritan Boston and Quaker Philadelphia: Two Protestant Ethics and the Spirit of Class Authority and Leadership* (1979)

Carl Bridenbaugh, *Cities in Revolt: Urban Life in America, 1743–1776* (1956)

——, *Cities in the Wilderness: Urban Life in America, 1625–1742* (1938)

Robert E. Cray, Jr., *Paupers and Poor Relief in New York City and Its Rural Environs, 1700–1830* (1988)

Dora P. Crouch, Daniel J. Garr, and Axel I. Mundigo, *Spanish City Planning in North America* (1982)

Sylvia D. Fries, *The Urban Ideal in Colonial America* (1977)

Joyce Goodfriend, *Before the Melting Pot: Society and Culture in Colonial New York City* (1991)

David G. Hackett, *The Rude Hand of Innovation: Religion and Social Order in Albany, New York, 1652–1836* (1991)

Hendrik Hartog, *Public Property and Private Power: The Corporation of the City of New York in American Law, 1730–1870* (1983)

Gary B. Nash, *Forging Freedom: The Formation of Philadelphia's Black Community, 1720–1840* (1988)

Darrett Rutman, *Winthrop's Boston: A Portrait of a Puritan Town, 1630–1649* (1965)

Jon C. Teaford, *The Municipal Revolution in America: Origins of Modern City Government, 1650–1825* (1975)

G. B. Warden, *Boston: 1689–1776* (1970)

Sam Bass Warner, Jr., *The Private City: Philadelphia in Three Periods of Its Growth* (1968)

Jean Parker Waterbury, ed., *The Oldest City: St. Augustine, Saga of Survival* (1983)

Lynn Withey, *Urban Growth in Colonial Rhode Island: Newport and Providence in the Seventeenth Century* (1984)

CHAPTER 3

Commercialism and Urban Life

in the New Nation,

1790–1860

✖

Between 1790 and 1860 the United States experienced unprecedented urbanization, and cities became indispensable to the national economy. Whereas in 1790 only four cities—New York, Philadelphia, Boston, and Baltimore—had populations over 10,000, by 1860 twenty-one cities contained populations of more than 40,000, and nine boasted over 100,000 residents. New York led with 814,000 people, but the urban network stretched across the continent to include interior cities such as Pittsburgh, Cleveland, Chicago, New Orleans, and Cincinnati and western cities including San Francisco. All these places, and countless small and middle-sized cities as well, developed environments that distinguished them from their surrounding rural areas and defined the preindustrial American city.

What did it mean for a community to be considered a city in this era? Historians interested in urban growth in the new nation have had to consider this question carefully in analyzing urban life at a time before cities existed in the form that we know them today. Several other questions flow out of the initial query: In what ways were there peculiarly "urban" institutions and problems? How did early cities differ in appearance from modern cities? Did they resemble modern cities in any ways? How did they organize their social and economic activities? What factors were likely to encourage or discourage growth?

✖ D O C U M E N T S

The first three documents give different contemporary perspectives on what early American cities were like in their physical features, economic activities, and social relations. Michael Chevalier, the author of the first excerpt, was a Frenchman who visited the United States between 1833 and 1835 to investigate the construction of canals and railroads but also to see how the French might learn from American institutions and habits. His description of Cincinnati highlights several key urban characteristics, including the importance of location, the mixture of commerce and infant industry, the role of leadership, the tendency toward pretension in arts and sciences, and the social emphasis on work. Federick Law Olmsted, the author of the second document, was a journalist before he became a famous landscape architect. His reports on his travels in the South in the mid-1850s contain observations on what he believed to be unrealistic economic attitudes and on the way that slavery discouraged the investment in commerce and industry that was necessary for urban growth. He gave low marks to Norfolk and other Virginia cities and tried to explain why they could not compete economically with New York City. The third document, by Anne Royall, a resident of Washington, D.C., and the writer of travel books, describes similarities between her city and any other young city, but it also reveals the special scale and problems of a city functioning as the nation's capital.

The fourth document presents excerpts from an early city charter, the first charter of the city of Providence, Rhode Island, which officially became a city—as opposed to a town—in 1832. The passages reveal various features included in the formal organization of a city, including the establishment of a government with a mayor and a city council of two legislative bodies; a definition of the duties of the government officers, especially the police powers of the mayor to quell disorder; the nature of local judicial courts; and a provision for certifying the property qualifications of voters.

A Frenchman's Impressions
of Early Cincinnati, c. 1833

Cincinnati has been made famous by Mrs. Trollope, whose aristocratic feelings were offended by the pork trade which is carried on here on a great scale. From her accounts many persons have thought that everybody in Cincinnati was a pork merchant and the city a mere slaughterhouse. The fact is that Cincinnati is a large and beautiful town, charmingly situated in one of those bends which the Ohio makes, as if unwilling to leave the spot. . . .

The architectural appearance of Cincinnati is very nearly the same as the new sections of an English town. The houses are generally brick, most often three stories high, with the windows shining with cleanliness, each designed for a single family and regularly placed along well-paved and spacious streets, sixty feet in width. Here and there the prevailing uniformity is interrupted by some more imposing edifice, and there are some houses of hewn stone in very good taste, real miniature palaces, with neat porticoes, inhabited by the aristocratic portion of Mrs. Trollope's hog merchants, and several very pretty mansions surrounded with gardens and terraces. . . .

In Cincinnati, as everywhere else in the United States, there is a great number of churches; each sect has its own, from Anglican Episcopalianism, which enlists under its banner the wealth of the country, to the Baptist and Methodist sects,

From *Society, Manners, and Politics in the United States: Letters on North America,* edited by John Williams Ward (Garden City: Anchor Books, 1961), excerpts from pp. 186–189, 194–200. Published by Bantam, Doubleday, Dell.

the religion of the laborers and Negroes. On another side stands a huge hotel which from its exterior you would take for a royal residence but in which, as I can testify, you will not experience a princely hospitality. Or a museum, which is merely a private speculation as all American museums are, and which consists of some few crystals; some mammouth bones, which are very abundant in the United States, an Egyptian mummy; some Indian weapons and dresses and a half-dozen wax figures, representing, for instance, Washington, General Jackson, and the Indian Chiefs, Black Hawk and Tecumseh; a figure of Napoleon afoot or on horseback; a French cuirass from Waterloo; a collection of portraits of distinguished Americans, including Lafayette and some of the leading men of the town; another of stuffed birds, snakes preserved in alcohol, and particularly a large living snake, a boa constrictor or an anaconda. . . .

The foundries for casting steam engines, the yards for building steamboats, the noisy, unwholesome, or unpleasant workshops are in the adjoining village of Fulton, in Covington or Newport on the Kentucky bank of the river, or in the country. As for the enormous slaughter of hogs, about 150,000 annually, and the preparation of the lard which follows, the town is not in the least incommoded by it; the whole process takes place on the banks of a little stream called Deer Creek which has received the nickname of *the Bloody Run* from the color of its waters during the slaughtering season, or near the basin of the great canal which runs from Cincinnati to Dayton in the center of the State and which they plan to extend much farther, all the way to Lake Erie. Cincinnati has, however, no square planted with trees in the English manner, no parks nor walks, no fountains, although it would be very easy to have them. It is necessary to wait for the ornamental until the taste for it prevails among the inhabitants; at present the useful occupies all thoughts. Besides, all improvements require an increase of taxes, and in the United States it is not easy to persuade the people to submit to this. Cincinnati also stands in need of some public provision for lighting the streets, which the repugnance to taxes has so far prevented. . . .

Cincinnati contains about forty thousand inhabitants, inclusive of the adjoining villages. Although founded forty years ago, its rapid growth dates only about thirty years back. It seems to be the rendezvous of all nations; Germans and Irish are very numerous and there are some Alsacians; I have often heard the harsh accents of Rhemish French in the streets. But the bulk of the population which gives tone to all the rest is of New England origin. What makes the progress of Cincinnati more surprising is that the city is its own creation. Other towns which have sprung up in the United States in the same rapid manner have been built on shares, so to speak. Lowell, for example, is an enterprise of Boston merchants who, after having raised the necessary funds, collected the workmen and told them, "Build us a town." Cincinnati has been gradually extended and embellished almost wholly without outside aid, by its own inhabitants, who have for the most part arrived on the spot poor. . . .

Cincinnati is, as I have said, admirably situated. This is true of its geographical position, but, if you follow rivers on the map and consider the natural resources of the soil, you will find that there are several points on the long line of the rivers of the West as advantageously placed, both for trade and manufactures, and that there are some even more favored. Pittsburg, which has within reach both coal and iron, that is to say, the daily bread of industry; which stands at the head of the Ohio, at the starting point of steam navigation, at the confluence of the Monongahela and the Allegheny, one coming from the south and the other from the north; Pittsburgh, which is near a great network of lakes, appears as the pivot of a vast system of roads, railroads, and canals, several of which are already completed. Pittsburg was marked out by nature at once for a great manufacturing center and a great mart of trade. Louisville, built at the falls of the Ohio, at the head of navigation for the largest class of boats, is a natural medium between the commerce of the upper Ohio and that of the Mississippi and its tributaries. In respect to manufacturing resources, Louisville is as well provided as Cincinnati, and the latter, setting aside its enchanting situation, seemed destined merely to become the market of the fertile strip between the Great and Little Miami rivers.

But the power of men, when they decide to will something and will it perseveringly, is sufficient to balance and conquer the power of nature. In spite of the superior advantages of Louisville as an *entrepôt,* in spite of the manufacturing resources of Pittsburg, Cincinnati is able to maintain a population twice that of Louisville and half as large again as that of Pittsburg in a state of well-being which equals, if it does not surpass, the average conditions of each of the other two. The inhabitants of Cincinnati have established this prosperity among themselves, by the instinctive reaction with which the sons of New England are filled by their eminently practical and calculating genius. . . .

The Cincinnatians make a variety of household furniture and utensils, agricultural and mechanical implements and machines, wooden clocks, and a thousand objects of daily use and consumption, soap, candles, paper, leather, etc. for which there is an indefinite demand throughout the flourishing and rapidly growing States of the West and also in the new States of the Southwest, which are wholly devoted to agriculture and in which, on account of the existence of slavery, manufactures cannot be carried on. Most of these articles are of ordinary quality; the furniture, for instance, is rarely such as would be approved by Parisian taste, but it is cheap and neat, just what is wanted in a new country where, with the exception of a part of the South, there is general ease but little wealth and where plenty and comfort are more generally known than the little luxuries of a more refined society. The prosperity of Cincinnati, therefore, rests upon the sure basis of the prosperity of the West, upon supplying articles to fill the basic needs of the bulk of the community; a much more solid foundation than the caprice of fashion upon which the branches of industry most in favor with us depend. The intellectual also receives a share of attention. In the first place, there is a large type-foundry in Cincinnati, which supplies the demand of the whole West and that army of newspapers printed in it. . . . The country trader who sells a little of everything is sure to find almost anything he wants in Cincinnati. Therefore he goes there before any other place in order to lay in his stock of goods. Cincinnati is thus in fact the great central mart of the West; a great quantity and variety of produce and manufactured articles flow through here, notwithstanding the natural superiority of several other sites, either in regard to the extent of water communications or mineral resources. . . .

. . . [I]n Cincinnati, there are no great factories or workshops. Industry is divided there, pretty much as the soil is among us. Each head of a family, with his sons and some newly arrived emigrants as assistants and servants, has his domain. Cincinnati is, therefore, as republican in its industrial organization as in its political. This subdivision of manufactures has hitherto been attended with no inconvenience because in the vast West, whose growth is visible to the eye, production cannot at present keep pace with consumption. . . .

The moral aspect of Cincinnati is delightful in the eyes of him who prefers work to everything else, with whom work can take the place of everything else. But whoever has a taste for pleasure and display, whoever needs occasional relaxation from business in gaiety and amusement, would find this beautiful city with its picturesque surroundings an impossible place to stay. . . . He would find himself denounced on political grounds, because men of leisure are looked upon in the United States as so many steppingstones to aristocracy, and anathematized by religion, for the various sects, however much they may differ on other points, all agree in condemning pleasure, luxury, gallantry, the fine arts themselves. . . . There is, therefore, no such thing in Cincinnati as a leisure class, living without any regular profession on their inheritance or on the wealth acquired by their own enterprise in early life, although there are many persons of wealth having one hundred thousand dollars and more. . . .

Frederick Law Olmsted Compares Virginia Cities with New York City, 1856

Norfolk is a dirty, low, ill-arranged town, nearly divided by a morass. It has a single creditable public building, a number of fine private residences, and the polite society is reputed to be agreeable, refined, and cultivated, receiving a character from the families of the resident naval officers. It has all the immoral and disagreeable characteristics of a large seaport, with very few of the advantages that we should expect to find as relief to them. No lyceum or public libraries, no public gardens, no galleries of art, and though there are two "Bethels," no "home" for its seamen; no public resorts of healthful and refining amusement, no place better than a filthy, tobacco-impregnated bar-room or a licentious dance-cellar, so far as I have been able to learn, for the stranger of high or low degree to pass the hours unoccupied by business.

Lieut. Maury has lately very well shown what advantages were originally possessed for profitable commerce [at Norfolk], in a report, the intention of which is to advocate the establishment of a line of steamers hence to Para, the port of the mouth of the Amazon. I have the best wishes for the success of the project in its important features, and the highest respect for the judgment of Lieut. Maury, but it seems to me pertinent to inquire why are the British Government steamers not sent exclusively to Halifax, the nearest port to England, instead of to the more distant and foreign port of New York? If a Government line of steamers should be established between Para and Norfolk, and should be found in the least degree commercially profitable, how long would it be before another line would be established between New York and Para, by private enterprise, and then how much business would be left for the Government steamers while they continued to end their voyage at Norfolk? So, too, with regard to a line from Antwerp to Norfolk . . .

New York City's South Street Port, 1828

Commerce, especially water-born trade, formed the economic base of U.S. cities in the early nineteenth century. Thanks to its broad, deep-water harbor, the best on the Atlantic coast, New York City grew rapidly and surpassed Philadelphia as the nation's largest city. This drawing shows the busy activity along the docks, with stores and warehouses nearby.

. . . [I]f a deadly, enervating pestilence had always ravaged here, this Norfolk could not be a more miserable, sorry little seaport town than it is. It was not possible to prevent the existence of some agency here for the trans-shipment of goods, and for supplying the needs of vessels, compelled by exterior circumstances to take refuge in the harbor. Beyond this bare supply of a necessitous demand, and what results from the adjoining naval rendezvous of the nation, there is nothing.

Singularly simple, child-like ideas about commercial success, you find among the Virginians—even among the merchants themselves. The agency by which commodities are transferred from the producer to the consumer, they seem to look upon as a kind of swindling operation; they do not see that the merchant acts a useful part in the community, or, that his labor can be other than selfish and malevolent. They speak angrily of New York, as if it fattened on the country without doing the country any good in return. They have no idea that it is *their* business that the New Yorkers are doing, and that whatever tends to facilitate it, and make it simple and secure, is an increase of their wealth by diminishing the costs and lessening the losses upon it.

They gravely demand why the government mail steamers should be sent to New York, when New York has so much business already, and why the nation should build costly custom-houses, and post-offices, and mints, and sea defences, and collect stores, and equipments there, and not at Norfolk, and Petersburg, and Richmond, and Danville, and Lynchburg, and Smithtown, and Jones's Cross-Roads? It seems never to have occurred to them that it is because the country needs them there, because the skill, enterprise, and energy of New York merchants, the confidence of capitalists in New York merchants, the various facilities for trade offered by New York merchants, enable them to do the business of the country cheaper and better than it can be done anywhere else, and that thus they can *command* commerce, and need not petition their Legislature, or appeal to mean sectional prejudices to obtain it, but all imagine it is by some shrewd Yankee trickery it is done. By the bones of their noble fathers they will set their faces against it . . . so they bully their local merchants into buying in dearer markets, and make the country tote its gold on to Philadelphia to be coined; and their conventions resolve that the world shall come to Norfolk, or Richmond, or Smithtown, and that no more cotton shall be sent to England until England will pay a price for it that shall let negroes be worth a thousand dollars a head, &c., &c., &c.

Then, if it be asked why Norfolk, with its immense natural advantages for commerce, has not been able to do their business for them as well as New York; or why Richmond, with its great natural superiority for manufacturing, has not prospered like Glasgow, or Petersburg like Lowell—why Virginia is not like Pennsylvania, or Kentucky like Ohio?—they will perhaps answer that it is owing to the peculiar tastes they have inherited. . . .

Anne Royall Observes the Nation's Capital, 1826

Washington City

As I before observed, the conveyance from Richmond to Washington, by way of Fredericksburg, is partly by land and partly by water. The steam-boat which takes you in at Potomac Creek, at 8 o'clock, P.M. lands at Washington about daylight—by which means we lost the pleasure of an approaching view of the city, which the river commands. When the steam-boat lands her passengers on the shore of the Potomac, they are a mile, at least, from the inhabited part of the city, with the exception of a few scattered dwellings. To remedy this inconvenience, the proprietors of the line have provided a large vehicle, something like a stage coach; it is called a carry-all, and would carry twenty persons. This vehicle soon brought us in view of the "mighty city," which is nothing more than distinct groups of houses, scattered over a vast surface, and has more the appearance of so many villages, than a city.

It was not long before the towering dome of the capitol met my eye: its massy columns and walls of glittering white. The next object that strikes the eye of a stranger, is the President's house, on the left, while the capitol is on the right, as you advance in an eastern direction. Another object of admiration is the bridge over the Potomac. The capitol, however, which may aptly be called the eighth wonder of the world, eclipses the whole. This stupendous fabric, when seen at a distance, is remarkable for its magnitude, its vast dome rising out of the centre, and its exquisite whiteness. The President's house, like the capitol, rivals the snow in whiteness. It is easily distinguished from the surrounding edifices, inasmuch as they are of brick. Their red walls and black, elevated roofs, form a striking contrast to the former, which is not only much larger, but perfectly white, and flat on the top. From the point just mentioned, it has the appearance of a quadrangular; it displays its gorgeous columns at all points, looking down upon the neighboring buildings in silent and stately grandeur. The War Office, Navy Office, the Treasury department, the Department of State, the General Post Office, and the City Hall are all enormous edifices. These edifices; the elevated site of the city; its undulating surface, partially covered with very handsome buildings; the majestic Potomac, with its ponderous bridge, and gliding sails; the eastern branch with its lordly ships; swelling hills which surround the city; the spacious squares and streets, and avenues, adorned with rows of flourishing trees, and all this visible at once; it is not in the power of imagination to conceive a scene so replete with every species of beauty. . . .

Manners and Appearance

With respect to the manners and appearance, no description can be given that would yield satisfaction. Perhaps no body of people can be found equal to the number, in which there is less similarity than in Washington. In their appearance scarcely any resemblance can be traced, and so of their manners. The cause of this is to be found in the nature of its population, which is derived from every part of the world. The inducements held out to all classes of people to settle the metropolis were many and lucrative. Here was much work to do, of all descriptions; a number of buildings to be erected, which required artificers of all sorts. These artificers were to be victualed and attended, which drew another species of emigrants [*sic*]. Anon, the Congress and a long train of public officers are to be furnished with accommodations, and foreign ambassadors and ministers swell the demand. These allurements, added to the eager desire of government to sell the lots donated to it by the proprietors of the city lands, produced a flood of emigration to the metropolis from all parts, both of Europe and the United States. These people brought with them different habits, religions, and customs; most of them, however, were from Ireland, and principally of the humblest class of citizens. This age must pass away before anything like assimilation of manners or characteristic traits can be assigned to the citizens of Washington.

The population of Washington may be said to consist of four distinct classes of people, whose pursuits, interests and manners, differ as widely as though they lived on opposite sides of the globe, viz. those who keep congress boarders and their mutual friends, and subordinate officers of government; these resemble in every respect and ought never to be separated; secondly, the labouring class; thirdly, what may be called the better sort; and fourthly, the free negroes. It may be observed briefly, that the first mentioned class are proud, ignorant, and many of them insolvent. The labouring class (of which there are a great number employed, both at the capitol and the navy yard, and improving the city,) are mostly very dissipated, and spend their earnings as fast as they obtain it. And as that class which may justly claim the appellation of the first citizens, unfortunately, they form but a small minority. In justice to Washington, however, it must be observed, that amongst these are to be found many men of worth, whose virtues and talents may justly rank them with the first men in the United States. The ladies of Washington are very handsome, they have delicate features, and much expression of countenance, and excel in the beauty and symmetry of the person; but (excepting the higher class, who are females of education,) are, withal, most detestably proud. As to the appearance of the men, as observed above, it is impossible to say what it is, differing so much as they do. . . .

General Remarks

No conception can be more fallacious, or any idea more wide of the truth, than that entertained by one who has never seen this city. Our hearts swell with national pride at the mention of its name—Washington! Washington city is repeated with a sort of holy enthusiasm; nothing evil or low mingles with the sound; it conveys sentiments at once the most elevated, the most pleasing. But how are we disappointed upon coming to this Idol of America! In every other country, in every other town or city, some semblance is maintained in that attention which is due to the poor and to the rich. But if you are poor, you have no business in Washington, and unless you are well dressed, you will have good luck if you be not kicked out of doors by the servants, should you attempt to enter a house. These servants, which are nothing more than so many bullies, swarm in every boarding house, and so much do they and proprietor resemble, differing only in slight shade of colour, that it would be difficult for one (if he were much frightened) to distinguish one side from the other. In point of politeness, the advantages are often on the side of the former. In short, ignorance, impudence, and pride are decided traits in the bulk of the citizens of Washington, particularly those mutual friends before mentioned. One is astonished upon going into the shops and stores, which are spacious buildings, to meet with the most unpolished, uncouth looking people, particularly the Irish women. They are certainly the most disgusting in their fierce, savage countenance, quite appalling to those unaccustomed to foreigners; though the Irish men are generous and humane, very much so. I have known them in a few minutes make a handsome collection for some indigent traveler, (who might happen to pass the work-shops) whom they had never seen before, and perhaps might never see again! . . .

The First City Charter of Providence, Rhode Island, 1832

Section 1. *Be it enacted by the General Assembly, and by the authority thereof it is enacted,* That the inhabitants of the town of Providence shall continue to be a body politic and corporate, by the name of the "City of Providence," and, as such, shall have, exercise, and enjoy all the rights, immunities, powers, privileges and franchises, and shall be subject to all the duties and obligations now appertaining to, or incumbent upon said town as a municipal corporation . . . ; may ordain and publish such acts, laws and regulations as shall be needful to the good order of said body politic, and inflict fines and penalties for the breach thereof, not exceeding two hundred dollars and six months imprisonment for any one offence; and may hold courts of judicature, with the powers and jurisdictions hereinafter mentioned.

Sec. 2.   *And be it further enacted,* That the administration of all the fiscal, prudential and municipal affairs of said city, with the government thereof, shall be vested in one principal magistrate, being a freeholder and freeman of said city, to be called the mayor; one council of six freemen, being also freeholders, to be called the board of aldermen; and one council of twenty-four freemen, being also freeholders, to be called the common council; which boards shall, in their joint capacity, be called the city council; together with such other magistrates or officers as by this act are, or hereafter may be, by the laws of this State and of said city, prescribed; . . .

Sec. 3.   *And be it further enacted,* That the major of said city shall be the chief executive magistrate, thereof, and shall be *ex officio* a justice of the peace within the city. It shall be his duty to be vigilant and active in carrying the laws to be executed and enforced; and in order to enable him more effectually to preserve the peace and good order of the city, all the powers given to sheriffs and other officers in and by an act entitled "An act to prevent routs, riots and tumultuous assemblies, and the evil consequences thereof," are hereby conferred upon him. He is hereby empowered to commit to prison, for a term not exceeding twenty-four hours, any dissolute person or persons who may be detected in revelling in the streets, committing any mischief, quarrelling, or otherwise behaving in a disorderly manner, to the disturbance or annoyance of the peaceable inhabitants of said city. He is also empowered to enter any house or building which he has reasonable cause to suspect to be inhabited by persons of ill fame, or to which persons of dissolute, idle, or disorderly character are suspected to resort; and if any dissolute, disorderly, or vagrant persons are found assembled in or about any such house or building, he shall command all such persons immediately to disperse, if in his opinion the good order of any portion of the city requires it; and in case of neglect or refusal to obey such command, he is hereby authorized to commit any person or persons so disobeying, to prison for a term not exceeding forty-eight hours; . . . He may call meetings of the boards of aldermen and common council, or of either of them, although one or both of them may have been adjourned to a more distant day. He shall, from time to time, communicate to both of them such information, and recommend such measures, as the business and interests of the city, may, in his opinion, require. He shall preside in the board of aldermen, and in joint meetings of the two boards, but shall have only a casting vote. . . .

Sec. 4.   *And be it further enacted,* That the executive powers of said city, generally, and administration of police, with all the powers now possessed by the town-council of the town of Providence, and of its members, by virtue of their offices, . . . except the power of passing by-laws and ordinances, shall be vested in the mayor and aldermen. All other powers now vested in, or by this charter, conferred upon the inhabitants or freemen of Providence, or in the town-council thereof, shall be vested in the mayor and aldermen, and the common council of said city, to be exercised by concurrent vote, each board to have a negative upon the other. . . . The city council shall take care that monies shall not be paid from the treasury, unless granted or appropriated; shall secure a just and proper accountability, by requiring bond, with sufficient penalty and surety or sureties, from all persons intrusted with the receipt, custody, and disbursement of moneys; shall have the care and superintendence of city buildings, and the custody and management of all city property, with power to let or see what may be legally let or sold, and to purchase and take, in the name of the city, such real and personal property as they may think useful to the public interest. All taxes ordered to be assessed by the city council, or by the General Assembly, shall be assessed, apportioned and collected according to the modes prescribed by the laws of the State; and the city council shall, as often as once a year, cause to be published, for the information of the freemen, a particular account of receipts and expenditures, and a schedule of city property. . . .

Sec. 6. *And be it further enacted,* That the judicial powers herein granted shall be exercised by a municipal court, to be holden by one judge, to be appointed by the city council; and by a police court, to consist of so many of the justices, assigned to keep the peace within said city by the General Assembly, not exceeding three, as shall be annually selected by concurrent vote of the city council, and oftener in case of vacancy; . . . The municipal court shall have original jurisdiction of suits for offences against the by-laws, ordinances and regulations of the . . . city-council of said city, in which the penalty or fine shall exceed two days' imprisonment, or twenty dollars. It shall have final appellate jurisdiction in suits originally brought at the police or justices' courts against inhabitants of said town or city, for offences against by-laws, in which the fine or penalty shall not exceed twenty dollars, or ten days' imprisonment. The judge of said court may empanel juries of freemen of the city, to be drawn by the board of aldermen in the same manner as heretofore by the town council. . . .

Sec. 7. *And be it further enacted,* That the police court of said city shall have exclusive original jurisdiction of suits for offences against the by-laws, ordinances and regulations of the freemen of the . . . city council of said city, in which the punishment shall not exceed two days' imprisonment, or twenty dollars fine, and shall be holden at such times and places in said city, as may, from time to time, be provided by the city council. The justices thereof shall have the same power and jurisdiction which other justices of the peace have in criminal cases; and all writs and process signed by any one of them, shall be valid to all intents and purposes. . . .

Sec. 8. *And be it further enacted,* That for the purpose of holding elections, the said city shall be divided into six wards, to contain, as nearly as may conveniently be, an equal number of freemen. And it shall be the duty of the city council, from time to time, not more than once in five years, to review, and, if it be needful, to alter said wards, in such manner as to preserve, as nearly as may be, an equal number of freemen to each. . . . In each ward there shall, annually, on the third Wednesday of April, be chosen a warden and clerk, who shall hold their offices for one year, and until others shall have been chosen to their places. The wardens shall preside at the meetings of the wards, with the power and duties of moderators of town-meetings; and the clerk shall record all the proceedings, and certify the votes given. Immediately after the choice of warden and clerk, the freemen present shall elect, by a majority of the votes given in each ward, four of the freemen of said ward to be members of the common council. As soon as the requisite number of common council men shall have been chosen, each freeman shall carry in his written or printed ballot, endorsed with his name, for one freeholder, being a freeman of said city, for mayor; and six such freeholders, being freemen, that is to say, one from each ward in the city, to be aldermen thereof, for one year from the first Monday of June, then next to ensue. . . . The said board of aldermen may, in the absence of the mayor, choose a president *pro tempore,* who shall preside at joint meetings of the two boards, and who shall also, in the absence of the mayor from the city, or in case of his inability, exercise for the time being all the powers and duties of mayor. . . . Each board may determine the rules of its proceedings, judge of the election of its own members, and in cases of failure of elections, or of vacancy by death, absence, resignation or disability, may order new elections. A quorum for the transaction of business shall in each board, consist of a majority of the members thereof. . . .

Sec. 10. *And be it further enacted,* That inhabitants of the said city of Providence, legally entitled to become freemen thereof, may be admitted as such by the board of aldermen and common council, in joint meeting; they having produced their deeds or other evidence of title, and been propounded on the records of said joint meeting, or in town meeting before the organization of the city government, at least three months before such admission, . . . and having otherwise conformed to the requisitions of law touching the admission of freemen. The names of all freemen shall be entered by the city clerk in a general list, alphabetically arranged; and it shall be his duty before making up the ward lists of freemen, hereinafter mentioned, to return to the board of aldermen the names of all persons, who having sold or been divested of their estates, shall be disqualified from voting. . . .

✳ *E S S A Y S*
_____

These essays address two important aspects of early urban growth and provide a general context for the topics introduced in the documents. The first essay, by Richard C. Wade of the Graduate Center of the City University of New York, represents one of the pioneering perspectives of the field of American urban history. Seeing western cities as vanguards of the frontier, Wade outlines the vital economic functions that cities of the Ohio River Valley, as centers of both commerce and industry, played in the early nineteenth century. The second selection, by Christine Stansell of Princeton University, illustrates the rise of new kinds of poverty as a result of urbanization between 1789 and 1820 and discusses the feminization of indigence in these years.

The Economic Base of New Cities in the National Period

RICHARD C. WADE

The towns were the spearheads of the frontier. Planted far in advance of the line of settlement, they held the West for the approaching population. . . . Whether as part of the activity of the French and Spanish from New Orleans or of the English and Americans operating from the Atlantic seaboard, the establishment of towns preceded the breaking of soil in the transmontane West. . . .

In a single generation this whole transmontane region was opened to settlement. In the process towns grew up along the waterways and in the heart of fertile farm areas. The names of many of these—such as Rising Sun, Vevey, and Town of America—were soon forgotten, but others—like Pittsburgh, St. Louis, and Cincinnati—became familiar words. This growth of urbanism was an important part of the occupation of the West, and it provided the central experience of many settlers who crossed the mountains in search of new homes. . . .

A city is many things: it is a cultural focus, a social resort, a political center, but before all—though not above all—it is a place where people earn a living. This priority is especially striking in young cities where a vigorous social and cultural life must await the establishment of a stable economic structure. . . . For this reason, during the first fifteen years of the nineteenth century the pulse of Western cities was their trade and manufacturing. Development along these lines was rapid, so much so that by the end of the [War of 1812] each town had erected an economy whose general outlines would not change substantially until the coming of the railroad.

The key to this economic growth was transportation. It determined the pattern of settlement, the direction and volume of commerce, and the ease and speed of the occupation of the West. Until the advent of the railroad and most important highways were rivers. Roads in the trans-Allegheny area were poor, and travel over them slow and expensive. . . . Hence, the clumsiness of land traffic put the major transport burden on the rivers. Until the adoption of the steamboat this was largely a southward movement, because the difficulty of ascending the Mississippi and Ohio made the cost almost prohibitive. . . .

The expense of this travel led to a search for speedier methods. Pittsburgh, Marietta, and Wheeling tried to meet the problem with sailing schooners, only to find that most of the vessels that reached the Gulf preferred to take their chances on the high seas rather than return up the tortuous inland rivers. In 1805 two Cincinnati firms rigged barges with sails, inaugurating a round-trip with New

Reprinted by permission of the publishers from *The Urban Frontier: Pioneer Life in Pittsburgh, Cincinnati, Lexington, Louisville, and St. Louis* by Richard C. Wade, excerpts from pp. 1–2, 39–72, Cambridge, Mass.: Harvard University Press. Copyright © 1959 by the President and Fellows of Harvard College.

Orleans which enjoyed some success for almost a decade. These expedients did little to disturb the downward commercial flow of the river, and in 1807 over 1,800 boats arrived in the Louisiana port, while only 11 went upstream. The war, however, accomplished what ingenuity could not. New Orleans' customary Atlantic routes broke under British pressure, and its merchants turned to the expensive interior waterways. By 1815 keelboats were reaching Pittsburgh daily from the South. . . . The new pattern, begun under war conditions, was later solidified by the steamboat, which for the first time permitted easy and regular upriver traffic.

Despite the attempts to equalize the flow of commerce on Western rivers, the great bulk of it moved toward New Orleans. On barges, keelboats, and flatboats the growing surplus of the new country floated to markets in the South. In 1801 the Gulf port's inland trade was valued at $3,649,000, six years later it had grown to $5,370,000, and in 1816 the West poured goods worth $8,062,000 into New Orleans. . . .

With a river system oriented to the South, and with awkward land contacts with the East, little bilateral exchange was possible. Instead, an extensive system of triangular trade arose. The new country imported Eastern goods across the mountains on credit extended by Philadelphia, Baltimore, or New York firms. Western merchants then found a market for their products in New Orleans, where, as a traveler described it, "their brokers . . . sell, as much as they can, for ready money; or rather take in exchange cottons, indigo, raw sugar, the produce of Low Louisiana, which they send off by sea to the houses at Philadelphia or Baltimore, and thus cover their first advances." This pattern was the best that the transmontane region could wring from an unfavorable situation, but soon cries of "extortion" and "colonialism" were raised. Payments to the East kept specie scarce, and prices in the West, absorbing the high transmontane costs, tended to move upward. This constant imbalance induced some cities to manufacture at home, and others to seek more favorable conditions in the New Orleans market. Thus arose the two most dynamic movements in the Western economy; and the towns, as the commercial nerve centers of the frontier, took the lead in the adjustment.

It was in the context of this relationship with the outside world that Western towns developed their basic economic structures. Though they shared a common dilemma, their responses to it varied. Peculiar locations, resources, and historic origins precluded uniformity and produced important differences. Some cities, such as Pittsburgh and Lexington, turned enthusiastically to industry; others, like St. Louis, maintained their reliance on commerce; while Cincinnati and Louisville experimented with both. By 1815, however, the direction of growth of each frontier city had been pretty well fixed, though the question of speed of development still held perils.

Pittsburgh, like other Western towns, was cradled in commerce; but while still very young it showed remarkable manufacturing promise. Indeed, this new interest spread so rapidly that by 1810 a native likened the town to "a large workshop." . . .

Its rise as a manufacturing center was accompanied by a population growth which made Pittsburgh by 1815 the largest city in the West. In that decade and a half the town increased more than fivefold, from 1,565 inhabitants in 1800 to an estimated 8,000 in 1815. . . . Much of this astonishing expansion was artificial, reflecting the prosperity occasioned by international complications and war, but few doubted the permanence of the boom, and pessimists were scarce. . . .

One of the sources of this optimism was the constant flow of immigrants across the mountains towards the interior. As the most publicized Western town, and situated on the best route to the new areas, Pittsburgh became the focus of the avenues of migration, "the Thermopylae of the West," as one observer put it. Travel over the Appalachians was so difficult and costly that most people converted their goods into cash before moving. When they arrived at the head of the Ohio, they needed nearly everything—food, furniture, and even clothing. Farm implements and building tools, too heavy to carry, would be indispensable in the next months. Hence migrants sold their horses and wagons in Pittsburgh, used up their cash, and moved down the river. . . . This transient immigration, along with Pittsburgh's own increase, made up a home market for local merchants and manufacturers that was of central importance to the town's economy.

The merchant could rely on a much broader demand, however, than that of the townsmen and migrants: the entire transmontane region offered opportunity. At first he was a middleman handling Eastern goods; indeed, initially he was usually a partner or factor of a Philadelphia or Baltimore firm. Wagons brought merchandise over the mountains to Pittsburgh, where it was either sold locally or sent by boat to the interior, often as far south as New Orleans. But this triangular trade was clumsy and sometimes inefficient. If Pittsburgh could manufacture some of these items itself, the expensive overland transit could be eliminated. This situation very early created an inducement to manufacture in the young city. The mountains formed a protective wall, or tariff, around new industries, allowing them to flourish even when their cost structure was relatively high. Hence for a time Pittsburgh got the best of both worlds; it remained an important link in the mercantile chain that bound Eastern cities to the frontier, and yet became a manufacturing center of increasing importance to the West. . . .

Most of the money invested in Pittsburgh manufacturing came from the town itself, very little being supplied from the East until the railroad era. This reliance on local capital makes the rapid growth of the city's industry even more remarkable. In 1803 the value of manufactured products was more than $350,000. Seven years later it had jumped to over $1,000,000, and by 1815, it exceeded $2,600,000. The progress was so startling that *Niles' Register* exclaimed, "Pittsburgh, sometimes emphatically called the 'Birmingham of America,' will probably become *the greatest manufacturing town in the world.*"

The principal factor in this development was iron, which by 1815 accounted for more than a quarter of the value of all goods manufactured in Pittsburgh. Though originally a rural industry, it very early become important in the town's economy. . . .

In 1815 Pittsburgh turned out over $750,000 in iron products, a fourteenfold increase in a dozen years. More important, however, than the statistics of expansion were the implications of the technological shift they denoted. Steam power quickly replaced water power, not only in Pittsburgh but in other Western cities as well. As it did so, settlement patterns were altered and the drive toward urbanization intensified. Water power had meant dispersion, the location of machines on many rivers and streams, and an emphasis on local markets. Steam power required concentration, location near reservoirs of raw materials and human skills, and large-scale production for extensive markets. Pittsburgh's iron industry set off this quiet revolution by making machinery available at reasonable prices and leading in the adoption of new methods.

While Pittsburgh's iron manufacture grew because metal goods were too heavy and costly to carry across the mountains, its glass industry flourished because that material was too fragile for rough overland conveyance. Colonel James O'Hara began making glass in 1795 in the first such factory in the United States to use coal for fuel. In 1803 the town's two houses produced $13,000 in white and green glass. By 1810 this figure had jumped to $63,000, and five years later a half-dozen firms valued their product at $235,000. . . .

Success in manufacturing did not cause Pittsburgh to neglect commerce. Indeed, industrial expansion lent new urgency to the young city's economic connections with the outside world. Located at the head of water navigation in the West, the town turned down river where it found outlets either in settlement along the Ohio or in New Orleans. . . .

By 1815 Pittsburgh surpassed Lexington as the largest town in the West, and was unchallenged in importance. Travelers had early recognized it as "the key to the Western territory," but now it was more than a gateway. Pittsburgh merchants traded on the Mississippi as well as on the Atlantic seaboard, while ships built on its wharves frequented the West Indies and Europe. "Iron City" manufacturing was already as famous as its smoke was notorious. . . .

Lexington, like Pittsburgh, owed its early importance to commerce, but in the first decade of the century it turned increasingly to manufacturing. Though landlocked, in a country where the main highways of travel were rivers, the city grew so rapidly that in 1815 *Niles' Register* predicted it would be "the greatest inland city in the Western world." Situated on an "extensive plain of the *richest land*," it had been Kentucky's central mart since its savage days. The road from Limestone connected Lexington with the Ohio by a trip of only two and a half days, and the Wilderness Road tapped Virginia and the Carolinas by a land passage which, though long and difficult, was much traveled. The town's merchants, using Eastern goods brought over the water route, supplied "not only their own state, but that of Tenasse [*sic*] . . . and part of the Indiana territory." As the hemp industry grew, however, traders turned to manufacturing cordage, bagging, and sail, and, later, under the impact of embargoes and war, expanded into other industrial areas as well.

During the resulting prosperity, Lexington's population speedily increased. It expanded from 1,795 to 4,326 in the ten years following 1800, and by 1815 travelers estimated it at from 6,000 to 7,000. . . .

Though an increasing number of Lexingtonians sought employment in industrial enterprises, and the newspapers constantly encouraged the immigration of skilled tradesmen, the town's basic business was commerce. Like Pittsburgh in the Ohio Valley, it became the pivotal dispatching point for Eastern goods needed on Kentucky and Tennessee farms, and, in turn, the merchandiser of the hemp, grain, and tobacco that increasingly flowed from Western soil to outside markets. . . .

Consistent profits from mercantile ventures enabled some Lexingtonians to accumulate sizable capital reserves. Though most of these earnings went into land speculation and opulent living, many merchants invested heavily in manufacturing. The continued unfavorable trade balance with the East combined with huge hemp surpluses on the Blue Grass to promote large-scale production of cordage and bagging. Merchant-manufacturers like Thomas Hart and the January brothers, forseeing the increasing demand for cloth and rope in the West, opened factories in the 1790s. The beginnings were modest until the commercialization of cotton in the South created a new market for both rough cloth and twine. By 1809 there were "13 extensive rope-walks, five bagging manufactories, and one of duck," with a total output of over $500,000. . . .

While processing hemp was Lexington's principal industry, it [composed] only a part of the general movement toward manufacturing. . . . A group of merchants formed the Lexington White Lead Company, and Thomas Copeland opened a factory for making steam engines. By the end of the hostilities the town boasted no fewer than six steam mills engaged in grinding grain, making paper, or spinning and weaving textiles. . . .

Lexington's industrialization was stimulated not only by an unfavorable trade balance and the proximity of such materials as hemp and wool, but also by a chronic shortage of labor. "The want of hands excites the industry of the inhabitants of this country," observed a traveler. . . . The deficiency led to the widespread adoption of slave labor in the new factories, especially in hemp operations where the work was uncomplicated and special skills readily acquired. Though some operators owned enough Negroes to man their ropewalks, most of them were "hired out" by other slaveowners on a monthly or yearly basis. Many factories were extensive, a cotton and a woolen one each employing over 150 hands.

In 1815 Lexington's optimism about its economic future exceeded even that of Pittsburgh. . . . Yet a cloud drifted lazily toward the town. The steamboat *Enterprise*, docking at Louisville in 1815 after a successful run against the Mississippi and Ohio rivers, demonstrated a new dimension of trade. Kentucky newspapers hailed this as a new and exciting era in the West's unfolding history. Few realized then that the next chapter of this story contained the economic ruin of Lexington, and that the steamboat, which liberated the new country from an unfavorable trade predicament, would be the agent of the disaster.

Increasingly diversified economies accompanied the growth of Pittsburgh and Lexington, but their most ambitious rival, Cincinnati, remained essentially commercial. . . . Cincinnati's strategic position in the Ohio Valley set it astride the great highways of travel and exchange, and around it lay the fertile farm lands of a considerable part of Ohio, Kentucky, and Indiana. . . . As the mercantile heart of this vast hinterland, Cincinnati grew in two decades from a "remarkable sprightly, thriving town" to the West's most dynamic city.

Though the whole Miami region attracted large numbers of settlers after the crushing of the Indians in 1794, the proportional increase was greater in Cincinnati than in the surrounding country. With about 500 in 1795, the town doubled its residents during the next decade. This was merely a prelude, however, to the striking expansion of the next ten years. By 1810 there were 2,540 inhabitants, and four years later the population had reached 4,000. In the next 24 months more than 2,000 additional people crowded into the budding city to make their homes. . . .

Cincinnati, however, did not grow because immigrants stopped there; rather, settlers disembarked at the "Queen City" because it was the most important trading center between Pittsburgh and the Falls of the Ohio. Merchandise from Philadelphia, Baltimore and New York was sold there, and the older inhabitants of the region bought European and Indies imports in Cincinnati stores. In addition, an increasing number of artisans fashioned household and farm implements for their fellow townsmen and the rapidly filling hinterland. Farmers on both sides of the Ohio took advantage of the port's wharves and shipping facilities, or found a market for their surplus grains in its mills and breweries. Lines of barges carried on a lively trade with New Orleans, taking Western produce to the Gulf and bringing back sugar, cotton, and molasses. These trade patterns, established early, remained essentially unaltered until the coming of the steamboat. . . .

Cincinnati's major commercial problem stemmed from its remoteness from the manufacturing East and the great expense of transporting merchandise across the mountains. Prices in the West reflected this added cost, all of the increase being passed on to the consumer. The war years, 1812–1815, aggravated conditions by creating constant shortages of Eastern goods and raising prices still further. Two movements arose to cope with this situation. One hoped to make New Orleans not only the receiver of Western goods but the import center for Eastern products as well. . . . The other sought to relieve the dependence on Atlantic cities by encouraging local manufacturing. Both of these drives enjoyed limited success, though neither disturbed Cincinnati's basic commercial matrix.

Upriver trade with New Orleans developed only slowly until the introduction of the steamboat, though rigged barges reduced freight charges from eight and nine dollars a ton to five and six. . . .

More spectacular and articulate was the campaign to encourage manufacturing in the city. Though travelers often predicted industrial expansion, and an increasing number of wood and iron objects were made in Cincinnati's shops, little manufacturing on a substantial scale developed in the first decade of the nineteenth century. Occasionally a successful merchant like Martin Baum invested in an iron foundry or a brewery, but this scarcely altered the commercial orientation of the town. Wartime scarcities, however, caused many to consider the advantages of local manufacturing. "It is well known," asserted a letter in *Liberty Hall,* "that a great city can be raised and an immense population supported, by extensive manufacturing establishments," so long as a home demand existed. . . .

This manufacturing drive represented the major economic current in Cincinnati during and immediately following the war with Great Britain. Behind the campaign were the town's most important people, many of whom invested in some industrial project. Though much of the talk was merely speculative, the achievements were substantial. In 1815 [Daniel] Drake pointed to a steam sawmill, driven by a twenty-horsepower engine, capable of cutting two hundred feet of board an hour. . . . The breweries had always been the city's greatest pride, and in 1815 they consumed 40,000 to 50,000 bushels of barley from the countryside. . . .

The symbol of the crusade, however, was the mammoth steam mill built on the river's edge and rising nine stories and 110 feet above the water—a monument alike to the "enterprising genius of the West" and the bumptious optimism of its entrepôt. . . . Half of the structure housed a seventy-horsepower engine designed by Oliver Evans, which could grind 700 bushels of flour a week, while the other half was reserved for a woolen factory. . . .

These manufacturing schemes, however, overextended local financial resources, causing many new firms to collapse in the postwar depression. As a result, this campaign probably retarded the city's industrial development, for throughout the twenties capital hesitated to invest in fields which had so recently proved fruitless. Cincinnati's economy turned again to commerce, though many citizens continued to preach diversification. . . .

Unlike other Western towns, St. Louis in the first decade of the nineteenth century still had an Indian problem, which reduced immigration and retarded its economic development. . . . Farther east, where Indian warfare was now a memory, St. Louis was regarded as a savage place. . . .

The fear, though greatly exaggerated, kept many immigrants away from St. Louis. Indeed, a petition to Congress in 1812 complained that some people were moving back across the river for safety. In the first decade of the nineteenth century only about five hundred residents were added to the town's population. Ironically, however, the outbreak of war with Great Britain in 1812 created the security needed to attract the hesitant by bringing troops into the area, and in 1815 St. Louis had around two thousand inhabitants. . . . The somnolent capital of Spanish Upper Louisiana suddenly became a boom town in the center of a rapidly expanding region.

Under the American flag as well as under Spanish or French authority, St. Louis's most important economic activity remained the fur trade. As early as 1769 an official Spanish report stated that "the sole and universal trade consists in furs." . . . Not only was this trade the core of St. Louis's economy, but the river metropolis was the commercial heart of America's fur empire. Almost all expeditions organized and outfitted there; all the principal companies centered in St. Louis, or had important branches there; most of the skins seeking markets in the East and Europe passed through there. It was the focus of activities that stretched north to the Canadian border and west almost to the Pacific. . . .

Though fur was the town's main economic prop, lead continually gained in importance. The most productive mines were in Wisconsin and Missouri, and initially Ste. Genevieve became the chief shipping port because of its proximity to those mines. However, the same considerations which made St. Louis the center of the fur trade ultimately combined to establish it as the central mart for lead. It was the only town on the river which could assure a constant stream of supplies into the digging areas, and which could provide the capital needed for equipment and land. . . .

Commerce in both lead and furs depended less on the size of St. Louis than on its advantageous location. The emergence of the town as a mercantile center, however, was connected with its growth in numbers and wealth. While nearly all merchants engaged in fur and lead trading to some extent, many turned increasing attention to the local market. A dozen general stores lined Main Street in the heart of the business district, serving the mounting population of the young city and the surrounding area. Most of their merchandise came from Philadelphia and

Baltimore, though some came up the Mississippi from New Orleans. A few merchants dealt on a grander scale, like Charles Gratiot, who was "better known in Paris, London and Geneva than on this continent."

Regional trade developed rapidly. As [one observer] noted in 1811, the "settlements in the *vicinity* on both sides of the Mississippi, resort to this place as the best market for their produce, and to supply themselves with such articles as they may need." . . . Newspaper advertising constantly catered to St. Louisians with Philadelphia and Baltimore stylings. As the city grew, many merchants came to recognize the townsmen as their most regular customers. . . .

By 1815 the outlines of St. Louis's economy had been established. Though manufacturing existed on a limited scale, commerce was the fundamental activity. The town was both the distributing center for Eastern goods on the Mississippi frontier and the dispatching point for Western produce to the outside world. Though but a new community of two thousand people, its trade stretched across much of the continent. Trappers from St. Louis gathered fur in the Rockies, while its traders haggled over prices in New Orleans, New York and London. Lead dug in Wisconsin and processed on the town's edge was sold in Pittsburgh and Philadelphia. Farmers from both sides of the Mississippi brought their surplus to the rising metropolis, whence it was forwarded to New Orleans. Watching the almost imperial extent of this trade, Henry Marie Brackenridge prophesied in 1811 that "St. Louis will become the Memphis of the American Nile."

Louisville, like St. Louis, grew with river trade. Its strategic location "at the head of ascending and the foot of descending navigation," a contemporary observed, meant that "all the wealth of the western country must pass through her hands." Its major business was the transshipment of goods around the Falls when the water was low and the rapids treacherous. Wagons carried merchandise two miles south to Shippingport, or brought them to Louisville from there, while passengers dined and purchased in the town's taverns and stores. Though the introduction of the steamboat made "the prosperity of Louisville . . . a fixed fact," its wharves already reflected the increased river trade of the West. . . .

This mercantile prosperity and promise attracted a growing number of people to Louisville. Gilbert Imlay had found "upwards of two hundred houses" at the Falls in the 1790s, though the official census listed only 359 inhabitants at the end of the century. By 1810 that figure jumped to 1,357, and it doubled again in the next five years. . . .

[G]enerally favorable prospects brought forth a lively manufacturing interest. As early as 1810 Richard Steele proposed to build an iron factory at the Falls, where he would have "the advantage" of "working with slaves." Two years later Paul Skidmore's iron foundry turned out steam engines on a modest scale. In 1815 the Tarascon brothers began work on the Merchant Manufacturing Mill, one of the most ambitious industrial projects of the time, which was six stories high and ultimately cost $150,000. At the same time a New England company erected an immense distillery to carry on its business "in a much more extensive mode than any hitherto established in the United States." . . .

Though each town evolved an economy peculiar to its own location and

resources, some elements were shared by all. The central nexus of the urbanization of the West was commerce. All towns sprang from it, and their growth in the
early years of the nineteenth century stemmed from its expansion. The Ohio
River was the chief agent of this development, and the towns on its banks were
the initial beneficiaries. Remoter places did not participate in this prosperity, and
even Lexington found its landlocked situation an increasing handicap. But other
factors too played an important part in laying the economic foundations of frontier urbanism, notably the influence of the army, the tide of immigration, the
emergence of manufacturing, the development of banking, and, most spectacular
of all, the coming of the steamboat.

Though the army was never popular in Western towns except in time of danger, its influence on the economies of these communities was immense. Not only
did the troops protect infant settlements against Indian raids and foreign incur-
sion, but, more important, their purchases provided a constant stimulus to urban
expansion. . . . Throughout the nineties Pittsburgh served as a supply headquarters for troops in the Northwest, and when war came in 1812 the young manufacturing city provided Western forces with ordnance and shot. For better than two
decades the army was the town's best customer, and many local fortunes were
built on this trade.

Cincinnati, too, from its very first days, profited from federal military spending. Since it served as an outfitting depot for operations against the Indians and
later the British, the army leaned heavily on the town's merchants. . . . The role of
the military in the economic development of other Western towns is a similar
story. . . .

In 1815 most adults in Western cities were immigrants. They came largely
from the older sections of the country, but an increasing number arrived directly
from Europe without loitering in the East. The population growth of these urban
centers reflected the magnitude of the human stream that moved across the mountains into the West. The immigrant impact on their youthful economies, however,
is not encompassed merely in numerical increase. These people did more than
create an expanding local market; they also brought with them skills to perform
new jobs and capital to invest in new enterprises. Choosing cities as carefully as
farmers selected land, mechanics and entrepreneurs sought the place of maximum
opportunity and brightest future. And Western towns competed for these urban
migrants, advertising openings for profitable enterprise and specific types of employment.

As the cities grew, some turned to industry. By 1815 manufacturing had
transformed the economic structure of Pittsburgh, made great strides in Lexington, and found advocates in Cincinnati and Louisville. Other towns, more modest
in their hopes, embarked only on limited projects, usually for local purposes.
Travelers, however, were astonished to see this remarkable development in an
area so recently rescued from the wilderness. Some of this industrial growth
proved artificial, having been stimulated by embargoes and war which kept foreign goods off the American market. In the depression that rocked the West at the
close of hostilities many business firms failed, factories closed down, and widespread distress resulted. Yet even after this fat had been pared away, an impressive achievement remained. And the increasing adoption of steam power in

Western factories strengthened the establishing urban pattern by concentrating manufacturing in the large towns where labor and capital could be readily secured.

This development, remarkable as it was, might have been even more extensive if so much urban capital had not been drained off into land speculation. Most of the towns were older than the surrounding country, and capitalists tended to invest in nearby tracts, low in price, whose value was "certain to rise." Only in Pittsburgh, where much of the hinterland was either already appropriated or of poor quality, did commercial profits readily seek industrial channels. . . .

The towns were not only the commercial and industrial centers of the West, but its financial leaders as well. Though capital constantly streamed across the mountains into land or commercial enterprises, the new areas continually complained of a kind of colonial status, in which money always seemed to be moving eastward. Soon commercial interests began to demand some kind of banking facilities to increase the volume of money. But banks were unpopular, and new states hesitated to grant charters for issuing notes. Hence banking came to the West through the back door as part of the operations of insurance or trading companies. In 1802 the Kentucky Insurance Company at Lexington was given certain privileges of note issue in connection with its marine insurance, and subsequently put out a large circulation. Similarly, the Miami Exporting Company in Cincinnati, capitalized at $150,000 in 1803 as a trading company, turned four years later exclusively to banking. . . . All these companies were composed of leading merchants, an indication of the intimate relationship between commerce and early financial institutions.

Soon Western states chartered banks directly. By 1815 Cincinnati had three, one without a charter, and all seemed thriving. . . . In the same period Pittsburgh supported four banks. Indeed, during the war the whole West outgrew its antagonism to banks and developed a policy of easy incorporation. The issues of these institutions broke the logjam of scarcity and soon flooded the Western country with paper, most of whose value was questionable.

Nothing, however, accelerated the rise of the Western cities so much as the introduction of the steamboat. Expanding commerce offered attractive opportunities in new towns, and manufacturing created an increasing demand for skilled labor, but steam navigation, by quickening transportation and cutting distances, telescoped a half-century's development into a single generation. . . . The steamboat, observed James Hall, "has contributed more than any other event or cause, to the rapid growth of our population, and an almost miraculous development of our resources." . . .

Though developed in the East, the steamboat had a peculiar importance for the West. "The invention of the steamboat was intended for us," observed the editor of the *Cincinnati Gazette*. "The puny rivers of the East are only as creeks, or convenient waters on which experiments may be made for our advantage." The successful run in 1815 of the *Enterprise* up the Mississippi and Ohio from New Orleans to Pittsburgh established the practicability of steam navigation on inland waters, though the trip of the *Washington,* a larger ship, two years later, seemed more conclusive to contemporaries.

The flow of commerce downriver was now supplemented by a northward and eastward movement, giving trade and manufacturing new opportunity for expansion and growth. "To feel what an invention this is for these regions," wrote Timothy Flint, "one must have seen and felt . . . the difficulty and danger of forcing a boat against the current of these mighty rivers, on which progress of ten miles a day, is a good one." . . .

The coming of the steamer in 1815 wrought such basic changes that it might be said to have ended the first era in the urban history of the West. The watershed might be fixed a little earlier or later, but this technological innovation altered all the conditions of transmontane development. That year, moreover, saw the end of wartime prosperity and the beginning of the painful adjustment to a new economic situation. . . .

Women's Work and Poverty, c. 1789–1820

CHRISTINE STANSELL

To imagine New York City in 1789 is to conjure up the figures of the eighteenth-century picaresque: tattered beggars, silk-stockinged rich men, pompadoured ladies and their liveried footmen, leather-aproned mechanics and shabby apprentice-boys, sleek coach horses, pigs. It was a volatile, contentious, politicized place, where the riotous world of the laboring poor surrounded a small, self-enclosed enclave of the wealthy and urbane. New York was still only an outpost of international commerce, but its inhabitants already displayed some of the traits of the metropolitans they would become in the next half century: stylishness, high self-esteem and an awareness of social tensions barely held in check.

The economic and social changes that swept the city after the Revolution and transformed it into the leading port and, then, manufacturing center of America greatly altered the lives of its laboring people. Poverty increasingly defined the experience of many of those living in the dark, dirty, overcrowded little plebian neighborhoods along the East River. Poverty was closely connected to economic development. The successes of New York's early manufacturers were in no small part due to the ready availability of the cheap labor of the working poor. Earlier in the eighteenth century, poverty had usually been associated with the *inability* to work—with the crippled, the aged and the very young. By the early nineteenth century, poverty was becoming connected to the changing structure of work itself—to the difficulties laboring people had in supporting themselves in manufacturing employments that paid insufficient wages and gave insufficient work.

These rearrangements also involved changes between men and women. Within the swelling ranks of the laboring poor, urban migration and the beginnings of urban manufacturing spelled the disintegration of the customary household economies that had formerly absorbed the energies and loyalties of women. The growing uncertainty of employment for many men eroded the older, familiar configuration of male provider and female household manager, an actuality for many laboring families up to the Revolution and a reasonable expectation for many more. The disruption of household economies fostered new forms of

"Poverty in the Early Nineteenth-Century City," from *City of Women* by Christine Stansell, excerpts from pp. 3–18. Copyright © 1982, 1986 by Christine Stansell. Reprinted by permission of Alfred A. Knopf, Inc.

insecurity: for women, uncertainties about men's support and commitment; for men, the loss of accustomed kinds of authority within their households and workplaces.

The City

By 1820, New York had become a center of capitalist development, a staging ground for the great transformation of the industrial wage system. The 1790s saw the first stage of this phenomenal expansion, as American neutrality gave the city's merchants the opportunity to corner the Atlantic shipping trade between European belligerents. New York shipping flourished throughout the series of events that eventually drew all Europe into war. With profits from their newly won preeminence on the Atlantic routes, New York shippers turned a modest provincial harbor into a hub of international commerce. The population more than doubled between 1800 and 1820, from 60,000 to more than 123,000 people.

Merchant capitalism shaped the social geography of the city. Lining Broadway, the street of fashion, were the fine town houses of wealthy shippers and financiers. . . . Many trans-Atlantic visitors remarked on the pampered tastes so evident on Broadway, decidedly at odds with the Europeans' preconceptions of republican simplicity. Dressed to the hilt in the latest British styles, trailed about by servants, the New York rich showed a flair for fashion that led travelers to compare the Broadway throng to that of London's Bond Street. . . .

Although the merchants were ambitious, their search for profits did not extend to the new factories with which their New England counterparts were experimenting. The beginnings of the city's manufacturing sector, already evident by 1820, lay rather with men of more modest means, master artisans who, beginning in the 1790s, produced goods for the merchant capitalists' distant markets. Proximity to the seaport gave these entrepreneurs connections to the lucrative export trade; the necessity of furnishing goods in bulk encouraged them to abandon traditional methods of handicraft and to implement rudimentary methods of mass production. In their workshops, they began to use their journeymen as hired wage laborers rather than as craftsmen due an accustomed price for their work. In changing around their workshop arrangements, the masters laid the groundwork for urban industrialization.

This flourishing economy pulled into it people from all across the Western world; international turmoil cast up poor people as well as riches on Manhattan's shores. Because the city was the main point of debarkation for immigrant ships, it became a way station of Atlantic misery, an asylum for all kinds of survivors looking for another chance. "Vagrants multiply on our hands to an amazing degree," lamented Richard Varick, soon to be mayor, in 1786. The term "vagrants" dates back to the Elizabethan poor law; with its connotation of an undifferentiated class, it can mislead us. These people were not a homogeneous group but rather the motliest of crews, bound together by the one common circumstance of having arrived in New York with little or no position in life. Some were born wanderers, children or grandchildren of the rootless proletarians who drifted about the English empire: soldiers and sailors, prostitutes and peddlers, beggars, thieves and rogues. . . .

Other poor people had once been settled folk. English and Irish farmers, squeezed by enclosures and a run of bad harvests, came by the thousands searching for ways to turn their luck. Land shortages in the nearby countryside and in lower New England sent young men and women to the city searching for some means to establish themselves in life. Politics had motivated others to set sail from home: wealthy planters and their mulatto supporters who sought refuge from the Santo Domingo Revolution in 1801, Irish patriots who had fled the repercussions of the failed rebellion of 1798, English radicals in flight from Pitt's repression. Other British working people migrated for the rumored high wages of the New World. All contributed to "the prodigious influx of indigent foreigners" which the Almshouse superintendent lamented in 1796.

The immigrant poor were castaways set adrift by the storms of distant places, other "vagrants" were insiders, laboring people from New York with their own troubles to bear. Beginning in the early eighteenth century, long-term factors of economic distress pushed increasing numbers of urban artisans out of taxable status—one index of a decent livelihood—into the ranks of the propertyless. The growth of the colonial seaport cities did little or nothing to benefit the great majority of their residents; urban prosperity between 1700 and the eve of the Revolution took the form of a redistribution of wealth toward the wealthiest residents. . . . By 1776, as many as a third of the residents of America's large towns lived in poverty.

The trend continued after the Revolution. Although wage rates rose for journeymen and unskilled laborers between 1790 and 1830, seasonal and intermittent unemployment undercut these gains. High prices made periods of unemployment all the more difficult, especially since saving was nearly impossible. In those trades where the shift to entrepreneurial, profit-accumulating methods of production was pronounced, journeymen suffered increased competition for work, irregularity of employment and a lowering premium on skill (which resulted in the breakdown of apprenticeship and the hiring of semiskilled and unskilled workers). In other words, they experienced what Marxist economists call the casualization of labor. . . .

As in other eighteenth-century cities, the situation in New York does not bear out the oft-repeated assumption that laboring people profited by some fabled scarcity of labor in America. Seasonal unemployment kept sailors, unskilled laborers, many small masters and most journeymen at the margins of poverty and liable to periods of indigence. During the winter, cold weather and harbor ice brought shipping nearly to a standstill and threw dock laborers, artisans in the maritime trades and sailors out of work. With good luck and a moderate winter, these men worked about two-thirds of the year. Severe winters, however, disrupted the delicate balance of employment and idleness and created serious hardship. In the hard winter of 1817–18, for instance, when the adventurous could walk on solid ice from Manhattan to New Jersey, poor relief soared. Seasonality also affected the building trades, which depended on the weather, and the consumer finishing trades, especially shoemaking and tailoring, which as mass production proceeded apace, followed yearly cycles of demand. The journeymen masons in 1819, appealing for public support during a strike, calculated they worked about 213 days a year and estimated their surplus income (what was left over for clothes, recreation, illness and emergency) at $27; the journeymen carpenters, in a similar statement in 1809, estimated their wages allowed them to maintain only the smallest margin above subsistence. In the slow seasons, unemployed men made do by using any small savings they had accumulated or, more typically, by turning to odd jobs and migration to pull themselves and their families through. Journeymen sometimes went tramping for work; laborers set off for the docks of Charleston, Savannah, and New Orleans. . . . A rise in the price of necessities could mean widespread distress for those whose livelihoods were so shaky. Some 600 journeymen in the winter of 1797, for instance, requested assistance from the Common Council because of high prices. "By reason of large families," they claimed, they could not buy enough wood for their fires.

The result was a spartan standard of living. Accident and disease spelled disaster, and both were rife in late eighteenth-century cities. Poor sanitation and crowding made disease endemic; dock work and streets teeming with horses and wagons posed considerable hazards to life and limb. The relatively primitive state of medical care meant that simple injuries—a broken leg, for example, or a laceration—could be permanently crippling. . . . Likewise, the common respiratory diseases and persistent infections brought on by cold weather could also reduce the able-bodied to dependence on charity. . . .

The hostilities with Britain precipitated a full-scale social crisis and ushered in a sustained visitation of economic ill fortune. The disastrous embargo of 1807–9 on Atlantic trade badly damaged an economy geared to maritime commerce and caused widespread suffering among the unemployed. The War of 1812, which again paralyzed merchant shipping, pushed the numbers of those who sojourned in the Almshouse in 1813 and 1814 up to 1,430 people. In the winter of 1813, as many as 1,000 people a day sought municipal relief. The end of the war brought little respite, since once trans-Atlantic shipping resumed, immigrants poured into the city. In 1817, a conjuncture of circumstances—an unusually severe winter, an economic slump and the arrival of over 7,000 immigrants—created what amounted to a state of emergency. An estimated one-seventh of the population—15,000 people—depended on relief that winter. Over the next few years the crisis continued, sustained by more heavy immigration, another bad winter in 1820–21 and an outbreak of yellow fever in 1822. . . .

The character of the poverty-stricken population was changing. Certainly the traditional poor of the colonial period still figured among New York's dependents: orphans, cripples, the blind and deaf, widows, disabled soldiers, the aged, the sick, and again slaves freed by their masters because they were infirm. There had always been an admixture of able-bodied men and women among the strolling poor: landless young sons, sailors, failed farmers, women outcast for illegitimate pregnancies. But after the turn of the century, the proportion of the able-bodied among those dependent on relief seems to have climbed. The numbers of the "outdoor poor"—those who were able to or insisted upon maintaining themselves outside the Almshouse—were, by 1809, "already incalculable and rapidly increasing," the Almshouse superintendent noted. Between 1813 and 1815, the numbers of persons granted outdoor relief doubled, from 8,253 people to 16,417. These indigent people, dependent on relief but able to work—indeed, often working—were too closely identified with the laboring classes for officials to dismiss them as vagabonds. The problems the working poor posed were becoming, by 1820, critical issues of political economy, public welfare and public health.

Those problems were most evident in the living conditions of the laboring classes, which deteriorated visibly in this period. Although visitors to New York always lauded the New World splendor of airy Broadway, most of the city was cramped, gloomy and noisome, not much different from the humble quarters of an English provincial port like Liverpool or Bristol. . . . The sharp class segregation that would mark residential patterns of the nineteenth century was only beginning. But as newcomers crowded into these already congested districts, the east side came to be more identified with the poor, while the wealthy began to withdraw from the streets where they had once lived to move uptown to country houses or to more homogeneous elite districts. Boardinghouses for sailors, day laborers, journeymen and their families became wedges for the movement of masses of the poor into the east side streets. In response to rising rents, laboring people doubled and tripled up in what had once been single-family dwellings and packed into town houses abandoned by their wealthy owners and subdivided into tenements and boardinghouses. In 1819 at one address in Corlears Hook, 103 people lived in one building. In the outer wards at the city's edge, too, journeymen and laborers crowded, two and three families together, into little cottages strewn along the dirt roads and open tracts of ground. But it was the area between Broadway and the eastern waterfront that comprised the main quarter of the working poor, those without "Even a stool to sit on, nor a bed to lie upon" and the journeymen and laborers one step removed from their lot.

Overcrowding aggravated already serious sanitation problems. Methods that had served the modest Dutch town collapsed. Garbage and waste collected in open sewers that ran down the middle of the streets and congealed into a fetid mire around the street pumps and docks where servants, slaves and the municipal scavengers dumped refuse and slops every night. Horses, dogs, cattle and pigs compounded the problems of street sewage. Water was in short supply. To some degree, the stench and filth oppressed all classes of citizens, but the laboring classes, predictably, suffered the most. In the households of the prosperous, servants provided some of the amenities of cleanliness, and the affluent could retreat to the country during epidemics and the especially foul summer months. Moreover, their houses stood on the airiest and most salubrious spots on the island, while the tenements of the working poor lay close to unhealthy and low-lying land. . . .

Yellow fever was the most ominous consequence of overcrowding and bad sanitation. The first cases appeared in the summer of 1791 in a poor neighborhood near the waterfront, "a part of the city thickly inhabited, its houses generally small, and badly ventilated." By the fall, the "malignant fever" had subsided, only to appear again for the next three summers. In 1795 it broke out into an epidemic that, by its end, had killed some 750 people. The poor, unable to flee, were its chief victims. It swept through again in 1798 and then in 1803, 1805, and 1822. Its etiology was a mystery to the baffled city fathers. They knew that it came from ships in the West Indies trade, but how and why it took root in their once healthful port was a mystery. Theories abounded, but those who mulled over the question agreed there was some relationship between the epidemics and the influx of poor people.

Eighteenth-century people were no strangers to squalor. The affluent and the poor alike were accustomed to bodily discomfort and uncleanliness. What was new by 1820 was not dirt and disease but their heavy concentration in some districts. The yellow fever epidemics were the most startling images of this process, as the quarters of the laboring poor became literal threats to public health. In subsequent decades, the New York bourgeoisie would conflate the problems of poverty with those of disease. For the moment, it is enough to note that by 1820, few New Yorkers could fail to perceive either the increasing bounty or the deepening misery of their city.

Women's Work

The growth of merchant capitalism, the spread of wage relations in manufactories and artisan workshops and the decline of living standards all altered the ways in which laboring women worked for a living. The disappearance of productive households, in both the city and the rural areas from which many newcomers came, pushed women into new employments. As the livelihoods of many men became less dependable, families increasingly needed women's cash earnings to get by.

To analyze the disintegration of productive household economies is a complicated enterprise. This extremely uneven process spanned at least a century, perhaps 150 years. It occurred in different parts of America at different times. In the seaboard cities, household economies could be characterized as mixed— partly depending on men's cash earnings and commercially purchased goods, partly depending on women's produce—as early as 1750. Except for the rural hinterlands, there were no "pure" household economies—where women themselves crafted all domestic necessities—by the time of the Revolution. In many families, domestic production was only makeshift (a bit of spinning here, a little soap making there), as family resources in land and household declined. Finally, women of the strolling poor were entirely uprooted from household production.

Still, domestic production in one form or another would have been an experience that remained within the living memory of most laboring people in turn-of-the-century New York. Many of them did come directly from family farms in the American countryside and from tenancies, freeholds and peasant plots in the British Isles. In such rural societies, household production prevailed. Even women who had grown up in the city would probably have worked as servants or daughters in households where mistresses tended gardens and kept chickens, pigs, and cows. . . .

The working poor, however, lacked such domestic resources. Some poor journeymen's wives who lived on the outskirts of town might still keep gardens and poultry. But the well-stocked larder of the respectable artisan's wife was unattainable for the wives of poor artisans and casual laborers crowded into the tenements and for the many destitute female immigrants who had once kept their own pigs and spun their own yarn in Irish and English villages.

The causes of female poverty were both economic and familial. Some women, of course, were born paupers: destitute daughters of indigent mothers, driven from one country village to another until, in the Revolution and its aftermath, they drifted into the comparatively secure harbor of the city. Others came on hard times with the declining fortunes of the men in their families. For others, poverty ensued from a sudden loss of male support. Widowhood was virtually synonymous with impoverishment. So was the sudden disappearance of a man, for one reason or another. Sailors' women, for instance, suffered great hardship while their husbands and lovers were at sea. The exodus of men to the Revolution and, later, to the War of 1812 precipitated a crisis of female poverty from which many of those who were subsequently widowed by the wars—or deserted by roving men—never recovered. . . . Male absence and desertion may also have generally increased. The difficulties men experienced in supporting their families made it more likely they would leave them, either permanently or temporarily, in the perennial search for work that took migrating laborers and tramping artisans up and down the East Coast. Women, one New York charity noted in 1818, were generally more vulnerable to impoverishment than men, being "more exposed to a sudden reverse of circumstances."

As much as they could, these women tried to hold together disintegrating family economies. Some kept pigs or bits of gardens. Others gave up altogether any lingering ambitions toward the role of household mistress and dedicated their energies instead to the makeshift housekeeping of the city, the catch-as-catch-can routine of the destitute. Whatever their relationship to older forms of domestic production, cash became crucial to many women, either to support themselves or to supplement men's wages.

Domestic service was probably the most common waged employment. "Helps" (a more common term than "servant" in the early nineteenth century) worked alongside mistresses in the demanding routines of household crafts and the labor-intensive tasks of housekeeping in an age before utilities like running water and gaslight were available. . . .

Other kinds of paid employment were extensions of household work. Providing lodging was one way for women to bring in money. There was always a demand for lodgings in a seaport, since so many transients passed through, but the need grew greater as immigration increased after the War of 1812 and as growing numbers of employers eschewed the old practice of lodging their employees in their own houses. Taking lodgers could be as simple a matter as letting someone sleep on your floor for a few pence a week; it could also be a more formal operation, as it probably was for the seventy-nine women who identified themselves in the 1805 city directory as boardinghouse keepers. Laundressing work was available year round. Washing clothes was an onerous task that required strength and submitting to extremes of hot and cold. Black women often took on this lowly labor, one of the few paid employments they could obtain. In the late summer and fall, women could also venture out into the country—to rural New Jersey, Connecticut, Long Island, Westchester County and the Hudson Valley—where farm families took them on to help with the harvesting, canning and preserving.

The provisioning trades also offered women some foothold. In a growing city where householders might live some distance from the markets and stores, where growing numbers of workplaces were separate from households, and where some transient people had no households at all, women could make a living by hawking and vending foods and domestic supplies. Street peddling was work for black women, the very poor and women too frail to work at service. It required only the strength to carry a basket about and a shilling or two to invest in a day's wares. The numbers of street peddlers increased after 1800 along with the numbers of poor people who bought from them. Female hucksters sold fruits and vegetables, candies and cakes door-to-door, on busy corners and around the docks and count-inghouses. Their cries gave a special flavor to city life. . . .

More fortunate women had some chance to establish a small proprietorship. A bit of money could go toward building a little stand on some frequented spot in the business and workshop districts or on the docks, where women owners then sold refreshments to passersby and workingmen. Some women rented stalls in the public markets where they vended fresh produce and dairy products. A few owned small food shops of their own. In the census of New York occupations in the 1805 city directory, 18 women were counted among the city's 793 grocers, 5 among 27 fruit sellers, 2 cookshop owners out of a total of 7, a confectioner . . . and 7 tavern or coffee-house keepers out of 113 in the city. Prosperous enough for the city directory to notice them, these were probably widows—like Mrs. Grover, the confectioner—who had inherited already established businesses. Widowhood was a common road to female proprietorship.

On a more modest scale, the easy movement of people between households and streets allowed women to set up accommodations for eating and drinking in their own rooms, where they sold fruits, candies, cakes and liquor. Thus the Society for the Relief of Poor Widows (SRPW), the earliest female charity in the city, agreed to loan five dollars to a Mrs. McLeod "to assist her in setting up a little shop." In 1804, however, with an eye sharpened toward improving as well as relieving the poor, the society's ladies resolved to withhold their help from any widow who was found vending liquor. They wished to discourage their charges from running "disorderly houses," as they were known to the authorities. Called "bawdy houses" by the public, these little places sold cheap liquor to patrons of the "lowest" sort: free blacks, journeymen, apprentices, sailors, and women on the loose—courting girls, prostitutes and runaway wives. The bawdy houses ca-tered to sexual license, male rowdiness and *bonhomie* and to working people's love of drinking and dancing. High times went on there, "dancing, kissing, curs-ing and swearing" until all hours of the night, to the great disturbance of neigh-bors, who periodically took their grievances to court. Raucous patrons collected about their doors, catcalling at passersby and brawling among themselves. At one end of the spectrum, bawdy houses shaded into groceries, retreats where people stopped to relax and gossip; at the other, into brothel-like establishments that rented rooms for illicit sex. Here, too, black women could earn money, since bawdy houses often catered to an interracial clientele.

The realm of commodity production generally excluded women, except inso-far as its employments overlapped with those of families. The only women counted among the city's artisans in 1805—a female hatter and the Widow Har-ris, a shoemaker—had probably learned their trades as helpers to their husbands.

The exceptions were those sewing trades that were traditionally female. In dressmaking and millinery, women followed the regular artisan sequence of training and mastery, as apprentices, journeywomen and mistresses. Only in these trades were women a substantial presence. . . .

In most craftwork, women received no formal training, and their position was marginal. Their employments were either an extension of tasks they performed as helpers to men—shoe binding, for instance—or continuations of domestic crafts they learned in family households. The "putting-out" or "giving-out" system, which encompassed most of the women who did work in commodity production, drew on both artisanal and domestic arrangements. In the years after the Revolution, city merchants and village storekeepers along the Northeastern seaboard began distributing raw materials to women to work up at home into ready-made goods, which the entrepreneurs then sold: flax and wool to spin into yarn, yarn to weave into cloth and stockings, stockings to seam, straw to braid into the makings of hats, shoes to bind, cloth to sew into gloves and shirts. Although putting out flourished mostly in rural New England, some give-out work was also available in New York. . . .

Most commonly, poor women worked at different employments throughout the year. Two women charged by authorities in 1820 with keeping a disorderly house, for example, also did washing and sewing on the side. A street seller might turn to laundressing in cold weather; a laundress might supplement her earnings with put-out work. When all else failed, laboring women turned to poor relief, either "outdoor"—cash, wood or food—or institutional "indoor" relief in the Almshouse or Almshouse hospital. For old women, the shift to relief was often permanent. Many Almshouse inhabitants would live out their days there, although hardly happily. . . .

Younger women seemed to have used the Almshouse as a temporary resort during the winter, when expenses were highest, or when men were absent, out of work, or ill. With good fortune, a woman could leave when circumstances eased; with a run of bad luck, she might be in and out for some time, forced to piece together ragged employments with indoor relief. . . . Periods of precarious dependency on a man alternated with hand-to-mouth self-sufficiency; both were coupled with the ongoing struggle to fend off disasters like a child's death.

The disruptions of the early national period made women's subsistence from male-headed households shaky, but New York's economy as yet provided them almost no other ways to make a living. When Edward Livingston, mayor in 1803, proposed a municipal workshop to employ the indigent, he was able to specify some tasks for men, but could propose nothing more for women than vague "labours suited to their strength." Even the stern gentlemen of the Society for the Prevention of Pauperism, ever vigilant against the idle propensities of the poor, acknowledged that it was difficult for women to making a living: "throughout the country, it may be said, there is often a defect of profitable employment for women and children of indigent families" . . . "women have fewer resources than men; they are less able to seek for employment." Paid work was sparse and unstable. Laboring women were confined within a patriarchal economy predicated on direct dependence on men, although that system was severely strained. The hardest-pressed of the working poor, they formed a vast reserve of labor that enterprising employers had only to tap.

※ *F U R T H E R   R E A D I N G*

Carl Abbott, *Boosters and Businessmen: Popular Economic Thought and Urban Growth in the Antebellum Middle West* (1981)

Robert G. Albion, *The Rise of the New York Port, 1815–1860* (1939)

Thomas Bender, *Toward an Urban Vision: Ideas and Institutions in Nineteenth Century America* (1975)

Barbara Berg, *The Remembered Gate: Origins of American Feminism—Women and the City, 1800–1860* (1978)

Elizabeth Blackmar, *Manhattan for Rent, 1825–1860* (1989)

Stuart M. Blumin, *The Urban Threshhold: Growth and Change in a Nineteenth-Century American City* (1976)

Paul Boyer, *Urban Masses and Moral Order in America, 1820–1920* (1978)

Michael Feldberg, *The Philadelphia Riots of 1844: A Study in Ethnic Conflict* (1975)

Lori D. Ginzberg, *Women and the Work of Benevolence: Morality, Politics and Class in the Nineteenth-Century United States* (1990)

Anita Shafer Goodstein, *Nashville, 1780–1860: From Frontier to City* (1989)

Leroy Graham, *Baltimore: The Nineteenth-Century Black Capital* (1982)

Hendrik Hartog, *Public Property and Private Power: The Corporation of the City of New York in American Law, 1730–1870* (1983)

Suzanne Lebsock, *The Free Women of Petersburg: Status and Culture in a Southern Town, 1784–1860* (1984)

Diane Lindstrom, *Economic Developments in the Philadelphia Region, 1810–1850* (1978)

Roger Lotchin, *San Francisco, 1846–1856: From Hamlet to City* (1974)

William H. Pease and Jane H. Pease, *The Web of Progress: Private Values and Public Styles in Boston and Charleston, 1820–1843* (1991)

Mary P. Ryan, *Women in Public: Between Banners and Ballots, 1825–1880* (1990)

Carroll Smith-Rosenberg, *Religion and the Rise of the City: The New York City Mission Movement, 1812–1870* (1971)

Jon C. Teaford, *The Municipal Revolution in America: Origins of Modern Urban Government, 1650–1825* (1975)

Richard C. Wade, *Slavery in the Cities: The South, 1820–1860* (1964)

Kenneth Wheeler, *To Wear a City's Crown: The Beginnings of Urban Growth in Texas, 1832–1865* (1968)

Shane White, *Somewhat More Independent: The End of Slavery in New York City, 1770–1810* (1991)

CHAPTER 4

Urban Services and Public Order in Young Cities, 1800–1870

✕

Between 1830 and 1860, the United States' urban population grew by 552 percent, from 1.1 million people to 6.2 million, the fastest urbanization the country has ever experienced. The streaming of so many people into relatively small places—cities were still compact—exacerbated the problems common among densely packed populations, among them crowding, disorder, disease, crime, fire, and poverty.

In some instances, technology could relieve the pressure, at least partially or temporarily. The development of water systems, with steam pumps, masonry aqueducts, and underground piping, helped most cities provide safer, more copious water supplies to aid in fighting fires and in reducing threats to health—though it took many cities many years to resolve whether water supply should be the responsibility of government or of private enterprise. Extending police protection, too, presented problems. Traditions of republicanism and voluntarism, left over from the colonial and revolutionary periods, militated against establishing a permanent armed force for preserving order. For a long time, many Americans feared the potential tyranny and abuses of a professional police force. Only when their concerns about social disorder overcame their other fears did they begin to accept a permanent professional police force. The ravages of epidemics constantly reminded urban dwellers of their inferior knowledge of the origin and contagiousness of diseases. And desires to preserve open spaces in their midst often conflicted with economic considerations reflecting the profitability of real-estate development. Today we take for granted many of the means used to provide services to urban dwellers, but just how cities would meet these needs in the nineteenth century was not always obvious and often more complicated than one might assume.

Each of these documents pertains to a different kind of urban service, meeting the needs for health, protection, and open space that early American urban dwellers faced as their cities grew. The first document, by Lemuel Shattuck, one of the earliest officials to collect demographic data, provides fascinating statistics on Boston's death rates and reveals the primitive state of medical science and urban health care in the mid-nineteenth century. Readers should note that Shattuck lived in an era in which the germ theory of disease had not yet won acceptance; thus he attributed high death rates both to unhealthy conditions in the city and to "unacclimated foreign emigrants." The second document is a plea for better police protection in New York City, written in 1853. It illustrates how fear of social disorder intensified in the mid-nineteenth century and gave rise to appeals for a professional, uniformed, and well-staffed police force that presumably would duplicate the functions and effects of London's professional police force, which became the model for police reform in American cities. The third document, from Frederick Law Olmsted, the United States' premier landscape architect and park planner of the nineteenth century, exemplifies the belief that trees and open spaces served as ventilators and "lungs" for cities, and asserts that parks should provide healthful benefits to urban dwellers, not only cleansing them physically but also relieving them of emotional stresses.

Lemuel Shattuck on Death Rates and Health in Boston, c. 1810–1840

In Table VII we have given the aggregate number of deaths, and calculated the . . . per cent. of the deaths at each specified interval of age. It appears that 2698, or 33.64 per cent., of the whole deaths in 1811 to 1820 were under 5 years of age, and that 14.13 per cent., the next greatest proportion, was between the ages of 20 and 30. In the next column of this table we have presented the number who survive each specified age, and in the fourth column the. . . per cent. of the surviving. It appears from this table that 5322, or 66.36 per cent., of the deaths in 1811 to 1820 survived the age of 5 years; 1624, or 20.25 per cent., survived the age of 50 years; and 222, or 2.77 per cent., survived the age of 80 years. In the fifth column we have presented the law of mortality calculated from the deaths alone, and given the . . . per cent. of the number of those who were alive at the beginning of each specified age, and who died before the next specified age. Of the whole deaths, 33.64 per cent. were under 5 years; of those who survived 5 years, 5.33 per cent. died before they attained 10 years; of those who survived 10 years, 8.53 per cent. died before they attained 20 years; and so on for each successive period, as appears in the table. We have presented these four different kinds of facts concerning the other periods, 1821 to 1830, and 1831 to 1839. A comparison of these facts presents some very important considerations.

It has been repeatedly said that the great improvements in the science of medicine—in the nature and treatment of disease, and other causes, have increased the average longevity of mankind; that life is more valuable now than it formerly was; and that these improvements are constantly going on. The value of life is estimated by the number of years we live. A long life is more valuable than a short one. It is said to be improved in value, when the various circumstances, which surround us, add to the number of years of existence, as compared with other causes, which have existed in other places or periods of time. No correct conclusion can be made in regard to such comparison, except by a careful examination of the facts. A sufficient number of these is not, however, as yet, attainable in this country to enable us to investigate the subject so fully and satisfactorily as could be desired. We can present some important ones in relation to Boston. . . .

It appears from this table that the value of life has slightly improved between the ages of 30 and 60 and over 80, the chances being somewhat greater than they were twenty years ago, that a person of these ages will live to the next higher age. Under 30 the mortality has increased; the greatest however is under 5. The mortality for 1838 was greater than in any other year, being 47.65 wanting but 2.35 per cent. of half the whole deaths, showing in that year a greater mortality under 5, than the average eight previous years. . . .

The causes of this increasing and alarming mortality should be investigated, and, if possible, removed. We have endeavored to ascertain some of these causes. Allowance should, we suppose, be made for the customs of the times. More luxury and effeminacy in both sexes prevail now than formerly; and this may have had some influence in producing constitutional debility, and the consequent feeble health of children. The nursing and feeding of children with improper food is another cause. The influence of bad air in confined, badly located, and filthy houses, is another and perhaps the greatest. Epidemic diseases which are particularly prevalent among children have increased. It will hereafter be shown that scarlet fever has prevailed very much the last nine years, and has increased the mortality. . . . Other infantile diseases have also increased. . . .

We had supposed that a greater mortality prevailed in certain localities, and in certain classes of our population than in others, and we have endeavored to ascertain how far the supposition is founded on fact. Though the records do not specify, as they ought, the place of residence of those whose deaths are recorded, they do give, in all cases, the places of burial. We have compiled the following statement from a list of all those who were buried from Boston in the South Boston and Charlestown Roman Catholic burial grounds.

Of the 1987 Catholic burials during the six years, 1833 to 1838, comprising 1028 males and 958 females, 61.39 per cent. were under 5 years. The still-born during the same time, and in the same religious denomination, not included in the above, were 125, or 5.77 per cent. of the whole burials; 112, or about 5 1/2 per cent. only, lived to see 50 years of age, and 30, or less than 2 per cent. lived to 70. During the year 1838 there were 439 burials; of whom 303, or 171 males and 132 females, were under 5; and 136, or 57 males and 79 females, were over 5. This is a mortality of 75 per cent. of the whole male deaths, and 60 per cent. of the whole female deaths under 5; leaving 25 per cent. only of the males and 40 per cent. of the females, or 31 per cent. of both sexes, to survive that early age. This shows a great increase in mortality, and will account for the increase of the deaths under 5 years of age. The influx of unacclimated foreign emigrants, and the great number of families crowded into the houses in Broad street, Ann street, and other densely populated parts of the city, render the air very impure, and expose the lives of infants, who are compelled to breathe it, to almost inevitable death. The influences of such circumstances are not confined to the places where they exist, but are extended to the population in the neighborhood, and epidemics are generated, which are no doubt injurious to the general health of the city.

A Plea for Better Police Protection in New York City, 1853

I have traversed the highways and byways of London, at all hours of the day and night, to watch the workings of its police. I . . . knew them by their *uniform,* walking their ceaseless round, at every turn I took. There is something assuring . . . in their steady, solemn tread of two miles an hour, resounding in the quiet street—a signal to the law-breaker to beware, and to the peaceful inhabitant that the eye of the policeman is watching over his safety. You do not see there, as you will nightly in our broad thoroughfares, four or five rowdies walking arm in arm abreast, filled with liquor and deviltry, with segars in their mouths elevated at an angle of 45 deg. and their hats cocked sideways at 30 deg. cracking their coarse jokes, or singing their ribald songs, and who if you come too near them, may jostle you in the way, and if you say a word in reply, or prepare to defend yourself, if a knife is not drawn you are well off; the chances are much in favor of your being knocked down. . . .

Look any and *every* day in the week, at your morning paper, and see what a black record of crime has been committed in your public streets the day and the night before, what *stabbings,* what shootings, what knockings down, what assaults by slung shots and otherwise; insults to women and other disgusting details of violence! . . . It is very commonly answered, that these acts are done by foreigners recently come here, and not by our citizens: granted, and what is the commentary? Why do not these foreigners commit these acts of violence in their own countries? . . . The answer is . . . found in the weakness of our police. It shows that . . . they fear the police of Europe, for they know them to be efficient and numerous; they do not fear our own, because from their small number and other reasons, there is neither a physical nor a moral power about it. . . . New York is the house of refuge for a large proportion of thieves and housebreakers, as the police of London make that city too hot for them. . . .

Look also at our sister city of Philadelphia, which used to be called the city of brotherly love, from the quiet of its streets, and the order and propriety of its population. And what has Philadelphia been for the last ten years? Misrule and riot have reigned there, to the defiance of its magistrates, and have made its streets hideous. Assaults, and shootings, and murders, arising among other causes, from the gangs of rowdies attached to, or running with their engines . . . so that the fire-alarm bell there has been for years, a signal for a deadly fight.

Look at Baltimore, and what scenes have been presented there for the last six months? Violence of the most savage kind, so frequent, so daring, and by such powerful gangs, as to overawe the citizens, to protect themselves, go armed; and, if they are compelled to go out at night, do so with a fair chance of a personal encounter. Such was the daring of the disturbers of the public peace in Baltimore, that it was currently circulated in the papers, that the Mayor of that city had determined to resign, in despair, of being able, with all the aid of the police, to put down rowdyism. . . . If New York, Baltimore, and Philadelphia will only take a few practical hints from the experience of London, they will soon give a moral power to their police, which it does not now possess. . . .

I appeal to the experience of every man for the truth of what I say, that there is no *moral* power in our police—there is nothing in their dress that strikes any terror into the thief or felon—there is nothing in the dress of our policemen to distinguish them from the mass of people among whom they are mingling. You cannot tell them by day, unless you are near enough to see the twinkling little star, and when night comes, that little star does not shine out, but is in *total eclipse.* I ask, if you want a policeman in the night time, how are you to know him or find him? How can you tell at night whether the man whom you see standing at a corner, of walking slowly along, is a policeman or a robber?

Frederick Law Olmsted Advocates Parks as Cures for Urban Malaise, 1870

There can be no doubt . . . that in all our modern civilization . . . there is a strong drift townward. . . . It also appears to be nearly certain that the recent rapid enlargement of towns and withdrawal of people from rural conditions of living is the result mainly of circumstances of a permanent character. . . . Now, knowing that the average length of . . . life . . . in towns has been much less than in the country, and that the average amount of disease and misery and of vice and crime has been much greater in towns, this would be a very dark prospect for civilization, if it were not that modern Science has beyond all question determined many of the causes of the special evils by which men are afflicted in towns. . . . It has shown . . . that . . . in the interior parts of large and closely built towns, a given quantity of air contains considerably less of the elements which we require to receive through the lungs than the air of the country . . . and that . . . it carries into the lungs highly corrupt and irritating matters, the action of which tends strongly to vitiate all our sources of vigor . . . and very seriously affect the mind and the moral strength. . . . People from the country are even conscious of the effect on their nerves and minds of the street contact—often complaining that they feel confused by it; and if we had no relief from it at all during our waking hours, we should all be conscious of suffering from it. It is upon our opportunities of relief from it, therefore, that not only our comfort in town life, but our ability to maintain a temperate, good-natured, and healthy state of mind, depends. . . .

Air is disinfected by sunlight and foliage. Foliage also acts mechanically to purify the air by screening it. Opportunity and inducement to escape at frequent intervals from the confined and vitiated air of the commercial quarter, and to supply the lungs with air screened and purified by trees, and recently acted upon by sunlight, together with opportunity and inducement to escape from conditions requiring vigilance, wariness, and activity toward other men—if these could be supplied economically, our problem would be solved. . . .

What I would ask is, whether we might not with economy make special provision in some of our streets—in a twentieth or a fiftieth part, if you please, of all—for trees to remain as a permanent furniture of the city? . . . If such streets were made still broader in some parts, with spacial malls, the advantage would be increased. If each of them were . . . laid out with laterals and connections . . . to serve as a convenient trunk-line of communication between two large districts of the town or the business centre, and the suburbs, a very great number of people might thus be placed every day under influences counteracting those with which we desire to contend. . . .

We come then to the question: what accommodations for recreation can we provide which shall be so agreeable and so accessible as to be efficiently attractive to the great body of citizens, and . . . also cause those who resort to them for pleasure to subject themselves . . . to conditions strongly counteractive to the special enervating conditions of the town? . . . If I ask myself where I have experienced the most complete gratification of [the gregarious and neighborly] instinct in public and out of doors, among trees, I find that it has been in the promenade of the Champs Elyses. As closely following it I should name other promenades of Europe, and our own . . . New York parks. . . . I have several times seen fifty thousand people participating in them; and the more I have seen of them, the more highly [do] I . . . estimate their value as means of counteracting the evils of town life. . . .

If the great city . . . is to be laid out little by little, and chiefly to suit the views of land-owners, acting only individually, and thinking only of how what they do is to affect the value in the next week or the next year of the few lots that each may hold at the time, the opportunities of so obeying this inclination as at the same time to give the lungs a bath of pure sunny air, to give the mind a suggestion of rest from the devouring eagerness and intellectual strife of town life, will always be few to any, to many will amount to nothing. . . . We want a ground to which people may easily go after their day's work is done, and where they may stroll for an hour, seeing, hearing, and feeling nothing of the bustle and jar of the streets. . . . Practically, what we most want is a simple, broad, open space of clean greensward . . . as a central feature. We want depth of wood enough about it . . . to completely shut out the city from our landscapes. The word *park,* in town nomenclature, should, I think, be reserved for grounds of the character and purpose thus described. . . . The park should, as far as possible, complement the town. Openness is the one thing you cannot get in buildings. Picturesqueness you can get. Let your buildings be as picturesque as your artists can make them. This is the beauty of a town. Consequently, the beauty of the parks should be the other. It should be the beauty of the fields, the meadow, the prairie, of the green pastures, and the still waters. What we want to gain is tranquility and rest to the mind. . . .

A park fairly well managed near a large town, will surely become a new centre of that town. With the determination of location, size, and boundaries should therefore be associated the duty of arranging new trunk routes of communication between it and the distant parts of the town existing and forecasted. . . . I hope you will agree with me that . . . reserves of ground for the purposes I have referred to should be fixed upon as soon as possible, before the difficulty of arranging them, which arises from private building, shall be greatly more formidable than now . . . for want of a little comprehensive and business-like foresight and study.

✖ E S S A Y S

The two essays reflect upon the broad political, social, and economic issues involved in the establishment of urban services. In an essay taken from his book *American Law Enforcement* (1981), David R. Johnson of the University of Texas, San Antonio, uses a unique approach, comparing London and American cities, to discuss the political and social questions being debated as professional "preventive" police forces were set up in nineteenth-century cities. In the second essay, David R. Goldfield of the University of North Carolina, Charlotte, traces the growth of southern cities in the early nineteenth century and discusses the problems of health in these cities, especially the interaction of epidemics with the impulse for business growth.

Police Reform: A Comparative View

DAVID R. JOHNSON

Changes in local law enforcement in England and America were caused by two powerful trends in both countries. The first of these trends was urbanization; the second, industrialization. Over a long period of time, these developments increased the standard of living for both western Europeans generally and for Americans. Such beneficial trends would seem to have little relationship to law enforcement, but in fact they made vast changes in the police necessary.

The need for changes in the police arose from the fact that industrialization and urbanization created a new kind of society. Old ways of thinking and behaving became obsolete, but the effort to replace them provoked a great deal of protest. Factories, for example, needed sober, punctual workers who could be trusted with machines. At the beginning of industrialization such workers did not exist in sufficient numbers because they were accustomed to less demanding schedules; they regarded drinking as an important recreation; and they feared machines which they thought would deprive them of jobs and destroy their status in society. In order to create what they regarded as a reliable work force, factory owners became enthusiastic advocates of many social reforms such as temperance. Workers resented these reform efforts and resisted them whenever possible. Likewise, urbanization promoted unrest by bringing together people from diverse class, ethnic, and (in the United States) racial backgrounds who resented each other. Conflicts between these competing groups over such issues as whose version of morality would dominate society were another source of trouble.

Crime, as distinct from collective protest, also appears to have increased in this period. Urbanization and industrialization both enhanced the material prosperity of many individuals and concentrated enormous numbers of less fortunate people who turned to crime to support themselves. Petty thievery abounded, and more serious offenses such as burglary, highway robbery, and swindling

"The Problems of Establishing a Police Force," by David R. Johnson, *American Law Enforcement: A History* (St. Louis: Forum Press, 1981), excerpts from pp. 17–33. Reprinted by permission of Harlan Davidson, Inc.

proliferated. The diversity and persistence of criminals frightened the inhabitants of cities who wanted their property and lives secured against these depredators.

Social change, unrest, and crime made the old system of law enforcement obsolete. Watchmen had never been effective in dealing with crime and violence; now their situation became even more impossible. Constables had overseen many activities which made urban life possible, but they were too few in number, too overworked, and too little interested in preventing crime to be effective in a rapidly changing society. A new kind of police was needed, one which would maintain order and pursue criminals in the altered circumstances of the early nineteenth century. In the three decades prior to 1860, reformers on both sides of the Atlantic set out to transform the nature of law enforcement. Although their efforts succeeded, the police forces they created were not comparable in spite of the fact that a single model—that of crime prevention—was the basis for reform in both countries.

English Police Reform

Social problems in England after the end of the Napoleonic Wars in 1815 eventually led to the creation of the world's first preventive police force. Workers' protests against new machines, food riots, and an apparent increase in crime generally alarmed Parliament. The army had traditionally been the only force able to disperse rioters, but it was now having greater difficulty doing so because the mobs seemed more willing to resist. . . . In 1822, when the prime minister appointed Robert Peel as home secretary (an official responsible for internal security), he ordered Peel to establish a police which would deal with rioting as well as with ordinary crime. . . .

Peel finally achieved his objective . . . when Parliament passed the Metropolitan Police Act of 1829. Under this Act, the home secretary was to appoint two men as police justices (later, they were called commissioners) to command the new organization. These men were to recruit "a sufficient number of fit and able men" as police constables, and they were to be responsible for the overall administration of the police as well as for the conduct of their men. The English preventive police thus began, and have remained, a highly centralized organization administratively.

The success of London's preventive police was due entirely to the good sense of the men whom Peel chose to lead the new organization. Peel had decided that one commissioner should be a military man who would have practical knowledge of discipline and organization; the other should be a lawyer whose knowledge would be invaluable in defining the appropriate limits of police power. Accordingly, Peel chose Colonel Charles Rowan and Richard Mayne, an Irish barrister, as the first commissioners. Both men turned out to be superb choices whose long service . . . provided the continuity of command which enabled the London police to develop into a superlative organization. . . .

Mayne and Rowan worked out the organizational details of the new police together. They carved London into a number of divisions. . . . The size of these divisions varied according to the amount of crime within each. Divisions which had a higher rate of crime than others had smaller boundaries, thereby enabling constables to cover their beats more frequently. Each division had a commander called a superintendent; each superintendent had a force of 4 inspectors, 16 sergeants, and 165 constables under him. . . . The commissioners also decided to put their men in a uniform (a blue coat, blue pants, and a glazed black tophat), and to arm them with a short baton (or truncheon) and a rattle (for raising an alarm). Finally, each constable was required to wear his personal number on his collar where it could be easily seen. Once these details had been arranged, the men had been recruited, and the force had received its instructions, the new police took to the streets in late September 1829.

The new police quickly discovered that they would have to overcome tremendous public hostility to their very existence. . . . Many people feared the new police would undermine liberty; others resented any interference in their personal freedoms or assumed rights; workers regarded policemen as enemies created to suppress their efforts to protect themselves from changes wrought by industrialization. . . .

Since public hostility threatened the very existence of the police, Commissioners Mayne and Rowan moved decisively to counter it. The policies they adopted emphasized a willingness to listen to all complaints and a patient forbearance of abuse. Constables received no help from their superiors in the form of public declarations of support. Instead, the men were constantly cautioned to be respectful and yet firm in dealings with the public. The commissioners, in the meantime, invited anyone with a complaint to submit it to their office. Each complaint received a full hearing, and if it was justified by the evidence the offending constable was removed from the force without further ado. . . . [The commissioners] hoped to create public support for their officers by stressing the reasonableness of their conduct. This policy exposed individual patrolmen to many problems, but it gradually worked to the advantage of the police. Public hostility began to lessen as the moderate conduct of the police became more widely known through countless personal experiences with constables on a daily basis. . . .

The Social Background for Police Reform in America

The reform of the London police attracted favorable attention in America shortly after the bobbies began patrolling their beats. But crime prevention was not permanently adopted as the basis for police reform in the United States for many years. The single most important reason for this delay was the fact that the negative social consequences of urbanization and industrialization had not yet become as serious as they were in England. America's cities had only begun to grow. In the years from 1830 to 1860 they would acquire new residents so fast and in such large numbers that problems with housing, city services, crime, and poverty became acute. Industrialization had not yet become an important economic development; there were only a few factories scattered in small towns along the east coast. Once industrialization began in earnest in the 1840s, it would contribute significantly to social problems and unrest among American workers. Thus, police reform began in England rather than in the United States because the British felt the need for a better police earlier than Americans did.

An absence of major problems caused by urbanization and industrialization does not mean that American society was free of strife. On the contrary, there were at least four important sources of trouble in the 1820s and 1830s which urbanization and industrialization aggravated: nativism, racism, social reform, and politics. All four caused a great deal of turmoil which occasionally turned violent.

Nativism, or prejudice against persons of foreign birth, became an important issue during the 1820s and remained so until the Civil War. Catholic immigrants (especially the Irish after 1840) were especially suspected of being incapable of loyalty to the United States. Native Americans thought Catholics could not understand the principles of democracy and would work to undermine our cherished institutions. Prejudice of this sort usually took the form of social and economic discrimination. Catholics found it difficult to obtain decent jobs and housing, and their children had to attend public schools in which reading from a Protestant Bible was part of the daily routine. But nativism did not always confine itself to these forms of discrimination. A number of riots can be traced to nativist origins, including the burning of a Boston convent in 1834, the Philadelphia riots of 1844, and the Louisville riots of 1855. In many cases property damage was extensive and several people lost their lives.

Racism could also be a deadly source of turmoil. Most blacks lived in the South as slaves, but several northern cities such as Cincinnati, Philadelphia and New York contained small populations of free Negroes. These people lived in generally wretched conditions and were the victims of intense prejudice. They eked out minimal livings by taking the worst paid jobs available. Casual and organized violence made their lives even more miserable. In Philadelphia during the late 1830s and early 1840s, white thugs armed with knives frequently stabbed any black who had the misfortune to be walking on the same street. Race riots erupted on the slightest pretext. Between 1829 and 1850 Philadelphia had five major race riots which required military intervention.

Violence also derived from some aspects of social reform during the antebellum era. Many Americans supported a wide range of reforms which they felt were necessary to the well-being of society. Practically everything, from eating habits to slavery, came under close and critical scrutiny. Two of the most important reforms, and ones which caused considerable turmoil, were the abolition of slavery and the temperance crusade. . . . Antagonism toward abolitionists frequently took the form of mob action, especially in the 1830s, and thereby contributed to the widespread rioting of that decade. The temperance crusade also angered many people, particularly immigrants and workers. . . . For a change, however, the temperance crusade did not provoke mass violence. Instead, temperance was a critical political issue which influenced the outcome of many local elections. It also became a major law enforcement problem which significantly affected the development of American policing.

Politics became a source of social turmoil because urban politicians lacked stable party organizations which could provide a framework for settling public issues. In order to build stable organizations, the politicians had to appeal to the sympathies and prejudices of the voters in ways which would make these voters remain loyal to their parties. Thus a local party might adopt a platform favoring nativist principles; voters who favored those principles flocked to this party, while those who did not stampeded to another which announced its opposition to nativism. Parties also tried to create enthusiasm for their principles and candidates by adopting techniques which would create mass participation in their rallies. Parades were a favorite tactic which soon became a major source of violence. When the parades of opposing parties met in the street, riots followed. Elections were also a fruitful source of trouble. Rival parties often clashed at the polls, as their adherents struggled to stuff a ballot box or to prevent their opponents from doing so. . . .

Threats to social order were only one problem facing urban residents. Crimes of a different sort also alarmed them. Highway robberies on poorly lit city streets attracted increasing concern. Pedestrians risked their lives as well as their pocketbooks walking home at night. Daring thieves prowled the business districts seizing anything from a pair of boots to a sack of gold coins as opportunities presented themselves. In an era when an attempt to collect accurate crime statistics had not even been made, it is extremely difficult to determine whether crime was actually increasing. We can say, however, that concern over property offenses had become widespread. Citizens arming themselves to defend their homes and persons was only one indication of this growing fear. Such measures had been unthinkable prior to the 1830s. Fear about this kind of crime, combined with dismay over the decay of social order, therefore made a powerful argument for police reform.

American Police Reform

When the movement to improve law enforcement did begin in the 1830s, the reformers' motives reflected the diversity of their concerns. Some wanted a new police which would restrain the behavior of "undesirable" citizens such as the Irish; others were concerned about the effect of disorder and crime on the safety of property and property values; and finally there were those who felt that the amount of crime, rioting, and general social conflict threatened the basis of civil society. It is impossible to say which group, if any, dominated the movement for a new police. All three shared the desire to alter existing police arrangements to cope with new needs, and representatives of each group could be found in every large city by the late 1830s. Their problem was how to convince a majority of their fellow citizens that police reform had become necessary to the future well-being of their communities.

This problem was not as easy to solve as many reformers first assumed. One central theme emerged as the crucial issue in every city: the reformers had to devise a police system which would conform to the ideology of republicanism. No reform plan could succeed unless it embodied the cardinal virtues of that ideology, especially its emphasis on decentralization of power (or checks and balances) and accountability to the voters. Any plan which advocated a police controlled by a single person, or a small number of people, immediately provoked cries of despotism. Similarly, proposals that policemen serve during good behavior, or that they wear a uniform (two features of the London police) aroused fears that the reformers wanted to tyrannize their fellow citizens. Uniforms were un-American in principle, and service during good behavior would encourage policemen to think they were not answerable to the public they served. Partisan politics made the reformers' task considerably more difficult. Local politicians wanted to be sure that their opponents would not use a new police to harass them at the polls by arresting their supporters. . . .

New York was the first American city to adopt a lasting version of a preventive police. While the exact details of New York's reform movement were not duplicated elsewhere, the general situation was fairly typical of the obstacles the reformers faced and the solutions they used to overcome their opponents. The campaign began in 1836 when New York's mayor sent the Common Council a report advocating police reorganization to better cope with civil disorders. In rejecting the mayor's recommendations, the councilmen made it clear that republicanism was the basis of their refusal to act. Their own report concluded that: "The nature of our institutions are [sic] such that more reliance may be placed upon the people for aid, in case of any emergency, than in despotic governments." Police reform disappeared as a major issue until 1841, when a spectacular murder case once more revealed the deficiencies of local law enforcement. Mary Cecilia Rogers was the victim in this case. She left home to visit her sister on July 25; three days later her body was found in the Hudson River. This murder, which was never solved, caused a sensation. Local newspapers clamored for police action, and when the police displayed an unwillingness to investigate unless a sufficient reward was forthcoming, the press began to campaign for reform. The demand for a new police received so much public support that all political parties endorsed reform. Unfortunately, the politicians could not agree on a plan. The campaign for a preventive police only succeeded when the Democrats mustered enough power to dominate decisions regarding reform. In 1844 the New York state legislature, then controlled by Democrats, passed a law establishing a preventive police for New York City.

Under the provisions of the New York law, preventive policing came to America in a dramatically different form than that adopted in Europe. The most important difference was readily apparent: in the American version, the police were deliberately incorporated into politics. Two provisions of New York's reform law made the police part of the political process. First, the law provided that each ward in the city would be a separate patrol district. This meant that in order to gain public acceptance the police would have to be responsive to the law enforcement view of the people in the wards they patrolled. In this situation, uniform enforcement policies which dealt with city-wide problems would be impossible. One ward might favor keeping saloons open on Sunday, for example, but another might not. Controversies over police behavior, therefore, became inevitable as special interest groups fought among themselves to extend their version of law enforcement over the whole city. The process for selecting policemen was the second means by which they became involved in politics. New York's mayor chose the police from a list of names submitted by the aldermen and tax assessors of each ward. He then had to submit his choices to the city council for approval. This system applied the theory of republicanism to preventive policing. No one person had control over appointments, and the politicians who made the appointments were all accountable to the voters. In practice, however, this selection process gave most power over the police to the ward aldermen. Those politicians had no interest in finding capable men to serve as policemen. They regarded the new police as a great opportunity to reward their friends and supporters regardless of their qualifications. Patronage politics was thus built into preventive policing at the outset and quickly became another source of controversy. . . .

In spite of these problems, the new force did have some resemblance to a preventive police. All police functions, from maintaining order to arresting criminals, had finally been centralized in a single body of men. Competing groups, such as watchmen and constables, were disbanded. The new police would patrol the city around the clock, not just at night or at their own convenience. Pay scales were high enough to attract competent recruits (although the politicians' control of nominations guaranteed that competence was not always a primary consideration). These were important advantages over the old police, and they at least provided the basis for further improvements when and if the public would demand them.

Police reformers in other cities did not adopt every feature of New York's plan. But there were enough similarities to say that New York served as a kind of model for the campaigns to establish preventive police elsewhere. New Orleans and Cincinnati adopted plans for a new police in 1852; Boston and Philadelphia did so in 1854, Chicago in 1855 and Baltimore in 1857. By the 1860s, preventive policing had been accepted in principle, properly modified to meet American conditions, in every large city and in several smaller ones. This was an important achievement.

Critical Issues in American Policing

Several issues critical to success of this new police emerged quickly, however, and helped determine their future development. The original American model of a police founded on the principle of crime prevention had several failings aside from the fact that politics was to play so large a role in the departments. Three important problems confronted the first police officials in the early years of policing, between 1845 and 1860: 1) a controversy over the adoption of uniforms; 2) a concern about arming the police; 3) and the issue of appropriate force in making arrests. The uniform was an important issue for a variety of reasons. First, the lack of a uniform undermined one of the principal ideas associated with crime prevention. In theory, people would be deterred from committing crimes when they knew that an officer was nearby. This was the uniform's purpose—it made a patrolman visible. Without this visibility, so the theory went, people would be more inclined to commit crimes. Other considerations also affected the uniform issue. The victim of a crime, for example, usually wanted to find a policeman in a hurry. How was he to do so if the police dressed, and therefore, looked just like everyone else? . . . These, then, were some of the reasons why many people insisted that the police should be uniformed.

Policemen themselves had other ideas. A uniform smacked of subordination and tyranny to many of them. These officers denounced uniforms as un-American liveries which would destroy their sense of manliness and democracy. . . .

Opposition from the ranks thus made the uniform issue difficult to resolve.

The tactics which eventually succeeded in uniforming the police varied from one city to another and depended upon the intensity of opposition as well as the means available to overcome it. Officials in New York took advantage of the fact that their police served four year terms of appointment. When those terms expired in 1853, the city's police commissioners announced that they would not rehire any man who refused to wear a uniform. The commissioners remained firm in their determination through a subsequent storm of protest, and New York became the first city with a uniformed police. . . . Both in Boston (1858) and in Chicago (1861) the police seemed less inclined to protest and uniforms were adopted in those cities with little incident.

Arming the police was a far more sensitive issue than the dispute over uniforms. The personal safety of officers and citizens alike was at stake, and problems could equal the threat of death for dramatic impact. . . .

However unhappy the critics of an armed police might be, they had to face one unavoidable fact. Americans, unlike the British, had a long tradition that every citizen had the right, even the duty, to own firearms. Guns were part of the American culture. Nativism, racism, and antagonisms among immigrant groups complicated the problem of gun use and control considerably. Beginning in the 1840s, people in cities began to use firearms against one another systematically for the first time. Street fights, riots among firemen, and various other sorts of social conflict became occasions for the use of pistols (and occasionally muskets). When the newly organized preventive police began patrolling the streets, they were armed only with nightsticks. During the late 1840s and early 1850s, newspapers began to carry stories about officers shot in the line of duty. A few of these incidents appear to have been ambushes, but most occurred when a policeman intervened in a fight in which one of the assailants was armed with a pistol.

The problem facing the police had now become critical. Patrolmen never could be sure when a rowdy might have a gun, yet the officer knew he had to intervene in disorder quickly or risk having a small dispute between a small number of people grow into a serious problem. Tactical considerations, such as when and how to use force, became more complicated in these circumstances. Officers who misjudged these questions could pay a severe penalty. The solution to these difficulties emerged during the 1850s as individual policemen began to carry firearms regardless of official orders and public opinion. In some cases, as in Philadelphia, the city councils authorized their police to carry pistols, but such authorization only recognized what was becoming standard, if informal practice. The public accepted an armed police because there appeared to be no other alternative at the time. One of the most significant changes in American policing thus developed from the conditions which officers confronted on the city streets.

One of the most admired characteristics of the London police was, and is, their restraint in using physical force to make arrests. American policemen, however, have been notorious for their readiness to use force, and this trait has attracted a great deal of criticism over the years. The attitudes toward, and the use of firearms in the United States helps explain our police's willingness to employ force, but the presence of guns does not completely account for it. There were at least two other reasons why policing in this country has often been so physical.

The explanation for this behavior on the part of the police lies first in American attitudes toward law and law enforcement and second in the social turmoil of the mid-nineteenth century.

American attitudes toward law and law enforcement are full of contradictions. Many citizens believe that laws against certain kinds of behavior are necessary, but that those laws should not be enforced against them. (Traffic regulations are good examples of this attitude.) Some people want to use the law as a way to regulate conduct which they think is offensive; but there are others who oppose using the law in this manner because they are not offended by that same behavior. (Laws against drinking or keeping saloons open on Sundays are examples of controversial legislation.) In too many cases, then, there is no consensus that a particular law, or a group of laws, should be uniformly enforced. This becomes an extremely difficult problem for an officer who is, for instance, under orders to arrest drunks when he is patrolling a neighborhood where drinking and drunkenness are seen as normal activities. The officer knows that if he arrests a drunk who then resists him, he cannot rely on bystanders to assist him because they disapprove of his actions. But he cannot back down from making the arrest; such an act would make him look ridiculous to onlookers who are already inclined to disrespect him anyway. Faced with these circumstances many patrolmen in the mid-nineteenth century resorted to force as a means of establishing their personal authority over the people they policed. In effect, law enforcement was often reduced to a question of whether a particular officer had the physical strength to dominate a situation requiring his intervention.

The social turmoil of the era between 1840 and 1870 also helped explain the use of force. Violence had become commonplace, and many people who supported police reform did so in the expectation that a more effective police would reestablish order on the streets. These people did not always care overly much exactly how the police accomplished that goal. If a few heads got broken in the process, that was a cost they were willing to pay. . . .

Although no one probably intended it, the use of force became a permanent legacy once the police discovered how useful it was in solving many of their problems. Violence, after all, did decline, but it did not disappear in the social life of American cities. Uncertainty whether an offender was armed, and a continuing lack of consensus over the enforcement of some laws, perpetuated the policeman's need to rely on his physical prowess as a means of dealing with incidents on the streets.

English and American Policing in Comparison

America's version of preventive policing thus developed quite differently from its British cousin. The contrast between the London bobby and the American cop appalled many people in the United States who had hoped to duplicate the polite, presumably efficient Britisher in a New World setting. But those who were disappointed or uneasy over the differences between the new police in each country failed to understand that the English model for crime prevention could not work in the United States. It could not for three reasons: the politics of English and

American policing were extremely different; the law enforcement policies which each police adopted differed dramatically; and the social environment in which each police worked contrasted sharply.

Politics affected the organization and the behavior of the police in both England and America. The difference in political influence became apparent, however, in the effect which politics had. In England, politics contributed to the success of the new police; in America politics severely hindered police effectiveness. London's police commissioners, Rowan and Mayne, answered for the conduct of their men to only one politician, the home secretary. That official consistently supported them in their efforts to establish a disciplined police force free from outside interference. London's police therefore had a highly centralized command structure in which the commissioners had the authority and responsibility necessary for the success of their work. By contrast, an American chief of police had many masters. So did his patrolmen. Mayors and aldermen interfered often and without thought about the consequences in matters of appointments, discipline, and law enforcement policies. In this situation there was no single standard of behavior which would have helped the patrolmen and the public to understand what was expected of the new police. A great deal of the public's disappointment with the police, and the police's inability to overcome their negative image, can be traced to the ways in which American politicians mismanaged their law enforcement responsibilities.

. . . The second important area in which contrasts in style became apparent had to do with law enforcement policies. In general, law enforcement was much more uniform in London than in American cities. Temperance regulation provided a classic example of the difference. If a law said all taverns had to close by midnight on Saturday, Commissioners Rowan and Mayne expected their officers to see that the law was obeyed. In the United States, however, saloonkeepers with political connections could use their influence with the patrolman's superiors to avoid closing laws. . . . The seesaw battle between reformers and saloonkeepers became a major source of problems for the police. No matter what they did, someone was angry at them. The absence of standard policies led to a situation in which people with an interest in questions of morality constantly tried to manipulate the law and the police to achieve their own ends.

The social environment was the final reason why the British and American police developed in such different ways. Policemen in both countries encountered violence against them when they first began patrolling the streets. But the attack on English constables decreased considerably within a few years while assaults on American officers remained at a rather high level. The reason for this trend in the two countries seems to be that American cities had more volatile problems than those in London. London was already an extremely large city; most American cities were just becoming modern metropolises. It may be that Londoners of conflicting views and from competing classes simply had learned to live together more effectively than had American citizens who had not had so many years to familiarize themselves with the demands of urban life. Violence was therefore more typical in America because people had not yet discovered other ways to deal with their problems. The attitudes toward the ownership and use of guns further complicated matters. . . .

Contrasting conditions thus created different traditions in England and America during the formative years of preventive policing. The bobby learned to enforce laws uniformly by the impersonal authority which resided in his official position as a lawman. American patrolmen learned that laws could be manipulated to serve the interests of various powerful groups and that they had to rely upon their personal authority and ability to impose their will on a populace which regarded them with suspicion and hatred. Thus the reform of law enforcement which had become so necessary due to the consequences of urbanization and industrialization produced two very different police forces.

The Business of Health Planning: Disease Prevention in the Old South

DAVID R. GOLDFIELD

Epidemic disease was the scourge of nineteenth-century American cities. Plagues of cholera, typhoid, and yellow fever transformed bustling cities into ghost towns, optimism to despair and prosperity to decay and depression. Epidemics victimized southern cities with particular severity. Killing frosts arrived later in that section, and the hot, humid summers characteristic of some southern cities provided a fertile atmosphere for the contraction and transference of disease.

Health planning was one of many urban services undertaken by local government during the first half of the nineteenth century. A relatively small group of businessmen controlled most aspects of urban life during this period. They formed an interlocking directorate in religious, social, economic, and political life that oversaw the development of their town into a city. The years between the War of 1812 and the Civil War witnessed the most rapid period of urbanization in the nation's history. As cities built railroads and canals across the hinterland, a vast commerce developed that stimulated growth. In order to facilitate orderly growth as well as to ensure future advances, civic leaders looked increasingly to their government to regulate this newfound prosperity.

Local government became an effective device of the business community to promote growth. The financial resources of government, obtained through taxation and the issuance of bonds, were utilized in a variety of projects designed to stimulate the urban economy. Cities invested heavily in railroads and canals, especially in the Old South. City officials also sought to make the urban environment a more attractive place to conduct business. Police and fire services, while still voluntary, came under increasing government scrutiny in the form of council-appointed commissioners and direct subsidies to upgrade equipment and performance. A safe city was attractive to visitor and resident alike.

While safety was a traditional concern of government, rapid growth created new responsibilities in the public-service sector. By 1830 local governments throughout the country were spending more for street repair than for any other public service. Once again, the city's image for potential customers was a major

From "The Business of Health Planning: Disease Prevention in the Old South" by David Goldfield, *Journal of Southern History* 42 (November 1978), excerpts from pp. 557–70. Copyright 1978 by the Southern Historical Association. Reprinted by permission of the Managing Editor.

motivating force in developing this service. As one Alexandria, Virginia, journal observed: "There are few things which operate against a city more than bad streets, and especially when they are the principal ones." Street lighting was another service that appealed to civic leaders. Gas lighting was a sign of modernity, and it impressed visitors. . . .

In addition to the cosmetic services there were education, poor relief, and recreational facilities. If urban growth seemed to generate an infinite number of services, tax dollars were finite. Since the property tax was the primary revenue source, civic leaders—usually among the city's most propertied individuals— were not eager to burden themselves unnecessarily. Urban governments therefore struck a balance in the provision of urban services. City councils determined expenditures on a simple cost-benefit calculation. If the business and growth generated by the service outweighed the cost in taxes on the leadership, the service would receive appropriate funding. Thus, police and fire protection, paved roads, and street lighting rarely extended beyond the business district. Since visitors did not venture into the city's poorer residential districts, the business generated by services in these areas would be inconsequential compared with the cost of providing the services. Education and poor relief relied mainly on private largesse with occasional financial crumbs from the city council. These services were not "visible" and were, therefore, unlikely candidates for city appropriations.

When American cities and their governments turned their attention to disease prevention, they viewed it as an urban service within the context of other services vying for appropriations. Civic leaders applied the cost-benefit analysis to disease prevention with results similar to those on poor relief and education: health planning was minimal, and funding was sporadic. Given the impact of epidemic disease on lives and on prosperity, such parsimony seems especially strange. Viewing the provision of health services through the eyes of the business community, however, reveals that their cost-benefit surveys were accurate, if not humanitarian.

Disease prevention and treatment provoked annual debates in southern cities. While civic leaders agreed generally on the best methods of street paving, there was no unanimity on the nature of epidemic disease. Ignorance spawned a proliferation of opinions, most of which were useless, and some of which were harmful. Until the discovery of the germ theory of disease in the late nineteenth century, discussion of disease etiology involved more of intuition than science. With the origin of disease a mystery, it is not surprising that epidemics struck at will and often with devastating force. Yellow fever attacked Charleston two dozen times during the antebellum era; within a twenty-seven-year period (1810–1837) New Orleans experienced fifteen yellow-fever epidemics. Disease produced a frightful death toll. Yellow fever killed 20,000 New Orleanians during the 1850s—enough to populate a medium-sized city of that era. Since treatment included "cures" ranging from sniffing rags dipped in vinegar to firing cannons, it was evident that flight was the only realistic remedy.

. . . The primitive state of medical knowledge compounded the problem of finding solutions to epidemic disease. There was some consensus, though, that cleanliness and quarantine were effective weapons in preventing disease. Even as city governments in the South went about implementing sanitation and quarantine policies, the evidence of the benefits of these plans was not compelling. The business leadership, inseparable from the government, was concerned about the costs of such procedures—both in terms of expenditures and the adverse impact on the urban economy. This concern would result in only a partial introduction of public health services in antebellum southern cities.

. . . The task confronting civic leaders was considerable. Garbage collected in the streets, fetid pools festered in the hot summer sun, human excreta trickled down open gutters, and drainage from privies and water supplies mixed frequently. Here was obviously a serious problem for a growing urban government and its business leadership.

Private contractors were the major street-cleaning agents in antebellum cities. Contracts were political rewards, and performance was an inconsequential feature of the arrangement. Occasionally, southern urban governments embarked on strenuous street-cleaning campaigns, but these were usually short-lived, and the results were mixed. Baltimore attempted to clean its own streets in the mid-1840s, but the system proved too expensive, and the city returned to private contracting in 1848. . . .

Other southern cities were more diligent in providing public street cleaning. Charleston appropriated funds for street cleaning and the draining of cellars flooded by rains. Savannah installed a rudimentary sewer system to replace the foul open ditches. Norfolk's Board of Health, a body appointed by the City Council began to conduct cellar inspections during the 1840s. Alexandria officials, after a detailed study of a similar system in Philadelphia, instituted regular garbage-collection service in 1856. Before then, one scavenger handled the city's garbage-collection chores.

Savannah evolved the most elaborate system of disease prevention through sanitation. Between 1817 and 1820 local officials placed large tracts of land surrounding the city—mostly low wetlands with stagnant pools—in dry culture. The City Council appointed a Dry Culture Committee to ensure that proper drainage and irrigation maintained the land in a dry condition. The city government paid planters forty dollars an acre to grow within a one-mile radius of Savannah only those crops which required dry culture. The government financed this plan by floating a bond issue for two-thirds of the $200,000 required to implement dry culture. The "sanative cordon" of dry-culture land around the city was Savannah's major defense against yellow fever.

Savannah was unique among southern cities in implementing a sanitation plan that went beyond street cleaning and inspection of dwellings. Even these minimum efforts of health planning, however, were probably selective in their application. There is no evidence that Savannah deviated from the more general urban pattern of confining street-cleaning activities to the major business thoroughfares. Business considerations apparently were predominant in Alexandria's heralded garbage-collection system. Citizens outside the business district rarely saw the garbage carts. . . .

The impact of business on health planning was even more evident with the second preventive measure, the quarantine. Most antebellum southern cities recognized the efficacy of such a policy, and by 1850 almost all cities had ordinances establishing a quarantine. Studies of earlier epidemics had convinced numerous officials that outside agents, usually vessels from infected European and Caribbean ports, were responsible for many of the outbreaks of disease. By establishing a specified time period (usually twelve days) for incoming vessels to remain off the port, cities hoped to avoid crippling epidemics. Charleston leaders, for example, attributed the absence of cholera in Charleston in 1832 to an effective quarantine. Despite quarantine laws, however, epidemics still occurred in Charleston in later years and in other cities as well.

The difficulty with quarantine lay in its implementation. Some ships and passengers eluded quarantine, and some cities enforced quarantine so haphazardly that it was virtually useless. The attitude of the business community was important in directing quarantine policy. Most merchants viewed quarantine as a restraint of trade. A Charlestonian in 1858 urged that the city forgo plans for invoking quarantine and concentrate on sanitation instead: "If a committee be appointed to inspect cellars, drains, yards, streets, lots . . . it will prove more conducive to the health of Charleston than all the quarantine . . . systems which may be invented, and by leaving our trade to itself, unfettered by restrictions, we may look forward to health and wealth combined." . . .

It would be erroneous to depict the business community—dominated by merchants in antebellum southern cities—as the unrelenting ogres of health planning. It was problematic whether protection from epidemic disease increased in direct proportion to the rigor of sanitation and quarantine procedures. Despite Savannah's impressive and expensive experiment with dry culture, yellow fever frequented that city about as often and with as much severity as in other southern cities. Charleston's tight quarantine may have saved the city from cholera in 1832, but it was of no value in the 1836 cholera epidemic, not to mention the periodic assaults of yellow fever during the interim. If business leaders were unable to conquer disease in antebellum southern cities, they could at least attempt to modify its adverse impact on the community's economic growth. It was at this point—when disease seemed imminent in the form of a serious epidemic—that health planning became a matter of public relations rather than a series of preventive measures.

Since cities were powerless to retard the relentless course of an epidemic, the mere rumor of pestilence was sufficient to send shock waves of fear throughout the community. In Richmond in 1849 the publication of a casual reference to the existence of a few cases of cholera in that city sent the entire state legislature scurrying to northern Virginia for refuge. Six years later the relative proximity of Richmond to yellow-fever-stricken Norfolk caused Lynchburg to urge the permanent removal of the state capital to a healthier location. Civic leaders understood that in the context of trade and prosperity health was an asset and disease anathema. Rivals lay waiting to seize upon a city's temporary distress for economic advantage.

The urban press was the businessman's primary protection against the erosion of his city's image in the wake of disease. It was an unwritten rule that the press should ignore or deny the existence of an epidemic, even if the contrary were so. To do otherwise would give undue commercial advantages to rival cities. It was also possible that, given the diagnostic imperfections of contemporary medicine, a flurry of early cases could prove to be a false alarm. Editors, armed with such assurances and convinced that the community's future was at stake, published repeated denials and recriminations against rivals.

Charleston and Savannah, bitter commercial rivals, clashed over health on numerous occasions. In the summer of 1854 yellow fever raged in both cities, but the presses in each city refused to acknowledge their respective epidemics until they were virtually over. During the pestilence the cities exchanged a series of denials and assertions concerning the progress of the disease in each city. The Charleston *Mercury* reported a ravaging epidemic in Savannah on August 26. The Savannah *Georgian* scoffed at the *Mercury's* claim, implying economic motives had influenced the report. The *Georgian* in turn charged that yellow fever was raging in Charleston. The *Mercury* termed these claims a "great injustice" and suggested that Savannah physicians were both overworked and "incompetent." By the end of September, however, when the danger to both commerce and health was subsiding, both presses quietly admitted the presence of a yellow-fever epidemic earlier in the month. In the case of Charleston more than six hundred residents died of the disease. . . .

The climatic theme was a variation on the attempt to persuade potential customers that the stricken city was inherently healthy. Journals admitted that cases of yellow fever or cholera were appearing with alarming regularity but asserted that they were confined to the foreign-born or to northern visitors, those individuals who were not "acclimated." In the fall of 1858 the Charleston *Daily Courier,* having suppressed information about the city's yellow-fever epidemic all summer, finally admitted it had existed but advised " . . . the city is perfectly safe and healthy for any American, or visitor of American acclimation." Savannah published a similar admission with the same reassurance: "We have had a sickly season. . . . But we have had no epidemic, and very few deaths among our native Southern population."

Such admissions from the press were usually printed sufficiently late and in the context of enough medical and climatic advisories to prevent severe dislocation of a city's commerce. The time elapsing between the first reported cases and the concession of an epidemic by the press was considerable. When yellow fever attacked Norfolk in early June 1855 the local journals suppressed the information until July 30. In the New Orleans yellow-fever epidemic of 1853 the first cases appeared on May 17. When victims began appearing in local hospitals with increasing frequency in June one journal sought to discourage speculation by warning readers that such rumors would "produce a wrong impression both here and abroad." In mid-July, nearly two months after the introduction of the fever into the city, the press conceded its presence.

Civic leaders, in addition to utilizing the press as a means to minimize the economic impact of disease, manipulated the governmental bodies designed to prevent and to report on epidemics. Southern cities, like those elsewhere, maintained boards of health as part of their expanding governmental functions. The city council appointed the board, and thus, from the outset, independence from the business community was unlikely. The board typically consisted of physicians, who divided the city into health districts with each doctor being responsible for one district. Their duties included inspection, aid to the sick and the poor, and the reporting of conditions conducive to disease. The board's infrequent meetings, however, generally vitiated these admirable functions. The members sat only during the summer months when the danger of pestilence was greatest.

The business community ensured that the board's pronouncements would result in a reiteration of the city's healthfulness coupled with innocuous reminders on the importance of good diet and proper clothing. Any Board of Health member who had the temerity to announce the existence of an epidemic before the civic leadership was prepared to acknowledge the presence of an epidemic received a sound verbal thrashing. . . .

The importance of preserving a favorable urban image in health planning was simply a reflection of its importance to other public service areas. Since health planning literally touched upon life-and-death matters as well as on portentous economic issues the role of southern urban merchants was more heavy-handed here than elsewhere. The unwillingness to extend sanitation to outer areas and the early removal of quarantine were typical cost-benefit decisions by local government. The repression of information and the management of press and government bureaucracy, while also justified on an economic basis, revealed a deep fear in the business community. A rutted street was one thing, but a massive epidemic was another. Numerous examples of the catastrophic impact of epidemic disease on a city encouraged business leaders to keep information about them to a minimum.

The Norfolk yellow-fever epidemic of 1855 was an example of such practices. A brief recounting of the epidemic affords an opportunity to understand the leaders' distrust of traditional health-planning procedures and their emphasis on public-relations techniques as the best method of shielding the community from economic loss. In the spring of 1855 the Norfolk City Council launched a wide-ranging cleanliness campaign, concentrating on the draining of swamps and the removal of standing pools of water. When news of yellow fever in the Caribbean reached Norfolk the city imposed a twelve-day quarantine on vessels from that area. Local merchants did not object since most of their trade went coastwise to Philadelphia and New York. On June 7 the steamer *Benjamin Franklin* arrived off Norfolk from the Virgin Islands. After the requisite waiting period passed without report of disease city inspectors lifted the quarantine, and the vessel proceeded to the wharf. An investigation conducted several months later revealed that the captain had successfully concealed two sailors who were dying of yellow fever. The disease thus introduced into the unsuspecting city wreaked havoc for the next three months.

News of the epidemic spread quickly along the Atlantic Coast. By midsummer other Virginia cities, Baltimore, and New York issued interdicts against trade from Norfolk. Wharves, streets, and business establishments became deserted. The estimated loss of business during the four-month plague was over five million dollars. The charitable Howard Association hastily transformed Norfolk's major hotel into a hospital, one which in most cases proved to be simply a way station to the grave. Among the two thousand who perished were the mayor and more than half of the city's ministers and physicians. . . . During the first week in September, at the height of the pestilence, there were at least eighty deaths a day. Within a short time the supply of coffins in the city was exhausted. . . .

For cities engaged in their own fight for survival in a competitive urban society the Norfolk tragedy, which attracted national coverage, seemed to underscore the dilemma of business leaders in dealing with health planning. Expenditures on sanitation and the imposition of a quarantine were not guarantees against epidemic disease. Further, with every gruesome detail of the pestilence that reached the public forum the good image of Norfolk received a telling blow. It took Norfolk five years to recover the population and business lost by the epidemic. . . . The psychological damage was probably as great as the economic and human casualties. Newspaper editors wrote not of increased trade and prosperity but of a "plague spirit." In 1859 one journal admitted that the "advancement" of Norfolk was "slow, too slow." The plague had "melted away the population like snow" and had shaken the self-confidence of the city.

Even the most organized and persuasive business leadership could not have prevented knowledge of the Norfolk epidemic. If the Norfolk experience of 1855, as well as similar plagues in Mobile and Atlanta—cities that earned regional reputations for cleanliness—demonstrated the marginality of contemporary health-planning practices, leaders sought to minimize the economic impact of disease through their control of community affairs. Moreover, it is difficult to assess the benefits which would have been gained by permitting the Board of Health to divulge the presence of the period, and the leaders' claims that they were averting chaos, panic, and a premature blow to trade may have been more than a reflection of business self-interest.

Epidemic disease had its own course in southern cities, and neither the feeble health-planning procedures established by local government nor the efforts to control information flows had much of an impact on the path of pestilence. The course was deadly, and expensive as well. In 1850 Dr. Joseph C. Simonds estimated that the economic cost of disease to New Orleans from 1846 to 1850 amounted to $45,437,700. No metropolis could experience such a loss without some trauma. . . .

Despite the toll of disease cities exhibited a great resiliency. Businessmen, anxious to resume business as usual and to recoup economic and psychological health, led recovery efforts. Though Norfolk rebounded slowly from the effects of pestilence, larger cities like New Orleans and Baltimore regained their trade and their booster spirit even before the last voluntary hospital closed its doors. In late September 1832, for example, two hundred Baltimore merchants pronounced an end to the cholera epidemic then ravaging the city. The fact that cases continued to appear in Baltimore for the next several weeks was immaterial. If business leaders could orchestrate urban growth, they could, presumably, transcend epidemic disease.

The optimism of Baltimore merchants was understandable because the first frost was approaching. New Orleans businessmen exhibited exuberance at a most uncharacteristic time, however. At the height of the worst epidemic in American history, when graveyards were gorged with corpses and victims fell at the rate of a hundred per day, the New Orleans press attempted to rally the city by calling attention to the bright economic prospects of the Crescent City. One journal recounted "a season of general prosperity," and another even touted the city's healthfulness. Such bravado was natural to cities engaged in the competition for trade. An epidemic could haunt a city long after the last case appeared. Civic leaders rallied the city and urged citizens to think of the promising future and forget about the dismal present. The ability of most southern cities to recover quickly after a deadly pestilence resulted from the activities of the business leadership in restoring confidence in the city's future.

The aggressive commercial elite that ruled antebellum southern cities planned policies and initiated services with a view toward maximizing profits and growth. As a disgruntled New Orleans health reformer asserted in 1854: "The leading idea has always been convenience for commerce." Disease-prevention mechanisms existed for convenience, and when they were no longer convenient wealth triumphed over health. . . .

❋ *F U R T H E R   R E A D I N G*

Nelson Manfred Blake, *Water for the Cities: A History of the Urban Water Supply Problem in the United States* (1958)

John Duffy, *A History of Public Health in New York City, 1625–1866* (1968)

Irving D. Fisher, *Frederick Law Olmsted and the City Planning Movement in the United States* (1986)

David Johnson, *Policing the Urban Underworld: The Impact of Crime on the Development of the American Police, 1800–1887* (1979)

Carl F. Kaestle, *The Evolution of an Urban School System: New York, 1750–1850* (1973)

Roger Lane, *Policing the City: Boston, 1822–1885* (1967)

Judith Waltzer Leavitt, *The Healthiest City: Milwaukee and the Politics of Health Reform* (1982)

Alan I. Marcus, *Plagues of Strangers: Social Groups and the Origin of City Services in Cincinnati, 1819–1870* (1991)

Raymond A. Mohl, *Poverty in New York, 1783–1825* (1971)

Eric H. Monkkonen, *America Becomes Urban: The Development of U.S. Cities and Towns, 1780–1900* (1988)

Fern I. Nesson, *Great Waters: A History of Boston's Water Supply* (1983)

Harold L. Platt, *City Building in the New South: The Growth of Public Services in Houston, Texas, 1830–1910* (1983)

James F. Richardson, *The New York Police: Colonial Times to 1901* (1970)

———, *Urban Police in the United States* (1974)

Laura Wood Roper, *FLO: A Biography of Frederick Law Olmsted* (1973)

Charles Rosenberg, *The Cholera Years: The United States in 1832, 1849 and 1866* (1962)

David J. Rothman, *The Discovery of the Asylum: Social Order and Disorder in the New Republic* (1971)

Stanley K. Schultz, *The Culture Factory: Boston Public Schools, 1789–1860* (1973)

Elizabeth Stevenson, *Park Maker: A Life of Frederick Law Olmsted* (1977)

Charles H . Weidner, *Water for a City: A History of New York City's Problem from the Beginning to the Delaware River System* (1974)

CHAPTER
5

Industrialization and
the Urban Working Class

✖

Although the earliest incidences of industrialization in the United States occurred in small towns or the rural countryside, where textile mills could utilize water power, after 1830 the processes of industrialization and urbanization began to wind together more tightly, until they reinforced each other. Cities had both the capital to invest in machines and the big factories necessary for the new kinds of production, and they contained large agglomerations of people to fill industrial labor needs.

The two processes spawned the growth of new classes of workers. One of these comprised urban laborers who no longer could characterize themselves as artisans controlling the pace and income of their work but who instead worked for wages paid by large-scale employers. A second new group was a class of middle- and upper-class owners and managers whose lifestyles diverged from those of their employees. Historians realize that this new urban-industrial system did not emerge overnight but rather developed in different places and different industries at different speeds. The workers and owners caught up in it, struggling to adjust to industrialization, encountered a variety of problems. How did the city facilitate—and exacerbate—the growth of new social classes, and how did workers, who once had considered themselves independent producers, react to the city and to the displacements of the factory system?

✖ DOCUMENTS

The following documents feature first-person accounts illuminating the early effects of industrialization on urban working classes. The first document, a reminiscence from David Johnson of his apprenticeship as a shoemaker, reveals both the complexity and the informality of shoemaking before the processes of industrialization changed the craft. It shows how the world of the urban artisan depended on proficiency with a variety of hand tools, well-developed skills, and close master-apprentice relationships, all of which disappeared when the factory system spread. It also reveals that urban laborers did not always work according to a regimented, clock-oriented schedule. The second document includes excerpts from letters written by Mary Paul, a New England woman who left home in 1830 at age fifteen and, after a few brief jobs, worked in the Lowell textile mills for the next four years. Her letters to her father illustrate the tension between the personal independence sought by a rural youth who moved into factory labor in the city, and family ties that, despite her separation, she was intent on maintaining. The third document contains excerpts from a series of letters written to the editor of the Rochester, New York, *Workingman's Advocate* in 1840. The letters portray an exchange between a carpenter and a master builder. They vividly illustrate the diverging interests of emerging working-class industrial employees, represented by the "mechanic," who is complaining about arbitrary reduction of wages, and emerging middle-class employers, represented by Mr. Bassett, who, while defending the prerogatives of his class, claims to remain a friend of laborers.

David Johnson Recalls His Apprenticeship in a Lynn Shoe Shop (c. 1830), 1880

A boy [apprentice] while learning his trade was called a "seamster"; that is, he sewed the shoes for his master, or employer, or to use one of the technicalities of the "craft," he "worked on the seam." Sometimes the genius of one of these boys would outrun all limits. One of this kind, who be called Alphonzo, worked on the seam for a stipulated sum. He seemed to regard his work as an incidental circumstance. When he left the shop at night he might be expected back the next morning: but there were no special grounds for the expectation. He might drop in the next morning or the next week. He left one Saturday night and did not make his appearance again until the following Thursday morning. On entering the shop he proceeded to take off his jacket as though there had been no hiatus in his labor. His master watched him with an amused countenance to see whether he would recognize the lapse of time. At length he said, "Where have you been, Alphonzo?" Alphonzo turned his head in an instant, as if struck with the preposterousness of the inquiry, and exclaimed, "Me? I? O, I've been down to Nahant." The case was closed. . . .

In almost every one of these shops, there was one whose mechanical genius outran that of all the rest. He could "temper wax," "cut shoulders," sharpen scrapers and cut hair. The making of wax was an important circumstance in the olden time. To temper it just right so that it would not be too brittle and "fly" from the thread, or too soft and stick to the fingers, was an art within the reach of but few, or if within reach, was attained only by those who aspired to scale the heights of fame, and who, "while their companions slept, were toiling upward in the night." Such a one eyed his skillet of melted rosin as the alchemist of old viewed his crucible wherein he was to transmute the baser metals into gold. When the rosin was thoroughly melted, oil or grease was added until the right consistency was supposed to be nearly reached, the compound being thoroughly stirred in the meantime. Then the one having the matter in charge would first dip his finger in cold water and then into the melted mass, and taking the portion that adhered to his finger, would test its temper by pulling it, biting it, and rolling it in his hands. If found to be too hard, more oil or grease would be added, but very cautiously, as the critical moment was being reached. Then the test would be again applied. When the right result was supposed to be nearly gained, a piece of wax would be passed around among the crew for a confirmatory verdict. If the judgment of the master of ceremonies was indorsed, the experiment ended, and the mixture was poured into a vessel of cold water—usually the "shop-tub"—to cool sufficiently to be "worked." . . .

The shop-tub was an indispensable article in every shop. In early times, before the manufactures of wooden ware had become plenty and cheap, some rudely-constructed wooden vessel of home manufacture served the purpose. Afterwards a paint-keg or a firkin with the top sawed off, and still later a second-hand water-pail, was made to do service.

The theory was that the water of the shop-tub was to be changed every day. As this water was used for *wetting* the "stock"—which meant all the sole leather put into the shoe—and also often used for washing hands, it was somewhat necessary that it should be changed occasionally. The shifting of the "tub" often devolved upon the boy of the shop, except when he was too bright. In that case he "shirked" with the rest of the crew. This was the sort of boy that looked out of the attic window of the dormitory where he slept, to see if the smoke was gracefully curling from the shop's chimney, in the gray of the morning as he stretched himself for a supplementary snooze.

The man who had an "eye" for cutting "shoulders" occupied a niche of distinction among his fellow-craftsmen. If it was not necessary that he should have a "microscope eye"—which Mr. Pope [the eighteenth-century English poet] tells us man does not need because he "is not a fly"—it was needful that he should have a "geometric eye" when called upon to adjust the "shoulder" to "convex" and "concave" edges. To do this successfully required little less than a stroke of genius. Two cents was the usual price for cutting a "shoulder," and an experienced cutter would gather in each week quite a pile of the larger-size coppers of those days, whose purchasing power of many things was twice as great as at present. . . .

Perhaps one of the sorest experiences a boy had in old times in learning the "craft," was that which came from *breaking awls.* In order to fully appreciate the situation, the reader must take a survey of the whole field. It was a period of low wages. Awls were the most expensive "kit" used by the shoemaker. . . .

The awls were of two kinds, diamond and round, so called from the shape of their points. The diamond-shaped were usually preferred, as they were thought to be less liable to become dulled by use; but the so-called round awls—these were rather flatted at their points—were often used by "don" workmen, as they were less liable to "cut" the "upper." The awls first in use in this country were of English manufacture. The name of the manufacturer was stamped upon each awl, and there were three kinds, more or less in use, some fifty or more years ago when those of American make began to take their place. These were known as the Allerton, Wilson, and Titus awls, respectively. After the introduction of the American awl, the English article was not held in very high esteem by workmen employed upon ladies' shoes. They were badly shaped, and the points were left unfinished. The Allerton and Wilson had usually too long a crook, while the Titus was faulty in the opposite direction, being too straight, especially for certain kinds of work. They had, however, two important recommendations—they were better tempered, and therefore less liable to break, and their cost was only one-half, or less, that of the American awl.

Before the English awl was used, it was necessary to finish the points. This was sometimes done by grinding, sometimes by filing, and sometimes by sandpaper; and the points were smoothed off on a "wheel-board," or by rubbing them on the pine floor. The man who could do this job skillfully was considered something of a genius. As already intimated, a boy could spoil a day's wages by breaking a few awls. If he was working on the seam on "long reds," and had a lot of extra hard soles on hand—some *hemlock tanned leather* for instance—he had gloomy forebodings of the period of the situation. If the master was a "hard" one, and the boy somewhat careless, there would most likely be an appeal to the "stirrup," whenever accidents of this kind rose above the average in frequency. . . .

Mary Paul on the Lowell Textile-Mill Experience, 1845, 1846

Lowell Nov 20th 1845

Dear Father

An opportunity now presents itself which I improve in writing to you. I started for this place at the time I talked of which was Thursday. I left Whitneys at nine o'clock stopped at Windsor at 12 and staid till 3 and started again. Did not stop again for any length of time till we arrived at Lowell. Went to a boarding house and staid untill Monday night. On Saturday after I get here Luthera Griffith went round with me to find a place but we were unsuccessful. On Monday we started again and were more successful. We found a place in a spinning room and the next morning I went to work. I like very well have 50 cts first payment increasing every payment as I get along in work have a first rate overseer and a very good boarding place. I work on the Lawrence Corporation. Mill is No 2 spinning room. I was very sorry that you did not come to see me start. I wanted to see you and [brother] Henry but I suppose that you were otherways engaged. . . . Had to pay only 25 cts for board for 9 days after I got here before I went into the mill. Had 2.50 left with which I got a bonnet and some other small articles. Tell Harriet Burbank to send me paper. Tell her I shall send her one as soon as possible. You must write as soon as you receive this. Tell Henry I should like to hear from him. If you hear anything from [brother] William write for I want to know what he is doing. I shall write to Uncle Millers folks the first opportunity. Aunt Nancy presented me with a new alpaca dress before I came away from there which I was very glad of, I think of staying here a year certain, if not more. I wish that you and Henry would come down here. I think that you might do well. I guess that Henry could get into the mill and I think that [brother] Julius might get in too. Tell all friends that I should like to hear from them.

excuse bad writing and mistakes
This from your own daughter
Mary—

P.S. Be sure and direct to No. 15 Lawrence Corporation.

"Letters of Mary Paul, a Female Factory Worker," from Thomas Dublin, ed., *Farm to Factory: Women's Letters, 1830–1860*, excerpts from pp. 101–5. Copyright © 1981 Columbia University Press, New York. Reprinted with the permission of the publisher.

Lowell Dec 21st 1845

Dear Father

I received your letter on Thursday the 14th with much pleasure. I am well which is one comfort. My life and health are spared while others are cut off. Last Thursday one girl fell down and broke her neck which caused instant death. She was going in or coming out of the mill and slipped down it being very icy. The same day a man was killed by the [railroad] cars. Another had nearly all of his ribs broken. Another was nearly killed by falling down and having a bale of cotton fall on him. Last Tuesday we were paid. In all I had six dollars and sixty cents paid $4.68 for board. With the rest I got me a pair of rubbers and a pair of 50 cts shoes. Next payment I am to have a dollar a week beside my board. . . . Perhaps you would like something about our [winter] regulations about going in an coming out of the mill. At 5 o'clock in the morning the bell rings for the folks to get up and get breakfast. At half past six it rings for the girls to get up and at seven they are called into the mill. At half past 12 we have dinner are called back again at one and stay till half past seven. I get along very well with my work. I can doff as fast as any girl in our room. I think I shall have frames before long. The usual time allowed for learning is six months but I think I shall have frames before I have been in three as I get along so fast. I think that the factory is the best place for me and if any girl wants employment I advise them to come to Lowell. Tell Harriet that though she does not hear from me she is not forgotten. I have little time to devote to writing that I cannot write all I want to. There are half a dozen letters which I ought to write to day but I have not time. Tell Harriet I send my love to her and all of the girls. Give my love to Mrs. Clement. Tell Henry this will answer for him and you too for this time.

This from
Mary S Paul

Lowell April 12th 1846

Dear Father

I received your letter with much pleasure but was sorry to hear that you had been lame. . . . Last Friday I received a letter from you. You wanted to know what I am doing. I am at work in a spinning room and tending four sides of warp which is one girls work. The overseer tells me that he never had a girl get along better than I do and that he will do the best he can by me. I stand it well, though they tell me that I am growing very poor. I was paid nine shillings a week last payment and am to have more this one though we have been out considerable for backwater which will take off a good deal. [A spring flood had caused stoppage of the water wheel which ran the mill.] The Agent promises to pay us nearly as much as we should have made but I do not think that he will. The payment was up last night and we are to be paid this week. I have a very good boarding place have enough to eat and that which is good enough. The girls are all kind and obliging. The girls that I room with are all from Vermont and good girls too. Now I will tell you about our [summer] rules at the boarding house. We have none in particular except that we have to go to bed about 10 o'clock. At half past 4 in the morning the bell rings for us to get up and at five for us to go into the mill. At seven we are called out to breakfast are allowed half an hour between bells and the same at noon till the first of May when we have three quarters [of an hour] till the first of

September. We have dinner at half past 12 and supper at seven. If Julius should go to Boston tell him to come this way and see me. He must come to the Lawrence Counting room and call for me. He can ask some one to show him where the Lawrence is. I hope he will not fail to go. I forgot to tell you that I have not seen a particle of snow for six weeks and it is settled going we have had a very mild winter but little snow. I saw Ann Hersey last Sunday. I did not know her till she told me who she was. I see the Griffith girls often. I received a letter from a girl in Bridgewater in which she told me that Mrs Angell had heard some way that I could not get work and that she was much pleased and said that I was so bad that no one would have me. I believe I have written all so I will close for I have a letter to write to William this afternoon.

Yours affectionately
Mary S Paul

P.S. Give my love to all that enquire for me and tell them to write me a long long letter. Tell Harriet I shall send her a paper.

A Carpenter-Employee and a Builder-Employer Debate the Control of an Industrial Worker's Wages, 1840

March 16, 1840

MR. EDITOR—Emboldened by the spirit of kindness and liberality which you have so repeatedly manifested towards the Mechanics of this city, through the medium of your useful and interesting paper, I beg leave to confide in the same disinterested feelings for the publicity of a few remarks which I am constrained to make, respecting the present condition of a large class of the Mechanics of Rochester, with the hope of rendering them (and the public generally) sensible of our grievances.

In the first place, therefore, I am enabled to state, from circumstances that have recently transpired, that our rights, as Mechanics, are now assailed, and that too by an individual who has hitherto lived upon the labor of the journeyman mechanic, and accumulated the principal part of widespread possessions by grinding the faces of the poor, who, through absolute necessity, are obliged to submit tacitly to his imposition. . . . In order to develop more fully my paramount object in addressing my fellow Mechanics, I must intimate to them, that the celebrated architect above referred to is now actually engaged in the most unprincipaled and despotic enterprise that can sufficiently characterize or define a tyrant—namely, of trying to depress the mechanics of this city, by depriving them of a fair and adequate remuneration for their daily toils, or, in other words, to reduce their wages immediately, because, as he states, the price of flour is now so extremely low! But can it be possible that my fellow Mechanics of this city, will suffer themselves to be gulled by this "*plausible*" pretext and become the voluntary dupes of this tyrannical nabob, whose predominant propensity is to correct those in his employment into profitable serfs and thus keep in a state of abject and cringing dependence? If, however, they should cower down beneath the awful displeasure of this *humane* and *philanthropic* aristocrat, let me ask them, if, in doing so, they are not deceiving themselves, ruining the interest of the

Workers and Building of Brown and Sharpe
Manufacturing Company, c. 1860

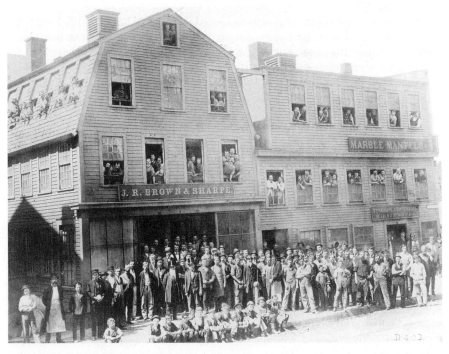

This photograph shows an early factory established in 1833 in Providence, Rhode Island, by clockmaker and mechanic David Brown and his son Joseph. Early urban factories mass-produced products by combining a large number of artisans, journeymen, and laborers under one roof. By the eve of the Civil War, when this picture was taken, mechanization and the use of interchangeable parts were reducing the need for skilled employees and undercutting workers' sense of autonomy.

Mechanics, and at the same time acting incompatible with the spirit of freedom which pervades this republican country, and which is perpetually ringing in the ears of every American freeman?

. . . Although it is our pride and privilege to be constituted citizens of this vast Republic, to inhale the invigorating air of freedom, and bask in the glorious sunshine of "civil and religious liberty," still, we have to regret that the clanking chains of despotic power are frequently heard throughout our land, and even the ghastly features of the tyrant, on many occasions, exhibited where *liberty* and impartial justice should *alone* preside.

A Mechanic

March 18, 1840

MR. EDITOR—I observed in the Advocate of Monday evening last, an attack upon some person whom the author styles "The Celebrated Architect." The writer charges the individual with "oppressing" the Journeyman Mechanics of this city—also, of monopolizing all the business of his profession (building). In the first place, I know of only two individuals, besides myself, in this city who claim to be Architects. . . . If your correspondent alludes to me, his long rigmarole of complaints and abuses are but one continued tissue of falsehoods. The long and short of the business is, there are a few individuals in this city who are dissatisfied with everything that is not in accord with their own views; they wish to dictate to the Master Mechanic how much he shall pay his men, and in what manner he shall conduct his business, and how much he shall do. . . .

I have always been in favor of paying the laboring man a full compensation for his services, and that his wages should be regulated according to the time and prices of provisions, &c. The writer seems to argue, that because provisions and everything else has fallen in price, that is no reason why his wages should decline. . . . If men are dissatisfied with their wages, they have all the privileges of freemen; and if they are not under any special contract, they can at once seek employment in shops in other towns and states, or establish themselves in business. I hope the author alluded to, will be manly enough to give his own signature, and identify the person whom he alludes to, by inserting his name.

Yours respectfully,
J. Bassett

March 21, 1840

MR. EDITOR—I sincerely regret that in consequence of intervening circumstances, which I need not mention, I have been rendered totally incapable of responding with promptness to some incoherent remarks which one of our citizens considered necessary to make upon a communication of mine, which appeared in the Advocate a few days since—yet, notwithstanding this, I am induced, even at this *unseasonable* period, to reply to some of the gentleman's unexpected, uncalled for, and indeed, undeserved animadversions. . . . My powerful antagonist has been *strangely* infatuated in the course he has adopted relative to this affair, conscious as I am that he must have seen *at once,* from the general tenor of my remarks that he is not the Celebrated Architect alluded to. . . .

I have no desire to enter into a paper war with my worthy friend B. . . . But still I feel it to be a duty incumbent on me to inform him of the general opinion entertained respecting his injudicious interference in this matter. And first, it is presumed that he will ultimately rest satisfied that he has *too* hastily applied my remarks to himself. Secondly, that he has *prematurely, impolitely* and consequently *injudiciously* accused a large class of the Mechanics of Rochester of being liars, without having any just or *even* presumptive authority for this illiberal and unfounded accusation. . . . [H]e is decidedly mistaken in asserting that I "seem to argue, because the price of provisions and everything else has fallen, that is no reason why his wages should decline." Now, I am prepared to state, without fear of successful contradiction, that such is not my argument. . . . We, as a class of laboring Mechanics, consider it unjust and oppressive to have our wages immediately curtailed if only one or two articles of consumption are fallen in price. At the present time, I know of *no* article worth mentioning that sells at the reduced price but flour, and yet, strange to say, our celebrated Architect and puritanical fellow-citizen contends, that this *alone,* is sufficient, and that *his* fiat will ultimately accomplish the grand achievement of blending into one *undistinguishabled* wreck, the Mechanic's wages and the price of flour! O astonishing revolution, deplorable calamity! . . .

Before I terminate, I feel it due to Mr. B. to state, that I never considered him as being inimical to the interest and welfare of the Mechanics of Rochester. . . . I am satisfied he has been, in a great measure, instrumental in establishing our rights, and hope therefore, his conduct on this occasion will be in strict conformity with the influence which he has previously extended in our behalf. . . .

A Mechanic

March 25, 1840
MR. EDITOR—I once more ask permission to trespass upon your liberality, by asking of you the privilege of appropriating a few brief remarks in reply to my friend S., under the signature of "A Mechanic." . . .

He says I prematurely, impolitely, and injudiciously, have accused a large class of mechanics of Rochester of being liars. In this assertion, he will see by reflection that he is in error, unless he insists that his first communication was intended for me, which he denies in the plainest terms. . . . If there are any individuals in this community who are disposed to oppress the laboring class, let him be pointed out and the mark of indignation be stamped upon him. . . . The march of intelligence among the laboring portion of the community fully indicates a successful permanent protection for their rights and interests. The intelligent American Mechanic (native or adopted) will never submit to any infraction of his social rights and privileges, and will repel, with the power of the mighty elements, any attempt to level his condition with the humble peasantry of the European powers. Therefore it is the imperative duty of every Mechanic and workingman to watch with a jealous eye those who hold influential and exalted stations, in order that their invaluable privileges may not be infringed upon, or their interests treated with contempt by those, who, from the influence of vanity and folly, would assume to themselves the appellation of being the better part of the community.

In conclusion, as my worthy friend has paid me a compliment which would do honor to the most honorable—that of being the friend and benefactor of the Mechanic and laboring man. . . . There are many things yet to be accomplished, which would be highly beneficial to the laboring man, and I would assure the worthy gentleman that I am ever ready to lend a helping hand in the hour of need.

Your obdn't servant,
J. B.

ESSAYS

These two essays consider antebellum urban industrialization. The opening piece, by Sean Wilentz of Princeton University, examines the development of the "sweating trades"—the production of clothing, shoes, and furniture in dismal garrets and lofts in New York City by low-skilled, low-paid workers. The second essay, by Susan E. Hirsch of Loyola University in Chicago, illustrates the different paces of industrialization as it occurred in specific industries in a specific city—Newark, New Jersey, the nation's most industrialized city in 1860.

The Rise of Sweatshops in New York City

SEAN WILENTZ

In 1845, the New York *Daily Tribune* prepared a series of reports on the condition of labor in New York. What the *Tribune* reporters found shocked them, and they groped for explanations—especially to account for the outrageous underbidding and exploitation that riddled the city's largest trades. A few years later, after he had read the works of the greatest urban journalist of the age, a *Tribune* correspondent named George Foster had found the right term: it was "sweating," "the accursed system . . . so thoroughly exposed in the recent investigations of Mr. Mayhew in the 'Morning Chronicle,'" a system that had come to prevail "proportionally to as great an extent in this city as in London." One or another variation of sweating emerged in almost all New York's early industrial trades. It arose in its purest forms in the consumer finishing trades, and most notoriously in the production of clothing.

It took only ten years, from 1825 to 1835, for New York's clothing revolution to conquer the local market; by 1850, it had created and captured the lion's share of a national trade in ready-made clothes for men. The original instigators were the city's cloth wholesalers, auctioneers, and jobbers, whose command of the English import market and broadening avenues to New England invited further adaptation and expansion of the contracting schemes of the early slopshop entrepreneurs. Their success, and that of the master tailors turned manufacturers whom they supplied with cloth and credit, was neither an act of Providence nor an inevitable working-out of the growth of commerce. Of all of New York's middlemen and manufacturers, the clothiers were the most astute at perfecting aggressive merchandizing methods; more important, it was the clothiers who first mastered the art of extending liberal credit to local retailers and country dealers, to expand their own contacts and squeeze their competitors in other cities (and smaller New York dealers) out of the market. By 1835, they had turned the New York trade in ready-mades into one of the nation's largest local industries, with some firms employing between three and five hundred hands each. A large portion of their output was for the "cheap" trade—in precut apparel for southern customers (as well as the "Negro cottons" for southern slaves), dungarees and hickory shirts for western farmers and miners, and shoddy clothing for the urban poor. Beginning in the early 1830s, the clothiers also entered the respectable market, introducing superior lines, fiercely promoted by the jobbers and retailers, for clerks, shopkeepers, and wealthy patrons who lacked the time or money to patronize a custom tailor. There was some initial resistance to this noncustom work among the most cosmopolitan customers—but by the late 1840s the clothiers had

From *Chants Democratic: New York City & the Rise of the American Working Class, 1788–1850* by Sean Wilentz, pp. 119–29. Copyright © 1984 by Robert Sean Wilentz. Reprinted by permission of Oxford University Press, Inc.

changed people's minds. In 1849, a breathless report in *Hunt's* noted with admiration that the clothing of one ready-made firm was "adapted to all markets and for all classes of men, from the humblest laborer to the fashionable gentleman." With this democratization of product and the continued growth of the southern market, the New York clothing trade became an antebellum manufacturing giant. By 1850, the largest New York firms hired as many as five thousand tailors and seamstresses to turn out goods "with a degree of precision that would astonish the negligent observer."

The rise of the ready-mades metamorphosed New York tailoring at every level of production. Some of the old-fashioned master craftsmen did survive, largely in the fancy trade: New York business directories from the 1850s still boasted of Broadway's rows of custom fitters and gentlemen tailors. After about 1830, however, even the finest custom masters began to feel the competitive pinch. Some large custom firms like Brooks Brothers' entered the ready-made market for themselves and divided their shops into separate departments for custom work and the cheaper lines; as early as 1835, master tailors' advertisements stressed the availability of ready-mades as much as the skills of the proprietor and his journeymen. Some small custom masters who lacked the funds to finance a ready-made operation set aside defective work and tried to sell it off as "precut." Others went to work for the manufacturers, either as foremen or as semi-independent retailers, vending a specific firm's ready-mades and doing a bit of custom tailoring on their own. A few of these men went on to become large employers themselves; they, and the clothing merchants, oversaw not enlarged craft firms but entirely new kinds of enterprises.

The focal point of the clothing outwork system was the New York version of the central shop—often an attractive structure when seen from the street, its shapely lines and graceful columns beckoning customers to inspect the stock. Once inside, a patron would see only the ample stores and the retinue of clerks; behind the scenes, the elite of the clothing work force, the in-shop cutters, prepared the predesigned patterns. The head cutters, the overseers of that elite, numbered about fifty in all in the city. With an average annual income of between $1,000 and $1,500 each, they were probably the best-paid craft workers in New York. Certainly they were the most privileged. Apart from their power to discipline workers, the head cutters (sometimes called "piece masters") were in charge of giving out all work to the journeymen, outworkers, and contractors. On the basis of their appraisal—or whims—a cutter or stitcher could earn a decent living or an excellent one. Impartiality in these matters was not among the head cutter's virtues. "Generally," the *Tribune* reported, "he has his favorites, perhaps a brother, or cousin, or a particular friend, who gets the 'cream of the shop' and is thus frequently able to make $30 or $40 per week." With their incomes, with their close control over the daily operations and the lives of their subordinates, and with the confidence of their manufacturer-employers, head cutters could reasonably expect one day to open their own businesses.

The cutters enjoyed relatively high wages (roughly $10 to $12 per week) and regular employment, but none of the foremen's powers. Rapid, regular work schedules prevailed in the cutting room. At the Devlin and Brothers' firm, cutters were divided into bureaus for coats, pants, vests, and trimmings, while the entire production process, one reporter observed, "was reduced to a system," in which every piece of work had its own number and a ticket with the workman's name. Emphasis fell on speed and accuracy in cutting predetermined designs; "Southern-trade cutting," a term synonymous with rapid rather than artful work, was the most common task in New York's major clothing firms at least as early as the mid-1830s. Any slip, momentary slowdown, or simple disagreement with the foreman could deprive a cutter of the best work in the shop; if he could not adjust to the pace, he was fired.

From the cutting rooms (again, out of sight of the customers), the head cutter or piece master distributed the cut cloth to the outworkers and contractors, and it was here that the worst depredation of sweating began. A variety of outwork schemes existed. While most contractors were small masters unable to maintain their own shops, or journeymen looking for the surest road to independence, some cutters and in-shop journeymen also managed to subcontract a portion of their work on the sly. Major firms dealt directly with outworkers. In all cases, the system invited brutal competition and a successive lowering of outwork piece rates. At every level of the contracting network, profits came from the difference between the rates the contractors and manufacturers received and the money they paid out for overhead and labor. Two factors turned these arrangements into a matrix of unremitting exploitation: first, the successive bidding by the contractors for manufacturers' orders (as well as the competition between manufacturers) depressed the contractors' income; second, the reliance of the entire trade on credit buying by retailers and country dealers promoted postponement of payment to all workers until finished work was done—and, hence, chronic shortages of cash. The result: employers steadily reduced the rates they paid their hands and often avoided paying them at all for as long as possible. To middle-class reformers, the great villain of the system was the contractor himself, the "sweater," the "remorseless sharper and shaver," who in league with the cruel landlord fed greedily on the labor of poor women and degraded journeymen. But the contractors and manufacturers had little choice in the matter, as they tried to underbid their competitors and survive on a wafer-thin margin of credit. "If they were all the purest of philanthropists," the *Tribune* admitted in 1845, "they could not raise the wages of their seamstresses to anything like a living price." Hounded by their creditors, haunted by the specter of late payment and bankruptcy, the contractors and garret masters lived an existence in which concern for one's workers was a liability and in which callousness (and, in some recorded cases, outright cruelty) became a way of life. Some were not above underhanded tricks to earn the extra dollar (the most widespread complaints concerned contractors who withheld wages on the pretense that an outworker's handiwork was not the proper quality); all maintained their independence from the only source available to them, the underpaid labor of the outworkers and garret hands.

The sufferings of the outwork and garret-shop hands—the vast majority of clothing-trade workers—taxed the imaginations of even the most sentimental American Victorians; if the reformers' accounts sometimes reduced a complex situation to a moral fable, they in no way falsified the clothing workers' conditions. All pretensions to craft vanished in the outwork system; with the availability of so much cheap wage labor, formal apprenticing and a regular price book had disappeared by 1845. At any given moment in the 1830s and 1840s, the underbidding in the contracting network could depress outwork and garret-shop piece rates so low that stitchers had to work up to sixteen hours a day to maintain the meanest of living standards: in 1850, some of the largest southern-trade clothing firms in the Second Ward paid their *male* workers, on the average, well below subsistence wages. Housing was difficult to come by and could amount to no more than a cellar dwelling or a two-room flat, shared with two or more families; single men crammed into outwork boardinghouses. During slack seasons or a bad turn in trade, the clothing workers struggled harder to make ends meet, with a combination of odd jobs, charity relief, and the starchiest kinds of cheap food. Poor journeymen tailors had little recourse but to sweat themselves and their families or, if they were single, to strike informal arrangements with girls and widows to work beside them, while they handled the negotiations with the head cutters or contractors: as a German immigrant later recalled, one New York adage from the 1850s ran, "A tailor is worth nothing without a wife and very often a child." The seamstresses and tailors' wives—consigned the most wearisome work (shirt sewing worst of all) and subjected to the bullying and occasional sexual abuse of the contractors—bore the most blatant exploitation; the men, working either as petty contractors or the patresfamilias of the family shops, enjoyed, by comparison, a measure of independence—but only that, as unionists noted in the 1850s. By themselves, such conditions were difficult; they were aggravated by the tendency for outwork and garret-shop wages to diminish further as workers tried to increase their earnings by intensifying their labor and by taking on larger lots of work, thus causing short-term gluts in the labor market and still lower piece rates—what Mayhew elaborated as the principle that "overwork makes for underpayment." Even more, the rise of the ready-mades accentuated the seasonal fluctuations in labor demand. In April and October, when manufacturers prepared for the spring and fall sales seasons, regular work was relatively plentiful; for the rest of the year, as much as two-thirds of the clothing work force had to string together temporary work in an already overstocked labor market.

Life for most New York shoeworkers was no better. Like clothing production, the boot-and-shoe trade changed dramatically with the expansion of the city's trade contacts and the wholesalers' pursuit of markets. By 1829, four major footwear jobbers had opened in Manhattan; by 1850, the number had increased tenfold. The most enterprising major concerns kept pace with the clothing dealers and extended their inland markets southward to Alabama and as far west as Texas. Unlike the clothiers, however, New York firms never took the national lead in the production of respectable ready-mades; most either relied on established firms in shoemaking capitals like Lynn or Haverhill or hired their own workers in outlying towns, where, the *Tribune* reported in 1845, "the workmen can live for almost half the sum it costs our city mechanics." What remained in New York, apart from a busy custom trade, was repair work, ladies' shoemaking, bootmaking and production of the cheapest lines of shoes, either for government military contractors or for wholesale exporters in the southern trade. The shoemakers were left either to what the English writer Joseph Sparks Hall called "the cheapening system" or to an endless competition for custom orders.

The transforming effects of credit, competition, and mercantile sponsorship were dramatized in one of the trade's success stories, the rise of John Burke.

Burke, an Irishman, had learned the shoemakers' craft in Dublin, where he also dabbled in radical, anti-British politics. Disgusted with postfamine conditions and with Ireland's inability to break British rule, he determined to try his fortune in "the Great Republic," and in 1847 he arrived in New York. Having landed jobs in the leather-cutting rooms of some of the best custom shops, Burke quickly learned that the New York trade was very different from the Irish: to earn his competence, he would have to curry favor and credit from his employers' customers. The erstwhile radical craftsman became an entrepreneur. Within two years of his arrival, he proudly reported that "all the customers were my friends"; by 1852, thanks to a timely loan from Moses Beach, the editor and chronicler of the city's mercantile fortunes, Burke opened his own shop. Over the next ten years, Burke expanded his business (eventually buying out one of his former employers, an event he noted with blustery pride) and with Beach's backing eventually began to "gain first place in the shoe trade." He readily admitted that without the help of his "good friends," his life would have remained "a fight against mishaps, disappointments, and adversity." For the thousands of journeymen who lacked Burke's combination of skills, contacts, and charm, such a life of adversity was unavoidable: those who would gain their independence had little choice but to become contractors, to be stigmatized as "the greatest tyrants in the entire trade," in a competitive shoemakers' world where, as Hall remarked, "money *bulk* and not money *worth* becomes the only standard of business."

The division of labor in boot- and shoemaking followed the same general pattern as in the clothing trade. Work in the custom shops and in the shops of the ladies' shoemakers and the bootmakers was divided into the very few skilled cutting chores (handled by men like Burke) and the simpler, more repetitive tasks of the crimpers, fitters, and bottomers. Most journeymen could expect to earn at best six dollars per week from the easier work; to supplement their incomes, they completed an array of ornamental "extras," the most time-consuming and exacting chores in the better branches of the trade. In the shops, apprenticeship, in decline even before 1825, was reported "pretty much done away with" by 1845. Outside of the shops, the demands of garret work and outwork led the *Tribune* to reckon in 1845 that no class of mechanics averaged so great an amount of work for so little money as the journeymen shoemakers. Chronic unemployment and underemployment were even more severe in shoemaking than in tailoring, leaving the journeymen to labor at a breakneck pace whenever work came their way. Family-shop arrangements like the one that had shocked the Reverend Ely thirty years earlier became ever more common:

> We have been in some fifty cellars in different parts of the city [the *Tribune* reported], each inhabited by a Shoe-maker and his family. The floor is made of rough plank laid loosely down, and the ceiling is not quite so high as a tall man. The walls are dark and damp and a wide desolate fireplace yawns at the center to the right of the entrance. There is no outlet back, and of course no yard privileges of any kind. The miserable room is lighted only by a shallow sash, partly projecting above the surface of the ground, and by the little light that struggles down from the steep and rotting stairs. In this apartment often live the man and his work bench, his wife, and five or six children of all ages; and perhaps a palsied grandfather and grand-

mother and often both. . . . Here they work, here they cook, they eat, they sleep, they pray. . . .

Outwork binders, almost all of them women, were placed in backstairs chambers, where they worked from before sunrise until after sundown for piece rates that brought in as little as fifty cents a day. Small masters, in a losing battle against the wholesalers and the Lynn trade, made the cheapest grade of shoes and survived, the *Tribune* claimed in 1845, on "the chance job of gentlemen's or children's mending brought in by the rich people above ground in the neighborhood who are not celebrated for paying a poor cobbler high prices."

Sweating assumed different forms and took slightly longer to develop in the furniture trades. The shift began in about 1830, when the larger master furniture makers, hoping to reduce their wage bills and circumvent the existing price books, solicited British and European artisans to emigrate to New York. Within five years, hundreds of cabinetmakers had settled in Manhattan, many of them Germans from declining craft towns, creating the oversupply of hands the masters wanted; one English cabinetmaker, upon his arrival in Manhattan in 1834, was advised to leave the overcrowded city as soon as he could, since steady furniture work was hard to find and since most available work was poorly paid. In their search for cheap labor, however, the masters also undercut their own position, as some of the Germans began entering the business for themselves and managed to undersell the established firms by hiring other Germans at low wages. Small German shops soon dotted the shores of the Hudson and East rivers, producing inexpensive goods for the wholesalers and paying piece rates well below those expected by native-born journeymen. In response, the established masters—including Duncan Phyfe himself—turned out cheaper lines (so-called butcher furniture) and cut some of their journeymen's wages accordingly, which only led the furniture jobbers to order more goods from the small garret-shops. By the early 1840s, garret contracting operations had inundated the trades; agents prowled the city's wharves looking for immigrants to steer to the cheap shops. Furniture making, though immune to the usual forms of outwork, became a sweated contract trade.

The majority of furniture workers divided into a small elite corps of custom workmen and the contract suppliers to the wholesalers and retailers. First-rate hands continued to turn and fashion elegant designs for the likes of Phyfe and Company and earned as much as fifteen dollars for a sixty-hour week, but by the mid-1840s such work was scarce, open to fewer than one in twenty furniture employees. Apprenticeship continued, although by one investigator's estimate in 1853, not one in fifty cabinetmakers was an apprentice; those who remained were taken on for periods of two to four years, a span [that] the *Herald* claimed "those who have had an experience in the trade say is almost impossible to obtain a complete practical knowledge of it." The "second-class" or "botch" workers labored at restricted, repetitive tasks, either in the larger manufactories along the Hudson or in the colonies of cabinetmaking garret shops on the Lower East Side, places where, as the cabinetmaker Ernest Hagen remembered, the work was strictly divided and masters "generally made a specialty of one piece only." Their plight, as reported in the *Herald,* was quite similar to that of the tailors, as intense competition between contractors and small masters led to a system of underbidding "in which the contending parties seem to lose all sense of honor or justice." By 1850 the furniture journeymen complained that most furniture workers could not expect to earn as much as "the common standard prices paid to hod carriers and sewer-diggers, little better than starving prices."

Tailoring, shoemaking, and furniture making were the most dramatic examples of consumer finishing trades beset by similar problems. In others—hat and bonnet making, umbrella making, and many more—one form or another of piecework, outwork, and sweating arose between 1825 and 1850; in still others, such as cigarmaking, the full force of the bastardization of craft would be felt within a generation. In all of them, we confront, in the most extreme way, the divided legacy of early-nineteenth-century capitalist growth. There can be little question that the transformation of New York consumer finishing improved material life for millions of Americans, in the form of cheaper clothes, cheaper shoes, and cheaper furniture, in greater quantities (and of higher quality) than ever before. For those at the very bottom of the outwork network—especially, after 1845, the famine-ravaged Irish—even work in the sweatshops and outwork cellars and the driven life of a petty contractor were preferable to rural disaster and, for some, starvation; for the fortunate few like John Burke, it was still possible to expect to earn, by one means or another, an independent estate. But none of this alters what was the harder truth in the sweated trades—that the cost of productivity, of salvation from agrarian calamity, and of opportunity for some was the collapse of the crafts and their replacement with a network of competition, underbidding, and undisguised exploitation—all in a city where the mercantile elite and the more successful manufacturers accumulated some of the greatest fortunes in America. These changes were invisible to most customers and chroniclers, hidden from view in the back-room cutters' bureaus and in the outworkers' cellars. To upper- and middle-class New York, the onset of metropolitan industrialization appeared mainly as a dazzling cavalcade of new commodities, "suited to every market." To the craft workers, it was the intensity of labor, the underpayment, and the subordination to the rule of another that was most apparent. Above all else, it was the very transparency of exploitation, the self-evident inequalities of power and material expectations at every level of production, that made the sweated consumer finishing trades the most degraded crafts in New York. It would also make these trades the most troubled of all during the city's labor upheavals after 1825.

The Process of Antebellum Industrialization: The Case of Newark, New Jersey

SUSAN E. HIRSCH

Industrialization was a motive force in the physical growth of Newark, producing a large city from a town, but it also created an industrial city, the home of a new working class and the graveyard of the artisan class. . . .

From *Roots of the American Working Class: The Industrialization of Crafts in Newark, 1800–1860* by Susan E. Hirsch, excerpts from pp. 15–36. Copyright © 1978 by Susan E. Hirsch. Reprinted by permission of the author.

In its most narrow terms, industrialization consisted of innovation in the methods of production: task breakdown and mechanization. Such innovation was related to the development of markets; manufacturers producing for wholesale rather than retail markets were the first to introduce new techniques. But wholesale production did not sweep all before it in the first half of the nineteenth century. A luxury market of middle and upper-class urbanites who desired quality products developed as the cities grew and allowed some skilled workers to continue using the old hand methods. Neither did early industrialization end the old seasonality and irregularity of production, since manufacturers had had little practice in calculating and controlling demand for their goods.

Industrialization was more than a technological process, however; it was also a social process because of its effects on workers. As manual skills became obsolete, apprenticeship waned, and a worker no longer spent his boyhood in a master's home. Mechanization removed work from the household to the factory, and household production became less prevalent. One aspect of mechanization, the introduction of sewing machines, also specifically undercut family labor by decreasing the number of females working in those crafts in which women had done sewing. Industrialization thus made new demands on the families and households of craftsmen; at the same time, it changed the concept of work. Working was more dangerous around machines, so workers' lives were less secure. The pace of the machines and the institution of the wage system led workers to conceive of their jobs in terms of time spent, not tasks accomplished, and thus to demand a limitation of their hours.

Ultimately, industrialization destroyed the artisan class. Workers lost control over their wages when they had fewer skills, and competition caused employers to cut wages whenever possible. The old unity of masters and journeymen disappeared, and workers often formed unions to oppose their employers. . . .

Newark's Economic Development

Industrialization began to revolutionize Newark's crafts in the 1830s, and by 1860 a tremendous spurt of economic and physical growth had made Newark America's major industrial city. Craft workshops had become large factories, and the population had increased more than six-fold. Expansion in Newark was grounded in manufacturing rather than in finance or commerce, and it commenced when other crafts followed the path shoemakers had begun earlier and moved toward the modern factory form of production.

Economic development began in the early 1830s in the increased demand for Newark's specialties and the creation of wholesale markets. Newark's goods had a reputation for high quality, a reputation publicized throughout the East at Mechanics' Fairs, where Newark products won many prizes. To meet this demand, masters in several crafts—shoemaking, hatting, saddle making, and carriage making—expanded their workshops to factory scale. These were rarely mechanized mills; most work was still done by hand, and in many mills the differentiation of tasks was just beginning. But even those "factories" that were simply large accumulations of craftsmen and raw materials under one roof created a new efficiency in production and marketing and thus greater profits. Although there were many large factories in Newark, many small traditional shops remained in those crafts producing for the local market. The average firm in Newark employed only about twenty people in 1836.

The expansion of the early 1830s created hundreds of jobs every year, and Newark's population expanded rapidly. The demand for hands was so great that even a hundred workmen left unemployed by a fire that destroyed their work place were assumed to be able to find work quickly. People flocked to Newark to take advantage of the new opportunities, and the population soared. Prior to the 1830s, Newark had been smaller than the average city in the Northeast. By 1836, with a population of 19,732, it was of average size. . . .

To develop as a manufacturing center, a city needed both markets and raw materials, access to which varied in the early nineteenth century because of the immature canal and railroad network. Newark was one of the towns that enhanced its transportation facilities and thereby created a stimulus to production. In 1832, the Morris Canal opened, connecting Newark with the Delaware Valley. This new, easy access to natural resources stimulated the range of iron-dependent and leather-dependent industries, since coal, ore, hides, and wood bark could now reach Newark in large quantities. Improvements in transportation connecting Newark to New York also aided industrial expansion. The opening of the railroad to Jersey City in 1834 reduced travel time between Newark and New York to approximately one hour.

Even prior to this increase in accessibility, Newark had become a satellite of New York, relying on the capital supply, labor force, and customers there to facilitate production. . . .

Although the New York area possessed a common labor pool and adequate transportation, and businesses could choose to locate within it at many sites, many found Newark especially attractive. Both employers and employees moved to Newark because rents and the cost of living were cheaper there than in New York City. This advantage may have been especially important in an age when employers were often but a year or two or a few hundred dollars removed from employee status. Newarkers were aware of the possible advantages of their city, and they did their best to enhance them: the government kept taxes low to attract businessmen, Newarkers promoted and invested in the improvements in transportation, and local speculators invested both in factory buildings and in new industries.

. . . The sharp panic of 1837 stopped business in its tracks, and the wholesale shoe firms collapsed. The depression that followed destroyed firms, large and small, in every field, The factories were empty, and people began to leave the city to find subsistence elsewhere. By 1840 the population had declined to 17,290—a loss of 2,500 from the recorded peak in 1836. The depression that began in 1837 lasted for six long years. Newark's economy stagnated, and no further strides toward industrialization were made.

When the national economy revived, in the 1840s, Newark grew once more as industrialization accelerated the evolution of crafts toward modern production methods. In response to further economic growth Newark broke through the ranks of the national urban hierarchy in the 1840s to become twice as large as the average city and one of the larger cities in the country. Newark's population increased by 125 percent between 1840 and 1850, so that it stood at 38,894 at midcentury. By 1860, Newark was a thriving industrial center of 71,941 with 74 percent of its labor force employed in manufacturing, and the value of its manufactured products ranked sixth in the nation. . . .

Newark's strong commitment to manufacturing was the foundation for the economic recovery on which population growth and urban development rested; in 1840, 80 percent of Newark's labor force worked in the manufacturing sector. The diverse industries, which had produced the boom of the 1830s and cushioned the shock of the loss of the shoe market, formed a base for recovery. New markets for some of Newark's specialties—patent leather, coach springs, prefabricated steps—appeared, even in the Far East, and army contracts during the Mexican War, especially for harnesses and wagons, underwrote industrial expansion.

Not only the demand for Newark's products, but also a greater productivity made possible by industrialization stimulated economic recovery. The initial commitment to manufacturing made the introduction of the new technology possible. The use of steam power to drive machinery was the most important innovation. By 1846 more than one hundred factories used steam power; in 1840 none had. . . .

Newark's evolution into a major industrial city, however, meant it could no more resist national economic trends in the 1840s and 1850s than it had in the 1830s. If anything, with more and more firms and workers producing for regional and national rather than local markets, Newark was increasingly vulnerable. In Newark, as in the nation at large, the prosperity of the late 1840s did not continue through the 1850s. There was periodic unemployment throughout the mid-1850s, and in the winter of 1854–55 soup kitchens had to be established. The panic of 1857 hurt many of Newark's industries, and by October perhaps half of all manufacturing workers were unemployed. While production resumed in some lines within three months, a year later overall production had yet to reach the heights attained in 1856. Industrialization had obliterated the self-sufficiency of the mechanic's town.

Industrialization as a Social Process

Industrialization was the mainspring of economic development and population growth in Newark, but it functioned as a social process because of its effects on mechanics—a complex social process, since its impact varied from craft to craft. Many trades industrialized between 1830 and 1860, but others like carpentry and blacksmithing remained in their traditional forms throughout the mid-nineteenth century. The pace of technological change was faster in some crafts than others. Two extreme examples in Newark were shoemaking and trunk making. Shoemakers failed to use even simple machines before the late 1850s, although they had begun to break down the tasks of their trade by the early nineteenth century. Trunk making, on the other hand, evolved in less than twenty years from a traditional craft into a factory-based industry using steam-powered machinery. Because industrialization did not affect all crafts equally, at any one time the work experience and the prospects of mechanics differed considerably from one trade to another. There was, however, a regular sequence to the process of industrialization as it affected craftsmen, a sequence revealed by viewing industrialization as the transition between two ideal states. At one end of a continuum lies the traditional craft; at the other lies the modern factory-based industry making the same product.

The traditional craft had two basic characteristics:

1. Every workman made the product in its entirety and learned all production techniques in a long apprenticeship;
2. Only hand tools were used.

These characteristics determined the large amount of independence each worker had since:

3. Workmen owned their tools, and master craftsmen owned the materials and the product as well;
4. By owning their tools and monopolizing knowledge of the techniques of production, journeymen controlled their remuneration;
5. Journeymen had realizable expectations of becoming masters, i.e., self-employed, themselves.

At the other end of the spectrum lies the modern factory-based industry. In it the work characteristics have completely changed, at least for the major phases of production. In many industries, one or two minor processes may have escaped great changes, but this does not affect most workers or the overall organization of the industry if the structure is "modern." The factory-based industry has these basic characteristics:

1. The process of making a product has been broken down into myriad tasks. Each worker knows but one task and needs little or no training to master it;
2. Mechanized production using nonhuman energy sources predominates.

The worker in the modern factory lacks independence because:

3. The workers do not own the tools or materials used nor the product;
4. Possessing neither tools nor skills that are not generally available, the workmen cannot directly control their remuneration;
5. There is little likelihood that workers can rise to ownership or even managerial positions in the field. . . .

Three broad stages can be defined in the transition from craft to modern industry. The first stage began with task differentiation—breaking down the craft into a series of simpler jobs. . . . As a result of such differentiation, part of the total work force had fewer skills than all had formerly. Those who already possessed skills were not always superseded, however; owners or foremen still had to know the entire process in order to teach others the separate tasks, and some apprentices continued to be trained to take their places. Often, however, the boys hired were apprentices in name only, exploited as cheap labor and not taught all the tasks of the trade. In the first stage of industrialization workers often still owned their tools but usually did not own the materials used nor the finished product. The wage system, typically in the form of piece rates, was established. Without as much skill, the workers' control over their remuneration lessened, and unions often arose because of wage disputes. Those who were already skilled could still become self-employed by exploiting the semi-skilled labor of others, although the new recruits had less chance of such advancement. The aim of task differentiation was to increase the volume of production per workers, and the techniques led to an increase in the size of shops or the establishment of the putting-out system.

The second stage of industrialization arrived with the introduction of simple machines for some tasks. These were mainly human powered, although a few used a nonhuman power source. Work places became incipient factories, larger on the average than those of the earlier stage because of the centralizing effect of machinery. . . . Because of mechanization, the skill level of the labor force as a whole decreased further, and few if any apprentices were trained. More importantly, the workers ceased to own the tools of production, and their wages declined further. . . . Although those with skills might still become supervisors or foremen, the increasing capital requirements of mechanization decreased the chance for self-employment. . . .

The third stage in the process of industrialization began when machines using nonhuman power sources were introduced for some important phases of production. Skill was gone from all but a few tasks. At this point apprenticeship was dead, and wages in the industry were near those for other unskilled occupations. . . . Factories at this stage were large (several hundred workers), and the high capital requirements of power-driven machinery made rising to self-employment unlikely for any worker. . . .

The Industrialization of Eight Crafts

The stages of industrialization progress neatly in the abstract, but the variation on the theme were many in reality. In general the factory with a large and varied work force replaced the household in which the craftsman, his family, and his apprentices had labored. Skill levels declined, apprenticeship disappeared, and wages decreased. Unskilled men, but rarely women, appropriated the new jobs; women were confined to their traditional tasks—sewing and textile production. Craftsmen formed unions in an attempt to assert control over their work, raise wages, and restrict their hours. The casual work day of old became obsolete as mechanization increased the pace of labor, but because of the primitive state of production planning, employment continued to be sporadic or seasonal in nature.

But few crafts fit this mold exactly. Some resisted change, and technological advance occurred mainly in those that engaged in production for wholesale rather than retail markets. When a local retail market continued to flourish, skilled craftsmen used their customary techniques and maintained high wages without unionizing. The new unskilled workers in the modern factories often had not personally experienced a downward trend of wages or skills and therefore might also be slow to unionize. Furthermore, wage levels and crafts at the same stage of industrialization differed considerably because the crafts had varied in profitability while in their traditional states and wage cutting had begun from different bases.

Carpentry and blacksmithing both relied on local markets, and these trades did not industrialize throughout the mid-nineteenth century. Population growth produced the demand for housing, and the number of carpenters fluctuated with the population. Between 1836 and 1845, for instance, there were many years of depression and little population growth in Newark; with only a minimal demand for housing then, the number of carpenters remained stationary. As the population soared in the late 1840s and 1850s, however, so did the number of carpenters.

Since they produced for a local market, carpenters had no competition from craftsmen elsewhere, and so they had little incentive for making changes in their techniques to reduce costs. Through 1860 carpenters went about their work much as earlier generations had; the carpenter's skills were unchanged, and apprenticeship remained necessary for entry into the craft. Carpenters worked in small groups, usually in shops that had fewer than ten employees. They owned their tools, and, consequently, they retained control over their wages and kept them high in comparison to other workers. No major technological innovations were made in carpentry, perhaps because carpenters resisted all attempts to implement them. . . .

Blacksmithing also retained a traditional structure before 1860, but a shrinking of the scope of the craft created real differences between the experiences of blacksmiths and carpenters. Quite early, forges and machine shops began to take over the heavier tasks once done by the neighborhood blacksmith, and consequently the number of blacksmiths in the United States decreased by 37 percent between 1850 and 1860. In Newark, factories producing articles like hardware for wholesale distribution usurped part of the traditional blacksmith's role, and less and less remained of what the craft of blacksmithing once had encompassed. . . . Blacksmiths did the remaining work, primarily horse shoeing and repairs, in the traditional ways in small shops. But unlike carpenters, the blacksmiths received low wages; only shoemakers, trunk makers, and hatters in the most mechanized factories made less. Apprentices and journeymen in blacksmithing did not form unions to protest their relatively low wages, however. This suggests that the traditional character of the craft, including the personal relationship between master and apprentice and the real chance for self-employment for the journeymen, operated to counter discontent. . . .

Crafts that had begun task breakdown did not necessarily mechanize quickly. Newark's shoemakers had introduced task differentiation—the three-person teams—early in the century, but shoemaking did not follow the pattern of increasing industrialization between 1830 and 1860. Shoemaking was in the first stage of industrialization in the mid-1830s. There were fourteen large shoe factories in Newark with an average of fifty-two employees each; skill was needed for the making of high quality goods, and some apprentices were still being trained. But Newark's shoe manufacturers experienced severe competition in the wholesale market from the products of New England factories. . . . As wholesale markets evaporated, the size of the average shop in shoemaking decreased. . . .

The stagnant quality of the industry continued in the 1850s, and there was, consequently, little growth in the labor force. In the late 1850s, however, mechanization began as some manufacturers bought sewing machines for their plants. This led to a decrease in the proportion of women employed because the machines were used, at first, only for binding uppers—women's work. By 1860, however, less than 50 percent of all shoemakers worked in establishments using sewing machines, and no other machines were introduced in this period. . . .

Even in the first stage of industrialization—with task breakdown—workers lost control over wages. What had once been prices agreed on by both master and journeymen became piece rates dictated by the manufacturer. Inflation made these piece rates ever more inadequate but manufacturers refused increases in order to maintain their competitive positions in the wholesale market. . . . A carpenter could make $275 in seven months, but a male shoemaker could earn that only if he worked for fifty weeks, an unlikely possibility since production was irregular and lay-offs were frequent. Besides, most businesses suspended operations for many weeks every summer to settle accounts and rest. To combat low piece rates, workers typically took joint action. In Newark five unions of male journeymen shoemakers and one of women binders and fitters formed between 1834 and 1836. . . . The formation of these unions signaled the arrival of the cleavage between worker and manufacturer that occurred with even the first steps of industrialization. The existence of a separate union for women also suggests that the days of domestic manufacture were long gone in shoemaking. The women binders and fitters hired out as individuals and were not wives and daughters helping craftsmen who worked within households. . . .

When manufacturers maintained wholesale markets, however, and unions were weak, industrialization was more rapid. Like shoemaking, saddle and harness making was a leather-working trade that had entered the first stage of industrialization prior to 1840. There were eleven factories in Newark by the mid-1830s, but the domestic system continued to some extent in saddle making as craftsmen took work home for female relatives to sew. As in shoemaking a few apprentices were still in training, but in 1835 the male craftsmen formed a union, the Journeymen Saddlers, Harness Makers and Trimmers, because of wage disputes with their employers. In 1833 the average yearly wage of a saddler was $257, slightly more than a shoemaker earned, but much less than a carpenter. In saddle making as in shoemaking, the techniques of production remained much the same throughout the 1840s. But in response to a growing national market for their products, saddle makers continued to work in large groups. The Journeymen Saddlers and Harness Makers Union disappeared after 1837, however, and the saddle manufacturers more easily introduced mechanization in the 1850s than the shoemakers did. Sewing machines, among others, were used by the companies employing most of the workers, and the largest firm was using some steam-powered machinery by 1860. Some skilled craftsmen were still working, however, because custom order work was done even in the large plants. As skill levels decreased in the 1850s, no further calls for apprentices were made, and if apprenticeship continued it was on a small scale. Thus after two decades in the first stage of transition, saddle making inched into the second stage.

In these four crafts, lack of technological innovation, some worker resistance, or subdivision of the industry meant that many craftsmen experienced little or no change in their work over long periods of time. But in other crafts in Newark, like leather making, new inventions were made and adopted swiftly, and workers had to adapt quickly to mechanization. Leather making had always been odious, dirty work, even if it was a skilled craft. Industrialization only compounded the situation. . . . By the 1830s leather making had entered the first stage of industrialization. While large factories did not develop prior to the 1840s, new processes such as patent leather making and the great demand for leather by shoe and saddle makers led to task differentiation. Firms often specialized in tanning, currying, morocco dressing, or japanning, and men specialized in less complicated operations within these subdivisions.

Leather manufacturers introduced new processes continually in the 1840s and 1850s. By the mid-1840s, they had divided the making of a piece of leather into six or eight separate steps. Because of the new processes the leather was ready in approximately six weeks rather than the year or two necessary with the traditional technology. Machines were available for such processes as splitting leather, and by 1850 one-third of all workers were employed in plants that had some steam-powered machinery.... Leather making had entered the second stage of transition to a modern form in the late 1840s, and it had progressed to the third stage by 1860.... By 1860 two-thirds of the leather makers worked in factories with more than one hundred employees, and 78 percent worked in factories that had steam-powered machinery....

Jewelry making was [a] remunerative craft that continued to pay well even as it industrialized. Newark's jewelers were not numerous in the 1830s, and they began to introduce task differentiation only in the mid-1840s. In 1849 manufacturers introduced the first steam-powered machinery, but mechanization was confined to a few operations, such as gold chain making and watchcase making. The best jewelry was made by artists who executed the complete process. Manufacturers hired girls to do polishing, but men held most of the jobs.... In a luxury trade like jewelry making, costs were more easily passed on to the consumer, so wages could remain high.

Even in such a trade, however, industrialization created adverse working conditions. In the 1850s jewelry making moved from the first to the second stage of industrialization with the introduction of small machines such as circular saws, lathes, and the like. Manufacturers hired more female workers and differentiated more tasks: diamond mounters, diamond cutters, and ring makers joined chain makers, watchcase makers, and engravers. Steam-powered machinery was still used for only a few tasks, but industrial accidents became much more common; ...

Factories of one hundred to three hundred workers were not rare in the late 1850s, but many medium-sized firms also arose in response to the growing demand for luxury goods by the new urban wealthy class. Many of these firms did custom-order work, such as the $1,800 diamond-studded watchcase made for a customer by Baldwin and Company in 1855. This gave employment to jewelers who possessed the old skill and encouraged boys to apprentice themselves for five years to them. Despite these vestiges of the old wages, however, industrialization destroyed the traditional relationship between employer and journeyman jeweler.... With the increase in mechanization and the separation of showroom from factory, the division between manufacturers and journeymen became more pronounced, and in 1859 the first union of journeymen jewelers was formed....

As the craft of trunk making industrialized, skilled and unskilled workers existed simultaneously as they did in jewelry making, but more rapid technological advance in the former shifted the balance drastically toward the unskilled. In the 1830s Newark's few trunk makers, like its jewelers, used traditional methods to produce goods for the local market. No conflicts arose between journeymen and masters, and the trade union movement of 1835–36 did not touch trunk makers. Beginning in the mid-1840s, however, trunk manufacturers overturned the old methods of production. By 1846 some trunk making companies had begun to produce a wholesale line of trunks of lower quality, simplified design, and cheaper price, in addition to filling custom orders for ornate baggage. While the latter employed the skilled workers, the cheaper products were made by less skilled personnel, each doing one task. . . . Most workers were employed in two large firms where wages were lower than those in any of the other crafts. No unions arose among the trunk makers though, perhaps because the few older skilled workers could still do custom work in the big factories or produce luxury goods for the growing urban wealthy class.

In the 1850s such great changes were made in the production of trunks that trunk making moved from the first into the third stage of industrialization in a decade. The large companies, employing two-thirds of all workers in the field, introduced steam-powered machinery for many tasks. Although smaller establishments did not use steam-powered machinery, they did follow the larger ones in using sewing machines, which lowered the percentage of women employed. Apprenticeship disappeared as skill levels declined, and wages remained low in comparison to other trades. . . .

In the most completely mechanized crafts like hatting all the major effects of industrialization appeared by 1860. Hatting in Newark had reached the second stage of industrialization by 1836 with the existence of eight hat factories averaging seventy-six employees each; task differentiation was well advanced, and the putting-out system was prevalent. Many small machines were used in the larger factories, such as those for ironing and finishing hats and for stiffening hat bodies. One man using a machine for stiffening hat bodies could do the work five had done by hand. Because of these innovations, apprenticeship had broken down and become a cloak for exploitation. Manufacturers hired men over twenty-one years of age as "apprentices" to hide their employment of unskilled labor. . . . To protest inadequate wages and the competition of adult "apprentices," the journeymen hatters formed a union in the mid-1830s and conducted strikes. In the 1830s only a few crafts had changed to this extent, but these were the industries that were the basis for Newark's economic growth.

The industrialization of the hatting trade was well under way in the 1830s, and technological changes continued in the 1840s, so that by the end of the decade, hatting had entered the third stage of transition. A silk hat could be made from a rough hat body in two hours and five minutes in 1850. At mid-century, two-thirds of all hat makers worked in factories with more than one hundred employees each. A small local retail market for hats continued to exist, however, and a few skilled craftsmen still made hats by hand. The tremendous difference in wages paid the vast majority who worked in the mechanized plants and the few who continued to use the old manual technology reveals the magnitude of the skill loss caused by mechanization. While wages were low for the majority, unemployment was also common. Ten months per year was considered steady employment in hat factories. In the large factories, moreover, working conditions were often dangerous, as hatters sometimes suffered from mercury poisoning, although this hazard predated industrialization. On the other hand, the large modern factories with steam heat and gas lighting had some comforts the older cramped workshops lacked.

Technological changes in hatting continued in the 1850s with the invention of the hat wire brim and the inflexible hat. The introduction of sewing machines displaced many of the women who had been trimmers or binders, and, as in the other trades in which women had done needle work, they faced a narrowly constricted job market, for few new tasks were open to them. But the modern factory form was not reached in hatting at that time. Some tasks were still done by hand, and some machines had yet to be steam-driven. Much labor was involved, and some skill was needed in hat finishing. In the mid-1850s the finishers formed an association that demanded a closed shop to limit the number of apprentices. They were successful in some shops, even some large ones, but not in others. By mid-century few, if any, industries were more advanced than Newark's hat making industry, but none had reached the modern stage of constant-flow processes and homogenized work force.

The history of these eight crafts, despite the similarities of general development, reveals the diversity of mechanics' experiences with industrialization. Charting the course of industrialization in the crafts emphasizes the progress from homogeneity to heterogeneity. . . .

※ *F U R T H E R   R E A D I N G*

Stuart Blumin, *The Emergence of the Middle Class: Social Experience in the American City, 1760–1900* (1989)

Alan Dawley, *Class and Community: The Industrial Revolution in Lynn* (1976)

Thomas Dublin, *Women and Work: The Transformation of Work and Community in Lowell, Massachusetts, 1820–1860* (1979)

Paul G. Faler, *Mechanics and Manufacturers in the Early Industrial Revolution: Lynn, Massachusetts, 1780–1860* (1977)

John Gilkeson, *Middle-Class Providence, 1820–1940* (1986)

Brian Greenberg, *Worker and Community: Response to Industrialization in a Nineteenth-Century American City, Albany, New York, 1850–1884* (1985)

Herbert Gutman, *Work, Culture, and Society in Industrializing America* (1976)

Michael B. Katz, Michael J. Doucet, and Mark J. Stern, *The Social Organization of Early Industrial Capitalism* (1982)

Bruce Laurie, *Working People of Philadelphia, 1800–1850* (1980)

David Montgomery, *Workers' Control in America* (1979)

Howard Rock, *Artisans of the New Republic: The Tradesmen of New York City in the Age of Jefferson* (1979)

Mary P. Ryan, *The Cradle of the Middle Class: The Family in Oneida County, New York, 1790–1865* (1981)

Christine Stansell, *City of Women: Sex and Class in New York, 1789–1860* (1986)

Daniel J Walkowitz, *Worker City, Company Town: Iron and Cotton-Worker Protest in Troy and Cohoes, New York, 1855–1884* (1978)

CHAPTER
6

Cities of Migrants
and Immigrants, 1870–1920

✕

From the beginning, the United States was a nation of immigrants, and after the Civil War immigration became a central supportive factor of urbanization and industrialization. The waves of immigrants from Germany, England, Ireland, and Scandinavia before 1880 swelled to a flood with the addition of newcomers from Italy, Austro-Hungary, and Russia in the early twentieth century. At the same time, others were arriving from Mexico, Canada, and Asia. Although some immigrants moved on from the ports of entry into the rural interior, the majority found residences in cities. By 1920 foreign-born residents composed 40 percent of the population in places as diverse as Milwaukee, San Francisco, Buffalo, Jersey City, and Detroit, and they made up a majority when combined with those who were native-born of foreign parents.

Historians have examined immigrants in several ways. The first studies viewed newcomers as helpless, disoriented pawns of the U.S. urban-industrial system, whose only recourse was to assimilate as quickly as possible into the host population. More recently, historians have recognized that immigrants retained their native cultures and used their traditions and customs to aid in adapting to the American environment. But just how much independence they retained, how much they influenced urban society, and how much they were affected by it remains open to debate.

The foreign-born were not the only newcomers to American cities in the late nineteenth and the early twentieth centuries. Native-born whites and African-Americans also moved to the city in large numbers. African-Americans provide a special comparison with foreign immigrants. Both groups arrived with few resources, low skills, and unfamiliarity with modern technology. Both experienced poverty, a low level of services such as schools and health care, poor housing, and various kinds of social and economic discrimination. But how far did the similarities between black migrants and white immigrants go? Did race make a difference?

✖ D O C U M E N T S

The first several documents contain dramatic personal accounts of the immigration experience and of immigrants' adaptation to the American city. The first four
testimonies, originally published in 1906 in *The Independent* magazine, include
the stories of a Lithuanian worker in the Chicago stockyards who gave his name
as Antanas Kaztauskis; a Polish sweatshop girl named Sadie Frowne, who lived
and worked in the Brownsville section of Brooklyn; an Italian bootblack named
Rocco Corrersca, known to his friends as Joe, who worked in Brooklyn; and a
Japanese servant who lived on both the West and East coasts. Most of these accounts reproduce the actual grammar used by the immigrants; the testimony from
the Japanese man especially contains unedited Japanese idioms and bookish English. The fifth document features excerpts from entries for the years 1875 and
1876 from the diary of Frank Roney, an Irish immigrant to San Francisco. Roney,
who later became active in the labor movement, experienced severe poverty in his
early years in San Francisco, and his diary portrays the precarious existence that
immigrant laborers experienced in their constant struggle to obtain and retain employment in the city. Constantly borrowing money to sustain his family, Roney
finally found a more secure job that allowed him to get out of debt and to enjoy
simple urban pleasures with his family.

The final document pertains to African-American migrants who moved
northward at the same time that immigrants were streaming into American cities.
The excerpt is from a 1913 article by George Edmund Harvey, a professor of
social science at Fisk University, who also served as the director of the National
League on Urban Conditions Among Negroes. Harvey, an African-American
himself, used the article to appeal for self-help as well as national acceptance for
African-Americans migrating to cities, and he tried to analyze contrasts between
black migrants and white immigrants.

Immigrant Testimonies, c. 1900

Story of a Lithuanian

[After I arrived in the United States] Everything got quicker—worse and worse—
till then at last I was in a boarding house by the stockyards in Chicago with three
Lithuanians, who knew my father's sisters at home.

That first night we sat around in the house and they asked me, "Well, why did
you come?" I told them about that first night and what the ugly shoemaker said
about "life, liberty and the getting of happiness." They all leaned back and
laughed. "What you need is money," they said. "It was all right at home. You
wanted nothing. You ate your own meat and your own things on the farm. You
made your own clothes and had your own leather. The other things you got at the
Jew man's store and paid him with sacks of rye. But here you want a hundred
things. Whenever you walk out you see new things you want, and you must have
money to buy everything."

Then one man asked me, "How much have you?" and I told him $30. "You

Immigrant Family, Ellis Island, New York Harbor, c. 1900

Like thousands of other families, this immigrant mother and her children arrived at Ellis Island wary but determined. Most likely, the husband and father had immigrated earlier and worked for money to pay for his family's passage to the United States.

must buy clothes to look rich, even if you are not rich," he said. "With good clothes you will have friends."

The next morning three of these men took me to a store near the stockyards to buy a coat and pants. ... "You stand still. That is all you have to do," they said. So the Jew man kept putting on coats and I moved my arms and back and sides when they told me. We stayed there till it was time for dinner. Then we bought a suit. I paid $5 and then I was to pay $1 a week for five weeks. ...

The next night they took me for a walk down town. We would not pay to ride, so we walked so long that I wanted to take my shoes off, but I did not tell them this. When we came there I forgot my feet. We stood by one theater and watched for half an hour. Then we walked all around a store that filled one whole block and had walls of glass. Then we had a drink of whiskey, and this is better than vodka. We felt happier and looked into cafes. We saw shiny carriages and automobiles. I saw men with dress suits, I saw women with such clothes that I could not think at all. Then my friends punched me and I turned around and saw one of these women, and with her was a gentleman in a fine dress suit. I began looking harder. It was the Jew man that sold me my suit. ... Then we walked home and I felt poor and my shoes got very bad. ...

The next morning my friends woke me up at five o'clock and said, "Now, if you want life, liberty and happiness," they laughed, "you must push for yourself. You must get a job. Come with us." And we went to the yards. Men and women were walking in by thousands as far as we could see. We went to the doors of one big slaughter house. There was a crowd of about 200 men waiting there for a job. They looked hungry and kept watching the door. At last a special policeman came out and began pointing to men, one by one. Each one jumped forward. Twenty-three were taken. Then they all went inside, and all the others turned their faces away and looked tired. I remember one boy sat down and cried, just next to me, on a pile of boards. Some policemen waved their clubs and we all walked on. I found some Lithuanians to talk with, who told me they had come every morning for three weeks. Soon we met other crowds coming away from other slaughter houses, and we all walked around and felt bad and tired and hungry.

That night I told my friends that I would not do this many days, but would go some place else. "Where?" they asked me, and I began to see then that I was in bad trouble, because I spoke no English. Then one man told me to give him $5 to give the special policeman. I did this and the next morning the policeman pointed me out, so I had a job. I have heard some big talk since then about my American freedom of contract, but I do not think I had much freedom in bargaining for this job with the Meat Trust. My job was in the cattle killing room. I pushed the blood along the gutter ... One Lithuanian who worked with me, said, "They get all the blood out of those cattle and all the work out of us men." This was true, for we worked that first day from six in the morning till seven at night. The next day we worked from six in the morning till eight at night. The next day we had no work. So we had no good, regular hours. It was hot in the room that summer, and the hot blood made it worse.

I held my job six weeks, and then I was turned off. I think some other man had paid for my job, or perhaps I was too slow. The foreman in that room wanted quick men to make the work rush, because he was paid more if the work was done cheaper and quicker. . . .

The Republican boss in our district, Jonidas, was a saloon keeper. A friend took me there. Jonidas shook hands and treated me fine. He taught me to sign my name, and the next week I went with him to an office and signed some paper, and then I could vote. I voted as I was told, and then they got me back into the yards to work, because one big politician owns stock in one of the houses. Then I felt that was getting in beside the game. I was in a combine like other sharp men. Even when work was slack I was all right, because they got me a job in the street cleaning department. I felt proud, and I went to the back room in Jonidas's saloon and got him to write a letter to Alexandra to tell her she must come soon and be my wife.

But this was just the trouble. All of us were telling our friends to come soon. Soon they came—even thousands. The employers in the yard liked this, because those sharp foremen are inventing new machines and the work is easier to learn, and so these slow Lithuanians and even green girls can learn to do it, and then the Americans and Germans and Irish are put out and the employer saves money, because the Lithuanians work cheaper. This was why the American labor unions began to organize us all just the same as they had organized the Bohemians and Poles before us.

. . . I had been working hard in the cattle killing room and I had a better job. I was called a cattle butcher now and I joined the Cattle Butchers' Union. This union is honest and it has done me a great deal of good. . . .

With more time and more money I live much better and I am very happy. So is Alexandra. She came a year ago and has learned to speak English already. Some of the women go to the big store the day they get here, when they have not enough sense to pick out the clothes that look right, but Alexandra waited three weeks till she knew, and so now she looks the finest of any woman in the district. We have four nice rooms, which she keeps very clean, and she has flowers growing in boxes in the two front windows. We do not go much to church, because the church seems to be too slow. But we belong to a Lithuanian society that gives two picnics in summer and two big balls in winter, where we have a fine time. I go one night a week to the Lithuanian Concertina Club. On Sundays we go on the trolley out into the country.

But we like to stay at home more now because we have a baby. When he grows up I will not send him to the Lithuanian Catholic school. They have only two bad rooms and two priests who teach only in Lithuanian from prayer books. I will send him to the American school, which is very big and good. The teachers there are Americans and they belong to the Teachers' Labor Union, which has three thousand teachers and belongs to our Chicago Federation of Labor. I am sure that such teachers will give him a good chance.

Story of a Polish Sweatshop Girl

I lived at this time with a girl named Ella, who worked in the same factory and made $5 a week. We had the room all to ourselves, paying $1.50 a week for it, and doing light housekeeping. It was in Allen street, and the window looked out of the back, which was good, because there was an elevated railroad in front, and in summer time a great deal of dust and dirt came in at the front windows. We were on the fourth story and could see all that was going on in the back rooms of the houses behind us, and early in the morning the sun used to come in our window.

We did our cooking on an oil stove, and lived well, as this list of our expenses for one week will show:

Ella and Sadie for Food (one week)

Tea	$0.06
Cocoa	.10
Bread and rolls	.40
Canned vegetables	.20
Potatoes	.10
Milk	.21
Fruit	.20
Butter	.15
Meat	.60
Fish	.15
Laundry	.25
Total	$2.42
Add rent	1.50
Grand Total	$3.92

Of course, we could have lived cheaper, but we are both fond of good things and felt that we could afford them.

We paid 18 cents for a half pound of tea so as to get it good, and it lasted us three weeks, because we had cocoa for breakfast. We paid 5 cents for six rolls and 5 cents a loaf for bread, which was the best quality. Oatmeal cost us 10 cents for three and one-half pounds, and we often had it in the morning, or Indian meal porridge in the place of it, costing about the same. Half a dozen eggs cost about 13 cents on an average, and we could get all the meat we wanted for a good hearty meal for 20 cents—two pounds of chops, or a steak, or a bit of veal, or a neck of lamb—something like that. Fish included butter fish, porgies, codfish and smelts, averaging about 8 cents a pound.

Some people who buy at the last of the market, when the men with the carts want to go home, can get things very cheap, but they are likely to be stale, and we did not often do that with fish, fresh vegetables, fruit, milk or meat. Things that kept well we did buy that way and got good bargains. I got thirty potatoes for 10 cents one time, though generally I could not get more than fifteen of them for that amount. Tomatoes, onions and cabbages, too, we bought that way and did well, and we found a factory where we could buy the finest broken crackers for 3 cents a pound, and another place where we got broken candy for 10 cents a pound. Our cooking was done on an oil stove, and the oil for the stove and the lamp cost us 10 cents a week.

It cost me $2 a week to live, and I had a dollar a week to spend on clothing and pleasure, and saved the other dollar. I went to night school, but it was hard work learning at first as I did not know much English.

Story of an Italian Bootblack

We were all landed on an island and the bosses there said that Francesco and I must go back because we had not enough money, but a man named Bartolo came up and told them that we were brothers and he was our uncle and would take care of us. He brought two other men who swore that they knew us in Italy and that Bartolo was our uncle. I had never seen any of them before, but even then Bartolo might be my uncle, so I did not say anything. The bosses of the island let us go out with Bartolo after he had made the oath.

We came to Brooklyn, New York, to a wooden house in Adams street that was full of Italians from Naples. Bartolo had a room on the third floor and there were fifteen men in the room, all boarding with Bartolo. He did the cooking on a stove in the middle of the room and there were beds all around the sides, one bed above another. It was very hot in the room, but we were soon asleep, for we were very tired.

The next morning, early, Bartolo told us to go out and pick rags and get bottles. He gave us bags and hooks and showed us the ash barrels. On the streets where the fine houses are the people are very careless and put out good things, like mattresses and umbrellas, clothes, hats, and boots. We brought all these to Bartolo, and he made them new again and sold them on the sidewalk; but mostly we brought rags and bones. The rags we had to wash in the back yard and then we hung them to dry on lines under the ceiling in our room. The bones we kept under the beds till Bartolo could find a man to buy them.

Most of the men in our room worked at digging the sewer. Bartolo got them the work and they paid him about one-quarter of their wages. Then he charged them for board and he bought the clothes for them, too. So they got little money after all. . . .

We were with Bartolo nearly a year, but some of our countrymen who had been in the place a long time said that Bartolo had no right to us and we could get work for a dollar and a half a day, which, when you make it *lire* (reckoned in the Italian currency) is very much. So we went away one day to Newark and got work on the street. Bartolo came after us and make a great noise, but the boss [said] that if he did not go away soon the police would have him. Then he went, saying that there was no justice in this country.

We paid a man five dollars each for getting us the work and we were with that boss for six months. He was Irish, but a good man and he gave us our money every Saturday night. We lived much better than with Bartolo, and when the work was done we each had nearly $200 saved. Plenty of the men spoke English and they taught us, and we taught them to read and write. That was at night, for we had a lamp in our room, and there were only five other men who lived in that room with us. . . .

When the Newark boss told us that there was no more work Francesco and I talked about what we would do and we went back to Brooklyn to a saloon near

Hamilton Ferry where we got a job cleaning it out and slept in a little room upstairs. There was a bootblack named Michael on the corner and when I had time I helped him and learned the business. Francesco cooked the lunch in the saloon and he, too, worked for the bootblack and we were soon able to make the best polish.

Then we thought we would go into business and we got a basement on Hamilton avenue, near the Ferry, and put four chairs in it. We paid $75 for the chairs and all the other things. We had tables and looking glasses there and curtains. We took the papers that have the pictures in and made the place high toned. Outside we had a big sign that read:

THE BEST SHINE FOR TEN CENTS

Men that did not want to pay 10 cents could get a good shine for 5 cents but it was not an oil shine. We had two boys helping us and paid each of them 50 cents a day. The rent of the place was $20 a month, so the expenses were very great, but we made money from the beginning. We slept in the basement, but got our meals in the saloon till we would put a stove in our place, and then Francesco cooked for us all. . . .

We remembered the priest, the friend of Ciguciano, and what he had said to us about religion, and as soon as we came to the country we began to go to the Italian church. The priest we found here was a good man, but he asked the people for money for the church. The Italians did not like to give because they said it looked like buying religion. The priest says it is different here from Italy because all the churches there are what they call endowed, while here all they have is what the people give. Of course I and Francesco understand that, but the Italians who cannot read and write shake their heads and say that it is wrong for a priest to want money.

We had said that when we saved $1,000 each we would go back to Italy and buy a farm, but now that the time is coming we are so busy and making so much money that we think we will stay. . . .

At first we did not know much of this country, but by and by we learned. There are here plenty of Protestants who are heretics, but they have a religion, too. Many of the finest churches are Protestant, but they have no saints and no altars, which seems strange.

These people are without a king such as ours in Italy. It is what they call a Republic, as Garibaldi wanted, and every year in the fall the people vote. They wanted us to vote last fall, but we did not. A man came and said that he would get us made Americans for 50 cents and then we could get $2 for our votes. I talked to some of our people and they told me that we should have to put a paper in a box telling who we wanted to govern us.

I went with five men to the court and when they asked me how long I had been in the country I told them two years. Afterward my countrymen said I was a fool and would never learn politics.

"You should have said you were five years here and then we would swear to it," was what they told me.

I and Francesco are to be Americans in three years. The court gave us papers and said we must wait and we must be able to read some things and tell who the ruler of the country is.

There are plenty of rich Italians here, men who a few years ago had nothing and now have so much money that they could not count all their dollars in a week. The richest ones go away from the other Italians and live with the Americans.

Story of a Japanese Servant

The desire to see America was burning at my boyish heart. The land of freedom and civilization of which I heard so much from missionaries and the wonderful story of America I heard of those of my race who returned from here made my longing ungovernable. Meantime I have been reading a popular novel among the boys, "The Adventurous Life of Tsurukichi Tanaka, Japanese Robinson Crusoe." How he acquired new knowledge from America and how he is honored and favored by the capitalists in Japan. How willingly he has endured the hardships in order to achieve the success. The story made a strong impression on my mind. Finally I made up my mind to come to this country to receive an American education.

I was an orphan and the first great trouble was who will help me the expenses? I have some property my father left for me. But a minor has not legally inherited, hence no power to dispossess them. There must be at least 200 yen for the fare and equipment. While 200 yen has only exchange value to $100 of American gold, the sum is really a considerable amount for a boy. Two hundred yen will be a sufficient capital to start a small grocery store in the country town or to start a prospective fish market in the city. Of course, my uncle shook his head and would not allow me to go to America. After a great deal of difficulty and delay I have prevailed over his objection. My heart swelled joy when I got a passport. Government permission to leave the country, after waiting thirty days investigated if really I am a student and who are the guardians to pay money in case of necessity. A few days later I found myself on board the *Empress of Japan* of the Canadian Pacific Line. The moment steamer commences to leave Yokohama I wished to jump back to shore, but was too late and I was too old and ashamed to cry.

After the thirteen days' weary voyage we reached Victoria, B.C. When I have landed there I have disappointed as there not any wonderful sight to be seen not much different that of foreign settlement in Yokohama. My destination was Portland, Ore., where my cousin is studying. Before I took a boat in Puget Sound to Tacoma, Wash., we have to be examined by the immigration officer. To my surprise these officers looked to me like a plain citizen—no extravagant dignity, no authoritative air. I felt so envious. I said to myself, "Ah! Indeed this is the characteristic of democracy, equality of personal right so well shown." I respect the officers more on this account. They asked me several questions. I answered with my broken English I have learned at Yokohama Commercial School. Finally they said, "So you are a student? How much money have you at hand?" I showed them $50. The law requires $30. The officers gave me a piece of stamped paper—certificate—to permit me go into the United States. I left Victoria 8 p.m. and arrived Tacoma, Wash., 6 a.m. Again I have surprised with the muddy streets and the dirty wharf. I thought the wharf of Yokohama is hundred times better. Next morning I left for Portland, Ore.

Great disappointment and regret I have experienced when I was told that I, the boy of 17 years old, smaller in stature indeed than an ordinary 14 years old American boy, imperfect in English knowledge, I can be any use here, but become a domestic servant, as the field for Japanese very narrow and limited. Thus reluctantly I have submitted to be a recruit of the army of domestic servants of which I ever dreamed up to this time. The place where I got to work in the first time was a boarding house. My duties were to peel potatoes, wash the dishes, a few laundry work, and also I was expected to do whatever mistress, waitress and cook has told me.

When I first entered the kitchen wearing a white apron what an uncomfortable and mortifying feeling I experienced. I thought I shall never be able to proceed the work. I felt as if I am pressed down on my shoulder with loaded tons of weight. My heart palpitates. I did not know what I am and what to say. I stood by the door of kitchen motionless like a stone, with a dumfounded silence. The cook gave me a scornful look and said nothing. Perhaps at her first glance she perceived me entirely unfit to be her help. A kindly looking waitress, slender, alert Swedish girl, sympathetically put the question to me if I am first time to work. She said, "Oh! well, you will get learn and soon be used to it!" as if she has fully understand the situation. Indeed, this ordinary remarks were such a encouragement. She and cook soon opened the conference how to rescue me. In a moment I was to the mercy of Diana of the kitchen like Arethusa. Whistling up the courage I started to work. The work being entirely new and also such an unaccustomed one. I felt exceedingly unpleasant and hard. . . .

After I stay there about ten days I asked the old lady that I should be discharged. She wanted me to state the reason. My real objection was that the work was indeed too hard and unpleasant for me to bear and also there were no times even to read a book. But I thought it rather impolite to say so and partly my strange pride hated to confess my weakness, fearing the reflection as a lazy boy. Really I could not think how smoothly I should tell my reason. So I kept silent rather with a stupefied look. She suggested me if the work were not too hard. It was just the point, but how foolish I was; I did positively denied. "Then why can you not stay here?" she went on. I said childishly, "I have nothing to complain; simply I wants to go back to New York. My passion wants to." Then she smiled and said, "Poor boy; you better think over; I shall speak to you tomorrow." Next day she told me how she shall be sorry to lose me just when I have began to be handy to her after the hard task to taught me work how. Tactfully she persuaded me to stay. At the end of second week I asked my wages, but she refused on the ground that if she does I might leave her. Day by day my sorrow and regret grew stronger. My heavy heart made me feel so hard to work. At that moment I felt as if I am in the prison assigned to the hard labor. My coveted desire was to be freed from the yoke of this old lady. Believing the impossibility to obtain her sanction, early in the next morning while everybody still in the bed, I hide my satchel under the bush in the back yard. When mistress went on market afternoon, while everybody is busy, I have jumped out from the window and climbed up the fence to next door and slip away. Leaving the note and wages behind me, I hurried back to Japanese Christian Home.

Since then I have tried a few other places with a better success at each trial and in course of time I have quite accustomed to it and gradually become indifferent as the humiliation melted down. Though I never felt proud of this vocation, in several cases I have commenced to manifest the interest of my avocation as a professor of Dust and Ashes. . . .

An Irish Laborer Confronts Hardship in San Francisco, 1875, 1876

[April, 1875]

I began work on the 12th instant in the Pacific Works. Ed Jones [is] foreman. What my wages is, I don't yet know and may not for some 6 weeks yet. If I could have what is coming to me each week, as it [is] earned, in a very little time I would have things all O.K. But, while I want money very badly, I cannot afford to forfeit my job. I have asked Lowell for the loan of some money which he has promised to let me have to-day. And, if he does, it will help to straihten matters a little. I must have money this coming week, come from where it may, because I have no fuel, and that alone is most indispensable. . . .

I am now indebted $3.25 for wood and coal, $15.00 for groceries and milk, $1 for bread, $5 on [the] stove, and $1 borrowed, making a total of $26.25. I have drawn $10 on my 1st weeks payment which is now due. Two [are] being kept back. This will render it impossible for me to settle up all I could wish, but still I shall struggle through as well as I can. I shall have another month's rent to pay and probably $5 more for groceries which makes $48.25, not to speak of meat and other little eccteras. I shall then have only coming to me on the 15th [of] May [wages] for 14 days and 6 1/2 hours.

May, 1875

Sunday [the] 2nd is the molders' picnic. Would like to go but cannot for want of funds. Lowell is to call on that day, and [I] may get some money from him. [I] rely upon him but may again be disappointed. . . .

My wife's anticipated sickness (parturition) is not yet arrived which will leave me better prepared for the event when it does take place. Though, even then, I won't be as well off for her sake as I could wish, but, as it is, God be thanked for what we have. . . .

June, 1875

Business still continues to get dull, and but very little prospects of it being much better.

On the 17th my wife was confined, and at 7:15 A.M. another boy was born. Everything turned out all right. Mrs. McDevitt is evidently both skillful and considerate as a midwife.

Joe Whalley from Omaha called upon me on the 19th on his way to Seattle, W.T. [He] gives very discouraging accounts of that place and hopes largely from

From Neil L. Shumsky, "Frank Roney's San Francisco—His Diary: April, 1875–March, 1876," *Labor History* 17 (Spring 1976), excerpts from pp. 251–64. Reprinted by permission of *Labor History*.

his new home. Since then, two molders, [the] Tenny brothers, have gone to Seattle, but Wharburton gives very discouraging accounts from that place. . . .

July, 1875

Moved to another house, No. 225 Perry St., owned by a man named Murphy. Rent $17.00. I got laid off at the "Pacific" and began work in the "City" Iron Works. . . .

The crowds on the streets of persons from Salt Lake City would give me the impression of it being a doomed city.

It seems as if this climate was not going to agree with me. The variety of weather one gets in San Francisco in a day is enough to satisfy the most fastidious for almost a season.

I want still another change and again think it is for the better. Of one thing I am satisfied. Moulding is not the business for me to follow. While out of it, I can always do without drinking. And [I] can, too, for a time after returning to it. But, gradually, the feeling grows upon me, and I again begin to taste. I want to quit that practice if possible. And the only remedy I know of is to secure a position outside of the business altogether. . . .

August, 1875

Moved to No. 3 Margaret Place; rent $13 per month.

Was laid off in [the] City foundry. I disliked the place all the time I was in it most thoroughly. . . .

During the month of August I did nothing, but [I] made $11.50 on the election. This, with some credit and $10 from Charley Butterfield, carried me through. . . .

September, 1875

Borrowed $5 from A. Sloan, $10 from G. McClelland, and $10 from C. Lowell, also $1 from E. Jones. Began work on Friday afternoon [the] 10th. . . .

On the last of the month, contrary to all expectations, [I] was laid off. . . .

[9] December, 1875

. . . With this month ends a year I had hoped from its auspicious beginning to terminate in a far different manner. But, while we hope still for the silver lining to the dark cloud of adversity, and as we think, we hope and work and toil for it, yet as time revolves on his unerring axis and brings not the mildest tinge of our fanciful lining, our hopes become tinctured with despair. . . . And, with the beginning of another year, [so also] does our hopes ascend till perhaps, by patient, constant toiling [and] hopeful, steady perseverance [which is] never wholly subdued by any obstacle, there comes a day in some bright year when we may gaze back on our labor and enter into the enjoyment of their results.

I began the year with very mild expectations, that of being out of debt by this time and of having my family, still increasing, better provided for. But, instead of clearing off my past indebtedness, I have added to it. And, while I still hope that another year will see me clearly out of debt, I confess I am somewhat doubtful. . . .

January, 1876

2nd In order to begin the New Year in a lucky, if not a more Christian manner, my wife insisted upon getting both Willie and the baby Christened today. Accordingly, I accompanied her to St. Mary's Cathedral for that purpose and accomplished it notwithstanding it was very cold for this climate and rained exceedingly. On our return home, we ate dinner and really felt happier than we had done for some[time] notwithstanding our poverty. The names given are William John and Edward Alfred.

3rd, 4th, and 5th Attended the Odd Fellows' Employment Office each day with no result.

6th & 7th Met Mr. Douglas, [the] freight agent [of the] Southern Pacific Railroad, who sent me to work at the Company's wharf where I helped to load cars with coal from noon till Friday night and earned $5. . . .

13th and 14th No success thus far. As usual, I have visited those shops where I might reasonably hope to get a job, but the ill fortune which has persistently followed me for 25 months still clings to me as tenaciously as ever.

While I regret my circumstances, I am aware [that] others are a good deal worse off. I still keep house. Of course, in a poor fashion, but yet I manage to eat some and secure enough warmth and sleep. But, my wife and children [are] pent up from week to week, without a sufficiency of warmth or of warm clothing. They feel the effects of this mode of living, and it begins to tell upon them.

20th Began work this day in the Union Iron Works. I was afraid I was not going to begin work, but after a little [while], the foreman came to me and told me [that], if I wanted to work for $3.50 a day, I could start. And, further, [he said] that he had orders to start no new men at any higher price. And so, I started. Worked the full day of 9 hours and all night and next day till quitting time. . . .

23rd Sunday. A most disagreeably wet day. I could not have gone out if I had to in consequence of my boots being very bad. In fact, both my wife and children as well as myself are [at] a very low ebb in clothing. During all of this day, [I] felt generally well pleased and, of course, was in good humor. [This was] the result of being employed and having some prospect ahead of not only being out of debt but being in a position to save a little money. My wife also feels in better condition than I have seen her for a long time from the same cause. I believe, or at least sincerely hope, she will pull with me [so] that, by the end of the year, we may have begun some provision for our children. . . .

31st Worked today 10 hours and made two pipes weighing about 700 lbs. The month of January terminates this day and has been productive of some benefit. I hope it is the precursor of better times than I have experienced in a long time. . . .

February, 1876

16th I have been suffering for 3 weeks past with a severe cold and have had a terrible cough. But today, I have had an intense pain in my left lung which may, if it continues, render it necessary for me to take a rest to recuperate if it don't assume a more serious character which, with God's help, I hope not for the sake of my young family. Worked 10 hours and produced 1,000 lbs. . . .

29th . . . This records the second month of this Centennial Year of Grace 1876, during which I have earned $84.50 and produced 15 tons, averaging clear profit to the proprietors [of] $450. . . .

March, 1876

. . . *19th* Sunday. Visited Maguire's Opera House last night with the wife and today being a beautiful day took the family out to 26th St. on the horse car. . . .

George Edmund Haynes on the Problems and Prospects of Black Migrants to Cities, 1913

Fifty years after four millions of Negro slaves were made freedmen, there is still the responsibility upon the nation to make that seeming freedom really free. So many other national problems thrust themselves upon the attention of the people today that there is danger lest the nation grow forgetful of the tremendous portent of the special responsibility left it from the past. The present generation is doubt-less just as loyal to the principle of liberty and just as faithful to the ideals of democracy as were the fathers of the republic, but the principles and ideals of the American people are meeting the challenge of latter day problems, and the people may become unmindful of unfinished tasks. Thus the condition of the Negro may receive less attention from the nation; his economic and social difficulties may be less generally known; his migration and concentration in cities, North and South, are given less attention. The increasing segregated settlements and life of Negroes within the cities may excite less concern. The resulting intensified industrial, housing, health and other maladjustments and the Negro's heroic struggles to overcome these maladjustments are in these days likely to be little considered. These conditions demand thought.

I. The Urban Movement

But social changes do not frequently keep time with social thought, for they are usually the result of unconscious social forces. Many of the changes among Negroes, especially the change from country to city, have been of such a character.

The past half century has seen an acceleration of the urban migration of the entire population. The Negro has been in that population stream. At times and in places his movement cityward has been affected by special influences, but where influences have been similar his movement has been similar.

The Emancipation Proclamation not only abolished the ownership of the slave, but it also released him from the soil. With this breaking down of the economic system based upon slavery, many of the landless freedmen fell victims to the *wanderlust* which has usually affected the masses in times of sudden social upheaval. . . . In fourteen Southern cities between 1860 and 1870 the white population increased 16.7 per cent, and the Negro 90.7 per cent; in eight Northern cities (counting all the boroughs of New York City as now constituted as one) the Negro population increased 51 per cent. . . .

The causes, besides breaking down of the slave regime, that have operated to draw the Negro to urban centers have been those fundamental economic, social and individual causes which have affected the general population. Chief among these has been the growth of industrial and commercial activities in urban centers. From 1880 to 1900 Southern cities (according to the showing of the census figures of manufactures, which are only approximately exact) have increased 143.3 per cent in total value of manufactured products, and 60.9 per cent in the average number of wage-earners, exclusive of proprietors, salaried officers and clerks, in manufacturing enterprises. . . .

The divorce of the Negro from the soil after emancipation, and the growth of the industrial and commercial centers are causes which are supplemented by the effect of higher wages paid weekly or monthly in the city on the economic motives of workers; by the trend of legislation, especially labor laws, which favor the city and which, in practical effect in some parts of the South, make harder the uninviting lot of the land tenant; by improved education and amusement facilities, and by the contact with the moving crowds; while the paved and lighted streets, the greater comforts of the houses and other conveniences which the rustic imagines he can easily get and the dazzling glare of the unknown great world are viewed in decided contrast to the hard, humdrum conditions and poor accommodations on plantation and farm.

The available facts and figures bear out the conclusion that along with the white population the Negroes, under the influence of causes likely to operate for an indefinite period, will continue to migrate to the towns and cities, and that they will come in comparatively large numbers to stay.

Already the Negro urban population has grown to considerable proportions. In 1860 it is estimated that about 4.2 per cent of all the Negroes in the United States were urban dwellers (places of 4,000 or more). By 1890 it had risen to 19.8 per cent (places of 2,500 or more; the figures for 1890 and since are not, therefore, comparable with those for censuses preceding); in 1900 it was 22.7 per cent, and in 1910, 27.4 percent, or more than one-fourth of the total Negro population. In 1910 thirty-nine cities had 10,000 or more Negroes, and the following twelve cities had more than 40,000 Negroes each:

Atlanta, Ga.	51,902
Baltimore, Md.	84,749
Birmingham, Ala.	52,305
Chicago, Ill.	44,103
Louisville, Ky.	40,522
Memphis, Tenn.	52,441
New Orleans, La.	89,262
New York, N.Y.	91,709
Philadelphia, Pa.	84,459
Richmond, Va.	46,733
St. Louis, Mo.	43,960
Washington, D.C.	94,446

Negroes constituted one-fourth or more of the total population of twenty-seven principal cities (25,000 or more total population), and in four of these cities—viz., Montgomery, Ala., Jacksonville, Fla., Savannah, Ga., and Charleston, S.C.—the Negro population was something more than one-half.

II. Segregation within the City

Migration to the city is being followed by segregation into districts and neighborhoods within the city. In Northern cities, years ago Negro residents, for the most part, lived where their purses allowed. With the influx of thousands of migrants from the South and the West Indies, both native Negro and newcomer have been lumped together into distinct neighborhoods. In Southern cities domestic servants usually still live upon the premises of their employers or near by. But the growing Negro business and professional classes and those engaged in other than domestic and personal service find separate sections in which to dwell. . . .

This segregation within the city is caused by strong forces at work both within and without the body of the Negroes themselves. Naturally, Negroes desire to be together. The consciousness of kind is racial, family and friendly ties bind them closer to one another than to their white fellow-citizens. But as Negroes develop in intelligence, in their standard of living and economic power, they desire better houses, better public facilities and other conveniences not usually obtainable in the sections allotted to their less fortunate black brothers. To obtain these advantages they seek other neighborhoods, just as the European immigrants who are crowded into segregated sections of our cities seek better surroundings when they are economically able to secure them.

But a prejudiced opposition from his prospective white neighbors confronts the Negro, which does not meet the immigrant who has shuffled off the coil of his Continental condition. Intelligence and culture do not often discount color of skin. Professions of democratic justice in the North, and deeds of individual kindness in the South, have not yet secured to Negroes the unmolested residence in blocks with white fellow-citizens. In Northern cities where larger liberty in some avenues obtains, the home life, the church life and much of the business and community life of Negroes are carried on separately and apart from the common life of the whole people. In Southern communities, with separate streetcar laws, separate places of amusement and recreation, separate hospitals and separate cemeteries, there is sharp cleavage between whites and Negroes, living and dead. With separation in neighborhoods, in work, in churches, in homes and in almost every phase of their life, there is growing up in the cities of America a distinct Negro world, isolated from many of the impulses of the common life and little known and understood by the white world about it.

III. The Sequel of Segregation

In the midst of this migration and segregation, the Negro is trying to make a three-fold adjustment, each phase of which requires heroic struggle. First, there is the adjustment that all rural populations have to make in learning to live in town.

Adjustment to conditions of housing, employment, amusement, etc., is necessary for all who make the change from country to city. The Negro must make a second adjustment from the status of a chattel to that of free contract, from servitude to citizenship. He has to realize in his own consciousness the self-confidence of a free man. Finally, the Negro must adjust himself to the white population in the cities, and it is no exaggeration of the facts to say that generally today the attitude of this white population is either indifferent or prejudiced or both.

Now, the outcome of segregation in such a serious situation is first of all to create an attitude of suspicion and hostility between the best elements of the two races. Too much of the Negro's knowledge of the white world comes through demagogues, commercial sharks, yellow journalism, and those "citizens" who compose the mobs, while too much of the white man's knowledge of the Negro people is derived from similar sources, from domestic servants and from superficial observation of the loafers about the streets. The best elements of both races, thus entirely removed from friendly contact, except for the chance meeting of individuals in the market place, know hardly anything of their common life and tend to become more suspicious and hostile toward each other than toward strangers from a far country.

The white community is thus frequently led to unjust judgments of Negroes and Negro neighborhoods, as seen in the sobriquets of "little Africa," "black bottom," "Niggertown," "Smoketown," "Buzzard's Alley," "China-row," and as indicated by the fact that the individuals and families who live in these neighborhoods are all lumped by popular opinion into one class. Only here and there does a white person come to know that "there are Negroes and Negroes just as there are white folks and white folks." The most serious side of this attitude and opinion is, that the Negro is handicapped by them in securing the very things that would help him in working out his own salvation. . . .

IV. Suggestions for Solution

The recital of the foregoing facts and conclusions would be of little consequence unless it led somewhere. The summary of the discussion presents a clear case of a large nation-wide Negro migration to towns and cities, such as is taking place among the entire people; a segregation within the city of Negroes into distinct neighborhoods with a decreasing contact with the larger community and its impulses; accompanying housing, economic, health, moral, educational and other conditions which are more critical and are receiving less attention than similar problems among the white people. With such a problem before us, what should be done?

1. There should be an organized effort to acquaint the Negro in the country with the desirability of his remaining where he is unless by education and training he is prepared to meet the exactions of adjustment to city life. The roseate picture of city existence should be corrected. Simultaneously with the agricultural and other improvements of country life calculated to make its economic and social conditions more attractive should go an effort to minimize the activities of labor

agents, employment agency sharks and the other influences that lure the rustics from home.

2. Recognizing that already more than two score cities and towns have large Negro populations in the first stages of adjustment, organized effort should be made to help the Negro to learn to live in town. The thoughtful white and colored people in each community will have to break the bonds of this increasing segregation and come into some form of organized community cooperation. The danger most to be feared is antagonism between the better element of both races, because they may not know and understand each other. The meeting on the high levels of mutual sympathy and cooperation will work wonders with prejudices and conventional barriers.

3. The cooperative movement of the white and colored citizens of each locality should work out a community program for the neighborhood, housing, economic, educational, religious and other improvement of the Negro. The time is at hand when we should not let this matter longer drift.

4. Such a movement should sooner or later become conscious of the national character of the problem and the towns and cities should unite for the exchange of plans, methods and experience and for general cooperation and for developing needed enthusiasm.

5. The Negro must have more and better trained leadership in these local situations. Slowly but surely we are listening to the lesson of group psychology and common sense and are beginning to use the most direct way of influencing the customs and habits of a people by giving them teachers and exemplars of their own kind. If the Negro is to be lifted to the full stature of American civilization, he must have leaders—wise, well-trained leaders—who are learned in the American ways of thinking and of doing things. And it should never be forgotten that the Negro himself has valuable contributions to make to American life.

6. The final suggestion is that the white people of each locality can best foster mutual confidence and cooperation of Negroes by according them impartial community justice. This means "a square deal" in industry, in education and in other parts of the common life. It means equality of opportunity.

These conditions among Negroes in the cities arise as much from the many changes which are taking place in the life of the Negro as from the changes taking place in the life of the nation. The Negro is awakening to a race consciousness and to the consciousness of American citizenship. His migration is a part of his groping efforts to better his condition; he is trying to engage in industry and commerce and is accumulating wealth. Above the ruins of the slave cabin he is building homes. Upon the ash-cleared hearth of the chattel he is developing the sacredness of family relationships. Where once he toiled that the children of others might have leisure and learning, he is trying to erect schools and colleges for the education of his own. In lieu of the superstition and ignorance which savagery and serfdom had made his daily portion, the Negro is trying to cultivate an ethical and religious life beautiful in holiness and achieving in service. In these efforts for self-realization in the city the Negro needs the fair dealing, the sympathy and the cooperation of his white brother. For the problem of his adjustment is only a part of the great human problem of justice for the handicapped in democratic America.

✕ *E S S A Y S*

The three essays present different perspectives on immigration and migration and raise several possibilities for comparison and contrast. The first selection, by John Bodnar of Indiana University, Roger Simon of Lehigh University, and Michael P. Weber of Duquesne University, complements the immigrant testimonies above by interpreting the ethnically and racially varied migration experiences and expectations of urban newcomers in early-twentieth-century Pittsburgh. The second essay, by Ricardo Romo of the University of Texas, Austin, examines a different immigrant group and its community: Mexicans who moved into Los Angeles between 1910 and 1930. The third essay, by James Grossman of the Newberry Library, Chicago, offers a perspective on the migration of African-Americans, not only outlining the process of their movement from the rural South to the northern city of Chicago in the early twentieth century but also analyzing internal divisions within the urban black community. Like the document on black migration, the excerpt from Grossman's book compares the conditions of black migrants and white immigrants.

Immigrant Newcomers in Turn-of-the-Century Pittsburgh

JOHN BODNAR, ROGER SIMON, and MICHAEL P. WEBER

During the first two decades of the twentieth century, Pittsburgh's population increased by nearly one-third. Such an increase was not the result of growth in all sectors of its population, however, but resulted basically from a massive infusion of unskilled and semiskilled workers and their families from largely agricultural areas. City residents emanating from Poland increased 39 percent from 1900 to 1920; Italians saw their ranks more than double, and blacks expanded their ranks by 85 percent. It is true that the increase in immigrant population took place largely during the century's first decade, and the foreign-born count declined somewhat between 1910 and 1920 when war in Europe restricted emigration. Indeed, black expansion exceeded that of any immigrant group after 1914. But overall it was from the ranks of this aspiring proletariat that Pittsburgh could count its new citizens. Simultaneously, the flow of newcomers from the areas of migration in the nineteenth century—Germany, Ireland, and England—declined considerably. Between 1890 and 1910 the number of residents from the older immigrant stock declined 10 to 20 percent. In effect the German, English, and Irish stock consisted mainly of second and third generations as the pioneers were slowly dying out.

While these newcomers all perceived certain benefits to be derived from the jobs that were available to them in the industrial city, an easy assumption should not be made that they pursued common objectives or possessed similar experiences before emigration. Generalizations about destitute individuals abandoning a rural world in search of golden opportunity in growing cities have pervaded

From *Lives of Their Own: Blacks, Italians, and Poles in Pittsburgh, 1900–1960* by John Bodnar, Roger Simon, and Michael P. Weber, excerpts from pp. 29–48. Copyright © 1982 The University of Illinois Press. Reprinted by permission of the publisher.

both scholarly and popular thinking about American urbanization in the twentieth century. But such abstractions have obscured the complex origins of urban new-comers and the attitudinal posture they carried from their ancestral homes. Certainly similarities existed. Blacks were clearly dissatisfied with political ex-clusion in the South, and Poles resented their subservience to Germans, Austri-ans, and Russians. But such similarities should not obscure fundamental differ-ences that characterized the experiences of blacks, Italians, and Poles prior to their arrival in Pittsburgh. Without acknowledging the specific condition of pre-urban existence, a full understanding of later developments in the industrial city is simply not possible.

Industrialization not only weaned ordinary people away from the land, but also it altered the nature of the workplace. The need to acquire specific skills before entering factory work lessened as corporations sought ways to improve efficiency and production. Mechanization and streamlined production modes, in fact, opened up thousands of manual operations that could be quickly learned by newly arrived workers from rural or considerably less industrialized regions. Fac-tory and mill production also undercut the household and traditional manufactur-ing in agricultural areas and began to force land dwellers to supplement their wages in industrial areas rather than at home. Landholding itself became a grow-ing problem as various factors conspired to make it more difficult to own land in sufficient quantities to support agricultural activities. This was particularly true in Russian Poland and Galicia, where agriculture suffered from an uncontrolled parcelization of estates. On the other extreme, blacks and Italians had difficulty in obtaining land at all. When industrialization began dislocating the worker in the countryside, the stage was set for the black, Italian, and Polish movement to Pittsburgh. . . .

The gradual movement of southern blacks from farms . . . was confirmed in oral interviews conducted for this study among migrants who came to Pittsburgh before 1917. Most blacks interviewed in Pittsburgh were raised on small farms in Alabama, Georgia, and Virginia. Migrants recalled their parents working as sharecroppers for larger farmers who were in a few instances black. About one-fifth of the respondents came from farms owned by their fathers. . . .

. . . While black settlement in western Pennsylvania was frequently attrib-uted to the importation of blacks as strikebreakers, nearly all blacks interviewed for this study came to Pittsburgh on their own volition as part of an expanding migratory process that had no other foundation than friends and kin. Essential services such as information about wage rates and job selection were provided by fellow blacks already in the city. An important distinction, however, was evident. While black migrants were able to supply information concerning wages and jobs, they appeared unable to assist other migrants in obtaining work regularly.

The movement of friends and kin from southern farms generated informal dissemination of knowledge about industrial employment. As a teenager Jean B. began working at a sawmill near Mobile, Alabama, while living on his parents' farm. It was at the sawmill that he heard mention of Philadelphia, New York, and Chicago. Such conversation prompted him to come north. He decided upon Pitts-burgh because two friends were already there. After saving $45, he took a train from Mobile through Cincinnati to Pittsburgh, where his friends obtained a room for him. William H. was working for a railroad in Alabama. His wife's uncle, who had worked in coal mines near Pittsburgh, informed him of higher wages. Although he initially intended to seek employment in the mines, a friend in Pittsburgh drew him to the Jones and Laughlin plant where wages appeared even "better." . . .

It should not come as a complete surprise that blacks were not tied wholly to the land and were beginning to loosen the ties they had. Black migration was not simply a direct transfer of people from an agricultural to an urban environment. Even prior to migration blacks were being weaned from the land and slowly being drawn into a wage-labor economy. To be sure, the vast majority of blacks still lived on farms, but a discernible trend away from agriculture had begun in the South in the late nineteenth century. By 1900 about 18 percent of all southern blacks were living in southern towns and cities. Among the remainder still living on the land only about 17 percent were owners; the rest were tenants or sharecroppers despite government programs such as the Southern Homestead Act that attempted to stimulate black land ownership. Compounding the problem of deriving a living from the land was the overall decline in southern agriculture, including the reduction in sizes of farms in the five decades following the Civil War and the difficulties blacks encountered in securing farm loans and mortgages. By 1900 blacks owned only about 8 percent of all farms and about 6.5 percent of all farmland in the five major cotton-producing states. Small gains made in ownership prior to 1892 were halted by 1900 because of depressed cotton prices. The resulting ties of most blacks to the land were based upon a system of sharecropping that facilitated further exploitation of black farmers by owners who alone knew the amounts crop sales brought and could easily distort the percentage earned by black and white tenants.

Already in the South by the 1870s the blacks were manifesting an outlook toward wage labor and a disposition to quit the land. Northern industrial firms such as the Pennsylvania Railroad did not begin active recruitment of blacks until 1917, an indication that much of the impetus for "quitting the land" came from blacks themselves. This should not be surprising in light of their tenuous ties to the land in the first place. By 1890 over one-quarter of the nonwhite males in the five largest cotton states worked in nonagricultural pursuits; among females the figure reached 34.8 percent. . . .

But beyond the economic and social difficulties which intensified the desire to quit the land, blacks were developing specific goals and aspirations that caused them to pursue eagerly what Arna Bontemps and Jack Conroy described as the "lure of the North." . . . Woven through numerous accounts of black migration northward was an indication of high motivation and hopes for the future. . . . In 1919 the *Chicago Defender* reported on fifteen black families who left Huntsville, Alabama, for Pittsburgh because they had received letters from friends in the city who had already "made good." Similar inclinations have been found in recent studies of black workers in western Pennsylvania. . . .

The high hopes blacks possessed for social improvement expressed themselves most cogently in their school attendance rates. An examination of blacks moving to Chicago, for instance, stressed the widespread desire of black parents to place their children in better schools as a reason for abandoning the South. By 1920 in Pennsylvania 84.5 percent of black males aged fourteen and fifteen enrolled in school compared to only 72 percent of adolescent males of foreign-born parents. Among females, blacks were more likely to be in school by their midteens than were immigrant girls. In New York and New Jersey black attendance rates also exceeded those of immigrant children. Among black high school students in Pittsburgh in 1928, moreover, occupational goals were anything but modest with over 43 percent indicating a desire to enter teaching, dentistry, pharmacy, law, or some other profession.

Expectations were equally high among blacks coming to Pittsburgh before 1917. Explanations that blacks simply abandoned the political oppression of the South seem less viable in the face of evidence that suggests they were slowly being weaned away from farming by industrial opportunities. Jasper A. left a farm near Albany, Georgia, at age twenty because his father and a job at a cotton seed mill simply did not "give me enough of everything I should have." Harrison G. initially aspired to be a "bigger farmer" than his father. Eventually, however, he grew tired of "bad years" and "bad raps" and decided to see if work could be better somewhere else. At age sixteen he began a search that took him to Tennessee, Cincinnati, and ultimately to the Oliver Steel plant in Pittsburgh. . . .

Black aspirations were not simply vague dreams, moreover, but consisted of specific occupational goals that were anything but modest. Sadie A. came to Pittsburgh to become an interior decorator. Freeman P. hoped to become a physical education instructor and even managed to attend Wilberforce University before his financial resources were exhausted. Harrison G. came to Pittsburgh to open a grocery store. John W. intended to become a social worker. Numerous migrants expressed a desire to become teachers, although Pittsburgh would not hire black (or even Slavic) teachers before the 1930s. That socioeconomic obstacles frustrated black goals made their initial intentions no less real.

Closely related to the high expectations of southern migrants was the importance attached to formal schooling and education. One scholar has even detected a black "folk tradition" that linked schooling and personal advancement. In fact, in 1910 a larger proportion of blacks than of American-born children of immigrants between the ages of fourteen and eighteen were in school. Pittsburgh was no exception to this trend. At age fifteen, 48 percent of immigrant children were in school as compared with 63 percent of black children. By age sixteen only 30 percent of immigrant children remained in school; the figure for blacks was 41 percent. A decade later, black attendance still exceeded that of foreign-born and second-generation children in Pittsburgh. Middle-class black publications like the *Pittsburgh Courier* reinforced this sentiment. The *Courier,* for instance, continually urged black youth to seek "educational advantages" and criticized the exclusion of black teachers from the public schools.

Black migrants were explicit when it came to education. William H. recalled that his farming parents stressed the importance of acquiring as much education as possible. Indeed, his father wanted William and his two sisters to become teachers and sent them away for training. . . . Sadie A. related that her mother insisted that her sister attend business school. "We were a poor family," Sadie related, "but we always aspired to higher things." Freeman P. remembered that one of the reasons his parents brought their children northward was to secure a "better education" for them. . . .

Like southern American blacks, Poles also began to loosen their ties to the land by the late nineteenth century. Population pressure on existing landholdings increased in all three divisions of Poland but especially in the Russian controlled sector (Congress Poland), which experienced a population growth of 179 percent in the four decades before 1900. Villages were overpopulated and one Polish source estimated that the Polish territories had a surplus population of four to eight million. Consequently, the migration of Polish workers on both a seasonal and permanent basis intensified as families sought to supplement their income. Migrants traveled to Prussia, Bosnia, and Brazil as well as the United States, often returning with their earnings to purchase additional land. . . .

Like blacks coming at the same time, Poles were obviously mobile before movement to Pittsburgh. A popular poem by Walenty Rozdziewsky, a Polish foundry worker, perhaps best illustrates the tradition of mobility among Polish workers.

> Freedom is our sole delight, the sole reward
> Of our misery, not treasures, not money!
> Since the Cyclops time we have never been
> Slaves to any tyrant, free to come
> And go as we please, after one year
> In one place we can move to another. . . .

Industrial Silesia, Polish cities such as Poznan and Warsaw, and even Russia attracted temporary wage earners by the 1870s and the 1880s. . . .

Land reform and emancipation of the peasantry also influenced the social and economic position of workers in Polish-occupied lands. In Prussian Poland, for example, emancipation and the right to own land began earliest, with peasants on state-owned lands gaining rights to their landholdings as early as 1807 in Pomerania, Silesia, and Poznania. Subsequent development in Prussia, however, led to a gradual polarization of peasant society rather than a wide distribution of land ownership. Wealthier peasants purchased so much land that by 1880 a full 80 percent of the agricultural population were wage earners working for larger estates or migrating to the industrial area of Silesia. The gradual monopolization of land by a few made it increasingly difficult for most farming families to pass land to progeny or survive. After nearly seventy years of steadily losing their ability to live off the land, this rural proletariat had little choice but to move. Traveling largely in family units they settled in midwestern agricultural areas such as Wisconsin. Some, however, settled in cities as early as the 1870s and became the least likely of all Polish groups to return to Europe.

Emancipation and land reform came later in Russian Poland but also led to heightened social stratification, although not as extensively as in Poznania. Because laws allowed peasants to divide their holdings primarily among their children, a somewhat wider distribution of land ownership occurred. Emigration began in the 1880s when systematic Russian oppression intensified growing economic difficulties caused by unequal land distribution and an increasing surplus labor force. Since land could be inherited, however, emigration was more typical of individuals than family units. As in Prussia, the emigrant came from families who had owned land for several decades and were faced with further declines in status if additional land or wages were not obtained.

If land reform and emancipation led to varying degrees of polarization in Prussian and Russian areas, Galicia (or Austrian Poland) experienced pervasive pauperization after emancipation. Small holdings proliferated in this most impoverished of Polish lands, and landholding quickly became a common tradition. Between 1850 and 1890 the amount of peasant-owned tilled land increased by 750,000 acres. Inevitably, parents could not pass sufficient land to their sons to support agriculture. Obsessed with the value of land, these sons emigrated as individuals to Brazil and America after 1890 to earn wages that would allow them to return to Galicia to purchase additional acreage. It was no accident that more money was sent from America to Galicia than to any other section of Poland. These immigrants left home to stave off a decline in status by acquiring the means to purchase more land. Indeed, the widespread ownership of land in Galicia and the encounter with land ownership experienced by so many Poles in the Russian and Prussian sectors offered a sharp contrast to southern blacks in America, 17 percent of whom were landowners by 1900. If blacks had glimpsed an opportunity to abandon their position at the bottom of southern society, Poles, despite their various regional origins, had already flirted with social improvement after various emancipation acts. While emancipation benefited some, however, others grew disillusioned and sought to avoid any further decline in economic status. If blacks coming to Pittsburgh exhibited some hope for what they might find, it should seem reasonable that Poles were considerably more skeptical.

While mobility was not unfamiliar to Poles prior to emigration, they did not appear to acquire the range of nonagricultural skills characteristic to blacks and, as shown below, Italians. Those who had migrated to Prussian Polish villages did acquire some expertise in mining and textile production. But those moving overseas were typically neither established very well nor long in either industrial, village, or agricultural sectors. Rather they were recent refugees from areas where agriculture was in decline. They had never really had the opportunity to learn a skill or, for that matter, own land for any length of time, although many still harbored notions of eventual proprietorship. . . .

But if migration of blacks to Pittsburgh originated within a framework of gradually rising expectations and individualism, Polish newcomers were considerably more tentative about the promise of the "steel city" and still susceptible to the larger claims of their families of origin. . . . [I]f blacks were rapidly becoming aware of new possibilities and seeking survival largely on their own, Poles were reluctantly realizing that continued existence on the land was becoming more difficult. Their initial experiences in industrial work, however, underscored their precarious economic situation. The working day, normally twelve or more hours, sustained life but gave little cause for rising expectations. . . . If blacks had even a hint of an elevation in social status, Poles were desperately trying to resist what seemed a precipitous decline.

As in most instances of urban migrations, kinship was an essential element. This was as true for Poles as well as blacks. The mother of Joseph D. was brought from Gdansk (Prussia) to "Polish Hill" by an uncle who ran a grocery store. Indeed Polish migration from Prussia consisted heavily of family units as opposed to the more individualistic migration from Galicia, Georgia, Alabama, or Virginia. Valerian D. was brought to McKeesport, Pennsylvania, by his father in 1906. Peter L. avoided service in the Russian army by following a brother to the "steel city." The parents of Joseph B. were brought from Russian Poland by relatives. With two sisters and a brother already working in the city, the father of Stephanie L. left German Poland in 1899 with his wife and Stephanie herself. Joseph B. sent passage for two brothers and a sister to come to the Southside. Joseph Z. attracted two brothers to the Oliver Steel plant.

The extent of the influence of the kin migration may be seen in the early settlement patterns of each group of Poles. Generally they entered Pittsburgh in successive waves from provinces under the control of Germany, Russia, and Austria. Beginning in the early 1870s German Poles began settling in the Strip District along Penn Avenue. Russian Poles settled along Penn Avenue and further north in Lawrenceville. Those from German-held territories predominated in Herron Hill (Polish Hill) and the Southside before 1900. After the late 1890s Austrian Poles from Galicia joined German Poles on the Southside and Russian Poles in the Lawrenceville section.

Perhaps most important, kin and friends could supply vital, practical information on migration to perspective newcomers. . . .

If black migrants left for Pittsburgh with positive occupational goals, Poles were considerably less optimistic. The goal of most immigrant Poles was simply "to get a job, any job." The variety and specificity of occupational goals expressed by black migrants were nowhere to be found among the Polish newcomers. The Polish pattern was consistent. Mike B. entered a Southside mill because he felt the nature of a job was unimportant as long as he was working. "You've got to work because you've got to live whether you like it or not," he reasoned. Walter B. did not particularly like his work on a labor gang, but it satisfied his major occupational goal: "to stay out of debt." Joe R. kept a position finishing freight cars because it allowed him to play in a band on weekends. Mike M. took the first job that seemed "steady" because "there was no other way out." Women such as Stephanie W. sought only employment that would allow her to "walk to work and bring home money."

Once a job was secured, it was not easily abandoned. While blacks would frequently walk away from a job over personal dissatisfactions, Poles endured— unless economic dislocation necessitated a move or enough funds were accumulated to return to their homeland. As Ignacy M. exclaimed, "When you're in the mill, where are you going to go?" Thus, Joseph B. related that his father was a boiler mechanic at the Jones and Laughlin plant for fifty years. John K. estimated that his father worked in the same rolling mill near Polish Hill for over fifty years. . . .

The modest thrust of Polish orientation and the high value placed upon steady work within the status system of the Polish community did not foster strong support of extensive secular education. To be sure, religious instruction was important, and a few Polish children progressed through the American educational system. But Polish support for secular education seemed less pronounced than that of blacks. In the hierarchy of Polish values, work and family came before educational nourishment of the individual. . . . Stephanie W. was removed from school by her father at age thirteen to work and remembered only two of ten brothers and sisters completing high school. Stanley N. left high school because his teachers continually made him self-conscious and uncomfortable by erroneously pronouncing his name. "That was one of the things that bothered me and caused me the hell to drop out," he emphasized. Another immigrant child described his parents' views on schooling: "Well, to tell you the truth most of the old people came from the old country and all they believed was in sending their children to work. . . . I had only one brother that finished school and no sisters." . . .

Poles and blacks certainly did not represent the full range of premigration experience. Italians as well showed similarities and differences in their prior experiences that would influence their settlement in the "steel city." If the decline of feudal arrangements heralded widespread land ownership in most areas of Poland, the result in southern Italy was significantly different and more nearly resembled that of the American South. Most land in the Mezzogiorno, which included Abruzzie Molise, Campania, Puglia, Basilicata, Calabria, and Sicily, had been in the possession of royalty or government. An 1806 law finally encouraged the division of public land among serfs, but the edict was rarely enforced. Consequently, a small group of independent landowners obtained land that was inferior in quality. Lacking the necessary capital needed for improvement, the peasants or "contadini" eventually sold their large pieces to wealthier owners. The result was that by the late nineteenth century large estates (latifondi) were increasingly significant.

The implication of the inability of southern Italian peasants to cultivate the soil profitably and to own land led to patterns of survival that differed from those of both the American South and Poland. The counterpart of the black tenant or the small Polish landowners was usually a villager who tended to walk several miles daily to perform his agricultural tasks in the fields of a large owner. . . . The classic, self-sufficient farmer rarely appeared in the Mezzogiorno. Rather, . . . villages held small owners, day laborers, and even tenants who made the daily trek to the fields. Emotional attachments to land and work were giving way to economic ones. Not surprisingly, after 1882 land ownership among south Italian peasants declined.

The growing inability of the small landowner to retain his property and the evolution of his status as a laborer dependent upon an employer initiated gradual changes in southern Italian society. As with blacks and Poles, Italians began moving in a wider area for supplemental wages, especially because agriculture was seasonal and unpredictable. Some followed the harvests in other regions of Italy. Others migrated much further. As early as 1858 an Italian government official noted considerable movement to the Americas. . . . Diminishing opportunities in agriculture particularly intensified the desire to acquire a skill or trade that could provide either additional income or regular employment by itself. In addition, the social structure of southern Italy already possessed a significant class of artisans and wage laborers, including fishermen, peddlers, shoemakers, tailors, carpenters, and masons. With the periodic uncertainty of agricultural employment and declining child mortality after 1890, more individuals were competing for wages offered by these alternative forms of employment. This search would eventually take many abroad.

Because of their experience with wage labor and skills, Italians who were eventually forced to extend their job search to America were more than simply impoverished, tradition-bound peasants. Invariably they came from the middle or upper reaches of the Italian working class and were eager for capital to acquire more land in Italy or to assist their sons in entering a business or trade. . . .

The exact nature of the goals and expectations of Italians leaving for America is still debated. Older interpretations stress that immigrants hoped to avoid a "slow decline in status by pursuing industrial wages even in areas where language and culture were unfamiliar," much like the Polish model. Recent accounts have indicated that Italians were ready for improvement and had high expectations of social mobility. . . . What is clear is that despite a heavy incidence of return migration, Italians' association with the land had been severely reduced by 1900. Italian workers seemed intent on improving their social condition, whether in Italy or America, by avenues other than farming. Many crossed the ocean semi-annually in search of suitable work. . . . To the extent that Italians had loosened their ties to the land and had elevated their future expectations, they more nearly resembled blacks coming to the "steel city" than Poles.

Interviews with Italians in Pittsburgh, conducted mostly with families emanating from Abruzzi, suggest that Italians saw Pittsburgh as a definite opportunity for improvement. Most of those interviewed indicated little intention ever to return. Since interviews were conducted only with those who did persist in the city, this is not unusual. Thousands, of course, did return to Europe with savings that enabled them to improve their life in Italy. . . . Nevertheless, the interviews with Italians were noticeably different from those of persisting Poles, who invariably indicated an initial desire to return. Nicholas R. had no intention of returning because he felt Pittsburgh afforded "greater opportunity" than Italy. The father of Felix D. came to Saffire Alley in the city because he was "mad" that as an apprentice in Italy he was only allowed to sweep floors. In disgust he left for America, "where everyone was making money." As a young woman in Abruzzi, Domenica M. was impressed by letters from Pittsburgh that described the earnings and acquisitions of emigrants. "The people were smart," she reasoned. "They saved the money. They built the houses. They got what they needed."

Like blacks and Poles coming to the city, Italians structured their entire migration around kinship. Beginning in the late 1880s a steady stream of Italians poured into four blocks . . . in downtown Pittsburgh. Business expansion into the area forced both Poles and Italians outward, with Poles moving to the Lawrenceville section, where they were concentrating in factory jobs, and Italians moving into Bloomfield and especially East Liberty, where many found employment in the erection of the city's new filtration plant in 1905. It was in East Liberty that the first Italian Catholic church was opened in 1897. . . .

The Italian community in Bloomfield was built on a foundation of friends and kin already in the city by the 1890s. Most of the neighborhood's Italians came from a half-dozen villages in Abruzzi, especially Castel di Sangro, Rocca Cinque Miglia, Ateleta, and Pesco Costanza. The father of Michael M. settled in the Strip District around 1911, lived with a brother, and worked in his brother's small produce business. Eventually another brother and sister followed them to the city. Precisely because all of his brothers and sisters settled in the city, Michael's father reluctantly abandoned his intention of returning to Italy in 1925 to open a dry goods store. Felix D. had worked in Pittsburgh between 1888 and 1890 before returning to Abruzzi. After marrying a girl from his village in 1890, he contacted relatives in Bloomfield, who secured a construction job that allowed him to return to Pittsburgh with his bride. Tom B. was brought to the city in 1912 by a grandfather who had worked in Wisconsin a decade before with Tom's father. After

Tom's father died from an illness that he contracted while loading coal barges, his grandfather brought three other grandchildren, Tom's mother, and several uncles and aunts to Bloomfield. . . .

All Italians, of course, were not coming to Pittsburgh in a feverish search for improvement. Once immigrant networks were established, they offered solutions to familial and economic problems that existed at the time. A surprising number involved young girls whose parents had died and who were in need of a place to live. In many instances these female immigrants married as soon as possible, often before the age of eighteen, to stabilize their lives and secure their positions in America. Albina B. came to an aunt in 1913 and one year later married an Italian laborer who was living across the street. Domenica M. came to Bloomfield at the age of fourteen after her mother died in 1910. She lived with an aunt whom she assisted in caring for boarders until she was married in 1914. Lidwina P. came to Pittsburgh to live with her father after her mother's death.

Clearly newcomers to Pittsburgh had much in common. Blacks, Italians, and Poles had encountered a gradual loosening of their ties to the land, which allowed them to become familiar with various forms of wage labor. All groups, moreover, relied essentially on friends and kin in moving to the industrial city and finding a place to live. But important distinctions emerged in the evolutionary process of transforming agricultural laborers into industrial toilers. Leaving at a time when their ties to the land were still meaningful, most Poles looked upon Pittsburgh as a temporary necessity in achieving the larger goal of proprietorship in the homeland. Blacks and Italians, on the other hand, had never experienced widespread proprietorship and were rather optimistic about entering the "steel city." Italians, in particular, even brought numerous skills that promised to serve them well. . . .

Creating Los Angeles' Eastside Barrio, 1910–1930

RICARDO ROMO

Many Americans assumed that Mexicanos were casual laborers who, like "homing pigeons," returned to the old country after short work stints in the United States. This was a misconception, however, for in Los Angeles by 1930 Mexicanos had created the largest "Mexican city" in the United States, a stable and growing community that rivaled in size principal cities of most other states.

During the period 1910–1930, rapid suburbanization and industrial growth pushed Mexican residents of the old Plaza community to the east, where the barrio recorded spectacular growth. Four factors help explain the development of this Mexican residential concentration. First, rapid increases in migration from Mexico generated a need for new housing areas. In the years between 1910 and 1920, the city's Mexican population grew from 5,000 to more than 30,000; by 1930 that figure had more than trebled [to over 90,000]. Second, the introduction of industry and commerce in the old Mexican plaza crowded out the residential areas there. Following the construction of a deep-water harbor and completion of

From *East Los Angeles: History of a Barrio* by Ricardo Romo, pp. 61–88. Copyright © 1983 University of Texas Press. Reprinted by permission of the publisher.

the Panama Canal, the demand for industrial and commercial sites in the central business zone increased significantly. North and south of the Plaza, railroad depots attracted warehouses, wholesale distributors, and light industry. A third factor, the development of interurban transportation, contributed to the decentralization of industries and middle- and upper-class homes. Long Beach almost tripled its population, from 55,593 in 1920 to 142,032 in 1930, and Hollywood gained 150,000 residents during the same period. Finally, a rise in racial tension and subsequent efforts to segregate Mexican residents prevented the movement of these immigrants into the north and west sections of the city. In the postwar years, these forces drastically affected physical change in Los Angeles.

The new wave of Mexican migration during the first quarter of the twentieth century was part of a general migration that transformed small towns in the Southwest into urban industrial centers. Mexicans came to Los Angeles by train directly from Mexico through Nogales, Tijuana, or Mexicali, or indirectly from other southwestern points such as El Paso, Douglas, Laredo, and Del Rio. A few came by ship, landing at either San Diego or San Pedro, and a smaller number traveled by automobile. Industrial growth, which caused the expansion of rail services eastward and across international borders, figured heavily in attracting Mexican laborers.

The making of Los Angeles' population in the period 1900–1920 indicates that Mexicans constituted one of the few major foreign-born groups in the city. In 1900 only one of five residents (18 percent) of the city had been born in a foreign country, a figure considerably lower than that for most other large American cities. As migrants, however, Mexicans need not have felt out of place. Two-thirds of the population in 1900 were from other areas of the United States. While New England had been the birthplace of more California immigrants than any other section of the nation in 1880, by 1900 most newcomers to Los Angeles came from the nation's midwestern heartland. . . . Nonetheless, despite its image as an Anglo American town, Los Angeles had other ethnic communities. Northern and western European immigrants made up the largest foreign-born group in the city from 1900 to 1930, but the southern and eastern European population doubled between the years 1920 and 1930. Russians and Italians represented nearly 60 percent of the Europeans who settled in the city. Other ethnic communities, mainly Black, Jewish, and Mexican, could be found in the southern and eastern sections of town.

The evolution of a distinct Black district, like that of the Mexican barrio, may be traced to the first two decades of the twentieth century. Historians mark the real estate boom of 1887–1888 as the beginning of Black migration to the city. But Blacks were only 2.5 percent of the total population in 1890, numbering only 1,258. Over the next two decades the Black population grew to 7,599, still only 2.3 percent of the total population. There was then little indication that Blacks would concentrate in significant numbers in any one area. When Mexican construction workers went on strike in 1903, the Southern Pacific Railroad imported 2,000 Blacks to the area. But action by the railroad did not signify a trend, and by 1920 the Black population had increased to only 15,579 residents. . . .

Blacks living in Los Angeles during the 1920s found economic opportunities there superior to those they had known in the South. In some industries the new migrants found little resistance to their participation and advancement, and even skilled positions were not out of their reach. Perhaps because Mexican workers were more numerous and employers held stronger negative attitudes toward them, Blacks were preferred over Mexicans in certain industries. As one representative of a meat-packing company observed, "There is no opposition to Negro labor on the part of the company. They make better butchers than the Mexicans and there is no trouble between the various race groups." As their numbers grew, however, the opportunities for Blacks in the semiskilled and skilled industries lessened. In many instances, even in the unskilled jobs, they found the door closed to them. . . .

At the same time that Blacks were in the midst of creating an urban homeland on the West Coast, across town on the east side, Jewish immigrants had initiated similar efforts. Although the first Jews had settled in Los Angeles during the Gold Rush era, two historians of the Jewish community postulated that in 1900 "there were too few Jews to form a definitely Jewish district." Between 1900 and 1910, a period of considerable Jewish immigration, the Los Angeles Jewish population more than doubled, from 2,500 to 5,795. The Jewish community actually had its beginning in East Los Angeles over the years 1910–1920. It grew in response to industrial expansion in the downtown core region where many Jews had settled. In six short years, between 1917 and 1923, the Jewish community increased substantially, from 10,000 to 43,000. Although quota laws of 1921 and 1924 cut by more than half the influx of Jews to the United States, the Jewish community of Los Angeles still prospered in the twenties. . . .

Following the introduction of a modern interurban railway system, dispersion of the ethnic communities increased. As most European immigrants left their inner city dwellings for new single-family homes in the suburbs, new groups of immigrants, in many cases Mexicans, took the old immigrants' places in communities such as Boyle Heights, Lincoln Heights, and the adjacent community of Hollenbeck Park. The development of the interurban rail system thus contributed greatly to the process of change that occurred in communities absorbing Mexican residents between the years 1900 and 1930. . . .

Construction of these interurban lines provided jobs for thousands of unskilled Mexican workers. As one of the major industries of the city, [Collis P.] Huntington's Pacific Electric Railway introduced the practice of recruiting laborers from Mexico. The majority of these workers came through El Paso, where thousands of unskilled workers stood ready to accept jobs in railroad work. Although the railroad companies, including the Pacific Electric Company, paid wages slightly lower than other industries, they offered free transportation and provided the workers and their families with company housing. In southern California, the railroad companies paid their Mexican workers from $1.00 to $1.25 for a ten-hour day, while offering other nationalities up to $1.75 for similar work. In parts of southern California, Mexicans working for the Southern Pacific earned an average of $1.25 per day, while Greeks earned $1.60 and Japanese $1.45 daily for the same work. In Los Angeles, where Huntington had to compete with the

Southern Pacific and the Santa Fe Railroad companies for track hands, the Pacific Electric initially paid Mexican workers $1.85 per day.

Mexican laborers recruited to Los Angeles by the Pacific Electric became the first group of immigrant residents whose residential locations were directly related to interurban transportation. At every major junction or end of the line, the company constructed labor camps for track hands. In Santa Monica, a community promoted as a resort paradise, a labor camp at the outskirts of town kept the rail line operating from that location to downtown. In Pasadena, Long Beach, and Santa Monica, labor camps slowly grew in the postwar years. Many workers left their railroad jobs and joined other industries but maintained residency in the labor camp communities. As the communities around the labor camps grew, small oases of Mexican residents became surrounded by suburban residents of a different class and nationality. In the middle of suburbia these small Mexican communities evolved into isolated urban satellite barrios outside of the political and cultural mainstream.

The development of Watts as a Mexican enclave in Los Angeles had such a beginning in 1902. The railroads recruited four hundred Mexican laborers to work on track construction extending from central Los Angeles to Long Beach and Los Angeles Harbor at San Pedro as well as the expansion of two other lines to Santa Ana and Redondo Beach. According to a longtime Anglo American resident of Watts, the Mexican laborers "first lived in box cars with their families, later in tents, and finally in rows of four-room houses, each house occupied by two families with a common shelter for wash days for the women." This was the "Latin Camp." The railroad companies that owned the small houses later relocated the camp in another part of Watts. At the new *colonia,* investigators found that of seventy-six households, only one family lived "in good conditions." . . .

The majority of the Mexican population of Los Angeles, however, did not move to Watts and other suburbs until the twenties. Prior to the twenties, newcomers from Mexico continued to settle in the old Mexican Plaza area. This area also attracted a large share of the non-Mexican foreign-born population, representing more than twenty different ethnic groups. Mexicans and Italians emerged as the principal groups, accounting for approximately 76 percent of the population of the Plaza community. When World War I began, immigration from Europe came to a halt, and Mexicans began replacing Russians, Italians, Jews, and even Anglos in "Sonoratown." Thus they once again became the major ethnic group in this section, in effect reconquering the Plaza. . . .

Although Mexicans also lived in railroad camps, private homes, boarding houses, apartments, and low-cost hotels, investigators took special interest in the conditions of the Mexican residents in the house courts. In these quarters, three to thirty small houses occupied a common lot, and the residents shared a common yard as well as toilet and washing facilities. The courts of the Plaza community, for example, gave evidence of the cramped and poor conditions of such facilities in the city. A court there consisted generally of ten to twenty houses, half on each side of the lot, with toilet facilities in the center. Lots were usually 40 by 170 feet and offered only limited space for children to play or for social activities. In 1920 tenants paid six dollars per month for a 300-square-foot two-room house. Residents of a typical court had the use of ten hydrants with sinks and six toilets.

Overcrowding was prevalent: in one court, for example, fifty-seven residents made their home—twenty men, nineteen women, ten boys, and eight girls—although only nineteen of the twenty-seven houses were occupied.

One research project found the existence of some 630 courts in 1913 accounting for 10,000 residents, with the number of individual houses numbering about 3,700. "Mexicans, Russians, Italians, Slavonians, Austrians, Chinese, Japanese and a scattering of some 20 other nationalities" lived in these house courts. While not actually promoting the construction of house courts, city officials considered them the answer to the growing city housing shortage. In 1912, in the 700 block of New High Street, considered at the time to be the heart of the Mexican barrio, developers constructed twenty-two one-store habitations on a lot occupying a space of 44 by 171 feet. As required by law, the owners left 30 square feet of the lot vacant, but the court was jammed tightly against adjoining lots. On each side of the lot stood eleven houses, all of them two-room dwellings, 15 feet wide and 12 feet deep. The total cost of the house court was placed at $1,000 and rent for each house brought the owner $6 a month, or $132 in all. Families of four or more typically lived in these small habitations, which often sheltered eight or nine individuals each. City regulations required only that the house courts have at least one men's toilet for every ten men and one women's toilet for every ten women. Older house courts also existed where a hard rain or a cold night made the residents miserable.

Although adequate housing continued to be an issue, raising a family in Los Angeles was seen by many immigrants as desirable. Nonetheless, employer groups testified in Congress that Mexicans came as single workers. A January 1915 study of 1,202 house court units in the city, many of them occupied by Mexicans, revealed that they housed a total population of 6,490 men, 4,920 women, and 5,100 children. Elizabeth Fuller surveyed fifty Mexican homes in the Central Plaza district in 1920 and found an average of 5.78 persons per household (including 3.10 children under age ten). The Mexican, Fuller concluded, "comes here as a young husband and a young father," not as a single individual. The family, she believed, would find "steady improvement" under the "influence of church, school, mission or settlement." In the fifty homes in Fuller's survey, the Mexican tenants paid an average monthly rental of $9.80—a considerable amount when one takes into account their low wages and irregular employment.

The heavy new Mexican immigration during the war years resulted in an overabundance of unskilled labor in Los Angeles. State investigators examined the work pattern of residents of the Plaza community in 1915 and concluded that unemployment was high and those who worked held poor-paying jobs in occupations that called for hard manual labor. The investigators found, for example, that of 246 Mexican men eligible for employment, 106 held jobs, 131 were unemployed, and the remaining 9 were either unaccounted for or away from their homes. Exactly 100 of these workers earned their living in blue-collar jobs, 93 of them as unskilled laborers. Only a small percentage of the Mexican women in the community worked outside the home. Of the 25 Mexican women employed, 8 worked in laundries and 7 kept boarders as a means of earning a living. . . .

That the immigrant residents of the Plaza community were able to make ends meet, considering their meager income and irregular employment, was a credit to their fortitude and willingness to make great sacrifices. Even those who worked regularly earned low wages. The largest industries in the community in 1916 included two beef packing houses which employed 876 men, the Los Angeles Pressed Brick Company which employed 143 men, and the Los Angeles Gas Works with 182 men. Daily wages averaged $1.75–$4.00 at the beef packing houses, $2.00–$4.00 at the Los Angeles Pressed Brick Company, and $2.00–$2.40 at the gas company. By way of comparison, a machine and foundry company in the community which employed only a few Mexicans paid $.35 per hour, or $3.50 for a ten-hour day. The machine company, however, listed 40 of its 48 workers in the skilled categories. Civic leaders blamed unemployment and low wages for the increasing social problems in the Plaza barrio. . . .

Following the outbreak of World War I, Los Angeles' economy greatly expanded as a result of the growth of war-related industries. The wartime rise in production and sales of goods ranging from ships to fruits generated a new demand for workers. No longer able to find housing in the Plaza colonia, the Mexican newcomers went northeast in search of living quarters. Within a few years, the Elysian Park neighborhood (also called the Ann Street District) north of the Plaza . . . grew in reputation as a heterogeneous working-class community. Researchers found that by 1916 Mexicans and Italians constituted 80 percent of the ethnic groups in this neighborhood. In a survey conducted by the Los Angeles Society for the Study of Prevention of Tuberculosis, some 1,650 individuals in 331 homes were questioned about their health situation. Fifty-one percent of the respondents were Mexican and 30 percent Italian. As in other Mexican communities, youth was a common denominator. Only 2 percent of the Mexican residents were over thirty years of age, compared to 13 percent for the other groups. Although the average Mexican family consisted of five members, more than half of them lived in small apartments in house courts. The cramped living and recreational space especially affected the Mexicans, since 56 percent of the 855 members of this group were between the ages of five and nine. The move to this neighborhood illustrates the fact that the Mexican community moved in a northeast direction at the same time that it was beginning its major thrust to the east side. . . .

Jobs, inexpensive housing, and community life accounted for the move of Mexicans to the east side. This resettlement, however, would have been of small consequence without the regular service and inexpensive fares provided by the interurban railway system. The electric interurban trolley made it possible for Mexicans to spread to residential areas several miles from the central business district and industrial areas. The movement of Mexicans toward the "new" east side occurred at the time when the Los Angeles Pacific Electric Railway opened new lines to Brooklyn Heights, Boyle Heights, and Ramona. Indeed, the existence of rail service to outlying communities such as Maravilla and Belvedere made it possible for many working-class families to leapfrog the older Mexican communities immediately east of the Los Angeles River. These scattered communities of the east side soon became one. In contrast to the overall population of Los Angeles, which lived in a "fragmented metropolis par excellence," the Mexican community emerged by 1930 as a group tightly clustered residentially and socially.

Mexicans built the interurban railroad system, and they were its most consistent users. But while the Mexicans continued to rely on the Red Cars, the Anglo population turned toward the automobile in increasing numbers. The rise and popularity of this new mode of transportation had a remarkable impact on the urban structure of Los Angeles. Auto registration soared, especially in the years after World War I. By the middle 1920s, 1 of every 7 Americanos owned an automobile, 1 of every 4 Californians were car owners, and in Los Angeles, hailed as the auto capital of the world, the rate was 1 car for every 2.25 people. Car owners had greater mobility; and as auto registration increased, the population naturally gravitated toward outlying areas. Like other cities around the country, Los Angeles annexed many of the new communities. A city of 100 square miles in 1910, Los Angeles claimed 441 square miles by 1930. As the population of the city spread, vast tracts of single-family homes emerged. By the 1920s, the auto had contributed not only to a mass movement of families to outlying areas, but also to the increasing dispersal of manufacturing industries. . . .

As the Mexican population shifted eastward, so did many of the social and religious centers involved with this group. The Brownson House Settlement, the oldest center for Mexican immigrants in Los Angeles, relocated its facilities in 1928 to Pleasant Avenue on the east side in order to continue to serve the Mexican population. . . .

By the late 1920s the community of Belvedere, with thirty thousand residents of Mexican descent, had the largest concentration of Mexicans in the Los Angeles metropolis, surpassing other communities closer to the central core such as Boyle Heights and Lincoln Heights. Mexicans had begun to move to Belvedere in the late 1910s, a period when lots and houses there were significantly cheaper than in Boyle Heights, a Jewish and Italian district at that time. Like Santa Ana, this eastside community was served by an interurban railway system that made movement into the city inexpensive. . . . Unlike the southwest communities of Los Angeles, where Mexicans and Blacks together constituted a majority, in Belvedere there were only 13 Black residents listed in the 1930 census. In Belvedere in 1920, native White residents and Whites of mixed foreign parentage were equally represented. The fact that there were few Blacks on the east side presumably increased the job opportunities for Mexican workers, especially workers seeking jobs in the brick, lumber, clay, and heavy manufacturing plants in the adjacent districts.

As industries set up new locations in the communities east and south of Belvedere, Mexican residents filled an important labor void. Companies restricted to areas outside of the residential sections, such as meat packing, steel, and auto assembly, as well as those companies seeking to remain near the more extensive railroad lines of the east side, established manufacturing headquarters in Vernon, Maywood, Commerce, Bell, and Cudahy. These plants gave Mexicans employment opportunities in industry-related jobs. Yet, despite what seemed to be an abundance of employment options, social worker Mary Lanigan noted that second-generation Mexicans in Belvedere by the late 1920s remained disillusioned, having "become accustomed to segregation and (referring to) Americans as white people." They had come to understand, Lanigan wrote, "that there are certain types of jobs for Mexicans and certain kinds for Americans." As to integration, she concluded that "Americans have repulsed the Mexican immigrant in every step he has taken toward that goal." . . .

The rapid growth of Mexican businesses in the barrio, numbering about 239 in 1922, reflected a sense of permanency and dispelled the myth that Mexicans in Los Angeles contributed to the economy only through seasonal work. Most Mexican business establishments, at least up until World War I, operated in the Plaza community. As the Mexican community spilled over to the east side in the postwar years, many of the businesses followed, for they too faced the problem of higher rents and lack of space. Moreover, greater business opportunities awaited Mexicans in the new communities. This was especially true of neighborhood stores such as those selling groceries and tortillas. By 1920, ten of the sixty-six grocery stores owned by Mexicans were located on Brooklyn Avenue on the east side, and dozens more opened over the same period on streets near Brooklyn. The grocery business was the most popular one for Mexicans; grocery stores constituted one-fourth of all the commercial activity in the community. The next two most popular businesses for Mexicans in the twenties were restaurants and cleaning establishments. The popularity of these two businesses may have resulted from the presence of many single men in the barrios.

The Plaza area, however, continued to dominate in recreational and cultural activities. Mexican workers frequented pool halls, movie houses, and penny arcades of the downtown area. Mexican men especially favored the pool halls of North Main as gathering places. On a typical afternoon, some 150 men played pool or simply visited the pool halls of this area. The pool halls catered to particular ethnic groups; and although segregation policies did not prevail, as a rule, Mexicans preferred to gather in areas with others of their class and background. In the post-World War I period Mexicans frequently patronized four pool halls operated by Japanese. Additionally, five of the most popular Mexican theaters in the city were located on North Main. During the 1910s, the Hidalgo Theater drew the largest audiences. For one Saturday show, for example, an investigator reported that 525 customers packed the theater and that 75 percent of them were Mexican. . . .

While some of the outlying communities continued to attract Whites as well as Mexicans, district patterns of Mexican and White neighborhoods became clearly visible with increasing Mexican population. For example, in Watts, according to Clara G. Smith, "Main Street divided the community into two sections; north of Main Street became settled by white people, mostly those who segregated themselves, while the greater part south of Main Street was occupied mostly by the Mexicans and later by both Mexicans and Negroes." Although Mexicans resided in every district of Los Angeles, housing discrimination by Anglos against Mexicans prevailed in many southern California communities. Prior to World War I, Anglo residents of the Central Avenue District of the Plaza successfully resisted the "invasion" of Mexicans, as well as Blacks and Asians, through their own personal efforts or by the use of restrictive clauses in mortgage contracts. Further south in Watts, Smith concluded, "When the Mexican buys property in the white district, he becomes an outcast of his former group and is rejected by his American neighbors." . . .

In 1927 the Los Angeles Chamber of Commerce asked surrounding incorporated cities to report on such issues as population growth and industries. The responses recorded shed much light on the problem of segregation and the attitudes of community leaders toward the movement of Mexican residents to their districts. The coastal city of El Segundo stated in a boastful manner that its city "had no negroes or Mexicans." Lynwood, one of the new industrial areas southeast of the central area, reported in 1930: "Lynwood, being restricted to the white race, can furnish ample labor of the better class." Every city that wished to attract new settlers apparently felt compelled to congratulate itself on having few foreign-born or racially mixed groups. Long Beach, a community that in the late 1920s actually had a large Mexican population of nearly 13,000, advertised haughtily, "Long Beach has a population of 140,000—99 percent of whom are of the Anglo-Saxon race." . . .

The impact that segregation had on the Mexican residents is difficult to measure. Certainly some of the newcomers chose to live in ethnically segregated communities, and such selection may have made their adjustment to new lifestyles easier. At a conference dealing with the immigration question, Orfa Jean Shontz, a former referee of the Juvenile Court of Los Angeles, spoke about "Mexican Family Relations in a Changing Social Environment." In her opinion, raising children was certainly no easier in the United States than in Mexico and as a whole, she found Mexicans "as a class, the best mannered, the most obedient, and the least quarrelsome of the nationalities" in California. Mexican family life, under strain in a new urban industrial environment, seemed to hold together, because, as Shontz noted, "Mexicans have a universal respect for childhood and old age" and family relationships among them "are closer, warmer, and more sacred than with us." No doubt living in the barrio made it easier for Mexicans to maintain these relationships. . . .

With changing economic conditions, Mexicans also came to view their migration and settlement in new ways. In the pre–World War I years when jobs in industry were few and low-paying, many Mexicans discovered that only crowded and inadequate house courts accommodated their families. In the twenties, suburban developers found it profitable to cater to a lower-income market and pursued Mexican buyers. Although a smaller proportion of Mexicanos owned their own homes than native Anglo Americans and European immigrants, many nonetheless found in the new barrio of the east side at least a partial opportunity to make a better life for their families.

Southern Blacks' Migration to Chicago in the Early Twentieth Century

JAMES R. GROSSMAN

Busy caring for her elderly mother in early 1917, an Ellisville, Mississippi, woman paid little attention to the "mild stir about the North." Her husband left for Chicago in March, but few others in town were "taking seriously" the rumors concerning the migration. In May, however, a friend breathlessly returned from

From *Land of Hope: Chicago, Black Southerners, and the Great Migration* by James R. Grossman, excerpts from pp. 98–99, 123, 127, 138–40, 142, 145–50, 153–60. Copyright © 1989 University of Chicago Press. Reprinted by permission of the publisher.

An African-American Family Arriving in Chicago, c. 1915

Dressed in their best clothes and looking as resolute as any foreign immigrants, this family was one of thousands who took northbound trains out of Mississippi and other Deep South states to the North. In an environment in which social institutions discriminated against racial minorities, blacks often developed self-reliance within the context of family ties.

New Orleans, buzzing with news of "the rush there to get out of the city." Telling her of the "great promise of the North," he reviewed the reason people were giving for their departure. From her window she could see the northbound express trains "loaded with Negroes." She wrote to her husband, who confirmed that conditions in Chicago were "beyond belief." Unable to sell their property, she left anyway, organizing a club of twenty-six which accompanied her in mid-June. At the railroad station a policeman informed her group that they could not leave without permission. For the first time in her life she "talked back to a white person." Two days later she was in Chicago.

However idiosyncratic, this woman's experience highlights salient features of the migratory process. Many other migrants were as cautious as she and did not leave until they had corroborated early rumors. Others left as soon as the first piece of information reached town. Some made careful plans, writing to friends, relatives, or social agencies in Chicago; others left in haste, pausing only to raise money to purchase a railroad ticket. Some families migrated together, others temporarily separated. If some migrants left without incident, thousands of others had to evade obstacles created by southern whites reacting to the threat to their labor supply. Many black southerners journeyed directly to the North; others sojourned in southern cities. Not all migrants asserted themselves as immediately or forcefully as did the Ellisville woman when she "talked back" to a southern policeman; but more did something during the voyage or soon after arrival in the North to certify, if only symbolically, their sense of renewed hope. Whether they moved out of the Jim Crow car after the train crossed the Mason-Dixon line or sat next to a white rider in a Chicago streetcar, the migrants—sometimes quietly, sometimes exuberantly—tested and welcomed their new status.

 . . . The decision to go to Chicago, rather than to New York, Detroit, or one of many smaller northern communities, rested on a variety of factors, whose impact changed over time. The first from an area to leave for Chicago probably chose the city because of its position at the head of the Illinois Central [Railroad] and its particularly high visibility in the black South. Chicago's black baseball teams, its reputation as a center of black business enterprise, and its reputation based on visits from conventioneers, as well as mail-order catalogues which were found in homes in rural and urban communities, all complemented the monumental importance of the *Defender* [Chicago's black newspaper]. There were jobs in the city's mills and packinghouses, but there were jobs elsewhere too. Those who chose to go to Chicago went because they knew about those jobs and that particular city. This knowledge multiplied as migrants settled in Chicago. It is likely that eventually most black southerners who decided to go North—regardless of why they made that particular decision—chose a destination based largely on the presence of kin and townsfolk. . . .

Black southerners arriving in Chicago generally knew where to go once they walked out of the train station. Like their counterparts in New York who asked in Pennsylvania Station how to get to Harlem, most black migrants to Chicago upon alighting at the Illinois Central terminal requested directions to the South Side or to State Street. People whose friends, relatives, or townspeople had preceded them sought out specific addresses; those who had no idea where to go were likely to be directed to the South Side. Whites would assume that all blacks "belonged" in the ghetto; blacks would reason that bewildered newcomers might obtain assistance from black institutions while avoiding the danger of straying into hostile white neighborhoods. The logic of such advice suggests the significance—if not the visibility—of Chicago's color line, as well as the importance of various aspects of community within black Chicago. Shaped by both the circumscribing influences of the white city that surrounded it and the demands of the migrants and "Old Settlers" who inhabited it, the emerging "Black Metropolis" on the South Side divided along lines of class, region, and even age. But it remained a community nevertheless, unified by the implications of racial taxonomies.

In 1910, 78 percent of black Chicagoans lived on the South Side in a narrow strip of land known to whites as the Black Belt. Beginning at the edge of an industrial and warehouse district just south of the Loop (Chicago's central business district), black Chicago stretched southward along State Street for more than thirty blocks, remaining only a few blocks wide except at its northern end. The

1910 census counted 34,335 black residents in this growing ghetto, which was expanding slowly along its southern and eastern boundaries. . . .

. . . [B]lack institutional development contributed to the growing vitality and self-consciousness of the emerging black neighborhoods, making them attractive to blacks who preferred avoiding white people and their prejudices. What one historian of Detroit's black community has called the "push of discrimination" and "the pull of ethnocentrism" combined to impel black newcomers toward the ghetto. Exclusion aside, many migrants sought their first homes in areas populated by other blacks, where they could be more comfortable and find familiar institutions. This dynamic of choice and constraint, heavily influenced by economic factors, resembled the experience of European immigrants to Chicago during this period, but the differences were significant. Unfamiliarity with English made the ethnic neighborhood essential for many Europeans; blacks had no comparable imperative. White immigrants tended to live near workplaces; blacks dispersed in service occupations could not, and when they did obtain industrial employment they were excluded from neighborhoods adjoining Chicago's major industries. European newcomers lived near others of their nationality but usually in an ethnically diverse neighborhood that could hardly be described as a ghetto. Whether middle or working class, black Chicagoans were less likely than members of other ethnic groups to share public space across ethnic but within class boundaries. More than any other group, black Chicagoans occupied neighborhoods defined by permanent characteristics. Neither cultural assimilation nor economic mobility promised significantly wider choices.

The color line separated more than residence. State legislation prohibiting racial discrimination in schools, municipal services, and public accommodations was seldom enforced, and except on the streets and in the streetcars, blacks and whites seldom mingled. . . . On the whole, in 1915 black Chicagoans lived among black neighbors, sent their children to predominantly black schools, and were excluded from most establishments catering to whites.

Blacks occupied a similarly limited place in Chicago's booming economy. Fewer than one black male in twenty—and virtually no black females—worked in an occupation that might be described as managerial, professional, or proprietary; even many of these operated marginal businesses. Most workers were unskilled, and few worked in industry. . . . White immigrants from southern and eastern Europe had to accept the worst jobs in the city's industries, but blacks lacked access even to those positions. Sharing the racial attitudes of other Americans, industrialists in Chicago and other northern cities saw no reason to hire blacks when they had thousands of white immigrants to fill their factories. Blacks were considered to be useful as strikebreakers on occasion, but were generally discharged once the strike ended. . . . Chicago and other northern cities offered mainly service jobs to blacks, and between 1900 and 1910 the number of black servants in Chicago increased by six thousand, nearly half the city's increase in black population during that period. Men were likely to work as porters, waiters, servants, janitors, or elevator operators; two-thirds of all employed black women in 1910 were either servants or hand laundresses, with most of the others performing some other type of service.

Despite this apparent homogeneity, however, black Chicago—like other urban black communities—was divided along class lines. Severely truncated at the top, the class structure rested less on wealth or contemporary white definitions of occupational status (except at the highest levels) than on notions of "refinement" and "respectability" maintained by the upper and middle classes. The few professionals, some with professional connections to the white community, tended to dominate the highest rungs of the ladders, with businessmen close behind. Postal workers, Pullman porters, and servants employed by Chicago's wealthiest white families and best hotels constituted much of the solid middle class, which at its margins could also include other workers with stable incomes and some education. Stable income was at least as important as accumulated wealth, an uncommon phenomenon in the black community. "Respectability" frequently depended upon property ownership, membership in the appropriate organizations, and leisure habits. Church, club, or lodge activities conferred as well as signified status; symbols of respectability could include affiliation with one of the larger Baptist or African Methodist Episcopal Churches, a YMCA membership, or a Masonic identification card. Upper-class blacks, who considered themselves "refined" rather than merely "respectable," joined Episcopalian, Presbyterian, or Congregationalist churches, entertained according to specific rules of etiquette, and socialized only within a limited circle of acquaintances.

Until the late nineteenth century, this upper class—largely businessmen with white clientele and professionals who had won the respect of their white colleagues—dominated black Chicago's leadership and resisted attempts to organize alternative institutions catering to blacks. To do so, they argued, would imply their acceptance of segregation. . . .

Between 1900 and 1915 a new leadership emerged in black Chicago, one with an economic and political base in the black community. The emergence of the physical ghetto coincided with widening racial discrimination in Chicago and other northern cities, which forced blacks to make decisions circumscribed by their exclusion from a variety of social and economic institutions. Increasing separation opened new opportunities for business, professional, religious, and political leadership, and by the first decade of the twentieth century, a new middle class had begun to replace an older elite unwilling to sacrifice integrationist principles and therefore wary of separate black institutions and a ghetto economy. . . .

Adapting Booker T. Washington's doctrines of racial solidarity and self-help to the northern city, these business leaders and politicians deemphasized the fight to integration and dealt with discrimination by creating black institutions. Between 1890 and 1915 they established a bank, a hospital, a YMCA, an infantry regiment, effective political organizations, lodges, clubs, professional baseball teams, social service institutions, newspapers, and a variety of small businesses. . . .

Most black Chicagoans before the Great Migration, however, neither possessed . . . "cultivation and refinement" nor lived "shiftless, dissolute and immoral" lives. Laboring long days in menial occupations, they returned home tired. Women, especially, spent most of their waking hours working, as they had to combine traditional household chores with other employment. Nearly half of all black women in Chicago in 1910 worked outside the home (compared with slightly more than one-fourth of white women), and among poor families the proportion was even higher. Most of these people had migrated from the South and had found that whatever skills or hopes they carried with them, service occupations provided the only possibility of employment in Chicago. Their leisure activities offered respite from their backbreaking, low-status jobs. Enthusiastic worship and lively nightlife attracted the scorn of much of the middle class, but such activities already were central elements of what St. Clair Drake and Horace Cayton would later call "the world of the lower class" in black Chicago. By 1904 (if not earlier), the storefront churches later to be associated with the Great Migration had already begun to appear along State Street. Less spiritually inclined workers found release in petty gambling, the fellowship of the numerous saloons along the State Street "Stroll," or boisterous parties. . . .

It is difficult to determine what kind of reception migrants expected from this community. Most probably anticipated a warm welcome. Much of what they knew about Chicago had been filtered through sources that emphasized race consciousness and individual and racial accomplishment. Class tensions and divisions within the black community seldom found their way into the *Defender*. Similarly, information from friends and relatives who only recently had arrived in Chicago highlighted instead the contrasts between South and North, rural and urban. . . . Based on the information at their disposal, black southerners preparing to go to Chicago could logically envision a black community that was self-sufficient, fiercely militant, and eager to assist those of "the Race" in flight from southern oppression. Accordingly, many wrote hopefully to the *Defender*, Chicago Urban League, and Bethlehem Baptist Association for train fare, suitcases, and prearranged employment and housing. Chicago's black institutional leadership could not provide these resources, but it did offer useful assistance and services. The same network that had stimulated and facilitated migration could now smooth adjustment. As migration increased, the other part of the network—community and kin—would prove most useful to newcomers during their first days in the city.

This informal network helped many migrants to solve their first problem upon arrival—shelter. Earlier migrants, having provided essential information, and sometimes funds, to family and community members who followed them to Chicago, now supplied a different resource, as they helped newcomers find suitable temporary quarters. Frequently, they took friends, relatives, and former townsmen into their homes as lodgers. Women undertook the greatest part of this burden, continuing to play the connective and leadership roles that they had performed as visitors, correspondents, and club organizers. Some of these women did not need the extra rent money, but they felt obliged to assist friends and relatives whom they had encouraged to come north. Newcomers "stopping" at such houses not only secured interim housing, but spent their first few days in Chicago in a familiar social setting. The "lodger evil" frequently decried by reformers, who worried that households with too many adults threatened family morality, was also a crucial adaptive mechanism based on family and community ties. Given the economic strains on the urban black family, lodging could actually enhance family stability by permitting women to earn money while remaining home with their children.

Migrants arriving without such contacts, or whose friends either lacked the resources to help them or had themselves come to Chicago too recently to be useful as guides, had to rely on more formal channels in their initial search for housing. Some, especially women concerned about their vulnerability "in a large city by self among strangers," as one New Orleans woman put it, wrote ahead inquiring about housing or live-in domestic work. . . . These young women, like many others in their predicament, were sent by Travelers Aid representatives to the black YWCA branch. Many younger men, arriving destitute after riding freight trains north, ended up in a courtroom, where at least one judge . . . regularly referred them to the Chicago Urban League.

Although it distributed thousands of cards inviting any "Stranger in the City" to visit its office "if you want a place to live," the League did not operate any housing facilities. But it could provide institutional assistance by referring homeless migrants to appropriate institutions or offering them its "certified lodging list." . . .

It was fortunate that there were some black institutions to which migrants could turn in their search for interim lodging arrangements upon arrival, as they were denied access to the standard alternatives available to other newcomers to Chicago. Most lodging houses in the city, including the Salvation Army's Reliance Hotel, YMCA Hotel, Christian Industrial League, Dawes Hotel, and probably the Municipal Lodging Houses, turned blacks from their doors, despite stated policies of accepting anyone who could pay except "inebriated" applicants. . . .

If housing constituted one measurement of "bettering one's condition," Chicago was at best a flawed Promised Land. Migrants moved into houses and apartments in some of the city's most deteriorated neighborhoods. . . . But Chicago did seem to offer many migrants—especially those who arrived before 1919—better homes than they had left behind in the South. Although many newcomers never escaped the dilapidated dwellings located west of State Street, others somehow managed to secure more space, if only temporarily. . . . In some cases, however, migrants had to close off rooms to reduce heating costs in drafty old frame houses. A more popular alternative was to take in lodgers, which while easing the adjustment process by perpetuating kinship or community ties, could also cause overcrowding and tension. . . .

Although most migrants moved frequently after locating in Chicago, their ability to improve their housing facilities was limited. The small black ghetto expanded rapidly in 1917, but resistance soon formed along its eastern and western borders. . . .

The interaction of discrimination and rapidly rising demand for housing not only fueled racial tensions and frustrated migrants' hopes of progressively improving their living conditions; it structured the physical environment of blacks already resident in Chicago and contributed to their concerns over the impact of the Great Migration. Although most black Chicagoans recognized that the exodus from the South and the entrance into the industrial economy represented a step forward for black America, they were not necessarily eager to see the newcomers become their neighbors. Some of these Old Settlers tried to avoid the social consequences of the Great Migration by fleeing from neighborhoods affordable to newcomers. Housing discrimination, however, left most of the city inaccessible even to the few blacks whose incomes should have provided a wide range of alternatives. . . . Unlike white immigrants and their children who similarly worked to accumulate the resources to move to a "better" neighborhood, most black Chicagoans struggling for security, respectability, and an environment suited to raising children found their ambitions stymied. . . .

Whether more concerned about the welfare or the behavior of southerners new to their community, black Chicagoans could draw on only a limited fund of existing institutional resources to deal with problems posed by the influx. Even before the Great Migration, the *Defender* had justifiably rebuked the city's black leadership for insufficient attention to the development of social service and welfare organizations. The community did raise funds for the Phyllis Wheatley Association's home for stranded women, the Jane Dent Home for Aged and Infirm Colored People, Provident Hospital, the black YMCA, and two settlement houses, but few of these institutions existed primarily to serve the poor. . . .

The centerpiece of both black and white efforts to assist and influence the newcomers was the Chicago Urban League, which provided the bulk of the services most important to recent migrants. Established five years after its parent organization's founding in 1911, the Chicago chapter immediately focused on the "adjustment or assimilation" of the city's black migrants. . . . By 1919, the League could count more than twenty thousand people passing through its doors (not including repeat visits) in a twelve-month period, and statistics for the following year indicate that nearly half had "been in the city less than six months." . . . In the areas of employment, housing, social work, and relief, the Urban League quickly emerged as the leading social agency in the black community. . . .

Chicago's black middle-class residents assumed that the migrants had to be guided from the moment they stepped from the train. Mechanisms of social control in the South—church, lodge, gossip, and established customs—were weaker in Chicago, according to one Urban League official, and the migrants were thus more susceptible to dissolution and "disorganization." Ida B. Wells-Barnett lamented that migrants were first attracted to State Street, where "not a single uplifting influence" competed with the saloons, poolrooms, and cabarets. The attractions of State Street and the old vice district at the northern end of the Black Belt threatened the migrants' moral fiber and sobriety as well as the reputation of the community. For if the newcomers fell easily into degeneracy as many Old Settlers feared—and whites expected—they would reflect poorly upon the race. . . .

Mostly young men and women, the newcomers indulged in forms of public behavior characteristic of young urbanites, frequently antagonizing churchgoers with their apparent repudiation of conventional morality and attraction to the "gay life." They hung out on street corners, threw loud parties, dressed in the latest risqué fashions, and enjoyed the bright lights of the city's night life. Like the black alderman who wanted to "forbid loitering on street corners," community leaders objected to the tendency of young men and women to converse loudly, in language not entirely within the bounds of genteel respectability. Spending evenings in dance halls, and "dancing in a rareback fashion entirely too close to her partner to be anything other than VULGAR," aroused the *Defender's* ire as quickly as wearing tight or "abbreviated clothes." Young blacks could make a better impression on whites and improve themselves by partaking in the "wholesome recreation" available in community centers, churches, and the YMCA and YWCA. The propensity toward less acceptable forms of leisure activity probably had little to do with regional origins, but the conclusion that migrants were a large part of the "youth problem" was not unreasonable. The migrants were, on the whole, considerably younger than the adult black population already living in Chicago. Moreover, young blacks in Chicago were likely to be migrants, while older blacks were likely to have arrived before 1910. . . . The importance of bright lights and leisure opportunities had been central to migrants' image of Chicago as a "freer" environment than the rural or small town South. It seemed logical to the older, settled residents that recent arrivals would be particularly susceptible to the temptations of city life because of their unfamiliarity with its dangers and their supposedly undeveloped sense of self-discipline.

Much of what offended and embarrassed those concerned with maintaining standards, however, was identifiably southern. The Deep South origins of the wartime era migrants distinguished them not only from native Chicagoans, but also from those who had arrived earlier, usually from the Upper South. The differences were obvious to black Chicagoans: there was no mistaking the regional provenance of streetside barbecue stands and such icons as watermelon and head rags. Old Settlers grew particularly upset when newcomers publicly displayed their southern backgrounds. . . .

The reactions of migrants to these messages varied, especially according to class. Middle-class migrants sought acceptance into Chicago's black bourgeoisie and shared its attitudes toward street life, boisterous behavior, and the trappings of lower-class life. They no more wished to be associated with southern rural culture than did the Old Settlers. . . .

Other newcomers, however, found the lessons condescending and either unnecessary, unwelcome, or impractical. . . .

Migrants most actively resisted attempts to change aspects of their everyday life. Despite the pleas of Old Settlers to "give us more grand opera and less plantation melodies," the migrants did not leave their cultural baggage at the train station. "It's no difficult task to get people out of the South," the Chicago *Whip* remarked, "but you have a job on your hands when you attempt to get the South out of them." Although they brought with them fewer "plantation melodies" than their fearful neighbors imagined, migrants did carry to Chicago a form of music equally disliked by many Old Settlers—the boogie-woogie, which probably had its origins in the Mississippi Delta and was closely related to southern revival music. Newcomers also continued to sing southern blues and work songs. . . .

Along with retaining some of their southern customs, migrants also established their own institutions in Chicago. Many southern business and professional people followed members of their community to Chicago, hoping to retain their patronage. In 1919, approximately two-thirds of all black-owned businesses in Chicago were operated by what the *Whip* called "newcomers" and an Urban League spokesman called "migrants." Appealing to the newcomers' affinity for "down home" cooking, Ira Buy and R. L. Mason opened the Southern Home Cooking and Southern Lunch Room restaurants, while another establishment advertised "Good Things to Eat: Southern Cooking." . . .

Migrants also created more formal institutions that brought them together with others from their former homes. By 1921, newcomers from at least nine southern states could join clubs comprising natives of their home state. Many of these clubs met regularly or held social affairs. Frequently dominated by men and women who had migrated to Chicago before the Great Migration, the clubs also sometimes served as sources of organized support for black politicians, many of whom were among those earlier migrants. . . .

The most important institutions founded by the migrants were their churches. At first, the city's established black churches exerted special efforts to recruit newcomers, and thousands of migrants readily accepted the invitations. During 1917–18, each week's *Defender* carried messages from churches claiming that "newcomers are welcome," "strangers welcome," or "everyone is welcome and made to feel at home." . . .

The enthusiasm, however, was often temporary. Many migrants felt distinctly uncomfortable in Chicago's churches, because of both the size of some congregations and the style of worship acceptable to their ministers and laity. Migrants, especially those from the rural South, were accustomed to services accompanied by improvisational singing, "shouting," and other forms of active participation and demonstrative enthusiasm. These men and women reacted coolly to the intellectual sermons of such ministers as Reverend William Bradan of Berean Baptist Church, who refused to hold revivals and prohibited standing in his church during services. . . .

Migrants not only objected to the general atmosphere and style of worship characteristic of Chicago's "old line" churches, but also found that they did not receive the individual recognition to which they were accustomed. . . . In response, some chose to organize their own congregations, frequently joining with former townsmen or other dissatisfied migrants seeking an alternative. A church founded by a small group of migrants provided an additional link to their southern backgrounds and to other newcomers. . . .

This process of joining churches, splitting off, and starting new institutions was part of the adjustment process for many newcomers. By first entering large churches, newcomers could receive assistance in finding jobs and homes, meet other southerners, and perhaps glean useful information from announcements during services. Eventually migrants could decide whether to leave the large church for a more intimate congregation or try a different—but established— church. Chicago offered a seemingly endless variety, not only of denominations but of styles and sizes. . . . On the whole, migrants tended to stick with traditional denominations, although by 1919, twenty Holiness storefront churches presaged a trend which would increase that sect's membership to one-fifth of all black churchgoers within the next decade. . . .

As a mode of adaptation to the new environment, choosing a church—or starting a new one—symbolized the hopes of many migrants. Migration not only had increased the number of available options; those options included the chance to adjust to the urban North while still retaining aspects of one's southern cultural heritage. In addition, many could realistically look forward to "bettering their condition" either by joining a more prestigious church or by organizing and leading a new congregation. And all this took place within institutions controlled by blacks, relatively insulated from oppressive race relations. . . .

Indeed, religious life in black Chicago suggests the complexity of the

relationship between migrants and the city's established black community. If
many migrants felt alienated from Chicago's black religious institutions, others
remained within the large churches. The hostility that existed in individual
churches along lines of class and geographic origin was partially bridged by the
fact of membership in a single institution and the leadership of the minister. The
divisions both within and between churches existed alongside a significant degree of cohesion based upon identification as part of Chicago's black community
and its institutions. Although the fissures were significant, they were neither as
deep nor as wide as the gap separating whites and blacks. Migrants found a black
community that seemed snobbish and condescending at times; but nevertheless
the established community and the migrants shared one thing which set them all
off from the rest of Chicago—race.

✕ F U R T H E R   R E A D I N G

Josef Barton, *Peasants and Strangers: Italians, Rumanians, and Slovaks in an American
City, 1890–1950* (1975)

John Bodnar, *The Transplanted: A History of Immigrants in Urban America* (1985)

James Borchert, *Alley Life in Washington* (1980)

John Briggs, *An Italian Passage: Immigrants to Three American Cities, 1890–1930*
(1978)

Alberto Camarillo, *Chicanos in a Changing Society: From Mexican Pueblos to American
Barrios in Santa Barbara and Southern California, 1848–1930* (1979)

Dino Cinel, *From Italy to San Francisco: The Immigrant Experience* (1982)

Elizabeth Ewen, *Immigrant Women in the Land of Dollars: Life and Culture on the Lower
East Side, 1890–1925* (1985)

Mario García, *Desert Immigrants: The Mexicans of El Paso, 1880–1920* (1981)

Caroline Golab, *Immigrant Destinations* (1977)

Victor Green, *For God and Country: The Rise of Polish and Lithuanian Ethnic Consciousness in America* (1975)

Oscar Handlin, *The Uprooted* (1951)

Tamara Hareven, *Family Time and Industrial Time* (1982)

Kenneth Kusmer, *A Ghetto Takes Shape: Black Cleveland, 1870–1930* (1976)

Ewa Morawska, *For Bread with Butter: Life-Worlds of East Central Europeans in John-
ston, Pennsylvania, 1890–1940* (1985)

Gary R. Mormino and George E. Pozzetta, *The Immigrant World of Ybor City: Italians
and Their Latin Neighbors, 1885–1985* (1987)

Gilbert Osofsky, *Harlem: The Making of a Ghetto* (1966)

Thomas Philpott, *The Slum and the Ghetto: Neighborhood Deterioration and Middle-
Class Reform, Chicago, 1880–1920* (1978)

Elizabeth Pleck, *Black Migration and Poverty: Boston, 1865–1900* (1979)

Judith E. Smith, *Family Connections: A History of Italian and Jewish Immigrant Lives in
Providence, Rhode Island, 1900–1940* (1985)

Alan Spear, *Black Chicago: The Making of a Negro Ghetto* (1967)

Joe William Trotter, Jr., *Black Milwaukee: The Making of an Industrial Proletariat,
1915–1945* (1985)

Olivier Zunz, *The Changing Face of Inequality: Urbanization, Industrialization and Immigrants to Detroit, 1880–1920* (1982)

CHAPTER 7

Bosses and Reformers
at the Turn of the Century

※

The topic of urban politics has long fascinated historians, and no other period has provided more drama in urban politics than the closing decades of the nineteenth century and the beginning years of the twentieth, when notorious bosses supposedly battled for power with righteous reformers. Some scholars have even concluded that urban bosses and their political machines were uniquely American institutions; no other society, these historians argued, developed this kind of political organization, which was built by professional politicians on a base of popular loyalty, personal favors, and, according to some, mass fraud and thievery. Historians also have concluded that revulsion by the so-called better classes against the vulgarity and venality of machines spawned a moralistic, economy-minded reform movement dedicated to rooting out bossism and reclaiming the democratic process.

At first, bosses were seen as villains catering hypocritically to immigrants and other residents of the inner city. Reformers, in contrast, were heroes battling against forces of evil to establish true democracy and fairness. By the mid-twentieth century, some historians reversed the assessment, seeing bosses and machines as providing necessary services such as jobs, welfare, and legal assistance to poor people when no other government agency was willing or able to do so, while at the same time criticizing reformers for their elitist and thinly veiled anti-immigrant biases. Lately, however, other historians have asserted that the significance of bosses and reformers alike has been exaggerated—that their influence was less effective and durable than the impact of others who labored inside and outside city government to create institutions that tended to urban dwellers' needs. The personality of bosses such as Tammany Hall leader Richard Croker—candid, blunt, even mischievous—impresses and entertains, but is urban politics as simple and pragmatic as he would have one think? Can students looking back on the era spanning 1870 to 1920 believe that the ideals of honesty, efficiency, and economy that motivated reformers were completely admirable? Given the complex ethnic, racial, religious, and socioeconomic composition of cities that previous chapters have confirmed, what factors had to be taken into account in urban policymaking during this period?

�֍ D O C U M E N T S

The documents in this section illustrate various aspects of and opinions about boss politics and reform. The first excerpt, from the assessment of American politics by the British writer and observer James, Lord Bryce, established the critical stereotype of bosses that galvanized reformers into action against political machines and influenced intellectual opinion of boss politics for the next several generations. Bryce's comments were published about the same time as the second document, taken from the famous investigation of police corruption in New York City chaired by New York State senator Clarence Lexow. The investigation revealed various forms of criminal and political corruption, much of it associated with the Tammany Hall machine, which reformers believed infested the city in the late nineteenth century. The selection includes testimony from an Italian merchant involved in police payoffs. The third document, written by Richard Croker, one of the most notorious bosses of the turn-of-the-century city, offers a defense of bossism from an insider's point of view. Croker explains his version of the machine's ability to prevail in the city despite the efforts of reformers, many of them rural Republicans, to discredit it. The final set of documents shows how reformers put much stock in changing the form of government so as to create administration based on expertise rather than on political connections. These documents, in describing reform efforts in two growing Texas cities, also reveal that movements for municipal reform, particularly changing the organization of city government, arose in other cities besides those in the Northeast and Midwest.

Lord Bryce on Rings and Bosses, 1895

In a Ring there is usually some one person who holds more strings in his hand than do the others. Like them he has worked himself up to power from small beginnings, gradually extending the range of his influence over the mass of workers, and knitting close bonds with influential men outside as well as inside politics, perhaps with great financiers or railway magnates, whom he can oblige, and who can furnish him with funds. At length his superior skill, courage, and force of will make him, as such gifts always do make their possessor, dominant among his fellows. An army led by a council seldom conquers; it must have a commander-in-chief, who settles disputes, decides in emergencies, inspires fear or attachment. The head of the Ring is such a general. He dispenses places, rewards the loyal, punishes the mutinous, concocts schemes, negotiates treaties. He generally avoids publicity, preferring the substance to the pomp of power, and is all the more dangerous because he sits, like a spider, hidden in the midst of his web. He is a Boss.

Although the career I have sketched is that whereby most Bosses have risen to greatness, some attain it by a shorter path. There have been brilliant instances of persons stepping at once on to the higher rungs of the ladder in virtue of their audacity and energy, especially if coupled with oratorical power. The first theatre of such a man's successes may have been the stump rather than the primary: he will then become potent in conventions, and either by hectoring or by plausible address, for both have their value, spring into popular favor, and make himself necessary to the party managers. It is of course a gain to a Ring to have among them a man of popular gifts, because he helps to conceal the odious features of their rule, gilding it by his rhetoric, and winning the applause of the masses who stand outside the circle of workers. However, the position of the rhetorical boss is less firmly rooted than that of the intriguing boss, and there have been instances of his suddenly failing, to rise no more.

A great city is the best soil for the growth of a Boss, because it contains the largest masses of manageable voters as well as numerous offices and plentiful opportunities for jobbing. But a whole State sometimes falls under the dominion of one intriguer. To govern so large a territory needs high abilities; and the State boss is always an able man, somewhat more of a politician, in the European sense, than a city boss need be. He dictates State nominations, and through his lieutenants controls State and sometimes Congressional conventions, being in diplomatic relations with the chief city bosses and local rings in different parts of the State. His power over them mainly springs from his influence with the Federal executive and in Congress. He is usually, almost necessarily, a member of Congress, probably a senator, and can procure, or at any rate can hinder, such legislation as the local leaders desire or dislike. The President cannot ignore him, and the President's ministers, however little they may like him, find it worth while to gratify him with Federal appointments for persons he recommends, because the local votes he controls may make all the difference to their own prospects of getting some day a nomination for the presidency. Thus he uses his Congressional position to secure State influence, and his State influence to strengthen his Federal position. . . .

It must not be supposed that the members of Rings, or the great Boss himself, are wicked men. They are the offspring of a system. Their morality is that of their surroundings. They see a door open to wealth and power, and they walk in. The obligations of patriotism or duty to the public are not disregarded by them, for these obligations have never been present to their minds. A State boss is usually a native American and a person of some education, who avoids the grosser forms of corruption, though he has to wink at them when practised by his friends. He may be a man of personal integrity. A city boss is often of foreign birth and humble origin; he has grown up in an atmosphere of oaths and cocktails: ideas of honour and purity are as strange to him as ideas about the nature of the currency and the incidence of taxation: politics is merely a means for getting and distributing places. "What," said an ingenuous delegate at one of the National Conventions in Chicago in 1880, "what are we here for except the offices?" It is no wonder if he helps himself from the city treasury and allows his minions to do so. Sometimes he does not rob, and, like Clive, wonders at his own moderation. And even he improves as he rises in the world. Like a tree growing out of a dust heap, the higher he gets, the cleaner do his boughs and leaves become. America is a country where vulgarity is sealed off more easily than in England, and where the general air of good nature softens the asperities of power. Some city bosses are men from whose decorous exterior and unobtrusive manners no one would divine either their sordid beginnings or their noxious trade. As for the State boss, whose talents are probably greater to begin with, he must be of very coarse metal if he does not take a polish from the society of Washington.

A city Ring works somewhat as follows. When the annual or biennial city or State elections come round, its members meet to discuss the apportionment of offices. Each may desire something for himself, unless indeed he is already fully provided for, and anyhow desires something for his friends. The common sort are provided for with small places in the gift of some official, down to the place of a policeman or doorkeeper or messenger, which is thought good enough for a common "ward worker." Better men receive clerkships or the promise of a place in the custom-house or post-office to be obtained from the Federal authorities. Men still more important aspire to the elective posts, seats in the State legislature, a city aldermanship or commissionership, perhaps even a seat in Congress. All the posts that will have to be filled at the coming election are considered with the object of bringing out a party ticket, i.e. a list of candidates to be supported by the party at the polls when its various nominations have been successfully run through the proper conventions. Some leading man, or probably the Boss himself, sketches out an allotment of places; and when this allotment has been worked out fully, it results in a Slate, i.e. a complete draft list of candidates to be proposed for the various offices. It may happen that the slate does not meet everybody's wishes. Some member of the ring or some local boss—most members of a ring are bosses each in his own district, as the members of a cabinet are heads of the departments of state, or as the cardinals are bishops of dioceses near Rome and priests and deacons of her parish churches—may complain that he and his friends have not been adequately provided for, and may demand more. In that case the slate will probably be modified a little to ensure good feeling and content; and will then be presented to the Convention.

. . . Discipline is very strict in this army. Even city politicians must have a moral code and moral standard. It is not the code of an ordinary unprofessional citizen. It does not forbid falsehood, or malversation, or ballot stuffing, or "repeating." But it denounces apathy or cowardice, disobedience, and above all, treason to the party. Its typical virtue is "solidity," unity of heart, mind, and effort among the workers, unquestioning loyalty to the party leaders and devotion to the party ticket. He who takes his own course is a Kicker or Bolter; and is punished not only sternly but vindictively. The path of promotion is closed to him; he is turned out of the primary, and forbidden to hope for a delegacy to a convention; he is dismissed from any office he holds which the Ring can command. Dark stories are even told of a secret police which will pursue the culprit who has betrayed his party, and of mysterious disappearances of men whose testimony against the Ring are feared. Whether there is any foundation for such tales I do not undertake to say. But true it is that the bond between the party chiefs and their followers is very close and very seldom broken. What the client was to his patron at Rome, what the vassal was to his lord in the Middle Ages, that the heelers and workers are to their boss in these great transatlantic cities. They render a personal feudal service, which their suzerain repays with the gift of a livelihood; and the relation is all the more cordial because the lord bestows what costs him nothing, while the vassal feels that he can keep his post only by the favour of the lord.

European readers must again be cautioned against drawing for themselves too dark a picture of the Boss. He is not a demon. He is not regarded with horror even by those "good citizens" who strive to shake off his yoke. He is not necessarily either corrupt or mendacious, though he grasps at place, power, and wealth. He is a leader to whom certain peculiar social and political conditions have given a character dissimilar from the party leaders whom Europe knows. It is worth while to point out in what the dissimilarity consists.

A Boss needs fewer showy gifts than a European demagogue. His special theatre is neither the halls of the legislature nor the platform, but the committee-room. A power of rough and ready repartee, or a turn for florid declamation, will help him; but he can dispense with both. What he needs are the arts of intrigue and that knowledge of men which teaches him when to bully, when to cajole, whom to attract by the hope of gain, whom by appeals to party loyalty. Nor are so-called "social gifts" unimportant. The lower sorts of city politicians congregate in clubs and barrooms; and as much of the cohesive strength of the smaller party organizations arises from their being also social bodies, so also much of the power which liquor dealers exercise is due to the fact that "heelers" and "workers" spend their evenings in drinking places, and that meetings for political purposes are held there. Of the 1007 primaries and conventions of all parties held in New York City preparatory to the elections of 1884, 633 took place in liquor saloons. A Boss ought therefore to be hail fellow well met with those who frequent these places, not fastidious in his tastes, fond of a drink and willing to stand one, jovial in manners and ready to oblige even a humble friend.

The aim of a Boss is not so much fame as power, and not so much power over the conduct of affairs as over persons. Patronage is the sort of power he seeks, patronage understood in the largest sense in which it covers the disposal of lucrative contracts and other modes of enrichment as well as salaried places. The dependents who surround him desire wealth, or at least a livelihood; his business is to find this for them, and in doing so he strengthens his own position. It is as the bestower of riches that he holds his position, like the leader of a band of condottieri in the fifteenth century.

The interest of a Boss in political questions is usually quite secondary. Here and there one may be found who is a politician in the European sense, who, whether sincerely or not, purports and professes to be interested in some principle or measure affecting the welfare of the country. But the attachment of the ringster is usually given wholly to the concrete party, that is to the men who compose it, regarded as office-holders or office-seekers; and there is often not even a profession of zeal for any party doctrine. As a noted politician happily observed to a friend of mine, "You know, Mr. R., there are no politics in politics." Among bosses, therefore, there is little warmth of party spirit. The typical boss regards the boss of the other party much as counsel for the plaintiff regards counsel for the defendant. They are professionally opposed, but not necessarily personally hostile. Between bosses there need be no more enmity than results from the fact that the one has got what the other wishes to have. Accordingly it sometimes happens that there is a good understanding between the chiefs of opposite parties in cities; they will even go the length of making (of course secretly) a joint "deal," i.e. of arranging for a distribution of offices whereby some of the friends of one shall get places, the residue being left for the friends of the other. A well-organized city party has usually a disposable vote which can be so cast under the directions of the managers as to effect this, or any other desired result. The appearance of hostility must, of course, be maintained for the benefit of the public; but as it is for the interest of both parties to make and keep these private bargains, they are usually kept when made, though of course it is seldom possible to prove the fact.

The real hostility of the Boss is not to the opposite party, but to other factions within his own party. . . .

It has been pointed out that rings and bosses are the product not of democracy, but of a particular form of democratic government, acting under certain peculiar conditions. They belong to democratic government, as the old logicians would say, not *simpliciter* but *secundum quid:* they are not of its essence, but are merely separable accidents. We have seen that these conditions are—

The existence of a Spoils System (= paid offices given and taken away for party reasons).

Opportunities for illicit gains arising out of the possession of offices.

The presence of a mass of ignorant and pliable voters.

The insufficient participation in politics of the "good citizens."

If these be the true causes or conditions producing the phenomenon, we may expect to find it most fully developed in the places where the conditions exist in fullest measure, less so where they are more limited, absent where they do not exist.

A short examination of the facts will show that such is the case.

It may be thought that the Spoils System is a constant, existing everywhere, and therefore not admitting of the application of this method of concomitant variations. That system does no doubt prevail over every State of the Union, but it is not everywhere an equally potent factor, for in some cities the offices are much better paid than in others, and the revenues which their occupants control are larger. In some small communities the offices, or most of them, are not paid at all. Hence this factor also may be said to vary.

We may therefore say with truth that all of the four conditions above named are most fully present in great cities. Some of the offices are highly paid; many give facilities for lucrative jobbing. The voters are so numerous that a strong and active organization is needed to drill them; the majority so ignorant as to be easily led. The best citizens are engrossed in business and cannot give to political work the continuous attention it demands. Such are the phenomena of New York, Philadelphia, Chicago, Brooklyn, St. Louis, Cincinnati, San Francisco, Baltimore, and New Orleans. In these cities Ring-and-bossdom has attained its amplest growth, overshadowing the whole field of politics.

The Lexow Commission on Criminal and Political Corruption in New York City, 1895

The results of the investigation up to this point may . . . be properly summarized in the general statement that it has been conclusively shown that in a very large number of election districts of the city of New York, almost every conceivable crime against the elective franchise was either committed or permitted by the police, invariably in the interest of the dominant Democratic organization of the city of New York, commonly called Tammany Hall.

. . . The testimony . . . showed . . . an extraordinary disinclination on the part of the police, so efficient in other respects, to display any desire or activity in the suppression of certain descriptions of vice and crime, a disinclination so strong that others attempting to perform that function found the police arrayed against them and experienced greater embarrassment from this circumstance than from any difficulty connected with the suppression of the vice itself. It indicated the amazing condition that in most of the precincts of the city, houses of ill-repute, gambling houses, policy shops, pool rooms and unlawful resorts of a similar character were being openly conducted under the eyes of the police, without attempt at concealment, so publicly, in fact, that the names of the persons and the street numbers of the houses were not only known throughout the community, but were published in the daily prints, and yet they remained open and ostentatiously flourished.

Some of the abuses which have been shown to prevail will now be specifically referred to.

Blackmail

. . . The nature of the offense is such as to render its proof by direct testimony a matter of great difficulty. The assumed bad character of the person paying blackmail, the difficulty of obtaining admissions, and then of substantiating such statements by corroborative evidence were elements of peculiar embarrassment. It is due largely to these circumstances that the police for many years have been able to ply this traffic with substantial impunity, and with a reckless disregard of decency, based largely upon the assumption that the only witnesses against them would receive no credence from either court or public.

Disorderly Houses

. . . The testimony upon this subject, taken as a whole, establishes conclusively the fact that this variety of vice was regularly and systematically licensed by the police of the city. The system had reached such a perfection in detail that the inmates of the several houses were numbered and classified and a ratable charge placed upon each proprietor in proportion to the number of inmates, or in cases of houses of assignation the number of rooms occupied and the prices charged, reduced to a monthly rate, which was collected within a few days of the first of each month during the year. . . .

The evidence establishes, furthermore, that not only the proprietors of disorderly houses paid for their illegal privileges, but the outcasts of society paid patrolmen on post for permission to solicit on the public highways, dividing their gains with them, and, often, as appears by proof, when brought before the police magistrates and committed to the penitentiary for disorderly conduct in default of bail, they compounded their sentence, and secured bail by paying $10 to $15 to the clerk of the court, or his agents, and were then released again to ply their calling and to become victimized as before. . . .

Gambling

The various forms of gambling testified to before your committee were pool-rooms, policy shops, and what is ordinarily understood as gambling.

The evidence is conclusive that with reference to this class of vice the police occupied substantially the same position as they did with respect to disorderly houses.

The policy business seems to have been conducted on a vast scale and under well-understood geographical limitations, each subdivision being assigned to certain favored individuals known as "policy kings," who backed with capital and ran the shops in the particular districts assigned to them. . . .

It seems clear from the evidence that this division of territory was largely for the benefit of the police, insuring a more rapid and easier collection of the tribute to be paid, the "policy king" to whom a particular district had been assigned paying in bulk at the rate of $15 per shop for all the shops running in such district or districts. . . .

Violation of the Excise Law

The position of those who violate the provisions of the excise law is somewhat peculiar. It appears that until some time in 1892 they paid a regular stipend to the police, either for protection in the violation of the law, or for immunity from police interference in respect to the conduct of their business on the border line between legitimate and illegitimate practice. . . .

Detectives, Pawnbrokers and Thieves

It has been conclusively shown that an understanding existed between headquarters' detectives, pawnbrokers and thieves, by which stolen property may be promptly recovered by the owner on condition that he repay the pawnbroker the amount advanced on the stolen property. In every such case, which appears in evidence, the detective seems to have acted rather in the interest of securing the pawnbroker's advances than of securing the absolute return of the stolen property. . . .

In almost every instance it also appears that the detective, acting between the owner and the pawnbroker, receives substantial gratuities from the owner of the property for the work done in his official capacity. . . . The reasonable conclusion deducible from the evidence, establishes the prevalence of the custom that in order to secure the return of stolen properties, a donation or reward must be paid to the headquarters' detective.

. . . Serapio Arteaga, called as a witness on behalf of the State, being duly sworn, testified as follows: . . .

Q. Mr. Arteaga, what countryman are you?

A. Sir?

Q. Where were you born?

A. In Cuba.

Q. How long have you lived in this city?

A. I have been here since 1851.

Q. In this city?

A. Yes, sir.

Q. In 1891 did you open a saloon in this city?

A. Yes.

Q. Whereabouts?

A. Three hundred and fifty-two Eighth avenue.

Q. And near what street is that?

A. Between Twenty-seventh and Twenty-eighth streets.

Q. Speak loudly, please.

A. Between Twenty-seventh and Twenty-eighth streets.

Q. Did you procure a license for the saloon?

A. Yes, sir.

Q. From the excise board?

A. Yes, sir.

Q. And you opened it as a billiard saloon and liquor store?

A. Yes, sir.

Q. Subsequently did you endeavor to secure a concert hall license?

A. No, sir.

Q. Did you try to secure one?

A. I did; yes, sir.

Q. Was it refused to you?

A. By Mayor Grant; yes, sir.

Q. After that did you run the place as a concert hall?

A. I did, sir.

Q. Before opening it as a concert hall, did you see any police official in that precinct?

A. I did, sir . . .

Q. Where did you see him?

A. At the station-house in the office.

Q. Was it Captain Price?

A. I could not be sure of the name; if I saw the gentleman I would know him.

Q. What time did you see him?

A. In the afternoon.

Q. How did you come to go there?

A. One of my customers told me if I saw him, he would arrange for me to open a concert saloon without a license.

Q. When you went there was the captain in?

A. Yes.

Q. Tell the committee the conversation you had with the captain, stating as fully as you can remember, what you said to him, and what he said to you?

A. I was there a very short time, because I asked him if he could help me get a license from Mayor Grant, he said he could not that he couldn't do anything for me in that respect, but I could see the ward detective and see what he could do for me.

Q. Did he name the ward detective.

A. Yes, sir.

Q. What was the name?

A. Wagner.

Q. What is the first name?

A. I don't know; a tall man of middle age.

Q. Go on and tell what the captain said.

A. Of course I left the station house. . . .

Q. Then what did you do?

A. He came to me without my looking for him.

Q. Wagner came to your place of business?

A. Yes, sir; and he took me into Twenty-eighth street, and I had a conversation.

Q. In the street?

A. In the street; yes, sir.

Q. What did he say to you?

A. Well, I asked him if he could procure the license for me; and he said, "No," that I should open the concert.

Q. Without a license?

A. Without a license.

Q. What did you say to that?

A. He wanted to know how much I could pay for it, and I said, I could not pay very much, and that I could pay about $50 a month; and of course in a few days I was ready to open, and I gave him the $50, and he came again, and I gave him the $50. . . .

Q. Did you give it to him in the place, or how?

A. In the place.

Q. In an envelope?

A. No; I shook hands with him, and left it in his hand.

Q. You had the bills in your hands, and came up and shook hands with him, and when you got through shaking hands, he had the bills and you did not?

A. I had nothing.

Boss Richard Croker Defends Tammany Hall, 1892

No political party can with reason expect to obtain power, or to maintain itself in power, unless it be efficiently organized. Between the aggressive forces of two similar groups of ideas, one entertained by a knot of theorists, the other enunciated by a well-compacted organization, there is such a difference as exists between a mob and a military battalion. The mob is fickle, bold, and timid by turns, and even in different portions it is at the same time swayed by conflicting emotions. In fact, it is a mere creation of emotion, while the drilled and compacted battalion is animated and supported by purpose and scientific plan. It has leaders, and these leaders are known to every man in the ranks and possess their confidence. It is thus that a single company of infantry is able to quell almost any popular outbreak in a city; and a regiment is completely master of the situation,

Tammany Hall Clubhouse, 14th Street, New York City

This building served as the headquarters for Richard Croker and other Tammany bosses. Supervising a well-oiled political machine required not just a strong personality but highly developed administrative skills and loyal subordinates. Croker drew on these qualities to build a powerful political organization in the early twentieth century. He used this building as his palace and required his aides to treat him with utmost deference.

even if it be outnumbered by the malcontents in the proportion of ten or twenty to one.

The City of New York to-day contains a political organization which, in respect of age, skillful management, unity of purpose, devotion to correct principles, public usefulness, and finally, success, has no superior, and, in my opinion, no equal in political affairs the world over. I mean the *Tammany Democracy.* I do not propose to defend the Tammany organization; neither do I propose to defend sunrise as an exhibition of celestial mechanics; nor a democratic form of government as an illustration of human liberty at its best. In the campaign of 1891 almost the only argument used by the Republicans against the Democrats was the assertion that Flower was the candidate of a corrupt political club, and that club was named Tammany. Tammany was accused of every vice and crime known to Republican orators; it was a fountain-head of corruption; it was because of it that every farmer throughout the State could not at once pay off his mortgages; it took forty millions annually from the citizens of New York and gave them nothing in exchange for it. To the credit of the Democrats let us note the fact that, while this torrent of abuse was being poured upon the heads of voters, Democrats did as the inhabitants of Spain are said to do when the clouds are opened,—"they let it rain." Nobody apologized for the misdeeds of the alleged malefactor; the Democrats went before the people on legitimate issues, and the result of the affair was expressed in the figures, 47,937 majority. I doubt if the Democracy would have fared anything like as well if they had defended or apologized or explained away. "He who excuses himself accuses himself" is a time-worn proverb. They let Mr. Fassett shout himself hoarse over "Tammany corruption," and they won the victory.

In fact, such a defensive attitude would have been wholly at variance with the basis on which the Tammany Democracy acts. A well-organized political club is made for the purpose of aggressive warfare. It must move, and it must always move forward against its enemies. If it makes mistakes, it leaves them behind and goes ahead. If it is encumbered by useless baggage of half-hearted or traitorous camp-followers, it cuts them off and goes ahead. While it does not claim to be exempt from error, it does claim to be always aiming at success by proper and lawful methods, and to have the good of the general community always in view as its end of effort. Such an organization has no time or place for apologies or excuses; and to indulge in them would hazard its existence and certainly destroy its usefulness.

The city and county of New York comprise a population of nearly two millions and furnish the business arena for near-by residents who represent two millions more. The political party, then, that is uppermost in New York legislation locally for the largest municipal constituency on the planet, except one. The task is clearly one of enormous magnitude, and demands a combination of skill, enterprise, knowledge, resolution, and what is known as "executive ability," which cannot be at once made to order, and cannot be furnished by any body of theorists, no matter how full may be their pockets or how righteous may be their intentions. Since the Whig party went out of existence the Democrats have administered the affairs of New York County, rarely even losing the mayorality [*sic*] except on personal grounds; always having the majority in the Board of Aldermen, and as a rule the Sheriff's and County Clerk's offices. And at the same time the guiding force of the New York Democracy has proceeded from the Tammany organization.

As one of the members of this organization, I simply do what all its members are ready to do as occasion offers, and that is, to stand by its principles and affirm its record. We assert, to begin with, that its system is admirable in theory and works excellently well in practice.

Coincident with the plan that all the Assembly districts shall be thoroughly looked after by experienced leaders who are in close touch with the central committees, is the development of the doctrine that the laborer is worthy of his hire; in other words, that good work is worth paying for, and in order that it may be good must be paid for. The affairs of a vast community are to be administered. Skillful men must administer them. These men must be compensated. The principle is precisely the same as that which governs the workings of a railway, or a bank, or a factory; and it is an illustration of the operation of sophistries and unsound moralities, so much in vogue among our closet reformers, that any persons who have outgrown the kindergarten should shut their eyes to this obvious truth. Now, since there must be officials, and since these officials must be paid, and well paid, in order to insure able and constant service, why should they not be selected from the membership of the society that organizes the victories of the dominant party?

In my opinion, to ask this question is to answer it. And I add that the statement made by the enemies of Tammany that "Tammany stands by its friends," is, in fact, praise, although intended for abuse. Tammany *does* stand by its friends, and it always will until some such change occurs in human affairs as will make it praiseworthy and beneficial that a man or an association should stand by his or its enemies. We are willing to admit that the logical result of this principle of action would be that all the employees of the city government, from the Mayor to the porter who makes the fire in his office, should be members of the Tammany organization. This would not be to their discredit. And if any one of them commits a malfeasance, he is just as responsible to the *people* as though he were lifted bodily out of the "Union League" or some transient "Citizens' Reform Association," and he will at once find himself outside of the Tammany membership also.

Fearfully and wonderfully made are the tales that are sent out into the rural districts touching the evil effects of "Tammany rule." The trembling countryman on arriving in New York expects to fall into a quagmire of muddy streets, and while struggling through these quicksands he fears the bunco man on one side and the sandbagger on the other. Reaching some hotel, he counts on being murdered in his bed unless he double-lock his door. That his landlord should swindle him is a foregone conclusion. And when no adventure happens, and he reaches home in safety, he points to himself, among his neighbors, as a rare specimen of a survival of the dangers that accompany the sway of a Democratic majority in New York.

The facts are that New York is a centre to which the criminal element of the entire country gravitates, simply because it offers at once a lucrative field for crime and a safe hiding-place. Therefore, to preserve social order and "keep the peace" in New York demands more ability and more policemen than are required in country solitude. It is safe to say that any right-minded citizen who attends to his own affairs and keeps proper company and proper hours is as safe in New York as in any part of the globe, the most violently Republican township of St. Lawrence County not excepted. Our streets are clean and are in good order as to the paving, except where certain corporations tear them up and keep their rents gaping. Our city is well watered, well lighted, and well parked. It is conceded that we have the best police and fire departments in the world. Our docks are being rapidly improved, and will compare, when completed, with the Liverpool and London docks. Our tax-rate is lower than that of dozens of other American cities whose affairs are not nearly so well administered. Nor is the tax-rate low because the assessed values are high. If any real-estate owner claims that his property is overvalued, you can silence him at once by offering to buy it at the valuation. Practical real-estate owners know that the county of New York does *not* over-assess its property-owners.

That the Tammany Hall Democracy will largely aid in organizing victory for the national ticket next November is beyond question. The national Democracy is free to choose whatever candidate it may prefer. Tammany has no desire to dic-tate or control the choice; its part in the conflict is to elect the candidate after he shall have been named. No matter what Republican majorities may come down to the Harlem River from the interior of the State, we propose to meet and drown them with eighty-five thousand majority from New York and Kings.

Municipal Reform in Two Texas Cities, 1914

City-Commission Government in Houston

Simplicity may very properly be regarded as the cornerstone of the commission form of municipal government. A concise, easily understood frame of govern-ment takes the place of a complicated one, or, what is worse still, a long series of conflicting, overlayering, often antiquated and usually complex, acts of assembly. . . .

Simplicity and directness beget efficiency in the hands of competent men. Mayor H. B. Rice, of the Houston Commission, one of the oldest commissioners in point of service, having been inaugurated in 1905, in an address a few years since, showed how a simple form of government worked out in practice.

"Here is one of, if not the strongest points in the commission government. In the city of Houston, with a majority of the aldermen always in session, business of the people can be, and is, attended to at a moment's notice. To show the prac-tical applications of the system, there is really no need of petition to the city coun-cil at their regular weekly meetings. Any citizen, or citizens, who want a street paved, taxes adjusted, nuisances abated, etc. have only to call at the mayor's of-fice and have his or their matters promptly adjusted. After a patient hearing, the matter is decided by the council in presence of the applicant. . . .

"To demonstrate, I will cite an incident that happened several months ago. A gentleman, a nonresident of Houston, whose home was in a Western state, owned some property in our city, and the property had been recently taken into the city limits. Investigating his assessment, he found that his property had been placed at a much higher valuation than that of his neighbors. Being a stranger, he called upon one of Houston's leading attorneys and asked his advice how to proceed for relief. The attorney suggested that they step over to the mayor's office and have the matter corrected. The owner of the land thought it would be wiser for the lawyer to get some of his friends to sign a petition to the council, so that it would have some weight with the authorities. The attorney replied that this mode of procedure was entirely unnecessary, as Houston now had a business government.

They called at my office, stated their mission. I sent for the tax collector, and in an hour the stranger had his matter adjusted and his tax receipt in his pocket."

Such a result would not be possible under the complicated system of checks and balances based on a more or less, and usually less, accurately determined division of powers. The commission form of municipal government tends, if properly administered, to eliminate the middleman, whether the lawyer, the lobbyist, or the professional politician, who, under the old order, and still in the large number of places, is a necessity. We have the middleman of these several classes now because we need at hand some one who "knows the ropes," and some one who knows how to unravel the red tape and the complications in the interest of getting things done. . . .

In an address before Chicago Association of Commerce, Mayor Rice . . . describes the results of commission rule in his city thus:

"I call your attention to the fact that during more than five years of this government in Houston, no alderman or commissioner has ever made a speech or addressed the council. The business of the city is conducted daily like any other business concern, and when they meet in public session on Monday afternoon, comfortably to law, it is merely to legalize and make record of their weekly business transactions. The length of the public meetings ranges from five to fifteen minutes."

In 1905 the price of gas was $1.50 per thousand. To-day it is $1.05 and next year $1, and the company pays one per cent annually upon its gross receipts. In 1905 the price of arc lights was $80 per year; now it is $70 per year. The telephone companies claimed that they did not need a franchise from cities in Texas, yet they were made to conform to the law, and they pay one percent to the city upon their gross receipts.

In 1906 the city of Houston purchased the water plant from a private corporation, the Houston Water Works Company, and paid $901,000 for it. The source of supply is artesian wells in the heart of the city. At the time of purchase the private corporation was charging 50 cents per thousand meter rate for water, and often pumping from the stream which flows through Houston, thus not giving to the community pure water.

To-day, under municipal ownership, Mayor Rice pointed out, the city of Houston charges only 15 cents per thousand gallons for water, on a meter basis, and it is all from artesian wells and absolutely pure. The plant is worth to-day three times its cost to the city. The street car company pays annually one per cent upon its gross receipts, has more than doubled its facilities, and will compare favorably with any other electric system in the country. The tax rate has been reduced from $2 to $1.70. . . .

In concluding his Chicago address from which these facts are taken, Mayor Rice said:

"After years of study and experience I find that nothing will bring forth the energies and progress of a people so much as a municipal government that fights for business methods, who are progressive themselves and demonstrate to the taxpayers that they are going to have a 'day's work for a day's pay.' Houston is a practical demonstration of this. In 1905 everyone was 'down in the mouth,' building had stopped and men of means refused to make any improvements."

An illustration of the manner in which the business administration of the city was reorganized by the commission government on its advent to power is afforded by an innovation which it introduced in the office of city treasurer. Under the old system there had been a city treasurer on a salary of $2,500 per year. Nothing was said about interest on city deposits, so these also went to the treasurer. The city commission abolished the office of city treasurer and appointed one of the national banks city depository. Now the city handles its business through the bank the same as any other corporation, the city paying the bank $50 per month clerk hire and the bank paying the city interest on all balances to the credit of the city in the bank. In this way the city annually receives $6,000 to $10,000 which formerly went to the city treasurers.

City-Commission Government in Dallas

Dallas claims to be the best-governed city in the United States, and backs up its claim by citing the results she has achieved under commission government. Whether any one city can reasonably claim such a distinction, certainly the results in Dallas have been highly satisfactory to the people. . . .

Speaking in New York before a meeting of business men, September 30, 1909, C. B. Gillespie, commissioner of finance and revenue, said: "In the two years' experience of Dallas, under the commission form of government, many miles of streets have been substantially paved; the enforcement of sidewalk construction is general throughout the city; four new parks have been acquired, numerous public buildings have been erected, extensive additions to the waterworks system are under way, and many reforms have been brought about; among which was the reduction of the city's street lighting from $73 per arc light per year to $60. In a financial way the city has shown a decided improvement. Its books are maintained up to date in every respect and the status of any fund or account can be ascertained at any hour as easily as a bank can show a depositor's balance. New method and systems have been invoked, daily itemized reports of all collections are required, together with a deposit daily with the treasurer of all funds collected, all of which is followed by regularly systematic checking of all departments. The city of Dallas operates thirty-three departments under what is known as its general fund, and which does not include the school, park, library, water and sewerage, street improvement, and interest in sinking funds. Of May 1, 1907, one month before the present board of commissioners assumed control, the general fund of the city was overdrawn $122,575.27. . . .

"During the two years ending May 1, 1909, the board of commissioners maintained these departments at a net saving under the cost of the former administration, and by enforcing the collection of all revenues it was enabled to liquidate the above overdraft and close the fiscal year with a credit balance in its general fund of $10,290.02.

"The affairs of the city are treated as a business proposition, and are handled about the same as a bank's directory would manage its affairs, and during the two and a fraction years of the Dallas board of commissioners no disruption of any kind has occurred. Nor has a single speech been made by the mayor or any member of the board at any of its meetings."

✳ *E S S A Y S*

The four essays in this chapter represent differing analytical approaches to bossism and reform. The first essay starkly illustrates how scholars elaborated on Bryce's theme of the predatory and unprincipled nature of boss politics. The author, Thomas Harrison Reed, also illuminates the way in which some scholars attributed the success of bosses to their manipulation of the "ignorant" masses of immigrants, unprepared for universal suffrage. The second essay, by Elmer Cornwell, a political scientist at Brown University, articulates the "functional" interpretation of machine politics, by which the author explains the mutually beneficial relationship between immigrants in need and politicians in quest of power. Cornwell also notes how machine politics provided avenues of mobility to immigrants who found other avenues closed to them. The third essay, by Samuel P. Hays of the University of Pittsburgh, affords insights into the nature of municipal reform and offers some provocative opportunities for debate, not only about the effectiveness of reformers but also about Hays's assumption that municipal reform was a man's activity. The final essay, by Jon C. Teaford of Purdue University, presents a recent critique of the interpretation that views urban politics of the late nineteenth century as a dialogue between bosses and reformers. Instead, Teaford sees others, particularly engineers and other professionals, as involved in the most far-reaching decisions involving urban growth and everyday life. His essay thus minimizes the importance of bosses and reformers and in this sense offers a transition to issues raised in the next chapter.

A Critical Appraisal of Machine Politics
THOMAS HARRISON REED

Probably the greatest single influence on the character of municipal government in the nineteenth century was the enlarged electorate which the progress of democratic ideas made inevitable. . . . To understand the full effect of universal suffrage, one must keep in mind the fact that about 1832 there began to pour into the United States a mounting flood of immigration and that our naturalization laws were not only liberal but most laxly enforced. . . . Most of [the] immigrants were untutored peasants, ignorant of the practices of representative government, separated from the bulk of the native population by religion, language, habits of thought. At the same time, our naturalization and election laws admitted the alien almost immediately to full participation in the privilege of universal suffrage. Since 1802 only five years' residence has been required for the acquisition of citizenship, a preliminary "declaration" being made two years before the final act

From Thomas Harrison Reed, "The Triumph of the Machine," chapter viii, *Municipal Government in the United States,* revised edition (New York: Appleton-Century Company, 1934), pp. 104–6, 110–16. Reprinted by permission of the Simon & Schuster Education Group.

of naturalization. . . . [M]any aliens were not obliged to wait even the brief period provided by law before having placed in their hands the sacred privilege of the ballot.

It is obvious that the enlargement of the electorate opened the way to new forms of political activity. Without attempting to deny that in the long run the votes of all the people are the surest basis of good government, we cannot doubt that the broadened suffrage and the introduction into it of hundreds of thousands of foreigners imperfectly adjusted to American life gave an opportunity to the political organizations of the period which they had not enjoyed among a smaller and more homogeneous group of voters. Impelled by the urge of immediate self-interest, the politicians quickly developed means of controlling the votes of the populace, and it took the slower resolution of the community itself more than half a century to devise methods of partially counteracting them. Universal suffrage alone might have occasioned little difficulty had it not been accompanied by the influx of aliens, the rapid growth of cities, a demand for wider city services, the development of great national parties, and the rise of the so-called democratic principles of checks and balances, popular election of administrative officers, and rotation in appointive office. It was the concurrence of all these forces that brought city government into disrepute. In this result, however, there can be no doubt that the existence of a large, ignorant, and inexperienced electorate played a great part. . . . With universal suffrage, the old type of office-holder and the old standards went out. The politicians of the new regime were held to no standards, for the new electorate had none. The city politicians of the period belonged largely to the predatory classes, and their ethics were those of the bartender, the gambler and the gang leader. . . .

The term *machine* is very often loosely applied to almost any kind of political party organization which is vigorous and effective. It is better, however, to confine it to those organizations in which the primary interest is not the propagation of the principles of a political party but the profit of the organization itself. It is an equally significant characteristic of the machine that it is not controlled by the members of the party. Whatever concession it offers to appearances, it is the machine itself which makes nominations, distributes patronage, dictates the conduct of mayors and councilmen. It may be described as an abnormal or perverted political organization, in which the normal functioning of a party is reversed. Edmund Burke defined a political party as a "body of men united, for promoting by their joint endeavors the national interest, upon some particular principle in which they are all agreed." According to this definition, a machine is not a political party, for it is a body of men united for promoting by their joint endeavors their personal interest without regard to any principle at all. Of course, in actual practice, most so-called machines are somewhere between this drastic definition and an ideal party organization. Even the worst ones have never been utterly disregardful of the popular will.

In their organization early political machines differed in no essential respect from the machines which exist to-day. A machine's chief prerequisite is a comparatively small group of voters in each election district who can be counted on to vote as directed by the leaders. In each such unit, there is a precinct captain or leader, who is responsible to a ward or district leader, who, in turn, is responsible to the big boss. The necessities of vigorous political warfare have evolved this one-man type of organization. It would not do to say that every machine has always had a boss. Sometimes the supreme power is shared by a number of leaders. But most of the successful machines have been ruled by a boss most of the time. The precinct captain has always won his position by his ability to deliver the necessary votes. He holds it by a like tenure; when some one else proves that he can deliver more votes, the job changes hands. The votes which the captain controls are, first of all, those of his own family and its connections; second, the office-holders or would-be office-holders and their families and connections; third, other recipients of favors, who may range all the way from protected thieves and gamblers to the innocent proprietors of street-corner newsstands. The precinct captain usually acts as the mediary in securing these favors; for example, a boy is arrested, charged with some infraction of the penal code; the precinct captain speaks to the ward leader; the ward leader speaks to the judge; the boy is released; his father, his uncles, his older brothers become followers of the precinct captain. This kind of work on the part of a machine has been praised by some writers as the humanizing of city government. There can be no doubt that there has to go into the composition of a successful precinct captain a lot of rough good-nature and a liking for his fellow-man. On the other hand, it should never be forgotten that the motive with which these virtues are employed is the perversion of popular government and the misdirection of the community's resources. . . .

Machines never could have been built to their full perfection without the spoils system, i.e., the practice of distributing appointive offices as reward for political service. To this no legal bar existed in any American city until 1883. In the colonial period and for nearly fifty years thereafter, practically all appointive offices were held for very short, fixed terms—one or two years—but there was a strong habit of reappointment. With the rise of the democratic movement, however, the doctrine of rotation in office came into vogue. The popular thought of the Jacksonian era regarded office not as a trusteeship for the public but as a privilege of the office-holder. . . . From this foundation, it was but a step to the principle expressed by Senator Marcy of New York, during a debate in the United States Senate, "To the victor belong the spoils of the enemy." The ruthless application of this idea for the next half-century corrupted politics and ruined administration. From heads of departments to street-sweepers and ditch-diggers, city job-holders were primarily interested in serving a machine and only secondarily in the performance of their work for the city. . . .

That the boss and his satraps were not in politics for their health is a truism. Some were doubtless attracted by the opportunity for the exercise of power, but with most of them the motive was the more sordid one of fattening their pocketbooks. The corruption of the old days was crude and open. There were three great sources of municipal graft. The first of them centered in the police department. It was a matter of withholding the hand of the law for a consideration—a species of blackmail made infinitely easier by the American practice of enacting moral aspirations into law with little regard to their enforceability. From a very early date in our municipal history, saloon-keepers, gamblers, prostitutes, and even thieves were made to contribute to the financial well-being of the machine. . . .

A second source of municipal graft was the desire of business men for favors at the hands of the city government. This ran all the way from the evasion of ordinances against unloading goods on the sidewalk to the pursuit of public utility franchises valued at many millions of dollars. One unfamiliar with the ways of municipal politics might have been surprised at the favorable attitude of presumably reputable business men toward the machine. It was due to the fact that they found it easier and cheaper to deal with the boss than with the regular city authorities acting openly in the public interest. . . .

A third source of graft was the direct raid on the city treasury, and this was graft's characteristic form in the middle years of the nineteenth century. Sometimes the officers entrusted with city funds stole them. Still more frequent were frauds in connection with contracts for the construction of public buildings and other works and the purchase of supplies and materials. It was by such means that the members of the notorious Tweed ring in New York enriched themselves. In the construction and furnishing of the county court house, for example, contractors put their bids at such a figure that they could turn over to the ring fifty to sixty per cent of the payment made by the county and still make an exorbitant profit. . . .

The results of the development of city government in the United States to 1888 are indeed best summed up in Bryce's often quoted statement, "There is no denying that the government of cities is the one conspicuous failure of the United States." The era was one of confusion and irresponsibility. The organization of municipal government was complicated to the point where responsibility could scarcely be fixed for misconduct, however glaring. The doctrine of checks and balances had done its work. Political conditions were favorable to the domination of machines and bosses. The heat of partisanship, the spoils system, defective nominating and election machinery, the presence of great numbers of ignorant voters without roots in the cities of their residence—all contributed to make the task of the boss easy. The rapid development of cities, with vast profits for the holders of public utility franchises, enormous public works, and constantly mounting municipal expenditures, provided unexampled opportunities for graft which were shamelessly accepted.

The disgraceful conditions which prevailed were, however, less the fault of the people of the cities themselves than the result of a remarkable combination of circumstances set in motion by the rapid exploitation of a continent. If one considers that the half-century from 1840 to 1890 was a long period for the grosser abuses of nominating and election procedure to remain uncorrected, it may be alleged in palliation that universal-suffrage democracy was being given its first trial on a large scale under conditions of the greatest difficulty. It must be remembered, too, that a machine, once in power, is difficult to dislodge. The predatory politicians were thoroughly entrenched in their organization and it was not until the effrontery of their corruption became unbearable that the interest of the public could be diverted from national to local politics sufficiently to search for and seize upon the remedy. In the meantime, cities had grown in population, had flourished economically, and had developed in culture. Machine government, bad as it was, had not been able to check the natural forces of progress. . . . But when all excuses have been made, it remains true that in 1888 our city governments were burdened with debt, and sodden with corruption and inefficiency. There is no blinking the fact that the United States had made a "conspicuous failure" of municipal government.

The Immigrants and Machine Politics

ELMER E. CORNWELL, JR.

[I]t was the succeeding waves of immigrants that gave urban political organizations the manipulable mass bases without which they could not have functioned as they did. And, until immigration dried up to a trickle in the 1920s, as one generation of newcomers began to espouse traditional American values of political independence, there was always a new group, often from a different country of origin, to which the machine could turn. As long as this continued to be possible, machines persisted, and once the immigrant base finally began to disappear, so did most of the bosses of the classic model. In a very real sense, then, the one phenomenon was dependent on the other. . . .

. . . [W]hatever else may be said about the conditions and forces that spawned the classic machine, this kind of disciplined political entity must rest at bottom on a clientele which has felt it necessary to exchange political independence—its votes, in a word—for something seen as more essential to its well-being and security. In general, such a group will be the product of some kind of socioeconomic disequilibrium or cultural tension which finds its members in an insecure or seriously disadvantaged situation. Thus, the immigrant was willing to submit to the boss in exchange for aid—real or imagined—in gaining his foothold in the new environment. . . .

The Classic Machine in Operation

It cannot be assumed that the process of machine exploitation of succeeding groups of newcomers was a smooth and simple operation. Any formal organization, political or otherwise, must maintain a continuing balance among a series of often contradictory forces. Its very existence rests on the success with which it achieves its objective—in the case of a political party, the winning of elections and, thus, power. In the long run, this success depends on the organization's continuing ability to tap fresh sources of support as time goes on and old reliances dwindle and may at times depend on keeping newly available resources away from its rival or rivals. For the machine, this has meant wooing each new ethnic contingent. Yet this process of growth and renewal will inevitably threaten the very position of many of the proprietors of the organization itself by recruiting rivals for their roles. Any organizational entity must not only achieve its corporate goals but, to survive, it must also satisfy the needs and desires of its members as individuals. If it fails in this, its supporters will vanish and its own objectives remain unattainable. . . .

Usually the machine did yield in the long run to the political imperative that all groups of potential supporters must be wooed, if for no other reason than to

Reprinted from "Bosses, Machines, and Ethnic Groups" by Elmer E. Cornwell, Jr., in volume no. 353 of *The Annals of the American Academy of Political and Social Science.* Copyright © 1964.

keep them from the enemy. The short-term risk to the present leadership often must have appeared minimal. The plight of the newcomers was so pitiful, their needs so elemental, and their prospects of achieving security and independence so problematical in the foreseeable future that they must have appeared like a windfall to the machine proprietors. Thus, after initial hesitancy, the Irish were taken into Tammany and found their way into the ranks of the clientele of other big city party organizations.

The ways in which immigrant political support was purchased are familiar and need no elaborate review here. They had at least three kinds of needs which the ward heeler could fill on behalf of the party leadership. Above all, they needed the means of physical existence: jobs, loans, rent money, contributions of food or fuel to tide them over, and the like. Secondly, they needed a buffer against an unfamiliar state and its legal minions: help when they or their offspring got in trouble with the police, help in dealing with inspectors, in seeking pushcart licenses, or in other relations with the public bureaucracy. Finally, they needed the intangibles of friendship, sympathy, and social intercourse. These were available, variously through contact with the precinct captain, the hospitality of the political clubhouse, the attendance of the neighborhood boss at wakes and weddings, and the annual ward outing.

As has often been noted, these kinds of services were not available, as they are today, at the hands of "United Fund" agencies, city welfare departments with their platoons of social workers, or through federal social security legislation. The sporadic and quite inadequate aid rendered by the boss and his lieutenants thus filled a vacuum. Their only rivals were the self-help associations which did spring up within each ethnic group as soon as available resources allowed a meager surplus to support burial societies and the like. . . .

Some of the later arrivals following the pioneering Irish were in at least as great need of aid. The Irish did speak English and had had some experience with political action and representative institutions at home. This, plus the fact that they got here first, doubtless accounts for their rapid rise in their chosen party, the Democracy. The groups that followed, however, usually did not know English and bore the additional burden of a cultural heritage that had less in common with the American patterns they encountered than had been the case with the Irish. And, too, almost all groups, the Sons of Erin included, differed religiously from the basic Protestant consensus of their Anglo-Saxon predecessors. . . .

The Machine as Social Integrator

There is another side to the coin of machine dependence on the continuing flow of immigrants. The "invisible hand"—to use an analogy with Adam Smith's economics—which operated to produce social benefits out of the *quid pro quo* which the ward heelers exchanged for votes was at work in other ways, too. . . .

This process has had several facets. In the first place, the mere seeking out of the immigrants in quest of their support, the assistance rendered in getting them naturalized (when it was necessary to observe these legal niceties), and so forth were of considerable importance in laying the foundation for their more meaningful political participation later. In addition, the parties have progressively drawn into their own hierarchies and committee offices representatives of the various ethnic groups. The mechanics of this process were varied. In some cases, there doubtless emerged leaders of a particular group in one ward or neighborhood who, if given official party status, would automatically bring their followings along with them. On other occasions, new ethnic enclaves may have sought or even demanded representation in exchange for support. Perhaps prior to either of these, the machine sought to co-opt individuals who could speak the language and act as a cultural bridge between the party and the newcomers. . . .

These general patterns can to some extent be documented, at least illustratively. The tendency for the urban machines to reap the Irish vote and later much of the vote of more recent arrivals is well known. The process of infiltration by group representatives into party structure is harder to identify precisely. With this in mind, the author did a study of the members of party ward committees in Providence, Rhode Island, the findings of which may reflect trends elsewhere. Analysis of committee membership lists or their equivalent going back to the 1860s and 1870s, showed initial overwhelming Anglo-Saxon majorities. For the Democrats, however, this majority gave way, between the 1880s and 1900, to a roughly 75 per cent Irish preponderance, while the Republican committees stayed "Yankee" until after the First World War. Then, in the 1920s, both parties simultaneously recruited Italian committeemen to replace some of the Irish and white Protestants, respectively. . . . In other cities, the timing of shifts and the ethnic groups involved will have differed, but the general process and its relation to local patterns of immigration were doubtless similar.

It is incredible, viewed now with hindsight, how reckless the American republic was in its unpremeditated policy of open door and the implied assumption that somehow, without any governmental or even organized private assistance, hundreds of thousands of immigrants from dozens of diverse cultures would fit themselves smoothly and automatically into a native culture which had its own share of ethnocentrism. The fact of the matter was that the process did not operate smoothly or particularly effectively. There were tensions and incidents which accentuated cultural differences and engendered bitterness. These ranged, chronologically, all the way from the abuses of the more militant Know-Nothings to the Ku Klux Klan activity of the 1920s.

Economically, most occupational doors that did not lead to manual labor jobs were closed to the Irish and later arrivals and were only gradually pried open after much time had passed and many lasting intergroup enmities had been engendered. Here again, the party organization represented one of the few mechanisms, public or private, that lubricated a process of integration which, in its very nature, was bound to generate enormous amounts of friction. Besides drawing group representatives into its councils, party work also was one of the few career ladders available to the immigrant and his ambitious sons. Here, status could be achieved, as well as a comfortable income, one way or another, when few other routes were open. . . .

Politics for the machine politician never was an ideological enterprise or a matter of beliefs and principles. As someone once said, the boss had only seven principles, five loaves and two fishes. Rather, politics was an entrepreneurial vocation like any other business. . . . The politician's aim was and is so to invest his supply of capital—jobs, favors, and the like—as to earn a profit, some of which he will take as "income" and the rest reinvest in quest of larger returns. In other words, the immigrant political leader took the one vocation open to him, politics, and made it into as close an approximation as he could of the more valued business callings in the society, from which he was effectively barred. He acted out the American success story in the only way open to him.

Obviously, the foregoing is not designed to portray the machine as a knight-errant rescuing American society from its willful folly. In the first place, the folly was not willful, and perhaps not folly. In the second, the boss's contribution toward making the melting pot melt should not be overrated. At the same time, many have testified—as does the record itself—to the almost unique ability of party as organization to bring people together across cultural and similar barriers. . . . Ticket-balancing, or United Nations politics, as it is sometimes called, is perhaps symbolic of the ultimate step in the process of granting group recognition and confirming the fact that something approaching intergroup equality has been achieved. . . .

In short, the classic urban machine rested upon the immigrants, while at the same time it fostered their integration into American life. . . . [A] political style which stressed personal obligations, and placed strong personal loyalties above allegiance to abstract codes of law or morals was congenial to the machine politicians and their followers, and they made it their own, developing its full implications in the process. At the same time, the immigrant versus old stock cultural cleavage prompted the latter to espouse the more vigorously the typically middle-class, reformist style which stresses honesty, impartiality, and efficiency. These two styles or ethics, since the late nineteenth century, have, by their interaction, shaped both the evolution of urban politics and the machinery of urban government.

Municipal Reform in the Progressive Era

SAMUEL P. HAYS

In order to achieve a more complete understanding of social change in the Progressive Era, historians must now undertake a deeper analysis of the practices of economic, political, and social groups. Political ideology alone is no longer satisfactory evidence to describe social patterns because generalizations based upon it, which tend to divide political groups into the moral and the immoral, the rational and the irrational, the efficient and the inefficient, do not square with political practice. Behind this contemporary rhetoric concerning the nature of reform lay patterns of political behavior which were at variance with it. Since an extensive gap separated ideology and practice, we can no longer take the former as an accurate description of the latter, but must reconstruct social behavior from other types of evidence.

Reform in urban government provides one of the most striking examples of this problem of analysis. The demand for change in municipal affairs, whether in terms of over-all reform, such as the commission and city-manager plans, or of more piecemeal modifications, such as the development of city-wide school

From "The Politics of Reform in Municipal Government in the Progressive Era" by Samuel P. Hays, *Pacific Northwest Quarterly* 55 (October 1964), excerpts from pp. 157–63. Reprinted by permission of the *Pacific Northwest Quarterly*.

boards, deeply involved reform ideology. Reformers loudly proclaimed a new structure of municipal government as more moral, more rational, and more efficient and, because it was so, self-evidently more desirable. But precisely because of this emphasis, there seemed to be no need to analyze the political forces behind change. Because the goals of reform were good, its causes were obvious; rather than being the product of particular people and particular ideas in particular situations, they were deeply imbedded in the universal impulses and truths of "progress." Consequently, historians have rarely tried to determine precisely who the municipal reformers were or what they did, but instead have relied on reform ideology as an accurate description of reform practice.

The reform ideology which became the basis of historical analysis is well known. . . . The urban political struggle of the Progressive era, so the argument goes, involved a conflict between public impulses for "good government" against a corrupt alliance of "machine politicians" and "special interests."

During the rapid urbanization of the late 19th century, the latter had been free to aggrandize themselves, especially through franchise grants, at the expense of the public. Their power lay primarily in their ability to manipulate the political process, by bribery and corruption, for their own ends. Against such arrangements there gradually arose a public protest, a demand by the public for honest government, for officials who would act for the public rather than for themselves. To accomplish their goals, reformers sought basic modifications in the political system, both in the structure of government and in the manner of selecting public officials. These changes, successful in city after city, enabled the "public interest" to triumph.

. . . [Historians] George Mowry, Alfred Chandler, Jr., and Richard Hofstadter have modified this analysis by emphasizing the fact that the impulse for reform did not come from the working class. This might have been suspected from the rather strained efforts of National Municipal League writers in the "Era of Reform" to go out of their way to demonstrate working-class support for commission and city-manager governments. We now know that they clutched at straws, and often erroneously, in order to prove to themselves as well as to the public that municipal reform was a mass movement.

The Mowry-Chandler-Hofstadter writings have further modified older views by asserting that reform in general and municipal reform in particular sprang from a distinctively middle-class movement. This has now become the prevailing view. Its popularity is surprising not only because it is based upon faulty logic and extremely limited evidence, but also because it, too, emphasizes the analysis of ideology rather than practice and fails to contribute much to the understanding of who distinctively were involved in reform and why. . . .

The weakness of the "middle-class" theory of reform stems from the fact that it rests primarily upon ideological evidence, not on a thorough-going description of political practice. Although the studies of Mowry, Chandler, and Hofstadter ostensibly derive from behavioral evidence, they actually derive largely from the extensive expressions of middle-ground ideological position, of the reformers' own descriptions of their contemporary society, and of their expressed fears of both the lower and the upper classes, of the fright of being ground between the millstones of labor and capital.

Such evidence, though it accurately portrays what people thought, does not accurately describe what they did. The great majority of Americans look upon themselves as "middle class" and subscribe to a middle-ground ideology, even though in practice they belong to a great variety of distinct social classes. Such ideologies are natural phenomena of human behavior. But the historian should be especially sensitive to their role so that he will not take evidence of political ideology as an accurate representation of political practice.

In the following account I will summarize evidence in both secondary and primary works concerning the political practices in which municipal reformers were involved. Such an analysis logically can be broken down into three parts, each one corresponding to a step in the traditional argument. First, what was the source of reform? Did it lie in the general public rather than in particular groups? Was it middle class, working class, or perhaps of other composition? Second, what was the reform target of attack? Were reformers primarily interested in ousting the corrupt individual, the political or business leader who made private arrangements at the expense of the public, or were they interested in something else? Third, what political innovations did reformers bring about? Did they seek to expand popular participation in the governmental process? . . .

Available evidence indicates that the source of support for reform in municipal government did not come from the lower or middle classes, but from the upper class. The leading business groups in each city and professional men closely allied with them initiated and dominated municipal movements. . . .

The character of municipal reform is demonstrated more precisely by a brief examination of the movements in Des Moines and Pittsburgh. The Des Moines Commercial Club inaugurated and carefully controlled the drive for the commission form of government. In January, 1906, the Club held a so-called "mass meeting" of business and professional men to secure an enabling act from the state legislature. P. C. Kenyon, president of the Club, selected a Committee of 300, composed principally of business and professional men, to draw up a specific proposal. After the legislature approved their plan, the same committee managed the campaign which persuaded the electorate to accept the commission form of government by a narrow margin in June, 1907.

In this election the lower-income wards of the city opposed the change, the upper-income wards supported it strongly, and the middle-income wards were more evenly divided. In order to control the new government, the Committee of 300, now expanded to 530, sought to determine the nomination and election of the five new commissioners, and to this end they selected an avowedly businessman's slate. Their plans backfired when the voters swept into office a slate of anticommission candidates who now controlled the new commission government.

Proponents of the commission form of government in Des Moines spoke frequently in the name of the "people." But their more explicit statements emphasized their intent that the new plan be a "business system" of government, run by businessmen. The slate of candidates for commissioner endorsed by advocates of the plan was known as the "businessman's ticket." J. W. Hill, president of the committees of 300 and 530, bluntly declared: "The professional politician must be ousted and in his place capable business men chosen to conduct the affairs of the city." I. M. Earle, general counsel of the Bankers Life Association and a prominent figure in the movement, put the point more precisely: "When the plan was adopted it was the intention to get businessmen to run it."

Although reformers used the ideology of popular government, they in no sense meant that all segments of society should be involved equally in municipal decision-making. They meant that their concept of the city's welfare would be best achieved if the business community controlled city government. As one businessman told a labor audience, the businessman's slate represented labor "better than you do yourself."

The composition of the municipal reform movement in Pittsburgh demonstrates its upper-class and professional as well as its business sources. Here the two principal reform organizations were the Civic Club and the Voters' League. The 745 members of these two organizations came primarily from the upper class. Sixty-five per cent appeared in upper-class directories which contained the names of only 2 per cent of the city's families. Furthermore, many who were not listed in these directories lived in upper-class areas. These reformers, it should be stressed, comprised not an old but a new upper class. Few came from earlier industrial and mercantile families. Most of them had risen to social position from wealth created after 1870 in the iron, steel, electrical equipment, and other industries, and they lived in the newer rather than the older fashionable areas.

Almost half (48 per cent) of the reformers were professional men: doctors, lawyers, ministers, directors of libraries and museums, engineers, architects, private and public school teachers, and college professors. Some of these belonged to the upper class as well, especially the lawyers, ministers, and private school teachers. But for the most part their interest in reform stemmed from the inherent dynamics of their professions rather than from their class connections. They came from the more advanced segments of their organizations, from those in the forefront to the acquisition and application of knowledge. They were not the older professional men, seeking to preserve the past against change; they were in the vanguard of professional life, actively seeking to apply expertise more widely to public affairs.

Pittsburgh reformers included a large segment of businessmen; 52 per cent were bankers and corporation officials or their wives. Among them were the presidents of fourteen large banks and officials of Westinghouse, Pittsburgh Plate Glass, U.S. Steel and its component parts (such as Carnegie Steel, American Bridge, and National Tube), Jones and Laughlin, lesser steel companies . . . the H. J. Heinz Company, and the Pittsburgh Coal Company, as well as officials of the Pennsylvania Railroad and the Pittsburgh and Lake Erie. These men were not small businessmen; they directed the most powerful banking and industrial organizations of the city. They represented not the old business community, but industries which had developed and grown primarily within the past fifty years and which had come to dominate the city's economic life.

These business, professional, and upper-class groups who dominated municipal reform movements were all involved in the rationalization and systematization of modern life; they wished a form of government which would be more consistent with the objectives inherent in those developments. The most important single feature of their perspective was the rapid expansion of the geographical scope of affairs which they wished to influence and manipulate, a scope which was no longer limited and narrow, no longer within the confines of pedestrian communities, but was now broad and city-wide, covering the whole range of activities of the metropolitan area.

The migration of the upper class from central to outlying areas created a geographical distance between its residential communities and its economic institutions. To protect the latter required involvement both in local ward affairs and in the larger city government as well. Moreover, upper-class cultural institutions, such as museums, libraries, and symphony orchestras, required an active interest in the larger municipal context from which these institutions drew much of their clientele.

Professional groups, broadening the scope of affairs which they sought to study, measure, or manipulate, also sought to influence the public health, the educational system, or the physical arrangements of the entire city. Their concerns were limitless, not bounded by geography, but as expansive as the professional imagination. Finally, the new industrial community greatly broadened its perspective in governmental affairs because of its new recognition of the way in which factors throughout the city affected business growth. The increasing size and scope of industry, the greater stake in more varied and geographically dispersed facets of city life, the effect of floods on many business concerns, the need to promote traffic flows to and from work for both blue-collar and managerial employees—all contributed to this larger interest. The geographically larger private perspectives of upper-class, professional, and business groups gave rise to a geographically larger public perspective.

These reformers were dissatisfied with existing systems of municipal government. They did not oppose corruption per se—although there was plenty of that. They objected to the structure of government which enabled local and particularistic interests to dominate. Prior to the reforms of the Progressive Era, city government consisted primarily of confederations of local wards, each of which was represented on the city's legislative body. Each ward frequently had its own elementary schools and ward-elected school boards which administered them.

These particularistic interests were the focus of a decentralized political life. City councilmen were local leaders. They spoke for their local areas, the economic interests of their inhabitants, their residential concerns, their educational, recreational, and religious interests—i.e., for those aspects of community life which mattered most to those they represented. They rolled logs in the city council to provide streets, sewers, and other public works for their local areas. They defended the community's cultural practices, its distinctive languages or national customs, its liberal attitude toward liquor, and its saloons and dance halls which served as centers of community life. . . . In short, pre-reform officials spoke for their constituencies, inevitably their own wards which had elected them, rather than for other sections or groups of the city.

The ward system of government especially gave representation in city affairs to lower- and middle-class groups. Most elected ward officials were from these groups, and they, in turn, constituted the major opposition to reforms in municipal government. In Pittsburgh, for example, immediately prior to the changes in both the city council and the school board in 1911 in which city-wide representation replaced ward representation, only 24 per cent of the 387 members of those bodies represented the same managerial, professional, and banker occupations which dominated the membership of the Civic Club and the Voters' League. The great majority (67 per cent) were small businessmen—grocers, saloonkeepers, livery-stable proprietors, owners of small hotels, druggists—white-collar workers such as clerks and bookkeepers, and skilled and unskilled workmen.

The decentralized system of urban growth and the institutions which arose from it reformers now opposed. Social, professional, and economic life had developed not only in the local wards in a small community context, but also on a larger scale had become highly integrated and organized, giving rise to a superstructure of social organization which lay far above that of ward life and which was sharply divorced from it in both personal contacts and perspective.

By the late 19th century, those involved in these larger institutions found that the decentralized systems of political life limited their larger objectives. The movement for reform in municipal government, therefore, constituted an attempt by upper-class, advanced professional, and large business groups to take formal political power from the previously dominant lower- and middle-class elements so that they might advance their own conceptions of desirable public policy. These two groups came from entirely different urban worlds, and the political system fashioned by one was no longer acceptable to the other.

Lower- and middle-class groups not only dominated the pre-reform governments, but vigorously opposed reform. It is significant that none of the occupational groups among them, for example, small businessmen or white-collar workers, skilled or unskilled artisans, had important representation in reform organization thus far examined. . . .

The most visible opposition to reform and the most readily available target of reform attack was the so-called "machine," for through the "machine" many different ward communities as well as lower- and middle-income groups joined effectively to influence the central city government. Their private occupational and social life did not naturally involve these groups in larger city-wide activities in the same way as the upper class was involved; hence they lacked access to privately organized economic and social power on which they could construct political power. The "machine" filled the organizational gap.

Yet it should never be forgotten that the social and economic institutions in the wards themselves provided the "machine's" sustaining support and gave it larger significance. When reformers attacked the "machine" as the most visible institutional element of the ward system, they attacked the entire ward form of political organization, and the political power of lower- and middle-income groups which lay behind it.

Reformers often gave the impression that they opposed merely the corrupt politician and his "machine." But in a more fundamental way they looked upon the deficiencies of pre-reform political leaders in terms not of their personal shortcomings, but of the limitations inherent in their occupational, institutional, and class positions. In 1911 the Voters' League of Pittsburgh wrote in its pamphlet analyzing the qualifications of candidates that "a man's occupation ought to give a strong indication of his qualifications for membership on a school board." Certain occupations inherently disqualified a man from serving:

Employment as ordinary laborer and in the lowest class of mill work would naturally lead to the conclusion that such men did not have sufficient education or business training to act as school directors. . . . Objection might also be made to small shop-keepers, clerks, workmen at many trades, who by lack of educational advantages and business training, could not, no matter how honest, be expected to administer prop-erly the affairs of an educational system, requiring special knowledge, and where millions are spent each year.

These, of course, were precisely the groups which did dominate Pittsburgh gov-ernment prior to reform. The League deplored the fact that school boards con-tained only a small number of "men prominent throughout the city in business life . . . in professional occupations . . . holding positions as managers, secretaries, auditors, superintendents and foremen" and exhorted these classes to participate more actively as candidates for office.

Reformers, therefore, wished not simply to replace bad men with good; they proposed to change the occupational and class origins of decision-makers. To-ward this end they sought innovations in the formal machinery of government which would concentrate political power by sharply centralizing the processes of decision-making rather than distribute it through more popular participation in public affairs. According to the liberal view of the Progressive Era, the major political innovations of reform involved the equalization of political power through the primary, the direct election of public officials, and the initiative, ref-erendum, and recall. These measures played a large role in the political ideology of the time and were frequently incorporated into new municipal charters. But they provided at best only an occasional and often incidental process of decision-making. Far more important in continuous, sustained, day-to-day processes of government were those innovations which centralized decision-making in the hands of fewer and fewer people. . . .

A Reappraisal of Bosses and Reformers in City Government

JON C. TEAFORD

In 1888 the British observer James Bryce proclaimed that "there is no denying that the government of cities is the one conspicuous failure of the Unites States." With this pronouncement he summed up the feelings of a host of Americans. In New York City, residents along mansion-lined Fifth Avenue, parishioners in the churches of then-sedate Brooklyn, even petty politicos at party headquarters in Tammany Hall, all perceived serious flaws in the structure of urban government. Some complained, for example, of the tyranny of upstate Republican legislators, others attacked the domination of ward bosses, and still others criticized the greed of public utility companies franchised by the municipality. Mugwump reformer Theodore Roosevelt decried government by Irish political machine hacks, the moralist Reverend Charles Henry Parkhurst lambasted the reign of rum sellers,

From "Trumpeted Failures and Unheralded Triumphs" by Jon C. Teaford in *The Unheralded Triumph: City Government in America, 1870–1900,* 1984, excerpts from pp. 1–10. The Johns Hopkins University Press, Baltimore/London, 1984. Reprinted by permission.

and that pariah of good government advocates, New York City ward boss George Washington Plunkitt, also found fault, attacking the evils of civil service. . . .

Likewise, many twentieth-century scholars passing judgment on the development of American city government have handed down a guilty verdict and sentenced American urban rule to a place of shame in the annals of the nation. In 1933 a leading student of municipal home rule claimed that "the conduct of municipal business has almost universally been inept and inefficient" and "at its worst it has been unspeakable, almost incredible." That same year the distinguished historian Arthur Schlesinger, Sr., in his seminal study *The Rise of the City,* . . . recount[ed] tales of corruption and describ[ed] municipal rule during the last two decades of the century as "the worst city government the country had ever known." . . .

Younger historians of the second half of the twentieth century were further removed from the scene of the supposed municipal debacle and could evaluate it more dispassionately. By the 1960s and 1970s, negative summations such as "unspeakable" and "incredible" were no longer common in accounts of nineteenth-century city government, and historians professing to the objectivity of the social sciences often refused to pronounce judgment on the quality of past rule. Yet recent general histories of urban America have continued both to describe the "deterioration" of city government during the Gilded Age and to focus on political bosses and good-government reformers who were forced to struggle with a decentralized, fragmented municipal structure supposedly unsuited to the fast-growing metropolises of the 1880s and 1890s. . . .

. . . Though many have recognized the elitist predilections of Bryce and his American informants, the influence of Bryce's words still persists, and the image of nineteenth-century city government remains tarnished. Historians have softened the harsh stereotype of the political boss, transforming him from a venal parasite into a necessary component of a makeshift, decentralized structure. Conversely, the boss's good-government foes have fallen somewhat from historical grace and are now typified as crusaders for the supremacy of an upper-middle-class business culture. But historians continued to aim their attention at these two elements of municipal rule, to the neglect of the formal, legal structure. They write more of the boss than of the mayor, more on the civic leagues than on the sober but significant city comptroller. Moreover they continue to stage the drama of bosses and reformers against a roughly sketched backdrop of municipal disarray. The white and black hats of the players may have shaded to gray, but the setting of the historian's pageant remains a ramshackle municipal structure.

Nevertheless, certain nagging realities stand in stark contrast to the traditional tableau of municipal rule. One need not look far to discover the monuments of nineteenth-century municipal achievement that still grace the nation's cities, surviving as concrete rebuttals to Bryce's words. In 1979 the architecture critic for the *New York Times* declared Central Park and the Brooklyn Bridge as "the two greatest works of architecture in New York . . . each . . . a magnificent object in its own right, each . . . the result of a brilliant synthesis of art and engineering after which the world was never quite the same." Each was also a product of municipal enterprise, the creation of a city government said to be the worst in Christendom. Moreover, can one visit San Francisco's Golden Gate Park or enter

McKim, Mead, and White's palatial Boston Public Library and pronounce these landmarks evidence of weakness or failure? Indeed, can those city fathers be deemed "unimaginative" who hired the great landscape architect Frederick Law Olmsted to design the first public park system in human history? And were the vast nineteenth-century water and drainage schemes that still serve the cities the handiwork of bumbling incompetents unable to cope with the demands of expanding industrial metropolises?

. . . Only recently has an admirable group of studies begun to explore the work of . . . municipal technicians who were vital to the formulation and implementation of public policy. But prior to the 1970s accounts of dualistic conflicts between political bosses and good-government reformers predominated, obscuring the complexities of municipal rule and the diversity of elements actually vying to power and participating in city government. And such traditional accounts accepted as axiomatic the inadequacy of the formal municipal structure. Critics have trumpeted its failures, while its triumphs have gone unheralded.

If one recognizes some of the challenges that municipal leaders faced during the period 1870 to 1900, the magnitude of their achievements becomes clear. The leaders of the late nineteenth century inherited an urban scene of great tumult and stress and an urban population of increasing diversity and division. During the midcentury, thousands of Roman Catholic immigrants from Ireland and Germany had flooded American metropolitan areas, threatening the traditional Protestant dominance and ignoring sharp ethic conflicts. . . . The melting pot was coming to a boil, and yet throughout the 1870s, 1880s, and 1890s waves of newcomers continued to enter the country, including more and more representatives of the alien cultures of southern and eastern Europe. . . .

The rush of migrants from both Europe and rural America combined with a high birth rate to produce another source of municipal problems, a soaring urban population. New York City, Boston, Baltimore, and Philadelphia were dynamic centers, expanding rapidly and increasing their populations at a rate of 30 percent to 40 percent each decade. Chicago, on the average, doubled its population each decade between 1870 and 1900, and elsewhere, growth rates of 50 percent or 60 percent were not unusual. During the last thirty years of the century, the nation's chief cities absorbed thousands of acres of new territory to accommodate this booming population, and once-compact cities sprawled outward from the urban core. This expansion and sprawl produced demands for the extension of services and the construction of municipal facilities. The newly annexed peripheral wards needed sewer lines and water mains; they required fire and police protection; and residents of outlying districts expected the city to provide paved streets and lighting. Municipal governments could not simply maintain their services at existing levels; instead, they had to guarantee the extension of those services to thousands of new urban dwellers.

Improved and expanded municipal services, however, required funding, and revenue therefore posed another challenge for city rulers. Municipalities markedly extended their endeavors during the midcentury, purchasing waterworks, creating paid fire brigades, establishing public school systems, and forming modern police forces. To pay for this, taxes rose and municipal indebtedness soared. Taxpayer revolts were common as early as the 1850s, with angry citizens in New

York City, Chicago, Philadelphia, and Milwaukee complaining of public extravagance and corruption and already urging a more frugal, businesslike administration of municipal government. . . . And throughout the 1880s and 1890s city governments faced the difficult problem of meeting rising expectations for services while at the same time satisfying demands for moderate taxes and fiscal conservatism. This was perhaps the toughest task confronting the late-nineteenth-century municipality.

During the last three decades of the century, American city government did, however, meet these challenges of diversity, growth, and financing with remarkable success. By century's close, American city dwellers enjoyed, on the average, as high a standard of public services as any urban residents in the world. . . . Moreover, America's cities achieved this level of modern service while remaining solvent and financially sound. No major American municipality defaulted on its debt payments during the 1890s, and by the end of the century all of the leading municipalities were able to sell their bonds at premium and pay record-low interest. Any wise financier would have testified that the bonds of these purported strongholds of inefficiency and peculation, the municipal corporations, were far safer investments than were the bonds of those quintessential products of American business ingenuity: the railroad corporations.

Not only did the city governments serve their residents without suffering financial collapse, but municipal leaders also achieved an uneasy balance of the conflicting forces within the city, accommodating each through a distribution of authority. Though commentators often claimed that the "better elements" of the urban populace had surrendered municipal administration to the hands of "low-bred" Irish saloonkeepers, such observations were misleading. Similarly incorrect is the claim that the business and professional elite abandoned city government during the late nineteenth century to decentralized lower-class ward leaders. The patrician, the plutocrat, the plebian, and the professional bureaucrat all had their place in late-nineteenth-century municipal government; each staked an informal but definite claim to a particular domain within the municipal structure.

Upper-middle-class business figures presided over the executive branch and the independent park, library, and sinking-fund commissions. Throughout the last decades of the nineteenth century the mayor's office was generally in the hands of solid businessmen or professionals who were native-born Protestants. The leading executive officers were persons of citywide reputation and prestige, and during the period 1870 to 1900 their formal authority was increasing. Meanwhile, the legislative branch—the board of aldermen or city council—became the stronghold of small neighborhood retailers, often of immigrant background, who won their aldermanic seats because of their neighborhood reputation as good fellows willing to gain favor for their constituents. . . .

At the same time, an emerging body of trained experts was also securing a barony of power within city government. Even before the effective application of formal civil service laws, mayors and commissioners deferred to the judgment and expertise of professional engineers, landscape architects, educators, physicians, and fire chiefs, and a number of such figures served decade after decade in municipal posts, despite political upheavals in the executive and legislative branches. . . .

Such extralegal participants as political parties and civic leagues also exerted their influence over municipal government, attempting to tip the uneasy balance of forces in their direction. The political party organization with its ward-based neighborhood bosses was one lever that the immigrants and less affluent could pull to affect the course of government. Civic organizations and reform leagues, in contrast, bolstered the so-called better element in government, the respected businessmen who usually dominated the leading executive offices and the independent commissions. Emerging professional groups such as engineering clubs and medical societies often lent their support to the rising ambitions and growing authority of the expert bureaucracy and permanent civil servants. And special-interest lobbyists like the fire insurance underwriters also urged professionalism in such municipal services as the fire department. Municipal government was no simple dualistic struggle between a city-wide party boss with a diamond shirt stud and malodorous cigar and a good-government reformer with a Harvard degree and kid gloves. Various forces were pushing and pulling the municipal corporations, demanding a response to petitions and seeking a larger voice in the chambers of city government.

State legislatures provided the structural flexibility to respond to these demands. The state legislatures enjoyed the sovereign authority to bestow municipal powers and to determine the municipal structure, but when considering local measures, state lawmakers generally deferred to the judgment of the legislative delegation from the affected locality. If the local delegation favored a bill solely affecting its constituents, the legislature usually ratified the bill without opposition or debate. . . .

Local delegations, however, responded not only to the requests of the formal rulers of the city—the board of aldermen and the mayor; they also considered the petitions of extralegal agencies eager to obtain favors and reforms. Recourse to the state legislature became an alternate route for those seeking action, a detour around the obstruction of city authorities. . . .

Why, then, all the complaints? . . . Why was municipal government so much abused? The answer lies in a fundamental irony. The late-nineteenth century municipal structure accommodated everyone but satisfied no one. It was a system of compromise among parties discontented with compromise. It was a marriage of convenience, with the spouses providing a reasonably comfortable home for America's urban inhabitants. But it was not a happy home. The parties to the nuptials tolerated one another because they had to. Nevertheless, the businessman-mayors and plutocrat park commissioners disliked their dependence on ward politicians, whom they frequently regarded as petty grafters, and they frowned upon the power of the immigrant voters. Likewise, the emerging corps of civil servants was irked by interference from laypersons of both high and low status. And the plebian party boss opposed efforts to extend the realm of the civil servants who had performed no partisan duties and thus merited no power. None liked their interdependence with persons they felt to be unworthy, incompetent, or hostile.

Enhancing this dissatisfaction was the cultural absolutism of the Victorian era. The late nineteenth century was an age when the business elite could refer to itself as the "best element" of society and take for granted its "God-given" superiority. . . . It was also an age when most Protestants viewed Catholics as papal pawns and devotees of Italian idolatry, while most Catholics believed Protestants were little better than heathens and doomed to a quick trip to hell with no stops in purgatory. The late nineteenth century was not an age of cultural relativism but one of cultural absolutes, an age when people still definitely knew right from wrong, the correct from the erroneous. . . . Although the prefix *poly* and the term *relativism* were alien to the guiding principles of the nineteenth century, they are basic to any description of urban government in that era.

Some leaders of the period could, without troubled conscience, act as broker and bargainer, and these figures thrived in urban politics. For example, the highborn Mayor Carter Harrison, Sr., of Chicago, was a master of municipal government and a pragmatic politician who seemed to enjoy the heterogeneity of his city. Likewise, in New York City the low-born Tammany boss Richard Croker commanded his motley metropolis, though he was unable to master the mechanism sufficiently to prevent the ouster of his organization twice in a decade. And a number of high-minded gentlemen seemed capable of playing the game of politics and winning the mayoral office, though they might turn to reform periodicals and lambaste in print the very system they exploited. Still, the idea of reaching an accommodation with grafters, saloonkeepers, and other social pariahs seemed reprehensible, especially among the upper middle class. Through its control of executive offices and independent commissions, the upper middle class was usually the dominant force within city government, and America's municipalities proved especially effective in providing services for that class. . . . No other group, however, proved more hostile in its attacks on the existing system of municipal rule. Though often effective, city government was, according to upper-middle-class critics, almost always dishonorable.

Late-nineteenth-century urban government was a failure not of structure but of image. The system proved reasonably successful in providing services, but there was no prevailing ideology to validate its operation. In fact, the beliefs of the various participants were at odds with the structure of rule that governed them. The respectable elements believed in sobriety and government by persons of character. But the system of accommodation permitted whiskey taps to flow on the Sabbath for the Irish and for Germans, just as it allowed men in shiny suits with questionable reputations to occupy seats on the city council and in the municipal party conventions. The ward-based party devotees accepted the notions of Jacksonian democracy and believed quite literally in the maxim To the victor belong the spoils. But by the 1890s they faced a growing corps of civil servants more devoted to their profession than to any party. Although new professional bureaucrats preached a gospel of expertise, they still had to compromise with party-worshipping hacks and the supposedly diabolical forces of politics. Likewise, special-interest lobbyists such as the fire insurance underwriters were forced to cajole or coerce political leaders whom they deemed ignorant and unworthy of public office. Each of these groups worked together, but only from necessity and not because they believed in such a compromise of honor. There was no ideology of heterogeneous polyarchy, no system of beliefs to bolster the

existing government structure. Thus late-ninteenth-century city government survived without moral support, and to many urban dwellers it seemed a bargain
with the devil.

※ *F U R T H E R   R E A D I N G*

John M. Allswang, *Bosses, Machines, and Urban Voters: An American Symbiosis* (1977)
Blaine A. Brownell and Warren E. Stickle, eds., *Bosses and Reformers: Urban Politics in
America, 1880–1920* (1973)
John D. Buenker, *Urban Liberalism and Progressive Reform* (1973)
William A. Bullough, *The Blind Boss and His City: Christopher Augustus Buckley and
Nineteenth-Century San Francisco* (1979)
Alexander B. Callow, Jr., ed., *The City Boss in America: An Interpretive Reader* (1976)
James B. Crooks, *Politics and Progress: The Rise of Urban Progressivism in Baltimore,
1895–1911* (1968)
Lyle Dorsett, *The Pendergast Machine* (1968)
Michael Ebner and Eugene Tobin, eds., *The Age of Urban Reform: New Perspectives on
the Progressive Era* (1977)
Kenneth Fox, *Better City Government: Innovation in American Urban Politics, 1850–
1937* (1977)
David C. Hammack, *Power and Society: Greater New York at the Turn of the Century*
(1982)
Carl V. Harris, *Political Power in Birmingham, 1877–1921* (1977)
Leo Hershkowitz, *Tweed's New York: Another Look* (1977)
Melvin G. Holli, *Reform in Detroit: Hazen S. Pingree and Urban Politics* (1969)
William Issel and Robert W. Cherny, *San Francisco, 1863–1932: Politics, Power, and
Urban Development* (1986)
Terrence J. McDonald, *The Parameters of Urban Fiscal Policy: Socioeconomic Change
and Political Culture in San Francisco, 1860–1906* (1986)
Seymour Mandelbaum, *Boss Tweed's New York* (1965)
William D. Miller, *Mr. Crump of Memphis* (1964)
Zane L. Miller, *Boss Cox's Cincinnati* (1968)
Bradley R. Rice, *Progressive Cities: The Commission Government Movement in Amer-
ica, 1901–1920* (1977)
Martin J. Schiesl, *The Politics of Efficiency: Municipal Administration and Reform in
America, 1880–1920* (1977)
Bruce M. Stave and Sondra Stave, eds., *Urban Bosses, Machines, and Progressive Re-
formers,* 2d rev. ed. (1972)

CHAPTER 8

Urban Professionals

in the Progressive Era

⁂

The closing decades of the nineteenth century and opening decades of the twentieth have attracted more attention from urban historians than any comparable period in American history. These were years not only of extraordinary social change through migration and immigration, economic change from industrialization, and political turmoil from bosses and machines, but also of exciting ferment from various reform movements. The last chapter introduced issues and personalities of civic reform—the attempts to root out corruption and alter the form of local government. This chapter focuses on institutional and social reform—efforts by men and women to improve the urban environment with new, often professional, methods.

Two kinds of professions developed to respond to particular urban problems. One, dominated by men, involved the application of technology and scientific expertise to the structural and environmental needs of cities. This group of reformers consisted of engineers, medical professionals, and planners who did not consider themselves politicians but who often were employed by government officials and public agencies. The other group of professions, primarily the domain of women, emerged from women's attempt to transfer their traditional functions of nurture and service to public institutions such as schools, charities, and settlement houses. Excluded from politics by voting laws that, before 1920, allowed only men to participate in the electoral process, these service-minded women developed strategies of urban reform that enabled them to make major contributions to progressivism, the reform spirit that swept the nation in the early twentieth century.

⁂ DOCUMENTS

The following three documents illustrate the gender divisions between urban administration and social reform in the late nineteenth and early twentieth centuries. The first document, by the well-known sanitary engineer George Waring, shows the emergence of engineering as an important influence on urban administration, in this case, on addressing the mounting requirements of sanitation and public health. The second selection comprises two excerpted articles illustrating the role of women in social reform and in what at the time was called municipal house-keeping, the application of domestic skills to the needs of cities for better cleanliness, health, and safety. The third document is a noted essay by Jane Addams, the founder of Hull House in Chicago and the most famous of settlement-house reformers. The treatise reveals several themes of settlement-inspired social reform: the impulse of educated young people who sought an outlet for their desires to apply their knowledge to social problems; the frustrations of young women who had been discouraged from moving into public life and aiding society; the religious motivation of service upon which settlements rested; and the belief that settlement-house reformers should cooperate with inner-city laboring classes, not impose their own values upon them.

Engineer George E. Waring on Modern Sewage Disposal, 1891

The life of man involves both the production of food, directly or indirectly by the growth of plants, and the consumption and destruction of the organized products of such growth. The production and the destruction are constant. Between consumption and renewed growth there intervenes a process which prepares what we reject for the use of plants.

It is this intervening process that we have to consider in applying the comparatively new art of sewage disposal. The process itself has gone on from the beginning of the world, but it has been left to unguided natural action, which takes no account of the needs and conditions of modern communities.

In the primitive life of sparse populations, it was comparatively safe to disregard it; but, as population became more dense, and, especially as men gathered into communities, it became increasingly important to bring it under control, for it then involved a serious menace to the safety of the people. So long as our off-scourings could be scattered broadcast over the ground, their destruction was attended with little danger; but when it became necessary to concentrate them in underground receptacles, a capacity for real mischief was developed. As these receptacles increased, with the growth of communities, the menace increased, until, in the light of modern knowledge as to the conditions of healthful living, the need for radical measures of relief became obvious. It is the application of these measures that we are now to consider.

The sewerage of towns, and the drainage of important buildings, are now controlled by expert engineers, and they rarely fail to be reasonably well done. The economy of good plans is understood, and especially the vital necessity for good construction. In fact, it may be said that the adoption of excellent methods and appliances for removing liquid wastes from houses and towns is becoming general. It will in time become universal.

This, however, is only the first step in sanitary improvement. It is only the step of removal. It gets our wastes out of our immediate neighborhoods; it does not destroy them. It is now recognized that quick and complete removal is only the beginning of the necessary service, and that proper ultimate disposal is no less important to health, to decency, and to public comfort. The organic wastes of

A City Street Before and After Sanitation Reform

Street cleaning was one of the major accomplishments of urban engineers in the late nineteenth century. These photographs show two views of New York City's Fifth Avenue before and after the appointment of George C. Waring as sanitation commissioner in 1893.

human life must be finally and completely consumed. It is not enough to get them out of the house and out of the town; until they are resolved into their elements, their capacity for harm and for offense is not ended. It does not suffice to discharge them into a cesspool, nor does it always suffice to discharge them into a harbor, or into a water-course, leaving them there to the slow process of putrefaction.

The need for improving the conditions of sewage-disposal has long been recognized, and, especially in connection with large foreign towns, efforts of the most costly character have been made to obviate accumulations due to the discharge of sewers. The floods made foul with the wastes of the huge population of London have been poured into the Thames, until, in spite of years of effort to relieve that river, its condition has become, in the language of Lord Bramwell, "a disgrace to the Metropolis and to civilization." The millions expended since 1850 on the still unsolved problem have not thus far effected more than a mitigation of the evil. London is today, apparently, as far as ever from its ultimate solution, though of course the former direct discharge of sewage all along the river front, and the resulting local stench, have been suppressed. The case grows in gravity with the growth of the population, and measures which promise success when adopted are not able to cope with the greater volumes produced later. . . .

In our country, New York City and the towns on the Mississippi, and on other very large rivers, have such tidal and flood conditions as to secure satisfactory disposal by dilution and removal. At Boston, Philadelphia, and Chicago, the needed relief can, under the methods adopted, be secured only by works of the greatest magnitude and cost, while the smaller towns have, as a rule, yet to devise methods by which, unless they are exceptionally well placed, they can destroy their wastes at a practicable cost. The importance of relief is being more and more realized, but the means of relief are little understood by the people. A wider appreciation of the efficiency of these means is a necessary condition precedent to general improvement.

Systematic works, chiefly by removal through intercepting sewers, have, until recently, been confined to cities. Smaller towns are now perfecting their methods of removal, and there is a growing desire to find means for purifying the outflow which will not cost more than can be afforded. Interest is also growing among householders, who are becoming convinced of the dangers of cesspools, with their retention of putrefying wastes within contaminating reach of houses and of their sources of water-supply.

In its progress thus far, the art of disposal has worked itself out mainly by progressive practice. It began in the instinctive desire to get offensive matters out of sight. As new difficulties presented themselves, and as the requirements of a better civilization arose, new methods were devised for better concealment in the ground, or better removal by sewers. . . . It is hardly half a century since the dangers of incomplete sewage removal were appreciated and radical measures of relief were attempted. In London, large brick sewers, not only in the streets, but under and about houses, which had long existed as the seats of foul deposits, now had their condition pointed out, and a "Blue Book" of the British Parliament, published in 1852, set it forth in a manner to secure effective attention. It was shown that these sewers and drains were so large that they could not be kept clean by their natural flow. It was then that the movement for the use of pipes for sewerage and house drainage received its first general impetus.

In 1857 there was presented to Parliament a report by Henry Austin, C.E., on the means of deodorizing and utilizing the sewage of towns. There followed, not only an improvement of much of the local drainage on London, but the carrying out of a plan for keeping foul sewage out of the Thames, by collecting it in reservoirs some miles down the river, to be discharged at the beginning of the outgoing tide. As has already been intimated, this work was ineffective, so far as the main purpose of purifying the Thames was concerned, and the problem seems still to be overtaxing the capacity of English engineers.

There was, at that time, little knowledge of the proper means of relief in such cases, and the enormous sums spent in works for the discharge of the sewage on the outgoing tide soon proved to have been a misdirected expenditure. The art of sewerage had, for many years, confined itself to an improvement of the means for distant removal, and the world accepted and still accepts, as a part of the policy of its great cities, the inevitable construction of majestic and costly engineering works for this service, carrying not only foul sewage, but floods of storm water as well. It is now demonstrated that, even at London, and in all but a few exceptional conditions, like those of New York, where the whole harbor is flushed twice a day by the great tides coming in through Long Island Sound and passing out at Sandy Hook, and of towns on great rivers, the effect of such works is, largely, to remove the point of deposit, not to prevent deposit, and that the great volume of their discharge has often added to the difficulty of final disposal. . . . Sooner or later, the provision of some means of purification, or, at least, of the removal of the grosser impurities of the sewerage, becomes imperative, and the question of sewage disposal is assuming greater importance year by year.

The tendency of legislation, here as well as abroad, is toward the prohibition of the fouling of rivers, thus far mainly for the protection of sources of water-supply. This is doing much, and promises to do more, in the way of restricting the free discharge of sewage into streams. There is also a growing sentiment in favor of cleanliness, and causes of offence which have hitherto been disregarded are now attracting attention. Those who occupy lands past which streams flow are beginning to assert and to enforce their undoubted right to have them flow in their natural unfouled condition. . . .

So, too, on the larger streams, villages are growing to towns, towns are growing to important cities, and conditions which were formerly tolerable are now becoming intolerable. The Schuylkill River, for example, which is the most important source of water-supply for Philadelphia, is lined with populous and growing manufacturing towns, which have only this river for an outlet, and which also take their water-supply from it. The same conditions exist along many of the rivers of New England, and throughout the older parts of the country generally, and they are extending westward. It is therefore clear that, in the case of towns not lying on the larger rivers, public sentiment and the rights of riparian owners will demand the increasing adoption of means for withholding crude sewage from them.

The following was written [by Waring] in 1888: "It is not likely that towns situated on great rivers or on the seacoast will, for a long time to come, give thought to any other disposal of their sewage than its discharge directly into the river or into the sea. As the country fills up, and as towns situated on small streams, or on no stream, increase in size and in wisdom, they must, perforce, seek for some means to get rid of the copious flow of water, made foul by its passage through the houses and shops of the people. The indications are clear that legislative control of this matter cannot long be delayed, and there is no more intricate or more interesting problem now presented to the sanitarian than the correct solution of this great question of the future. . . ."

During the years that have since elapsed, the most important investigations of the Massachusetts State Board of Health . . . have confirmed the theories then held, and have thrown much light on the methods by which they may best be reduced to practice. It was only after this clear definition and demonstration of the processes involved, and of the methods of their application, that we were in a position to work with real knowledge. Then only could empiricism be made to give place to well-established theory.

Could we now set aside the influence of long years of practical work, the atmosphere would be greatly cleared; but practical work has a very persistent influence, and the art of purifying sewage will long feel the effect of experience with methods which would not have been devised in the light of what is now known. When the first attempts were made to get rid of the impurities of sewage by artificial means, great importance was universally attached to their manurial value, and promise was held forth of great profit to result from their development into a useful form. The obstacle of extreme dilution was not appreciated, and it was long before the discovery was made that, as with the gold said to exist in sea water, the attempt to separate these matters by artificial methods would cost more than they were worth.

The belief also prevailed that the chief source of offensiveness of sewage lay in the solid fecal matter that it contained, and this belief still finds much popular acceptance. One of the most prominent sanitary exhibits at the World's Fair in Chicago, a Russian invention, has the separation of this matter for its chief end, and the description accompanying it urges such separation as the *sine qua non* and the chief need of hygiene improvement. Even in Paris, where the purification of sewage is being carried out on a very large scale, and where its requirements are well understood, the use of the *tinette filtre,* which holds back the solid parts of house drainage until they putrefy, and then allows them to flow to the sewer, in this worst possible form, has within recent years been allowed to come into extensive use. At Newport the old rule still prevails largely, that house drainage shall be retained in cesspools until it can, after decomposition, overflow as a foul liquid into the public sewers. The fact is, that fecal matter is of far less consequence than urine and the waste of the kitchen sink.

Then, too, it was long thought that if sewage could be purged of its suspended matter,—of that which clouds it and colors it,—purification would be effected. An imperfect clarification by mechanical or chemical processes is still applied in some cases where a high degree of purification is really needed, although it is now well known that such clarification does not and cannot remove from sewage its most putrescible matters, nor its minute living organisms. Imperfect results, which have satisfied legal requirements in Europe, are in such cases accepted as sufficient, in spite of a recognition of their incompleteness.

The purification of sewage is surely on the eve of great extension in this country, and it is necessary to its success that the importance of making it as thorough as possible be made known, as well as its conditions and requirements. If the work is to be done at all, it is worth while to do it well. Half-way measures, like chemical precipitants, may satisfy present legal demands, and they may, in exceptional cases, be advisable, but they will not meet the requirements of the better-informed public opinion that is now growing up. The means for entire purification are within reach, and imperfect results will not long be accepted as sufficient.

In practical work, two cardinal principles should be kept in view, and should control our actions:—

(a) *Organic wastes must be discharged at the sewer outlet in their fresh condition,—before putrefaction has set in;* and

(b) *They must be reduced to a state of complete oxidation without the intervention of dangerous or offensive decomposition.*

Two Views of Women's Role in Social Reform, c. 1900

Hester M. McClung on Women's Work in Indianapolis

In 1893, the year of the cholera scare, Mrs. R. S. McKee and Miss Catherine Merrill conceived an idea which materialized into the Indianapolis Sanitary Association, the first group of women in the city to deliberately reach forth into the realm of municipal affairs. The aim of the organization is to render assistance to the city officials in their efforts to secure cleanly and healthful conditions.

At first, meetings were held in different parts of the city, where sanitation was discussed, and people of all classes awakened to the importance of cleanliness as a health measure. These meetings, in connection with brief but frequent press articles calling attention to the subject, marked the beginning of an era of steady advancement in the city's ideals of cleanliness. Reports of nuisances discovered are passed upon by the executive board, copied upon blanks furnished by the city, signed by the secretary and forwarded to the Board of Health, which proceeds to take action.

The work of the Association has been distributed principally among the following standing committees: markets, hospital and dispensary, schools and school buildings, garbage, clean streets, clean sidewalks and buildings, parks, literature and emergency. Unremitting attention has also been given to the inspection of meats, milk, wells, cellars, cesspools, vaults, etc.

In the newness of the work, the garbage problem appeared impossible of solution, but in due time it was successfully attacked. Collection of garbage at the city's expense and a crematory to destroy it, were two plans persistently advocated by the Association, until now after these many anxious years, no stale garbage lurks in the back yard of even the veriest hovel. The committee and the city superintendent fully understand each other's methods and work hand in hand to keep solved this most obstinate question. Of course, the possession of a crematory and collection at the city's expense, are not due to the efforts of the sanitary association alone, but it has played a most important part.

Every school building in the city has been personally inspected by a committee of the association, and reports on lighting, heating, ventilation of rooms and basements, disinfection of floors and desks, condition of closets, etc., are from time to time made to the health board, with suggestions for improvement. Largely through its efforts, individual drinking cups have been provided, and invaluable service has been rendered in the prevention of contagious diseases.

Through the vigilance of another committee, considerable has been done towards keeping the streets clean. A personal acquaintance with the sweeping inspector exists, and reports of ineffective work receive attention at once. Directly through the suggestion and plan of the Association, smoke-stacks of the pneumatic sweepers were re-adjusted to prevent the flames from injuring the foliage of shade trees.

In view of the difficulties which the anti-expectoration committee encountered, its work may be considered preeminently successful. Placards reading, "Gentlemen will not spit in this car," have been placed in all of the street cars. At the request of the Association, police powers have been granted to the janitor of the city library in order to prevent its defilement. Ordinances prohibiting expectoration in theatres, public places of amusement and street cars have been passed by the city council at the solicitation of the Association. These ordinances are not strictly enforced, but considerable advancement has been made and a strong public spirit aroused in this direction.

The park committee through petitions signed by hundreds, and by many other means, has persistently worked against the pollution of streams, and advocated purchase of land for parks along the water courses. The purchase of dumps and other unhealthful waste places for park purposes has also been urged, the city thus securing both beauty and healthful conditions with but slight expense.

Park Memorial Tree Association. The ladies of this Association, which was called into existence by the gentlemen of the Commercial Club and the Board of Park Commissioners, have interested themselves in the improvement of street lawns and shade trees. Through their influence dead and unsightly trees have been removed, living trees properly trimmed, and the hideous work of the advertising fiend has been torn from trees, telephone poles, bridges and other public structures. Memorial trees have been planted with appropriate ceremonies; the subject has been kept before the public through the press articles and various other means have been used to increase the city's interest and care for its trees. An ordinance, in whose construction the Association had its influence, is now pending. It gives to the park superintendent a partial control of the planting and removal of street shade trees, and it prohibits the placing of advertisements thereon. The Association formed a club of boys who were thoughtlessly ruining a fine stretch of street lawn. The boys were consulted regarding plans for its preservation, and each was given some specific task for which he was responsible. A more neatly-kept strip of lawn is not now seen in the city, and each of those eight boys holds his head higher, because of the sense of citizenship engendered by the possession of responsibility in the city's improvement.

Some years ago the Meridian Street Woman's Christian Temperance Union, realizing the treatment to which women, girls and little boys were subjected while in detention at the police station, asked and gained permission from the proper city officials to try, at their own expense, the experiment of placing a matron in charge of a "woman's department" for the term of six months. At the end of this period the progress toward refinement was of such perceptible proportions that the authorities gladly adopted the idea, and the office of the police matron has since been an important feature in the city's system of government. Out of this movement grew the office of jail matron and also a state law creating the office of police matron in cities of a certain size throughout the state.

The Society of Hygiene confines its interests chiefly to personal and household hygiene, but the city is indebted to its influence for the readjustment of an alley crossing in the center of the business district where thousands of pedestrians had been subjected to an enormous waste of physical force necessitated by the long and awkward step required to descend and arise from the alley grade.

The agitation of the wine room evil by the Local Council of Women, first fixed the attention of the author of the "Nicholson Bill" on that phase of the temperance question, and as Mr. Nicholson says, the passage of his bill was the result. The Local Council has also been instrumental, together with other organizations and individuals, in securing compulsory school attendance and the curfew ordinance, both of which measures add greatly to the progress and safety of the city.

Several years ago, Miss Florence Fay established a sewing school (the first of its kind) in a section of the city where employment for young children was sadly needed. When Mrs. Eliza Blaker, the pioneer apostle of Froebel, came to the city, this little manual training school was given to her as a foundation for what has grown to be extended system of free kindergartens. To the Free Kindergarten Society, which was formed for the support of these schools, the city is indebted for the advanced ideas of citizenship held by the rising generation.

Through the efforts of Miss Lydia Blaich, a vacation school was maintained in the summer of 1897. Its fascination for the children, who would otherwise have been in the street, was so markedly beneficial that the school was reopened this summer, under the auspices of the Local Council of Women—an organization composed of fifty or more of the woman's societies of the city.

The Woman's Club, a pioneer and select organization which has hitherto been devoted to purely literary interests, has now donated funds for the purchase of the outfit of this vacation school, and have permission from the school board to introduce this industrial work, as an experiment, in one of the ward buildings this school year.

The Young People's Circle, composed of young ladies of Plymouth Congregational Church, during the last two summers, has maintained a playground for children in one of the school yards. The circle bears the expense of swings, games and the maintenance of a kindergartner in charge.

Indeed the air seems rife with all manner of projects for the improvement of citizenship which is certainly one way of securing better municipal conditions.

Martha A. B. Conine on Women's Work in Denver

The work in municipal affairs of the women of Denver dates back only to the organization of The Woman's Club of Denver, which began its work in the autumn of 1895. It was founded upon the lines of the well-known Chicago Women's Club, and at the present time has a membership of over one thousand names. It is divided into six departments, one of these being the department of reform. This department is again subdivided into various committees, one of the most popular of these being the city improvement committee, under the chairmanship of Mrs. Jaspar D. Ward. Its work has been and will continue to be largely educational. The following extracts from its report at the end of its first year, gives a very good idea of its scope and progress:

On April 8th the chair appointed a committee to interview the shopkeepers on Sixteenth street, between Curtis and Arapahoe streets, asking them to hire a man to keep that block clean. They did so. That hired man went to work with brush and dustpan on Thursday. On the following Monday the city had six men at work in the same manner, and by the end of the month, we left the city to do the work and pay the men. That was brought about by the force of example and the hearty co-operation of the street cleaning department, Mr. Northington and city officials. The abatement of nuisances, the hearing of complaints, and all attempts to secure the enforcement of much needed but neglected ordinances, is the province of the ordinance committee. The difficulty of finding men of sufficient leisure for the work, and the urgent advice of leading citizens that it be kept in the hands of women, led to this result.

Through the health commissioner, Dr. Munn, notices against expectoration on the sidewalk and in all public places have been posted whenever people would permit it. A committee was appointed to wait upon street car officials, asking them to put these notices in their cars. Col. Randolph of the Cable Line at once placed them on his line, at his own expense. The tramway lines are just now putting them in all their cars. When Mrs. Trautman of the Health Protective Association of New York visited Denver this summer, she said to the chairman of this committee: "You have accomplished more in two years along the line of prohibiting promiscuous expectoration in Denver, than we have been able to in seven."

Two dozen rubbish cans were put upon the corners of the down-town streets. This was accomplished by a persistent visiting of the city hall, and we are indebted to Mr. Northington, of the Street Cleaning Department, for these cans.

Trees for Public Ways.   During the past year, the club has worked to save Thirteenth avenue from a proposed widening of the block between Grant and Logan avenues, thereby helping to save a fine row of trees. Our study of methods prevailing in the Eastern cities as to the care and disposal of unlicensed dogs, and our continued protests against the ineffective law of Denver, aroused such interest among city officials that an excellent ordinance was framed, and after long agitation, was passed by the council. The study of Shaw's "Municipal Government of Continental Cities," was continued through the summer under the direction of Miss Sarah Spalding. Such loud outcry was raised by the severe pruning of trees around public buildings, that we arranged a conference on trees with the city officials and those citizens who have shown special interest in the subject. After long study of methods adopted in the older towns and cities, the appointment of a city forester was advocated, to whom shall be given the sole right to prune the trees outside the lot line along our streets. Recently the matter of a more uniform and complete method of planting trees around the public schools was presented by us to the school board, through the chairman of buildings and grounds, Dr. Mary Barker Bates. The gratifying announcement has been made by her, in consequence, that the board has voted to spend $500 on trees on next Arbor Day. A committee from this society has visited every school and presented in detail the needs of each school yard.

Vacant Lot Cultivation.   Another branch of work carried on by the Women's Club may, perhaps, more properly be said to belong under the head of philanthropy rather than of municipal improvement, but it certainly has been productive of much good. This work is the "Pingree Gardens," under the supervision of the philanthropic department. Denver, being a young city with a widely extended area, has, in consequence, large tracts of unoccupied ground. The conversion of many of these vacant lots from fields of flourishing noxious weeds into well-kept vegetable gardens, is an improvement even from the artistic point of view. And the material and moral benefit which the city has received by converting a dependent and indolent class, into self-respecting industrious citizens, is incalculable. This work has been under the immediate supervision of Mrs. Fred Butler. Nearly every morning during the past three seasons, she has mounted her wheel and covered ten or fifteen miles in overseeing the labors of the "Pingrees" before returning to lunch.

Seventy gardens have been cultivated during the present season. The use of the lots is donated by their owners. The county authorities pay for the plowing and provide the tools and a superintendent. The Charity Organization furnishes the seeds, and the city the water, which is quite an important factor owing to the fact that in Colorado agriculture is carried on only by irrigation. For the last six months these seventy gardens have provided a livelihood for no less than sixty-five families, or the very considerable number of three hundred and ninety persons; and before the season closes a supply will have been stored away sufficient for winter use, and a surplus exchanged for other necessities.

The Civic Federation.   Coming now to the question of reform in municipal governments, the most palpable results in that line have been effected by the Civic Federation of Denver. This is the only political working organization of women in the state aside from partisan clubs. It is composed entirely of women who are like all the other women of Colorado, full-fledged citizens. It has a central council of one hundred and sub-organizations in each ward of the city. Its membership is divided into four departments: educational, philanthropic, municipal and county affairs, and public morals. The Federation was organized in 1895 by a few members of the reform department of the Woman's Club, and grew out of the need which had been felt by them while attempting to secure legislation upon certain desirable measures. Chief among these was a new primary law based upon the principle of direct nomination of candidates by the voter, without the interruption of the convention, by means of registration and the Australian ballot. The bill was drafted upon precisely the same lines as the plan set forth in the June issue of *Municipal Affairs* by Mr. Record. The Civic Federation is organized on strictly non-partisan lines and immediately attracted to itself women from all parties who had been vainly endeavoring to secure municipal reform through party influence.

The situation as regards any attempt to secure governmental reform in the city of Denver, is a curiously complex one. Denver is not only the state capital, but it is also the county seat. Thus there are three sets of office-holders and would-be office-holders with their various projects and plans, and the frequently recurring elections. All the "public utilities" are in the hands of private corporations. To add to the complication, there is a charter which gives to the governor the power of appointing the fire and police board, and the board of public works. One can readily see, therefore, that although Denver boasts of one of the best street car systems, and one of the finest water supplies of any city in the world, there are many occasions when the interest of the citizen is lost sight of in the scramble for profits and spoils among these various corporations and circles of professional politicians.

The Civic Federation has aimed to cultivate a civic conscience, and to give an opportunity to the lay-citizen to make known his wishes and exercise his political rights in a way which could not be subverted by the schemes of interested ward heelers. It had not intended to become a political party, or to put a ticket in the field, but was forced by circumstances to do so.

A Political Campaign. At the last city election, the Civic Federation, acting in conjunction with the Tax-Payers, a similar organization of men, called a convention in the following manner. Invitations were sent to representative citizens in every line of profession, business or trade, ministers, lawyers, physicians, manufacturers and laborers, regardless of sect, party or sex. A nominating committee appointed jointly by the executive boards of the two afore-mentioned organizations had prepared a list of candidates in accordance with the plan set forth in the primary bill above mentioned. This list was submitted to the convention and quite fully adopted, but no one was pledged to support this list, and any member was privileged to propose a substitute for any name if he wished to do so. The ticket thus nominated rolled up a majority of six thousand at the ensuing election. Not only this, but suspected ballot-box frauds were probed and their perpetrators indicted by the grand jury—a[n] instance unheard of before.

Of course such an overwhelming defeat for the usual manipulators of the city elections awakened the most violent antagonisms. Every effort of time and money was put forward to defeat the reform forces at the next—a county election, which was in many ways as important to Denver as the city election itself.

Although the Federation's candidates were not elected, the election was in one sense a success, and had been productive of one great reform. For during a contest over the election of sheriff, the ballot boxes were opened in the usual manner and a thorough investigation disclosed that in no case was there evidence of fraud. The election so far as the ballots were concerned, had been an honest one.

The Federation is in no sense daunted by one defeat and is pursuing its usual course. It expects the support and confidence of the better class of citizens in the future as in the past, and will not be dismayed by defeat nor calumny.

Jane Addams on What Lured Women to Settlement Houses, c. 1910

This paper is an attempt to analyze the motives which underlie a movement based, not only upon conviction, but upon genuine emotion, wherever educated young people are seeking an outlet for that sentiment of universal brotherhood, which the best spirit of our times is forcing from an emotion into a motive. These young people accomplish little toward the solution of this social problem, and bear the brunt of being cultivated into unnourished, oversensitive lives. They have been shut off from the common labor by which they live which is a great source of moral and physical health. They feel a fatal want of harmony between their theory and their lives, a lack of coordination between thought and action. I think it is hard for us to realize how seriously many of them are taking to the notions of human brotherhood, how eagerly they long to give tangible expression to the democratic ideal. These young men and women, longing to socialize their democracy, are animated by certain hopes which may be thus loosely formulated; that if in a democratic country nothing can be permanently achieved save through the masses of the people, it will be impossible to establish a higher political life than the people themselves crave; that it is difficult to see how the notion of a higher civic life can be fostered save through common intercourse; that the blessings which we associate with a life of refinement and cultivation can be made universal and must be made universal if they are to be permanent; that the good we secure for ourselves is precarious and uncertain, is floating in mid-air, until it is secured for all of us and incorporated into our common life. . . . Nothing so deadens the sympathies and shrivels the power of enjoyment as the persistent keeping away from the great opportunities for helpfulness and a continual ignoring of the starvation struggle which makes up the life of at least half the race. To shut one's self away from that half of the race life is to shut one's self away from the most vital part of it; it is to live out but half the humanity to which we have been born heir and to use but half our faculties. We have all had longings for a fuller life which should include the use of these faculties. These longings are the physical complement of the "Intimations of Immortality," on which no ode has yet been written. To portray these would be the work of a poet, and it is hazardous for any but a poet to attempt it. . . .

"It is true that there is nothing after disease, indigence, and a sense of guilt, so fatal to health and to life itself as the want of a proper outlet for active faculties." I have seen young girls suffer and grow sensibly lowered in vitality in the first years after they leave school. In our attempt then to give a girl pleasure and freedom from care we succeed, for the most part, in making her pitifully miserable. She finds "life" so different from what she expected it to be. She is besotted with innocent little ambitions, and does not understand this apparent waste of herself, this elaborate preparation, if no work is provided for her. There is a heritage of noble obligation which young people accept and long to perpetuate. The desire for action, the wish to right wrong and alleviate suffering haunts them daily. Society smiles at it indulgently instead of making it of value to itself. . . . Parents are often inconsistent: they deliberately expose their daughters to knowledge of the distress in the world; they send them to hear missionary addresses on famines in India and China; they accompany them to lectures on the suffering in Siberia; they agitate together over the forgotten region of East London. In addition to this, from babyhood the altruistic tendencies of these daughters are persistently cultivated. They are taught to be self-forgetting and self-sacrificing, to consider the good of the whole before the good of the ego. But when all this information and culture show results, when the daughter comes back from college and begins to recognize her social claim to the "submerged tenth," and to evince a disposition to fulfill it, the family claim is strenuously asserted; she is told that she is unjustified, ill-advised in her efforts. . . . The girl loses something vital out of her life to which she is entitled. She is restricted and unhappy; her elders, meanwhile, are unconscious of the situation and we have all the elements of a tragedy.

We have in America a fast-growing number of cultivated young people who have no recognized outlet for their active faculties. They hear constantly of the great social maladjustment, but no way is provided for them to change it, and their uselessness hangs about them heavily. . . . They tell their elders with all the bitterness of youth that if they expect success from them in business or politics or in whatever lines their ambition for them has run, they must let them consult all of humanity; that they must let them find out what the people want and how they want it. It is only the stronger young people, however, who formulate this. Many of them dissipate their energies in so-called enjoyment. Others not content with that, go on studying and go back to college for their second degrees; not that they are especially fond of study, but because they want something definite to do, and their powers have been trained in the direction of mental accumulation. . . .

This young life, so sincere in its emotion and good phrase and yet so undirected, seems to me as pitiful as the other great mass of destitute lives. . . . Mr. Barnett, who urged the first Settlement—Toynbee Hall, in East London—recognized this need of outlet for the young men of Oxford and Cambridge, and hoped that the Settlement would supply the communication. It is easy to see why the Settlement movement originated in England, where the years of education are more constrained and definite than they are here, where class distinctions are more rigid. The necessity of it was greater there, but we are fast feeling the pressure of the need and meeting the necessity for Settlement in America. Our young people feel nervously the need of putting theory into action, and respond quickly to the Settlement form and activity.

Other motives which I believe make toward the Settlement are the result of a certain renaissance going forward in Christianity. The impulse to share the lives of the poor, the desire to make social service, irrespective of propaganda, express the spirit of Christ, is as old as Christianity itself. . . .

That Christianity has to be revealed and embodied in the line of social progress is a corollary to the simple proposition that man's action is found in his social relationships in the way in which he connects with his fellows; that his motives for action are the zeal and affection with which he regards his fellows. By this simple process was created a deep enthusiasm for humanity, which regarded man as at once the organ and the object of revelation; and by this process came about the wonderful fellowship, the true democracy of the early Church, that so captivates the imagination. . . .

I believe that there is a distinct turning among many young men and women toward this simple acceptance of Christ's message. They resent the assumption that Christianity is a set of ideas which belongs to the religious consciousness, whatever that may be. They insist that it cannot be proclaimed and instituted apart from the social life of the community and that it must seek a simple and natural expression in the social organism itself. The Settlement movement is only one manifestation of that wider humanitarian movement which throughout Christendom, but pre-eminently in England, is endeavoring to embody itself, not in a sect, but in society itself. . . .

I believe that this turning, this renaissance of the early Christian humanitarianism, is going on in America, in Chicago, if you please, without leaders who write or philosophize, without much speaking, but with a bent to express in social service and in terms of action the spirit of Christ. Certain it is that spiritual force is found in the Settlement movement, and it is also true that this force must be evoked and must be called into play before the success of any Settlement is assured. There must be the overmastering belief that all that is noblest in life is common to men as men, in order to accentuate the likenesses and ignore the differences which are found among the people whom the Settlement constantly brings into juxtaposition. . . .

The Settlement, then, is an experimental effort to aid in the solution of the social and industrial problems which are engendered by the modern conditions of life in a great city. It insists that these problems are not confined to any one portion of a city. It is an attempt to relieve, at the same time, the overaccumulation at one end of society and the destitution at the other; but it assumes that this overaccumulation and destitution is most sorely felt in the things that pertain to social and educational privileges. From its very nature it can stand for no political or social propaganda. . . . The one thing to be dreaded in the Settlement is that it lose its flexibility, its power of quick adaptation, its readiness to change its methods as its environment may demand. It must be open to conviction and must have a deep and abiding sense of tolerance. It must be hospitable and ready for experiment. It should demand from its residents a scientific patience in the accumulation of facts and the steady holding of their sympathies as one of the best instruments for that accumulation. It must be grounded in a philosophy whose foundation is on the solidarity of the human race, a philosophy which will not waver when the race happens to be represented by a drunken woman or an idiot boy. Its residents must be emptied of all conceit of opinion and all self-assertion, and ready to arouse and interpret the public opinion of their neighborhood. They must be content to live quietly side by side with their neighbors, until they grow into a sense of relationship and mutual interests. . . . They are bound to see the needs of their neighborhood as a whole, to furnish data for legislation, and to use their influence to secure it. In short, residents are pledged to devote themselves to the duties of good citizenship and to the arousing of social energies which too largely lie dormant in every neighborhood given over to industrialism. They are bound to regard the entire life of their city as organic, to make an effort to unify it, and to protest against its overdifferentiation. . . .

✳ *E S S A Y S*

The first essay, by Martin Melosi of the University of Houston, focuses on "municipal housekeeping" and the municipal engineers who figured as a third major influence (accompanying political bosses and reformers) on urban growth. In his analysis in the second essay, Stanley Schultz of the University of Wisconsin, Madison, offers further revision of the boss-reformer dichotomy by tracing the roots of urban planning in the crucial but underappreciated accomplishments of urban engineers. The subjects of Melosi's and Schultz's essays are male professionals, but the third essay, by Robyn Muncy of the University of Maryland, Baltimore County, asserts the primacy of women in urban reform, especially the enduring aspects of social reform such as human services. Muncy shows how, beginning in the urban settlement houses, women carved out a new dimension to professional life. She is particularly helpful in identifying the origins of government intervention in areas of reform and in examining the links between urban reform and the major components of national progressive reform.

Refuse as an Engineering Problem: Sanitary Engineers and Municipal Reform

MARTIN V. MELOSI

Sanitary engineers were the twentieth-century heirs of Colonel [George E.] Waring and his sanitary reforms. In one sense they were highly trained (or experienced) specialists in the increasingly complex field of public works. They were the experts upon whom reform politicians depended to solve the pressing problems of advancing industrialization. In a larger sense, however, sanitary engineers were generalists, when it came to broad questions concerning the maintenance of a viable physical environment. In the years before the appearance of professionally trained and academically educated ecologists, sanitary engineers were among the small minority of technocrats who possessed a comprehensive knowledge of the urban ecosystem. It is no wonder that they came to dominate refuse reform in the early twentieth century. Their efforts to measure more scientifically the extent of the refuse problem, to devise modern collection and disposal methods and technologies, and to implement business efficiency in administering public works departments went a long way in giving credence to Colonel Waring's claim that refuse was more than a simple nuisance—that it was a serious environmental problem.

In the early twentieth century sanitary engineers superseded health officers and sanitarians as the leaders of refuse reform in the United States. They accomplished this feat as much by default as their training or their environmental vision.

From *Garbage in the Cities: Refuse, Reform, and the Environment, 1880–1980* by Martin V. Melosi, The Dorsey Press, 1981, excerpts from pp. 79–90, 97–104. Reprinted by permission of Texas A & M University Press.

In the wake of the bacteriological revolution of the late nineteenth century, many in the health field came to regard environmental sanitation as inconsequential as a means of combating disease and virtually abandoned it. They placed their faith in the germ theory of disease and the widespread use of inoculation and immunization as the means of eradicating communicable diseases. . . . Doctors and health officials recognized the advantages of eradicating filth and cleaning the physical surroundings, but they had been frustrated for years by their inability to prevent communicable diseases through sanitary measures alone. As medical historian John Duffy wrote, "The discovery of specific pathogenic organisms enabled public health workers to understand for the first time precisely what they were fighting."

The transition from the widely accepted miasmic theory to the germ theory was not a simple one. Through the mid-1880s anticontagionists offered strong resistance to the germ theory. Most people were unable to comprehend that something unseen or unfelt could be the cause of disease. In 1878 even *Scientific American* chided the advocates of the new theory for accepting such a farfetched notion. Impressive reduction in the mortality rate between 1860 and 1880, attributable in some measure to good sanitation practices, further weakened the case for bacteriology. The death rate in most cities fell from twenty-five to forty persons per thousand in 1860 to sixteen to twenty-six per thousand in 1880. Rates were especially low in cities with sound sanitary practices. Nonetheless, the tenacity of the germ-theory advocates and the inconsistent results of environmental sanitation perpetuated the controversy. Not until the turn of the century did the contagionists successfully topple the miasmic theory. The veritable successes of immunization and inoculation and the advances credited to the bacteriological laboratories far exceeded the erratic record of "municipal housecleaning" and other sanitation practices.

The contagionists' victory over the anticontagionists was only a qualified success. Adherents of the germ theory too easily accepted bacteriology as offering the means of preventing disease and too quickly dismissed environmental sanitation as a valuable practice in disease prevention. In the eyes of many in the health field the emphasis on the "environment" as a root cause of disease had been misplaced, or at least exaggerated. The scientific base of environmental sanitation had been seriously flawed, but its goal—removing potential breeding cultures of disease from the range of human senses—had validity. Too often in the zeal to promote new ideas much is lost in abandoning the old. That is what happened when health officers relinquished their leadership in promoting and providing environmental sanitation in the cities.

The demise of the filth theory led to a critical appraisal of environmental sanitation as a function of health departments. With respect to the refuse problem several public-health officials questioned the necessity for health workers to supervise or direct the collection and disposal of waste. They recognized that refuse was in some respects a health problem, but few believed that its solution required the active involvement of municipal health departments. The view of Dr. Charles V. Chapin, superintendent of health of Providence, Rhode Island, and one of the pioneers in the American public-health movement, . . . led him to conclude that the "filth nuisance" should not be a health-department responsibility. The health officer, he asserted, "should be free to devote more energy to those things which he alone can do. He should not waste his time arguing with the owners of pig-sties or compelling landlords to empty their cesspools." . . .

Irrespective of the controversy over responsibility, the trend in the early twentieth century was decidedly away from health-department control. A survey of eighty-six cities, conducted by the American Child Health Association and published in 1925, showed that in forty-seven cities operating their own collection service only nine (or 19 percent) gave the responsibility to departments of health. . . . In most cities where health departments did not oversee collection and disposal, they did have enforcement power over nuisances and in some instances supervisory power over the selection of contractors. Such compromises, however, often led to jurisdictional disputes among municipal departments and failed to resolve the question whether health departments should retain full or at least partial control. The outcome of the trend away from health-department responsibility was that health officers lost much of their influence over defining and controlling waste.

The engineer was the obvious choice to assume responsibility for sanitation problems. The growing assumption that environmental sanitation was a task primarily requiring effective administrative and technical expertise, supplemented by some basic medical and scientific knowledge, pointed directly to the engineering profession. Professionally trained engineers were products of the industrial age, and, as Edwin T. Layton, Jr., suggests, they were to be the "stewards of technology." In an increasingly mechanized and technically advanced world, engineers were recognized as the agents of material progress. . . .

By 1900 engineering was the second-largest profession in the United States, following close behind teaching. In that year there were about 45,000 engineers in the United States. By 1930 their ranks had swelled to 230,000. The vitality of the profession was apparent not only in the increasing numbers of engineers but also in the diversity of its activities, which reflected the impact of technology. Civil engineers were the first progressional engineers. They emerged in the great canal- and railroad-building era of the early nineteenth century. By 1900 professional civil engineers had been joined by professionally trained mining, mechanical, electrical, and chemical engineers. . . .

Inevitably large numbers of engineers looked to the cities as their primary arenas of enterprise and opportunity. Rampant urban growth created massive physical problems which engineers were often best trained to address. By the late nineteenth century engineers were playing major roles in American cities as consultants to city officials or as administrators and employees of various municipal departments. . . .

As the growing concentration of people in the central cities in the nineteenth century strained the meager city services, and as suburban residents clamored for the extension of these services to their communities, municipal authorities called on engineers to improve existing conditions and often deferred to them in the making of policy on these matters. The need for safe water supplies, adequate sewerage, well-ventilated housing, and efficient refuse collection and disposal required the engineer's technical expertise and the public-health officer's knowledge of sanitation. A hybrid profession—sanitary engineering—emerged to try to meet the environmental challenge of the burgeoning industrial cities. . . .

Like their European counterparts American sanitary engineers received their first practical education in developing public water supplies and constructing city-wide sewerage systems. In the post–Civil War years most large cities were forced to abandon many of their local water sources—wells, cisterns, and local springs—for less-contaminated and larger-volume sources usually far from the city limits. By 1896 engineers were helping to provide more than three thousand new water sources, and by 1910 more than 70 percent of cities with populations over thirty thousand were maintaining their own waterworks. The introduction of running water into urban residences and business establishments led to tremendous increases in water use. Per capita water consumption increased from about two to three gallons a day to between fifty and one hundred gallons a day. The convenience of running water also led to the widespread adoption of water closets; by 1880 about one-third of all urban households had them. This sanitary innovation added greatly to the growing consumption of water. The dramatic increases in water use placed excessive burdens on existing cesspools and privy vaults, since waste water had no place to go but into the soil or into the yards of adjacent houses. The health hazards implicit in this phenomenon and the inconvenience of overflowing water led city officials to support the construction of city-wide waste-water systems. After 1880 most major cities adopted sewerage systems to accompany or combine with their storm-water systems (in the form of underground sewers or sometimes open gutters). Naturally sanitary engineers were given the task of designing and constructing them.

The efforts of the sanitary engineers produced impressive results. In 1860 there were only 136 municipal waterworks in the country; by 1880 there were 598. Increases in sewer lines of all kinds were no less extensive. The miles of sewers increased from 8,199 (in cities of more than ten thousand population) in 1890 to 24,972 (in cities of more than thirty thousand population) in 1909. The central role of the sanitary engineers in the construction of abundant and effective water- and waste-water carriage systems propelled the profession into the forefront of environmental sanitation in the United States. Sanitary engineers seemed to offer the best balance between technical and health expertise in dealing with the water problem.

The widespread recognition of the accomplishments of sanitary engineers and the simultaneous abandonment of environmental sanitation by health departments encouraged municipal officials to look to them to resolve another pressing urban problem—refuse collection and disposal. The growing faith in sanitary engineers as protectors of the urban environment also led to the assumption that solid waste was primarily an engineering problem. Faith in technology fostered the belief that since the water-carriage problem had been solved by technical means, refuse could likewise be mastered through the skills of the engineer. . . .

Confidence in sanitary engineers to find immediate solutions to the refuse problem, resting as it did on a too-optimistic faith in technology, placed a heavy responsibility on their shoulders. Refuse had always been more than an engineering problem. Despite growing adherents to the germ theory, refuse remained a health problem to be reckoned with. . . . It presented even more confounding administrative problems than sewerage had raised. If engineers had relied solely on their technical expertise, their contribution to refuse reform would have been minimal. Instead, trained as environmental generalists as well as technical specialists, sanitary engineers, while failing to provide the quick solutions expected of them, did advance refuse management significantly. Having developed a more comprehensive understanding of the refuse problem than had those who grappled with it in the nineteenth century, they capably defined the range of issues associated with refuse collection and disposal. Opportunities for thoughtful solutions, therefore, were greatly improved. . . .

Imbued with a penchant for the systematic and the orderly, sanitary engineers understood the importance of gathering and collating data about past and present collection and disposal practices as a necessary prelude of offering possible solutions. . . . Sanitary engineers were not satisfied simply to collect statistics, however. Implementing new programs or revising old ones was a necessary second step, which required effective administration. Sanitary engineers advised municipalities on ways of placing their public-works departments on a business footing. . . .

Careful record keeping came to be regarded as one of the best ways to improve municipal refuse management. Itemizing costs, recording the quantity and composition of wastes, and evaluating seasonal variations in collection and disposal practices proved to be effective ways of monitoring a city's sanitation program. . . .

In the sanitary engineers' recommendations for efficient refuse management was almost universal support for municipal control of sanitation functions. Although commitment to community responsibility in street cleaning and garbage removal was spotty during the 1880s and 1890s, the increasing emphasis on "home rule" in the larger cities and the subsequent expansion of municipal bureaucracies made municipal control of sanitation seem more practicable. At first glance it might seem that a large portion of the engineering community would disapprove of municipal control, especially since many sanitary engineers made their living as itinerant consultants, selling their advice and expertise to city officials throughout the country. Also, some engineers . . . channeled their engineering expertise into entrepreneurial ventures, such as manufacturing and marketing collection and disposal equipment. Yet the itinerant consultant and the engineering entrepreneur had vested interests in municipal control of sanitation. After all, municipal control provided a greater degree of permanence than contracted services. New sanitation programs required a large investment as well as considerable time to produce the complex management systems required, especially in the large cities. Furthermore, city-provided sanitation services ensured jobs for sanitary engineers, jobs which afforded them substantial responsibility, authority, and power. The sense of permanence and stability which municipal control implied offered the best atmosphere for the sanitary engineer to promote his career and the necessary reforms required to produce a well-organized program of sanitation. . . .

Surveys conducted from the 1890s to the outbreak of World War I indicate a substantial shift away from the contract system and toward increased municipal responsibility in street cleaning and garbage collection and disposal. By 1880 a significant number of American cities (approximately 70 percent) had made important strides in the municipal control of street cleaning, and a survey of 150 cities taken in 1914 indicated that about 90 percent of the cities had assumed responsibility for street cleaning. In collection and disposal, which had traditionally lagged far behind street cleaning, surveys from the 1890s onward indicated a steady rise in municipal responsibility. By World War I at least 50 percent of American cities had some form of municipal collection system, as compared with only 24 percent in 1880. Whether the sanitary engineers influenced this trend is difficult to determine, but there is little question that municipal control of sanitation provided them with a solid base of operations in municipal government.

Once sanitary engineers began exploring the magnitude and complexities of the refuse problem, they came to realize, more than any other group had before them, that tinkering with the existing programs would be insufficient. Consequently they advocated centralization of refuse management through municipal departments operating under the newest managerial techniques. Their administrative and organizational programs borrowed heavily from private industry as well as from successful water- and waste-water carriage programs. While the administrative methods and organizational techniques of these bodies had validity for refuse management, solutions to the problem of collection and disposal required further examination and study. As William T. Sedgewick, a leader in water-pollution control, suggested, "Doubtless one reason why the refuse problem is still so vexing in most communities is because the collection, of necessity, must be intermittent, and yet the system must function smoothly and without interruption." Sedgewick, of course, revealed only the tip of the iceberg, since no single method of collection and disposal could be universally applied.

If sanitary engineers were unable to find the ultimate technological methods of collection and disposal, they did make strides in placing in perspective the relative strengths and weaknesses of primitive methods and the potential applicability of new techniques. With the luxury of hindsight they understood many of the limitations of nineteenth-century methods. They almost universally condemned or at least criticized such practices as land and sea dumping, open burning, and filling with untreated wastes. In an informal discussion at the annual meeting of the American Society of Civil Engineers in 1903, John McGaw Woodbury, the street-cleaning commissioner of New York, asserted, "It is of the utmost importance that dumping at sea be stopped, not simply because it makes the beaches unsanitary and unsightly, but because it is a waste of valuable material."

Woodbury and other critics of primitive methods failed to take into account ecological considerations, but the ever-increasing quantities of refuse convinced sanitary engineers that in the selection of methods more comprehensive criteria had to be devised. As pragmatists, sanitary engineers placed emphasis on the need to examine local conditions thoroughly before advising about appropriate collection and disposal methods for a given community. In planning new systems, they tried to take into consideration not only the types and quantities of waste but also the quality of local transportation facilities, the composition of the agency in charge of the work, and physical characteristics of the city that might determine the type and location of the disposal system. Engineers also began considering

political and social factors that might indicate the receptivity of the local government and citizenry to changes in sanitation practices. The reliance of sanitary
engineers on a technological solution to the problem of refuse, therefore, was
increasingly being tempered out of necessity by considerations which were
broader in scope and not directly related to refuse as an engineering problem. In
a sense, sanitary engineers, as implementors of new systems, began adapting to
the complexity of the issue, relying more on their roles as environmental generalists than on their positions as technical specialists.

Because of their low regard for primitive methods of collection and disposal,
sanitary engineers focused their attention on newer methods which they hoped
would fulfill the sanitary and financial requirements of the various cities. Inciner-
ation and reduction were most often discussed as the logical alternatives to the
older methods. Each method had its advocates and detractors, but both came
under greater scrutiny than they had when they were first introduced in the late
nineteenth century. Gone was the naive view that either method offered the final
answer. The maturity of the sanitary-engineering profession and the knowledge
gleaned from hasty implementation of poorly tested equipment brought a more
measured response to the unqualified advocacy of a single method. . . .

The days of haphazard collection and disposal practices appeared to be ending with the rise of sanitary engineers. The careful accumulation of data, the design and evaluation of new equipment, and the organizational structure of public-
works departments were the kinds of improvements admired in an increasingly
complex—and confounding—age. In the chaos of the newly emerging urban-
industrial society, dependence on experts seemed imperative. Not only technical
expertise but managerial skills and efficiency were especially prized talents. As
Samuel Haber suggested, many Americans were having a love affair with efficiency; ". . . the progressive era gave rise to an efficiency craze—a secular Great
Awakening, an outpouring of ideas and emotions in which a gospel of efficiency
was preached without embarrassment to businessmen, workers, doctors, housewives, and teachers, and yes, preached even to preachers."

Yet the impact of sanitary engineers on refuse management depended at least
as much on the ability to perceive the totality of the urban environment as on their
skill in tinkering with its parts. Had there been greater cooperation between health
departments and public-works departments during the period, that perspective
might have been broader yet. Nonetheless, sanitary reform came a long way
under the guidance of the sanitary engineers. They effectively refined Colonel
Waring's rudimentary environmentalism and formalized it through their young
profession. . . .

The Engineered Metropolis

STANLEY K. SCHULTZ

At the heart of the engineered metropolis stood a new and expanding profession
of municipal engineers. During the post–Civil War years, they were the principal
promoters of technological solutions to urban ills. Virtually the only problems

---

From *Constructing Urban Culture: American Cities and City Planning, 1800–1920* by Stanley K. Schultz,
pp. 183–205. Copyright © 1989 Temple University Press. Reprinted by permission of the publisher.

successfully attacked by nineteenth-century urban leaders were those susceptible to engineering expertise. . . .

Municipal engineers solidified their growing reputation as problem-solvers in three ways. First, they made themselves indispensable to officials eager to boost their city's expansion. Second, they proclaimed (and apparently persuaded the public) that they were neutral experts who stood above partisan politics. Third, within their own ranks, they created a professional bureaucracy that outsiders came to admire as a model of efficiency. As an often-cited early twentieth-century text on sanitation and planning observed about the construction and administration of all types of public works, "details have been wisely left to the engineers."

That affirmation was partly wishful thinking, partly admonition. On numerous occasions, urban partisan politics and short-sighted efforts to cut corners and save money had interfered with public works construction. Still, if city officials had not left everything to the engineers, they had often entrusted the details of planning and construction and most of the details of administration to them.

By doing so, officials recognized and supported the growth of a new profession in the United States—municipal engineering—and set in motion processes that would ultimately help restructure municipal government. For local governments and the public at large had come to accept the concept of city planning, if not always the actual practice. . . .

Engineers shepherded remarkable innovations in technology, helped shape the directions of city planning thought and practice, and laid the groundwork of modern municipal administration. Scrutiny of the emerging profession and its part in reshaping the urban physical environment underscores the importance of engineers in the developing urban culture of the United States.

Engineering and Bureaucracy

The functions of modern municipal administration were inherent in water and wastewater technologies. Sewerage and water supplies required permanent construction and thus necessitated some kind of long-range planning. If engineers did not plan systems to accommodate future growth, the city would have to lay new aqueducts and trunk sewers each time the population increased even slightly or began to move into new subdivisions. A system that met present needs and anticipated future growth might be expensive in the short run but economical over time. City officials quickly learned these facts and also that disastrous health and financial consequences ensued if they ignored the advice of experts.

Consider several examples. During the early 1870s Alexander Shepard, boss of the District of Columbia, wasted a $5 million bond issue when contractors hired for political reasons built lateral sewers that had to run uphill to empty into the main sewers. In the absence of effective pumping mechanisms (most systems at the time depended upon gravity flow rather than steam pumps), Shepard's system was worse than useless. Partly because of this fiasco, the District lost home rule and became subject to a federally appointed commission that had to include at least one officer of the Army Corps of Engineers. St. Louis had to reconstruct its water-supply system and Cincinnati its sewer system within ten years after completion; both city administrations had rejected engineers' proposals in favor of politically popular decisions to cut costs. Partisan politics and graft counted more than engineering considerations in the construction of Detroit's sewer system, as the city's reform mayor, Hazen Pingree, complained when its concrete pipe began to crumble into dust during his regime in the 1890s. And so the story went from city to city.

Water and sewer systems required centralized construction and administration. There were economies of scale in building only one reservoir and one main aqueduct. An integrated sewer system with a receiving sewer at the lowest grade level and an outfall at a site that minimized pollution also considerably reduced costs over the long haul. The new technologies thus demanded a permanent bureaucracy to acquire land, oversee construction, administer on a day-to-day basis, and plan for long-term needs. Technological and managerial experts who could survey topography, choose appropriate construction materials, and draw readily upon the experiences of their counterparts in other cities gradually gained recognition as the most efficient builders of public works. . . .

Engineers and their projects served to centralize metropolitan administration of public works vital to the health and safety of city dwellers. A substantial minority of engineers active late in the century (almost 28 percent of those born before 1820) had had some legal training, and engineers often advised other city officials on broadly defined administrative and legal questions. In Boston during the 1870s, for example, engineers instigated, drafted, and oversaw enforcement of public welfare laws. Thanks to their success in public works construction and management, engineers often found city councils receptive to their requests for additional responsibilities. In late nineteenth-century Chicago, the Public Works Department added garbage collection and street cleaning to its specified duties. Gradually, the offices of city engineers and public works boards acquired the reputation of being wise managers who could streamline government operations.

Engineers were apparently the first officials of the emerging administrative bureaucracies to attain anything resembling job security. Ellis Chesbrough, chief engineer of the Chicago Board of Sewerage (1856–61), served as that community's first city engineer from 1861 to 1879, an amazing longevity at a time when most municipal jobs changed hands with every election. Others had equally long terms. . . . Their political caution, growing stature as problem-solvers, and reputation for fairness all worked to the engineers' advantage.

They bolstered their claim to be neutral experts by institutionalizing the role of consultant. Operating in a cosmopolitan context, engineers were as responsive to their professional peers as to local pressures. George Waring and Rudolph Hering, the two most prominent sanitary engineers of the period, worked almost exclusively as consultants, moving from one city to another. Chesbrough, [George] Benzenberg [of St. Louis], Moses Lane of Milwaukee, Joseph P. Davis of Boston, and Colonel Julius W. Adams of Brooklyn were home-based but traveled widely to consult on major projects in other cities. The consultant role reflected both the status of engineers and their aloofness from the pendulum swings of partisan politics. . . .

Engineers secured job tenure through professionalization. At a time when few if any clearinghouses for the exchange of ideas and practices benefited cities nationwide, the engineers built up a remarkable communications network among themselves. Their common training, whether in engineering schools or apprenticeships (usually on the major railroads), bound them together. . . . Engineers belonged to local and regional professional clubs that corresponded with one another, publishing and exchanging reports about conditions in their respective cities. Numerous professional journals provided forums for discussion and debate. . . . Finally, engineers belonged to the same national organizations. The majority held memberships in the American Society of Civil Engineers, which frequently published papers on municipal engineering projects with appended comments from experts throughout the nation. In 1894 professionals involved principally with urban problems formed their own specialized national organization, the American Society for Municipal Improvements. . . .

. . . Engineers' growing importance as managers of the physical city involved them intimately with elected officials and raised the potential for abuses of power. Yet there is in fact little or no evidence of city engineers' being "on the take," embroiled in the numerous political scandals, large and small, that amused, bemused, or outraged post–Civil War city dwellers. Although they served the immediate interests of local boosters and elected officials, the engineers could claim that over the long run their work benefited all citizens. . . .

The engineers offered city governments a corps of individuals skilled in the technology and management of large-scale enterprises, experts who could solve the physical problems of the cities. Decades before early twentieth-century political reformers depicted their ideal bureaucrat, municipal engineers embodied all of the characteristics: efficiency, expertise, and professionalism. . . .

Engineering and City Planning

Over the last half of the nineteenth century, engineers repeatedly demonstrated the value of long-range planning to municipal administration. Not only did the profession offer solutions to such physical problems as water and sewer supply; it also contributed comprehensive planning schemes that illustrated the interaction of technology with the social, economic, and political structure of cities. . . . Frequently working with landscape architects and sanitarians, many engineers showed great sensitivity to and a deep understanding of the health needs of the populace. . . .

The sanitarians' image of the city as an organic being stirred sympathetic response in the engineers. Such metaphors were common in the engineering press. Sewerage works, one engineer rejoiced, had created "an entire urinary and intestinal tract, and . . . an artificial anus" for the city. Using the same imagery, a writer observed in 1894 that "the city engineer is to the city very much what the family physician is to the family. He is constantly called upon to advise and direct in all matters pertaining to his profession. . . . He does know the character, constitution, particular needs and idiosyncracies of the city, as the family physician knows the constitution of the family." Engineers, accustomed to thinking about unified systems, joined with sanitarians in viewing the city as a vast, integrated unit within which the efficient functioning of one part depended upon the efficient functioning of all the parts.

Belief in their "physician" role led some engineers to advance comprehensive planning schemes focusing on all the interconnected parts of the urban system. During the post–Civil War years, a number of plans of this type appeared. . . . Three plans that enjoyed varying degrees of success illustrate the scope of the planners' vision.

In the late 1850s, Boston undertook a massive landfill operation and development project for its Back Bay area. Other historians have recounted the full story of this two-decade-long operation, but for present purposes several elements need emphasis. The city enforced restrictive covenants in deeds for lots in the newly filled land. These covenants limited nonresidential use of land, imposed building height restrictions, and dictated the distance that houses must be set back from the street. In other words, they constituted an early effort at what in the twentieth century would be called zoning legislation. The entire area pivoted around a principal traffic artery, Commonwealth Avenue. On the model of European boulevards, the paved road included a strip of park down the middle. Land-use restrictions and the boulevard enhanced the attractiveness of the new residential area. . . . Boston also began a major reconstruction of its sewer system so that wastes drained into the South Bay, rather than the more stagnant waters of the Back Bay. The city forced railroad lines to relocate from the Back Bay to a freight yard on newly filled land in the South Bay, thereby turning that district into an attractive site for industrial activities.

In the late 1870s, when engineers had finished most of the Back Bay development, the city sought to complete the project with yet another engineering scheme. To further reduce pollution and provide recreational and health amenities, the city hired Frederick Law Olmsted to design and oversee construction of a park system (the Back Bay Fens) along the Muddy River, which drained into the bay. Working with William Jackson, Boston's city engineer, Olmsted produced a plan that the city accepted and implemented quickly. . . . This carefully engineered project sparked enthusiasm for similar planning efforts in other cities.

Our second example takes us to New York City. Between 1865 and 1877, Olmsted and John J. R. Croes, a civil engineer, surveyed and prepared a thorough plan for a portion of the Bronx recently annexed to New York City. Initially charged with planning a street system and a rapid-transit steam railroad to connect the annexed wards to Manhattan, Olmsted and Croes instead proposed comprehensive development of the area as a suburb *before* potential residents could purchase property. Their design implicitly argued for thorough planning of all the undeveloped areas that one day would make up greater New York City.

The Croes-Olmsted plans, presented in three reports, called for the development of a business district bordered by a residential section on the high ground around the center of the area, with suburban homes on the northern and western edges. They offered street patterns that would provide gravity drainage, thereby lessening the costs of subsurface water and sewer facilities. They urged construction of wide north-south avenues along valleys and the tops of the ridges that dominated the topography. These avenues would cover water and sewer lines and also accommodate elevated railroads built up the middle to minimize disturbance to the surrounding environment. Linear parks would protect creeks and the Bronx

River from pollution, and parkways would facilitate travel to the downtown area. . . .

Throughout their reports the planners minimized private development decisions and elevated the comprehensive planning role of the public authority, in this case the Board of Commissioners of Public Parks. Those suggestions proved to be the plan's undoing. The desire of board members and real-estate speculators to populate the area quickly by the traditional means of unrestricted private development won the day. . . . The new sections of the Bronx grew in the helter-skelter fashion that typically resulted from private land-use decisions.

Bits and pieces of the Back Bay scheme and the Bronx plan soon appeared in other cities. Between the mid-1880s and the turn of the century, Chicago, Kansas City, Boston, and Buffalo, among others, had built or had under way multipurpose park systems that went far beyond the provision of recreational land usage. Each of these plans protected rivers and streams from inordinate industrial pollution. Each provided new transportation networks that eased travel in and about the city. Each promised a solution to public health problems. Each projected improved housing facilities for large numbers of city residents.

Yet another example of the comprehensive approach was a sort of anthology of public works proposals prepared by the Engineers' Club of Philadelphia during the early 1880s. Lewis Haupt, professor of engineering at the University of Pennsylvania, presented a number of papers on street layout and the need for rapid transit. He even tried to devise an accurate method of forecasting population growth. . . . Throughout the 1880s and the following decade, other local engineering clubs in St. Louis, Chicago, Cleveland, Kansas City, and elsewhere prepared similar reports.

Each of our three examples produced at least a kernel of accomplishment for the comprehensive planning viewpoint and presaged its greater success and greater popular acceptance in the twentieth century. Perhaps the most telling way to evaluate success, however, is to examine the costs of failure. The experience of Baltimore during the 1890s and early 1900s encapsulated all that had gone before.

The City as Sewer

Among major American cities, Baltimore alone put off construction of the kinds of public works projects that sanitarians, landscape architects, and engineers had called for since the 1840s. In 1859, 1881, and again in 1893, commissions appointed by the mayor and led principally by engineers had urged planning and construction to remedy the city's problems. On each occasion the public's reluctance to spend tax dollars, along with partisan politics, had sunk the proposals. Baltimore alone had ignored mounting evidence of the ties between the cleanliness or filth of the environment and rates of disease and mortality among city dwellers. Its citizens paid dearly for the delay. Although the census of 1890 judged Newark, New Jersey, the nation's unhealthiest city, the Chesapeake Bay community did not lag far behind—and Baltimore was two-and-a-half times as populous as Newark, with vastly larger financial resources.

In 1890 Baltimore was one of only seven cities in the United States with a population of 400,000 or more. During the eighties it more than doubled its physical size through annexation, a tool used by every large American city in this period. Annexation, coupled with immigration, boosted Baltimore's population during the eighties by more than 102,000 people. This sudden spurt, paralleled in every other metropolis in the United States, placed stress on Baltimore's ability to provide adequate urban services. Unlike the other large American cities, it would not respond to the problems of development until the close of the first decade of the twentieth century. Between 1890 and roughly 1910, Baltimore remained one of the nation's prime examples of the city as sewer.

Baltimore lines the banks of the Patapsco River, an arm of Chesapeake Bay, with a peninsula splitting the river into a Middle and a Northwest Branch. Along the latter branch as it stretched northward in the city stood factories, grain elevators, warehouses, and the wharves of the nation's third-largest port. Beyond these stood the central business district. Bisecting the city from the north and ending at a harbor formed by the Northwest Branch ran a ravine threaded by a foul stream called Jones Falls. Industrial wastes fed into the stream and poured into the harbor. On one side of Jones Falls lay East Baltimore, housing most of the city's working-class population. Slum tenements huddled in rows along the harbor and the lower sections of the falls. To the north of East Baltimore was most of the land annexed during the 1880s, containing some of the wealthiest sections of the city as well as rapidly growing middle-class suburbs. Immediately west of the core of the city, on the other side of Jones Falls, was the principal black ghetto (next to Washington, Baltimore had the largest Negro population of any American city in 1890). North of the ghetto was a district called Bolton Hill, where lived many of the city's professional and business families. Frequent rainfall, the rolling topography of the city, and the geographic separation of different sections had long hindered provision of an adequate water supply and an effective sewage-disposal system.

During the first half of the nineteenth century, the private Baltimore Water Company supplied the community with water from a number of small reservoirs along Jones Falls. In 1854 the city purchased the water company and expanded service while still depending on Jones Falls for its supply. As population grew and indoor plumbing became popular, that source became inadequate. Between 1875 and 1881, city engineers constructed a new reservoir that tapped a different water source. Although expanded, however, the water supply system, which depended largely on gravity flow, was far from perfected. The houses built during the eighties on hillsides surrounding the Jones Falls valley stood above the reach of existing reservoirs. Baltimore met the problem by building new reservoirs in various districts of the city and installing pumping mechanisms to fill them with water. The pumps often broke down, resulting in water shortages. That was not unusual; other cities at that time faced the same difficulties with the new technology. Nor was it unusual that the new supplies of water were hardly pure. In many large cities thorough filtration and purification of water did not become standard practice until the early 1920s.

Thus, with regard to water supplies, Baltimore's experience was typical—in provision of a municipal water system and in the timing of construction, Baltimore was on track with the rest of urban America. That decidedly was not the case for the city's handling of sewage disposal.

For most of the nineteenth century, Baltimore relied upon "natural" disposal. Rainwater soaked the soil of backyards and the largely unpaved streets, eventually running off through streams. Householders customarily dropped kitchen refuse and domestic wastewater into surface street gutters. Cesspools drained the excrement from privies; in the rainy seasons seepage turned backyards into putrid marshes. As the century wore on, the problems of sewage pollution increased. In some of the wealthier sections, private citizens contracted for the construction of storm drains. There was little or no coordination of these scattered efforts, which served only a small proportion of the city's citizens and polluted nearby streams. Some 15,000 homes owned by the city's elite had privately built sewer lines that funneled raw household wastes into Jones Falls.

. . . The streams, the surface gutters, the private lines, and cesspool seepages all finally dumped their burdens into the harbor, with the predictable result that in spring and summer that body of water was afloat with rotted garbage and the flotsam and jetsam of urban wastes, smelling like "a billion polecats." . . . Since most of those who lived on the harbor's fringe were slum dwellers, however, the better classes of Baltimoreans turned up their noses at the pollution. . . .

Wastewater disposal, from all sources, had become a problem of epic dimensions by 1890. . . . In 1890 the death rate from all physical ailments of residents of the nation's twenty-eight largest cities averaged 23.3 persons per thousand. Newark, with a population of 182,000, had a mortality rate of 29 per thousand, highest among American cities with populations of 100,000 or more. Among major cities—those with 400,000 or more citizens—only New York had a higher death rate than Baltimore. By 1900 matters had improved little. Newark's death rate had fallen to 19.8, while Baltimore's had declined to 21 per thousand. Philadelphia, with a rate of 21.2, barely edged the Chesapeake Bay community in the death race, or Baltimore would have stood alone at the top of the heap. . . .

By the turn of the century, conditions had become so wretched that even well-to-do Baltimoreans could tolerate them no longer. Engineers and sanitarians were no longer alone in calling for the construction of a citywide integrated sewer system. Organizations of prominent, reform-minded citizens, such as the Municipal Art Society and the Reform League, demanded action. . . .

Finally, in 1905, through a series of intricate political maneuvers, a new mayor appointed a blue-ribbon sewerage commission empowered to oversee the building of a comprehensive system. Construction began in 1906 and concluded in 1915. By then, nearly 500 miles of integrated sanitary sewers served more than 100,000 homes. Once stirred into action, the city moved with efficiency and dispatch. In less than a decade, Baltimore transformed itself into one of the best-sewered cities in the nation.

Demands for a host of other public improvements brought about street widening and paving projects, park planning schemes, new transportation networks, and new schools, police stations, and firehouses during the first decade and a half of the twentieth century. In all cases, new administrative procedures governed implementation of city planning proposals. The city charter adopted in 1898 had provided for a five-person Board of Estimates to conduct Baltimore's financial affairs. One of the five was the city engineer, appointed by the mayor. His task was principally to coordinate the activities of several boards charged with administration of various public works and oversee plans for future public improvements.

By the early years of the new century, the city had joined the rest of urban America, which had long since recognized the importance of engineering expertise in the construction and administration of public works projects and city planning. . . .

Planning and Managing the Cities

In May 1909 a large group of prominent individuals met in the nation's capital to convene the First National Conference on City Planning and the Problems of Congestion. Among them were engineers, landscape architects, public health officials, conservationists, economists, lawyers, social workers, journalists, corporate leaders, and public officials. A sense of urgency pervaded the gathering.

John Nolen denounced present trends in city development as "fatal" and called upon cities to investigate their problems, promote cooperation between public authorities and private individuals, and achieve "prompt and courageous execution of the plan found to be best for all concerned." Benjamin C. Marsh, the era's leading proponent of comprehensive city planning, demanded surveys, publicity, and new legal weapons "against which corporate interests cannot contend." Representing some of those corporate interests (presumably the "responsible" ones) was the financier Henry Morgenthau, who identified congestion as "an evil that breeds physical disease, moral depravity, discontent, and socialism—and all these must be cured and eradicated or else our great body politic will be weakened." Frederick Law Olmsted, Jr., reflecting the views of many other participants, described the glories of town planning in Germany, pointing out that German plans included not only street layouts "and so forth, but the whole code of building regulations, health ordinance, police rules, and system of taxation in so far as they have a direct influence upon the physical development of the city." Some participants sought to encourage purely local responses to problems, while others called for federal action. But the conference was in full agreement about its final goal—comprehensive planning in and for urban America.

At that first meeting, the noted landscape architect, Robert Anderson Pope, emphasized the pressing need for "a profession equipped to make city planning the social and economic factor it ought to be." The National Conference on City Planning continued to meet once a year, in a different city each time, advertising principles of comprehensive planning to countless thousands of urban Americans. . . . In short, the conference sparked commitment to the formal creation of the profession Pope had called for.

The role of engineers in the emerging profession was considerable. New York City's chief engineer, Nelson P. Lewis, author of one of the earliest and most widely consulted texts on city planning, dedicated his 1916 volume "To the Municipal Engineers of the United States, the first men on the ground in City Planning as in City Building." Of the fifty-two charter members of the American Institute of Planners (first called the American City Planning Institute) in 1917, thirteen were engineers. Only landscape architecture provided more members (fourteen), and several of them had some engineering training. The newly formed AIP included the individuals who had prepared most of the comprehensive city plans advanced since 1905. . . .

The direct contributions of engineers to municipal administration during the early years of the twentieth century were even more impressive than their role in the growth of the city planning profession. However much political reformers disagreed about the details of structural change, they agreed that the professionalization and bureaucratization of government were steps in the right direction. . . .

. . . Characteristic of progressive-era structural reform was an emphasis on efficiency, specialized training, and administrative accountability. No single political change better reflected those values than the managerial revolution in urban government.

In brief, the progressives wanted to replace ward bosses and corrupt machine politicians with trained, nonpartisan professionals who could carry out the day-by-day administration of government without regard for the vicissitudes of the political arena. An elected commission or council—having gained office through an at-large, citywide election rather than through the traditional ward-by-ward process—should establish public policies and appoint a skilled professional to handle executive functions. Such a centralized administration would manage municipal services with businesslike efficiency. Reformers repeatedly charged that machine politicians cared not about efficiency but about staying in office to loot the public treasury. Machine leaders controlled elections by garnering the votes of ignorant immigrant dwellers living in the urban core. A favor given here, a job secured there—these were the coins of the realm for exploiting the immigrants for their votes. Meanwhile, the machines failed to represent the interests of the "better sort" of citizens, the middle- and upper-class people who had left the city for the suburbs in an effort to escape the corruption of the core. Or, so the reformers asserted. A city-manager form of government would reduce the voting power wielded by the lower-class central wards while elevating the influence of the business and professional elites living on the urban periphery and in the suburbs. To critics who warned about the dangers to democracy inherent in the scheme, supporters retorted that "democracy need fear no setback through the introduction of this new form of administration, and efficiency . . . can come into her own at last."

The new city-manager form of government first surfaced in Staunton, Virginia, in 1908. The city council appointed Charles E. Ashburner, charging him with improving the community's streets while also holding the line on public expenditures. Within three years, Ashburner had placed the city on a sound financial basis, improved the water and sewage systems, directed installation of effective street lighting, and accelerated the street-paving process tenfold, lifting the community, as one contemporary put it, from "mud to asphalt." Other cities, including communities in both Carolinas, Oregon, and Michigan, soon followed suit. For the most part, these were small cities, and their problems therefore appeared easier to treat than those of larger, more industrialized communities. A more dramatic example was needed.

One came in Dayton, Ohio, in 1913. That city of some 110,000 citizens had governmental problems akin to those of the largest cities. A devastating flood in March focused national attention on Dayton while also revealing the inability of local machine politicians to respond efficiently. Led by John H. Patterson, the wealthy head of the National Cash Register Company, a group of Dayton professionals and businessmen succeeded in gaining election to office, whereupon they drafted a city-manager charter that they sold to the electorate. Early in 1914 the new council appointed Henry M. Waite to the post of city-manager. He not only solved the immediate problems of rebuilding municipal services, but also engaged in social engineering, providing free legal aid, a milk-inspection program in the city's schools, and free medical examinations for children. The "Dayton Plan," as contemporaries called it, spread rapidly throughout the nation over the next few years. . . .

It is not my purpose here to describe in detail the impact of the managerial revolution. Rather, I want to sketch a profile of these new technocrats and look at how their efforts reflected growing public acceptance of the necessity of expertise in planning and managing cities.

A profile of the new profession reveals common backgrounds. The first city managers of Staunton and Dayton, for example, were both practicing civil engineers. Ashburner had worked for railroad and electric companies and for the Public Roads Administration of the federal government. Waite came to his Dayton post directly from a highly successful career as city engineer of Cincinnati. The 1919 *Yearbook* of the new City Managers' Association showed that 48 percent of the total membership were engineers. In 1920 a survey of California city managers stated that of the twenty-one listing their backgrounds, thirteen were engineers. Surveys taken during the 1920s and 1930s demonstrated that of those managers with bachelor's degrees, 75 percent had trained as engineers. By the time the "typical" manager assumed his job, he had engaged in practical engineering work and had held one or more posts in government, usually as a department head. As late as 1940, a major nationwide survey related that more than 63 percent of city managers over the previous quarter-century had trained as engineers.

Many contemporaries saw the establishment of the new profession of city manager as the high-water mark of progressive reform in municipal administration. The managers themselves were recruited primarily from another profession that had long since proved its central importance to the orderly functioning of cities. Over the half-century preceding the progressive era, the job of municipal engineer had developed into a profession that had helped reshape the physical landscape of urban America. Of equal significance, it had provided a corps of experienced experts and a model of administrative skill that latter-day progressives would use as a basis for the structural reform of urban government.

In both the technological and the political arenas, municipal engineers played an increasingly important part. Over the last half of the nineteenth century, they stamped their long-range visions of metropolitan planning on the public consciousness. Their demands for political autonomy in solving the physical problem of cities contributed to an ultimate insistence on efficient government run by experts. At the center of physical and political changes in the administration of American cities—indeed, at the very core of city planning by the first decade of the twentieth century—stood the work of municipal engineers.

The Hull House Settlement and Female Urban Reform

ROBYN MUNCY

"There's a power in me, and will to dominate which I must exercise," wrote Jane Addams in 1889, "they hurt me else." In late-nineteenth-century America, frustrated ambition was injuring other college-educated women as well. Consequently, when Addams eased her own pain by founding a social settlement in Chicago, her venture attracted a group of women similarly bruised by constraints on their aspirations and ready to unfetter their capacities for personal independence and public authority. The desire to unlock the shackles that would have bound them to obscure, private lives provided Addams and her followers with a motive for creating a female dominion within the larger empire of policymaking; their experiences at Hull House supplied the values and strategies that made their creation possible.

The precondition for opening Addams's settlement in 1889 lay in a transformation of female experience that had occurred during the previous half-century. Middle-class Americans had, in the early nineteenth century, invented a set of prescriptions for female behavior and assumptions about women's nature that largely excluded women from the competitive arenas of politics and business. Called the cult of true womanhood, this belief system proclaimed women the natural harbors of spiritual and moral values in the wildly acquisitive seas of Jacksonian America and further apotheosized women as that half of the human race motivated only by concern for others. In all she did, woman was to sacrifice individual ambition in order to serve. She served best through childrearing, charitable activities, and nursing the wounds sustained by both individual men and communities in battles for political and economic advantage. To fulfill this responsibility for preserving familial and social relationships, women were to cultivate piety, purity, submissiveness, and domesticity. But the first two of these qualities almost immediately subverted the latter two: If men tended to corruption and women to moral perfection, some women reasoned, then the Republic needed women for duties other than cooking and cleaning and even childrearing. . . .

Such aspirations burned in the souls of Jane Addams and Ellen Gates Starr, two women who met in 1877 at Rockford Female Seminary in Rockford, Illinois. . . . Both Addams and Starr originally tried to enter professions through the same doors that admitted men, and both failed. Illness and family obligations blocked Addams's approach to medical school. Harvard's discriminatory rules obstructed Starr. . . . Supposing a change of scenery might at least lift their spirits, the two women set out for a European tour with a mutual friend—Sara Anderson—in December 1887. . . .

While in London, they visited the first settlement house in the world. Toynbee Hall, founded by Samuel A. Barnett in 1884, invited university men to live in the midst of a working-class neighborhood. The purpose of the settlement was to bridge the gap between London's educated and laboring classes, to

From *Creating a Female Dominion in American Reform, 1890–1935* by Robyn Muncy, excerpts from pp. 3–4, 6, 8–9, 11–14, 17–18, 20–22, 24–25, 27–28, 30, 37. Copyright © 1991 by Robyn Muncy. Reprinted by permission of Oxford University Press, Inc.

promote understanding between those groups, and especially to provide education and culture to working people. Though Addams and Starr had surely witnessed similar poverty in American cities, the very unfamiliarity of London permitted them to see the suffering of working-class life with new eyes. So impressed were the two women by both the living conditions of working-class London and the settlement's response to those conditions that they determined to open their own settlement in Chicago.

Addams and Starr were not the first American women to be intrigued by the settlement idea. Also inspired by trips to Toynbee Hall, a group of graduates from Smith College founded the Settlement Association in 1887. Chapters of the Association formed at Vassar, Smith, Wellesley, Bryn Mawr, and Harvard Annex. Opening its first settlement on Rivington Street in New York City, the Association began with seven female residents, and received over eighty applications by the end of the first year.

Relocating in working-class neighborhoods attracted educated women in America because it offered them wholly new opportunities in public life that could be justified as an extension of accepted female activities. On the conventional side, settlement appeared simply to extend female philanthropic activities. After all, the cult of true womanhood had slated women for leadership in charitable service, and because settlements required women to surrender themselves to the needs of others, they seemed to fulfill the imperative to female self-sacrifice. On the innovative side, settlements promised women independence from their families, unique possibilities for employment, and the sort of communal living arrangements they had cherished in college.

. . . In her famous essay, "The Subjective Necessity for Social Settlements," Addams argued that America's middle-class women were "taught to be self-forgetting and self-sacrificing, to consider the good of the whole before the good of the ego." But "when the daughter comes back from college and begins to recognize her social claim . . . the family claim is strenuously asserted. . . ." As a result, according to Addams, "the girl loses something vital out of her life to which she is entitled. She is restricted and unhappy; her elders, meanwhile, are unconscious of the situation and we have all the elements of tragedy." Settlement life offered a worthy vocation for these tragic figures, who otherwise languished in a society that had little use for them. The success of the settlement movement at the turn of the century thus represented the middle-class female quest for a new place in American life.

In addition to the subjective necessity for settlements, Addams identified an objective need: the great chasm that separated America's working and middle classes. In fact, Addams defined a settlement as "an experimental effort to aid in the solution of the social and industrial problems which are engendered by the modern conditions of life in a great city." And in 1889, when Addams and Starr were recruiting for their settlement, Chicago certainly exhibited all of "the social and industrial problems" that "the modern conditions of life" could hope to produce. Many problems of housing, transportation, and sanitation stemmed directly from Chicago's phenomenal rate of growth in the late nineteenth century. Representative of urban centers all over the country, Chicago more than doubled its population in the decade between 1880 and 1890. Mushrooming from 503,000 to over a million inhabitants, the midwestern city admitted immigrants from Germany, Scandinavia, Poland, and Italy to such an extent that by 1890 almost 78 percent of Chicagoans were either born abroad or were children of parents born abroad. Also indicative of national trends, Chicago had become an industrial center with almost one-half of its working population engaged in manufacturing and mechanical trades. . . . Chicago's immigrant working classes crowded around factories and stockyards in tenements often unsafe and always lacking the amenities enjoyed by Chicago's elite.

It was especially the contrast between these groups that concerned Jane Addams, Ellen Starr, and growing numbers of middle-class Americans. As railroads, mail-order houses, and business mergers brought America's far-flung communities closer together, those same advances seemed to split individual communities into hostile classes. America, once divided by distance and region, now appeared to be dangerously divided by economic class. Embroiled especially in over 23,000 strikes that punctuated the country's last two decades, class conflict seemed constantly to threaten national unity. Perhaps the most famous and anxiety-producing conflict of all occurred right in Chicago, where several police and workers were killed in the Haymarket Riot of 1886.

Thus, driven by their own need for meaningful work and drawn by the social problems they might solve, Addams and Starr opened their settlement at 335 South Halsted Street on September 18, 1889. Located in an immigrant neighborhood on the southwest side of Chicago, the mansion of the late Charles Hull provided enough space for a start and promised more room in the future. . . .

When Addams and Starr first settled into the Hull mansion, their plans were vague. No one knew exactly how the women intended to bridge the gulf between classes or provide a "people's parlor." Addams herself referred to the first year as "experimental," a time during which she and Starr would get to know their neighbors' needs. Until familiarized with the neighborhood, the women followed Toynbee Hall's example: they organized social clubs for the young according to age and sex; parties for all according to nationality; lecture series for adults; concerts and exhibits. From the beginning, the settlement housed a kindergarten and sponsored a visiting nurse.

During the next few years, the settlement provided a remarkably flexible institution, devoted especially to serving women and children. As Addams and Starr acquainted themselves with immigrants from southern and eastern Europe, who constituted the bulk of their neighbors, they witnessed the problems encountered by these newest groups of America's working class. When the women became aware of a specific problem, they endeavored as best they could to solve it. Having discovered by 1891, for instance, that mothers in these families often worked outside the home, Addams and Starr opened a day nursery. By then familiar with the vagaries of wage-paying employment, they started a free labor bureau for men and women. Remembering with nostalgia the fresh air and wide-open spaces of their rural childhoods, the women opened Chicago's first public playground. Growing concerned about the horrid working conditions and low pay suffered by working-class women, Addams began to invite female labor unions to meet at the settlement, and she raised funds to build a cooperative living club for working women just down the street from Hull House. . . .

By fall 1891, . . . Addams and Starr had taken over the entire Hull mansion, and several other women moved in with them. Two years later, with more property and programs, the settlement housed 15 permanent residents, and in 1896, it boasted 25. After the turn of the century, that number more than doubled. Throughout the 1890s, women dominated the residential force: in 1894, it comprised 13 women and two men; in 1896, 20 women and five men; in 1899, 18 women and six men.

. . . [F]emale relationships also supported work in Addams's settlement. These were collaborations with rich matrons who helped Addams to pay for the services of settlement workers. The kindergarten at Hull House, for instance, depended on funding from Chicago's Kindergarten Association. Women of means formed the Association and raised funds for kindergartens all over the city. Although the Association's primary interest was the education of children from disadvantaged homes, its financial support not only helped children but also paid the salaries of aspiring kindergarten teachers. . . .

Where there were not existing organizations to support a resident's work, Addams sought individual patrons. At first Addams had drawn from her own independent income to pay the salaries of a few workers, but as the settlement grew, she began to ask wealthy friends to help finance the work of individual residents. By 1895, Addams had ordered the process. Whenever she identified a need in the community and found a woman ready to meet the need, Addams went in search of an individual donor to pay the worker's monthly salary. This Addams called the fellowship system. . . .

The fellowship system allowed women to experiment with and to begin defining new professions. Many of the services provided by fellowships were supplied previously by volunteers in charitable organizations or not at all. Before 1890, no one could have earned her living by reading to sick children or minding the neighbor's kids. Schools did not yet hire teachers specifically to offer music or art lessons or to exercise their students. Unemployment did not earlier provoke the intervention of a professional devoted to nothing else save finding one a job, and few homeless women could have sought shelter in a lodging home whose director received a salary. Often, after a period of definition and testing, women convinced established institutions to incorporate these services into their regular programs. During the early twentieth century, public schools, for instance, began to hire kindergarten teachers, art teachers, and gym teachers as part of their permanent educational staffs. Municipalities and state governments established employment bureaus, and even charitable organizations replaced volunteers with salary-earning professionals. . . .

In the 1890s, women were thus creating a professional culture different from that of the older, male professions. One reason for the difference was that women entered the professional world most successfully when they carved out wholly new areas of expertise in which they did not compete with men for jobs or training. Their successes increased when they could justify their professional ambitions as fulfillments of the Victorian imperative for women to serve children and the poor. Because this clientele could not afford to pay for services, female professionals looked to wealthy women for financial support. The incomes of female professionals, unlike those of men in law, medicine, or business, consequently came not from a fee-paying client but from wealthy benefactors who vicariously fulfilled their own missions through the professionals they supported. This peculiar position required professionals to draw nonprofessional women into their work and to convince both client and patron that their services were important. Under these circumstances, the female professions could not develop the exclusivity of the older male professions. At precisely the time when those traditional male professions were seeking to increase their fees and status by emphasizing their esoteric knowledge, women were creating professions that depended on the cooperation of lay people. Though specialization and specific training increasingly characterized those female professions, the women who claimed expertise had continually to interpret that knowledge to their lay sisters. They had to be popularizers as well as professionals. . . .

In addition to popularizing scientific knowledge, the emerging female professional ethos valued self-sacrificing service. Whether in male- or female-dominated professions, women could not escape the cultural imperative to submerge their egos in service to others. While male professionals were also expected to serve, their professional culture did not define service as self-sacrificing. . . .

This peculiar element in the female professional ethos arose not only from turn-of-the-century constructions of femininity but also from the social positions of women creating professions. In order to maintain the sponsorship of their benefactors—those wealthy women funding the professionalization process—professional women had to direct their individual ambitions toward service. After all, the true object of the patronage of elite women was to aid the downtrodden—not to subsidize individual careers. Only by justifying an occupation in terms of service to the dispossessed could professional women solicit such support. . . .

. . . [T]he service ideal itself exacted a price. Serving a clientele that could not pay for professional services, the women at Hull House constantly searched for sources of funding. Because voluntary contributions continued only at the pleasure of the individual donors who might at any time find a more attractive cause for their largesse, female professionals began to look for more constant and reliable funds from the very beginning of their occupational experiments at Hull House. Usually, their patrons searched with them, and often the most obvious source of continuous support was government. Soon after the settlement opened its employment bureau, for example, it began to lobby the state government for the establishment of publicly funded bureaus. In 1899, such legislation passed. Services to young legal offenders finally found a continuous source of funding through the county government, and recreational specialists won municipal support for playgrounds. . . .

Because their professional situations thus predisposed them to see government intervention as the solution to social problems, women at Hull House counted among America's first progressives. Historians refer to the first two decades of the twentieth century as the Progressive era because they constituted a period of vital response to the social and economic changes wrought by industrialization in the previous half century. Literally millions of Americans organized in local, state, and national bodies to push for reforms of the industrial order.

Though members of many of those bodies would unite in the new and temporary Progressive party in 1912, there existed no truly unified progressive movement in these years but rather a hodgepodge of coalitions working for changes that often contradicted each other. Different social groups had different ideas about how the new industrial order should look, and in many cases, the same individual lobbied simultaneously for changes that now seem antithetical to each other. For example, in an effort to democratize government, reformers mounted campaigns for the direct election of senators, women's suffrage, the use of referenda, and the right to recall representatives thought to betray voters' interests. At the same time, groups of reformers sought to streamline local governments by replacing political machines with expert administrators ostensibly responsible to no other bosses than efficiency and economy. Rule by unelected experts, of course, flew in the face of democratic ideals and in many instances represented the attempt of native-born middle classes to wrest control of city government from immigrant groups.

As problematic for reformers as democracy were the gigantic corporations that had engulfed the American landscape during the late nineteenth century. While some progressives—convinced that huge corporate entities threatened the economic competition on which American mobility and democracy depended—devoted themselves to busting trusts, others—cherishing the efficiency of larger enterprises—urged various levels of government simply to regulate industries so as to prevent rank exploitation of either consumers or workers. From the latter motive came legislation to guarantee the purity of food and drugs, to regulate railroad rates, and to ensure the sanitation of manufacturing establishments and city streets. . . .

Toward the plight of industrial workers progressive reformers took wildly different approaches as well. Some believed that government should take the lead in ameliorating the suffering of the working classes by requiring unemployment and disability insurance, public employment agencies, and legal safety standards for industries. Others saw the salvation of the workers in unionization; yet others, in the ever-increasing scientific management of industry, which would reputedly so increase productivity that every worker would earn a decent wage under clean and safe conditions. Distrustful of management's good will, still other reformers organized consumers who, through socially conscious buying, would force employers to do justice to their workers. Some progressives advocated all of the above, attesting to the difficulty of identifying any unifying motive or political agenda for the various people agitating for change between 1900 and 1920. . . .

Insofar as progressive reform meant the expansion of government especially into areas of social welfare, women loomed large in progressive reform. As the early years at Hull House show, female participation in that area of reform grew out of a set of needs and values peculiar to middle-class women in the late nineteenth and early twentieth century. Settlement workers did not set out to become reformers. They were rather women trying to fulfill existing social expectations for self-sacrificing female service while at the same time satisfying their need for public recognition, authority, and independence. In the process of attempting to weave together a life of service and professional accomplishment, they became reformers as the wider world defined them.

Indeed progressive reform cannot be fully understood without the specific study of female reformers. Even if middle-class women worked closely with and shared many ideals with their middle-class male counterparts, women and men came to those common enterprises from different motives and with different experiences. Surely the peculiar situation of aspiring professional women in the 1890s—as exemplified by the women at Hull House—should be counted as one of the causes of Progressive reform and as one explanation especially for the early twentieth century's enthusiasm for government solutions to social problems. . . .

During the 1890s, middle-class American women developed values and strategies that would permit them to build their dominion. They formed female communities bound together by a common commitment to new roles for women in the larger society. They proved themselves tireless social researchers and publicists. They made public issues of private matters that had always fallen under female authority and thus convinced men that they had a right to positions of power. To support their initial excursions into professional life and policymaking, professional women called on their wealthier sisters for support and grew accustomed to working with and depending on lay women. But at the same time, professionals were seeking to end their dependence on private benevolence and to convince established institutions, often governments, to fund their services to an indigent clientele. This professional need led them to combine their search for individual opportunities with campaigns for the expansion of governmental involvement in social welfare, and through the national networks they formed, these women were gaining the strength of numbers and perspective needed to move these strategies from the local to the national level.

※ *FURTHER READING*

Ruth Bordin, *Women and Temperance: The Quest for Power and Liberty. 1871–1900* (1981)

Louis P. Cain, *Sanitation Strategy for a Lakefront Metropolis: The City of Chicago* (1978)

Charles W. Cheape, *Moving the Masses: Urban Public Transit in New York, Boston, and Philadelphia* (1980)

Carl W. Condit, *Chicago, 1910–1929: Building, Planning, and Urban Technology* (1983)

Doris Groshen Daniels, *Always a Sister: The Feminism of Lillian D. Wald* (1989)

Allen F. Davis, *American Heroine: The Life and Legend of Jane Addams* (1973)

————, *Spearheads for Reform: The Social Settlements and the Progressive Movement, 1890–1914* (1967)

Lori Ginzberg, *Women and the Work of Benevolence: Morality, Politics, and Class in the Nineteenth-Century United States* (1991)

Ann Durkin Keating, *Infrastructure and Urban Growth in the Nineteenth Century* (1985)

Judith Waltzer Leavitt, *The Healthiest City: Milwaukee and the Politics of Health Reform* (1982)

Roy Lubove, *The Urban Community: Housing and Planning in the Progressive Era* (1967)

Clay McShane, *Technology and Reform: Street Railways and the Growth of Milwaukee, 1887–1900* (1974)

Martin V. Melosi, ed., *Pollution and Reform in American Cities, 1870–1930* (1980)

Elisabeth Israels Perry, *Belle Moskowitz: Feminine Politics and the Exercise of Power in the Age of Alfred E. Smith* (1987)

Joel A. Tarr, *Transportation Innovation and Changing Spatial Patterns: Pittsburgh, 1850–1910* (1982)

Meredith Tax, *The Rising of the Women: Feminist Solidarity and Class Conflict, 1880–1917* (1980)

Judith A. Trolander, *Professionalism and Social Change: From the Settlement House Movement to Neighborhood Centers, 1866 to the Present* (1987)

CHAPTER 9

Leisure Time and
Popular Culture, 1890–1930

✳

Throughout American history, the city has been fertile ground for the development of various leisure-time activities that have attracted all groups of people. From the colonial period onward, recreation and amusement offered urban dwellers diversions from work and religious observance while prompting moralists to complain about the alleged depravity inherent in leisure-time pursuits. By the end of the nineteenth century, the large numbers of people concentrated in cities became consumers for new, commercial mass amusements such as dance halls, vaudeville, and sports. Business entrepreneurs enriched themselves by catering to people's leisure-time preferences. Moreover, urbanization significantly shaped these leisure institutions, which in turn offered various types of urban dwellers opportunities to cultivate and express new kinds of behavior.

Several controversies, however, surrounded the spread of such establishments as dance halls and movie houses, and debates raged over the moral value of sports. Certain questions proved especially vexing to contemporaries. How much control should be exerted, either by families, organizations, or government, over the entertainment centers, particularly those frequented by young people? What sports were appropriate for working-class people who needed self-discipline in order to be productive factory laborers? With urban space becoming increasingly contested and limited, who should control the buildings, lots, and playgrounds where leisure activities took place?

✳ D O C U M E N T S

The first selection, written by a noted turn-of-the-century social reformer Belle Israels Moskowitz, illustrates the rise of leisure-time consumerism among young working-class women, the institutions of mass leisure (especially the dance hall), and the attempts by reformers to regulate those institutions and the behavior they allegedly encouraged. It is followed by a survey and treatise written by a Toledo, Ohio, clergyman, presenting a moralist's view that motion pictures had an unhealthy influence on local patterns of amusement. It also reveals the extent to which concerned citizens feared movies' effects on children. Note the alleged connection between movie houses on the one hand and dance halls and saloons on the other. The third document is an article on athletic clubs, forerunners of the popular health clubs of today. The article shows that athletic clubs served not only as places where middle- and upper-class urban men could restore their bodies through physical exercise, but also as centers for the promotion of new interest in sports and athletic competition. The final document describes the extraordinary popularity of baseball and how city youths adapted the sport to their narrow streets and cramped vacant lots.

Reformer Belle Israels Moskowitz on the Leisure Activities of Young Working-Class Women, 1909

The girls say that "carfare" is all it costs for a summer day at North Beach, admission fees the only "price" for a winter evening at a dancing academy. "With a voice of joy—with a multitude that kept holiday," they come and go at both places. In the summer the problem is what to do during enforced idleness; in the winter it focuses on where to go for relaxation. The beaches are summer types of amusement. The dancing academy of the winter months is at one end of a slide, with stops *en route,* to the saloon where dancing is allowed as a thirst accelerator—where girls are an asset only in proportion to the amount of liquid refreshment that they can induce the men to buy.

The amusement resources of the working girl run the gamut from innocent and innocuous vacation homes and settlement dancing schools, sparsely furnished for those "well recommended," to the plentiful allurements of the day boat, with its easily rented rooms, the beach, the picnic ground, with its ill-lighted grove and "hotel," to numberless places where one may dance and find partners, with none too scrupulous a supervision.

Having made accusations, let us proceed to substantiate them.

It is an industrial fact that the summer months find thousands of working girls either in the position of compulsory idleness through slack season in the trades with which they are familiar, or attempting "to kill time" through one or two weeks of a vacation, unwelcome because it bears no definite recreative fruit. The general aspects of the amusement problem of the working girl bear certain undetermined relation to the undercurrents besetting society in a large city, in proportion as opportunities for healthful outlet for social desire are adequate or inadequate. Industrial activity demands diversion. Industrial idleness cries out for rational recreation. As these are provided wisely and freely, the population of the underworld decreases. As they are neglected, the tide rises. Like Janus, the problem looks two ways—towards an escape from enforced idleness and relaxation from necessary labor. Active participation in athletics gives a natural outlet for the boy. The recreative desire of the young girl leads not to Sunday baseball—except as "he" may be playing—nor is it able to content itself with a comparatively expensive and therefore infrequent visit to the theater. Her aspirations demand attention from the other sex. No amusement is complete in which "he" is not a factor. The distinction between the working woman and her more carefully guarded sister of the less driven class is one of standards, opportunities, and a chaperon. Three rooms in a tenement, overcrowded with the younger children, make the street a private apartment. The public resort similarly overcrowded, but with those who are not inquisitive, answer as her room.

There is no need to dwell on what have come to be almost axiomatic statements of the uncomfortable home surroundings of the average working girl in a large city. It is perhaps equally ineffectual to harp on her natural desire for amusement. These things taken for granted, we must survey the field which spreads itself before her, first for the summer months and then for the indoor season.

The range of summer amusements around New York city covers first, beach resorts; second, amusement parks; third, the picnic park utilized for the outing, the chowder and the summer night's festival; fourth, the excursion boat; fifth, the vacation home or camp provided by settlements, churches, and girls' clubs.

Of the beach resorts, Coney Island and Rockaway are naturally in the van of public thought. Rockaway is expensive to reach. Its *clientele* is of the upper class of saleswomen and office workers. They enjoy the ocean bath and spend a comparatively simple day at the beach; and, being better provided with the world's goods than the average girl whom we wish to consider, are not seeking the same kinds of excitement.

Coney Island—the people's playground—where each year "everything is new but the ocean" is the most gigantic of the efforts to amuse.

A dancing master said: "If you haven't got the girls, you can't do business! Keep attracting 'em. The fellows will come if the girls are there."

Coney Island does attract them. It only costs fare down and back, and for the rest of it the boys you "pick up," "treat."

When the girl is both lucky and clever, she frees herself from her self-selected escort before home-going time, and finds a feminine companion in his place for the midnight ride in the trolley. When she is not clever, some one of her partners of the evening may exact tribute for "standing treat." Then the day's outing costs more than carfare. With due recognition of the simpler amusement places on the island—such as Steeplechase Park, where no liquor is sold, and also of the innocent pleasure along the beach front, not even belittling the fact that "nice" people dance in the Dreamland ball room, the fact remains that the average girl has small powers of discrimination. So many hundred places abound on the island to counter-balance the few safe ones, that "careers" without number find their initial stage in a Raines law hotel at this resort.

The danger is not in the big places on the island, where orderly shows and dance halls are fun, and where young persons may go unattended. But the greatest number of music halls and dance resorts are along the side streets of the Bowery, and, with the exception of one or two semi-respectable places, are thoroughly disreputable. On Saturday and Sunday nights many young working girls are attracted to these places. They know the bad reputation of some of them, but the dancing floor is good, there are always plenty of men, and there are laughter and liberty galore. . . .

Girls do not of intention select bad places to go to. The girl whose

temperament and disposition crave unnatural forms of excitement is nearly beyond the bounds of salvation; but ninety out of one hundred girls want only what
they are entitled to—innocent relaxation. The moving picture show is on the
wane. The skating rink had its day long ago. The dance is destined to be the next
feature in popular amusement.

Let us provide it plentifully, safely, and inexpensively. . . .

We must recover from the idea that the public is intrinsically bad. It needs
instruction in the fine art of using, not abusing its privileges, and a little faith in
the great American proletariat will develop a marvelous return.

Let us frankly recognize that youth demands amusement. When the cities
begin to see their duties to the little ones, playgrounds come. Youth plays too.
Instead of sand-piles give them dance platforms; instead of slides and seesaws,
theaters; instead of teachers of manual occupations, give them the socializing
force of contact with good supervising men and women. Replace the playground,
or more properly, progress from the playground to the rational amusement park.

Denial of these privileges peoples the underworld; furnishing them is modern
preventive work and should be an integral part of any social program.

The Reverend John J. Phelan Assesses Movies in Toledo, Ohio, 1919

1. The Number of Motion Picture Houses in Toledo

In spite of the fact that the population has increased thirty per cent, or more, during the past five years, the number of picture houses is marked by a relative uniformity. The greater number, 66, was in the year 1914. . . . At the close of 1918,
and the beginning of 1919, there are 58 places inspected by the City Department
of Public Buildings, which are equipped for possible exhibition of motion pictures. Of this number, however, only 42 are active operating houses; ten houses
have recently suspended business; while six others, although equipped, are used
primarily for other amusement purposes. . . .

Three others are planned for a near future and are as follows: . . .

Incorporation of the Pantheon Theater Co. with a capital stock of $100,000
assures Toledo the erection of one of the finest motion picture houses in the
country.

The new company has taken over the property formerly occupied by the
Kaiserhof cafe.

The exterior of the building will be glazed terra cotta.

A large foyer, which will accommodate more than 300, will be utilized as a
dance hall on special occasions, and the dances may be made a regular feature of
the program. Back of the lobby will be a large reception and music room, elabo-
rately furnished, where concerts may be held. . . .

There will be no balcony, but the theatre will have a seating capacity of
1,200. A $25,000 Hope Jones organ will be installed.

A large canopy will be built over the street and there will be a double ticket
window. A new lighting system, on the order of the "flood light," will be used.

Rest rooms, a private projection room and dressing rooms for the ushers and performers will be located in the basement. A play room for children will also be down stairs. . . .

The construction of a $60,000 three-story brick moving picture building on Lagrange street, near Central avenue, will be started July 1, according to Walter L. Grudzinski of the county clerk's office. . . .

The Sun & James Amusement Co. of New York, has leased the property now occupied by the Arcade theatre, St. Clair and Jackson streets, and will construct a $300,000 theatre building.

The deal was closed Monday, through Thomas Davies, of the Thomas Davies Realty Co. The building, it is expected, will seat 3,000. It probably will be used for both vaudeville and moving pictures.

The building will be 90 by 170 feet, brick and concrete. . . .

2. Site and Location

Forty-eight, or 82.7 per cent of the picture houses are located near or within the **Middle** of the block. The remaining ten, or 17.3 per cent, are located on street corners, which permit of a fair ventilation from three sides. The buildings situated within the block, however, permit of ventilation from only two sides—the front and rear. Twelve of the houses have provisions for both gallery and floor accommodations.

It is noted that many of the clubs, society and labor halls are used for both public and private dances, in addition to the four dancing academies of the city. Strong inducement is made to the public to patronize many of these dances, even though termed "invitation" dances. Fifty-four rooms used for dancing purposes were noticed in the neighborhood of the picture houses—principally in the downtown district. From personal observation, it was noted that a hasty and promiscuous acquaintance is often made at the picture shows which later develops in patronage of these dances.

Toledo has many rooming houses. These are largely occupied by unmarried young men and women who work in the various local industries. Many of these young people come from out-of-town and are away from the restraining and refining influences of the established home. The moral dangers, therefore, are extremely acute, especially as the City has no organized Community centers, Field houses or City recreation centers. Honorable mention is here made of the excellent work of the Y.W.C.A. and the Y.M.C.A. in the providing of play facilities and group gatherings in their well-equipped plants, but, as is too often the case, the persons who ought to be under the influence of these splendid organizations—are "outside the fold." Consequently, "cheap" popular shows—in all that the name implies—and the many unsupervised and commercialized forms of amusement are greatly patronized. It is estimated that at least 20,000 young persons live in the 300 rooming houses which are located within walking distance of the picture houses. An authority in the business, states that "the larger part of these persons attend two or three times a week, and a considerable number, nearly every night in the week and Sundays."

There are 408 saloons in Toledo. Over one-third of these are situated in or near the Sixth Ward—the downtown section, where the larger and greater patronized shows are operated. Saloons are strategically located . . . where both the young and old assemble. A previous study of the liquor industry revealed a large number of young persons as patrons in the saloons which are located in the neighborhood of picture houses and theatres. Subtle suggestions, due to the vivid portrayal of the underworld life, vampire life, sex problems and exhibition of scantily clad, together with stirring scenes of "shooting" and "stabbing"—necessarily make for added stimulation and resort to the "drink." . . .

4. Seats and Seating Capacity

The seating capacity of the fifty-eight houses is 47,997 seats—a general average of 827 seats to a house. Fifteen places, however, or more than one-fourth have a seating capacity of 31,488, or more than 66 per cent of the whole number. . . . In nearly every house stationary chairs or seats are used, and narrow, uncomfortable accommodations, both as to seats and floor spaces is tolerated by the pleasure-seeking patron. The general dangers, due to close seating, are as follows:

> Promiscuous mingling with undesirables (moral.)
> Physical contact with the unclean (physical.)
> Inhaling of disease germs and offensive odors (sanitary.)
> Possibility of theft and personal insult (social.)

5. Sanitary Conditions

He who enters the average picture house in Toledo, is seldom favorably impressed with the sanitary conditions. The ventilation is entirely inadequate—the air being stagnant and contaminated with offensive odors, particularly after the second audience comes in. This is largely due to the following factors:

The location of the playhouse itself, which is usually within the middle of a block, thus permitting the ingress of a comparatively limited amount of fresh air, and then only at the front or rear.

Uncleanness, due to lack of daylight—the darkness of the room making it impossible to detect with the naked eye the exact condition of either the seats or floor.

Inadequate ventilating system, and, in rare cases when provided, characterized by slovenly inattention.

Prevalence of bacteria germs and dry dust—caused largely by the heat of picture machines, poor ventilation, stamping feet and expectoration of tobacco juice.

Odors from garments and persons of mixed patronage.

Insufficient, and in many cases, inefficient janitor service. . . .

The Moral and Social Effects of the Movies

The social effects are not entirely of an incalculable quantity. In fact, many arguments, both of a positive and negative nature can be advanced as to their use. The advantages are as follows:

1. The providing of a reasonable-priced and highly entertaining form of amusement.
2. Convenience both as to accessibility and continuous play hours.
3. The promotion of family unity—as seen in attendance of the entire family.
4. The counteraction against the influence of the brothel, saloon, public dance hall and other questionable forms of amusement.
5. A provision for amusement and relaxation.
6. The supply of information in regard to travel, history and world events.
7. The treatise of high moral and educational themes.
8. The movies as an "art."

To these items serious attention must be given. No true educator can deplore in a busy age—the opportunity for recreation and amusement that is afforded persons of limited means. Proper recreation and amusement are as necessary as food and raiment. The person who makes his boast, that "he has no time or disposition to play" is, or will prove to be, a dangerous factor to society. . . .

Again, it is a matter of great convenience to be able to "drop into" one of these picture houses and spend but a couple of hours' time, free from the necessity of "fixing up" and "losing time," so characteristic of the days of the speaking drama. . . .

Whether the patronage of saloons, public dance halls and other forms of questionable amusement has decreased within the past twenty years . . . , there is no definite dependable data. There are two communities, however, one at Washington, D.C., and a county in Pennsylvania of which it is stated that the patronage of the saloon has decreased forty per cent. Of course the man who takes his family with him to the movies is not at that particular time patronizing the saloon, whatever his conduct may reveal later.

There can be no question but what there are many really fine pictures which possess marked educational merit, but that the "movies" either at present or in the remote future can function as a final substitute for text-books and the cultural advantages derived from a long and sustained period of study, not even the most ardent promoters affirm. . . .

Much is heard of the "movies as an art" and it is well to heed an authority on this particular phase, William A. Brady, a famous play producer. He says: "The movies are handicapped in an artistic competition with the stage. The majority do not command the best authors and few picture actors take themselves or their work seriously." . . .

Is the average performance of such a nature as to shape and develop moral fibre? Many persons are "visual-minded," that is, their sensations, emotions and impressions are derived for the greater part from what they "see" or "feel," rather than from what they read and think through from standard sources. This large class of non-readers secure snap-shot ideas of life from the screen—ideas of religion, morals, ethics, government, domestic life, forms of amusement, liberty and personal license. Little or no discrimination is made between the travesty and the real—the comic and the serious—the genuine and the superficial. . . .

The specific dangers to children—due to an indiscriminate patronage of public picture houses are as follows:

Physical Dangers

1. Injury to the eyes.
2. Development of neurasthenia.
3. Loss of sleep to growing children.
4. Danger of disease.
5. Substitute for physical exercise.

Social Dangers

1. Laxity of home-control.
2. Promiscuous mingling with feeble-minded.
3. Formation of loose-spending habits.
4. Incapacity of sustained mental application, especially in school work.
5. Creation of adult standards for immature youth.

Moral Dangers

1. Exaggerated viewpoints of life.
2. Awakening of morbid curiosity.
3. Lack of discrimination of what constitutes travesty and serious.
4. False conceptions of sin.
5. Development of an abnormal imagination.
6. Creation of sickly sentimentalism.
7. Creation of a desire to imitate plots.
8. The false depicting of true art.
9. Vivid portrayal of loose ethics as affecting home-ties, relation to state and society.
10. False delineation of what constitutes true Americanism.
11. Evils incident to the entire system of "commercialized" and unsupervised forms of public amusement.

The whole question in a nutshell, is one of control. It is freely granted that the movies possess great educational, social and entertainment possibilities. But, when the so-called "great movies" are brought down to clap-trap and balderdash, an insult is rendered every one whose intellect is above the dime-novel stage. . . . The legitimate drama and stage all come in for drastic criticism, but the press is strangely silent about the malicious distortions, and moral incongruities of many picture plots. . . . Why not also have a dramatic critique of the aesthetic element of the plot and the educational and moral values to be derived? . . .

Local Observations

From an observation extending over two years in Toledo, and making a reasonable allowance for some truly great plays, it is estimated that at least sixty per cent . . . will have interwoven, either in plot or execution, some "suggestive" touch before their completion! Frequently, it is the presentation of a prolonged passionate love scene which is freely mixed with excessive kissing—the graphic depicting of domestic infidelity ending in the elopement with another man's wife, or, the vivid presentation of the scenes of a life that has gone wrong, but is now acceptable to society, quite immune from the scars and penalties of sin, and with little or no clear-cut evidence of repentance or restitution. . . .

It ought to be a matter of concern to any community, if a great army of boys and girls in their "teens" are increasing in number before the Juvenile Courts each year. This is the condition in Toledo and in many other rapidly growing cities. . . . The chief offences are Stealing, Truancy and Immorality. . . .

Fifty per cent of these delinquents are mentally defective and hence, particularly susceptible to suggestions and impressions. Two-thirds of all juvenile delinquents come from homes where the parents are likewise delinquent—due to feeble-mindedness. It is estimated that two-thirds of the girls who appear before the Court charged with immorality, owe their misfortune to influences derived directly from the movies, either from the pictures themselves, or in the "picking up" of male acquaintances at the theatre!

The offences for stealing include robbery, swindling and playing the part of the "hold-up" man.

A small boy was brought before the local Juvenile Court. He had been accused of shooting a revolver at his playmate's feet. When asked "why he did so?" he replied: "I saw the stunt pulled off at the movies, and I thought it was great." . . .

A few are asking, "Where do the young secure these ideas of life? At least seventy per cent (according to their own testimony) derive their ideas from the movies. How could it be otherwise? The children do not make the plots for the pictures, and lacking discrimination meekly accept them as ideals for conduct. . . .

4. The Complexity of the Problem

That the business is utilized chiefly for gain, no one cares to deny. The spirit of unalloyed altruism is not the spirit of commercialized amusement. To be sure, since the war began, the Government has found the movies an excellent medium to promote bond sales, encourage enlistment campaigns, deliver messages of the Food Commission, and to disseminate democratic principles. This is work of a truly educational character. The indiscriminate presentation of the eternal "blood and sex" problems, however, with their intricate dramatic treatment is of a distinctly different category. The whole subject also becomes peculiarly acute from the fact that the National Board of Censors "VINDICATES the dramatic presentation of life in even its most dangerous relationships." It pleads to be "permitted to portray life AS IT IS LIVED in the various stratas of society," and asks "not to be condemned when it SHOWS THE BAD in order to emphasize the good!" This is asking for too much privilege—the laboratory test reveals the weakness of its plea.

First of all, it will be seen that modern educational methods make serious objections to such logic. Moral science also teaches that the good is accentuated and developed only by the considerations of its kind, namely, the pure and clean. Surely not by undue emphasis and lurid portrayal of the subtle intrigues and working of the evil mind. The primary purpose of going to the movies is not to take a lesson in moral training—the effect of evil can be seen, and all too well, in any morning newspaper. People go to the movies to be entertained, and while there become affected by whatever ideals are presented. The proper place for the teaching of morals is through regularly organized channels, such as the home, church and school. . . .

In the light of the discussion and the evident need of control in some form, the following suggestions are submitted. They are not intended as a "cure-all," but as a reminder of the many ways social service can aid in one of the greatest problems confronting the American city. If unity of community action is secured in but one feature alone, the advisability and necessity of the others will become increasingly evident.

5. A Proposed Solution

1. The increase of parental responsibility, as seen in intelligent and sympathetic guidance, regarding the evils of promiscuous, excessive and indiscriminate attendance at picture-shows, burlesque and vaudeville—care to be exercised against "over-control" as well as "under-control."

2. The possible creation of a Department of Public Morals as a branch of the City Government. This department to supervise all of the public amusement places of the city; co-operate with the various charitable, philanthropic, social, religious and educational agencies, and enforce the present City Ordinance regarding the attendance of unchaperoned minors at theatres. To give it legal status, this department could be made a branch of the Department of Public Welfare or Public Safety.

3. The immediate appointment of a local Board of Film Censors to co-operate with the Ohio Board of Film Censors as to the type of pictures most desirable for children. The number, personnel and all matters of detail to be worked out carefully by the Social Service Commission of the Inter-Church Federation, Catholic and Jewish churches. The censorship of all picture posters and advertising schemes outside of theatres and picture houses is also necessary.

4. The insertion in the local press (each week) of the bulletins issued by the Committee of Better Films for Young People.

5. The development of a Children's Theatre in the city wherein clean, wholesome and proper plays may be shown to both children and parents. . . .

6. Immediate instruction to be given to theatre managers and all employees regarding enforcement of present city ordinance as to attendance of unchaperoned minors.

7. Request for the appointment of a Federal Board of Film Censors. . . .

8. The creation of a law to prevent children from attendance at shows after nine o'clock in the evening.

9. A reasonable and efficient method devised, whereby "movies" may be shown with comfort, little expense and safety in the home.

10. The need of co-operation between the educator and film-maker to build up a film library as complete and comprehensive as in the school library.

11. A civic awakening on the part of the public, that only the best pictures be allowed to be exhibited, and the determination to patronize only the best show-houses.

Harper's Weekly Looks at Athletic Clubs in New York City, 1890

There is a season for rowing, and a season for base-ball; a season for tennis, and a season for foot-ball; but for general athletics there is no particular season. Gymnastics may be practised the year round. Men can walk and run and jump almost as well in-doors as out, and swimming-tanks have made exercise in the water as practicable in winter as in summer. Most clubs now have both winter and summer "meetings"—competitions, that is to say, open either to members of the club or to all amateurs. In winter their energies are apt to be mainly directed to bowling and general gymnastics; in summer more attention is paid to base-ball, rowing, yachting, and tennis. The late fall is the season for foot-ball, and in a winter like the one just past cross-country runs may be held every week.

The past ten years have seen a most remarkable development of athletics in this neighborhood. Twenty years ago only two of the present athletic clubs were in existence. . . . Now there are in this city, Brooklyn, and the neighborhood, within fifteen miles, including Newark, Orange, and Elizabeth, some thirty clubs recognized by the Amateur Athletic Union, not to mention the hundreds of separate bowling and tennis and base-ball clubs. It has become fashionable to be an athlete, and there is many a man who would be called a dude east of the Bowery that is prouder of his muscles than of his clothes, and that could "put up his hands" with any of the brawny denizens of the east side. It is said by those who know that New York has more active members of athletic clubs, both absolutely and in proportion to population, than any other large city in the world. . . .

Of all our indigenous athletic associations the New York Athletic Club is the oldest, as it is about the largest and best established. It was founded twenty-four years ago by William B. Curtis, John C. Babcock, and Henry E. Buermeyer in a back parlor on Sixth Avenue. It was in this year that amateur athletics began to become prominent in England. The first Oxford Cambridge athletic contest was held in March of that year, and the first amateur championship meeting was given in the same month. It was the accounts of these competitions that inspired the young athletes already mentioned to renewed efforts.

The first public contests of the New York Athletic Club were held in the American Institute building, on Third Avenue, November 11, 1868. Since that time its progress has been rapid. It now has over two thousand members; it owns one of the largest, best-appointed, and most complete club houses in the world, and besides that has a country house at its summer resort of Travers Island which is itself as fine a club-house as could be desired. . . .

The only rival of the New York Club in numbers, wealth, and influence is the Manhattan. . . . The club was not legally incorporated until 1878, but it took a prominent place from the start. Its leaders secured a track and grounds within the city limits, and made the track one of the very best and fastest in the country. They devoted much energy to the development of athletes who would make records and bring glory to the club. They gave handsome prizes and held frequent meetings. . . .

One of the best "all-round" clubs is the Staten Island. Most of the clubs, especially the smaller ones, confine their efforts largely to one or two branches of sport. Thus the Palmas are mostly given to shooting and bowling, the Crescent to foot-ball and base-ball, the Star and National to boxing, the Jersey City to bowling, the Elizabeth to bowling and base-ball, the Turnverein to gymnastics proper; but the Staten Islanders do a little of everything, and do it pretty well. They have some good performers on field and track athletics; they have a good crew; they keep up canoe races and yacht races; they have tennis tournaments every year; their lacrosse team is one of the best in the country; and they are making a fine record as base-ball players. Their club property is valued at $100,000. . . .

The Pastime Athletic Club, founded in 1878, early earned for itself the title of the "Nursery," because it produced so many good athletes who afterward joined larger and wealthier organizations. The social feature is perhaps not quite so prominent in the Pastime as in some of the others. Its club-house is an old church, more or less surrounded by gravestones, and it has not the advantages of some other clubs. . . .

Of the younger athletic organizations none is now more prominent tha[n] the New Jersey Athletic Club, which has its headquarters at Bergen Point. It was incorporated two years and a half ago, the Bergen Point Base-ball Club, and the Argonauta and Viking rowing associations joining in its formation. Since the Olympic Athletic Club and the Claremont Cricket Club have cast in their fortunes with it. It has about 550 members, a good club-house, a fine field and track, and an excellent rowing course on Newark Bay. . . .

The Acorn Athletic Club is only a year old, but is already prominent. Its club-house and grounds are in South Brooklyn. . . . It has a good cross-country team, and cultivates general athletics. . . .

The Crescent Athletic Club is devoted mainly to foot-ball and base-ball. Its house and grounds are at Bay Ridge on Narrows Avenue, between Eighty-third and Eighty-fifth streets. . . .

The growth of athletics has been nowhere more clearly manifest than in our militia regiments. The building of such immense armories as those of the Seventh in New York and the Thirteenth in Brooklyn has given the regimental athletes room enough to hold games in-doors, and has greatly stimulated winter exercise of all sorts. Nearly all the regiments now have athletic clubs, the most nostalgic of which are those of the Seventh, the Twenty-second, and Twelfth, and the Thirteenth. The Seventh contains many members who belong also to the New York or Manhattan or other local clubs. An idea of the variety and excellence of its games may be had from a mere list of the events and some of the principal competitors in the meeting of Saturday, April 5th. Here is the programme: 1000-yard run, 220-yard run, half-mile walk, putting 10 pound shot, 440-yard run, 220-yard hurdle, running high jump, wheelbarrow race, half-mile roller-skating race, three-legged race, and 2 mile bicycle race. . . .

It is easily seen that the encouragement of athletic sport among members of the National Guard is an excellent thing for this important branch of the service. Young men who keep "in condition," and who are trained to walk and run and jump and play ball, are certainly capable of better service in the field than they could render without such training. . . .

The "Y.M.C.A.'s" deserve a separate article to themselves. Almost every well-organized Young Men's Christian Association in the city and neighborhood has now its athletic department, and many of them have gymnasiums. It is the muscular form of Christianity that seems to take best among young men. The New York Y.M.C.A. is the oldest and best known, and its gymnasium has been celebrated these fifteen years. Last year there was a flourishing Y.M.C.A. base-ball league of some twenty or thirty clubs, and this year the interest bids fair to be still greater. . . .

The bad feeling which once existed between the New York and Manhattan clubs, and which led to the formation and the maintenance for several years of separate national organizations is now happily gone. All the clubs have come together in the Amateur Athletic Union—the "A.A.U.," as it is generally called for short—and harmony prevails throughout the United States. Such an organiza-tion is desirable and necessary for many reasons, but mainly because of the good fellowship it cultivates among athletes everywhere, and because it prevents any conflict of the dates of open meetings. Individual clubs are often dissatisfied with the action of the A.A.U. on some particular point, but the advantages of union are too great to be overbalanced by any temporary injustice, either fancied or real; and there seems to be no reason why the A.A.U. should not live many years. . . .

After all, . . . the real object of athletic organizations should not be, and in most cases is not, to break records and to produce champions. Their main purpose should be the development of healthy bodies in all their members. That club is really the most successful which benefits the most of its members, whether it also and incidentally produces champions or not. These facts are recognized far more generally to-day than they were even as lately as ten years ago. All the good clubs now have their gymnasiums, with varied apparatus for the development of all parts of the body. Some of them have swimming tanks; all have bath-rooms. The better-appointed club-houses contain bowling alleys, billiard-rooms, rooms for fencing and for boxing, a good running track, rowing machines, and all sorts of gymnastic appliances. Most important of all, a few have regular instructors who are at the club-house every day, and conduct classes and give private advice and instruction to the members. Without such advice and instruction novices nearly always overdo, and so either injure themselves or become disgusted and stop ex-ercising.

Of all such instructors no doubt the best known is Mr. George Goldie, of the N.Y.A.C., formerly instructor in gymnastics at Princeton College. . . . Mr. Goldie has been at his present post for about seven years, and to him in no small degree the success of the club is due. Certainly it is mainly due to him that the club is one of the best institutions of the world in which men of ordinary build and no espe-cial athletic proficiency build up their strength and improve their general health. It will astonish any one who has never been inside the club-house to examine the ingenious apparatus—some of it devised by Mr. Goldie himself—for strengthen-ing the neck, the back, the fingers, the wrists, the abdominal muscles—in fact, all parts of the body. The N.Y.A.C. is celebrated for the number of its champions, but it deserves to be still more celebrated for the excellence of its provision for help-ing its ordinary members. . . . As the clubs become larger and richer, all will be provided with houses containing as good facilities as are now enjoyed by members of the New York, the Manhattan, and the Berkeley. There will be a more general diffusion of athletic education among young men. The result can hardly fail to be the gradual evolution of a higher and better type of physical manhood.

Collier's Magazine on How City Children Adapted Baseball, 1911

See the picture first: A chasm, its walls the fronts of tall tenement buildings: at the bottom a street too narrow for the volume of traffic or for pedestrians. Over the slippery asphalt scores of children are swarming. Their shrill voices sound above the pounding of street-car wheels and the rumble of heavy wagons. By instinct— since they appear neither to see nor to hear the cars and the trucks—those children at play sometimes dodge danger in the latest possible fraction of time.

To discover what a new outdoor game, such as a modified form of baseball, may mean to these street children is a fascinating quest for any one with an interest in common sense sociology. Only think for a moment how few games are possible in a space so limited as a city street. Recall, further, what happens when games are lacking—that is to say, what *is* happening all the time. A picture of two boy gangs at war like savages, may flash first to the mind, or some memories of the very literal sense in which tenement children play with fire. Sometimes, on a walk in New York's East Side, it seems as if every chasm of the whole district has a bonfire, with children dancing around it, jumping over the flames. . . . For another case, there is the continual destruction of property by tenement children the moment it is left unguarded.

Children Playing Baseball in a Chicago Street, c. 1910

Baseball, traditionally played in open areas, proved adaptable to cluttered city streets. Evading adult supervision and using only the most fundamental equipment, children created their own rules to have fun in the urban environment.

When you see street children risking their lives with bonfires, or pulling a chair from a van to smash it to pieces with the avidity of a pack of wolves, or when you hear the crash of window glass followed by a patter of boys' feet and an enraged baker sprinting down the avenue, scattering flour and profanity by the way, you behold the pathological symptoms of a lack of good games. There is no inbred viciousness in tenement children: there simply are the evidences of an unsatisfied hunger for play.

No easy matter is it to find a game adapted to the needs of the street playground. First, it must be exciting enough to be attractive to a real boy. Next it must be something suited to the most limited sort of space. As a final necessity, the equipment must be cheap enough to be reached by the possessor of an extremely lean purse. Does it sound like an easy problem?

If any sport could furnish attraction enough to constitute an insurance against youthful disturbers of the peace, it would be the national game of baseball: and balls and bats and gloves are cheap enough to be within reach of all. Field baseball, however, requires too much space to be the right sort of game for a playground of the bottom of a chasm. If there were only some way to adapt and modify baseball to the needs of a narrow street or a cramped little vacant lot! That thought, no doubt, has with many a social worker become almost a fervent prayer.

Give all due credit, then, to those unsung adventurers among the boys of Chicago who first dared to disregard a label and play indoor baseball outdoors. In gymnasiums for a good many years the indoor game has been popular because it is so well adapted to a small area of floor space: but it was only three or four years ago that Chicago boys began to adopt this form of play for street use. So fast has the idea spread that today nearly every small boy in the city has at one time or another practised the modified style. In the thickly populated sections, particularly, it is rapidly becoming one of the most popular of boys' games.

Few spectators who have watched one of these contests in the streets fail to remark on the combination of picturesqueness and danger involved. On the floor of an artificial cañon, in a faint fog and the rumbling traffic, behold some wildly animated small athletes pitching a grotesquely large ball, swinging a bantam-sized bat, with an iron manhole cover for home plate, and first base the gridiron of a sewer catch-basin. Trolley-cars dart and clang near the players' backs, unheeded: the batters knock out liners under the very noses of draft horses: or sometimes an eager base-runner nimbly skips across the course of a motor truck. Any rather wide intersection of streets furnishes a temporary ball ground pending the appearance of a patrolman from around the corner. In an alley in the very heart of the loop district, at the noon hour, I once saw four office-boys playing indoor baseball with all the dead earnestness of league athletes in a post-season series for the world's championship. Their luncheons wrapped in newspapers waited on a near-by window sill. Likely you will find yourself wondering first at the incongruities in such animated pictures and then go home debating whether the boy's danger from being run down by the traffic is not a better risk than the peril of being run in for the mischief he may find to do if his life is without good games.

By no means, of course, is the street the only place that the modified baseball game is popular in outdoor Chicago. The street is where the interest is most tense for the spectator: but for the player the vacant lot is more to be desired. The tiny bat cannot knock the big, soft ball far enough to require much space, so some of the smallest of lots serve as ball grounds.

In a large plot the indoor game's chief virtue is that it allows of many more contests at one time than are possible with field baseball. From noon until two o'clock on any sunny day of spring or summer the fascination of the revised form of the national game draws droves of office men and clerks and boys from adjacent buildings to play in Grant Park—Chicago's downtown athletic field and public outdoor noonday club headquarters. This strip of land lies between the Michigan Avenue hotels and shops, and the railway tracks that border the lake front. It is only a step or two away from their desks for hundreds of office employees. The gases from locomotives kill the grass and shrubs, so the park commissioners could find no valid objection to giving up some of the north end of the strip to the noonday athletes. The available space is large enough for perhaps two league baseball diamonds, or to give exercise to three dozen active players. But when the indoor game has the use of the grounds almost two hundred . . . can play: and it is not at all unusual to find a dozen games in progress at once.

✖ E S S A Y S

The essays below exemplify the recent explosion of historical interest in the leisure-time pursuits of ordinary urban dwellers in the past century. The first essay, by Kathy Peiss of the University of Massachusetts, Amherst, examines the role of dance halls in the leisure life of working-class urban dwellers. Peiss considers how dance halls not only provided young women with opportunities for independent social lives away from watchful parental eyes but also made them vulnerable to exploitation from predatory males. The second essay, by Steven A. Riess of Northeastern Illinois University, explores the interrelationships among urbanization, the rise of sports, and the cultures of different socioeconomic groups. Riess tries to show what sports were more common to—and more appropriate for—different ethnic and racial groups.

Women and the New York Dance Halls

KATHY PEISS

Of all the amusements that bedazzled the single working woman, dancing proved to be her greatest passion. After the long day laboring in a factory or shop, young women dressed themselves in their fanciest finery, put on their dancing shoes, and hurried out to a neighborhood hall, ballroom, or saloon equipped with a dance floor. The gaily decorated hall, riveting beat of the orchestra, and whirl of dance partners created a magical world of pleasure and romance. Thousands of young women and men flocked to such halls each week in Manhattan. By the 1910s, over five hundred public dance halls opened their doors each evening throughout

From *Cheap Amusements: Working Women and Leisure in Turn-of-the-Century New York* by Kathy Peiss, pp. 88–114. Copyright © 1986 Temple University Press. Reprinted by permission of the publisher.

greater New York, and more than one hundred dancing academies instructed 100,000 neophytes yearly in the latest steps. As one reformer exclaimed, "The town is dance mad."

The dance hall was the favorite arena in which young working women played out their cultural style. Their passion for the dance started early, often in childhood, as girls danced on the streets to the tunes of itinerant musicians. . . . By the time they were teen-agers, dancing had become a pervasive part of women's social life. The vast majority of women attending dance halls were under twenty years of age, and some were only twelve or thirteen. Their male dance partners tended to be slightly older; dancing was even more popular with them than were saloons and pool halls. For both sexes, going to the city's dance halls marked a particular stage in the life cycle. Participation rose during adolescence, when dance halls offered "the only opportunity in the winter for unrestrained, uncramped social intercourse between the young people of the two sexes." Attendance at the halls lessened considerably when girls started "keeping company" with a beau and ceased upon marriage. . . .

Young women's attendance at dance halls followed the general patterns of their participation in street life and social clubs. The evidence is too limited to show the specific social composition of the dancers—their ethnicity, family life, or work experience. No ethnic enclave seems to have had a monopoly on dancing. . . .

While dance hall culture is only a piece of working-class experience, and a relatively small one, it is a window on cultural issues and social dynamics that are usually obscured. Ethnographic description of dance halls—dance steps, ballroom etiquette, drinking customs, clothing styles—illuminate aspects of the cultural contrasts of gender among working-class Americans. These forms of expression dramatize the ways in which working-class youth culturally managed sexuality, intimacy, and respectability.

This dance hall culture, and its embodiment of sexual ideology and gender relations, must also be situated in a broader social context. The organization of dancing underwent important changes in the late nineteenth century, as the commercialization of leisure challenged older patterns of working-class recreation. Once a family amusement and neighborhood event, dancing was transformed as its setting changed. New ballrooms and dance palaces offered a novel kind of social space for their female patrons, enhancing and legitimating their participation in a public social life. The commercial culture of the dance halls meshed with that of working-class youth in a symbiotic relationship, reinforcing emergent values and "modern" attitudes toward leisure, sexuality, and personal fulfillment.

The Social Organization of Working-Class Dance

Dance madness thrived in the back rooms of dingy saloons, in large neighborhood halls, and in the brightly lit pavilions of amusement parks. The character of working-class dances from 1880 to 1920 varied considerably with the type of hall, the organization of the dance, and the social composition of the participants. The traditional working-class dance of the late nineteenth and early twentieth centuries, however, was the "affair" held in a rented neighborhood hall. . . . The affair not only raised money for charitable purposes, but strengthened group spirit for members and their families. . . .

Organization affairs and traditional balls took place in an environment controlled at least partially by familial supervision and community ties, although without the strict proprieties and chaperonage of a middle-class dance. This was particularly the case at smaller dances, observed one settlement worker, where "greater respectability is maintained because there is a closer acquaintance among those who attend." Usually the sponsoring organization issued formal invitations and sometimes appointed floor managers to oversee the dancing and drinking. . . .

Young women attended affairs . . . with their families or an approved escort, expecting to see friends and neighbors. With the exception of Italian immigrants, who sharply restricted the public activities of women, most parents considered these dances relatively safe for their daughters. . . . In the 1890s, however, new ways of organizing dancing, spurred by the growth of a working-class youth culture, developed alongside the traditional ball and affair. The "racket," a dance organized by social clubs and amusement societies, increasingly enticed young pleasure-seekers. . . .

Rackets differed greatly from the lodge affair or benefit society ball, in which dancing was associated with neighborhood supervision, philanthropy, and intergenerational sociability. Clubs evinced little interest in controlling admission and chaperoning the dance floor. . . . Extensive advertising and the indiscriminate sale of tickets often brought crowds of seven hundred to eight hundred dancers to a single event. . . . At such dances, proper working-girls in their neat shirtwaists might find themselves mingling with the flashily dressed and "tough." . . . Rackets offered not only pleasure but profit: the sale of tickets produced enough money to finance excursions and vacations for club members. The Rounder Social Club, for example, ran an affair every year in order to rent a bungalow at Rockaway Beach each summer. With these incentives, the club dance became increasingly widespread throughout the working-class sections of the city.

The Commercialization of Dancing

An interlocking network of commercial institutions and voluntary societies structured working-class dancing. Whether the dances were lodge affairs or club "blow-outs," the dance craze was intensified by the expansion and commercialization of Manhattan's public halls. For the working-class population packed into small tenement apartments, large halls that could be rented for dances, weddings, mass meetings, and other gatherings were a requirement of social life. The number of public halls in Manhattan rose substantially in a short period; business directories listed 130 halls in 1895 and 195 in 1910, an increase of 50 percent. . . .

The "liquor interests" spurred the growth of large public halls that could accommodate dances for hundreds of people. In the lower East Side, 80 percent of the dance halls surveyed in 1901 were adjacent to saloons, and the sale of alcohol formed the foundation of their business. . . . The club would sell tickets and hat checks to swell its coffers, while the hall owner dispensed liquor to enlarge his. Other halls based their rentals on a sliding scale, determined by the amount of alcohol consumed. . . .

By the 1910s, the old multiple-purpose neighborhood hall and saloon no longer could meet the demand for dance space, and huge metropolitan halls and ballrooms designed specifically for dancing sprang up. The first dance palace, the Grand Central, was built in 1911, and five others, including the Roseland Ballroom, followed in the next ten years. Ranging in capacity from five hundred to three thousand patrons, the large halls were usually located in the commercial amusement zones of the city, in such areas as 42nd Street and Broadway, 14th Street, and 125th Street, serving a city-wide clientele. Dance palaces attracted people of all nationalities, but they appealed more to factory and office workers than to middle-class and elite amusement seekers, who flocked to Gotham's cabarets and restaurants. Large working-class organizations often rented these halls for their yearly gatherings. . . .

In the large commercial halls, the continuing presence of a sponsoring club or organization conferred legitimacy on the dance, even as the activity moved away from its traditional working-class form. Hall managers even created their own clubs to encourage a steady clientele and add a veneer of respectability to the dance. . . . A popular strategy was to advertise the hall as a dancing academy, teach the latest steps during the day, and offer open public "receptions" in the evenings and on Sunday afternoons. . . .

Commercial dance halls remained morally suspect to some parents and their daughters. Irma Knecht, for example, differentiated between the respectable social evenings of the *landsmannschaft* societies and the promiscuous public halls: "We didn't go to these dance halls, [we] used to go to organization affairs." Others, however, had no qualms about attending the public halls. Ruth Kaminsky, for example, exclaimed, "As single girls we went dancing . . . in dancing halls, . . . we used to have a nice time, to meet fellows." Girls who were not closely supervised by their parents went to public dances and social club parties at least one evening a week, and some attended as many as three or four. . . . For these women, the emergence of the large commercial dance halls, whether run through general admission fees, through social club rentals, or as a dancing academy, created an alternative to the traditional affair of the fraternal lodge and benefit society. The intergenerational integration that was possible in the locally based dance rarely occurred in the new ballroom and dance palaces. Rather, this expanding network of commercial dance halls became the territory of working-class youth.

Dance Hall Culture

With the commercialism of dancing, hall owners and entrepreneurs especially promoted the participation of young women. Halls lowered their admission prices for unescorted women, charging ten to fifteen cents, as opposed to the usual fee of twenty-five or fifty cents per couple; some even admitted women free. Charges for checking hats and coats show a similar differential. . . . This policy implicitly recognized the subordinate economic status of women, at the same time that it urged them to attend ballrooms with or without an escort.

The hall owners' pitch was not primarily an appeal to thrift, however, but rather a promise of excitement, glamour, and romance. In the late nineteenth century, working-class dances had often taken place in small, dingy saloons, crowded with dancers who simply ignored the unpleasant surroundings. The new commercial dance halls, however, were large structures that enticed their patrons with bright lights, blaring music, and a festive atmosphere. . . . In the hall, a large, polished dance floor, bounded by a stage at one end and a bar at the other, drew crowds of youth. Often a balcony ringed the dance floor, containing chairs and tables for patrons to relax and watch the dancers. . . .

Dancing Styles

The sexual expressiveness of working-class youth at the commercial halls was particularly apparent in the styles of dancing. Anxious to maintain their good reputations with working-class parents and placate civil authorities, many hall owners sought to contain promiscuous sexuality by patrolling the dance floor. . . .

In the unrestrained commercial halls, however, dancing styles took less traditional forms. In the 1890s and early 1900s, "pivoting" or "spieling" captivated working women. . . . In this dance, the couple, held tightly together, would twist and spin in small circles on the dance floor. One observer at a Coney Island dance house described two stereotypical pivoters:

> Julia stands erect, with her body as rigid as a poker and with her left arm straight out from her shoulder like an upraised pump-handle. Barney slouches up to her, and bends his back so that he can put his chin on one of Julia's shoulders and she can do the same by him. Then, instead of dancing with a free, lissome, graceful, gliding step, they pivot or spin, around and around with the smallest circle that can be drawn around them.

Pivoting, which was a loose parody of the fast waltz, was diametrically opposed to the waltz in intention. In nineteenth-century high society, the waltz was initially scandalous because it brought the sexes into closer contact than in dances of previous eras, but the dance form itself countered that intimacy with injunctions toward stiff control and agile skill. The speed of the dance demanded self-control and training to achieve the proper form. The major innovation of the dance was that a woman and man placed their hands on each other, but instructors insisted that partners' shoulders be three to four inches apart and that the distance between their bodies should increase downward. . . .

The spieling dance, in parodying this form, was performed not with self-control, but as a dance out of control, its centrifugal tendencies unchecked by proper dance training or internalized restraint. Instead, the wild spinning of couples promoted a charged atmosphere of physical excitement, often accompanied by shouting and singing. . . .

The sexual emphasis of the dance was even more pronounced in a style known as "tough dancing," which became popular after 1905. Tough dancing had its origins in the houses of prostitution on San Francisco's Barbary Coast and gradually spread, in the form of the slow rag, lovers' two-step, turkey trot, and bunny hug, to the "low resorts" and dance halls of major metropolitan areas. . . .

Tough dances differed significantly from earlier dances like the waltz or two-step, in which partners held each other by the hands or around the waist. "Bodily contact has been conventionalized to an unprecedented degree," observed one reformer, while another elaborated, "Couples stand very close together, the girl with her hands around the man's neck, the man with both his arms around the girl or on her hips; their cheeks are pressed close together, their bodies touch each other." The dancers' movements ranged from a slow shimmy, or shaking of the shoulders and hips, to boisterous animal imitations that ridiculed middle-class ideals of grace and refinement. Performed in either a stationary or a walking position, such dances were appropriate for a small, crowded dance floor. Moreover, they were simple to learn, requiring little training or skill, while permitting endless variations on the basic easy steps. . . .

Tough dancing not only permitted physical contact, it celebrated it. Indeed, the essence of the tough dance was its suggestion of sexual intercourse. As one dance investigator noted obliquely, "What particularly distinguishes this dance is the motion of the pelvic portions of the body, bearing in mind its origins [i.e., in houses of prostitution]." What troubled such reformers was that the dance, whether wild or tame, became an overt symbol of sexual activity, which the dancers, operating outside the usual conventions of dance, were free to control: "Once learned, the participants can, at will, instantly decrease or increase the obscenity of the movements, lowering the hands from shoulder to the hips and dancing closer and closer until the bodies touch." More than other dances, the tough dance allowed young women to use their bodies to express sexual desire and individual pleasure in movement that would have been unacceptable in any other public arena. . . .

Constructing Heterosexuality in the Public Halls

Control over dancing styles was only one aspect of the larger problem of regulating heterosexual relations at dances. The popular middle-class resorts, cabarets, and cafes tended to mediate promiscuous contact by imposing elaborate rules on their clientele. . . . Moreover, as Lewis Erenberg cogently argues, the placement of tables and the stage in middle-class cabarets created a structure that limited contacts between unacquainted women and men. . . . The "couple on a date" became an increasingly important cultural construct for the middle class, since it provided a way to structure potentially promiscuous heterosocial relations at the new resorts.

The commercial dance halls frequented by working-class youth varied in the types of behavior their managers would tolerate, particularly those concerned with vice raids. Unlike the middle-class resorts, however, many hall owners simply ignored the unruly revelry of the crowds and the close physical contact of women and men. . . . Investigations by the Committee on Amusements and Vacation Resources of Working Girls cited numerous instances of dance halls with little supervision by the management, concluding that "the proprietors of these places not only permit the young men and women who visit the place to do about as they please, but often encourage their lascivious and immoral tendencies." Balconies, for example, were accepted zones of free behavior, and women could be observed on men's laps, hugging and kissing in the dark corners of the hall.

In contrast to the pleasure-seekers at middle-class cabarets, working-class youth often did not attend dances as heterosexual couples, heightening the problem of control. . . . Instead, young people arrived at the halls alone or with members of their own sex, expecting to "couple off" during the dance. . . . The halls themselves devised schemes to facilitate heterosocial interaction. A number of downtown dance academies and halls employed men called "spielers" who danced with unattached women. . . . Waiters were encouraged to play a role in matching up and introducing young women and men.

More commonly, finding a partner occurred through the custom of "breaking" women on the dance floor. At the beginning of a dance, women would dance together, with men watching them from the sidelines; then "the boys step out, two at a time, separate the girls, and dance off in couples—the popular form of introduction in the popular dance hall. . . .

The scorn for proper introductions reflects the widespread practice of "picking up" unknown women or men in amusement resorts or the streets, an accepted means of gaining companionship for an evening's entertainment. Indeed, some working-class social clubs apparently existed for this very purpose. . . .

Such social customs as "picking up" and "breaking" suggest the paradoxical nature of dance hall culture for women. Women enjoyed dancing for the physical pleasure of movement, its romantic and sensual connotations, and the freedom it allowed them. The commercial dance halls were public spaces they could attend without escorts, choose companions for the evening, and express a range of personal desires. Nevertheless, the greater freedom of expression women found in the dance halls occurred in a heterosocial context of imbalanced power and privilege. Picking up women and breaking dancers were more often male prerogatives in a scenario where women displayed themselves for the pleasure of male eyes. . . . Moreover, the custom of treating, which enabled many women to participate in the life of the dance hall, undercut their social freedom. Women might pay trolley fare out to a dance palace, or purchase a dance ticket and hat check, but they often relied on men's treats to see them through the evening's entertainment. Making a virtue out of economic necessity, young women learned to prize male gifts and attentions. . . . Under these conditions, the need to strive for popularity with men came to be a socially defined—and ultimately restricting—aspect of female expressiveness and desire.

To win male attention in the dance halls, working women fully elaborated their eye-catching style. Chicago women, for example, placed powder puffs in their stocking tops and ostentatiously flourished them to attract male attention on the dance floor. Their New York sisters could hardly be outdone, wearing high-heeled shoes, fancy ball gowns, elaborate pompadours, hair ornaments, and cosmetics. . . . This practice reinforced women's objectification, but it also allowed them an outrageous expressiveness prohibited in other areas of their lives. . . .

Women's popularity was also predicated on willingness to drink. In many dance halls and saloons, economic considerations militated against abstinence, and any women not drinking or encouraging others to imbibe was made unwelcome by the manager or waiters. In some places, prizes were offered the woman who had the most drinks to her credit. . . .

The approved cultural style of dance hall women involved other forms of uninhibited behavior as well. Loud talk, boisterous laughter, and cigarette smoking all helped women gain attention and status in the halls. Smoking was still a controversial form of female behavior in the 1910s, symbolic of the modern and somewhat risque woman. . . . Participation in kissing rituals was also emblematic of the "game girl." "Now the kissing parties are starting in," observed a waiter at Remey's New Year's Eve dance, "it appeared to be contagious, when one started kissing they all started." . . .

Treating and Sexuality

For these women, treating was not always a one-way proposition, but entailed an exchange relationship. In the male subculture of the saloon, treating rounds of beer asserted workingmen's independent status while affirming common ties among a group of equals. Women, however, were financially unable to reciprocate in kind and instead offered sexual favors of varying degrees. Most commonly, capitalizing on their attractiveness and personality, women volunteered only flirtatious companionship. "Pleasures don't cost girls so much as they do young men," asserted one saleswoman. "If they are agreeable they are invited out a good deal, and they are not allowed to pay anything." . . . Not all working-class women simply played the coquette, however. Engaging in treating ultimately involved a negotiation between the desire for social participation and adherence to cultural sanctions that strongly discouraged premarital sexual intimacy. One investigator captured the dilemma women faced in their dependency on men in their leisure time: "Those who are unattractive, and those who have puritanic notions, fare but ill in the matter of enjoyments. On the other hand, those who do become popular have to compromise with the best conventional usage."

The extent of sexual intimacy involved in treating and the nature of the social relations surrounding it are difficult to establish. Dualistic middle-class categories of "respectability" and "promiscuity" do not adequately describe the complexity and ambiguity of working-class sexual norms, norms that were complicated further by ethnic, religious, and generational differences. The Italian daughter who stayed out late at ballrooms or an unmarried Irish girl who became pregnant might equally be stigmatized by their respective communities. . . .

Working-class women received conflicting messages about the virtues of virginity in their daily lives. Injunctions about chastity from parents, church, and school might conflict with the lived experiences of urban labor and leisure. Working in factories and stores often entailed forms of sexual harassment that instructed women to exchange sexual favors for economic gain, while talk about dates and sexual exploits helped to pass the working day. Crowded tenement homes caused working-class daughters to pursue their social life in the unprotected spaces of the streets, while those living in boarding homes contended with the attentions of male lodgers. The pleasure and freedom young women craved could be found in the social world of dance halls, but these also carried a mixed message, permitting expressive female sexuality within a context of dependency and vulnerability.

Negotiating this world produced a range of responses. While many women carefully guarded their reputations, attended chaperoned dances, and deflected the attention of men, others engaged in looser forms of behavior. Women who had steady male friends they intended to marry might justify premarital sexual intimacy. . . .

Other women fully bought into the culture of treating, trading sexual favors of varying degrees for male attention, gifts, and a good time. These young women were known in underworld slang as "charity girls," a term that differentiated them from prostitutes because they would not accept money in their sexual encounters with men. As vice reformer George Kneeland found, they "offer themselves to strangers, not for money, but for presents, attention and pleasure, and, most important, a yielding to sex desire." A thin line divided these women from "occasional prostitutes," women who slipped in and out of prostitution when unemployed or in need of extra income. Many respectable working women apparently acted like Dottie: "When she needed a pair of shoes she had found it easy to 'earn' them in the way that other girls did." . . .

This evidence points to the presence of charity girls at dance halls, but it tells us little about their numbers, social background, working lives, and relationship to family and community. The vice reports suggest that the women were young, some not over fifteen or sixteen. . . . The jobs they held were typical of other working women—waitresses, domestic servants, garment-makers. While some lived alone, others resided with their families, which made sexual encounters difficult. One man, who picked up charity girls at a dance hall, remarked, for example, that "he sometimes takes them to hotels, but sometimes the girls won[']t go to [a] hotel to stay for the night, they are afraid of their mothers, so he gets away with it in the hallway." . . .

Whatever the specific numbers of charity girls, many more women must have been conscious of the need to negotiate sexual encounters if they wished to participate in commercial amusements. Clara Laughlin, for example, reported the story of an attractive but decorous working girl who could not understand why men dropped her after a few dates. Finally a co-worker gave her the worldly advice that social participation involved an exchange relationship: "Don't yeh know there ain't no feller gong t'spend coin on yeh fer nothin'? Yeh gotta be a good Indian, Kid—as we all gotta!" . . .

The culture of the commercial dance hall—the anonymity of its spaces, tolerance of uninhibited behavior, aura of romance, and peer pressure to conform—supported the social relationship of treating. It induced young women to engage in freer forms of sexuality and perhaps glamorized the notion of a sexual exchange. While treating gave some women opportunities for social participation they otherwise would have lacked, it remained a situation of vulnerability and potential exploitation.

One way women exerted some control over their interactions with men was by attending dances and other leisure activities in the company of a "lady friend." Young working-class women's friendships were structured relationships between girls who usually met at school, at work, or on the streets. Unlike their brothers, who often joined gangs or clubs, young women would cultivate a single friend or at most a small clique. . . . The lady friend enhanced social occasions, as a companion to share the fun of a dance and a confidante for whispered gossip. At the same time, she performed another function, serving as an implicit protector whose presence helped to deflect unwanted sexual attention. At a racket for the Drivers' Sick and Benevolent Fund, the Committee of Fourteen investigator "tried to get next to some of the women but couldn[' not]t, they travel in pairs and it['not]s hard for one man to pick any of them up." . . .

The lady friend symbolically drew the line of respectability at a time in women's lives when heterosexual contact was at its most promiscuous and dangerous, when meeting men in dance halls, amusement resorts, and the streets. The single woman alone might be taken for a prostitute, but hunting in pairs permitted women to maintain their respectability in the aggressive pursuit of pleasure. . . .

In the commercial dance halls, single working-class women found a social space that reinforced their emergent cultural style and offered an opportunity to experiment with unconventional sexual and social roles. In a few hours of dancing and camaraderie, they could seemingly escape the social relationships and expectations tying them to their household responsibilities, jobs, and ethnic communities. What mattered in the dance hall—popularity, dancing ability, fashionable clothes, and male attention—was a modern style that promised independence, romance, and pleasure. Nevertheless, the realities of working-class life persistently intruded; women's situation in the labor force and family undercut their social freedom, and treating underscored their material dependency. And within the halls, an ideology took shape that fused notions of female autonomy and pleasure with heterosexual relationships and consumerism. This formulation, which ultimately limited female possibilities and power, increasingly defined the cultural construction of gender in the twentieth century.

Sport and the Urban Social Structure

STEVEN A. RIESS

The development of the industrial radial city had a crucial impact upon the sporting pleasures of all urban social classes. The greatest impact was economic: the rise of industrial capitalism enriched a small number of people, improved the standard of living for the nonmanual middle class, weakened the position of the artisan class, and gave rise to a huge pool of poorly paid, semiskilled and unskilled industrial workers who worked long hours at a backbreaking pace. As widening income levels, substantial differences in discretionary time, and diverse social values resulted in different leisure options for different social classes, sport came to mark social boundaries and to define status communities. Spatial and demographic changes in the radial city also influenced the development of urban sport along class lines. The enormous physical growth of cities, accompanied by extraordinary increases in population, had major impacts on historic patterns of land use, which in turn influenced each class's sporting opportunities. In the era

From *City Games: The Evolution of American Urban Society and the Rise of Sports,* by Steven A. Riess, excerpts from pp. 53–85, 91. Copyright © 1989 The University of Illinois Press. Reprinted by permission of the publisher.

of the walking city, the countryside had been relatively accessible to most urbanites, who could enjoy there a wide variety of outdoor sports, but after the 1870s, empty lots, the woods, and unpolluted streams were harder to reach, especially for lower-class men who could not afford costly transportation fees. Furthermore, traditional playing fields and sports centers in the old urban core were displaced to make way for more valuable development, and consequently workingmen lost many traditional recreational sites. But the changing spatial patterns were far less of a problem for middle- and upper-income groups, who were more likely to live near sports facilities and could afford the cost of transportation to their favorite athletic sites.

Sport and the Urban Upper Class

In the Gilded Age a segment of the urban elite constituted a community of conspicuous consumers who built costly mansions and estates, held extravagant balls, belonged to prestigious men's clubs, and enjoyed costly sports. As Thorstein Veblen recognized, the elite watched and participated in sports not merely for the sake of having fun but also to be trend setters and to acquire the prestige associated with such exclusive sports as racing, yachting, and polo. The nouveaux riches were particularly prominent in elite sports through which they could certify their acceptance by the social elite whose lifestyles they admired and sought to emulate.

The elite found sport at a wide variety of athletic venues. They enjoyed spectator sports like horse racing and football at semipublic places and leisurely participatory sports like croquet and ice skating at public parks. . . . But the sporting venues most characteristic of this class were private sites like athletic clubs and country clubs, which fostered a heightened awareness of social exclusivity.

The "sport of kings" was dominated by the social elite, who raced expensive thoroughbreds, organized high-status jockey clubs, operated prestigious tracks, and governed the turf. The best breeding farms and stables were owned by very rich sportsmen, mainly members of the elite, although some wealthy men of lesser standing, like Tammany boss Richard Croker, also raced thoroughbreds in an effort to secure social status. . . .

Besides racing, another spectator sport that drew elite interest was college football. Intercollegiate sport had originated at elite eastern universities, and the sons of the elite were among the most prominent amateur athletes of the late nineteenth century. Collegians enjoyed sport because it was exciting, promoted community among the student body, and operated independently of adult supervision. Furthermore, they anticipated that athletic training in combination with fraternity life and the study of modern subjects would prepare graduates for the modern business world.

Football, more than any other intercollegiate sport, fit in with the needs of upper- and upper-middle-class urban youth at a time when America was ripe for a violent and virile sport that stood for honorable values in stark contrast to the corruption, greed, and materialism of the Gilded Age. A manly game played by gentlemen, it represented the higher ideals of Theodore Roosevelt's Strenuous Life philosophy. . . .

While the elite did not totally avoid public and semipublic sporting facilities, at least as long as they could enjoy themselves in privacy, most elite sport did occur at private sites and facilities owned and operated by status communities. At a time of declining urban space and rising property values, voluntary athletic associations constructed gymnasiums, boathouses, running tracks, and other facilities. Sports clubs arranged competition, including championships, formulated playing rules, and guaranteed the character of competition. Membership criterion was strict and candidates could be blackballed for no reason. High initiation fees and annual dues also discouraged undesirables from joining. Acceptance into such a restricted club proved certification of a candidate's high social standing.

Athletic clubs were among the first restricted sports societies to be formed after the Civil War. They emphasized participation in track and field contests which had been previously dominated by professional pedestrians and Caledonians. The first athletic club to gain widespread recognition was the New York Athletic Club (NYAC), incorporated in 1868 by three upper-middle-class sportsmen who modeled it after the London AC. They wanted to be able to compete in athletics with other men from the same social class. The NYAC facilitated the rise of track and field as an amateur sport by building the first cinder running track and by sponsoring the first American amateur championship in 1876. . . .

In addition to athletic clubs, elite sportsmen formed other participatory sports organizations that utilized private space. Cricket was an important elite sport in Philadelphia, where five major clubs, each with memberships of 500 to 1,300 had elaborate clubhouses located on large lots in prestigious Mainline neighborhoods. The new polo clubs used private sites like the original Polo Grounds located just north of Central Park. . . .

The most important sports organizations that utilized private space were country clubs, located in suburban areas where they provided members with a taste of English country life. The first was The Country Club, established in Brookline, Massachusetts, in 1882, and it became a model for future clubs. Its membership list constituted a veritable Who's Who of Boston, with names like Cabot, Forbes, Lowell, and Saltonstall. Half of the original 403 members were Harvard men, 30.5 percent were also in the Union Club and 67.2 percent in the Somerset, the city's most prestigious men's clubs.

. . . At the turn of the century golf was the most important country club sport, even though the first American course in Yonkers was just thirteen years old. It was not an exertive sport, but did require concentration and eye-hand coordination, and was suitable both for older men seeking an excuse to escape the city for the out-of-doors and for their daughters as well. . . . The other major club sport was tennis, which required expensive courts but far less space than golf. The first courts were often built expressly for country club wives and daughters who played leisurely doubles matches while garbed in full-length skirts. . . .

In the period from 1870 to 1920 the enormous size of cities and their populations, the growth in the number of the elite, and a high degree of impersonalization meant that urban elites could no longer know everyone of their class on a face-to-face basis. They relied on club membership to provide a comfortable and safe haven spatially segregated from the problems of the industrial city and to help them distinguish the proper people with whom to socialize and do business.

It became important to men of new money to join sports clubs to certify their level of status and to further advance into more restricted metropolitan clubs. . . .

The Urban Middle Class

In the antebellum era the development of a positive sports ideology that justified and encouraged participation in respectable sports, and the increased middle-class participation in those sports paved the way for the great postwar boom in bourgeois athletics. . . . Middle-class sportsmen had sufficient discretionary income and free time, and were psychologically prepared to take advantage of the social changes wrought by urbanization to enhance their athletic prospects. By the late nineteenth century, office workers were down to a forty-four hour week, including half-day on Saturday. Although they could not afford expensive elite sports staged at private resorts, they could utilize the new mass transit facilities to travel to respectable semipublic sporting sites and the new public parks located on the suburban fringe beyond the old boundaries of the walking city. This enabled them to physically separate themselves from the lower orders of society.

The rising middle-class interest in sport reflected a desire by workers in sedentary jobs to demonstrate physical prowess and manliness and to gain recognition which bureaucratic occupations did not always supply. . . . Middle-class men were also concerned about their courage, about becoming "overcivilized," about losing their sexual identity, and about the feminization of culture. . . .

Middle-class residents of the suburban fringe were among the first urbanites to use parks for sports. As public parks were built or purchased throughout the country, nearby residents used them for sports like sleigh riding and ice skating in winter and boating and croquet in summer. These were sociable sports, enjoyed by both men and women, which did not harm the beauty or serenity of the parks. In the 1880s municipalities began building tennis courts in suburban parks, making that relatively new elite sport available to the middle classes. . . .

The middle-class sporting rage in the 1890s was the bicycle, which enabled millions of middle-class men and women to leave behind the problems of industrial cities for relaxing pastoral landscapes, momentarily fleeing progress on a vehicle that was itself a product of that technological progress. . . .

In 1880 the League of American Wheelmen (LAW) was formed with local branches all over the country. The LAW promoted competitive racing and touring and fought for good roads and equal access with horses on municipal thoroughfares. Its *Bulletin,* one of eighty-five American cycling periodicals, had a printing of nearly 100,000 by the turn of the century. In 1883 the LAW achieved an important political victory when New York City opened Central Park and Riverside Drive for part of the day to bicyclists. Within the next few years few city streets and parkways were off limits to wheelmen.

The bicycle craze of the 1890s followed the invention of the safety bicycle, which had equal-size tires, chain gear drive, a diamond-shaped frame, and more efficient coaster brakes. It was still primarily a middle-class vehicle which cost $50 for a cheap bicycle and nearly $100 for a medium quality one. The introduction of installment buying and the resale of second-hand bicycles brought the cost down to where clerks and artisans could afford it. However, it was too expensive for unskilled workers. Residents of poor neighborhoods resented middle-class folk using their streets for riding paths, interfering with street life and endangering children at play as well as other pedestrians. . . .

In the 1890s cycling achieved considerable popularity as a spectator sport, with a number of important road races, most notably the fifteen-mile Chicago-to-Pullman Race held on Memorial Day that attracted from 200 to 400 competitors. Far more consequential were the professional indoor races, which were popular from the late 1870s through the 1920s and drew crowds of up to 10,000. But the key to the cycling fad was the enormous number of recreational cyclists. By 1893 there were over a million riders in the United States, and they quadrupled in three years. . . .

By the turn of the century there were ten million bicycles in the United States, but the bicycle fad had passed. The market was saturated, and innovative manufacturers were turning to a more sophisticated vehicle, the automobile, which enabled the tourist "to see more, faster, with urban comfort and social isolation built into his machine." While in other parts of the world the bicycle remained an important mode of transportation and a major sporting device, Americans increasingly regarded it as a child's toy. The car replaced the bicycle in the hearts of Americans because it was more exciting and ownership conferred greater prestige.

Baseball was the most important sport played by the middle classes in the period from 1870 to 1920. Despite its pastoral mythology, baseball was very much an urban game, first played in cities, and the best players were mainly urbanites. The first fully modernized American team game, the sport was rationalized and bureaucratized in cities, where its spirit of nationalism, wholesomeness, excitement, and drama made it the national pastime. The character of the team game was congruent with the work experience of bureaucrats. But in one important way the sport did not fit in with industrialized urban society: baseball was not controlled by the clock. . . .

In the post–Civil War period baseball was a democratic sport which lacked social prestige, but the ideology of the sport fit in nicely with the bourgeoisie's prevailing value system as well as their social experiences. The baseball creed—an extension of the positive sports ideology developed in the antebellum era in response to modernization and urbanization—fully touched base with the beliefs, values, and social needs of middle America, reassuring old-stock folk that their traditional small-town values were still relevant to the increasingly impersonalized bureaucratized, and urbanized society. . . .

While there is little evidence that baseball actually built character or provided a social catharsis, the baseball creed had a strong influence on contemporary thought and behavior because people perceived the ideology to be accurate. They regarded baseball as rural game played on a large verdant lot and through it identified with the values of a simple, pristine world. . . . Sportswriters and other journalists writing in mainstream middle-class periodicals like *American Magazine, Collier's, Harper's Weekly, The Independent,* and *Scribner's* all accepted the cultural fiction that baseball was a useful sport that promoted social integration by instilling hometown pride, providing a setting where people from all walks of life could come together, and enabling hard-working urbanites to release their pent-up emotions in such socially sanctioned rituals as booing opponents and cursing umpires. Playing baseball was regarded as a good exercise that also improved the mental health of participants; just attending games was even said to help urbanites improve their fitness by getting them out into fresh air, where they could wave their hands and exercise their vocal chords. The baseball creed further asserted that the sport was an educational game that taught modern values such as teamwork and certified traditional values like rugged individualism, honesty, hard work, temperance, and respect for authority—qualities that would make urbanites better citizens and disciplined workers. . . .

Fans became part of a community of like-minded spectators who rooted for the local club in a collective demonstration of hometown pride and boosterism. Baseball competition became a metaphor for interurban rivalries, and a victory over other towns in the league symbolized the superiority of your city. . . .

Blue-Collar Sportsmen

In the late nineteenth century, when middle-class white-collar men living in the industrialized radial cities were becoming avid sportsmen, a major segment of the manual work force was constrained in their leisure opportunities by the social impact of industrialization and urbanization. Until the 1920s working-class sportsmen were primarily drawn from the labor aristocracy or municipal service workers—groups that earned about twice as much as laborers, worked shorter hours, and had a tradition of participating in sports and physical culture. Most workingmen could afford only the simplest, cheapest pleasure. These employees—mainly the unskilled, new immigrant factory workers—had long working hours, few holidays, and little discretionary income. They were unfamiliar with sporting institutions, their crowded slum neighborhoods offered little outdoor space for athletics, and they could not afford the cost of frequent trips to outdoor facilities located at the increasingly distant urban periphery. . . .

Working-class attendance at spectator sports was limited by time, discretionary income, and access. In the days before cheap mass transit the easiest sites to reach were indoor gymnasiums located in slums or arenas in the Central Business District (CBD). Boxing matches that attracted a working-class clientele were usually held in neighborhood gymnasiums, often known as "athletic clubs"—firetraps that were "nothing more than a loft, with tiers of wooden benches to the ceiling." . . .

Outdoor sporting events like thoroughbred racing or baseball were more difficult to attend because of the cost and time. These events were held at distant sites that required public transportation. Professional baseball did not gear itself as much for the poor urban masses as for the middle classes, who paid higher admission fees and lent the sport an aura of respectability. Games were scheduled for times when most employed blue-collar men were on the job, the general admission ticket to a National League (NL) game was set at fifty cents in 1876, and the fields were far from the inner city. . . .

Unlike the NL, the American Association, the second major league, did try to cater to working-class fans. Founded in 1882, the AA charged just twenty-five cents for admission, sold alcoholic beverages, and scheduled Sunday games wherever possible. When the two leagues merged in 1892, the new NL adopted the AA policy of Sunday ball and gave each team the option to sell bleacher seats for a quarter to build up attendance, a pricing policy later adopted for one season by the new American League (AL) in 1901. . . .

Working-class sports fans unable to attend their favorite sporting events kept abreast of developments and read about their heroes through the media, which was very accessible. Even before the Civil War innovations in production had made newspapers affordable, and improvements in distribution made the penny papers widely available. Newspapers began to build up enormous circulations, topped by the morning and evening editions of the *New York World,* which reached 374,000 in 1892. These papers featured yellow journalism, which emphasized sports, crime, and sex, providing next-day reportage of even the most distant events. In addition specialized weekly sporting periodicals appealed to a primarily urban audience—the *New York Clipper,* one of the first popularizers of baseball and a leading defender of pugilism, and the *National Police Gazette,* which focused mainly on boxing. . . .

The athletic options of low-paid blue-collar workers in the late nineteenth century were further limited by the declining accessibility of outdoor play space. The growth of cities reduced the number of open lots available for ball games in the vicinity of the inner city and pushed far away the once accessible woods and polluted the old streams that had been used for field sports. . . .

Inner-city sportsmen used whatever space was available in their own neighborhoods. Young men who lived near rivers or lakes swam there, often in the nude, which resulted in considerable public outrage. Respectable citizens petitioned the city council to restrict the location and hours of such public bathing and to require clothing; spokesmen for the plebes demanded public swimming baths for recreational and health reasons. In the 1880s certain cities began to establish public swimming sites for their poorer residents. Urban youths also used city streets for their playing areas. Young boys played stickball, football, handball, and other games in the street. Local businessmen demanded the police keep the streets and sidewalks clear because they needed the roads to transport freight and feared that youths hanging around would scare away customers. . . .

To escape urban crowding and middle-class outcries, most slum residents had to rely on semipublic neighborhood sites like taverns and billiard parlors for their sporting pleasures. The saloons, or "workingmen's clubs," described by their leading historian as game rooms and quasi-gymnasiums, provided many sporting services, including some spectator sports such as boxing matches and cockfights. Saloons were also gambling centers where by the 1880s one could find neighborhood bookmakers who took wagers from men who could not afford, or did not have the time, to go to the racetracks. . . .

Billiard table games were enormously popular among urban males; they provided a cheap opportunity to display skill, kibbitz, gamble, and meet friends in a warm and accessible location. . . . At the turn of the century nearly 30,000 establishments had pool tables; in the mid-1920s the sport reached its peak, with about 42,000 poolrooms, 90 percent of which were semipublic places. . . .

Poolrooms had a very bad public image even though the sport of pool was not inherently evil. . . . However, the conventional wisdom held that pool halls were hangouts for loafing inner-city boys and men of immigrant stock who gambled, plotted crimes, drank heavily, and corrupted minors, and thus these gathering places should be stamped out. . . .

The character and quality of the billiard facilities in the early twentieth century city varied substantially. The finest rooms—professional billiard halls located in the CBD—were either resorts for downtown businessmen or center of that city's male bachelor subculture. They had as many as fifty or more tables, were located above street level, and were relatively well maintained. . . .

The poolrooms regarded as the greatest danger to the public welfare were the small rooms, located in slum neighborhoods, frequented by a "rough" element. . . . As in all poolrooms, about 80 percent of the patrons were spectators, but the general feeling was that at the rough rooms they were up to no good. Often these pool halls were operated by individuals with police records who were seldom interfered with by the police though everyone in the neighborhood knew what was going on inside.

Billiard parlors were probably more widely distributed than any other commercialized entertainment except perhaps the movies. In the nineteenth century, when pool tables were less likely to be found outside billiard rooms and in cigar stores and saloons than in the future, a greater proportion of facilities were in the CBD. . . . Billiard parlors were concentrated not only in downtown neighborhoods but also on just a handful of heavily travelled commercial streets where they could attract a walk-in clientele. . . . Subsequently, as the concentrations of facilities in the CBD declined, so did the proportion of rooms on those streets (23.5 percent in 1910 and 15.3 percent in 1936), but it was still quite high and very significant. . . .

As a popular commercialized urban entertainment bowling was similar to billiards—cheap and readily accessible to the working classes and historically heavily associated with saloons, gambling, and the male bachelor subculture. The sport, actually banned in cities like New York for several years because of the gambling nexus, was revived in the 1880s among members of German-American voluntary associations like the Turners and the *Schüzengesellschaft* (shooting clubs), who enjoyed Sunday bowling in outdoor parks and laid out lanes in their clubhouse basements. At the turn of the century alleys were usually located in restaurants or saloon basements, where they were the scene of considerable betting, and thus bowling was not regarded as a respectable sport for women. . . .

Bowling had a strong appeal among working-class ethnic sportsmen. In the early 1900s, for example, one-third of Chicago's alley owners were foreign-born, primarily German, and they catered to a large ethnic clientele. Later on in the interwar period, all of the city's poor and modest white neighborhoods had bowling lanes, and this was typical of all the major industrial cities along the Great Lakes. . . .

The bowling alley, like the poolroom, was an important adjunct for street-corner life in the interwar era. It provided young men with a hangout where they could socialize and demonstrate individual skills, but it was far more respectable than the poolroom. . . . Bowling also facilitated sociability with the opposite sex. Alleys provided a public, non-threatening environment where street-corner boys could meet groups of young women and enjoy their companionship without the awkwardness that often accompanied blind dates. . . .

Despite a tradition of working-class professional track and field athletes who participated in long distance races, sprints, and the Caledonian Games, few leading amateurs were manual workers. While training regimens were less rigorous than today's and athletes might not have to take too much time off from work, they still lacked regularly established free time to practice, suitable equipment, proper coaching, and sponsorship. . . .

In the late nineteenth century the most important sources for amateur working-class competition were the annual picnics arranged by businesses, unions, and ward heelers. . . . While companies sponsored outings to improve employee-management relations, political machines sponsored picnics as a service to their constituents and to raise money. . . . Tammany-sponsored outings attracted primarily Irish crowds who played and watched competition in track, baseball, football, bowling, and Gaelic football. . . .

Artisan fraternal organizations and unions sponsored sport to encourage a sense of community among men who shared the same work experience and the same social economic problems. . . . Union halls were the workers' private space that doubled as centers of sociability and camaraderie where men could enjoy pool matches with their peers. . . .

After the turn of the century, industrial corporations played an important role in sponsoring working-class sports through welfare capitalism, which sought to promote company loyalty, retain skilled workers, forestall unionization by promoting a sense of community at the workplace, increase profits, and improve the firm's public image. Athletic facilities, club rooms, and picnics were financed under the supervision of an industrial relations department. . . .

Welfare capitalism reached its height in the 1910s and 1920s. Big city firms did not stress athletic and other recreational aspects of the program as much as was done in isolated mill towns, where workers had less access to uplifting sports and other entertainments. Nevertheless, sports programs were an important part of welfare capitalism among industrial firms with over 500 workers. In metropolitan areas where workers could not readily go home for dinner and then return to the plant to participate in sports, companies like NCR in Dayton and Heinz in Pittsburgh organized lunch-hour sports programs. . . .

While most athletic programs emphasized mass participation, a lot of companies also sponsored high-quality baseball, soccer, and football teams that played before hundreds and sometimes thousands of spectators. The purpose was to exercise social control beyond the factory gates, to deflect labor unrest by providing a source of moral entertainment, and to advertise the name of the company. . . . Players on company baseball teams might include former professionals who get easy jobs, paid time off to practice, and travel allowances. . . .

Conclusion: Sport and the Urban Social Structure

The nature of the urban social structure and its dynamic interaction with such elements of urbanization as space, demography, economic development, social institutions, political structures, and ideology had an important bearing on the development of sport and sporting institutions in the industrialized radial city. Because of different economic situations, social and cultural environments, neighborhoods, and value systems, members of different social classes did not have the same opportunities or options to partake of sports. However, over time sporting choices did become more democratic; especially by the 1920s and 1930s as the standard of living improved and municipal and private institutions increased their sponsorship of mass sport.

※ *F U R T H E R   R E A D I N G*

Melvin L. Adelman, *A Sporting Time: New York City and the Rise of Modern Athletics* (1986)

Gunther Barth, *City People: The Rise of Modern City Culture in Nineteenth-Century America* (1980)

Domenic Cavallo, *Muscles and Morals: Organized Playgrounds and Urban Reform, 1880–1920* (1981)

Patricia G. Click, *The Spirit of the Times: Amusements in Nineteenth-Century Baltimore, Norfolk, and Richmond* (1989)

John T. Cumbler, *Working-Class Community in Industrial America: Work, Leisure, and Struggle in Two Industrial Cities, 1890–1930* (1979)

Perry Duis, *The Saloon: Public Drinking in Chicago and Boston, 1880–1920* (1983)

Lewis Erenberg, *Steppin' Out: New York Nightlife and the Transformation of American Culture* (1981)

Stephen Hardy, *How Boston Played: Sport, Recreation and Community, 1865–1915* (1982)

John Kasson, *Amusing the Million: Coney Island at the Turn of the Century* (1978)

Bruce Kuklick, *To Everything a Season: Shibe Park and Urban Philadelphia* (1991)

Roy Rosenzweig, *Eight Hours for What We Will: Workers and Leisure in an Industrial City* (1983)

Bob Ruck, *Sandlot Seasons: Sport in Black Pittsburgh* (1987)

Dale Somers, *The Rise of Sports in New Orleans, 1850–1900* (1972)

Robert V. Snyder, *The Voice of the City: Vaudeville and Popular Culture in New York City, 1880–1920* (1990)

Metropolitan Growth and

the Automobile in the 1920s

✕

The federal census figures for 1920, which revealed that for the first time a majority of Americans—51.4 percent—lived in cities (places with 2,500 or more people), symbolized that the United States had become a truly urban nation, with all the problems and opportunities of a modern urban society. During the 1920s urban growth continued. Certain industrial cities, among them Detroit, Birmingham, and Houston, registered large gains, and especially high growth occurred in warm-climate cities such as Tampa, Tucson, San Diego, and Miami. At the same time, however, suburban growth accelerated even faster. Bedroom communities surrounding places such as Chicago, Cleveland, and Los Angeles increased by as much as 500 percent over the decade.

Much suburban growth involved the migration of middle-class families, and it was made possible by the automobile. Car registrations climbed from 8 million in 1920 to more than 23 million by 1929. Hailed as "democratic transportation," "pleasure palaces on wheels," and "shaper of cities," the automobile became the principal means of transport for suburbanites, who now could drive to work, to stores, or to recreational sites. The car also introduced new problems: traffic jams, pollution from exhaust fumes, and mounting death rates owing to accidents. What exactly were the car's positive and negative effects on urban and suburban life? Was the automobile as powerful an influence as contemporaries and scholars have believed? Does it hold the key to understanding metropolitan development in the 1920s, or was it merely one of many factors determining the configuration of the city and its satellites?

✕ D O C U M E N T S

The four documents in this chapter pertain to the relationship between the automobile and suburbanization in the 1920s. The first document, by John Ihlder, a city planner and the manager of civic development for the U.S. Chamber of Commerce in 1924, explains how changes in forms of vehicular transportation altered spatial relationships in the city and argues for a more conscious effort to consider the automobile in future city planning. Ihlder's points illustrate how issues of parking, decentralization, and downtown decay—all of which came to plague American cities later—were emerging in the 1920s. His statements also afford an opportunity for comparing the establishment of streets and automobile-related services with the establishment of the city services treated in Chapter 4 and with the long-range-planning accomplishments of engineers considered in Chapter 8. The second document presents a perceptive contemporary account of suburban growth in the 1920s, focusing particularly on the influence of the automobile and the problems of traffic congestion in downtown areas. In the third document, J. C. Nichols, the famous developer of Kansas City's suburban Country Club district, describes how a sense of community, akin to the atmosphere in an idealized city neighborhood, can be created in the suburbs. He sees the developer and the realtor as playing major roles in building such an environment and stresses that the services and features created eventually pay for themselves; indeed, his scheme makes no allowance for public financing or authority. The final document is by Lewis Mumford, probably the most trenchant urban theorist of the twentieth century. Mumford's vision adapts the "greenbelt city" ideal of British thinker Ebenezer Howard to the United States' urban system. Mumford, as much as he dislikes modern cities, still would not do away with urban living; he only wishes to apply greater planning and size limitations.

A City Planner on the Automobile and Community Planning, 1924

The automobile found us in our customary frame of mind, resentful of an innovation which interfered with established habits. From the day when the drivers of horses cursed an occasional devil wagon to the present, when crowds of pedestrians, many of them car owners themselves, denounce the delays and hazards at busy crossings, our attitude has been negative. Probably if we had realized back in 1900 just how drastic are the changes which the automobile is forcing upon us we would have organized a crusade against it. For our lack of imagination, instead of being the handicap we usually consider it, is probably one of the chief factors in our progress; it gives us the courage or the indifference of ignorance.

But we have now reached a point where we can no longer progress backwards, seeking means of keeping things as nearly as possible as they were in the days of our fathers. Suppression has become the dream of a fanatic. We find it difficult to remember even back to the time when it was not good form to go to church in an automobile—the very thought suggests all manner of irrelevances—and when our feelings were outraged by the sight of an automobile at a funeral. And now regulation is proving a broken reed. So we have got to turn about and face a future in which adequate provision will be made for automobiles. This involves a revision of our practice of city building.

Reprinted from "The Automobile and Community Planning" by John Ihlder, in volume no. 116 of *The Annals of the American Academy of Political and Social Science*. Copyright © 1924.

Dreams in City Building and Results

For centuries, our cities have been closely built. An occasional Utopian dreamed of green and spacious cities, an even more occasional one sought to create them. William Penn had a vision of city dwellings set among green gardens and orchards. Yet before the Liberty Bell rang out its message his city had become red with its solid rows of brick houses. Washington and L'Enfant had the vision when they planned the Federal City [Washington, D.C.] and sought to safeguard it by making wide tree-lined avenues. Today, behind the building lines of private property the Federal City is almost as overcrowded with buildings as is Philadelphia, and proposals to cut down street trees and widen roadways are constantly being advanced.

This tendency to over-build has its root in the human desire for a minimum of effort, for conveniences, for companionship. When Benjamin Franklin first walked into Philadelphia, every step counted. Even in his later days when he could drive, distance was a matter to take into serious account. But the dream persisted. The mass of men had caught the vision of the Utopians and desired more spacious cities. Because of that dream they welcomed rapid transit—horse cars, elevated railroads, trolleys, subways—believing that each of these would make the dream come true. On the strength of the dream they made a radical change in their manner of life. More and more those who could afford it deserted the dwellings above the store or beside the printing office and set up their homes at a distance made accessible by the new means of transit. So our cities spread out.

But each of these means of transit had its counter effect. As it made the suburbs more accessible from the center of town, so it made the center of town more accessible from suburbs and what had once been distant communities. Consequently more and more people came in to the center to do their shopping, to attend the theaters, to consult their lawyers. And to serve these buyers, patrons, clients, more people were employed in the center of town, people whose hours of work or scale of pay made it inconvenient for them to live at a distance from their places of employment. So we had, as on the lower East Side of New York, constantly more numerous, more rapid, more expensive and more *crowded* means of transit provided in order that the workers of Manhattan might live in the green fields of the Bronx and Flatbush—fields and green when the means of transit were first provided, but quite different now—while at the same time the population of the thronging East Side increased steadily and rapidly. The dream did not come true.

Then city planning in its modern phase began. It had run true to form in its development. It looked backward for its inspiration. It saw Old World civic centers that put our haphazard locating of public buildings to shame. It saw broad boulevards which added to the dignity of cities. So we started out to beautify. We again began to dream and in some places this dream is coming true. Cleveland is about to realize its dream after some two decades of effort and fighting. . . . In other cities there is progress and promise.

With achievement our dream became more magnificent. From civic centers and a few great boulevards we advanced to visions of park systems with connecting parkways. We drew plans which included not only the whole city, but much of the surrounding country. And again some of our dreams are coming true. . . .

Increasing Congestion and Efforts to Avert

But so far we followed traditional lines. Except where parks or water or steep hills interfered, our cities grew solidly, the more open suburban development swallowed by advancing rows of buildings. And behind these rows came skyscrapers, most numerous in the center of town but sporadically shooting up in other sections.

It was the skyscrapers that finally aroused us and forced us to realize that ancient and medieval and even modern Old World examples, though supplemented by rapid transit, do not give us all we need, that we must do some thinking for ourselves. Old-time habits of concentrating nearly all the business life of the community were producing conditions that mean constant loss. High buildings crowded closely together darken each other's windows, cut off each other's air, turn streets into sunless canyons inadequate to carry the traffic demanded by the abutting population. Rapid transit instead of solving the problem has intensified it. Now comes the automobile.

The first obvious effects of the automobile's arrival are in our streets. These streets are crowded to a degree of which their dedicators could not conceive. Their death and casualty lists exceed those of battle field. But—much more important from the point of view of securing action—their inadequacy hampers us in our daily life. We are constantly annoyed and handicapped by the steady procession of cars that holds us chafing on the curb, or we are prevented from leaving our car where we wish to alight because someone else has already parked there. Our first and natural impulse is to widen the streets. Every day in every city there is discussion of the pros and cons of street widening, either by setting back the abutting buildings, or, as a less expensive compromise, narrowing the sidewalks and so securing more space for roadway.

Evidently such remedies as these, taken up piece-meal, are mere temporary palliatives. Any practicable increase of street or road width is immediately filled with more automobiles and the *status quo ante* is restored. So we have reluctantly begun to realize that we must be more thoroughgoing in our search for a remedy, must even examine anew some of our most firmly established practices in city building. This brings us face to face with what seems to be the fact that the automobile differs from our former methods of rapid transit in that it demands a good deal of space for itself. Instead of enabling us to crowd more people into a given area, it is forcing us to diminish the density of population. The alternatives seem to be, either fewer people per square foot or fewer automobiles. Assuming what again appears to be the fact, that we shall elect to have *more* automobiles, the problem is squarely before us.

Following our natural bent as an ingenious people who delight in complicated and expensive contrivances for getting things that nature is ready to give us for nothing—such as light and air which we first build out and then force in—

supplemented by our tendency to the spectacular, some of our cities are proposing to double-deck their streets or to dig automobile subways. . . .

A dim realization of the futility of such proposals is making us begin to ask some questions. For example, what is the most efficient width of roadway in terms of number of traffic lanes? Most of us, accustomed to rather narrow streets packed to capacity, now believe that widening will give relief and that "adequate" widening will give "adequate" relief. But some who have lived beside very wide streets with very wide roadways know from experience that they are not only very expensive, increasingly hazardous to pedestrians—for whom islets of safety must be made, so narrowing the effective roadway by a series of bottle-necks—increasingly difficult to police for traffic regulation; but that they are also comparatively inefficient for traffic flow because they tempt drivers to pursue a devious and traffic checking course. . . . Essentially similar to the proposal for widening streets and thereby diminishing abutting building sites, is the proposal to cut new streets through built-up areas. The principal effect is the same, more street area, less building area. . . .

So we incline to turn to zoning as offering the most promising way out of our dilemma. If a given bulk of building of a given character—industrial plant, retail store, theater, apartment house, one-family dwelling—originates a given amount of traffic of given character—heavy trucks, delivery cars, street cars and buses, taxis, private passenger cars, pedestrians—on the abutting street, we have a basis for computing the ratio which should be established between building bulk and street width or roadway width. If a given roadway width is most efficient for traffic flow, we have another factor which can be taken into account. Then we can decide whether to widen the street, to open a new street or to regulate the character and the bulk of abutting buildings. The last seems likely to prove the least expensive and the most effective.

But this, of course, takes account only of the first obvious effect of the automobile's arrival. The picture we have had before our mind's eye so far has been a busy business district with nearly continuous lines of moving cars. Except for those of us who live or work in the centers of a very few of the largest cities this picture is supplemented by one of even more continuous rows of parked automobiles. In the very few exceptional cities the parked car has almost disappeared downtown where the streets wear a comparatively deserted look to the visitor from a bustling town up state or out west. The revulsion against much too much has thrown them all out, with what effect upon the business of the downtown area is only just beginning to be indicated by stories of firms which have moved to sites where automobile customers can still get at them. This moving of business firms because of traffic congestion is one we must study with some care. Because certain chain stores were located on corners where traffic counts showed the greatest number of pedestrians passing, many of us jumped to the conclusion that these were the most valuable locations for business, or at any rate for retail business. Now because certain stores are moving from the center of town many of us are getting ready to jump to the conclusion that all businesses depend on an automobile trade. This jumping habit saves mental effort, but it does not lead to good city planning.

The Parked Car

The parked car, however, again raises the question of space and of a ratio. First, shall parking space be provided by the city, (a) on its streets, (b) on other public property, and if so, shall it be provided free or for a fee? Present practice is to provide it free and on the street until the situation becomes intolerable, then to seek other public space and perhaps to charge a fee. But except where streets are very wide or where considerable unbuilt-upon areas remain within easy reach of the city center, these expedients promise no adequate relief. New space invites more cars. So we return to the ratio. A given bulk of building of a given character draws to it cars the number and character of which can be fairly definitely determined. Shall the city provide parking space for these cars or shall the building itself make such provisions? Shall we widen the street and so diminish the building site, or shall we provide on the building site storage space adequate to meet the needs of its occupants? Indications are that the latter will prove our ultimate policy and that in those sections of the city where populous and expensive buildings cannot be remodeled, either near-by accommodations will be found for the cars of tenants or those sections will find themselves in a losing competition with sections more fortunately situated. . . .

Classifying Traffic

To the dweller in . . . crowded home neighborhoods has become increasingly important the question of segregation or classification of traffic. It is bad enough to have the curb before his house constantly occupied by the cars of strangers, but it is even worse to have his peace disturbed, his house shaken, by heavy lumbering trucks and to have his special assessments increased by bills for repaving the streets those trucks have broken up. Zoning classifies buildings by use, creates districts of distinctive character. City or community planning is called upon to supplement this by providing thoroughfares of like distinction. To build all streets strong enough to carry heavy trucks is extravagance. To pave and repave streets ruined by uses for which they were not designed is folly. To classify traffic and provide for the needs of each class is an economy upon which we are about to enter.

And this again will make for spaciousness in our cities. The cost of a house lot is not so much in the land as in the improvements. A light roadway, the medium priced roadway for which the engineers are now seeking, reduces the cost of the lot. Zoning, which not only determines for a long period the character of a neighborhood but sets a fairly definite limit to its population by determining the height and percentage of lot occupancy of its buildings, makes possible other economies. The size of sewers and water mains as well as the type of paving may be decided upon with some assurance. So space will not mean as it has, an undue burden of cost necessitated by an unprophesiable future.

The speed and flexibility of the automobile—for its owner is not bound to given routes or to a time schedule—makes possible not only greater spaciousness but better planning of new home neighborhoods. The great arterial highways which lead from center to center, the rapid transit lines gradually converted from local to through express routes with lower peaks and higher valleys in their daily schedules, will become boundaries far within which will be placed the schools and recreation places. Children will no longer cross lines of heavy traffic as part of their routine.

The human desires for a minimum of effort, for convenience, for companionship, are as strong and compelling today as they were in Franklin's day, but the automobile apparently has put them within our reach without our crowding. It is doing more, it is compelling us to cease crowding if we would take full advantage of what it offers. Apparently its arrival will introduce a new era in community planning, or to speak more accurately since we have long *planned* spacious communities, a new era in community building.

A Contemporary View of the "World's Greatest Migration," 1928

Press notices in the early part of the last century directed attention to the increasing numbers of people who were leaving the rural districts in favor of the cities, and expressed the fear that, should the movement continue, the nation, which then consisted largely of the northeast quarter of our present area, would find itself in an agricultural crisis. These remarks resemble many that we still read; but the nation seems to survive. The migratory movement is not so much one which we need to fear, as one which we need to study.

In 1880 our rural population was 71.4 per cent of the total, while today it is only 48.6 per cent. The urban population, on the other hand, has increased from 28.6 per cent of the total to 51.4 per cent. While a part of this shift has been due to the growth of villages from less than 2,500 persons to 2,500 or more, thereby classifying them as urban, the change in percentages is on the whole representative of the trek from the farm to the city. However, this migration becomes insignificant when compared with what is happening today when millions of people are moving from the heart of our metropolitan areas to their outermost limits and beyond.

The rate of growth of the suburban area of Boston exceeded that of Boston itself by 7.4 per cent during the decade 1910–1920. New York's suburban area exceeded the rate of growth of that city itself by 9.3 percent, while Philadelphia, long known as the city of homes, has had to trail its suburbs, the latter increasing in population 34.3 per cent, while the urban district grew only 17.7 per cent. Among interior cities, Detroit has shown a growth of 113.3 per cent, while its suburbs have climbed to the dizzy height of 254.9 per cent. Cleveland increased 42.1 per cent, but its suburbs attained a growth of 108.2 per cent. Recent tendencies point not only to a continuation of the suburban increase, but a further acceleration.

The suburban migration has come about, first, because of the development of the automobile and consequent good roads, and, secondly, because of the combination of the "Own your home" and the "Garden" movements. Rapid transit has changed our conception of distance. We no longer describe a suburban location as eight to twelve miles from the city, but refer to it as twenty-five to forty minutes. This transformation in viewpoint has moved our residential areas from a limited radius of about eight miles from the heart of the city to a range of from twenty-five to fifty miles.

Following upon the adoption of the automobile as a distance-reducer, the city-man's appreciation of the desirability of the invigorating fresh country air took a decided up-turn. The realtor capitalized the situation, and our national magazines contributed their effective influences to the new enthusiasm for the soil, the flowers and all of the out-of-doors. The end is not yet; in fact, we are still moving farther and farther out, beyond the confines of the political limits of the trade center, where we can communicate with nature's best, and increase the joy of living and even the span of life.

We are often reminded that there are two sides to every situation and this migration of millions of people from the heart of our cities to their periphery is no exception. It carries with it a trade problem of serious import to many retailers. Along with the local drug store, grocery and meat market, have come the dry goods shop, the hardware store, the garage and repair shop, the men's outfitters, and the miniature department store. Most of the immediate needs of the suburbanites are now being provided for within a stone's throw of their homes, in many cases dispensed from highly attractive shops. While all these conveniences are being offered, the failure of our streets in the central business districts of the cities to accommodate the increasing numbers of automobiles, discourages buying downtown and encourages local buying. In consequence, the sub-retail centers are growing by leaps and bounds at the expense of the central districts. This new situation has forced the larger establishments to set up branch stores to save themselves, and this action, in turn, presents a new form of competition for the subretail store whose buying power is less than that of the branch-store organization.

The whole movement has recast the city structure so rapidly that it has come upon us before we have had an opportunity to completely adjust ourselves to it. The periphery of our cities is ever widening, and what its limits shall be we hardly dare forecast, for the airplane is now upon us, and distance, which we have come to think of in terms of minutes, we shall soon be measuring in seconds. Is it not likely that many of these sub-retail communities will tend to completely decentralize our major retail districts or at least greatly modify the present size of the major establishments?

As the sub-retail center grows, it brings a source of supply close to satellite centers (communities sufficiently close to a major trade center to enjoy many of its advantages, but politically independent), many of which have heretofore depended upon the major business centers. The increased conveniences encourage some of the population to migrate from the suburbs to satellite centers, and help to insure the permanence of abode of those already resident in the latter centers.

In all this movement, the chambers of commerce and other civic-commercial organizations are, or should be, vitally concerned. They seek new industries and additional population. We may fairly question whether they should seek to make their cities larger at the expense of the satellites, and we ask whether it would not be well for them to make a serious effort to harmonize their own center with their satellites so as to promote the growth of the entire metropolitan area in the interests of all the area.

The current migration from the heart of the city to the suburbs and from the suburbs to the satellites, combined with the resistance offered by some satellites against political union with major cities, may be construed as a healthy sign. According to a few European and American city planners, large size is not essential to comfort and happiness. When a community attains a size which affords its members the normal amenities of life, it has fulfilled its purpose and the addition of numbers beyond this point contributes nothing. Just what the population number should be depends upon the location, the environment and the times. . . .

A Kansas City Developer Touts the Community Features of Suburbs, 1924

Developing suburban subdivisions with community features is a subject of constantly increasing importance to the real estate profession. Community features may be largely instrumental in first attracting the attention of that buying public to a subdivision. They may be the factors that largely create sales in the beginning. Community features can be the means of giving character and distinction to suburban property; the things that create enthusiasm for the property by its residents; the things that cause the tenants and owners in the property to enjoy living there.

Recreation for the Community

An annual community field day—bringing together all the school children in the district—can be made inexpensive and very effective. For several years we have held such events in the Country Club District of Kansas City, largely underwriting the expenses of the meet. In May of this year we had approximately 3,000 school children on the campus of one of our private schools. . . . All the events were carefully worked out in advance—each school having its own individual feature event, and also entering representatives in the general events.

And then again we have our hikes into the country—perhaps a "wienie" roast for the boys of a certain school. . . .

Other recreational and cultural features include a supervised playground; a community hall, where neighborhood dancing lessons, lectures, and community events may be held; neighborhood flower shows; community Christmas trees, and the singing of Christmas carols as a community activity; the encouragement of horseback riding and of bicycle clubs; and an organization of boys to keep the snow swept from ponds or streams for skating in winter.

We have four golf clubs in the Country Club District. Three of them we have built as an adjunct to our real estate development, organizing financing and developing the club from the beginning. In two of these organizations it is stipulated that no one can become a member unless an owner of property in our subdivisions. We generally provide a site for the course without any charge, on our unsold acreage in the beginning. We start the dues at, say, $30 or $40 a year, with no initiation; provide no club house, simply a little room for golf headquarters; and start out with 9 holes, adding others as the club grows. . . . When it has grown to a strong membership, a club generally begins establishing a sinking fund for the purchasing of its own real estate for a permanent course and the erection of a complete club house. These organizations have been able to reimburse us for the amount of money we advanced during the early period, and their value to us has been well worth the giving of the ground without rent during the formative years.

Community Homes Association

In every subdivision we have developed for many years, we have stipulated that the owner of each lot be obligated to pay not to exceed a mill per square foot per annum towards the organization and maintenance of a community homes association. This tax rests upon all unsold as well as sold sites. It is a tax on land, and not on improvements. Only residents can serve as directors, and without salary. It is an honor to be elected. An annual meeting is held of all the owners and the policy is prescribed, which the directors carry out.

Snows are cheaply plowed from the streets and walks, at a cost of only a few cents to every 50-foot lot. Street trees are sprayed and trimmed at a far less cost than the individual could do it, even if he would. . . . Vacant property is kept cleaned and mowed as a community expense; shrubbery, flowers and ornaments in all public places are maintained; street trees are replaced when necessary; trash is hauled away at community expense once a month from each home. This waste-removal service alone would otherwise cost the individual owner more than his entire expense of the community homes company assessment.

The directors of this homes association are also charged with the responsibility of enforcing restrictions—and have the funds to go to court, if necessary. They take over the control of any playgrounds, fountains, picnic ovens, or other community features. They become a united, powerful organization to present any cause to municipal authorities, or to any public utility. They develop a strong community feeling, a neighborhood pride and betterment of the physical condition as well as the community spirit of the entire section.

Architectural Standards

Stores and shops in a real estate subdivision should be of good architecture, not offensive to the surrounding home owners. All loading and unloading of trucks should be confined to courts in the rear. No overhanging signs or big lettered posters should be permitted. No ugly or filthy rear ends should be tolerated. Filling stations can be made unobjectionable, if proper control of design, color and maintenance is retained.

The design and location of the fire and police station is important and should be made inoffensive. Of course the location of schools, with ample playgrounds, and the distribution of churches and structures needed to meet community needs are important factors in community development.

Another important factor is the giving of character and distinction to certain neighborhoods and certain streets by a particular type of development. This may be done by the grouping of buildings of harmonious architecture; by a pleasing blend of the colors of the roofs of near-by houses; by the careful graduating of grade and floor elevation of one house with another; by the avoiding of the over-shadowing of low houses by tall ones. . . .

The curving of the streets, the placing of the trees, the planting of the shrubs, the walk design, and the various street furnishings may all be so arranged as to give a variety of character to various parts of a subdivision. Frequent triangular parks at street intersections give a cosy, domestic character to a residential street. They relieve monotony, they break the sweep of winds, they relieve the hot glare of a straight stretch of paving, they give ever-changing color and create a street scene of value to the entire neighborhood. . . .

The Opportunity of the Realtor

In the development of community features there is a great opportunity for the realtor. He is the man who creates and fixes the appearance of the city. It would be foolish for idealism to carry beyond the things that would pay. But as the realtor develops his properties and as the public appreciation will justify it, better and better community features may be successfully added. The community spirit will reflect itself in the architectural design of every home, in the garden side as well as the street side of the lawn, in the interior arrangement; hangings, paintings, and furniture of the owners, and in the mental attitude and spiritual attitude of the residents themselves.

Children will become interested. They will develop an art appreciation in the broad sense. They will become observant of the beauty of this great world around us. They will see greater beauties in the sunset, in the distant haze-covered hills. They will get a greater joy in the budding of the forest trees in the spring. They will be more thrilled by the singing of the birds in the early morn in the trees around their homes. They will gain an understanding of the miracle of the opening flower in the joyous springtime. They will learn to abhor ugliness and prize beauty. They will learn the value of good design in every physical object that exists. They will appreciate color harmony in our schools and homes, the streets, and the public buildings. Their eyes will be lifted beyond the more sordid things in everyday existence, and they will begin to dream dreams for the future achievement and beauty of their city.

Lewis Mumford Argues for Small, Planned Cities, 1926

Manifestly, the suburb is a public acknowledgement of the fact that congestion and bad housing and blank vistas and lack of recreational opportunity and endless subway rides are not humanly endurable. . . . The suburb is an attempt to recapture the environment which the big city, in its blind and heedless growth, has wiped out within its own borders. With the aid of the suburb, business and living are divided into two compartments, intermittently connected by a strip of railroad. . . . The sort of life the suburb aims at is of course only partial: inevitably the suburbanite loses many of the cultural advantages and contacts of a complete city; but even its limited effort to obtain two essential things—a decent home for children and a comely setting for life—is thin and ephemeral in its results. The suburb is not a solution. It is merely a halting place. So long as the big city continues to grow, the suburb cannot remain suburban. . . . Sooner or later it will be swallowed up and lost in the maw of the great city. . . .

Our technicians usually accept the fact of unregulated and unbounded urban

From "The Intolerable City: Must It Keep Growing?" by Lewis Mumford, *Harper's Magazine* 152 (February 1926), excerpts from pp. 287–93. Copyright © 1926 by *Harper's Magazine*. All rights reserved. Reprinted from the February issue by special permission.

growth as "given." So instead of attempting to remove the causes that create our mangled urban environments, they attempt only to relieve a few of the intolerable effects. They exhaust the devices of mechanical engineering and finance to provide palliatives for expanding cities and expanding populations, and they flinch, most of them, from asking the one question which promises any permanent and effectual answer—how can we provide a stable environment for a stable population? . . . How are we to obtain the physical foundations of a good life in our cities?

The problem would be utterly discouraging were it not for two conditions. One is that the growth of modern invention has diminished the necessity for urban concentration. The other is . . . that the more intelligent and sensitive part of the population is becoming a little bored by "greatness," and they are beginning to feel towards their skyscrapers the way an Egyptian slave perhaps felt towards the Pyramids. . . . During the railroad era the favored urban spots were at the terminals of trunk lines. . . . The result was vast urban agglomerations . . . at points where the traffic ended, coalesced, or crossed. Modern motor transportation and modern airplane traffic do not abet this tendency: They favor a more even distribution of population . . . ; for the net of motor roads makes it possible to serve any point in a whole area by car or truck, instead of simply those points "on the line." Economically, this works towards regional rather than metropolitan development; towards industrial decentralization rather than toward further congestion. . . .

The alternative to super-congestion is not "back to the farm" or "let things go." The real alternative to unlimited metropolitan growth is limited growth, and, along with it, the deliberate planning and building up of new communities. . . . Any effective effort to provide good living conditions within our existing cities rests upon achieving a fairly stable population: this can be accomplished only by building up new communities in the hinterland, which will hold back the flood . . . but also drain off some of the surplus from existing centers. What we need is a policy of "community afforestation." . . . Our present small towns and villages are unable to retain their young people because so many of them are scrub communities. . . . If we are to prevent congestion, we must deliberately create communities which will be fully equipped for work, play, study, and "living" . . . ; in other words, they must be, in English usage, complete garden cities.

How would these new communities differ from existing cities? First, in placement; they would be established in relation to the best remaining water and power resources, and in country districts where land values were still low. They would be surrounded by a permanent belt of agricultural land, to provide a continuous local food supply of green vegetables, and to preserve open spaces, without taking them altogether out of productive use. Second, provisions for all the institutions necessary for a community of a given size, say ten thousand or fifty thousand, would be made from the beginning. That is, the land needed for schools, churches, libraries, theaters, hospitals, municipal buildings, associations, playgrounds, and parks would be calculated, platted, and reserved; at the same time, the land needed for shops, factories, and offices would be allocated, with due respect to convenient access, to amenity, and—in the factory district—to prevailing winds and outlooks. The residential parts of the city, instead of being intersected by innumerable streets, would be planned for quiet, safety, and beauty. . . . In general, no houses higher than three stories, and no office higher than five, would be permitted; but that would not prevent the erection of a single tall building, or a small group, as high as, say, ten stories if the height served some direct purpose, such as the grouping of municipal departments, or medical services. The high building would not, however, be permitted as a mere rent barracks. . . .

The provision of gardens and playgrounds would likewise be made on the initial plan; and since the population would be definitely limited, their adequacy would be permanently insured. The time now wasted in subway travel would, since the area of the city is limited, be available for sport, rest, education, or entertainment. Land values increase in the business district of such a city; but the increase is kept for communal purposes. . . . If some potent institution, like an expanding industry or a great center of learning, caused such a city to attract more people than originally provided for, the further extension of the city, once it had filled its sites, would be taken care of by founding another city, similarly restricted in area and population, similarly surrounded by a rural belt. . . .

Here then is the choice—between growth by the "mechanical extension" of existing urban areas, and growth by the foundation of new communities, fully equipped for working, learning, and living. In the growth by mechanical extension we move inertly towards the intolerable city. . . . With a tithe of the constructive power we now spend on palliatives, we might found a hundred fresh centers in which life would really be enjoyable, in which the full benefit of modern civilization and culture might be had.

❋ *E S S A Y S*

These two essays feature different ways of interpreting the automobile's effects on urban and suburban development. In the first article, historian Joseph Interrante identifies the link between the rise of the automobile and metropolitan growth in the 1920s and 1930s. Interrante's focus is on how each reinforced the other, an interaction that gave cars an important and necessary function in urban society. In the second essay, Mark S. Foster of the University of Colorado, Denver, analyzes the process of decentralization in Los Angeles, the country's premier western city, and shows how both the rise of the automobile and certain policy decisions determined the direction of suburban growth. Foster's essay offers a provocative elaboration of the ideas expressed in the Van Cleef document.

The Road to Autopia: The Automobile and the Spatial Transformation of American Culture

JOSEPH INTERRANTE

In the 1920s, Robert and Helen Lynd, in their classic study *Middletown,* found that the automobile had become "an accepted essential of normal living." It had become the primary focal point of urban family life and had made leisure activity

"The Road to Autopia: The Automobile and the Spatial Transformation of American Culture" by Joseph Interrante, *Michigan Quarterly Review* 19–20 (Fall–Winter, 1980–81), excerpts from pp. 502–17. Reprinted by permission of the author.

a customary aspect of everyday experience. Indeed, the car had become so important to Middletown residents that many families expressed a willingness to go
without food and shelter, to mortgage their homes and deplete their bank savings,
rather than lose their cars. "We'd rather do without clothes than give up the car,"
a working-class mother of nine told the Lynds. "I'll go without food before I'll
see us give up the car," another wife said emphatically. Other observers found
that rural families were similarly attached to their cars. When a farm woman was
asked by a U.S. Department of Agriculture inspector during the 1920s why her
family had purchased an automobile before equipping their house with indoor
plumbing, she replied, "Why, you can't go to town in a bathtub!" For these urban
and rural Americans alike, the car had become a basic social necessity. This essay
will examine the nature of that need in the context of changes in urban and rural
space during the first half of the twentieth century.

More generally, this essay offers an alternative perspective for understanding
the history of Americans' "love affair" with the car. Previous scholarship on the
automobile has examined our consumption (purchase and use) of cars in terms of
the car itself and the effects of its use. Authors may disagree over the relative
importance of air pollution and traffic congestion versus privacy, freedom of
movement and "democratic" access to consumer goods like the car, but all authors discuss the automobile strictly in those terms. This kind of cost-benefit analysis (which to a great extent ends up trying to compare apples and oranges)
avoids the basic question, why people use cars. In examining the social and historical basis for our use of automobiles, scholars generally choose one of two
explanations. Some writers talk about the "intrinsic appeal" of car use; its flexible
and individual form of movement, as if this appeal were something which could
exist outside of history. Such accounts focus on the car in isolation from a social
context. Other writers explain the origins of automobile consumption in terms of
corporate manipulation of consumer needs. At its most simplistic level, this argument [asserts] . . . that automotive companies have abused the public trust
through false advertising and government influence. More complicated versions
attribute the success of corporate manipulation to people's social isolation and
feelings of powerlessness. However, both versions assume that our need for cars
is a "false" need created through the manipulation of consumer desire.

In contrast to these interpretations, this essay begins with the premise that our
consumption of cars satisfies a real need for transportation—a need as basic as
food, clothing and shelter—but argues that this need has changed as the social
and spatial patterns of American culture have changed. In other words, it looks at
the automobile as an historically specific form of transportation, one appropriate
to a particular stage in capitalist development. It examines the automobile as simultaneously a cause and consequence of the rise of consumerism—that is, the
corporate development of new markets designed to provide new goods and services to an enlarged buying public. When the automobile first appeared as a
mass-produced commodity after Henry Ford's introduction of the Model T in
1908, people bought automobiles because they met old transportation needs better than existing alternatives and offered new possibilities for movement. But use
of the car also altered urban and rural life in important ways, some of which I
shall describe in the following pages. These changes were part of a general reor-

ganization of the physical and social urban and rural environments which changed people's needs for transportation. This reorganization had already acquired a distinctive geographic form by 1933, when the Hoover Commission on *Recent Social Trends* christened it "metropolitanism":

> By reducing the scale of local distance, the motor vehicle extended the horizon of the community and introduced a territorial division of labor among local institutions and neighboring cities which is unique in the history of settlement. The large [urban] center has been able to extend the radius of its influence. . . . Moreover, formerly independent towns and villages and also rural territory have become part of the enlarged city complex. This new type of supercommunity organized around a dominant focal point and comprising a multitude of differentiated centers of activity differs from the metropolitanism established by rail transportation in the complexity of its institutional division of labor and the mobility of its population. Its territorial scope is defined in terms of motor transportation and competition with other regions. Nor is this new type of metropolitan community confined to great cities. It has become the communal unit of local relations throughout the entire nation.

"Metropolitanism" became, in other words, the geographic configuration of a consumer society based upon car travel. Initially made possible by the automobility of the car, metropolitan consumerism in turn made the automobile a transportation necessity. This essay will explore the growth of metropolitanism in pre–World War II America. In the history of these developments can be found the origins of our dependence upon automobiles.

Between 1900 and 1940, changes in the structure of business enterprise and the strategy of industrial and market relations drastically transformed economic life in general and the urban economy in particular. Business firms extended their existing lines of goods to a greater number of customers at home, sought new markets and sources of materials overseas, and created new markets by developing new products for different kinds of customers. The expansion and diversification of markets occurred through the combination and consolidation of firms into single multidivisional corporations like E. I. DuPont, General Motors, and Sears, Roebuck and Company. These corporations were distinguished from older industrial firms by their integrated structures and coordinated functions. Decisions and information flowed through a hierarchy consisting of a general office, divisional offices, departmental headquarters, and field units. Changes in business structure, which were designed to plan effectively for long-term and short-term market exigencies and to insure an undisrupted flow of production for those markets, substantially altered, in turn, the quality of industrial work experience. A new class of professional managerial workers was distributed among the various strata of the corporation to transmit instructions and information and to supervise directly the work process. The work process itself was broken down into numerous separate tasks, and synchronized through technological innovations like the automated assembly line as well as through the "scientific management" of individual and group worker behavior. As the work process intensified, the length of the work day was shortened and wage rates increased. The reorganization of factory work served the double purpose of rationalizing and increasing production, and investing workers with the financial capacity and the opportunity to consume the goods which they produced. Together, these changes . . . radically altered life in cities, where most industry had been located at the turn of the century.

Paradoxically, as multidivisional corporations integrated industrial and business relations, the spatial organization of manufacturing became decentralized. Corporations began to establish factories outside major urban centers in "industrial satellite cities" like Gary, Hammond, and East Chicago outside Chicago; Lackawanna outside Buffalo; East St. Louis and Alton across the Mississippi River from St. Louis; and Chester and Norristown near Philadelphia. Industrial growth in these satellite cities occurred at a faster rate than central city manufacturing: between 1899 and 1909, employment in the outlying districts around cities grew by 97.7 percent, while central city employment increased only 40.8 percent. Thus, while urban industrial employment continued to increase in absolute terms, the *proportion* of factory employment located within these cities declined. Between 1920 and 1930, it fell from 46 to 35 percent in New York City, and from 65 to 54 percent in Detroit. Indeed, every city with a population of at least 100,000 experienced this proportional decline in industrial employment. The decline was part of the increasing diversification of business functions, a diversification which manifested itself in specialized use of urban space. For as manufacturing declined in central cities, the proportion of communications, finance, management, clerical and professional services located there increased. Reflecting this specialization, downtown office space in the ten largest cities increased by 3,000 percent between 1920 and 1930. Tall skyscrapers mushroomed over the urban landscape: by 1929, there were 295 buildings 21 stories or taller in the five largest cities alone. These skyscrapers housed the general and divisional offices of the new corporations, as well as the banks, law offices, and advertising agencies which served them. They replaced and displaced factories, small retail businesses, apartments, and tenements. Thus cities became financial and administrative centers at the same time that they lost their older manufacturing functions.

Many residents displaced by the reorganization of economic activity and urban real estate within the city moved to outlying districts. This "suburban" boom, which began after World War I, peaked during the 1920s, and slowed but did not disappear during the 1930s, was based upon car travel. It was not simply an accelerated version of late nineteenth- and early twentieth-century streetcar movement into the suburbs. Unrestricted by a need for access to mass transit facilities, real estate speculators located subdivisions everywhere around the central city. By 1922, 135,000 suburban homes in 60 cities were already wholly dependent upon cars for transportation. Most of these suburbanites were wealthy families, but during the 1920s and 1930s the movement out of the central city expanded to include the middle class (who located in exclusively residential suburbs) and the working class (who located closer to work in industrial suburbs). These outlying districts together grew during the 1920s at a rate twice as fast as the cities around which they were located. Even though the rate of increase slowed during the depression years, it remained impressive when contrasted with the absolute decline of population in central cities during the same period. By 1940, 13 million people lived in communities beyond the reach of public transportation.

Moreover, the socio-economic relationship between suburbs and the central city changed. As downtown shopping districts were transformed into central government and corporate headquarters, small retail services—which could not afford skyrocketing rents and were losing customers unwilling to face downtown traffic snarls—relocated in the suburbs near their customers. . . . Likewise, large department stores set up branch stores in these satellite communities. Mail-order firms like Sears, Roebuck and Montgomery Ward turned into suburban chains. Banks also established branches in suburbs. Dentists and doctors opened offices near their clients' (and their own) homes. In short, many formerly centralized institutions and services were relocated outside cities. These outlying districts became the retail business centers of urban space—especially in smaller cities which had never developed extensive trolley networks. Indeed, the Hoover Commission noted in 1933 that the old "star" pattern of nineteenth-century urban development (a star whose rays ran along streetcar tracks) had been transformed into a veritable "constellation" of interdependent centers within a single metropolitan region. . . .

The dispersion of manufacturing and residential settlement was based upon car travel. The importance of the automobile varied, it is true, with the size of the city and the availability of public transportation. But even in cities with elaborate mass transit systems, like Boston, Chicago, Philadelphia, and New York, observers in the 1920s and 1930s noted that car travel was necessary for much of the business and recreation which took place in and around them. Moreover, the car's importance increased as streetcar service declined through mismanagement, overextension of services, and competition from jitneys and buses. Indeed, planners in these cities were deliberately reshaping the central city landscape by the late 1920s and 1930s in order to facilitate communication by car. In these large cities, cars accounted for 20 to 32 percent of the daily traffic into the central business district (CBD) by 1930. Cars became more important earlier in smaller cities like Kansas City, Milwaukee, and Washington, D.C. There car travel during the 1920s accounted for 50 to 66 percent of the daily commutation into the CBD. By 1930, 222 cities with at least 10,000 residents were entirely dependent on motor transportation.

Urban space was enlarged through automobile use. The further one lived from the city, the more advantageous car travel became. A 1930 traffic control study of Kansas City illustrated the savings in time during the evening "rush hour:" In the downtown area, trolleys and cars moved bumper to bumper. But outside the CBD [center of the business district], the car rapidly moved ahead of streetcars. Two miles from the CBD it had gained a five-minute advantage; at 7½ miles, it had gained 15 minutes. Along secondary trolley lines, on which service was less frequent, cars traversed the 7½ miles with a 35 minute advantage over streetcars. The same advantages were documented in Detroit in 1930. In addition to this daily flow of traffic into the city, automobiles made possible crosscurrents of movement throughout the outlying district—something streetcars could not do. In Los Angeles, this movement superseded commutation into the downtown area. The number of people entering downtown Los Angeles between 1923 and 1931 declined by 24 percent despite a population boom in the metropolitan area. But the most important point was that the reorganization of urban space made these crosscurrents of movement not only more possible but more necessary as well. Goods which families had purchased in old downtown shopping districts now had to be purchased at stores scattered throughout the suburbs. Many employees had to drive to decentralized workplaces, or from decentralized residences to the CBD. If the automobile first appeared as a convenience which permitted more frequent, faster, and more flexible transportation movement, metropolitanism gradually made that movement an inescapable feature of urban living. . . .

The geographic reorganization of urban and rural areas drew these regions into closer and more interdependent relationship with each other. This relationship was most evident in the cities and towns which lay in the outlying districts around urban centers. These towns attracted people from both central cities and the surrounding countryside. For example, a 1931 survey of 4,000 families that moved to Evanston, Illinois, during the 1920s found that 47 percent came from Chicago, while 46 percent had moved to Evanston from rural areas outside the immediate metropolitan region. . . . In addition, farm families that converted to truck farming were tied more closely into the urban market and urban culture. Many families held onto their farms during the Depression by taking advantage of the work opportunities in cities and satellite towns. . . . All of these activities necessitated new patterns of commutation based upon use of a car.

This change in people's habits of movement was a change in daily routine. Many of the goods and services—food, clothing, education, health care, entertainment—which people bought in village centers or suburban retail centers had formerly been produced or performed by members of these families, especially by women. This shift from the direct production of goods to the purchase of them in metropolitan markets changed people's habits of consumption. These new habits were a central aspect of life in metropolitan America. For rural and urban Americans alike, changes in consumption represented the other side of the geographic reorganization of the metropolitan landscape.

In the 1920s, metropolitanism began to change household activity and consumption habits by drawing women out of the household and into the marketplace. . . . Families also spent more money and time on recreation outside the home. Both urban and rural families consumed these goods and services. A 1930 study of bread consumption, for example, found that most families everywhere had shifted to store-bought goods: 66 percent of farm households, 75 percent of village homes, and 90 percent of urban households. These figures meant that most housewives were now traveling by car to a local baker or A&P to buy what they used to make in their own homes. . . .

. . . [W]hy did women and their families accept these changes so readily? The automobile originally offered new possibilities for movement. It especially liberated women from the home. The automobile was a *private* vehicle, and that characteristic made it safer and more acceptable than public streetcars or trains. Even the most genteel women began traveling alone; some wealthier women took cross-country trips together unescorted by male relatives. This "freedom," as many women described the experience of driving, was the positive side to the transformation of women's lives. . . .

But as the metropolitan market expanded to include commodities formerly produced at home, the necessity for finding them in village and town centers increased. Thus use of the car did not lessen women's household work; rather it helped to change it into many consumer duties. When the farm woman told the USDA inspector that she couldn't go to town in a bathtub, she was describing the changes in her life which made shopping in town part of her work. And when Middletown women told the Lynds that they would sacrifice food and clothing before they gave up the family car, they knew that giving up the car meant sacrifices in family consumption.

What began as a vehicle to freedom soon became a necessity. Car movement became the basic form of travel in metropolitan consumer society. However, there was nothing inevitable about metropolitan spatial organization or people's uses of cars upon that landscape. The car could have remained a convenience used for recreation and cross-movement outside areas serviced by railroads and trolleys, while people continued to use mass transit for daily commutation. Car travel could have remained an option offering certain distinct advantages; instead it became a prerequisite to survival. Moreover, this dependence upon automobiles was not the outcome of a corporate manipulation of consumer needs. Rather, it resulted from the *reconstitution* of transportation needs within the spatial context of metropolitan society—a reorganization of the physical and social environment which the car facilitated but did not require. Within this spatial context, automobile movement became the basic form of travel.

The Depression did not loosen the relationship between Americans and their cars. "If the word 'auto' was writ large across Middletown's life in 1925," the Lynds wrote in *Middletown in Transition* (1937), "this was even more apparent in 1935, despite six years of Depression." People clung so tenaciously to their cars, the Lynds observed, because car transportation had become a "must" close in importance to food, clothing, and shelter. . . . Automotive statistics reflected this dependence on car travel. Although annual car sales declined 75 percent, from 4.5 million to 1. 1 million, between 1929 and 1932, car registrations decreased only 10 percent, from 23 to 20.7 million, during the same period. People stopped buying new cars, but they gave up car ownership entirely only under the gravest economic circumstances. Moreover, both sales and ownership began to rise sharply after 1933, while the country was still in the depths of the Depression. Annual automobile sales increased to 3.7 million by 1940, and car registration rose to a new high figure of 29.6 million in 1941. . . .

Yet if automobile ownership and use had become a basic need by the 1930s, the Lynds also found that people experienced that need and valued car ownership in very different ways. The working class saw the automobile as "their great symbol of advancement. . . . Car ownership stands to them for a large share of the 'American Dream'; they cling to it as they cling to self-respect." The business class, in contrast, viewed the car as a luxury item which "it is more appropriate for well-to-do people to have . . . than for poor people." . . . These different attitudes reflected a structural dynamic in modern capitalist society. For if the mass production of goods had *democratized* consumption by enlarging the potential market for goods like cars and making ownership contingent solely on the ability to pay, it did not *equalize* consumption. A range of social and economic considerations—for example, the proportion of family income which could be spent on a car—shaped people's identities as consumers and their uses of cars. In other words, inequality continued to affect the ability to consume even though the opportunity to consume became more widespread. . . .

. . . [T]hese variations in consumption were social rather than individual differences. Take, for example, the experience of suburban residence. Although movement to outlying districts involved both middle-class and working-class urban residents, as well as some rural inhabitants, suburbanization was a diffentiated movement. Working-class suburbs and rural villages remained centers of work as well as residence, while middle-class suburbs were strictly residential areas. Indeed, this difference was protected through the use of housing covenants and zoning restrictions on land use, as well as through less formal factors such as the need for workers to remain within commuting distance of their scattered workplaces. In concrete terms the difference was manifested in the kinds and quality of institutions located within the particular suburb: the presence or absence of noisy and sooty factories, the proportion of single- versus multi-family dwellings, the location of a highway next to or even through a working-class community, and even the kinds of schools available for children. These institutions shaped the experience of everyday life in suburbs: the relation between work and leisure, the character of domestic life and the kinds of household goods purchased by a family, the senses of privacy and autonomy one felt in one's life, and the opportunities for and definition of personal achievement. In short, the degree to which suburban and village residents were able to exert control over their social environments infused these residents' attitudes toward their cars. . . .

In both urban and rural areas, then, automobile use was shaped by social and economic considerations which lay behind class status: control over income level, workplace, location, work hours, job tenure, choice of residence, consumption of household goods, and participation in leisure activities. . . . These differences characterized people's different needs for transportation within metropolitan society. They remained in the forefront of automobile use because the automobile was a private vehicle which people fit into the fabric of their day to day lives. Thus, if the automobile promoted the reorganization of American space, it did not homogenize the experience of automobile ownership and use within that space.

The Automobile and the Suburbanization of Los Angeles in the 1920s

MARK S. FOSTER

Although the automobile introduced a high degree of flexibility to twentieth-century urban transportation, it proved to be a mixed blessing. By the time urban planners realized the full implications of the enthusiastic acceptance of the automobile by the public, the automobile had been encouraging [urban] decentralization for years. Haphazard-appearing patterns of suburban development drew the attention of many social critics. In Los Angeles, they perceived one of the worst examples of unchecked horizontal growth. Noting that city's "cancerous urban

From "The Model-T, The Hard Sell, and Los Angeles's Urban Growth: The Decentralization of Los Angeles during the 1920's" by Mark S. Foster, *Pacific Historical Review* 44, no. 4, (November 1975), excerpts from pp. 459–83. Reprinted by permission of author and publisher.

Whittier Boulevard in a Los Angeles Subdivision, c. 1924

During the 1920s, automobiles and electricity greatly altered city life. Automobiles spurred decentralization, enabling those urban dwellers who could afford it to move to new homes on the outskirts and to escape dependency on streetcar lines. Electricity not only powered factories and lighted homes but also made possible a cornucopia of consumer goods such as vacuum cleaners, washing machines, radios, and phonographs.

sprawl," critics viewed with foreboding the unpleasant prospect of a 200-mile long megalopolis stretching from Santa Barbara to San Diego, or even beyond. One prevalent view that soon became a cliché held that Los Angeles was not a city at all; it was many suburbs in search of a city.

Although the symptoms of Los Angeles's decentralization were evident to all by [the mid-twentieth century], the causes were not. They have sparked controversy among knowledgeable observers for years. Several scholars have suggested that the impetus for the region's horizontal growth developed prior to the 1920s. . . . Despite their valuable insights, earlier studies have placed insufficient emphasis upon three important facets of Los Angeles's decentralization. First, a single decade, the 1920s, was a more dynamic period of horizontal growth than heretofore believed. During the decade, widespread acceptance of the automobile over the trolley as a preferred mode of urban transportation emphatically confirmed a tendency toward decentralization which had been emerging for some time. Second, the real estate boom of the 1920s profoundly affected the overall pattern of regional growth. By that decade, developers were no longer confined to building residential subdivisions within walking distance of streetcar lines. They responded by promoting thousands of homesites located miles from the nearest railway facilities. Third, the 1920s was a period when city leaders consciously and confidently committed themselves to a decentralized pattern of development as a positive goal. . . . This essay will demonstrate that a combination of events marked the 1920s as a crucial decade in the emergence of Los Angeles as a decentralized metropolis.

Although Los Angeles was founded in 1781, it remained a small provincial town for over a century. By its centennial, the community boasted only 11,183 residents. Although the land boom of the 1880s brought many newcomers to the region, Los Angeles's population of 102,379 in 1900 hardly ranked it among the nation's major cities. Not until the 1920s did Los Angeles experience the growth which perhaps most profoundly influenced its present day appearance. During the decade its population more than doubled, jumping from 576,673 to 1,238,047.

The population boom of the 1920s coincided with the start of the decline of the electric railways and with the widespread adoption of the mass-produced, low-priced automobile as the primary mode of urban transportation. . . . Though Los Angeles County's population doubled between 1919 and 1929, the number of registered automobiles in the country multiplied five-and-a-half times, from 141,000 to 777,000.

The concomitant rise of the automobile and decline of the trolley in the United States generally and Los Angeles in particular have been traced to a multitude of factors. A general increase in trolley fares may have driven away some public transportation patrons. In addition, . . . [i]ncreasingly efficient means of production [of automobiles] brought lower prices; and the enormous expansion of installment credit during the 1920s encouraged many middle-class American families to view what still had been a luxury for the affluent in 1920 as an absolute necessity by 1930.

The rise of the automobile may well have fostered a feeling of apathy on the part of both the general public and elected officials about the future of the street railways. This certainty appeared true in Los Angeles by the 1920s; people simply took the trolley for granted. At the same time, overconfidence on the part of local street railway officials probably contributed to that casual attitude. . . . [In 1928], the editor of the *Pacific Electric Magazine,* perhaps succumbing to a spell of wishful thinking, assured readers that

> time can never come when the city dweller can always rely upon his own private vehicle to supply him with all the transportation he and his family and guests may need. . . . It is true, also, that the automobile industry appears to have reached the peak of its productivity. We are told that all but a small percentage of the sales made nowadays are replacement sales. . . .

In retrospect, it is surprising that Los Angeles's worsening traffic situation during the 1920s did not severely temper this optimism. One of the earliest and most noticeable effects of the conversion to the automobile was traffic chaos, particularly in the downtown area. Several factors contributed to the problem. Automobiles required far more street space to transport a given number of passengers than did trolleys. As more and more automobiles jammed downtown streets, all traffic, trolleys included, was inevitably slowed. Los Angeles's downtown traffic congestion was aggravated by the fact that more automobiles entered its central district each day than entered the central districts of other cities, and its streets were also among the narrowest of any city in the United States. . . .

Even as the 1920s opened, downtown traffic congestion had reached crisis proportions. Traffic snarls created by shoppers during the 1919 Christmas season inspired front-page newspaper coverage. Predictably, those merchants having a large economic stake in the preservation of the central area pressured public officials to find a solution to the problem. Traffic officials reasoned that since most downtown streets contained four lanes, elimination of on-street parking during business hours would effectively double the rate of traffic flow. In hasty response to rapidly mounting pressures, the city council on February 7, 1920, enacted the required ordinance; it went into effect on April 10.

The strict no-parking ordinance was a drastic, short-lived failure. Downtown merchants were flabbergasted at the negative impact of the ordinance upon their sales. Deprived of the convenience of parking at the doorstep of their favorite stores, large numbers of shoppers avoided excursions to the central district. . . . Bowing to overwhelming opposition to the no-parking ordinance, the city council drastically revised the statute on April 26; thereafter, the ordinance applied only during the evening rush-hours. The original no-parking ban had withstood the test of public opinion for only sixteen days.

This was but the first of numerous attempts during the 1920s to solve the growing problem of downtown traffic congestion. Public officials and concerned civic groups engaged in protracted deliberations over the feasibility of providing some sort of comprehensive rapid transit system. While these discussions were unquestionably well intended and in some ways productive, they delayed positive action to solve the problem. This delay abetted the triumph of the automobile. By 1923, increased competition from the automobile, combined with numerous complaints about slow service in the downtown area, induced officials of the Pacific Electric Company to draw up plans for construction of a subway terminal. . . . Late in 1923, a hastily assembled committee, which included representation from several interested business groups, failed to reach agreement over where the subway terminal should be located. The committee could only agree upon a recommendation of the city council that it hire outside technical consultants for a survey of the region's entire transportation needs. In May 1924, the city council hired the planning firm of Kelker, De Leuw and Company for that purpose. . . .

Early in 1925, Kelker, De Leuw and Company presented its comprehensive transit proposal. The firm recommended that the city spend over $133 million to build a system which would contain 26 miles of subway lines and 85 miles of elevated tracks. However, instead of receiving enthusiastic public support and resolving the rapid transit question, the plan sparked a rancorous debate that continued for the rest of the decade. The proposal drew strong criticism from several civic organizations. Following extensive study, six of seven members on a special committee of the City Club opposed the plan. They contended that huge public outlays for subways and elevateds in such older cities as New York, Philadelphia, and Boston had intensified downtown congestion. The majority report further noted that widespread use of the telephone and public acceptance of the automobile had emerged after rapid transit systems were constructed in some eastern cities. By permitting almost instantaneous interpersonal communication, the telephone largely eliminated the need for businesses to remain in close proximity to each other. The automobile served to facilitate movement among outlying districts not directly connected by public transportation. Thus, the majority report suggested that these advances in technology presented Los Angeles with a golden opportunity to develop in a wholly different pattern. The committee envisoned the emergence of a decentralized metropolis, suggesting that

> the great city of the future will be a harmoniously developed community of local centers and garden cities, a district in which need for transportation over long distances at a rapid rate will be reduced to a minimum.

The majority report emphatically rejected the notion that rapid transit should be used for promoting and perpetuating a centralized city with a large downtown area. . . .

Mounting criticism of the rapid transit concept did little to ease the apprehensions of those who wanted to preserve the central district. Downtown merchants had hoped that a modern rapid transit system would stimulate patronage of their stores. By the mid-1920s, some merchants believed that public policy was directed toward virtual abandonment of the downtown area. Even worse from their standpoint was the endorsement by public officials of a massive street and highway building program in the outlying areas. . . .

In the early 1920s, downtown merchants had proposed large-scale street widening as one of the more promising solutions to the problem of traffic congestion. . . . Local planners soon discovered, however, that widening existing streets in the downtown area would be prohibitively expensive; one estimate placed the cost at a million dollars per mile. Therefore, some traffic planners suggested that the city council would employ its limited street funds more wisely by providing adequate streets and highways in outlying areas. . . .

The city council, pressured on all sides by competing interest groups, turned to professional planners for help. . . . [T]he Major Traffic Street Plan . . . was presented in 1924; it offered little comfort to downtown business interests. The plan suggested large expenditures of funds for construction of highways in outlying areas. More important, the plan implicitly endorsed the concept of decentralization. It envisioned the downtown area's future role in limited terms: as a center for theaters, government offices, corporation headquarters, and some "specialty" stores. The bulk of retail trade would be transacted in local neighborhood centers located miles from the central district. . . . The president of the Los Angeles County Planning Commission explained why the plan emphasized highway development in the outlying areas:

> When we faced the matter of subdivision in the County of Los Angeles[,] . . . subdivisions which were coming like a sea wave rolling over us . . . [,] we reached the conclusion that it would be absolutely necessary to go out into the country and try to beat the subdivider to it by laying out adequate systems of major and secondary highways and boulevards.

Thus, from its inception the Major Traffic Street Plan emphasized highway development on the region's periphery. . . .

This clear pattern of new street and highway development, combined with the decline of the trolley and intolerable traffic congestion downtown, convinced many people that central Los Angeles's future prospects were dim. During the 1920s, the area lost much of its vitality as almost all new businesses and professional offices located outside of the central district . . . .

This clear trend toward decentralization also represented a reaction to new directions of population flow. Businesses and professional offices followed the people to suburban locations. The influx of thousands of newcomers into the Los Angeles basin during the 1920s created a heavy demand for residential property. . . . The 1920s witnessed an enormous increase in the number of subdivisions opened. In 1920, only 346 new subdivision maps were recorded; the number rose to 607 the following year. In 1922, the boom really developed momentum as 1,020 new tract maps were filed, and it reached its peak in 1923, when 1,434 plans were presented. . . . [B]etween 1917 and 1928, property values in outlying areas rose twice as fast as did property values in the central district. . . .

Where the subdivider went, so did the building contractors. Construction activity dramatically revealed the extent of Los Angeles's decentralization during the 1920s. In 1924, only 14.2 percent of the land in the Los Angeles area had been converted to urban use; a decade later the percentage had increased to 24.4. . . . In 1924, only 13.4 percent of the ring of land located between 8.6 and 10.3 miles from the downtown area was devoted to urban use; a decade later the percentage had more than doubled to 27.8 percent. The primary reason for the remarkable increase in urban land use in outlying areas was the construction boom in single-family homes. . . .

This evidence also suggests that although the interurban railway provided the initial impetus toward real estate development in outlying areas, the public preference for the automobile confirmed and intensified the direction of that growth. While the trolley promoters established a number of subdivisions miles from the downtown area, they had developed only a tiny fraction of the land in the Los Angeles area by 1920. Pre–World War I residents were so dependent upon the trolley for transportation that developers made few attempts to promote single-family homesites more than a half-mile from the lines . . . .

As southern California became increasingly dependent upon the automobile during the 1920s, developers promoted property more and more remote from streetcar lines. . . . The development of the San Fernando Valley during the 1920s was, perhaps, the most spectacular example. The real estate boom of the 1920s witnessed the promotion of thousands of lots, many located miles from the nearest trolley line. The Encino tract, opened in 1923, contained several hundred single-family homesites. The development was located on the southwest corner of Balboa and Ventura boulevards, two miles from the nearest red car stop. The Girard tract—which contained several thousand single-family homesites—was situated even farther from the trolley lines, the nearest line being almost three miles distant. . . . Advertisements insisted that proximity to commodious highways was far more important than accessibility to trolley lines. A 1923 advertisement for the Cahuenga Park subdivision advised prospects to "come out today and see those wonderful half-acres—on Vernon Boulevard—a one hundred foot wide paved highway—at the corner of Sherman Way—a thoroughfare. . . .

Despite the myriad factors influencing Los Angeles's decentralization, that pattern of growth might not have been so spectacular had it not been that so few challenged the viability of population dispersal during the 1920s. To be sure, local planning agencies were not sufficiently well established to exert a strong countervailing influence against decentralization. The city planning commission was not founded until 1920; organizational difficulties hampered its first few years of operation. Although Los Angeles County created the nation's first regional planning commission in 1923, not until the late 1920s did that organization and the city planning commission begin to work together effectively. Even then, both commissions operated with small professional staffs and limited budgets throughout the crucial period of the 1920s.

Despite such handicaps, local planners might have exerted more influence upon the pattern of Los Angeles's growth had they disapproved of the effects of horizontal development. Such was not the case. They favored decentralization at least in part because they had had the opportunity to study the massive problems created by a high degree of centralization in many older eastern cities. . . . Clearly local planners desired to exert some control over the direction of growth throughout the region. They realized that their limited funds and staffs would force them to marshall their efforts carefully. Although they did not consciously abandon the downtown area, they concluded that since the most dynamic changes during the 1920s were occurring in the outlying areas, those areas were where they should concentrate their efforts. . . .

In retrospect, two factors distinguished Los Angeles's decentralization from that in other cities during the 1920s. No other major city in the United States approached Los Angeles's growth rate between 1920 and 1930. During a decade when the automobile won widespread public acceptance, Los Angeles's population more than doubled. In contrast, such "established" older cities as New York, Cleveland, Boston, and Pittsburgh all experienced population increases of less than fifteen percent. Those cities in the United States which rivaled or exceeded Los Angeles in size by 1930 had been shaped largely by the limits of nineteenth-century technology and had generally experienced their most dynamic growth before the 1920s. Consequently, the impact of the automobile upon those cities was far less dramatic than its impact upon Los Angeles. In contrast, cities such as Atlanta and Kansas City, which expanded in a manner similar to Los Angeles, had growth rates during the 1920s and populations by 1930 which were a fraction of those in the latter city. Just as important, residents of Los Angeles purchased more automobiles per capita than did residents of any other city in the country. By the end of the 1920s there were two automobiles for every five residents in Los Angeles, compared to one for every four residents in Detroit, the next most "automobile oriented" American city. Thus, the impact of the automobile upon Los Angeles's urbanization process compared to that in other cities is distinguished chiefly by its magnitude. The size and timing of the region's population boom, and the suddenness with which local residents adapted themselves to the automobile were major factors shaping Los Angeles into its highly decentralized form. Both critics and defenders of Los Angeles's decentralization generally concede that by 1930 the city was in many respects the prototype of the mid-twentieth-century metropolis.

※ *FURTHER READING*

Paul Barrett, *The Automobile and Urban Transit: The Formation of Public Policy in Chicago, 1900–1930* (1983)

Scott L. Bottles, *Los Angeles and the Automobile: The Making of the Modern City* (1987)

M. Christine Boyer, *Dreaming the Rational City: The Myth of American City Planning* (1983)

Lizabeth Cohen, *Making a New Deal: Industrial Workers in Chicago, 1919–1939* (1991)

Richard O. Davies, *The Age of Asphalt: The Automobile, the Freeway, and the Condition of Metropolitan America* (1975)

Donald Finley Davis, *Conspicuous Production: Automobiles and Elites in Detroit, 1899–1933* (1980)

Robert Fogelson, *The Fragmented Metropolis: Los Angeles, 1850–1930* (1967)

Mark S. Foster, *From Streetcars to Superhighway: American City Planners and Urban Transportation, 1900–1940* (1979)

Kenneth T. Jackson, *The Crabgrass Frontier: The Suburbanization of the United States* (1985)

Roy Lubove, *Community Planning in the 1920s: The Contribution of the Regional Planning Association of America* (1963)

Howard L. Preston, *Automobile Age Atlanta: The Making of a Modern Metropolis* (1979)

John Rae, *The Road and the Car in American Life* (1965)

Daniel Schaeffer, *Garden Cities for America: The Radburn Experience* (1982)

Jon C. Teaford, *City and Suburb: The Political Fragmentation of Metropolitan America, 1850–1970* (1979)

CHAPTER
11

The Great Depression and
the Federal-City Partnership

✻

Although many cities, particularly older manufacturing cities in the Northeast, began to suffer economic strains in the mid-1920s, the nationwide Great Depression that struck in 1929 hit cities with special force. The national unemployment rate, only 3.2 percent before the Depression, soared to 15.9 percent in 1931 and peaked at 24.9 percent in 1933. In individual cities, however, the rates were frighteningly higher. In Butte, Montana, 75 percent of the families were on relief by the early 1930s; the steel mills of Gary, Indiana, laid off almost 90 percent of their employees. The auto industry nearly shut down, devastating not only Detroit but also places like Toledo and Akron, centers of industries related to automobile production. In Chicago nearly 700,000 people were jobless; in New York the number approached 1 million. Everywhere, people were unable to pay their mortgages, rents, taxes, and even their food bills. And everywhere, city governments struggled to meet basic needs and to relieve misery with drastically declining revenues.

How could these problems be overcome? Who would provide the ideas and resources to solve them? Some urban officials steadfastly insisted that their cities could handle the situation without outside help. Others believed that government should not intervene; rather, private effort, from businesses and charities, would pull their community out of crisis. Still others turned to the federal government as the only agency with resources to help in such a dire emergency. Even though President Franklin D. Roosevelt did not have any special sympathy for the troubles of the cities, his New Deal programs did show compassion for the individual problems of urban dwellers and distributed millions of federal dollars and jobs to alleviate their plight. As this final step—aid from the federal government—became increasingly prevalent, a new relationship between city halls and Washington, D.C., developed that extended far beyond the exigencies of the Depression years.

The reactions of urban officials to the Depression's particular effects on cities changed as the economic crisis worsened. The first document, an article written early in the Depression by Frederick L. Bird, the assistant director of an organization called the Municipal Administrations Service, reveals the recognition that the Depression did indeed have serious effects, but Bird also expresses some hope that the cities will recover. The second document, written in 1936 by Morton Wallerstein, the executive secretary of the League of Virginia Municipalities, illustrates how the urban situation had changed after several years of struggle. Wallerstein recognizes cities' growing dependence on assistance and policy direction from the federal government, a trend that was to extend for the next half-century. The third document features three letters written to Franklin and Eleanor Roosevelt by urban dwellers suffering hardship and desperation as they tried to maintain themselves and their families amid the depths of the Depression. The letters, from two white women and one black man, dramatize not only the lengths to which people went but also the threats to personal and family dignity that the Depression posed.

Frederick L. Bird Views American Cities and the Business Depression, 1931

How are American cities weathering the financial storm? To secure specific and up-to-date information on this vitally important question the Municipal Administration Service has addressed inquiries to municipal officials or bureaus of governmental research in the 326 cities of over 30,000 population in the United States and Canada. Replies received from 135 cities form the basis for a comprehensive report issued by the organization. While the reporting cities constitute a representative cross section of all population groups it is probable that the cities which failed to reply included an abnormally large proportion of those which are in serious financial difficulties. Thus, the actual picture of the entire situation may be slightly less favorable than that presented in the report.

The questions which the survey sought to answer are primarily:

1. What is the trend in the assessed valuation of property and of tax rates?
2. To what extent is the amount of tax delinquency increasing?
3. What is the trend in annual municipal revenues, expenditures, and budgets?
4. To what extent are cities showing deficits through inability to meet expenditures from current revenues?
5. To what extent is unemployment relief imposing an additional burden on city treasuries?
6. What actions are cities taking to curtail expenditures?
7. To what extent has this involved the reduction of salaries and wages of municipal officials and employees?

From "American Cities and the Business Depression" by Frederick L. Bird, *National Municipal Review* 20 (November 1931), pp. 630–34. Reprinted courtesy of National Civic League Press.

8. To what extent are cities approaching the limit of their long-term borrowing capacity?

As the report is almost entirely statistical in form, its factual value is somewhat lost in any attempted summary, but the general trends indicated form a significant commentary on the present financial status of American cities.

Trends of Assessed Valuations, Tax Rates and Delinquent Taxes

So long as the general property tax continues as the major source of municipal revenue, property owners will continue to bear a disproportionate share of the financial burden of city government. The decline in property values is tending to increase this load at the present time. . . .

A large majority of these cities are confronted with a serious problem in the increase of delinquent and unpaid taxes. In all but 21 of the 105 cities from which information has been received, the percentage of delinquent taxes shows an increase from 1929, in many cases to a very serious extent. The average percentage of tax delinquency in sixty-nine cities has increased from 7.22 in 1928 to 11.32 in 1930. This widening discrepancy between the amount of taxes levied and total annual collections is . . . reducing revenues below expectations and needs. . . .

Revenues, Expenditures and Budgets

Drastic reduction of expenditures of most American cities seems rather improbable unless the public comes to favor the abandonment or curtailment of many services which they now enjoy. It is much more reasonable to believe that after the current crisis is passed, city governments will continue the expansion of the scope of their activities.

The immediate problem is that of adjusting expenditures to declining revenues. The available data indicate that thus far the majority of cities are doing this with a fair degree of success. . . .

From the very nature of a city's services, which are of a continuing nature not greatly influenced by a recession in business, it is not to be expected that declining revenues would be reflected immediately in falling costs. This is well illustrated by the fact that in 1930 the expenditures of 70 of 103 cities increased over the previous year. In 1931, however, the city governments were beginning to get the situation in hand and 45 of 77 municipal budgets showed a definite decrease. The indications are that marked accomplishments toward curtailment will be reflected in the budgets of 1932.

Special Action to Curtail Expenditures

The present demand for retrenchment offers an unrivaled opportunity for the elimination of waste and inefficiency through more businesslike budgeting and purchasing methods, greater foresight in long-term financial planning, improvement of personnel management, better administrative organization, elimination of antiquated taxation procedures and the like. Economies effected along these basic lines will be of lasting value. Indiscriminate curtailment of essential services at the request of panic-stricken citizens, however, will work inestimable harm.

"What action is your city taking to curtail expenditures?" was the specific question asked on this subject. Officials in 11 of the 135 cities who responded to the general inquiry for information failed to mention this subject and 18 more said that nothing was being done as yet. The replies of at least 51, however, indicate that the most careful attention is being given to budget control, with budgets kept within estimated revenues, careful adherence to schedules and general curtailment of expenditures. In a few instances, at least, there is danger that the curtailment is so drastic as to be inconsistent with continued efficiency. . . .

Salary and Wage Reduction

American cities in general have not as yet resorted to salary and wage reductions as a means of reducing municipal expenditures. Whether recent wage cuts by large industrial concerns will influence a change in policy is not as yet apparent, but present salary schedules thus far have been left largely intact. . . .

Unemployment Relief

Direct expenditures by city governments for poor relief and unemployment have been responsible for increased budgets or for failure to reduce budgets in a considerable number of cities during 1930 and 1931. An outlay of over $18,000,000 for this purpose by Detroit is largely responsible for its present financial difficulties. In a number of the smaller cities particularly, the demands of the unemployment emergency have more often offset their efforts for retrenchment. In Woonsocket, Rhode Island, for example, the increase in the poor relief appropriations for 1931 over normal years considerably exceed the saving effected by drastic salary reductions.

In general, however, unemployment and poor relief have not placed an excessive financial burden on city treasuries. In a majority of cities, poor relief is an obligation of the county or the township, and the major portion of unemployment relief funds has been collected and disbursed by non-governmental agencies. Direct municipal expenditures for these purposes, nevertheless, have gone far in offsetting economies effected in other lines. The total amount expended by 100 cities, not including the three largest, rose from $18,900,000 in 1929 to $40,700,000 in 1930. It is impossible to give a comparable budget total for 1931 but cities reporting, with a few notable exceptions such as Detroit, which has cut its appropriation from $14,000,000 to $400,000, have increased appropriations, in many instances several times those for 1930. . . .

Unused Margin of Bonded Debt Capacity

At the same time that the rapidly mounting bonded indebtedness of city governments is being severely criticized, cities are being urged to increase and speed up their public improvement programs as a partial solution of the unemployment situation. Curtailment of borrowing, decrease in current budgets and expansion of

public improvements are hardly compatible. Sound as a policy of increased public improvements in a period of depression may be, its adoption is impossible
without the further issuance of bonds on a large scale. If, as is widely claimed,
cities are approaching the limits of their bonding capacity as established by law
in most states, a large increase of bonded indebtedness for this or any other purpose is legally debarred. . . .

Summary

Viewing the situation in its general aspects, it is fair to say that the majority of
American cities are not thus far meeting the emergency in their financial affairs
with a sufficient degree of foresight and good management. While the predicament of Chicago is far from being characteristic of any but a comparatively small
number of city governments, serious difficulties are still in store for a number of
cities which have been lax in their financial management in the past and slow to
arouse themselves to the demands of the present crisis, and most city governments are confronted with the need for more economical and efficient management of their affairs than they have heretofore exercised if they wish to remain
solvent, continue to improve the quality of their services, and at the same time
lighten the burden of taxpayers. If, instead of indiscriminate cutting of salaries
and ruthless slashing of department appropriations, city authorities will look beneath the surface to the need for fundamental reorganization of administration,
elimination of wastes and the introduction of well-known, but too inadequately
tried, efficient methods of carrying on public business, the current depression
may prove in the long run to be a real boon to municipal government.

Morton L. Wallerstein Considers Early Federal-City Relations, 1936

Prior to the year 1932 with one possible exception no mention of city, for which
purpose we will include any incorporated community, appeared in the statutes of
the United States, it is believed, although hundreds of federal services were being
rendered to city governments. Up to that time local relationships with the federal
government were either with the state or with the federal divisions in those states
which the federal government itself had set up. Such a thing as the federal government dealing directly with the cities was absolutely unknown.

. . . During [1932] a desperate fight was made by the cities and towns of the
country, acting through the American Municipal Association, to secure in Congress an amendment to the federal highway act to require that at least 25 per cent
of the federal road funds be used for streets within the cities. An understanding
was reached with the congressional leaders whereby the department under whose
jurisdiction these matters were, would write that provision in its regulations. It
has been there ever since. This marked the definite beginning of federal-city relations, which although indirect showed the cities for the first time their real federal
political power.

From "Federal-City Relations—Whither Bound" by Morton L. Wallerstein, *National Municipal Review* 25 (August 1936), excerpted from pp. 453–57. Reprinted courtesy of National Civic League Press.

The Relief Problem

During the early summer of 1932, the cities of the nation suddenly realized that the relief burden, which they for several years had been handling without any assistance, had reached a point where they could no longer successfully carry it, due not only to the tremendous problem of unprecedented unemployment, but to the serious, financially-embarrassed condition of municipalities in many states and the breakdown of the market for municipal securities.

In this situation, a national emergency, it was to be expected that the cities and the states would look to the federal government for assistance. There were certain elements concerning the federal government's ability to cope with this problem which neither the states nor the cities had. One was that the federal government had at least some control over the banks and might be able to resuscitate an otherwise dead public bond market. Then, too, the credit of the federal government far exceeded that of the states and cities. Beyond all this, however, was the feeling that, because some of the states were unable to bear any of the burden, the fairest thing to do was for the federal government to step in and aid all states at least to some extent. In other words, we had developed the doctrine that Michigan's inability to handle its unemployment problem was not merely the problem of Michigan, but the problem of Virginia, in fact, it was a national problem.

The emergency program of 1933, as well as of 1935, concerned the municipalities in many phases in addition to the highway matter already discussed. The cities found themselves dealing with such federal organizations as the Federal Housing Administration, the Home Owners' Loan Corporation, and other new agencies of the government.

However, this paper will discuss the relationship between the federal government and the municipalities in connection with the activities of only several of the most important agencies, such as the Bureau of Public Roads, and Federal Emergency Relief Administration, Civil Works Administration, Public Works Administration, and the Works Progress Administration. . . .

In only one case out of the five different types of federal-municipal relationships were necessary, but it cannot be successfully claimed that any of them have been entirely satisfactory. Each relationship has had its weakness as well as its strength. The Civil Works Administration, one of the most urgent of the emergency programs, coming at a most acute time in our history, was set up in great haste, administered largely by inexperienced personnel, and, except in rare instances, wholly unplanned as to type and extent of projects. As a relief measure it put men to work quickly and thus saved the day, but it was very wasteful.

The Federal Emergency Relief Administration, first as a direct relief program and next as a limited work-relief program, and its successor, the Works Progress Administration, suffered from rapidly changing administrative rules, lack of planning, and lack of continuity of operation. Failure to assure completion of municipal projects once started has been and will probably continue to be the cause of much dissatisfaction.

From the viewpoint of the municipal official the Public Works Administration generally proved the most satisfactory federal agency because it was not wasteful, the projects it approved were useful, and completion and ultimate cost were assured from the beginning. Yet the strength of this program was its weakness, since in setting a new standard for public expenditures on a non-pork-barrel basis, it unfortunately surrounded its program with a centralization of administration in Washington, excessive red tape, and failure to admit that local administrations might be trusted. These, then, are examples of the way in which this new animal in the menagerie—the federal-city relations—has been built up.

Thus far most of us have attempted to develop our own abstract philosophy of federal-city relationships. Little if any effort has been made to study agencies of the type just noted in the light of three years of experience, and from their successes and failures to chart our future course. Yet it would seem that we can draw certain conclusions: (1) The relationship must be as direct as possible; (2) the program should involve a federal grant-in-aid, with a supplement of local funds; (3) the red tape must be eliminated; (4) there must be a sound local administrative setup; (5) the federal government must realize that municipal administration is just about as honest and efficient as federal administration; (6) assurance must be given that a program, once started, will not be left uncompleted by lack of funds; (7) a long-range plan backed by an enlightened local public sentiment should be adopted; (8) the United States should localize the administration of the program, placing federal responsibility for its execution on the municipal level; (9) recognition by the federal government that criticism made by local officials are usually intended as helpful and constructive; (10) we must stop picturing as an emergency what is a probable permanent condition. If it be a permanent condition, then it requires long-range planning in which the municipalities must assume their burden through skilled and adequately financed city planning boards. . . .

From the past experiences with federal-city relationship have come new theories of government. It is not easy to prophesy what the future may have in store.

In 1930 Dr. Charles E. Merriam, professor of political science at the University of Chicago, now also a member of the National Resources Committee, said: "I do not know what is going to happen to municipal government in the United States. I think increasingly you are going to see in this country an emphasis on the urban point of view. Through what instrumentality or agency that is going to be expressed, I do not know, but one of the normal channels for expressing the position of the cities of the United States is the life of these leagues of cities in the various states, and if they choose to exert their strength, they will be in a very powerful position." . . .

In any consideration of this problem of the further development of the dual relationship, we must realize that 56 per cent of the population of this nation in 1930 was urban, although only twenty-one states were predominantly urban. Yet the municipalities of the country have just found out in the last three years that they have the power to present and have the Congress and federal agencies understand their problems. Contrast this with the inability, even in the predominantly urban states, of the municipalities securing any semblance of justice from state legislatures and the handwriting on the wall can be seen. The states must, and this does not mean a decade from now, but now, begin to realize that cities are local government units entitled to fair treatment; otherwise, I believe that we will find the cities ignoring mother and looking to adopted grandmother for aid. Those who believe in more local handling of local problems, in home rule for cities, in a sympathetic relationship between the city and its mother, the state, can hardly help but deprecate these developments now taking place along national lines and realize the danger that the cities will turn more and more to the federal government if the states continue to be so slow in recognizing the seriousness of the problem.

Letters from People in Need to Franklin and Eleanor Roosevelt, 1935

Troy, N.Y.
Jan. 2, 1935

Dear Mrs. Roosevelt,

About a month ago I wrote you asking if you would buy some baby clothes for me with the understanding that I was to repay you as soon as my husband got enough work. Several weeks later I received a reply to apply to a Welfare Association so I might receive the aid I needed. Do you remember?

Please Mrs. Roosevelt, I do not want charity, only a chance from someone who will trust me until we can get enough money to repay the amount spent for the things I need. As a proof that I really am sincere, I am sending you two of my dearest possessions to keep as security, a ring my husband gave me before we were married, and a ring my mother used to wear. Perhaps the actual value of them is not high, but they are worth a lot to me. If you will consider buying the baby clothes, please keep them [rings] until I send you the money you spent. It is very hard to face bearing a baby we cannot afford to have, and the fact that it is due to arrive soon, and still there is no money for the hospital or clothing, does not make it any easier. I have decided to stay home, keeping my 7 year old daughter from school to help with the smaller children when my husband has work. The oldest little girl is sick now, and has never been strong, so I would not depend on her. The 7 year old one is a good willing little worker and somehow we must manage—but without charity.

If you still feel you cannot trust me, it is alright and I can only say I donot [*sic*] blame you, but if you decide my word is worth anything with so small a security, here is a list of what I will need—but I will need it very soon.

2 shirts, silk and wool, size 2
3 pr. stockings, silk and wool, 4 1/2 or 4
3 straight flannel bands
2 slips—outing flannel
2 muslin dresses
1 sweater
1 wool bonnet
2 pr. wool booties
2 doz. diapers 30 × 30—or 27 × 27
1 large blanket (baby) about 45" or 50"
3 outing flannel nightgowns

If you will get these for me I would rather no one knew about it. I promise to repay the cost of the layette as soon as possible. We will all be very grateful to you, and I will be more than happy.

Sincerely yours,
Mrs. H. E. C.

New Orleans, La.
City
Sunday October 27th 1935

Dear President Roosevelt i take the Pleasure of writing to you these few lines asking you could you help me Please i have 10 Children and i have 4 has to go to School and i cant get them No Clothe my husband is working for the City But he dont work every Day Some Days he makes 3 Days and Some Days he makes 4 Days and how could i Pay Rent and Buy Clothes for my Children other People get more than i do i use to get 5 Dollars a week from the fera and they cut me down to $405¢ and they are People Dont Need it and they get every thing i even told them i Need 3 quilts and they only gave me anorder to get only one theres a Woman only got 5 in her famliey and i got 12 in my famliey answer my Letter Soon as you can and She has her husband working and She get 2500 dollars every Month and i dont get that much Please answer my letter Soon i wouldn't mind if they Would give my Big Boy a job But they wont do it. if my Boy was working that would help a hole lot Please Do Something for me and my 10 Children half the time my Children has Nothing to eat at home. Please write to me Soon here is My address

[Anonymous]
New Orleans, La.
City
Please write to me Soon.

October 27, 1935
Marietta, Ga.

To President Roosevelt:—
    You honor sir and your royalty. Majesty. This is the one of the most honable Colored workers of America who has been faithful and true law abiding Citizens of this Cob County & the City of Marietta, Ga. Your honor sir I am down now is very feeble and isnt able to work for my living. Ive been keep up by the relief but now have fail They haven't help me any in a month I am very poor and needing Condition I am not able to support my self so dear sir you honor I begging you please sir for food and ramont dear sir. I am very much in need now. They are helping white but are not me poor Colored man my whife has been going there times after times but refused give her anything to eat. So I am hoping through your highness and good natural and kindness that I succeed. So dear sir I am thanking you in Advance and your benevolence will never be for gotten here after. For I know have the power to Correct such matters if you will.

Depression-Era Housing in an African-American Neighborhood, Atlanta, Georgia, 1936

Familiar with poverty long before the Depression, many black Americans in southern cities lived in shanties such as the one pictured here. Relief workers and housing reformers tried to develop local and federal programs to replace run-down housing, but the effort proved only marginally successful.

Those of the Community Chest and the state of Releif and the food Administration and distributors.

Your honorable
President Roosevelt
Colored
Cob Co. Marietta, Ga.

ESSAYS

The two essays below relate to the documents by showing how the Depression affected various urban groups and how different cities adjusted to the problems caused and exacerbated by the Depression. In the first essay, Julia Kirk Blackwelder of the University of North Carolina, Charlotte, presents two somewhat unusual foci in analyzing the Depression's toll at the local level: first, it shifts emphasis from the commonly studied Northeast to a southwestern city; second, it examines the particular circumstances of women, a group overlooked in most historical analyses. The second essay, by historian Douglas L. Smith, explores the conditions of southern cities and reveals that they, like their northern counterparts, attempted to adjust to the economic and social crises of the Depression by trying new policy tactics.

The Depression's Effects on Anglo and Minority Women in San Antonio

JULIA KIRK BLACKWELDER

This work recounts the experiences and describes the behavior of women who lived through the Depression in San Antonio, one of America's poorest cities. The Depression exacerbated problems of low wages, substandard housing, and poor health conditions that afflicted San Antonio before the crash. Separately and together San Antonio women experienced economic disasters and dislocations that were worse than those of most other American communities. Not all groups bore San Antonio's distress equally.

In a geographic sense the women of San Antonio's racial and ethnic groups frequently were separated from each other, residing in distinct enclaves. Anglos dominated the North Side, blacks clustered on the East Side, and Mexican Americans concentrated in West Side slums. Differences in wealth and surroundings reinforced the geographic separation. . . .

The economic and social life of San Antonio inevitably brought Anglo, black, and Mexican-American women in contact with one another, though they resided in separate neighborhoods. During the Depression such interaction often revealed the distances that separated life-styles, for San Antonio's ethnic and cultural complexity and the unequal distribution of wealth in the city made it a place of remarkable and frequently painful contrasts. . . .

Twin themes run through the stories of women in Depression San Antonio, ethnicity and family. Ethnic prejudices divided women into what were virtually three separate worlds. Women understood the Depression largely in the context of the collective experiences of Anglos, blacks, and Mexican Americans. Ethnicity was the most important single indicator of socioeconomic status in San Antonio, and the Depression reinforced the pattern of segregation. Anglos, who were predominantly middle class, saw the Depression as a difficult time, but as a group they were callous to the city's high death rate from disease and malnutrition that almost never touched them personally. Black San Antonians comprised a small, overwhelmingly working-class community who experienced high unemployment. The black community knew hunger but rarely starvation. A cooperative spirit helped many black families through the most difficult periods. In contrast, Mexican Americans lived daily with the specter of disease and death. It was an unusual Hispanic family that was not touched by the death of a child or young adult. Unlike middle-class Anglos, middle-class Mexican Americans could not

From *Women of the Depression: Caste and Culture in San Antonio, 1929–1939* by Julia Kirk Blackwelder, 1984, excerpts from pp. 3, 4, 7–8, 111–29. Reprinted by permission of Texas A & M University Press.

turn their backs on the misery in their midst. Unlike blacks, Hispanics found that community resources were too few for cooperation to provide substantial relief for their numbers. . . .

Among all ethnic groups family was the emotional anchor of female identity and the focus of female concern during the Depression. The attention to family and the interdependence of its members across generations gave most women emotional ballast and financial assistance. Some women, however, found themselves totally alone or alone with dependents. When unemployment struck and persisted, the latter group suffered intense feelings of isolation and helplessness. In a city with few social services, the Depression was a particularly terrifying experience for women alone and those with children to support. . . .

In a city like San Antonio, where the Depression reached so broadly and deeply, the FERA [Federal Emergency Relief Administration] and the WPA [Works Projects Administration] provided the margin of survival for many women and their families, though there was always more demand for work than either agency could begin to meet. Public works projects were late in coming to San Antonio, and women had an especially long wait for their meager share of emergency employment. Before the arrival of federal public assistance the legions of hungry and unemployed residents had few places to turn for help. Since neither San Antonio nor Bexar County dispensed local public relief funds, the unemployed could turn only to private charities during the early years of the Depression. The Salvation Army, the Junior League, the International Institute, Catholic and Protestant churches and convents, settlement houses, and other organizations helped feed and clothe destitute local residents and transients. The Bexar County Red Cross provided food, clothing, and shelter, and their relief expenditures increased 300 percent from 1928 through 1931. As San Antonian Veda Butler recalled, the relief commodities dispensed by the Salvation Army to the East Side black community were insufficient and barely edible, but many people waited in line for hours for these handouts because of their desperate need.

There were virtually no Anglo-financed private and social services other than the Salvation Army to which blacks could turn in times of need. However, a history of steady employment and the strong economic base of black churches provided the black community with some weapons to fight the ravages of the Depression. The Mexican-American community lacked the overall economic strength to see its members through hard times. A few private charities dispensed food and clothing on the West Side, but they could do little to mitigate the widespread starvation and disease. The concentration of poverty in San Antonio and its consequences are revealed in health statistics of the Depression years. In 1937, after public relief had alleviated some of the city's health problems, Mexican Americans suffered a death rate from tuberculosis of 310 per 100,000, blacks 138 per 100,000, and Anglos 56 per 100,000, giving San Antonio the worst record of any major American city. The infant death rate was 144 per 1,000 live births among Hispanics, 105 among blacks, and 51 among Anglos. For Mexican Americans housing conditions were as severe a threat as starvation. The high incidence of infant diarrhea and enteritis among Hispanic children testified to environmental dangers. Hundreds of mothers watched helplessly each year as their young children sickened and died.

Throughout the Depression local politicians and relief administrators discriminated against blacks and Hispanics. Racism was at the heart of the resistance to locally funded public relief, but early in the Depression, San Antonio leaders moved to improve the dispersal of private relief assistance. At the end of 1931, Mayor C. M. Chambers announced the formation of the Central Unemployment Relief Committee (CURC), which was authorized to collect private funds for relief efforts and to certify workers for the few public jobs funded by a recent bond issue. Encouraging charity was as far as either the city or the county would go in ameliorating local problems. The CURC exemplified Anglo antagonism to Hispanics in announcing that no aliens would be hired for jobs funded through contributions to the committee. The committee began providing make-work the following January, but the funds and foodstuffs the CURC could distribute made little impact, and by March the funds had been exhausted. . . .

Despite the obvious inadequacy of private funds to meet the local emergency, some civic leaders continued to oppose public relief. Commenting on President Hoover's plea in 1932 that relief administrators "make sure that no American this winter will go hungry or cold," the *San Antonio Express* argued that "Responsibility for that achievement rests, first of all, upon the individual citizen, who cannot evade his 'God-imposed obligation to look after his neighbor.' When that debt shall have been discharged, it will be time to appeal for government assistance, through the Reconstruction Finance Corporation." In fact, some RFC funds had already flowed into Bexar County, and in the fall of 1932 the city sought a $300,000 loan from the new corporation. The chamber of commerce estimated that twice that amount would be needed to sustain the unemployed through the winter. . . .

Both the city and the county benefited from expenditures of the NRA [National Recovery Administration], the CWA [Civil Works Administration], and the WPA. Local government first became directly involved in relief in June, 1933, when Harry Hopkins, director of the Federal Emergency Relief Administration, ordered that all relief funds must be administered by public agencies. The CURC had to be reorganized as a public board, and in the process it became a countywide committee under the guidance of the Texas State Relief Commission. In early August the committee, now federally funded, began making cash disbursements to relief clients. On August 5 more than one thousand persons lined up outside the Bexar County Courthouse to receive their payments of $4.50 per household head in exchange for two days' labor on relief projects. . . .

The WPA and NYA [National Youth Administration] provided the major sources of help for the unemployed from 1935 through 1939. With the beginning of the WPA in 1935, the relief board was again reorganized, with responsibilities only for relief of unemployables. By the end of 1936 federal funds for the relief of unemployables had come to an end, and direct relief again became the burden of private agencies. The city finally agreed to provide administrative assistance for the distribution of the available relief commodities, but neither the city nor the county would assume direct responsibility for relief in the final years of the Depression. City and county officials had maintained that code and charter provisions forbade the expenditure of local public funds for relief efforts, but other Texas communities had successfully circumvented similar charter complications.

Not until 1940, when the Depression was lifting, did San Antonio move to amend the city charter to provide for public welfare expenditures.

Federally funded relief provided the margin of survival for thousands of San Antonians, but there were never sufficient resources to meet the needs of all who qualified for assistance, and per capita relief expenditures in the city were low. In New Orleans, a city also hard-hit, monthly emergency relief expenditures under the FERA averaged $29.68 for a family of four, while in San Antonio the average was $15.74. Women workers in San Antonio, whether family heads or supplementary workers, faced special obstacles in obtaining emergency jobs.

Despite the establishment of women's divisions and the prominence of women in some New Deal agencies, women were second-class citizens under most work and relief programs. Under the operating procedures of the WPA and other agencies, job preference was given to male family heads. Separated or widowed female family heads received first-priority ratings only if there were no adult male children in the household. A married woman whose husband was present in the home achieved first-priority certification only if her husband was disabled. An applicant of second-priority status stood no reasonable chance of employment in public works. Although the NYA created jobs for youthful female workers who had been denied employment in the CCC [Civilian Conservation Corps], boys received preference over girls in NYA placement.

Overall, men dominated the better-paying emergency jobs. Among women the superior status of Anglos is revealed in statistics showing that a disproportionate number of women's jobs went to whites rather than blacks and no black or Hispanic women were prominent in the administration of federal programs for women in San Antonio. The general pattern of discrimination against women in the allocation of public or private relief jobs throughout the Depression also emerges in direct relief statistics. While needy men were given jobs, needy women were frequently extended only commodities. While men received most of the relief jobs in San Antonio, women comprised most of the direct relief clients. . . .

. . . In San Antonio separate relief projects were maintained for blacks and whites. Mexican Americans and Anglos were not administratively segregated from each other in the work programs of the FERA or the WPA, but Anglo and Mexican-American clients rarely crossed paths in applying for relief commodities or emergency jobs. A relief office on the West Side served most of the Mexican-American clients, channeling Mexican-American men and women into unskilled work and reserving the few white-collar positions for Anglos. Similarly, federal and local relief agencies respected the tradition of occupational segregation by gender. The establishment of the women's division under both the FERA and the WPA generated segregation by sex in federal emergency job programs throughout the nation.

Particularly in San Antonio relief administrators regarded women as temporary workers whose primary role was in the home. Relief programs were structured to equip female clients with domestic skills that they could utilize after the Depression had passed. Relief programs developed around the assumption that additional women had been propelled into the labor market by declining male employment and that these women would retire to the home when the work of fathers and husbands returned to normal. Administrators recognized that some women would always be in the work force, and these workers were rigorously segregated into "appropriate" occupations. . . .

Texas officials frowned on any works project that employed women at tasks that they perceived as nontraditional. Although Texas women had worked as migrant agricultural laborers for generations, the state WPA head vetoed projects that required heavy outdoor labor. The WPA employed women on grounds improvements in several southern cities, but the Texas office refused to approve a similar project in the state, and the WPA in Texas also objected to federal funding of laundry work for women, though women were already extensively employed in commercial laundries throughout the state. Women's projects of the CWA, the FERA, and the WPA in Texas were largely confined to sewing, food processing, and domestic service or health care.

Programs for black women functioned on the assumption that the destiny of the black woman was domestic work. In an economic environment in which opportunities for the employment of domestic workers in homes were declining, the FERA and the WPA reinforced occupational segregation and participated in a discriminatory educational system that denied black women the skills to compete for the few areas of female employment that expanded during the Depression. . . .

In seeking federal approval and funding of women's work projects, local administrators frequently revealed their racial, ethnic, or sex-role biases. In 1936 the San Antonio office successfully proposed the creation of a program to train black domestic workers, stating that "the Object of this Vocational Training School is to teach fundamental principles of service, courtesy, honesty, cleanliness, and efficiency as applied in the general household activities; and to fit them for duties which are in keeping with their mentality." . . .

The WPA office in San Antonio sought to assist nonworking as well as working women. The WPA attempted to help the housewife cope with a tightened budget by improving her home-management skills. A program to train housekeeping demonstrators and a center for homemaking involved Anglo, black, and Mexican-American women. . . . The WPA also conducted the housekeeping-aides program, in which women were trained to be visiting housekeepers in homes where mothers were ill or confined after childbirth. The aide project, which put Anglo women to work in private homes, drew considerable criticism. The aides complained that the work was dirty and exhausting. Their situation was taken up by the Texas Protective League, which complained to Washington that the aides were no more than slaves sent to work in the homes of the affluent. The league protested that the women, who were paid six dollars a week by the WPA, were considered servants by the women they assisted and that the WPA officials threatened to fire them if they criticized working conditions.

WPA officials took a broader view of the occupational possibilities of Mexican-American women than black women. The adult-education program of Sidney Lanier School, which enrolled more than three hundred Hispanic men and women, had Americanization as a unifying goal but presented various training and educational programs. Women were offered training in nutrition and home and child care. Clerical skills were another area of study, and some graduates of the school obtained employment as stenographers and bookkeepers. However, the majority of Hispanic WPA clients found jobs in sewing rooms and did not enter WPA classes.

Discrimination on the basis of marital status added to the liabilities of gender and ethnic origin that many women bore as they sought employment in Depression San Antonio. As Lois Scharf has documented with regard to the nation as a whole, the work rate among married women increased dramatically, but the increase occurred despite the disapproval of husbands, societal pressure, and some legal measures taken to deprive wives of employment. The Depression elicited unprecedented public pressure to drive women, particularly married women, from the work force. It did not matter that men were unlikely to prepare for or accept jobs as teachers, nurses, or secretaries; society demanded that married females withdraw from the work force. In 1931 the American Federation of Labor adopted a position endorsing discrimination in hiring against women whose husbands earned a decent wage. Depression divorce, the agreement of marital partners to terminate their marriage so that each could remain employed, was publicized by the press, though there is no persuasive evidence that the course was widely adopted. . . .

Nationally the unfounded fears that women competed with men for a limited number of employment openings and that they displaced employed male workers was translated into a law prohibiting a husband and wife from simultaneous employment by the federal government. Section 213 of the Economy Act of 1932 did not specify which partner in a marriage would be hired or continued on the federal payroll, but since wives almost universally had less earning power than husbands, it was women who gave up federal jobs. Only a few states adopted similar legislation during the 1930s. Most states left the matter of working wives to local governments. At the local level female public employees were most visible in the schools, and married women teachers were the most common targets of discrimination.

Depression San Antonio was a city without a strong voice for women's rights. Although women in Atlanta, Georgia, and some other cities successfully fought policies preventing the employment of married female teachers, the dismissal of married women from the San Antonio schools met little opposition. In August, 1931, the San Antonio school board announced that married women would receive low priority in hiring of new teachers. In June, 1932, all previously hired married women whose husbands earned a minimum of two thousand dollars a year were terminated. In 1931 offices in the Bexar County Courthouse began dismissing married women, a practice apparently opposed only by the victims. . . .

In drafting emergency employment programs for women, Texas relief officials were wary of drawing in married women. Texas officials balked at setting up household-worker projects in the state if second-priority female workers— women living with employed or employable fathers, husbands, or sons—were to be recruited. A Texas administrator reported that several organizations in San Antonio would donate space for conducting WPA training programs as long as no woman with an outside source of income was certified for entrance, because "the general feeling in this part of the country is that her husband and father should earn the livelihood for the family."

Although married women were discriminated against by the school board

and had difficulty obtaining emergency jobs, personal influence in local administrative offices could break down the barriers that had been erected against their
hiring. Anglo women, of course, were much more likely to have pull in city and
county offices than were black and Hispanic women. Throughout the New Deal
era citizens complained to officials in Washington about the hiring of wives of
local administrators on relief payrolls. In 1933 an investigation by the Texas Senate of the Bexar County Board of Welfare and Employment involved accusation
that wives of city and county employees were receiving emergency work wages
while other San Antonians went hungry. . . .

Women workers understood that their only competitors for emergency work
were other women. The most likely critics of working women were unemployed
women. Late in the Depression a widow with two dependents wrote Eleanor Roosevelt that her WPA salary had been cut while wives with no real need had experienced no reduction:

> I have been on the W.P.A. at a salarie of $57.60 per month for the past few years.
> Recently I was cut to a $40.00 a month salarie. Instead of cutting the women who had
> other income and husbands to support them, they have cut the widow women with
> children and no other income. If the W.P.A. had made this cut after an investigation
> to prove that people did not need their jobs, it would have been different, but they are
> taking the jobs away from the little people, while they have increased their own sal-
> aries. Why? Because the little fellow had no pull. It is not efficiency or education or
> refinement or need that counts in San Antonio, it is pull. I have none. . . . I could give
> you the names of W.P.A. women that have their own homes, cars, and working sons
> and husbands. They have their beer and cigarettes and all the luxuries of life, while
> others that do not do these things have a mear existence. . . .

In San Antonio as elsewhere in the nation, the administration of both public
and private relief entailed endless bureaucratic red tape. Caseworkers were
viewed with suspicion; almost all of them were Anglos and few were bilingual,
though Mexican Americans comprised more than half the relief population.
When Ruth Killing was appointed to oversee local relief operations, she was
characterized by the Bexar County Protective League as well seasoned in "the
kind of charity where a poor woman is asked a bunch of impertinent questions
and given a bunch of carrots and a bunch of beets and told not to eat it all at once."

Adela Navarro was the first Hispanic appointed as a caseworker in San Antonio, and it was more than a year before a second was hired. Often frustrated by
official procedures or policies, she found ways to circumvent the rules when it
seemed necessary. She refused to report to her superior that among her cases was
a couple living together out of wedlock because she knew that they would be
stricken from relief rolls if the information was divulged. However, said Navarro,
someone was "so damn mean" that the information reached the relief office despite her silence on the issue. When her supervisor asked whether she knew that
a particular couple were not married, she answered that she did not consider it her
place to sit in moral judgment and that what she did know was that the people
were hungry, and she could get them food. Satisfied with her response, the supervisor no longer interfered with her case reports.

Although public and private relief work was inconsistently administered and
always inadequate to meet women's needs, clear patterns of preference and discrimination characterized the programs. Women were regarded merely as tempo-

rary and secondary workers who needed help getting by in hard times. The content of training programs generally militated against occupational advancement for women and was frequently unsuited to the local economy. Although black women were perceived as permanent workers, they received the fewest opportunities for training. Mexican-American women fared better than blacks in the variety of public works that employed them, but many Hispanics were turned away from relief and employment offices because of their alien status.

Southern Cities and the Depression

DOUGLAS L. SMITH

It was overcast and humid in New Orleans, January 8, 1930, when late in the afternoon Alexander J. Heinemann stepped from a vacant storeroom at the baseball park bearing his name. A recent $300,000 loser in the stock market, and in poor health, the president of the New Orleans Pelicans had waited alone, preparing to follow a course of action he had rehearsed five days before. Someone must have suspected that all was not right. Earlier in the day, club officials later reported, they had seen the admired sports figure gazing from the grandstand at the home field of one of the South's most successful minor league franchises "as if watching the ghost teams of his memory." At 4:45 p.m., a despondent Heinemann inserted the barrel of a pistol into his mouth and pulled the trigger. Two hours later, the groundskeeper discovered his body lying in a deserted hallway under a sign that read: "A full stomach and a bankroll make a man tempermental [*sic*]; my daily prayer is to teach me to keep my nose out of other people's business." Apparently Heinemann's associates had respected the latter aphorism, and now their friend was dead.

Fortunately for most victims of the Wall Street crash, and for the millions of others also affected by the Great Depression, their situations never became so desperate. Yet between 1929 and 1933, what had seemed to be a flourishing economy plunged to unknown depths. And in few areas was economic collapse more catastrophic than in the South, including its major cities, where the upheaval adversely affected all residents and almost every facet of urban life. Unemployment soared, while agricultural and industrial production declined sharply. Local relief rolls were taxed to a maximum, and like everywhere in the country, the suffering of the jobless was most acute in the years prior to the New Deal and federal intervention because public relief stipends proved woefully inadequate. Perhaps worse, the unparalleled growth experienced by the southern cities during the 1920s had the effect of blinding most residents in the early depression months to the reality of an economic downturn.

Although northern cities had recorded greater economic gains in the immediate predepression years, the largest southern municipalities had expanded overall and had reached significant plateaus. The population of Memphis more than doubled during the Roaring Twenties, for example, while during the same period the

From *The New Deal in the Urban South* by Douglas L. Smith, 1988, excerpts from pp. 11–26. Reprinted by permission of Louisiana State University Press.

state reported a population growth rate of only 11 percent. Similarly, while Atlanta was expanding by nearly 50 percent, Georgia on the whole was growing by only 4 percent—the highest growth rate among the Deep South states. Throughout the Southeast, moreover, the urban areas expanded at a far greater rate than did the region as a whole. Thousands moved from small towns to large cities seeking work promised by new manufacturing.

Birmingham offers an excellent example of urban industrial expansion in the South during the 1920s. The city's iron and steel industry, its principal economic force, had never before operated at such high levels of output. By the late 1920s, experts in New York were calling the city the "Pittsburgh of the South." Because steel, iron, and coke production increased steadily throughout the decade, United States Steel in 1930 invested twenty-five million dollars and overhauled several mills owned by its subsidiary, the Tennessee Coal and Iron Company (TCI), which received all of the parent company's southern business. Expansion created jobs, and even during the first depression year, TCI maintained production and employment levels for a time because of advance orders to be filled. Clearly the enlargement of the steelworks supported community expectations of a bright future.

Birmingham's banking resources fared similarly in the 1920s. Late in the decade, the city's financial institutions had total assets up to three times greater than their holdings in 1915. Construction generally remained healthy throughout the twenties, and building contracts in all southern cities reached their highest levels ever in 1928 and 1929. . . .

Atlanta in the 1920s also experienced economic development. Threatened by a depression in 1925 because of a panic triggered by the Florida land bust, the city's prominent businessmen initiated the "Forward Atlanta Movement," part of the predepression southern "booster-mania." Supported by the chamber of commerce, the campaign raised $750,000, which during the ensuing five years advertised the city a total of 125 million times in nationwide business publications and major newspapers. The effort successfully lured several hundred new manufacturing and other business establishments to the Fulton County area, offering employment to more than 15,000 and an annual payroll of more than $30 million. . . .

Atlanta's financial institutions also prospered in the 1920s. As well, a thriving construction business continued for a time into 1930, with municipal officials believing that contract work would remain healthy for years to come. Throughout the 1920s, the federal government opened several offices in Atlanta, bringing white-collar employment while contributing building activity and the emergence of the city as the South's air travel center. The city's major steel producer, Atlantic Steel Company, showed a trend much like its rival in Birmingham, actually increasing its share of the southern steel trade between 1929 and 1932.

Perhaps more subtly, similar economic growth occurred in Memphis during the predepression period. The number of manufacturers located in the area increased throughout the 1920s, and by mid-1930, the city housed more firms than in any other period of its history. An active construction trade further signified economic well-being. Home and industrial building even during 1930 remained active, exceeding levels of 1929. Unemployment in Memphis, as reported by the federal census in mid-1930, stood at less than 4 percent of the city's work force.

In Atlanta and Birmingham, unemployment rates were a bit higher but still below 6 percent. Even in New Orleans, the exception to the regional urban boom, unemployment as of mid-1930 had yet to affect the bulk of the labor force.

While economic forces in at least three southern cities appeared healthy on the eve of the depression, the same was not evident in New Orleans. That city did not enjoy significant expansion during the 1920s, falling into second place behind Atlanta as the principal city and financial center of the lower South. Income from manufacturing and per capita output in New Orleans lagged far behind that in the other cities, while the city's overall standard of living was significantly lower. Despite the alluring French Quarter and an abundance of famous restaurants, the city was unable to attract conventions, perhaps best demonstrating its comparative lag. Atlanta, Memphis, and even industrial Birmingham attracted many more such gatherings, with the Tennessee and Georgia municipalities ranking among the ten American cities hosting at least ten thousand conventioneers each year.

Despite the economic differences, each of the cities in question faced the new decade with high hopes. Boosters in Atlanta, Birmingham, and Memphis, for example, proudly pointed to their cities' unparalleled growth, confident in their faith that expansion was irreversible. Yet in New Orleans—precisely because it had not shared in the boom of the twenties—residents also confronted the uncertainties of the 1930s with confidence. Crescent City civic leaders, as well as the local press, countered the first news of widespread misery in Chicago by suggesting that the stability of the New Orleans economy was its buffer against the downturn that was bringing adversity to areas that had earlier experienced rapid but unstable expansion. . . .

An attitude best described as the "sunshine syndrome" was the key ingredient in the urban South's initial optimism. Southern newspapers steadfastly maintained that layoffs would be temporary in the winter and that normal employment would return with the arrival of warm weather. Welcoming March, 1931, for example, the Atlanta *Journal* indicated that until then conditions had shown "a bright omen here and there against a gray sky" but the spring would bring a "getting down to business" and a "quickening at the roots as well as in the branches of economic life." The Atlanta chamber of commerce in 1930 initiated a "reawakening campaign," complete with parades and a civic pageant, to usher in warm weather. According to the Atlanta *Constitution,* the ceremonies demonstrated that the spring "business is coming back to normal and jobs for the unemployed are becoming available once more." The notion that sunshine would somehow cure economic ills was so entrenched that many of the first municipal relief agencies were active only during the winter. The "sunshine syndrome" suggests too that the urban South maintained much of its regional identity, feeling itself somehow isolated from national and international events.

Despite wishful rhetoric about the curing powers of sunshine, a serious economic downturn was evident even to the most hopeful by mid-1931. While many were shocked, believing that the collapse had somehow happened overnight, the subtle but steady erosion of local economies had been ongoing for many months, with conditions reaching their lowest ebb by late 1932. . . .

Late in 1930, urban manufacturers began experiencing the worse effects of the depression. Production cutbacks became routine, workers were released or their wages reduced, and many mills closed their doors. Some shutdowns were temporary, with industries functioning on a piecemeal basis, although too many proved permanent, as hard times and reduced work orders caused even established firms to remain idle for months at a time. Federal surveys showed that in New Orleans, by late 1931, all major industries had reduced work forces and that all were operating only a few days each week at best. In Memphis, by the middle of the same year, the total number of manufacturers had declined by more than fifty, and by 1933, Atlanta had lost nearly one hundred.

In cities throughout the United States, the industrial decline was severe. Between 1929 and 1933, the total number of manufacturing establishments in the nation decreased by one-third, while each of the southern cities lost factories in higher proportions. At the same time, the value of manufacturing output fell, with declines ranging from more than 50 percent in Atlanta and New Orleans to more than 70 percent in Birmingham. . . .

Declining fortunes in agriculture and related industries in turn meant the curtailment of commercial activity. Between 1928 and 1933 in New Orleans, the volume of foreign trade decreased by more than 50 percent. The total value of tonnage handled by the Crescent City port also fell sharply, declining by 1932 to the levels of 1918 through 1920. Limited activity on the waterfront meant fewer jobs for dock workers and caused a sharp increase in the number of nonresident sailors drydocked in New Orleans. The situation created a serious transient problem for the Gulf Coast city.

Of all the southern businesses, none suffered more than the large steelworks in one-industry Birmingham. Producers had entered the 1930s optimistically, but by 1931 and thereafter, steel mills were all operating on part-time schedules. In addition to TCI plants, Sloss-Sheffield Steel and Iron and the Woodward Iron Company at first functioned on three-day schedules, but all too soon workers were fortunate to realize a full shift's work every two weeks. From a peak of more than one and one-half million tons in 1929, production in the Birmingham mills declined by one-half in 1931 and by one-half again in 1932. In the coal fields as well, reverses were sharp, with area mines in mid-decade yielding less than nine million tons annually, the same amount produced in 1900 and two to three times less than the output in 1926. . . . The severity of conditions forced the Roosevelt administration later to designate Birmingham as the "worst hit" city in the nation.

The retail trade showed a similar downturn beginning in 1931. The number of stores and the value of sales declined significantly between 1929 and 1933, with reverses in the southern cities being more severe than the national average. In New Orleans, the retail volume by 1933 stood at only 60 percent of the level in 1928, reflecting a community with less buying power than before. Discouraged by the increasing number of unoccupied stores, the Atlanta chamber of commerce in 1932 urged remaining businesses to rent vacant windows for display to maintain the city's facade. . . .

Ultimately, manufacturing and retail cutbacks caused a sharp increase in unemployment. The official 1930 census showed minimal joblessness in the southern urban areas; however, little time elapsed between the federal count and the initial depression layoffs. By the end of that year, there was at least one jobless man or woman for every ten normally in the labor force, and thereafter the number rose. By late 1931, unemployment had doubled, with a like percentage working only part time. Industrial employment in Birmingham decreased by 52 percent between 1930 and 1933, while the number of retail jobholders fell by one-third. The nadir came in early 1933, when all communities reported at least 30 percent of their labor force unemployed, which directly affected between 100,000 and 150,000 individuals in each city. Throughout the early depression years, all of the southern states reported higher rates of joblessness than the national average of 25 percent.

Those who managed to keep their jobs suffered drastic wage reductions. Spendable income per capita in the cities under examination fell by more than half between 1928 and 1933—a figure equal to the national decline. In Birmingham, TCI by early 1933 had trimmed weekly pay envelopes between 50 and 75 percent and was threatening workers with dismissal if they questioned the policy. . . . Some firms reacted to the difficult times a bit differently. In Memphis, several thousand manufacturing jobs held by women in 1929 were lost to men by 1933. Other companies attempted to ease the impact of unemployment by opening soup kitchens or by providing seeds and plots of land for the jobless, displaying a regional sense of paternalism toward their employees. . . .

Segregated job patterns in most southern businesses at first caused joblessness among whites and blacks to increase equally, especially in the Birmingham steelworks, where "white" and "black" labor were well defined. Yet the trend was short-lived, and despite a handful of contractors who hired unorganized blacks instead of unionized whites, Negroes were soon suffering more than whites from unemployment and wage reductions. Whites began moving into traditionally black positions, becoming bellhops and porters, for example, and among industrial workers, blacks were indeed the first to be let go. By early 1931, the unemployment rate among black males in New Orleans and Birmingham was double that of white males. By 1932, the number of blacks without work in Atlanta and Memphis accounted respectively for 50 percent and 75 percent of the total number of unemployed in the two cities. And between 1931 and 1932, the absolute number of jobless blacks in Atlanta increased by more than 95 percent, while the real number of unemployed whites increased by only 25 percent. Clearly such percentages were disproportionate—as they remain today—with the percentage of blacks to total residents in the southern cities ranging from 28 percent in New Orleans to 38 percent in Birmingham. . . .

The economic downturn adversely affected local governments and civic institutions in addition to individual wage earners. Employment lost and manufacturing reverses meant a lower tax base and diminished operation revenue for all municipalities. In the face of increasing tax delinquencies, cities reduced public employment, cut services, and eventually turned to local banks for operating capital. The situation in Atlanta was representative. A municipal statute authorized officials there to borrow a maximum of two million dollars a year from financial institutions. As of 1933, the city had relied on loans for so many years that it no longer had total control of its annual expenditures. The Atlanta banking establishments reserved the right to approve the city's annual budget.

Like their counterparts in the private sector, municipal employees experienced difficult times. The workers remaining on Birmingham's payroll by 1933 had accepted four salary cuts of 10 percent each, with similar trends prevailing in Atlanta, Memphis, and New Orleans. In place of cuts, other employees reluctantly "donated" a number of workdays each month to city hall, without pay. Conditions also resulted in the curtailment of police, fire, health, and other municipal services. In Birmingham, the city's public health program, one of the first civic programs to be slashed, practically disappeared during the early 1930s. By 1934, the southern steel center was spending only seventeen cents per capita on health services, compared to a national per capita average of seventy cents. Cities turned to scrip in lieu of salaries as well. While some retailers accepted the substitute dollars, recipients often had to redeem their notes at local banks or with loan sharks, both of whom discounted the notes at least 20 percent. . . .

School systems fared no better than other public institutions. The city budgets in Birmingham, Atlanta, and Memphis allocated fewer dollars each year for education, and in New Orleans, the school board itself became indebted to local financial establishments. Teachers were the first to suffer. They saw their meager salaries reduced, while their classrooms became grossly overcrowded. Educators in Memphis, even more so than other municipal employees, received several payments in scrip, and when salary reductions failed to save sufficient funds, a more general austerity program resulted. By the 1932–1933 academic year, special programs had disappeared from the city schools, including adult night classes, guidance services, vision correction and testing programs, and hygienic and psychiatric counseling, as well as vocational training financed in part under the federal Smith-Hughes Act.

Retrenchment in education took its most serious twist in Atlanta, where school authorities vehemently opposed city council demands to cut programs. Rather, the Atlanta Board of Education demanded additional funding—it received not a cent from county coffers even though taxes paid by city residents accounted for 85 percent of the county treasury. The conflict became so heated that councilmen at one point began talking about replacing the board with a new group of trustees. Because state legislative concurrence was needed, the threat remained just a threat, although city administrators brought it up on several occasions thereafter. Even when Georgia lawmakers ordered that the city school receive an increased percentage of Atlanta's budget, a decision that only aggravated hostilities during difficult times that called instead for cooperation, most school service programs were curtailed anyway.

The many students whose parents were unemployed caused further problems for urban school systems. Full attendance was never assured, even though educators in all cities successfully operated schools for complete terms. According to public welfare officials in New Orleans, as many as ten thousand children lacked "apparel conforming to standards of comfort and decency; the majority are home because torn and ragged garments shame them before their fellows." The crisis in education, moreover, lasted throughout the decade. As late as 1937 and 1938, full teacher salaries in Birmingham and New Orleans remained unrestored, and officials still could not guarantee full terms without the aid of emergency funds.

Despite urban financial needs, local banks were neither able nor always willing to grant municipal loan requests. Total banking deposits and resources recorded sharp declines early in the 1930s, and like all depressed businesses, banking reached a low point in 1932 and 1933. Banking failures were apparently more frequent in the rural communities than in the southern cities, with the fate of urban financial institutions varying from place to place. In Memphis, there were no major closings—a loan from the RFC averted the one near-panic—while in Atlanta, a number of banking consolidations in the 1920s apparently kept financial establishments solvent throughout the depression period. When banks in both cities closed during the federal banking holiday in March, 1933, all reopened within a week, although federal and state banking authorities placed withdrawal restrictions on some for several months thereafter.

Neither the Birmingham nor the New Orleans banking community was so fortunate. As early as January, 1933, Hamilton Fish of the House Banking Committee charged that New Orleans financier R. S. Hecht, president of both Hibernia Bank and Trust and Continental Bank and Trust, had misused federal funds in covering debts that one bank owed the other. Intensifying concerns was the fact that Hecht was chairman of the regional RFC advisory committee. Disclosure of the charges caused many out-of-state depositors to begin withdrawing funds from Hibernia. Civic leaders next braced for a run on the bank by Crescent City patrons. Substantial RFC loans to the two institutions in the end halted the panic.

The short-lived run in February, 1933, proved only the first in a series of setbacks affecting banks in New Orleans. Within a year, the state banking commission had ordered into liquidation at least six major financial institutions, reporting only three banks operating normally. Although two of the troubled banks later reorganized, with one reopening as part of a merger, thousands of Crescent City residents lost all or part of their savings. Most of the banks that closed never reimbursed their patrons in significant amounts, and even when there was some repayment, only middle- and upper-class residents—the large, steady depositors—managed to recover anything at all.

Clearly the southern cities in the early 1930s were experiencing a period of severe economic upheaval. Based on previous growth, the municipalities had entered the depression decade optimistically and despite subtle reverses from the outset, communities had failed to perceive a crisis until late in 1931. Yet by the end of 1933, unemployment, wage reductions, and lost savings affected thousands, as did the curtailment of city services. Perhaps the larger industrial cities in the Northeast and Midwest endured greater business reverses and more jobs lost, but the thousands ailing in the southern communities were nonetheless desperate. While times were the harshest, moreover, all localities were left alone to meet the problems as best they could. The attempt to relieve depression miseries would demand a great effort and commitments by individuals and local institutions.

※ *F U R T H E R   R E A D I N G*

Carl Abbott, *Urban America in the Modern Age: 1920 to the Present* (1987)
Jo Ann E. Argersinger, *Toward a New Deal in Baltimore: People and Government in the Great Depression* (1988)
Roger Biles, *Big City Bosses in Depression and War: Edward J. Kelly of Chicago* (1984)
———, *Memphis in the Great Depression* (1983)

William W. Bremer, *Depression Winters: New York Social Workers and the New Deal* (1984)

Blaine A. Brownell, *The Urban Ethos in the South, 1920–1930* (1975)

Lizabeth Cohen, *Making a New Deal: Industrial Workers in Chicago, 1919–1939* (1991)

Lyle W. Dorsett, *Franklin D. Roosevelt and the City Bosses* (1977)

Mark I. Gelfand, *A Nation of Cities: The Federal Government and Urban America, 1933–1965* (1975)

Kenneth T. Jackson, *The Crabgrass Frontier: The Suburbanization of the United States* (1985)

Lawrence H. Larsen, *The Urban West at the End of the Frontier* (1978)

William N. Mullins, *The Depression and the Urban West Coast, 1929–1933: Los Angeles, San Francisco, Portland, and Seattle* (1991)

Gerald Nash, *The American West in the Twentieth Century: A Short History of an Urban Oasis* (1973)

Harvard Sitkoff, *A New Deal for Blacks* (1978)

Bruce M. Stave, *The New Deal and the Last Hurrah: Pittsburgh's Machine Politics* (1970)

Judith Ann Trolander, *Settlement Houses and the Great Depression* (1973)

Charles H. Trout, *Boston, The Great Depression and the New Deal* (1977)

Winifred D. Wandersee, *Women's Work and Family Values, 1920–1940* (1981)

CHAPTER
12

Redevelopment and Renewal in the 1940s and 1950s

The Great Depression and Second World War had a dampening effect on cities, especially their housing resources. First the lack of money and credit during the 1930s, and then the scarcity and diversion of materials to the war effort in the first half of the 1940s, left cities with housing shortages that, when combined with the deterioration of existing housing, created a near-crisis situation. The U.S. Housing Act of 1937, passed to energize the construction industry as well as to help relieve housing pressures, had committed the federal government to providing public housing for needy families, but real-estate interests and allies of private enterprise had managed to prevent the federal government from directly constructing housing. Instead, the government could only fund local agencies whose purpose was to clear blighted slum areas, and then subsidize the redevelopment of the land.

In 1945 senators Robert F. Wagner of New York, Allen J. Ellender of Louisiana, and Robert A. Taft of Ohio submitted a housing bill that set a goal of providing every American with decent housing and that specified the construction of 810,000 public-housing units for low-income families. After long delay and debates, the bill finally passed Congress in 1949 and was signed into law by President Harry Truman as the Housing Act of 1949. The act provided for several categories of urban redevelopment: slum clearance, public housing, and expanded mortgage insurance. In 1954 an amendment to the 1949 act gave increased attention to the rehabilitation of dilapidated structures and instituted the term urban renewal, which subsequently was used to refer to all forms of government-sponsored redevelopment and construction.

These measures essentially earmarked extensive federal assistance to relieve specific urban problems—aid that expanded dramatically over the next two decades and that has continued in various forms to the present. This closing of the partnership between cities and the federal government has provoked ongoing controversy. Have cities really been unable to solve their own problems, especially in the years of postwar prosperity? Is it the federal government's responsibility to involve itself in private housing markets? Whom did urban renewal help, and whom did it hurt? Have the effects of urban renewal been salutary, detrimental, or mixed? Have policymakers learned from the successes and failures of urban renewal? If so, what have they learned and applied?

※ *D O C U M E N T S*

These documents provide insight into the process and policies of urban renewal. The first selection presents excerpts from the U.S. Housing Act of 1949, the landmark legislation that created federally funded urban redevelopment. This document can be analyzed for a number of issues, most particularly the apparent commitment of the federal government to the goal of decent housing for every American; the extreme care taken within the act to promote and to protect private enterprise; the provision of funneling grants through local agencies so as to remove the appearance of federal intervention in local affairs; the emphasis on planning; the strict and careful criteria to screen potential occupants of public housing; and the preference given to veterans. Most important are the definitions in "Sec. 110," which use the term *predominantly residential.* This section was the cause of great misinterpretation in subsequent years. The second document is from a speech given to the National Planning Conference of the American Society of Planning Officials by Warren J. Vinton, the first assistant administrator for the Federal Public Housing Administration. Basking in the afterglow of the recently passed U.S. Housing Act of 1949, which gave policymakers great optimism about the possibilities of improving urban life, Vinton foresaw a rosy future for both redevelopment and public housing, a future that, as the essay below by John F. Bauman and others shows, brought more hardship than renewal.

The U.S. Housing Act of 1949

An Act

To establish a national housing objective and the policy to be followed in the attainment thereof, to provide Federal aid to assist slum-clearance projects and low-rent public housing projects initiated by local agencies, to provide for financial assistance by the Secretary of Agriculture for farm housing, and for other purposes. . . .

Declaration of National Housing Policy

Sec. 2. The Congress hereby declares that the general welfare and security of the Nation and the health and living standards of its people require housing production and related community development sufficient to remedy the serious housing shortage, the elimination of substandard and other inadequate housing through the clearance of slums and blighted areas, and the realization as soon as feasible of the goal of a decent home and a suitable living environment for every American family, thus contributing to the development and redevelopment of communities and to the advancement of the growth, wealth, and security of the Nation. The Congress further declares that such production is necessary to enable the housing industry to make its full contribution toward an economy of maximum employment, production, and purchasing power. The policy to be followed in attaining the national housing objective hereby established shall be: (1) private enterprise shall be encouraged to serve as large a part of the total need as it can; (2) governmental assistance shall be utilized where feasible to enable private enterprise to serve more of the total need; (3) appropriate local public bodies shall be encouraged and assisted to undertake positive programs of encouraging and assisting the development of well-planned, integrated residential neighborhoods, the development and redevelopment of communities, and the production, at lower costs, of housing of sound standards of design, construction, livability, and size for adequate family life; (4) governmental assistance to eliminate substandard and other inadequate housing through the clearance of slums and blighted areas, to facilitate community development and redevelopment, and to provide adequate housing for urban and rural nonfarm families with incomes so low that they are not being decently housed in new or existing housing shall be extended to those localities which estimate their own needs and demonstrate that these needs are not being met through reliance solely upon private enterprise, and without such aid; and (5) governmental assistance for decent, safe, and sanitary farm dwellings and related facilities shall be extended where the farm owner demonstrates that he lacks sufficient resources to provide such housing on his own account and is unable to secure necessary credit for such housing from other sources on terms and conditions which he could reasonably be expected to fulfill. . . .

Title I—Slum Clearance and Community Development and Redevelopment

Sec. 10. On extending financial assistance under this title, the Administrator shall—

(a) give consideration to the extent to which appropriate local public bodies have undertaken positive programs (i) for encouraging housing cost reductions through the adoption, improvement, and modernization of building and other local codes and regulations so as to permit the use of appropriate new materials, techniques, and methods in land and residential planning, design, and construction, the increase of efficiency in residential construction, and the elimination of restrictive practices which unnecessarily increase housing costs, and (ii) for preventing the spread or recurrence, in such community, of slums and blighted areas through the adoption, improvement, and modernization of local codes and regulations relating to land use and adequate standards of health, sanitation, and safety for dwelling accommodations; and

(b) encourage the operations of such local public agencies as are established on a State, or regional (within a State), or unified metropolitan basis or as are established on such other basis as permits such agencies to contribute effectively toward the solution of community development or redevelopment problems on a State, or regional (within State), or unified metropolitan basis. . . .

Capital Grants. Sec. 103. (a) The Administrator may make capital grants to local public agencies to enable such agencies to make land in project areas available for redevelopment at its fair value for the uses specified in the redevelopment plan: *Provided,* That the Administrator shall not make any contract for capital grant with respect to a project which consists of open land. The aggregate of such capital grants with respect to all the projects of a local public agency on which contracts for capital grants have been made under this title shall not exceed two-thirds of the aggregate of the net project costs of such projects, and the capital grants with respect to any individual project shall not exceed the difference between the net project cost and the local grants-in-aid actually made with respect to the project. . . .

Local Determination.   Sec. 105. Contracts for financial aid shall be made only with a duly authorized local public agency and shall require that—

(a) The redevelopment plan for the project area be approved by the governing body of the locality in which the project is situated, and that such approval include findings by the governing body that (i) the financial aid to be provided in the contract is necessary to enable the land in the project area to be redeveloped in accordance with the redevelopment plan; (ii) the redevelopment plans for the redevelopment areas in the locality will afford maximum opportunity, consistent with the sound needs of the locality as a whole, for the redevelopment of such areas by private enterprise; and (iii) the redevelopment plan conforms to a general plan for the development of the locality as a whole; . . .

(c) There be a feasible method for the temporary relocation of families displaced from the project area, and that there are or are being provided, in the project area or in other areas not generally less desirable in regard to public utilities and public and commercial facilities and at rents or prices within the financial means of the families displaced from the project area, decent, safe, and sanitary dwellings equal in number to the number of and available to such displaced families and reasonably accessible to their places of employment: . . .

Sec. 110. The following terms shall have the meanings, respectively, ascribed to them below . . .

(c) "Project" may include (1) acquisition of (i) a slum area or a deteriorated or deteriorating area which is predominantly residential in character, or (ii) any other deteriorated or deteriorating area which is to be developed or redeveloped for predominantly residential uses, or (iii) land which is predominantly open and which because of obsolete platting, diversity of ownership, deterioration of structures or of site improvements, or otherwise substantially impairs or arrests the sound growth of the community and which is to be developed for predominantly residential uses, or (iv) open land necessary for sound community growth which is to be developed for predominantly residential uses (in which event the project thereon, as provided in the proviso of section 103(a) hereof, shall not be eligible for any capital grant); (2) demolition and removal of buildings and improvements; (3) installation, construction, or reconstruction of streets, utilities, and other site improvements essential to the preparation of sites for uses in accordance with the redevelopment plan; and (4) making the land available for development or redevelopment by private enterprise or public agencies . . . at its fair value for uses in accordance with the redevelopment plan. . . .

Title III—Low-Rent Public Housing

Local Responsibilities and Determinations; Tenancy Only by Low-Income Families. Sec. 301. The United States Housing Act of 1937, as amended, is hereby amended by adding the following additional subsections to section 15:

"(7) In recognition that there should be local determination of the need for low-rent housing to meet needs not being adequately met by private enterprise—

"(a)The Authority shall not make any contract with a public housing agency for preliminary loans . . . for surveys and planning in respect to any low-rent housing project initiated after March 1, 1949, (i) unless the governing body of the locality involved has by resolution approved the application of the public housing agency for such preliminary loan; and (ii) unless the public housing agency has demonstrated to the satisfaction of the Authority that there is a need for such low-rent housing which is not being met by private enterprise; and

"(b) the Authority shall not make any contract for loans . . . or for annual contributions pursuant to this Act with respect to any low-rent housing project initiated after March 1, 1949, (i) unless the governing body of the locality involved has entered into an agreement with the public housing agency providing for the local cooperation required by the Authority pursuant to this Act; and (ii) unless the public housing agency has demonstrated to the satisfaction of the Authority that a gap of at least 20 per centum has been left between the upper rental limits for admission to the proposed low-rent housing and the lowest rents at which private enterprise unaided by public subsidy is providing . . . a substantial supply of decent, safe, and sanitary housing toward meeting the need of an adequate volume thereof.

"(8) Every contract made pursuant to this Act for annual contributions for any low-rent housing project initiated after March 1, 1949, shall provide that—

"(a) the public housing agency shall fix maximum income limits for the admission and for the continued occupancy of families in such housing, that such maximum income limits and all revisions thereof shall be subject to the prior approval of the Authority, and that the Authority may require the public housing agency to review and to revise such maximum income limits if the Authority determines that changed conditions in the locality make such revisions necessary in achieving the purposes of this Act;

"(b) a duly authorized official of the public housing agency involved shall make periodic written statements to the Authority that an investigation has been made of each family admitted to the low-rent housing project involved during the period covered thereby, and that, on the basis of the report of said investigation, he has found that each such family at the time of its admission (i) had a net family income not exceeding the maximum income limits theretofore fixed by the public housing agency . . . for admission of families of low income to such housing; and (ii) lived in an unsafe, insanitary [sic], or overcrowded dwelling, or was to be displaced by another low-rent housing project or by a public slum-clearance or redevelopment project, or actually was without housing, or was about to be without housing as a result of a court order of eviction, due to causes other than the fault of the tenant: *Provided,* That the requirement in (ii) shall not be applicable in the case of the family of any veteran or serviceman . . . where application for admission to such housing is made not later than five years after March 1, 1949.

"(c) in the selection of tenants (i) the public housing agency shall not discriminate against families, otherwise eligible for admission to such housing, because their incomes are derived in whole or in part from public assistance and (ii) in initially selecting families for admission to dwellings of given sizes and at specified rents the public housing agency shall . . . give preference to families having the most urgent housing needs, and thereafter, in selecting families for admission to such dwellings, shall give due consideration to the urgency of the families' housing needs; and

"(d) the public housing agency shall make periodic reexaminations of the net incomes of tenant families living in the low-rent housing project involved; and if it is found, upon such reexamination that the net incomes of any such families have increased beyond the maximum income limits fixed by the public housing agency . . . for continued occupancy in such housing, such families shall be required to move from the project."

A Housing Administrator Sees a Rosy Future for Redevelopment and Public Housing, 1949

Urban redevelopment projects should never again be conceived of as small isolated islands, surrounded by unrelated neighborhoods, and rebuilt in a single construction job. A redevelopment project should be conceived of as the rebuilding of a whole neighborhood or as much as should be rebuilt, with boundaries running out to natural barriers or to other unspoiled neighborhoods. In such large-scale projects, land would be acquired when opportunity offers; demolition be carried out when local conditions make possible the rehousing of displaced families, businesses, or industries; and rebuilding be done from time to time as different developers come forward or as the public interest warrants.

Such an organic redevelopment of a large area could be spread over a period of years. It might well constitute one redevelopment project, but the rebuilding of the area could be done in a number of different operations, all subject to one general plan. Indeed, if a redevelopment project is to be really satisfactory in scale, it will be next to impossible to find a single firm with large enough resources of capital and of experience to undertake the job of rebuilding the whole area. It will almost always be necessary, fortunately, to seek a number of redevelopers to rebuild different parts of an area, each in accordance with his own special interests: some undertaking stores, some developing light industries, others building houses for sale, and still others developing rental housing. The city itself will participate through the building of schools, health facilities, and other public buildings and parks.

Diversity Should Be Encouraged

A redevelopment project carried out over a period of years, with rebuilding done by a number of entrepreneurs, would have a diversity and variety in its related parts which would be lost if it were rebuilt in one gargantuan operation. It should

Construction and Demolition of the Pruitt-Igoe Housing Project, St. Louis, Missouri

Built in 1954, this vast low-income housing complex at first was heralded as a model of government-financed public housing. Yet lack of maintenance, rising crime, and the public and private sectors' failure to provide the means for tenants to earn sufficient incomes led to so much deterioration and so many other problems that the U.S. Department of Housing and Urban Development demolished the buildings in 1974.

be our purpose to foster such diversity and variety in the rebuilding of our cities, and avoid the dead monotony which is so easy a concomitant of large-scale operations. . . .

In the well-planned but diversified redevelopment of large urban areas, public housing will find its appropriate place. Most localities will decide that public housing and private housing can exist side by side to the mutual advantage of each. It is my personal hope that public housing in the future will never be concentrated in mammoth projects serving two, three, or four thousand families with uniform income levels, living in uniform dwellings, and subject to uniform administrative regulations. Regimentation is the inevitable result of such uniformity, and regimentation is repugnant to the free soul.

I, myself, have always thought it would be pleasant if the gridiron pattern of our cities were relieved by turning one block out of every six or eight into a public park. One side of such a square might well be occupied by a low-rent housing project, a couple of sides be devoted to middle-income housing, and the fourth side be occupied by higher-income families. . . .

It is already apparent that in most cities the new low-rent programs will have to start with projects on vacant sites, or on sparsely developed sites which involve little family relocation. It is important, moreover, that the first urban redevelopment projects in the various cities be initiated as soon as possible, so that the tenants to be displaced by slum clearance can be accommodated in the first low-rent projects. . . .

As families are taken out of areas selected for slum clearance, the dwellings which are vacated, if sufficiently substandard to warrant the use of the police power, can be closed up or ordered demolished. The amounts which must be paid for the land on which this worst housing is located will thus be lowered, and the cost of subsidy to the federal and local governments will be correspondingly reduced. Here again close cooperation between public housing and urban redevelopment is essential in the interests of both programs. . . .

Acquiring High-Priced Sites

The urban–redevelopment programs will be of assistance to public housing in connection with the acquisition of some high-priced sites which may lie within redevelopment areas and be suitable for low-rent housing use. Such sites, although they may constitute the worst slums in the locality, have in the past been avoided by public housing because overcrowding and the high rents derived thereby have run land costs to prohibitive levels. When such sites are used for the construction of either public or private housing, large write-downs in cost are necessarily involved.

In the administration of the subsidies which Congress has made available for the public-housing program, I believe that we should not use them for write-downs in the cost of such very high-priced slum clearance sites, but devote them primarily to the provision of low-rent housing. . . .

I do not believe that PHA [Public Housing Administration] would be justified in approving a project in which the entire cost of a very expensive slum site would be met exclusively with low-rent housing subsidies. When the use of such a site for low-rent housing is justified on sound planning considerations, funds other than low-rent housing subsidies should be used to meet the difference between the cost of the site, including site improvements, and the amount which could be reasonably justified for inclusion in the development cost of the low-rent housing project. While it might be possible for some cities to make up this difference through donation directly to the low-rent project, it would seem preferable that the write-down should be made as contemplated in Title I of the new Act with a two-third sharing by the Federal Government and a one-third sharing by the locality.

ESSAYS

The first essay was written in 1960, a decade after the passage of the U.S. Housing Act of 1949 that established urban redevelopment and subsequently urban renewal. The author, Richard H. Leach, a professor of political science at Duke University and an authority on American national and state governments, summarizes several aspects of urban renewal and describes conditions, especially with regard to relocation and housing, as they existed at the beginning of the 1960s. He also illustrates a contemporary point of view about the weaknesses of urban renewal in terms of government policy and planning. The second selection, by John F. Bauman of the California University of Pennsylvania and Norman P. Hummon and Edward K. Muller, both of the University of Pittsburgh, examines the impact of federal urban renewal and redevelopment on urban African-American families and provides a historical link to the current discussions of the underclass considered in the next chapter. The essay also presents a good summary of scholarly analysis of urban African-American life in the past twenty years.

The Federal Urban Renewal Program: A Ten-Year Critique

RICHARD H. LEACH

Urban renewal as a federal program began only in 1949 and has been emphasized only since 1954. It is important to keep these dates in mind when beginning an appraisal of the program. All new governmental processes require time for public support to be built up and public understanding gained, as well as for problems of operation to be worked out. Perhaps it is too soon to judge urban renewal. It should also be remembered that both the Congresses which have provided for federal assistance in urban redevelopment and the state legislatures which have passed acts enabling local agencies to launch urban renewal projects are, if not actually dominated by rural constituencies, bound by the rural tradition and orientation of American political life. Because urban renewal is new and because it demands for the first time concentrated attention on urban areas, it has been subjected to repeated attack. Every extension has been resisted; and there is still a heavy opposition to the whole idea. Under these conditions, an objective appraisal is seldom encountered.

Granted all this, it seems very possible that history may in the end demonstrate that the Housing Act of 1949, which launched urban renewal on its way, is the most significant piece of legislation placed on the federal statute books since World War II. Not only was federal involvement authorized in an activity which "touches practically every phase of the Nation's economy," and thus of its very life, but, what is more, the federal government was enlisted for the duration in the

From "The Federal Urban Renewal Program: A Ten-Year Critique" by Richard H. Leach, *Law and Contemporary Problems* 25 (Autumn 1960), excerpts from pp. 777–92. Reprinted by permission.

battle for "the elimination of substandard and other inadequate housing through the clearance of slums and blighted areas, and the realization as soon as feasible of the goal of a decent home and a suitable living environment for every American family. . . ." Perhaps no one foresaw in 1949 that the battle would be such a long one, for, despite the federal government's participation for ten years in the fight against it, the cancer of urban blight has spread since 1949. The life of urban America is still far from being saved. A recent analysis in Boston, for example, concluded that while "Boston's urban renewal program has made discernible progress . . . the rate of renewal activity still is being outstripped by the rate of decay. . . . [B]etween 1959 and 1960, it is estimated that . . . 22,000 more dwellings have fallen into the sub-standard category. This is nearly three times the amount of poor housing eliminated in the last ten years." What is true in Boston is true in virtually every urban area in the United States. What seemed to be merely a skirmish against slums has turned out to be a war for urban survival. Although the federal government is not fighting the war alone—the states, local governments, and private developers are all allied with her in the struggle—the federal government has come to bear an increasing responsibility for the successful outcome of the battle. In part, this is true because the costs of urban renewal are so great and the federal monopoly of the tax base so tight that effective action by the other governmental members of the team is made very difficult. In part, it is because postwar federal programs in urban areas—public housing, mortgage insurance, highway and airport construction, defense contracts and installations, for example—are creating unprecedented new problems for cities, for the solution of which the federal government cannot avoid assuming responsibility. And, in part, it is simply because two-thirds or more of the people of America live in the battle areas. What affects two-thirds of the nation's population obviously is of intimate importance to the national government.

For all these reasons, there can be no retreat for the federal government from its urban renewal objective. . . .

I

As already noted, the statutory authorization for urban renewal is to be found chiefly in Title I of the Housing Act of 1949, as amended. It is important to note that the very title of the Act implies an emphasis on housing rather than on urban renewal. Indeed, the broader subject has been treated all along as merely an aspect of the narrower one. When Congress decided to act in 1949, it saw slum clearance as an adjunct of the housing program, and that relationship has been maintained to the present day. In fact, however, urban renewal and redevelopment is the major task to be accomplished; improved housing is but one aspect of the broader program. Urban renewal means nothing less than full community development. . . . Unfortunately, but understandably in the context of pressure politics, Congress seems to see the matter the other way around, so that the focus of its attention—and of appropriations as well—has been on housing. The pressure for homes right after the war was easy to appreciate. No cause perhaps had more ardent or more politically powerful advocates. The need to save urban centers from progressive blight and eventual strangulation, on the other hand, was complex and hard to grasp; and it lacked persuasive political force. Thus, the resulting emphasis in legislation on the former and not the latter was a natural product of the situation. Not that improved housing was not then and is not still important. There was indeed a mounting housing crisis after World War II, and Congress properly acted to meet it. The difficulty is that in its concern to meet one need, it failed to understand that it was neglecting a greater one. To this day, urban redevelopment has not been brought to the center of the state where it belongs; and it suffers from the minor role it has been assigned.

One result of regarding urban renewal as an aspect of the housing program has been its emphasis on residential building and improvement. Yet residential areas obviously cannot be divorced from the commercial and industrial areas where the people shop and work. The federal program should be amended so as to demonstrate an understanding of this basic fact and to provide for the renewal of non-residential areas. . . .

The federal urban renewal program suffers, too, from the piecemeal way the housing program has been developed. Different aspects of the program have been handled at different times by different committees in Congress in response to different kinds of pressures. Over the years since 1949, statute has been piled upon statute, amendment on amendment, until considerable expertise is needed to comprehend the program. Over forty changes in the law were made by the Housing Act of 1959 alone. The very complexity of the legislation handicaps its effective application. As the mayor of Philadelphia recently testified, the law is "so full of 'provided thats' and 'notwithstandings' that it is a nightmare to track down just what is provided for. . . ."

Moreover, obscure and complicated legislation aids and abets delay and red tape, and a universal complaint about the urban renewal program since the beginning has been the "detailed and cumbersome . . . procedures and requirements" which it involves. Often five to seven years have been consumed in processing an urban renewal application. Such delays obviously cause the loss of many opportunities to handle particular urban renewal problems effectively.

The administration of the urban renewal program only makes the situation worse. Although the basic administrative unit is the Urban Renewal Administration, URA is only a child of the parent Housing and Home Finance Agency, not the Commissioner of the Urban Renewal Administration, with the responsibility for approving the Workable Programs developed by local communities under the terms of the act. Indeed, administration of the program is highly centralized in HHFA. All contacts outside of Washington must be made with regional HHFA offices, which are chronically understaffed. To be sure, HHFA and URA must protect the funds appropriated for urban renewal by determining the legal eligibility and the practical feasibility of project applications, and in doing so a certain amount of central control is demanded. Many observers feel, however, that far too much control is exercised. . . .

To make matters still worse, not all federal activities affecting urban renewal are subject either to the HHFA or the URA. The Bureau of Public Roads, the Veterans Administration, the Department of Defense, and the Department of Health, Education and Welfare all carry on activities with a direct impact on urban development, and the programs of a number of other federal agencies have a lesser degree of impact on it. . . .

II

The more important faults of the urban renewal program lie in other directions. First and foremost is the fact that urban renewal as a concept has so far been confined to the community, a concept now outmoded. Thus, the section of the law requiring a Workable Program specifies that the program shall demonstrate that it deals effectively "with the problem of urban slums and blight within the *community*" and that it is directed toward "the establishment and preservation of a well-planned *community.* . . ." Loans are authorized to assist local *communities* to eliminate slums, and the Act specifies that the "governing body of the *locality*" shall approve the acquisition of real property as the first step in the loan process. . . . Nowhere in the Act is a "community" defined. And although the Administrator is admonished to "encourage the operations of . . . public agencies . . . on a State, or regional (within a State), or unified metropolitan basis," no specifics are enumerated. . . .

The crux of the matter is that urban renewal cannot properly be considered as affecting only a community, a neighborhood or a locality, in other words, parts of much larger wholes. The effects of slum clearance and urban redevelopment—and of conservation and rehabilitation—reach far beyond the renewal areas themselves and touch the entire urban region of which they are a part. The impact of slums and redeveloped areas on the flight to the suburbs is manifestly a direct one. The economics of the whole urban complex are involved in every renewal project. Highway and street construction, water supply and sewerage, traffic and parking, mass transit, and a host of other activities must all be considered, along with urban renewal, as parts of a single metropolitan picture. . . .

There are admittedly legal difficulties barring immediate accomplishment of this objective. The whole metropolitan area problem is made hard to attack by the fact that metropolitan areas, with the exception of the Miami area, have no corporate existence in the United States. Having no legal foundation, they have no over-all governmental organization to which federal grants can be made. If at first blanch, however, it appears that this is a problem beyond the reach of the federal government and that under our federal division of powers it belongs to the states, there is, nevertheless, much the federal government could do through its own activities and through its grants-in-aid programs to encourage the creation by the states of larger units of government to fit present and future social and economic realities in metropolitan areas. The federal government might, for example, require all its grants-in-aid programs, housing and urban renewal among them, to be related to comprehensive metropolitan plans rather than, as at present, to comprehensive community plans. . . . It might require as a condition precedent for federal aid that the local public agency be representative of the entire area rather than of a single city or county. There is something to be said for saving trees; there is much more to be said for saving the forest.

Equally critical to the long-term success of urban renewal is its successful coordination with other urban programs of both the federal and state governments. It has even proved difficult in many cases to coordinate urban renewal and public housing projects in a single city, even though both are activities of the HHFA, for the law permits the public housing and redevelopment programs to be handled by separate local agencies and does nothing to require their coordination . . . .

Launched independently as each federal urban program is, there is seldom any effective provision for coordination between them. A common headline across the country in the last few years has been "Delay in Expressway Site Slows Urban Renewal Plan." In virtually every case, the article following the headline reveals a lack of coordination between the state highway department and the community with a projected redevelopment plan. . . .

Similarly, federal activities in the field of recreation, airport construction, water pollution control, civil defense, to name only a few, are all allowed to operate independently and under separate administrative auspices, without a mechanism for coordination. For the most effective operation of each of them, both national and local coordination should be required. One area in particular demands immediate attention. The federal government locates and enlarges its defense and military installations in urban areas virtually oblivious to the impact of such action on the problem of urban redevelopment. Indeed, in the negotiations to obtain a military installation or to enlarge an existing one, it is common for a representative of the chamber of commerce and the congressman from the district concerned to be consulted; but it is seldom that the city planning director or the head of the local urban redevelopment agency is called in. . . .

Once again the lack of coordination among federal programs in urban areas is rooted in the fact that metropolitan areas lack any responsible over-all governing body. Thus, urban renewal is parcelled out to the redevelopment agency, expressway construction to the state highway department, airport construction to the airport authority, civil defense to the director of civil defense, and so on. Each moves in the direction that seems best from its limited viewpoint. Perhaps there is no answer, at least no easy answer, to the problem of coordination—and thus to the improvement of this aspect of urban renewal—until some headway is made in attacking the problem of government in metropolitan areas. Here again, however, Washington might lead the way. There are few signs yet that it will do so.

III

Better coordination of the many government programs having impact on urban areas with urban renewal plans would constitute a major advance. However, the urban renewal program is handicapped in reaching its objectives by more than lack of coordination. To a large degree, the federal government's several housing and mortgage insurance programs work at direct cross-purposes to the urban renewal programs. Renewal is largely a matter of the central city. It is chiefly the downtown slum areas which need to be renewed and redeveloped (although slums have popped up already in an alarming number of new suburbs). Slums are primarily multifamily rental residences; and the great need in a redevelopment area is for replacement housing which will accommodate the large number of people being displaced at a rent they can afford, and constructed in a way that will meet their emotional and social needs satisfactorily. The federal mortgage insurance programs, however, operate in almost direct opposition to these requirements. The FHA and GI programs are far more favorable to the construction of single-family homes than to multifamily rental units. FHA regulations do not encourage renovation of old houses in run-down areas. Rather they show decided partiality to the new single-family dwelling. And since land for single-family dwellings inside the central city is generally limited, developers go to the suburbs and erect small houses there. The result of FHA emphasis is that from "every large urban center the suburbs spread out and out, without shape or grace or any centered form of civic life. Many are so built that they are the slums of tomorrow."

Meanwhile, the would-be apartment-house builder is restricted in many ways. To receive federal aid, he must file a cost certificate; if he manages to build below his estimate, he is penalized by having the amount of his mortgage loan reduced proportionately, regardless of the value of the property. Moreover, his profit rate is restricted, his rents are regulated, and he must manage the building over a period of years to get his profit out of the enterprise. All these factors make building needed multifamily rental housing much less attractive to developers than suburban houses and explain, to some extent at least, why so much of the housing built since World War II has been in single-family units.

Nor has the government's public housing program been an adequate substitute. More often than not, the only recourse has been to erect a public housing project in an urban renewal area, but such projects are seldom satisfactory. "These vast barracks-like superblocks [seem to be] designed not for people who like cities, but for people who have no other choice." Too many are cut off from city life. They are, to use a term frequently applied to them by their builders, "self-contained." But practice belies the assertion. There is no place in most of them for the development of a community life to replace the very strong sense of community which was characteristic of a great many slum areas. . . .

Moreover, in serving families low on the income scale, public housing has taken an unnecessarily large proportion of broken families, families without a wage-earner, or with family heads chronically unemployed or incapacitated. "As a result, projects have tended to become social and economic ghettos." Moreover, there is "an increasing tendency to locate projects in areas already occupied by nonwhite families, thus decreasing rather than increasing racial democracy."

All these factors lead to the conclusion that public housing projects should give greater consideration to the social needs of the people who are to live therein—both for the sake of their welfare and to assure that the broad objectives of urban renewal will in the end have any meaning. Public housing should be more attractively designed, should look less institutional, less like jails or hospitals—efficient, clean, but a social vacuum. More important they should be designed in recognition of the sociological factors which make for successful community living; they should provide play space for children, meeting places for adults, and recreational facilities for senior citizens, out of which a sense of community can be developed.

Emphasis on public housing for low-income groups has resulted in a failure by the federal government to recognize the nearly as great needs for better housing of the middle-class-income groups in urban centers. Building costs and property values in urban centers have risen faster than the ability of many middle-class-income families to meet them. Yet the public housing limitations on income are too low for them to qualify, even if they wanted that kind of housing. The only answer has been either to desert the central city and join the exodus to the suburbs, or to continue to live in deteriorating houses in deteriorating neighborhoods. . . . Once again, leadership from Washington would go far toward providing solutions to the problem.

The problem is not one, however, which can be solved by the Urban Renewal Administration alone. The solution lies deeper than that. It must proceed from a recognition of the fact that urban redevelopment depends on the successful relation of many different programs one to the others, and that the benefits of action by one agency to assist urban renewal projects may be cancelled by the action of others in building public housing units, encouraging suburban development, building new expressways, or planning a new military installation. . . .

Perhaps the Achilles' heel of urban renewal will turn out to be the relocation of the residents of areas to be renewed. In New York City alone, as many as 500,000 families—over one fifth of the city's population—will probably be uprooted as urban renewal needs are met in the next fifteen years. Such massive turnover in population has obvious implications for every facet of community life. Some relocation is temporary only. Slums must be torn down before replacement housing can be built. In the meantime, the people who are removed from the site must be housed. More often, relocation is permanent. Although statistics are not easily available, it appears that about a third of the people displaced from renewal areas leave those areas altogether. A movement of that proportion amounts in many cases to mass migration. Unfortunately, however, relocation has too often been treated as a minor problem of secondary importance. It is often handled by a separate agency rather than being coordinated with the urban renewal program. . . . The federal government could do a great deal toward eliminating the neglect of relocation on the local level if it would spell out in greater detail, and put teeth into, its requirement that a workable program should include a demonstration that families displaced by urban renewal and other governmental activities will be adequately rehoused. . . . Too often, relocation results in fact in moving from one substandard housing area to another. The present federal grant of $200 to individual family units and $3000 to businesses to aid in relocation is not enough in many cases to make a real difference. The whole relocation problem is one which has been neglected and seriously needs attention. Until it and the related problems of providing the type of housing actually needed in renewal areas are solved, the objectives of urban renewal will be frustrated.

IV

Certainly one of the major problems of the urban renewal program arises out of the fact that while the declared purpose of the program—to provide decent housing and a suitable living environment for all American citizens—is a long-term goal, appropriations have been made on a short-term basis. In the light of the estimates made earlier this year by ACTION that a grand total of $100 billion a year should be spent on urban renewal for the next ten years if the spread of urban blight is to be halted and overcome, as well as of the survey recently conducted by the American Municipal Association and the United States Conference of Mayors, which showed an estimated need of a total of $3,617.9 million in federal grants for urban renewal between now and 1970, it is obvious that the battle has only been begun. The same figures make it clear that there can be no cut-off date imposed on the program if it is to accomplish its objectives.

Successful planning of so massive a program as urban renewal cannot take place in fits and starts. . . . Putting the program on a long-term basis would remove many of the hardships of planning and would facilitate the operation of the program.

More important, perhaps, is the size of the federal contribution to the program. Federal resources are not without limit, and there is general agreement that both taxes and borrowing are already at uncomfortably high levels. On the other hand, in the latest federal budget, only 0.2 per cent of the proposed expenditures were for urban renewal. . . . [I]t is a truism that the automobile has depopulated the central cities and permitted both industry and upper-income families to migrate to the suburbs, taking with them a large part of the possible tax base. If the cities could develop a practical means of taxing suburban residents and industries who nevertheless receive benefits from their nearness to the central city, reliance on such a tax would no doubt be preferable to federal taxes and federal grants. But no such practical means have been developed. And few states are able to offer much help. The matter boils down very quickly to the fact that, if anything like the proper kind of action is to be taken, the federal government must support it. It is not a matter of choice; it is a matter of necessity. . . .

V

Perhaps the most serious weakness of the urban renewal program has been that it was set to work, and has operated since, in a vacuum. From the beginning, it has been marked by a lack of emphasis on research. Very little is known either about the effectiveness of its procedures or about the validity of its goals. In the last ten years, some good private research has been done in the field, and the literature about urban renewal is by now quite respectable. But little attempt has been made to apply what has been discovered to on-going programs. . . .

Thus, no one is sure what really is the impact of urban renewal projects on the over-all development of the cities in which they are located—to say nothing of the nature of their impact on surrounding metropolitan areas. Despite large federal expenditures over the last ten years and a great deal of organization and activity, no one is sure whether in the long run the result will be good or bad. The millions of dollars being spent for redevelopment are setting the pattern of metropolitan communities for years to come; yet the pattern may turn out to be far from ideal. Conducted, as the urban renewal program is, without necessary correlation with other federal programs in urban areas, it is entirely possible that the end product may be no improvement at all. The tragic thing is that no one seems concerned about finding the answer. . . .

The difficulty is that [a testing of urban renewal effectiveness] will probably not be taken, nor will any of the other recommendations made here and elsewhere be put to the test, without effective leadership. There is a pressing need in Washington for real leadership in urban renewal. . . . The fact is that urban blight is no longer a local problem. Washington has simply failed to wake up to the fact that this is no longer an agricultural country, but one composed chiefly of urban dwellers. The condition of the cities, in which the majority of American citizens work, live, and produce the bulk of the nation's economic wealth, is of grave and immediate concern to the federal government. The question of federalism and the distribution of powers between the nation and the states is really beside the point. Indeed, the point is that facts have made the theory irrelevant. The only issue today is whether the process of decay will be allowed to spread until any action is too late; or whether the federal government will accept its clear responsibility and act to make the objectives of the Housing Act of 1949 a reality. Only a determined leadership, based on an understanding of the real nature of urban renewal and of the defects of the present program, can translate those objectives into fact.

Public Housing, Isolation, and the Urban Underclass

JOHN F. BAUMAN, NORMAN P. HUMMON, AND EDWARD K. MULLER

The underclass is a timely issue. In the past decade at least five books and dozens of articles examining the subject have been published. Scholars define this inner-city population as physically and socially isolated. Individuals and families who experience sustained unemployment or may not even participate in the labor force, who may engage in criminal behavior, endure long-term poverty and are welfare dependent. These characteristics, moreover, are often associated with the large percentage of inner-city, minority families that are headed by women.

The debate over the causes of the underclass locates its origins in the 1960s. In his acclaimed *The Truly Disadvantaged,* William Julius Wilson distinguished today's underclass from post–World War II low-income black families, who lived in stable communities with strong social networks and little social disorganization. Indeed, many scholars, especially in the early 1970s, emphasized the black family as an adaptive institution that enabled ghetto residents to endure the depriving inner-city environment. They argued that historically in every generation the black family has been forced to contend against monumental social and economic barriers. In the face of these obstacles, black families have been resilient and have made necessary adaptations, including, for example, broadening kinship networks and reshaping male and female roles.

However, in our study of low-income black families living in the Richard Allen Homes, a large Philadelphia public housing project, we have evidence of a black population who, as early as the 1950s, displayed characteristics similar to the modern underclass. In the 1960s scholars and social commentators also described families in public housing whose ability to cope strained against the hardships of their ghetto existence. But these observers failed to recognize the importance of public housing policy itself, and the urban redevelopment program of

From John F. Bauman, Norman P. Hummon, and Edward K. Muller, "Public Housing, Isolation, and the Urban Underclass: Philadelphia's Richard Allen Homes, 1941–1965," *Journal of Urban History* 17 (May 1991), pp. 264–92. Copyright © 1991 Sage Publications, Inc. Reprinted by permission of the publisher.

which it was a part, as factors in this postwar era. They treated public housing projects merely as ghetto space, albeit federally designed space. In their conceptions these families confronted hardships common to all ghetto residents, including neighborhood segregation, labor market exclusion, inadequate education, and poor access to social services. We see postwar federal policy, particularly public housing and urban renewal policies, posing obstacles that intensified social isolation and impeded the adaptive strategies that had historically facilitated survival in the depriving world of the inner city.

The Low-Income Black Family in the Literature

It was not until the 1960s in the wake of the rediscovery of black urban poverty that psychologist Kenneth Clark's *Dark Ghettos,* and Assistant Secretary of Labor Daniel Patrick Moynihan's *The Negro Family* refocused scholarly attention on black life in the city and especially on the black family. If Clark's portrait of the socially stifling environment of the inner city, from which Moynihan borrowed, drew uniform praise, the young assistant secretary's call for government intervention in the black family attracted unmitigated controversy. . . . Moynihan's 1965 report expressly sought to explain why the civil rights victories of the late 1950s and 1960s would not be translated into black equality; why, that is, the 1964 civil rights legislation, the Manpower Training Act, and the Office of Equal Opportunity would not halt the breakup or diminish the number of black families on the welfare rolls. He asserted that the cumulative effect of historic discrimination (including the slavery-induced matriarchal family structure and the destructiveness of rapid urbanization) rendered the black family too impaired to seize the opportunities afforded by the civil rights victories. "The fundamental problem," he wrote, in 1965, "is that the Negro family in urban ghettos is crumbling." A middle class, Moynihan conceded, had saved itself, but the vast number of unskilled, poorly educated blacks had become enmeshed in a self-perpetuating cycle of poverty. Therefore, as early as 1965, Moynihan spotlighted the emergence of a black underclass, the same population that sociologists such as William Julius Wilson would rediscover in the 1980s.

. . . Following the lead of Kenneth Clark, Moynihan's report contained solid evidence about the state of the urban black family. He based his study on an analysis of 1960 census data that showed that blacks represented an increasingly large segment of the welfare population, that females headed 25 percent of black families, and that nearly a quarter of black babies were born out of wedlock. Therefore, despite gains during the 1950s in black employment, Moynihan revealed that the number of black female-headed families was rising ominously in tandem with black welfare dependency. He concluded that the black family was hopelessly entangled in a web of poverty. . . .

Moynihan's nod to the upwardly mobile black middle class notwithstanding, many scholars viewed his report as a scathing indictment of black families in general. Rather than producing a consensus on how to attack inner-city poverty as President Lyndon Baines Johnson had hoped, Moynihan's report on the black family stirred a decade of political and academic controversy. Not only were federal policies for achieving black equality at stake but also scholarly positions concerning the nature and history of the black family. Ethnologists and historians who wrote about the black family in the 1960s and early 1970s hardly disputed Moynihan's linkage of fatherlessness and deepening poverty. What they challenged was his conclusion that this represented a pathological condition rooted in twentieth-century urbanization and discriminatory employment, as well as in the ravages of slavery and post–Civil War Reconstruction. . . .

Elizabeth Herzog and Hylan Lewis denounced Moynihan's insinuation of the black family in a culture of poverty. Rather than being embedded in a dysfunctional culture, lower-class black family behavior, they argued, originated in the travail of poor people burdened by discrimination, joblessness, and low pay. According to Herzog and Lewis, the socioeconomic indicators that Moynihan had used to define the culture of poverty—poor employability, low wages, crowded living conditions, and poor education—defined poverty, not black culture. Moreover, they charged Moynihan with failing to recognize the great diversity of both incomes and life-styles among black families. When controlled for income, argued Herzog, black and white family structural difference largely disappeared. . . .

However, while rejecting his characterization of the black family as a "tangle of pathology," ethnographers of the 1960s seemed to concur with Moynihan that society had erected social and economic barriers to the attainment of middle-class status that many lower-class black families found increasingly impossible to surmount. Although viewing poverty as situational, not cultural, they saw the chronically poor internalizing lower-class behaviors that made dependency harder to overcome. This latter point of view was especially pronounced in the sociological writings of Lee Rainwater and Elliot Liebow. . . . Their studies described the form and operation of low-income black families as part of a subculture rooted in a depriving environment. In particular, this environment denied the black male the opportunity to perform effectively the crucial role of breadwinner. Liebow's ethnographic study of Washington, D.C., streetcorner men explored the world of inner-city black males whose low skills and pay foreclosed the kind of employment that would have enabled them to feed and clothe a family adequately. Work, marriage, fatherhood, even friendship, became occasions for failure, and this failure shaped their social interactions and behavior. . . . Rainwater, like . . . Liebow, and other Moynihan critics, rejected the idea of a black culture of poverty. Instead, they saw the black family adapting to historical discrimination and to a racially oppressive social and economic environment. But in this process, argued Rainwater, poor black families formed a worldview and set of behaviors that, while presenting a formidable obstacle, did not foreclose successful adaptation to the outside world. . . .

In a study of low-income young black women . . . Joyce Ladner forcefully stated the case for both the legitimacy and the viability of the black family. Employing what she called the "sociohistorical" perspective, Ladner charged that the black family had always endured the ravages of institutionalized racism that excluded blacks from full participation in social, economic, and political life. Blacks could not conform to social norms because society withheld from them the resources to accomplish basic material and social goals. In her *Tomorrow's Tomorrow,* Ladner dismissed middle-class family norms as irrelevant for blacks, thus ipso facto freeing the low-income black family from centuries of stigma. For Ladner . . . the black family was effective, resourceful, and resilient in the face of historic racism.

While ethnographers addressed Moynihan's assertion of a tangle of pathology, historians examined his theory that what he espied as black family defectiveness could be traced historically to slavery and urbanization. . . .

In the wake of the Great Depression, with black urbanization unabating and the rate of black joblessness and poverty appallingly high, [historian E. Franklin] Frazier questioned the very survivability of the urban low-income black family that he deemed too disorganized and demoralized to cope with modern city life. An assimilationist who feared that lower-class folkways impaired black progress, Frazier traced this flawed behavior historically to American Negro slavery that permitted only the loosest ties of sympathy between black family members and households. By casting the weak slave family adrift, even emancipation, insisted Frazier, proved a shattering experience. Nevertheless, despite being burdened by a loose familial structure, the black family weathered the serfdom of the Reconstruction era only to flounder following the great urban migration northward. Frazier blamed this perceived demoralization and breakup of the lower-class black family not only on a matriarchal family structure inherited from slavery but also on the economic discrimination blacks faced in the city.

Surmising that both Moynihan and Frazier had constructed their case for the pathological black family upon an untested assumption that slavery had demoralized the black family, in 1967 two historians, Lawrence Glasco and Herbert Gutman, set out to derive a more accurate picture of the black family. They theorized that if, as Frazier and Moynihan argued, slavery caused matrifocal black families, then such families should be visible in the census records of nineteenth-century cities. The two historians quantitatively assessed black families in nineteenth- and early twentieth-century Buffalo, New York. But, rather than broken families, they found that consistently for the years between 1855 and 1925 double-headed kin-related households prevailed among black families. Moreover, their research also disclosed strong evidence of lively black institutions, suggesting that contrary to the Frazier and Moynihan argument, urbanization had not destroyed the fabric of black social life.

Tantalized by the Buffalo findings, historians scoured nineteenth-century archival records in Boston and Philadelphia. Elizabeth Pleck, for example, looked at black households in nineteenth-century Boston and discovered that typical black families there in the 1880s included husband, wife, and children. . . . In their Philadelphia research, Frank Furstenberg, Theodore Hershberg, and John Modell pressed further the implications of Pleck's demographic findings. Comparing 1880 data on Philadelphia Irish, German, and African-American families, the authors found little variation in family composition; black families were slightly more extended and slightly more female headed. Therefore, the findings about nineteenth-century black Philadelphia, Buffalo, and Boston did not uphold Moynihan's and Frazier's slavery-specific hypothesis. Indeed, in the 1847–1880 era families of ex-slaves seemed more likely to be two-parent households. . . .

The historian's effort to vindicate the modern black family culminated in Gutman's highly acclaimed *Black Family in Slavery and Freedom.* Encompassing almost three centuries of black family history, 1620–1925, Gutman's opus concluded that the black family had survived both slavery and the initial process of urbanization intact. Despite the venality and malevolence of white slaveholders, slave husbands and wives acted often heroically to defend and preserve the bonds of marriage and family. Rather than causing disorganization, as Frazier contended, emancipation and the era of Reconstruction, in Gutman's view, confirmed the free black family's resilience and vitality. . . .

. . . James Borchert in *Alley Life in Washington* explored how the low-income black family functioned in the initial half of the twentieth century. Like Pleck, Furstenberg, Gutman, and Glasco, he also found little evidence that urban life spawned broken families and bred welfare dependency, rampant sexual promiscuity, and juvenile delinquency, as nineteenth-century reformers had charged . . . .

Borchert contended that black families molded rural folkways to the demands of urban living. He underscored the resiliency and adaptability that the poor black alley family displayed in forging strategies for survival amid the dire economic circumstances of low pay and high unemployment. . . . The "secret world" of the alley, argued Borchert, operated ideally as usable space, enabling dwellers to engage in cottage-type industries, fashion nurturing kinship systems, and in other ways support a viable community life. . . .

Social Change in the Richard Allen Homes

A quarter-century of scholarship has left the debate about the nature and origin of the black underclass unresolved. . . . During the years 1965–1990, from Moynihan to Rainwater, Ladner to Gutman and Borchert, scholars have wrestled with the issue of black culture versus the black situation in a racially oppressive socioeconomic system. Their studies either deplored the racist urban environment that compelled black families to shape a system of social norms different from those of the white middle class or celebrated the resiliency of the malleable black household. However, with the exception of those historians, such as Gutman, Pleck, and Hershberg, who sought to exorcise the curse of slavery, very few scholars of the urban black experience looked longitudinally at the forces molding the black family experience. None examined the critical period, 1945–1960, when heavy black urban migration, white suburbanization, the erosion of the urban industrial base, and the dual forces of urban renewal and public housing reshaped the physical and social contours of urban America.

Among the first cities to plan postwar urban redevelopment, Philadelphia as early as 1947 had targeted a sizable district north of downtown for large-scale renewal. This area of North Philadelphia was no newcomer to slum clearance. Several years earlier, in 1941, it had experienced demolition activity when it became the site for the building of the Richard Allen Homes, an impressive 1,324-unit human-scale housing complex for low-income black families.

Before clearance the site consisted of a maze of small streets, alleys, and ancient courts. The Richard Allen Homes, one of the original three housing projects built in Philadelphia following passage of the 1937 Housing Act, replaced this quiltwork of small businesses and residences with fifty-three three- and four-story, red and yellow brick apartment buildings arranged on eight quadrangles. In addition to the bright new housing, Richard Allen featured a community building, housing management offices, workshops, a nursery, an auditorium, and grassy courts planted with trees and shrubbery. Originally conceived in the 1930s as a way station, or community of opportunity for a temporarily submerged, but potentially upwardly mobile working class, the Richard Allen Homes like public housing projects across America welcomed applications for occupancy from hard-working, albeit low-income, two-parent families. Following a "neighborhood composition formula," Richard Allen was racially segregated.

World War II temporarily forced the Philadelphia Housing Authority to soften its rigid income limits for occupancy. Therefore, Richard Allen opened as housing for black war workers as much as homes for the poor. Indeed, the wartime environment at the project reflected the optimism of a working-class black community. . . .

The glow lingered two years after V-E Day, when a Philadelphia *Evening Bulletin* report praised Richard Allen as "a spic and span place so outstanding that the remainder of the city is extremely drab by comparison. What little trash [one sees there]," stated the article, "blows in from the outside, and the residents are justifiably proud of the appearance of the area."

However, only five years later the kudos and high expectations of the 1940s had vanished. The combination of housing authority tenant selection and occupancy policies, the 1947 federal directive forcing housing authorities nationally to purge from their projects households with incomes over the maximum allowable for continued occupancy, and regional economic forces, including a declining urban manufacturing base and the inception of urban redevelopment, produced a tenant population with a demographic and occupational profile much different from the wartime years.

Change in the demography of the Richard Allen Homes revealed itself most profoundly in family structure and size. In 1943, soon after the initial acceptance of tenants, couples headed approximately 70 percent of the Allen families. Almost half of these families had between three and four members; 40 percent had over five members. Committed to the way-station model of public housing (that is, a temporary shelter and moral environment for the uplifting of the submerged working class) and, therefore, to middle-class norms, management in the early postwar years (1945–1952) enforced a policy of admitting married couples. . . . The situation changed significantly over the next decade. Within five years only half of Allen households included a married couple, and by 1964 the percentage had dropped to under 40. A female headed 48 percent of Allen families that year.

Accompanying this increase in the number of female-headed families was a corresponding decrease in the size of Richard Allen households. While one- and two-person households accounted for barely 11 percent of the project population in 1943, two decades later they composed 28 percent, reflecting both an increase in female-headed families and the aging of the population.

These demographic changes corresponded to a pattern of steadily worsening employability among Richard Allen tenants, which emphasized diminished labor force participation and female rather than male employment. In wartime 80 per-

cent of Richard Allen Homes heads of households found good, stable employment in the booming Philadelphia job market. With the exception of the Korean
War years, the percentage of employed heads of households fell after 1945 to 60
percent in the 1960s. More ominously, the percentage of heads of household not
in the labor force doubled from about 11 percent in the 1940s to 23 percent in
1965. . . .

Tragically, as experienced in other large rust belt cities, the rate of black male
employment in Philadelphia's manufacturing, especially the skilled trades, plum-
meted in the wake of World War II. The Richard Allen data mirror the trend.
From a high of 54 percent in 1943, employment of Richard Allen workers in
manufacturing had slumped to 25 percent in the 1960s. . . . This precipitous
decline reflects especially the vacation of Richard Allen workers from
Philadelphia's metal-working industries. . . .

Likewise, an increasing number of Allen household heads labored in the retail, health, and other jobs of the city's growing service sector, a trend that attests
strongly to a changing urban employment structure. Similar to the garment and
needle trades, the service sector employed large numbers of women. . . . By the
1960s, over 60 percent of Allen breadwinners worked as maids in department
stores; as laundresses, orderlies, or aides in city hospitals; as matrons and teacher
helpers in city schools; or in other service trades. . . .

Therefore, by 1965 a clear pattern of project demography and employability
emerged in the Richard Allen Homes. From a place characterized in the 1940s
and early 1950s by working, two-parent families, Richard Allen became by the
1960s a place where women headed over 50 percent of Richard Allen homes, and
where nearly a quarter of all household heads were not in the labor force. This
change can in large part be attributed to weakening postwar employment opportunities for black males, which shattered the World War II illusion that
Philadelphia's black population had at last found a secure job niche in manufacturing. During this twenty-year period jobless or partially employed Richard
Allen males gradually disappeared from the labor force to be replaced as primary
breadwinners by females. Concomitantly, more and more Allen workers occupied the low-paid service sector of the economy. These facts belied the touted
way-station role of public housing and pointed instead to public housing projects,
such as the Richard Allen Homes, as unwitting nurseries of an embryonic underclass. Indeed, rather than bustling havens of opportunity for the suppressed working class, as originally conceived, after 1952 black housing projects such as
Richard Allen increasingly harbored families where breadwinners, who were
often underemployed or jobless, barely survived on abysmally low paychecks or
public assistance.

Making Postindustrial North Philadelphia

These portentous changes in project demography and employability can be understood by looking at both Philadelphia's postwar economy and the impact of
urban renewal and housing policy. One of the most striking facts was the extraordinary wartime and postwar growth of the city's black population, especially the

increase of the black population in North Philadelphia. Although by the 1970s the North Philadelphia black population had begun to decline, an inner-city ghetto had emerged there amid the decay of a deindustrializing economy.

During the 1940s Philadelphia's citywide black population rose by 125,161, a 50 percent increase. It continued to grow over the next two decades, while the city's total population declined by 123,000. Thus, by 1970 blacks composed fully one-third of Philadelphia's inhabitants. In North Philadelphia the black population became steadily more concentrated in a ghetto. . . .

At the same time that the black population was expanding, the postindustrial economic transformation was displacing traditional central city goods production and distribution activities with corporate headquarters and expanded university, legal, managerial, and investment banking functions. Many of the old industries moved to more spacious locations outside the city, while obsolete or noncompetitive industries disappeared altogether. . . .

North Philadelphia in particular felt the full brunt of the city's eroding traditional economic base. In fact, between 1928 and 1972 one study has estimated that the area lost between 20,000 and 50,000 manufacturing jobs. Not surprisingly, the number of North Philadelphians who reported employment declined by a half between 1950 and 1970, from over 143,000 to under 72,000 in 1970. Although total population declined during the same period, the ratio of employment to population also declined from 38 percent to 29 percent. . . .

Therefore, during the 1950s North Philadelphia experienced an ominous transformation. While the white population declined precipitously and the black population rose by almost a third, the city's manufacturing economy was disintegrating. Even though urban renewal in North Philadelphia spurred a black population decline in the 1960s, employment dropped even faster. Where once a white ethnic population built communities around thriving textile mills and metal manufactories, blacks now competed for a dwindling number of low-paying jobs in manufacturing and the service sector.

As elsewhere in America, urban renewal disproportionately affected the inner city's growing black population by clearing away thousands of low-rent units without providing sufficient replacement housing, or eradicating the patterns of residential segregation. North Philadelphia experienced the social cost of urban renewal. As early as 1939, Federal Housing Administration property assessors and local bank officials spotlighted it as a blighted area ripe for renewal. . . . But, while urban renewal between 1950 and 1965 scored some early successes, . . . large-scale demolition proved catastrophic for the neighborhood structure of the area. . . . [O]ver 6,250 families and single persons were dislocated, and between 1950 and 1970 the number of dwelling units in North Philadelphia declined from almost 114,000 units to under 90,000.

Urban renewal cleared businesses as well as residential structures. For example, during two years, 1962–63, 633 small laundries, repair shops, groceries, garages, ice yards, bakeries, junk shops, and other small businesses, which once dotted the North Philadelphia streetscape, vanished into rubble. . . . Renewal and code enforcement, along with the flight of business and industry, were eroding the already frail economy of these poor black communities.

While numerous businesses and residential structures disappeared from

North Philadelphia, the people did not. Over 90 percent of displaced families and single persons reportedly moved back into North Philadelphia, ordinarily within a mile of their demolished residences. Contemporary reports show that blacks composed two-thirds of the families and single persons displaced from North Philadelphia sites between 1958 and 1962. Most of these dislocated households were economically disadvantaged. Over 60 percent of these cases had annual incomes under $3,000, a third were either divorced, widowed, or separated, while 19 percent were single. A 1963–1964 study of 780 cases of displacement found almost half of these households dependent on welfare, child support, or pensions. Thirty-eight percent of the household heads were not in the labor force; 39 percent of the households were headed by a female. These displaced households, constrained by poor employability, low incomes, non-nuclear-family structures, and discrimination, formed part of the expanding pool of North Philadelphia families seeking shelter in places such as Richard Allen.

Public Housing and the Black Family

Between 1952 and 1970 uprooted low-income black families more and more frequently found refuge in public housing. However, housing policy created conditions in the projects that contrasted invidiously with the malleable world of the alley described by James Borchert. While before World War II these alley places facilitated adaptation to the harsh urban environment, after World War II public housing would systematically thwart it. . . .

Borchert argued that in the cloistered alley world common to twentieth-century Philadelphia and Washington, D.C., rural black migrants, like the transplanted European peasantry, adapted traditional rural culture and work routines to overcome limited economic opportunities and overcrowded living quarters. Historically, urban reformers had denounced tenement houses bulging with kin as socially disorganizing. However, the same reformers, explained Borchert, were just as fearful that urban life was destroying migrant family life, a process they saw beginning with the change from the extended to the nuclear family. Borchert argued that such alley families only appeared nuclear to reformers. In reality, observed Borchert, the situation was more complex. While many families were nuclear, others were either extended or augmented by both actual or fictive kin, as well as by boarders and even the children of hapless neighbors. Although the presence of outsiders in families could be seriously disruptive, expanded households often enabled economically embattled families to endure hardships while effectively performing vital family functions, such as nurturant socialization and the provision of adequate food, shelter, and member emotional support. Aunts, uncles, boarders, or even unwed fathers living within the household, supplemented household income, attended to young children, and helped with daily chores.

Public housing policymakers, on the other hand, described the ideal tenant family as two-parent without the cluster of kin who crowded the tiny ramshackle houses of urban courts and alleys. Project managers required prospective tenants to present a certificate as evidence of marriage and disallowed aunts, uncles, cousins, or other extended kin from even long stays in the apartments. The alley dwellings described by Borchert teemed with family members, including the off-spring of households temporarily incapable of caring for them. The overcrowding that resulted was anathema to nineteenth- and early twentieth-century middle-class reformers. So it was this extended family, and this familial overcrowding so vital to the socialization process and economic survival of alley households, that was actively discouraged in public housing. . . .

Paradoxically, public housing policymakers intended to create a strong community structure. In fact the ideological roots of American public housing can be traced in large part to the communitarianism of the 1920s. . . . However, post–World War II housing management policies, which enforced the eviction of tenants with over-maximum incomes, closely monitored tenant behavior, and even conducted unannounced inspections of tenant units to check on housekeeping practices or illegal residents, undermined the achievement of community. Rather than controlling their environment, public-housing tenants faced, and sometimes capitulated to, a host of regulations resisted only at the cost of eviction. Under management orders flower gardens were to be planted on time; hallways were to be swept daily. Required to disclose annually every penny of their income, spiteful tenants anonymously informed on neighbors suspected of concealing resources. . . . Within such an oppressive and socially distrustful environment, neither cooperation nor community leadership could endure for long before withering for want of nourishment. . . .

Finally, public housing policy dismantled the frail, but vital, structure of opportunity that had facilitated survival of families in the ghettos. . . . Borchert found that the black alley dwellers often successfully fashioned entrepreneurial strategies to cope with economic hardship. They kept boarders, repaired second-hand furniture for resale, took in laundry, and collected junk for sale to salvagers. Clandestine and illegal operations such as bootlegging, prostitution, and gambling also contributed to the alley economy.

However, management forbade the use of project apartments and grounds for commercial purposes. In the battle to maintain middle-class decorum, it would hardly permit the storage on the premises of junk or the hanging out to dry of excessive loads of laundry. Naturally, management banned all forms of vice, prostitution, numbers games, and even gambling for pennies. Nor were tenants allowed to have boarders, regarded as one of the most universally employed working-class strategies to make ends meet.

Therefore, while black migrants flooded into North Philadelphia, manufacturing, together with the white middle class fled, urban renewal demolished whole blocks of aging alley housing, and the contours of a new, more formidable urban environment appeared. Public housing made up an important part of this new environment, especially for the low-skilled, low-income black family. It was not the architecture or design of these housing megaliths that made them in Lee Rainwater's words fearful and forbidding places. After all, Philadelphia's Richard Allen Homes was a low-rise project whose brick design was not that unsympathetic to the carpet of two- and three-story brick houses covering the rest of North Philadelphia. Rather it was . . . the insensitivity of postwar housing policymakers to the uses and potential of the urban community, a failure to understand the need for malleable community structures that people could adapt to their social, political, and economic requirements.

Public Housing, Isolation, and the Underclass

The world that did evolve at the Richard Allen Homes in the postwar era has significance for illuminating the current debate about the underclass. For one, it rolls back the chronological boundaries of the debate by a full decade, from the early 1960s to the early 1950s. Current debate, as outlined earlier, has focused on the mid 1960s, when Moynihan conceived the "tangle of pathology" and when the boom in federal programs . . . spawned an insidious nexus between family assistance and family dissolution. . . . According to Wilson, federal programs of that period guaranteeing affirmative action in hiring, and prohibiting discrimination in housing, engendered the upsurge of the black middle class and the consequent isolation of an underclass in the black ghetto lacking the bulwark of an economically integrated community to provide direction and support.

But public housing had produced evidence of that phenomenon as early as 1952 at the Richard Allen Homes. By the early 1960s scholars failed to distinguish public housing from black housing and the black community in general. The housing projects in effect became a convenient surrogate for the black ghetto. These scholars neither underscored the uniqueness of public housing as a creature of public policy nor explained . . . that many black families outside public housing successfully utilized time-honored family strategies to cope with poverty and discrimination.

Public housing did not singularly create a black underclass. However, we do argue that midway through the postwar era it functioned to isolate, socially and spatially, a growing segment of the black poor whose manifold disadvantages— "low aspirations, poor education, family instability, illegitimacy, unemployment, crime, drug addiction and alcoholism, frequent illness"—eventually became hallmarks of the underclass.

The black poor have historically lived in American central cities and in physical proximity to both the black middle class and to many white ethnics. While the social interaction among these groups, especially white and black, was often fragmentary, it existed, nevertheless, in varying degrees. However, by the late 1950s social, political, and economic forces were unraveling the fabric of inner-city neighborhoods such as North Philadelphia. An increasing proportion of low-income black families were rendered unemployable and dependent, and routine interaction with the wider urban community diminished. Urban renewal and public housing helped shape the new environment of the evolving postwar ghetto.

Public housing in the 1950s, as we have argued, fostered a condition of isolation analogous to the process of isolation described by Wilson. Not only was it frequently concentrated in the black ghetto, but its tenant selection and retention policies had the unintended consequence of concentrating low-income black families away from the more socially and economically diverse black community surrounding it. Furthermore, its way-station mission foreclosed the use of traditional family strategies for economic survival. Therefore, because it left residents unable to include kin within the project household, or to use their residences for enterprising purposes . . . public housing, together with urban renewal and regional economic decline, became deeply implicated in the processes of underclass isolation and alienation that inexorably overwhelmed sections of the inner city after the mid 1960s.

※ F U R T H E R   R E A D I N G

Carl Abbott, *Urban America in the Modern Age, 1920 to the Present* (1987)

Leo Adde, *New Cities: The Anatomy of Urban Renewal* (1969)

Martin Anderson, *The Federal Bulldozer: A Critical Analysis of Urban Renewal, 1949–1962* (1964)

John F. Bauman, *Public Housing, Race and Renewal: Urban Planning in Philadelphia. 1920–1974* (1987)

Jewel Belush and Murray Hausknecht, eds., *Urban Renewal: People, Politics, and Planning* (1967)

Devereux Bowly, Jr., *The Poorhouse: Subsidized Housing in Chicago, 1895–1976* (1978)

Robert Caro, *The Power Broker: Robert Moses and the Fall of New York* (1974)

William W. Cutler III and Howard Gilette, Jr., eds., *The Divided Metropolis: Social and Spatial Dimensions of Philadelphia* (1980)

Richard O. Davies, *Housing During the Truman Administration* (1966)

Lawrence M. Friedman, *Government and Slum Housing: A Century of Frustration* (1968)

Philip Funigiello, Jr., *The Challenge of Urban Liberalism: Federal-City Relations During World War II* (1978)

Herbert Gans, *The Urban Villagers: Group and Class in the Life of Italian-Americans* (1962)

Mark I. Gelfand, *A Nation of Cities: The Federal Government and Urban America, 1933–1965* (1975)

Scott Greer, *Urban Renewal and Urban Cities* (1965)

Edward Haas, *De Lesseps S. Morrison and the Image of Reform: New Orleans Politics, 1946–1961* (1974)

Arnold Hirsch, *Making the Second Ghetto: Race and Housing in Chicago, 1940–1960* (1983)

Anthony Jackson, *A Place Called Home: A History of Low-Cost Housing in Manhattan* (1976)

Roger W. Lotchin, ed., *The Martial Metropolis: U.S. Cities in War and Peace* (1984)

John H. Mollenkopf, *The Contested City* (1983)

Mark Rose, *Interstate: Express Highway Politics, 1939–1989* (1990)

Peter Rossi and Robert Dentler, *The Politics of Urban Renewal* (1961)

Christopher Silver, *Twentieth-Century Richmond: Planning, Politics and Race* (1984)

Clarence Stone, *Economic Growth and Neighborhood Discontent: System Bias in the Urban Renewal Program of Atlanta* (1976)

Jon C. Teaford, *The Twentieth-Century American City: Problems, Promise and Reality* (1986)

James Q. Wilson, ed., *Urban Renewal: The Record and the Controversy* (1965)

Frederick W. Wirt, *Power and the City* (1975)

CHAPTER 13

Political, Economic,
and Spatial Factors in
the Postindustrial City

✖

In the past two decades, several forces of national significance have buffeted the economic fortunes of U.S. cities. In the 1970s and early 1980s, outmoded factories, high taxes, high labor costs, an inhospitable climate, and foreign competition brought about a decline in the old industrial cities of the Northeast and Midwest. At the same time, low taxes, low labor costs, an attractive climate (made especially comfortable by air conditioning), and federal support of defense and aerospace industries fueled explosive urban growth in the Sunbelt, the region stretching across the southern and southwestern tier of states. By the 1980s, however, Sunbelt cities were experiencing their own economic problems, caused in part by overexpansion and the end of the energy boom. These trends and others—notably, continuing suburbanization and the flight of middle- and upper-class people from the central cities—left cities across the country with declining economies, aging neighborhoods, decaying downtowns, and rising poverty.

Since the establishment of urban renewal and redevelopment in the 1940s and 1950s, city officials and federal policymakers have struggled to revitalize the economy of American cities. Schemes for joint efforts between private and public interests, such as the renaissance of Pittsburgh in the 1950s, the gentrification of inner-city neighborhoods by middle-class investors in the 1970s, and the special commercial and restoration projects inspired by planner James Rouse in the 1970s and 1980s, existed simultaneously with programs involving stronger government contribution, such as Model Cities in the 1960s, revenue sharing in the 1970s, and block grants in the 1970s and 1980s.

In 1981 Ronald Reagan became president and began a systematic effort to restore more responsibility to private enterprise and to reduce federal expenditures for subsidies to various urban-related programs. Reagan believed that tax cuts and reduced government expenditures would revive the national economy and that the effects would trickle down to cities and urban dwellers. His administration drastically cut or eliminated budgets for specific grant programs, public housing, job training, and other forms of federal assistance. Instead, Reagan and his supporters promoted the concept of the urban enterprise zone and exhorted—sometimes with tax credits— private businesses voluntarily to invest in urban redevelopment. When George Bush succeeded Reagan in 1989, he continued his predecessor's policies. The election of Democrat Bill Clinton in 1992, however, presaged a major shift in urban affairs. Whether Clinton and the Democrats can make good on a range of promises involving urban life remains to be seen.

Throughout the recent past, a flood of conferences, books, articles, speeches, projects, and policy statements has explored ways in which to "save" American cities. What has worked and what has not? What factors must be considered in designing urban policy? What impact will the shift from Republican presidents to a Democratic one make on urban affairs? Are our cities worth saving? Why or why not?

✕ D O C U M E N T S

The six documents in this chapter focus on economic patterns in recent urban development, as well as programs to deal with the needs of urban dwellers. The first selection, a report from the U.S. Bureau of Labor Statistics, analyzes government data and tries to explain the reasons for one of the most notable geographical and economic trends affecting metropolitan areas in the past quarter-century: the growth of the Sunbelt and the parallel decline of the Frostbelt. The article is especially provocative because, without frequent references to urban issues, it nevertheless includes various kinds of information that can be examined for their urban implications. The second document, from an article in a southern business magazine, gives a southern perspective on some of the issues of Sunbelt-Snowbelt competition, particularly over federal funds. It includes a discussion of how almost all federal funding programs in the 1970s had some relationship to urban growth and problems. The third document contains excerpts from an address given by planner and developer James Rouse, one of the most dynamic and influential advocates of private sector–public sector joint efforts to revitalize cities economically. Rouse's speech reveals the optimism that still makes him such an inspiration to those who believe that local businesses can succeed in revitalizing cities. The fourth document comprises excerpts from testimony given before a congressional committee by Jack Kemp, the Bush administration's secretary of housing and urban development. As a member of the House of Representatives prior to serving as HUD secretary, Kemp strongly advocated enterprise zones, a means of rejuvenating cities economically by using federal, state, and local government subsidies to encourage businesses to locate in depressed inner-city areas. Once George Bush was elected president and Kemp became secretary, enterprise zones were made the keystone of the administration's urban policy. The fifth document also includes testimony before Congress; it is given by a planning official from Norwalk, Connecticut, who describes his city's positive experiences with enterprise zones. The final document excerpts parts of the 1992 Democratic party platform, the policy statement on which Bill Clinton ran for president, and presents the issues that Clinton and his party promised to address, along with various policy proposals.

Moving to the Sun: Job Growth
in the Sunbelt (1968–1978), 1980

Interregional migration has been one of the dominant forces associated with economic progress in the United States. At the heart of the great interregional migration in this country has always been the search for economic advantage. This was true whether the search was made by the family moving to Ohio to farm in the 1800s, the entrepreneur leaving New York to drill for oil in Texas in 1900, or the children of poor blacks who left the South to work in northern factories during the 1940s.

The most recent major population shift also has had the search for financial reward as its principal catalyst and sustainer. But the causes and repercussions of the movement towards the sun—from the "industrial heartland" of the North to the South and West—go beyond economics. Many have moved for reasons that traditional human capital theory does not explain: for "quality of life" reasons. And the growth and development of the sunbelt States has both created and been nurtured by a shift in regional political power. The net result of these factors— economic, sociological, and political—has been a population and employment boom in the South and West, largely at the expense of the North Central and Northeast regions. . . .

Trends in industry employment for the Nation as a whole have been fairly well documented. . . . Not unexpectedly, the big losers [between 1968 and 1978] were agriculture, where almost half a million jobs were lost, and manufacturing, which added only 700,000 during a period when employment grew by almost 20 million. Industries with the fastest rates of growth were all outside of the goods-producing sector. Services experienced by far the most impressive rate of growth—from 12 percent of total employment to 15 percent. Medical and hospital services led the performance of this industry group, almost doubling its proportion of total employment. Other service industries also posted very strong gains, most notably "other" professional, business and repair, and entertainment and recreational services. Wholesale and retail trade, finance, insurance and real estate, and government all posted relative employment gains, with the last concentrated in State and local jurisdictions. . . .

All regions experienced absolute employment gains over the decade. But . . . the Northeast region experienced a large decline in its share of total employment, from 25 to 22 percent, reflecting relative reduction in virtually all of the major industry groups. The North Central region also experienced relative job losses; the South and West posted strong gains in overall employment as well as in most industries. . . .

The movement of firms from the industrial North to the sunbelt has been less important to regional employment growth than widely thought. Several studies have shown that, in the South, creation of new firms and expansion of existing

---

From "Moving to the Sun: Regional Job Growth, 1968–1978" by Philip L. Rones, in U. S. Bureau of Labor Statistics, *Monthly Labor Review* 103 (March 1980), excerpts from pp. 12–19. Reprinted by permission.

firms tend to be the dominant causes of employment growth. In the North, the closure of existing firms tends to be of primary importance. . . .

The allocation of Federal funds has been one of the most important factors contributing to economic development in both the South and West. Most notably, defense spending patterns over the last several decades have intensified the shift of both population and manufacturing out of the Northeast and North Central regions and into the South and West. This can be seen most dramatically from data on military prime contract awards. From 1951 to 1976, the South increased its share of these awards from 11 to 25 percent of the national total; the West's increase was just as dramatic, from 16 to 31 percent. . . .

These data reflect, to a large extent, changing defense requirements. Aerospace and other high technology industries have developed largely in California and in several areas of the South. The growing dependence on high technology industries for defense needs has led to the channeling of funds to these areas. Similarly, funds for the space program have gone largely to both the South and West: with program headquarters in Houston; the launching station in Cape Canaveral; the rocket center in Huntsville, Alabama; and the research arm in California. Research and development supported by defense and space program funds have led to many technological advances that have become commercially successful. Thus, the areas and firms that benefited from such Federal funds have become the manufacturing centers for products such as computers, calculators, semiconductors, scientific instruments, and many others.

Considerable publicity has been focused on the transfer of manufacturing jobs out of the older industrial area of the North and into the South and West. But if manufacturing employment were held constant, the relative job growth of the four regions would be affected only slightly. In general, manufacturing has been losing its dominance as an employer. Hence, although its relative demise is a key to the slow growth rate in the Northeast, manufacturing employment can only be seen as a relatively small part of the economic expansion of the South and West.

The activities of the service-producing sector are primarily concerned with local consumption. The rise of the trade and service industries in the South and West, for instance, is largely the result of population shifts to these areas; changes in employment in retail trade, as one might expect, closely matches the regional shift in total employment. . . .

Although construction is not a service, it, too, is an industry where demand is largely dependent on population pressures. It is, in fact, the industry that had the greatest relative decline in the Northeast and growth in the West; construction employment shifted less dramatically out of the North Central region and into the South. In both the South and West, expansion of the construction work force has resulted from rapid urban and suburban development, construction of interstate highways, as well as the need for industrial structures that accompanied growth in manufacturing. . . .

The factors that lead to an individual's decision to move to a new region certainly overlap with those that cause a business to either relocate or to expand in one area instead of another. Lower personal income taxes or good weather, for instance, might influence the decisions of both individuals and businesses to relocate. In fact, the two decisions are partly a function of each other; businesses may move to utilize a growing labor pool, and people may move to take advantage of new business opportunities. However, it may be useful to look at the relative employment growth in the South and West from the individual's (or family's) perspective, separate from the firm's perspective. The following discussion should be viewed as a summary only, borrowing from the extensive literature on interregional migration patterns.

As the rate of increase in total population (the excess of births over deaths) declined in recent years, interregional migration accounted for an increasing share of population change, particularly in the South. In fact, during 1970–75, net migration accounted for about half of the population gain in both the South and West. In the previous 5-year period, migration accounted for only about 12 percent of the population rise in the South; the West, on the other hand, experienced a strong inmigration throughout the postwar period. During 1968–78, the four major regions experienced the following net migration: Northeast (−2,284,000); North Central (−2,034,000); South (2,655,000); and West (1,763,000). . . .

On average, regional migrants (and migrants in general) tend to be better educated than the nonmigrants at both the place of origin and destination. Several hypotheses have been proposed to explain the relationship between migration and education: persons in professional occupations respond to a geographically broader job market than do those in blue-collar and service occupations; educated persons are better at obtaining and processing job market information and, thus, are better able to deal with economic disequilibria; the effects of distance tend to decline with higher levels of education; and investment in occupation-specific training often precludes occupational mobility as a method of increasing income, making geographic mobility more attractive. . . .

Age is another determinant of the propensity to move between States or regions. The highest rate of migration occurs at age 23, with rates steadily declining as persons age. (The propensity to migrate appears *not* to increase among the oldest age groups, despite the increased mobility often associated with retirement.) When migration is seen solely as an economic decision, the relationship between age and migration becomes clearer. A younger person has more time to maximize the benefits of migration. The costs of moving (actual moving expenses, loss of seniority or pension coverage, and so on) become more difficult to recoup the older the person becomes. And, certainly, the younger person faces less cost in moving to begin with—he or she is less likely to have a family, accumulated possessions, and, of course, job-related costs. It is not coincidental, then, that the peak migration age corresponds closely to the usual age of graduation from college. The migration of the young, which often follows an investment in human capital, is generally governed by the search for employment and is constrained by the fewest number of costs, both economic and personal. . . .

Economic factors are the most critical to the migration decision. Certainly the differences in propensity to migrate based on age and education are strongly linked to economic considerations. Long and Kristen Hansen, using results from the 1974, 1975, and 1976 Annual Housing Surveys, found that 59 percent of all interstate migrants cited job-related factors as their major reason for moving, when only their major reason could be reported. These job-related factors included job transfer, new job, looking for work, entering or leaving [the] Armed

Forces, and others. Although these results emphasize the importance of employment factors in the decision to move, they also demonstrate, as the authors note, that economic reasons fail to account for the movement of a sizable proportion of the population. . . .

If almost 60 percent of interstate migrants cited job-related factors as their major reason for moving, then, of course, 2 out of 5 persons moved principally for noneconomic reasons. . . .

Family considerations appear to be important to a sizable group of interregional migrants. Almost 2 out of 5 women who head households cited family factors as their primary reason for moving. Also, of interstate movers age 55 and over, one-third cited family reasons; 15 percent or less of the younger groups did so. Those moving for family reasons (whether females or males) were often return migrants. The South, which had a net outmigration until the late 1960s, most likely has received the largest share. In fact, it was the only region to have a net inflow of persons who cited family factors as their main reason for moving.

Climate is also an important noneconomic factor in the migration decision. . . . [T]he South and West have been net gainers among persons who move primarily because of a desire to change climate. Interestingly, in absolute numbers, more young persons (age 20–34) move for reasons of climate than do those age 55 and older.

Long and Hansen propose that people are becoming increasingly able to assign a high priority to environmental quality in deciding where they live. Some of the causal factors include smaller families and more single-person households and households comprising unrelated persons (large families and the presence of school-age children tend to impede migration). Also, in some cases, wives who work outside the home—whose numbers are growing rapidly—may give their husbands greater flexibility to choose their place of residence according to criteria other than maximization of his income (although, certainly, a wife's career may impede other families from moving). . . .

Regional growth and decline occur not only because of changes in comparative advantage between regions but also as a result of public policy, of which defense expenditures, mentioned earlier, are a primary example. Much of the regional impact of Federal policy, for example, results from programs and policies that are largely unrelated to regional development. Defense policies probably did more for recent economic growth in the West than did any other factor. Science and research policies also have resulted in providing economic advantage to selected regions. Federal welfare policy, energy policy, transportation and water resources policy, and virtually all Federal programs have definite regional impacts.

Thus, the migration of population and employment is much more than a demographic curiosity. With recent migration have come changes in the locus of both economic and political power, and a shift of concern from the future of the South to that of the North. The problem of urban decline in the northern industrial areas in the 1970s is just as compelling an issue as were the problems of poverty and economic backwardness in the rural South which have been a national concern throughout much of this century. To address adequately the regional imbalances in growth and development, policymakers must understand not only the economic, but also the personal or sociological factors that have resulted in this imbalance.

The South Responds to Attempts
to Diminish Sunbelt Influence, 1981

Alistair Dunn, a nattily dressed Scotsman, stood beside a beaming George Busbee one Thursday in August as Georgia's governor announced the location of yet another new business in the state. Thornwood Investments Limited, of which Mr. Dunn is the managing director, had chosen Atlanta as the headquarters for its fleet management subsidiary, Thornwood Leasing International, Inc. The governor said the Scottish firm "chose the Sun Belt region for this operation because of the South's economic strength and growth potential."

"We looked at Boston," Mr. Dunn said later. "The Northeast had natural attractions; it is much nearer Scotland, for example. But the Northeast is already highly developed. Here [Atlanta] the people were outgoing and more receptive to new business. We supply services and businesses that tend to be in a growth stage. Atlanta has a momentum in business, and our studies on the best location showed there were really no rivals at all."

. . . Thornwood's Southern decision is one more chapter in what has become a well-worn book for businesspeople and political leaders who have deep-pocket stakes in the economies of the aging North, especially in areas such as Boston, Detroit, Chicago, Cleveland, New York, Providence, and Philadelphia. Since 1970, the South had increased its share of the nation's total employment in every Bureau of Labor Statistics category except mining. The region had reaped over eight million new jobs, including healthy gains in manufacturing, the service industries, wholesale and retail trades and all levels of government. . . . Politicians and officials from the so-called Snow Belt . . . have grown jealous watching businesses sprout in the fertile business climate of the Sun Belt. At home, they are looking at idle factories, vacant storefronts and shabby, abandoned housing. They are comparing the anemic census of the region to the lusty growth of the Old South states and points West. Because of all this, they have, in effect, declared regional war, and the battlefield is the United States Congress.

Five years ago, Snow Belt representatives became fed up with seeing their constituents fleeing burdensome local taxes and gutters full of winter slush. That spring, they fired the first verbal shot in what has become known as the Second Civil War, a phrase coined by *Business Week* magazine in a special report that May. By September 1976, congresspeople from the Northeast and Midwest organized their own caucus confederacy to stop the flow of federal funds that for decades had been furnished into the South to help improve the region's economic standards which, since the first Civil War, had been marked by widespread poverty and a lack of economic development. This Yankee caucus called themselves the Northeast-Midwest Economic Advancement Coalition (NMEAC) and boasted 218 members from both parties, a significant representation of the 435-member Congress.

From "The Second Civil War" by Nick Taylor, *Business Atlanta* 10 (November 1981), excerpts from pp. 38–42. Reprinted by permission of *Business Atlanta*.

Rep. Michael J. Harrington, a Massachusetts Democrat, was credited with the NMEAC idea. He contended that the industrial states from the Northeast to the Great Lakes paid billions more in federal taxes than they got back from the government. He said, "Despite their growing need for relief, the industrialized states of the Northeast and Midwest continue to be called upon to finance the economic growth of other regions of the country.". . .

Southern congressmen were slow to pick up the latest Yankee gauntlet; therefore, retaliation fell to the Southern governors. . . . At its 1977 meeting, the Southern Governor's Conference set up the Southern Growth Policies Board, a research board funded by the member states dedicated to nosing out the economic effects of their Yankee adversaries, particularly in Congress.

What the Yankees were up to, the Southern Growth Policies Board concluded after some study, was an irreversible plan to revise the formula by which federal grant monies flow to the states. Instead of using poverty and growth potential as means of targeting federal funds, the Northeast Midwest Coalition wanted to recognize such factors as housing built before 1940 and the number of people on welfare. Its first target was Community Development Block Grants. Charging that the distribution formula favored new growing cities (like Atlanta, Birmingham, Columbia, Jackson, et al.), NMEAC successfully steered grants to the older cities of the Northeast and Midwest by adding a provision to the block grants act that would insure federal infusions of money to cities it believed needed rebuilding as badly as some Southern cities needed rebuilding. It meant an additional $412 million in community development grant funds for coalition states.

The response of the Southern governors to the game plan was predictably angry. Led by Governor Busbee, then Chairman-elect of the Southern Governor's Conference, the governor said, in effect, "Hell, No!" Mr. Busbee, in fact, met with the Yankee coalition's members in 1978 and warned that Southern congressmen would "do unto you what we perceive you are trying to do unto us." . . .

Since 1978, both sides have fought mainly rhetorical battles, accusing each other of eroding their region's economic base. A few meaningful skirmishes came and went with only the Northern coalition standing firm with its block grant victory under their belts. But during the summer of 1981, the coalition struck again and this time the Sun Belters were not only ready, but also spawned their first official hero of the conflict—Georgia's Fifth District representative Wyche Fowler. The issue was a cap to be placed on federal welfare funds, which go to states based on their average per capita income—the lower the income, the higher the federal contribution to welfare and vice versa. Southern states, where incomes have traditionally lagged behind, get a higher percentage of federal money. Georgia, for example, gets about two-thirds of the money it spends for welfare from Uncle Sam; Snow Belt representatives wanted to cut off the federal share at 57%.

The cap would have cost the Southern states $100 million in money earmarked for Aid to Families with Dependent Children. It would have cost Georgia alone $10.6 million, and a similar move to cap Medicaid funds would have cost Georgia another $62.3 million. Mr. Fowler halted the move in the Ways and Means Committee and won a citation for "distinguished and outstanding service to the Sun Belt states." . . .

President Franklin D. Roosevelt in 1938, 73 years after Appomattox, declared the South "the nation's number one economic problem." To help solve the problem, he began engineering a plethora of New Deal programs that began the southward flow of federal dollars the Northeast-Midwest Congressional coalition is now attempting to reverse.

"As long as the migration of industry and population was gradual from a relatively rich Northeast to what was a relatively impoverished South and Southwest, it helped to unify the nation," said *Business Week* in its 1976 report. "But within the past five years, the process has burst beyond the bounds that can be accommodated by existing political institutions." Between 1960 and 1975, manufacturing employment dropped 9% in New England and nearly 14% in New York, New Jersey and Pennsylvania, while increasing 43% in the Southeast and 67% in the Southwest. Real personal income rose 114% in the Southeast, while in New England and the Northeast income grew at a rate of 10 to 20 points below the national average of 77.5%.

The *National Journal*, a Washington, D.C., weekly focusing on trends in government, added fuel to the fire by reporting in June of 1976 that the Northeast and Great Lakes states had paid nearly $29 billion more in federal taxes the previous year than they received in return from the government. At the same time, according to the magazine, Southern states had a payment surplus of $11.5 billion. Politicians from the industrial states chose to ignore the magazine's caveat that "The inequities are almost entirely accidental." Waving the red shirt of regional indignity, the Snow Belt defenders birthed the NMEAC and began brandishing the power of their votes like so many cavalry swords.

Rep. Henry D. Reuss, a Wisconsin Democrat and chairman of the House Committee on Banking, Currency and Housing, said at the time, "Our task will be to see that the deterioration of the economic position of 16 states from Maine to Iowa is ameliorated." In the five years since, however, the rush to the Sun Belt has continued. The population shift has also eroded the coalition's voting strength. Andy Lang estimates congressional reapportionment will cost the coalition 16 or 17 votes in the Congress after the dust of the 1981 reapportionment settles. . . .

Gov. Busbee, Rep. Fowler and others, however, fret that the pending loss of seats has instead spurred a last-minute effort by the Northeast-Midwest representatives, aimed at bringing immediate parity, rather than continuing the battle with few forces over a period of years. . . . "I imagine that does give some incentive to their cause," says Gov. Busbee. "They felt (that since) we would be gaining in political strength . . . they would make one big push to write in these formulas that grossly discriminate against the Sun Belt."

Last summer, the Southern Growth Political Board identified "seven techniques which may be used in targeting federal funds away from the South." E. Blaine Liner, the board's executive director, met with Southern congressmen on June 18 and outlined the danger areas, including:

—Defining government assistance need, according to slow growth rates, rather than low-income population; a goal basically accomplished in the 1977 change to a dual formula for Community Development Block Grants. . . .

—Use of statistical data favorable to the Northeast and Midwest in allocation formulas, as in the unemployment/labor surplus rates used to target the

$3.4 billion in defense procurement contracts; and in the steering of Low In-
come Energy Assistance to areas where cold waves are more likely than heat
waves;

—Including cost-of-living adjustments in national allocation formulas, which
would shift federal funds from low-income to high-income states;

—Factoring regional differences in wage rates into General Revenue Sharing
allocation formulas;

—Using a device called the Representative Tax System, which attempts to figure out which local and state governments put a heavier load on their taxpayers
and reward governments accordingly with federal funds, a real bonus for
Northern states;

—Measure program participation instead of the total poverty population. Areas
where more people receive welfare would receive more federal assistance than
areas where larger numbers of people are in poverty. This would hurt the
South, since there are more people eligible for welfare in the region than actually receive it;

—Limiting the impact of poverty by putting floors or ceilings on allocations by
formula. This was the case in the effort, debated by Mr. Fowler, to cap AFDC
and Medicaid funds at a 57% federal share.

"I respect the coalition's ability to effect these changes," Mr. Liner admits,
but he and others, including Gov. Busbee, believe the NMEAC efforts are based
on a self-help view of Southern economic progress and the incorrect opinion that
federal formulas have favored the South. "That is not true," says Mr. Liner.
"We've been the beneficiary of the money, but not the formulas." Despite narrowing the gap in recent years, Mr. Liner points out, the South still lags behind
the rest of the country in many of the crucial economic indicators. Gov. Busbee,
the generally accepted general-in-chief of the Southern economic forces, isn't
nearly so diplomatic. "Things aren't really like what a lot of Northern researchers
and politicians claim," he says, adding their conclusions are "infuriating myths,
false testimony and poor thinking." In fact, he told a North-South regional sum-
mit meeting in 1978, "We [the South] still have the greatest percentage of people
in poverty . . . with less than five years of schooling . . . living in sub-standard
housing . . . lacking plumbing . . . and with more people per room than any other
section in the country. Our murder rates . . . the death rate for children under five . . .
the percentage of elderly receiving public assistance . . . these too are all dramatically higher in the South." In 1979, the South's per capita income still lagged 10
points behind the national average.

Despite such admonitions, Northern politicos continue to make electoral hay
from the southward flow of federal money. Senator Daniel Patrick Moynihan of
New York in July released the fifth in his annual series of reports contending that
the federal budget favors the Sun Belt at the expense of New York. Increased
defense spending under the Reagan administration will favor the Sun Belt, he
writes, while cuts in social service funds for food stamps, welfare and Medicaid
will also hurt his state. Mr. Liner responds that the location of military bases in

the South is no great bargain, since military personnel are relatively low-paid. He also points out that few of the Pentagon's research and development funds are spent in the South. . . .

Therefore, as the South continues to gain economic parity, it must work harder to convince the rest of the nation that its growth is not coming at the expense of the distressed industrial regions. As Gov. Busbee told the NMEAC in 1978, "I'm glad the catch-up growth we are experiencing today is being perceived as some kind of regional bonanza, which should be discouraged through official policy." Employment gains in the South, points out the Southern Growth Policies Board, have not been caused by the relocation of Northern firms in the South. According to a board publication, "Over the past few years the primary cause of declining employment in the North has been the 'death' or closure of existing firms. In the South, the primary cause of the increasing employment has been the expansion of existing firms."

Tax breaks available to businesses also are downplayed by the Southerners as a factor in inter-regional business movement. . . . Nonetheless, the Southern states offer a broad array of tax incentives for industry. Alabama leads the way with 11 forms of tax exemption and credit. . . .

Regardless of the significance of tax breaks in the overall equation, they contribute to the pro-business reputation of the South. Companies faced with the choice of relocating, or new business looking for a place to start, continue to be attracted by these and other Southern advantages. Construction, energy, and labor costs remain lower. Of perhaps equal importance in a decision to relocate is the fact that executive living costs are also lower in the South; a company's decision-makers generally can live better for less than in the Northeast and Midwest. The right-to-work laws so zealously guarded by Southern states contribute to the region's "healthy business climate." And that business climate draws firms like Thornwood Leasing International looking for an easy foothold in a growth economy instead of having to chip away at a more rigid business order.

As the South continues its economic gains, the available job mix reflects a widening employment base. Agriculture has long since ceased to be the major job provider. In 1979, wholesale and retail trade, 22.8% of the jobs, replaced manufacturing, with 22.4%, as the leading employment sector. Services and government employment also grew dramatically during the 1970s, which brings up a new point in the Sun Belt–Snow Belt competition—regional differences may eventually be erased by the mere fact of Southern growth. On the other hand, however, and certainly not out of the view of Northern leaders, their fight today may be meaningless as the Sun Belt continues to grow and usurps the North's traditional role as the national leader, placing it instead in much the same economic and political position the South—and to a lesser extent, the West—held for the first 200 years of the nation's existence. However, there are already signs that the region is nearing the saturation point, at least as far as some are concerned. While Kentucky Gov. John Y. Brown continues to tout Kentucky as "the state that means business," a disgruntled Dallas resident wrote *The Wall Street Journal* recently to discuss the changes business growth had wrought there. "Dallas used to be a very idyllic place to live, with plenty of housing, a very low cost of living, a friendly and leisurely lifestyle, and plenty of jobs," wrote E. R. Jackman. "Now, not only is Dallas becoming too crowded and rushed, the cost of living is out of sight and finding a job is becoming a cut-throat proposition . . . the message from Texas is "'Yankees Stay Home!'"

James W. Rouse on Opportunity Ahead for the American City, 1982

I had a letter that invited me to this meeting, and the letter raised the strongest set of questions, the most rational set of questions that I have seen with respect to the American city, and I just want to read them. The one that came first I put last because I think it's the most important.

"Can the American city be saved? Who and what will save it? What is the proper role of local and state government? Can public-private partnership command the human and financial resources to stem the decay in the cities? How can short-range efforts be extended over the long term?" And then, last and most important, "Who or what is the vehicle for social change?" If you've really been dealing with those questions, you've had to have a lot stirring in this hall.

From my experience, I find that there exists in this country a surging new spirit in the old city very different from anything that has existed in the past 40 to 50 years. I've lived and worked in the city and about the city and on the issues of the city all of my adult life. I've financed and been a part of suburban sprawl. . . .

I guess I've attended literally hundreds of meetings like this; but I can tell you today, it's a new world. There's a new spirit about the city. There's a hope. There's an expectancy. There's a determination on the part of people about their city that simply didn't exist until the last handful of years, three, four, five, six years. It's a feeling among people that the city can be better than it is, that something can be done about it, that something is being done about it elsewhere, and why can't it happen here? There's an impatience with respect to cities not working. There's an attitude of "Let's find out what to do and do it," and it is being done. It's happened in cities across the country. And cities that aren't really moving today are being left behind because it's no longer this static, drab, dead condition in our cities. There's life and movement and action and a powerful new growth in the center of the American cities.

Before looking to the future, which is what I was asked to talk about, I'd like to carry you with me for a minute into the past—because there are reasons we got where we are, or where we were. We didn't see them at the time; we should have but we didn't, and now we look back and identify. I won't probably be telling you anything you don't know but kind of pulling it together. There are reasons today for this massive change in the city. It is important to understand those reasons in order that we use them because we failed in the last 30 to 40 years to use the forces that were at work, and we allowed the city to disintegrate. And if we don't recognize the forces that are at work today, it could wind up in a kind of messy, disintegrated central-city instead of the well-organized one that we could have.

James W. Rouse, "Opportunity Ahead for the American City," a speech delivered at the conference, "Who Will Save the American City," a Public Affairs Conference, sponsored by the *Providence, Rhode Island Journal* and Brown University, Nov. 30–Dec. 2, 1982 at Brown University. Edited and reprinted by permission of Brown University.

The New Town of Reston, Virginia, c. 1975

Created as an alternative to both urban and suburban communities, Reston is a "new town" located outside Washington, D.C. Its developers, all private, intended it to be self-sufficient, with its own schools, shops, and places of employment, as well as open space and community activities—all for the purpose of nurturing a sense of community. However, the diverse activities of modern middle-class families have diverted the people of Reston and similar towns into a variety of loyalties, only one of which has been their community of residence.

The role of devil in the piece of the American city over the last 40 years has, without any question, been the automobile. The automobile came upon us after World War II as a brand new system of transportation; not really *brand new*, we all knew about the automobile, people had automobiles, but the real sweep of the automobile occurred after World War II.

Cities weren't equipped to handle it. The streets couldn't carry it. There was no place to park it. We responded slowly. We didn't know what to do about this monster. And what happened by the accident of a community doing nothing is that it became so inconvenient, so congested, so impossible that bit by bit, one thing after another moved to the suburbs and moved in a sprawling way that then caused the traffic in the suburbs, increased automobiles, widened the roads, put down the front lawns, put in filling stations and hot dog stands and all of the stuff that's scattered along the old highway.

They became so congested that then we built freeways, and we hacked them

through the landscape and then we came to an intersection with the old highway and there we built a shopping center and an office park and a motel. And
gradually, we just sucked the blood out of the center of the city because, during
that time, we were doing nothing really effective to make the center of the city
work.

At the same time, we were experiencing in America the worldwide phenomenon of farm-to-city migration. This was the new migration of the post-war years.
In America, this was different than other migrations. Lots of people had come to
the United States from central Europe, from the Orient, and they'd come into the
center of the city; and as they worked their way up, they went out. But this migration had a tag on it that no other migration had. It had a color. It was black, and it
could be seen and identified, and it was pushed into the center of the city, and
walls built around it didn't allow them to get out. Crowded into the center of our
city were people coming from the farm who wanted to experience urban life.

Out of that congestion, we gradually withdrew the quality and the level of
services that had been available in the old city to the people who lived there. We
created slums; we created jungles at the heart of our city, and we're still paying
for it. . . .

We're faced with the transformation of the American city over the next 20
years. We will look back on the '80s and '90s with the same kind of surprise that
we looked back with in the '60s and '70s on the suburban explosion. We're now
going to experience the explosion of the center-city. It's going to be as massive in
its impact on the city as the suburban explosion was—but very different.

How we handle it, what we do with this new potential for the city, is going to
measure the quality of life in the city by the end of the century. We've been living
so long with exhortation for people to do something about the city that we may
not realize that it's a different ballgame now. It really isn't so much exhortation
as it is identifying the resources the city has and using them well, managing this
change in a way that creates the kinds of cities we want.

What are the forces? Well, the first force working toward the center-city is
really not a force of the future; it's of the past. It's that we have done a lot of
things to the center of our cities over the last 30 years. Better highways—you can
get to the center of almost any city today quicker, easier than you could 25 years
ago. We have done a lot in the way of public squares, beautifying the center of the
city, new office buildings, more workers in the center of most cities today than
there were 25 or 30 years ago. Institutions have expanded—art museums, university hospitals, whatever—different in different cities. There has been a cumulative impact of bits and pieces not well thought through, not planned, not organized, not always good in their relationship to one another, but it's happened, and
it is a force to be used in the center of the city today. Secondly, and very important, is a change in lifestyle, a radical change in lifestyle. For millions and millions of young Americans of the '50s and '60s and into the '70s, the American
dream was the house on a quarter-acre lot, a picket fence, station wagon, an outdoor barbecue and a country club. This was the American dream.

That no longer is the American dream for millions and millions of young
American people who don't value that. In addition, it doesn't work for them.
They're more interested in a Volkswagen than a station wagon. They're more

interested in baking bread than an outdoor barbecue. They're more interested in a pair of skis than a set of golf clubs. There are two of them working, larger incomes, relatively, than 35 or 40 years ago, and they are postponing children.

Sixty-five percent of the households in America today have two people working. Fifty percent have no children. Think of those demographics as an opportunity for the center of the city. Suburbs don't fit that lifestyle. Here's the market, and that market is pressing against the center of the city—not being built to like we did in the suburban explosion—having to force itself in, buying old houses, rehabilitating them, new values. Young people today will move right into the middle of a black area and not be afraid, which is a wonderful change in American life.

This pressure expresses itself better in some cities than others. In Baltimore there have been 7,000 dwelling units rehabilitated to good condition in the last seven years within 10 minutes of the center of the city, 2,000 new units built in the center of the city.

You see more of this in some cities than in others, but it happened in every city across the country. The economic forces are favorable to the center of the city in housing. With gas costing more, travel is less in the center of the city. Heating is less in a city townhouse than it is in a suburban house; more space for less cost than in a suburban house. Economic forces of business and industry are favorable to the center of the city if we know how to use it. . . .

The environmental, historical forces favor the center of the city. A builder used to be able to go out and build anywhere he wanted, whatever he wanted, almost. Now, there are all kinds of constraints on what he can do. These are inhibiting, difficult and maybe more expensive, but they're right, and they're late, if anything. At the same time, at the center of the city the historical forces are preserving buildings that would have been bulldozed a few years ago. So, we're holding onto an inventory that is available for housing at lower cost than in the suburbs.

And, of course, the whole energy issue, with people becoming increasingly energy-conscious in the country, you use less fuel for travel, for heat, for whatever and, in turn, public transportation is going to continue to be supported and pushed. . . . We've got to provide federal assistance to effective public transportation. It's an absolute demand of our society, and we will. . . . That is the way it will be. Every city in the country has resources that it's not using to fulfill a potential that it is not realizing. There just are enormous things that we can do in the city that we're not taking hold of. Some cities are. You can see it in bits and pieces here and there.

Waterfront is one. Almost every city in America is on the waterfront. A hundred years ago, Chicago, under the leadership of an extraordinary man, Daniel Burnham, saw that this waterfront was a mess, and it ought to be corrected. Under the Burnham plan, they went in and covered over those railway yards, built the marinas, built Grant Park, made Michigan Avenue the magnificent boulevard that preserved, for the center of Chicago, the vitality and activity as really no city in the country has done. None of us learned from the Burnham plan. We didn't learn what that waterfront meant.

Nor did we learn from San Antonio, which couldn't have been more different. But here's a little city once, big city now, that had a storm sewer flowing through it, and the women's garden clubs of San Antonio, using WPA—Works Progress Administration—money in the middle of the depression, started reforming that storm sewer into an attractive little river. If you haven't been to San Antonio, you ought to go. It may be the most romantic city in America. That river now winds all through the city. The businesses that once backed on it now front on it, with walkways along the banks. It's a treasure, and it has a tremendous impact on San Antonio and on the center of the city. So different these two activities, but how powerful they've been and how little we've learned from them. . . .

Indianapolis took the resource of that center square that's rare in this country, and they've done everything they can to make that into a treasure and restore the city market. They are capturing their resources. They are bringing that coliseum and the stadium right into downtown. They are making that city thrive because they are capturing their resources. Baltimore, of course, has done this in an extraordinary way, and I'll come to that in a minute.

The Rouse Company has just opened in August a new center in Milwaukee. Milwaukee was not a bad city downtown, it was just a tired city. By going in and connecting two downtown department stores, they opened up a magnificent, old arcade built back in the 1890s—just an extraordinary building that sat right there all closed up, boarded over, not being used. They tied that in with a bridge into Gimbels, winding an arcade down through the other stores in downtown; the Grand Avenue is the name of it.

It opened on August 26. The crowds and everybody had their fingers crossed in Milwaukee. Was anybody going to come downtown? This is what they asked in Boston, this is what they asked in Baltimore. The crowds were so enormous, you couldn't get in the place and they stayed that way. . . .

The real thing we need to do today, when we're so conscious of less money and less available resources to do the things that have to be done, is to put a fine eye on the resources that are available in the city. The city needs to see itself as a business, and that's a new way to look. Cities have seen themselves as service, but they need to see themselves as business. They need to capture every opportunity they have. When they've got a piece of land that's for sale, they ought to demand a piece of the action on that land, 50 percent of the cash flow from what develops from it. They ought to be developing revenues all over the place.

This is a dangerous story I am going to tell; it's only illustrative, but it's significantly illustrative. Baltimore doesn't yet have cable TV, and it's about to; competition is now underway. Who gets the cable TV? I was asked many months ago to join a group, to be a part of one of the proposals, and I listened to it, and it was so profitable. What I was going to have the opportunity to make out of it was so enormous, I said, "There's something wrong with this." If there are these kinds of profits in cable TV, the profits ought to be going to the community, not to a lot of people coming in like you and me.

They went ahead, proposals are now in; and in yesterday morning's *Sun* was a long, featured article on the deal that has been made with what looks like the television company that's going to get it. There's nothing wrong in this at all—nothing illicit, nothing unethical. But the fact is, under what has been called the rent-a-citizen process, by which cable TV companies file their bids, 16 citizens, outstanding people in Baltimore, are being allowed, for $48,000 each, to have shares in this television company, and the television company agrees to buy them out in five years at four times what they paid—but it holds the prospect of buying them out at nine times what they paid. And on the average those 16 people putting in $48,000 will receive $543,000 for doing nothing but giving their name.

And that's only a part of it. The net result is that in the whole process, there will be somewhere between $10 and $16 million being paid by the successful company to win a TV franchise. Not robbery, not unethical, but a resource that the city didn't capture. You know, if that was there, the city ought to have it, not a lot of citizens who do nothing.

This kind of thing in one way or another exists through the city, and we've got to be resourceful in capturing those flows of money and using them. If the city sees itself as something in demand downtown, not having to exhort people to come, by gosh, then, it has these assets—old buildings, old, worn-out places, all the things we've looked upon as being discards but which are valuable, jewels. They need to be made available on the basis that the city gets a big return. And sometimes the city, as that business, has got to put money into realizing that.

The city of Norfolk [Virginia] wanted to do its waterfront. It had a marvelous but deteriorated waterfront and a devastated downtown. All the ships had gone, as has happened in most ports, gone out further, and we were asked in my new company, . . . Enterprise Foundation, to do the Norfolk waterfront. It will open June 1, and it will be a Harborplace equivalent, a Faneuil Hall/Harborplace-type activity of about half the size. But when that was approached originally by the Rouse Company, we were paid to make a study, and the study said this is not economical; and it wasn't. It would cost $15 million, and any reasonable forecast said it was worth $7½ million; and 80 percent financing would mean $6 million financing, $9 million equity. Absolutely no way it could be justified, so the project couldn't happen.

But I took it with me when I left the company and formed [Enterprise Foundation]. I know the people in Norfolk very well, and I sat down with the executive vice president of the Virginia National Bank and the mayor, and I said, "Let's all get on the same side of the table and figure out how we can make this work." So we devised what we've come to call the Norfolk Financial Plan, by which the city is putting up this uneconomic thing that couldn't be done, yet is of tremendous benefit to the city; revitalization of the waterfront, tremendous fallout for downtown, would create a thousand jobs in the center of the city the day it was opened. Based on our Harborplace experience, almost half of those would go to unemployed, young, black men and women. We would expect to create, again based on the Harborplace experience, 10 to 15 new black merchants in that center, increase taxes, favorably affect land and business all around, already before it's opened.

But how could you do it? We went through this economic forecast based on eliminating all construction money, which saved a lot of money, the city putting up all the money. We entered into a 50-50 joint venture relationship with the city, knowing the city was going to take losses for five years. The forecast, which we consider to be conservative, shows that it would make them up by the eighth year, and we would divide the cash flow thereafter.

The net result of that little project, extended over 30 years, by the executive vice president of the bank and the people in the city government and themselves, shows that the city over those 30 years will get $25 million in taxes it never would have gotten; it will get all its monies back at 11 percent interest, and we will make a profit of $48 million on the center. And, if it goes well, it will be doubled in the course of the next three to five years. That kind of opportunity is available in the city.

This is the way cities have to think, and cities that don't see themselves in business and having resources to capture and use are going to lose opportunities and are going to lose money. The most important resource of all is people, and the center of the cities have [*sic*] people. We have come to regard the people in the center of the city as a burden instead of a resource. This is backwards. . . .

There are two ways of thinking about a city. We're habituated to one way, and it's the wrong way. We're habituated to thinking about the city as a problem, that we've got a crisis to meet, we've got a problem to deal with, and so we're always patching up, repairing, maintaining, surviving, and that really is our frame of mind about the city. By and large, as American people living in cities, we don't expect them to be beautiful, efficient, humane, caring for the people in the city.

The other way of thinking about a city is to think what would it be like if it worked? Suppose we took Providence or Baltimore or any other city, and instead of looking at its problems and its crises, we looked at what this city would be like if it worked in the best possible way for the people here? . . . What would it be like physically? . . . How would the urban systems of education, health care, crime, justice, correction, employment—all the systems of the city—work? What would it be like?

We have the capacity in this country to do that. We can put a man on the moon. We surely can think through the urban systems well enough to contemplate the rational, working city. If we did that, then we've got that image, and we start back here and figure how we get there. Of course, we won't be able to do all those things. We'll have to make choices. We'll have to postpone some things. But we will be working toward a rational image, and everything we do will relate to that image; and that way of thinking can apply to a little part of the city, it can apply downtown, or it can apply to the whole city. It can apply to the physical form of the city, or it can apply to the whole social system, meeting human needs of the city.

But that's the way an American business, industrial corporation would face its future. And that's the way the city ought to face its future. It's raising up the rational image of what ought to be, and then figuring out how to get there. In doing that, we would leap right over a lot of the problems that bog us down today, in the life of the city. . . . We don't believe in the city enough to raise up images of its possibilities, and therefore raise up the expectancy of the people to want it. When that happens, then things begin to move. This is a cardinal mistake in the growth or non-growth or disordered growth of the American city downtown.

The second thing is organizing to carry out that big image. . . . Organization outside of city government, alongside city government, is indispensable I think.

The third thing, of course, is what has today come to be called the private-public partnership. Private-public partnerships have been going on for a long time in America, just in this manner—in Pittsburgh and in Philadelphia and Milwaukee, and a lot of other cities. But it's now getting a new expression because it's so important. . . .

There's another new force today that is very important—the new relationship between the federal government and the city. It's the budget cuts. This is painful—enormously painful.

But there is another side to this. The federal government has an important role to play with the city. But we don't yet know what it is because what America has expressed is a massive discontent with mindless programs, with big expenditures of money that don't produce adequate results, with inefficiency, with bureaucracy. . . .

I'm not normally a conservative Republican—my political bias tends to be in the opposite direction—but nevertheless, I find an enormous potential good out of the valley we're now in. That potential good is that the business community—particularly, that has been saying, "get the government off our backs"—now has the responsibility for recognizing these needs, and putting our backs to those needs.

We have the potential for creating a new relationship between business (and other elements of the private sector) and the city, that hasn't existed for 50 years. We have the way now, we've got the demand now, we've got the responsibility now to prove that this extraordinary free enterprise business system can deal effectively with human needs in ways we don't yet know.

Processes and systems and structures need to be newly created. There ought to be in every American city today a new committee, a new council—maybe community partnership doesn't adequately define it—and it doesn't have to be done by the big-shot business leaders either. A half-dozen bright young people who care about their city could organize this task force on human needs. It could then set up a staff, raise money, and recognize that we haven't had in our cities, nor in our federal government, any adequate process for research and development such as we have in most of our society. We don't really research our problems, we don't take a look at welfare really deeply in terms of its causes and how it can be dealt with. How can we care for the poor and the indigent without encouraging people to be poor and indigent? We need to examine these things in this country in a way we haven't done, and differently in all kinds of cities, so we're raising up different solutions.

But that task force and that budget and that staff, working with the city not against it, would come up with new answers. As it came up with new answers, it would be its job to propose, to negotiate, to advocate, to see that they get implemented. We'd create a new vitality in the city. . . .

We've got to find better new ways of doing things, and this is the valley in which we need to invent those new things. This is the necessity that should breed inventions that are important to this country. It's beginning to happen in an encouraging way, but not enough.

I'm going to end with a thing I tore off the wall of a man's office in England 15 years ago. I've held it ever since. I've used it once or twice. But it's very important to us in thinking about the city. And this said:

Until one is committed, there is hesitancy, the chance to draw back, always ineffectiveness, concerning all acts of initiative and creation. There is one elementary truth, the ignorance of which kills countless ideas and splendid plans: at the moment one definitely commits oneself, then Providence moves, too. All sorts of things occur to help one that would never otherwise have occurred. A whole stream of events issues from the decision, raising in one's favor all manner of unforeseen incidents and meetings and material assistance, which no man could have dreamt would have come his way.

And that is true. I have learned a deep respect for one of Goethe's couplets: "Whatever you can do or dream you can, begin it. Boldness has genius, power and magic in it."

HUD Secretary Jack Kemp Urges Enterprise-Zone Legislation, 1989

Chairman Rostenkoski, Congressman Archer and Members of the Committee, it is a pleasure to appear before you today on the topic of revitalizing our inner cities, rural areas, and Indian communities, a subject that is not only of critical interest to the Committee but a high priority of President Bush and mine as well.

The President has recommended enterprise zones in his budget, and he has forwarded his proposals to Congress which includes [*sic*] the elements we consider critical to success. . . .

The Ways and Means Committee recently reported a tax bill that reduces the capital gains tax—a provision which the Bush administration strongly supports. Yet the Committee ignored the opportunity to pass enterprise zones to help poor people in depressed urban and rural communities. . . . At a time when parts of our nation still suffer from poverty, despair and hopelessness, I believe that [it] would be a tragic and unfair mistake not to give poverty top billing on this nation's political agenda.

Mr. Chairman, while Washington has been bogged down over enterprise zones, 37 States and the District of Columbia have taken leadership on their own. State zones have saved or created an estimated total 180,000 jobs and spurred about $9 billion in private investment in poor areas. These State zones have worked quite well despite the fact that they lack the most powerful ingredients of Federal tax incentives, including the ability to reduce such large tax barriers as the Federal income tax, capital gains taxes, payroll taxes, and the corporate income tax, which together impose a far higher Federal tax burden than State taxes. I see no reason why we cannot turn the modest success of State enterprise zones into one of the most effective weapons our Nation can muster in the war against poverty. . . .

Learning from these State experiences, the Administration has identified some key objectives of Federal enterprise zones.

Focus on creating new small businesses since firms with 20 or fewer employees generated over two-thirds of all net new private sector jobs and virtually all the jobs in the Northeast. Development of a strong, local business community is also an important ingredient in successful revitalization of depressed neighborhoods. Small business owners have a direct stake in their community and strengthen the social fabric. And small businesses are often the most innovative and adaptive, likely to produce the sorts of products and services most in demand by the local neighborhood.

Avoid the type of complex, capital based tax incentives that appeal only to large businesses. Some States have failed to understand that small business tax incentives differ from those that appeal to large businesses. Federal incentives for small businesses should be designed to help attract seed capital, improve cash flow, and enhance entrepreneurial incentives since most small businesses usually have little or no tax liability in the initial years of operation.

Recognize that competition for designation is critical. Federal tax incentive should act as a catalyst for other State, local and private sector efforts to cooperate to restore vitality and economic buoyancy. In a competitive process, those States and localities which offered the strongest package of incentives and initiatives would receive preferential selection for zone eligibility.

For example, some preference for Federal enterprise zone designation could be given to States and localities that offer relief from land use regulations, zoning laws, and real estate taxes, building codes and rent control. Similarly, States and localities could toughen community drug enforcement, begin new anti-crime efforts or improve municipal services and neighborhood infrastructure.

Focus on neighborhood development, renovation, and indigenous businesses. Enterprise zones are not designed to tear down neighborhoods, lure big businesses into the area, or create huge industrial parks—all of which can displace local residents and gentrify neighborhoods. The social fabric of a community should be respected and protected so that economic development and job creation redound to the benefit of the poor people who live in the neighborhood.

Keeping three principles in mind, the Administration designed an Enterprise Zone bill with the following three major provisions:

The first incentive in President Bush's enterprise zone initiative is a zero capital gains tax rate on tangible zone assets. . . .

When the top capital gains tax rate was reduced from 49 percent under previous law to 20 percent, the number of small company startups more than doubled, rising to 640,000 from 270,000, creating 15 million new jobs. President Bush and I are confident that eliminating the capital gains tax in depressed areas can help "percolate" a whole new generation of small business entrepreneurs and community leaders, set in motion a process of self-improvement and job generation, but most of all restore hope for progress in America's future.

The second incentive is *expensing of investor purchase of newly-issued small zone corporate stock.* Because start up businesses typically have little or no tax liability in their first years, there is a limit to what direct tax reduction can do to help these firms. The Administration proposes giving investors an up-front deduction for up to $50,000 per year of new equity investment, with a $250,000 lifetime limit, for investment in corporations having less than $5 million of total assets.

In return for an up-front tax deduction, investors would provide inner city and rural entrepreneurs the kind of seed capital they need to start up retail stores, a printing shop, a delivery company, laundries, or workshops, just to name a few examples. . . .

The third incentive is a 5 percent refundable *income tax credit* for the first $10,500 of wages to individuals working in a zone and having total wages below $20,000. The maximum credit will be $525, and the credit will phase out between $20,000 and $25,000 of total wages.

Welfare recipients and other low-income people on government support often face effective tax rates that are steeper than for our highest income earners. As they enter the workforce, not only do they pay income and social security taxes on the earnings, but they also face higher effective marginal taxes from losing their AFDC, food stamps, Medicaid coverage and other government payment cuts as well as from new costs such as child care and other employment related expenses.

The Administration believes that giving employees greater incentives to leave welfare and take advantage of new job opportunities will help break the poverty trap. . . .

Questions About Enterprise Zones

Some people question whether zones will simply redistribute growth from outside the enterprise zone to inside the zone with no net increase in jobs or investment. I personally believe this concern is groundless. The 1981 and 1986 tax rate reductions helped generate nearly 20 million new jobs, over 4 percent economic growth a year, and rapidly rising productivity. U.S. progress was not stolen from or at the expense of economic growth in the rest of the world. . . .

Another criticism of enterprise zones can also be put to rest. Let me assure you that I do not consider enterprise zones to be a replacement for other Federal programs, although I think that over time, as enterprise zones succeed, we may well see them more efficiently accomplishing the goals of many Federal programs. I view enterprise zones as one major weapon in the arsenal of our war on poverty. It is a way to bring together the resources of all levels of government and the private sector in a productive partnership. . . .

A City-Planning Official on the Benefits of Enterprise Zones, 1982

Mr. Chairman, it is a great pleasure to have the opportunity to be here today. Coming from a state that will soon have operational enterprise zones, we would like to describe our experiences and plans for implementing them effectively. Norwalk's enterprise zone preparations have already afforded the city important opportunities to improve its economic climate—and have given us insights into ways of ensuring that neighborhood residents will participate in zone success. In the remarks that follow, we would like to review our progress in building innovative partnerships between businesses and neighborhood organizations, to the benefit of all concerned. We feel that our experience suggests the desirability of broadening the federal legislation to encourage self-help activities as well as business initiative.

When our preparations began six months ago, South Norwalk's conditions seemed to be as discouraging as those of many inner cities. Industries have been declining, unemployment rates in several census tracts have stubbornly stayed far above regional or national norms, housing has deteriorated in many neighborhoods, population has declined precipitously in two census tracts, and crime rates have been excessive. Traditional tools of urban revival had not resolved the underlying problems in the most distressed areas of South Norwalk.

Despite these formidable problems, Norwalk's City Council felt that enterprise zones were worth exploring. The State of Connecticut last July enacted the first enterprise zone legislation in the country, offering businesses in distressed areas unprecedented state tax relief. The prospect of additional federal incentives, as presented in HR.3824 of last year, was decisive in our decision to begin intensive preparations in February. At a time when communities throughout the country are struggling to maintain their local economies, and to give birth to industries of the future, we believe that enterprise zones offer a crucially needed set of tools.

Norwalk's overriding goal is to generate new economic activity on terms that benefit existing residents as well as business. To determine the potential contribution of enterprise zones towards these ends, we assembled in February a task force representing a large number of the potential participants in and beneficiaries of an enterprise zone in South Norwalk. . . .

One of the first jobs of the task force was to examine which areas can qualify for designation under the eligibility minimum specified by the Connecticut and the federal enterprise zone legislation. We focused our attention on two census tracts near the heart of downtown South Norwalk. . . .

The Norwalk Enterprise Zone Strategy

The task force quickly came to appreciate the essential attractiveness of the enterprise zone idea. In contrast to conventional programs designed to stimulate business activity, an enterprise zone will offer automatic cost-savings to any entrepreneur who creates jobs or makes new investments. By avoiding uncertainty and delay for businesses regarding enjoyment of benefits, an enterprise zone has the potential to create a climate of opportunity for all entrepreneurs. . . .

At the same time as Norwalk was reaching agreement on the need for a comprehensive approach to improving the business climate, task force members became concerned about a problem of another sort—the potential effects of a successful enterprise zone upon residents of the area. When conditions for investment greatly improve, property values in an area can rise substantially. Some gentrifying inner city areas in other communities have experienced massive displacement of existing residents because property values doubled or tripled in a short time. In general, we have accepted the principle that residents should have an equity or other beneficial interest in the appreciation of property values. This can help protect residents who now lack ownership against being displaced from their homes. . . .

Specific Elements of the South Norwalk Enterprise Zone

The Norwalk Enterprise Zone task force has proceeded in a way that we believe embodies the spirit as well as the letter of the proposed federal legislation. In preparing our local commitment, we have reached agreement in a number of areas to reduce governmentally-created obstacles to economic development. Some of these reforms have been already adopted; others are imminent; and still others await federal and state designation.

I. Tax Relief. On the strength of recent favorable reviews by the task force and Norwalk's legal counsel, the city will soon approve the strong package of local tax incentives required in the state enterprise zone legislation. The tax incentives to be offered include the following:

—A fixed assessment on properties improved after enterprise zone designation. Propertyowners will enjoy a fixed assessment on their properties, regardless of the improvements made, for two years. Over the next five years, the improvements will be assessed at a fraction of their market value.

—In special cases, the ordinance will authorize the Norwalk Common Council to approve a fixed assessment for up to a full seven years. This provision makes it possible for the city to ensure that highly desirable investments are given all possible reason to come to South Norwalk.

The ordinance specifically rules out development of upper-income housing from receiving benefits of the assessment freeze. Developers of low and moderate income housing, however, will be welcome to make use of the tax incentive.

II. Neighborhood Initiatives. Recognizing that crime and the perception of crime are leading barriers to business activity in South Norwalk, the task force has recommended that community "block watches" be a key part of the enterprise zone. In studies of ways to reduce crime, block watches have shown abilities to dramatically reduce victimization rates of residents by criminals. Residents take turn looking out windows at allotted times, reporting any incipient crimes or crimes-in-progress to police. . . .

The effectiveness of neighborhood self-help efforts depends on mobilizing enough volunteers to ensure that the initial organizers do not "burn out"—and on developing a source of continuing funds for the associations to operate. I am pleased to say that the South Norwalk enterprise zone will help on both counts. For residents who join—and remain active in—self-help groups, we will set aside a share of the money earned through lease of city-owned properties in the zone to business. Neighborhood associations that cooperate in crime-prevention and clean-up activities, under this approach, will gain increasing revenues as property values rise in the South Norwalk area. . . .

III. Service Improvements. A number of moves are underway to improve delivery of basic services for residents and businesses within the enterprise zone area, particularly through alternative methods of delivery. Voluntary sector providers will assume increased responsibilities in service areas ranging from job brokering to park management.

Perhaps the most innovative initiative originated with a leading community organization, Norwalk Economic Opportunity Now. NEON has been especially concerned about the availability of jobs for teenaged youths. Many businesses have been reluctant to hire youths, particularly for short-term employment, because of concern about the possibility that workers will claim unemployment compensation. NEON will soon supply short-term workers to several local employers in a breakthrough agreement that will open new job opportunities by reducing employer concerns about unjust unemployment compensation claims.

The enterprise zone task force has begun to explore ways of releasing new energies for skill development. Job training is essential if many of the unemployed residents of South Norwalk are to enjoy the employment opportunities generated by the zone. . . .

Another promising area for private initiative consists of the "adopt a park" program. Because of municipal budgetary and staffing limitations, upkeep of parks has been less than desired in South Norwalk. . . .

South Norwalk also intends to explore opportunities for contracting out responsibilities for basic service delivery. We have taken initial steps to contract out responsibilities for maintenance of school buildings, and will soon examine the desirability of contracting out park maintenance and refuse collection in conjunction with the enterprise zone.

IV. Deregulation/Streamlining of Red Tape.   Among the most trying problems for businessmen around the country are the difficulties of contending with a mass of overlapping and sometimes conflicting local regulations. Our task force has been particularly sensitive to the need for improvements in this area, without jeopardizing public health and safety. Reducing unproductive regulations promises to be of special benefit to small businesses and propertyowners, who often lack the professional skills of larger businesses to deal effectively with city hall.

In the past few months, important strides have been made to loosen zoning constraints in the South Norwalk area. Half of the zone area has been recently designated for high-density residential/industrial use, permitting significant flexibility for zone propertyowners and manufacturers alike. . . .

A second major area for improvement now underway is in the permitting process. Until recent months, a developer seeking to begin a significant project in South Norwalk was forced to fill out paperwork for seven governmental departments and agencies. Coordinating the permit process proved to be an exhausting task even for major developers. In its place, Norwalk is instituting a "one-step" permitting procedure, using a master form in place of the seven forms previously in effect. . . .

A third area for administrative streamlining is with code enforcement. At present, developers are vulnerable to complications arising from fragmented inspections. Fire, health, and building code inspectors can slow up major projects by being inaccessible at critical times. The city is now investigating the prospects for cross-training inspectors, so that a single inspector can apply the needed evaluation.

In addition to the above elements of our local commitment, Norwalk is using a number of existing developmental tools to improve conditions for businesses and residents of the zone area. Major infrastructure improvements are planned, including widening of access roads for businesses in the area, upgrading of sewers, and improvement of drainage. To give existing residents more of a stake in their community, Norwalk has already begun to offer tenants the ability to own their own homes. . . .

As these examples indicate, we believe that the approach taken by South Norwalk embodies the innovative and practical spirit of enterprise zones. Reducing barriers to investment on a comprehensive basis ensures that an enterprise zone in the city stands an excellent chance of becoming an economic success. Similarly, creating a beneficial interest in zone development for community organizations has the potential to generate revenues for residents who help reduce crime and improve the physical appearance of the inner city. Creating jobs and stimulating neighborhood improvements in the most depressed part of the city, moreover, can strengthen the economic health of the entire community. . . .

Urban Policies of the Victorious Democratic Party, 1992

Preamble

Two hundred summers ago, this Democratic Party was founded by the man whose burning pen fired the spirit of the American Revolution—who once argued we should overthrow our own government every 20 years to renew our freedom and keep pace with a changing world. In 1992, the party Thomas Jefferson founded invokes his spirit of revolution anew. . . .

The Revolution of 1992 is about putting government back on the side of working men and women—to help those who work hard, pay their bills, play by the rules, don't lobby for tax breaks, do their best to give their kids a good education and to keep them away from drugs, who want a safe neighborhood for their families, the security of decent, productive jobs for themselves, and a dignified life for their parents. . . .

The Revolution of 1992 is about facing up to tough choices. There is no relief for America's frustration in the politics of diversion and evasion, of false choices or of no choices at all. Instead of everyone in Washington blaming one another for inaction, we will act decisively—and ask to be held accountable if we don't.

Above all the Revolution of 1992 is about restoring the basic American values that built this country and will always make it great: personal responsibility, individual liberty, tolerance, faith, family and hard work. We offer the American people not only new ideas, a new course, and a new President, but a return to the enduring principles that set our nation apart: the promise of opportunity, the strength of community, the dignity of work, and a decent life for senior citizens.

To make this revolution, we seek a *New Covenant* to repair the damaged bond between the American people and their government, that will expand *opportunity*, insist upon greater individual *responsibility* in return, restore *community*, and ensure *national security* in a profoundly new era.

We welcome the close scrutiny of the American people, including Americans who may have thought the Democratic Party had forgotten its way, as well as all who know us as the champions of those who have been denied a chance. With this platform we take our case for change to the American people.

I. Opportunity

Our Party's first priority is opportunity—broad-based, non-inflationary economic growth and the opportunity that flows from it. Democrats in 1992 hold nothing more important for America than an economy that offers growth and jobs for all. . . .

The Cities. Only a robust economy will revitalize our cities. It is in all Americans' interest that the cities once again be places where hard-working families can put down roots and find good jobs, quality health care, affordable housing, and decent schools. Democrats will create a new partnership to rebuild America's cities after 12 years of Republican neglect. This partnership with the mayors will include consideration of the seven economic growth initiatives set forth by our nation's mayors. We will create jobs by investing significant resources to put people back to work, beginning with a summer jobs initiative and training programs for inner-city youth. We support a stronger community development program and targeted fiscal assistance to cities that need it most. A national public works investment and infrastructure program will provide jobs and strengthen our cities, suburbs, rural communities, and country. We will encourage the flow of investment to inner-city development and housing through targeted enterprise zones and incentives for private and public pension funds to invest in urban and rural projects. While cracking down on redlining and housing discrimination, we also support and will enforce a revitalized Community Reinvestment Act that challenges banks to lend to entrepreneurs and development projects; a national network of Community Development Banks to invest in urban and rural small businesses; and microenterprise lending for poor people seeking self-employment as an alternative to welfare. . . .

II. Responsibility

Sixty years ago, Franklin Delano Roosevelt gave hope to a nation mired in the Great Depression. While government should promise every American the opportunity to get ahead, it was the people's responsibility, he said, to make the most of their opportunity. "Faith in America demands that we recognize the new terms of the old social contract. In the strength of great hope we must all shoulder our common load." . . .

Strengthening the Family. Governments don't raise children, people do. People who bring children into this world have a responsibility to care for them and give them values, motivation and discipline. Children should not have children. We need a national crackdown on deadbeat parents, an effective system of child support enforcement nationwide, and a systematic effort to establish paternity for every child. We must also make it easier for parents to build strong families through pay equity. Family and medical leave will ensure that workers don't have to choose between family and work. We support a family preservation program to reduce child and spousal abuse by providing preventive services and foster care to families in crisis. We favor ensuring quality and affordable child care opportunities for working parents, and a fair and healthy start for every child, including essential pre-natal and well baby care. We support the needs of our senior citizens for productive and healthy lives, including hunger prevention, income adequacy, transportation access and abuse prevention.

Welfare Reform. Welfare should be a second chance, not a way of life. We want to break the cycle of welfare by adhering to two simple principles: no one who is able to work can stay on welfare forever, and no one who works should live in poverty. We will continue to help those who cannot help themselves. We will offer people on welfare a new social contract. We'll invest in education and job training, and provide the child care and health care they need to go to work and achieve long-term self-sufficiency. We will give them the help they need to make the transition from welfare to work, and require people who can work to go to work within two years in available jobs either in the private sector or in community service to meet unmet needs. This will restore the covenant that welfare was meant to be: a promise of temporary help for people who have fallen on hard times. . . .

III. Restoring Community

The success of democracy in America depends substantially on the strength of our community institutions: families and neighborhoods, public schools, religious institutions, charitable organizations, civic groups and other voluntary associations. In these social networks, the values and character of our citizens are formed, as we learn the habits and skills of self-government, and acquire an understanding of our common rights and responsibilities as citizens. . . .

Combatting Crime and Drugs. Crime is a relentless danger to our communities. Over the last decade, crime has swept through our country at an alarming rate. During the 1980s, more than 200,000 Americans were murdered, four times the number who died in Vietnam. Violent crimes rose by more than 16 percent since 1988 and nearly doubled since 1975. In our country today, a murder is committed every 25 minutes, a rape every six minutes, a burglary every 10 seconds. The pervasive fear of crime disfigures our public life and diminishes our freedom.

None suffer more than the poor: an explosive mixture of blighted prospects, drugs and exotic weaponry has turned many of our inner-city communities into combat zones. As a result, crime is not only a symptom but also a major cause of the worsening poverty and demoralization that afflicts inner-city communities.

To empower America's communities, Democrats pledge to restore government as the upholder of basic law and order for crime-ravaged communities. The simplest and most direct way to restore order in our cities is to put more police on the streets. America's police are locked in an unequal struggle with crime: since 1951 the ratio of police officers to reported crimes has reversed, from three-to-one to one-to-three. We will create a Police Corps, in which participants would receive college aid in return for several years of service after graduation in a state or local police department. As we shift people and resources from defense to the civilian economy, we will create new jobs in law enforcement for those leaving the military.

We will expand drug counseling and treatment for those who need it, intensify efforts to educate our children at the earliest ages to the dangers of drug and alcohol abuse, and curb demand from the street corner to the penthouse suite, so that the [United States], with five percent of the world's population, no longer consumes 50 percent of the world's illegal drugs.

Community Policing.   Neighborhoods and police should be partners in the war on crime. Democrats support more community policing, which uses foot patrols and storefront offices to make police officers visible fixtures in urban neighborhoods. We will combat street violence and emphasize building trust and solving the problems that breed crime. . . .

Housing.   Safe, secure housing is essential to the institutions of community and family. We support homeownership for working families and will honor that commitment through policies that encourage affordable mortgage credit. We must also confront homelessness by renovating, preserving and expanding the stock of affordable low-income housing. We support tenant management and ownership, so public housing residents can manage their own affairs and acquire property worth protecting. Operating assistance would be continued for as long as necessary.

✖ *E S S A Y S*

The first essay, by Richard M. Bernard of Bethany College and Bradley R. Rice of Clayton State College, discusses the political and economic forces behind the rise of Sunbelt cities as they existed in the early 1980s. The generally positive assessment of the two authors did not foresee the economic stagnation that struck in the mid-1980s when the boom in the energy industry collapsed. The second essay, a sympathetic magazine article on James Rouse, complements the document by Rouse above. Chosen by the magazine as its "Man of the Year," Rouse is portrayed as having a unique approach to urban housing and redevelopment problems. The third essay is taken from another magazine article, this one on Jack Kemp and enterprise zones, and it complements the two documents on enterprise zones above. The article describes the plan proposed by Kemp and other (mostly) Republican government officials and tries to identify its positive and negative aspects.

Politics, Economics, and the Rise of Sunbelt Cities

RICHARD M. BERNARD and BRADLEY R. RICE

Between 1940 and 1980, the Sunbelt, which stretches from coast to coast below the 37th parallel, increased its population by 112.3 percent. Over the same period the combined northeastern and midwestern regions, often called the Frostbelt,

From *Sunbelt Cities: Politics and Growth Since World War II,* edited by Richard M. Bernard and Bradley R. Rice, excerpts from pp. 1–26. Copyright © 1983 University of Texas Press. Reprinted by permission of the publisher.

grew by only 41.9 percent. Most of the difference between these two rates of population expansion results from a mass movement of northern Americans to the emerging metropolitan areas of the Sunbelt. . . . This demographic explosion has reversed the century-old movement of young people and blacks from the South to the North and represents one of the greatest population shifts in American history. . . .

The very concept of a Sunbelt is a novel and somewhat controversial notion in American geography. Political strategist Kevin Phillips coined the term "Sunbelt" in his 1969 book *The Emerging Republican Majority*. He used the concept to focus attention on the increasing electoral strength of the region and how the Republican party could benefit from it. Ironically, the term caught on before the Republicans did. The election of southern Democrat Jimmy Carter to the presidency in 1976 served as a catalyst for a mid-decade outpouring of journalistic and scholarly analysis of the South in particular and the Sunbelt in general. Both during the campaign and after the balloting, the *New York Times, Nation's Business, Business Week, Fortune, Saturday Review*, and numerous other periodicals ran stories extolling the growth of the Sunbelt. These articles had the effect of legitimating the term "Sunbelt" as a part of the nation's intellectual as well as popular vocabulary.

General usage, however, has not led to a common definition of the American Sunbelt. . . . The most widely circulated early description was probably that of freelance journalist Kirkpatrick Sale, who assailed the rise of the Sunbelt as a threat to the nation's progressive political tradition. Sale actually used the term "southern rim" rather than Sunbelt, but he discussed the same phenomenon. With some minor adjustment, his definition of the region's boundaries is still the best. "It hardly seems an accident," Sale wrote in his 1975 polemic *Power Shift*, "that there is indeed a cartographic line that sets off this area almost precisely: the boundary line which runs along the northern edges of North Carolina, Tennessee, Arkansas, Oklahoma, New Mexico, Arizona, or generally the 37th parallel." He extended the line to the Pacific to catch lower Nevada and Southern California.

Subsequent writers, both those who agreed with Sale's alarmist tract and those who challenged him, have not been so confident about the Sunbelt's exact perimeter. Much of their confusion has its origin in the failure of the United States Census to recognize the Sunbelt as a separate region and to list statistics for it as a unit. . . . Given this lack of official guidance, some authors have chosen one set of boundaries and others have redrawn them. The resulting lack of consistency in terminology has made it quite difficult for scholars . . . to generalize about the findings of previous inquiries. Different writers have, in fact, written about different Sunbelts.

The areas that have caused the most definitional difficulty are the upper South, the Pacific Northwest, the Rocky Mountain states, and the state of California. A typical approach in the Sunbelt literature has been to generalize about the region by drawing figures from the Census Bureau's South and West regions. Writers who follow this pattern end up including the rainy Northwest and the snowy Rockies in the western half of what must surely then be misnamed the "Sunbelt." In the South, the use of census regions results in the addition of Kentucky, West Virginia, and the Chesapeake Bay region. With the possible exception of Virginia, however, none of this territory lies within the Sunbelt as popularly conceived. . . .

One simple technique for measuring regional perception was demonstrated by sociologist John Shelton Reed, who sought a common definition for the South. Working with the assumption that the South is "that part of the country where people think they are Southerners," he used business entries in telephone directories to plot the geographic incidence of the terms "South," "southern," and "Dixie." Dixie turned out to be, in Reed's words, "more attitude than latitude." A similar technique can be applied to the Sunbelt, assuming that it is that part of the country in which people believe that they live in the Sunbelt. The result is a fairly neat convergence of attitude and latitude that tends to endorse Sale's 37th parallel definition, with the exception of the San Francisco Bay area. . . .

One factor that draws [the cities of the Sunbelt] together is substantial postwar growth. Among them, Phoenix's forty-year metropolitan growth rate of 1,137.8 percent was most impressive. San Diego, Houston, Dallas–Fort Worth, Tampa, Miami, and Atlanta all showed better than fourfold increases. New Orleans grew slowest, but even this Sunbelt laggard more than doubled its size.

Why have these metropolitan areas experienced such significant population growth? Some of the reasons are intangible and some overlap, so it is not easy to identify with precision just why these areas grew so rapidly, but four influences stand out: defense spending (especially that generated by World War II), other federal outlays, a favorable business climate, and an attractive quality of life. Certain sections of the region have also benefited from other economic activities, notably oil and gas exploitation in Texas, Oklahoma, and Louisiana; the building of retirement centers in Florida and Arizona; and the emergence of the recreation and tourism industries in Southern California, Florida, New Orleans, and Las Vegas. These factors and others have combined to make the Sunbelt attractive to migratory individuals and to the companies that employ them. In fact, across the southern rim of the United States, economic opportunities snowballed . . . as postwar migrants moved westward and southward.

A common theme that runs through [the rise of Sunbelt cities] is the positive impact of World War II on metropolitan growth. Federal defense policy before the war had not been especially favorable to the South and the West when it came to the allocation of military installations and the letting of contracts for weaponry and other hardware. Most bases, and to an even greater extent most production contracts, had gone to the great industrial areas of the Northeast and Midwest. With war clouds overhead, however, the armed forces made deliberate efforts to relocate their personnel and training facilities around the country and to spread out defense contracts in order to make bombing and even invasion more difficult for the enemy.

The South and the West were the big winners in this policy shift. Warm weather coastal cities became centers of naval construction and land-based operations, causing such places as Mobile, San Diego, and Tampa to suddenly overflow with shipbuilders and sailors. . . . Inland cities of the South and Southwest offered wide-open spaces for ground force training and airplane production and maintenance and clear skies for airplane testing and flight training. New Orleans, Atlanta, Fort Worth, Oklahoma City, San Antonio, Albuquerque, and Phoenix were among the many locales to prosper thanks to the construction of aircraft production facilities and the location or expansion of military bases.

It was the cities of the South and the West that experienced the greatest in-migrations as a result of the war effort. Between 1940 and 1943 defense contractors issued calls for massive numbers of new workers, and the military inducted and trained its first waves of fighting men. In those early war years the metropolitan counties of the South grew by 3.9 percent and those in the West expanded by 2.7 percent. In contrast, such areas in the North Central section were up by only 2 percent, and the metropolitan counties of the Northeast actually suffered a net loss of .6 percent.

Immediately after the war, most of these burgeoning centers suffered predictable economic downturns, but usually only briefly. Military spending slowed down, but it certainly did not stop. One journalist remarked that only increasing cold war expenditures saved San Diego "from the ravages of peace." Much the same could be said about San Antonio and to a lesser extent about most of the cities of the Sunbelt. . . . Through the efforts of southern, and to a lesser extent western, congressmen, the Sunbelt has continued to garner far more than its proportional share of defense dollars. . . .

A recent study prepared by Employment Research Associates of Lansing, Michigan, quantified the drain on the Northeast and Midwest at $27 billion per year. They reported that while the Pentagon spent only $44 billion in the Frostbelt the region contributed over $70 billion in taxes toward the military budget. Defense spending, the report concluded, "is by far the most important factor in accounting for the now massive shift of resources from the Northeast and Midwest to the South and West.

Nondefense federal spending has also stimulated Sunbelt development, although in this case the region's relative advantage vis-à-vis the Frostbelt is less pronounced. A 1976 article in the limited-circulation but influential *National Journal* clearly delineated the Sunbelt's advantages in federal allocations, including defense. The article's conclusions sparked such a hot debate between congressional, academic, and economic spokesmen of the two sections that *Business Week* labeled the exchange "The Second War Between the States." . . .

Although offering advantages to all sections of the country, some federal spending programs have proved especially helpful to the South and Southwest. Interstate highway construction and urban redevelopment, for example, came into being at a time that was crucial in the development of Sunbelt cities. The age of massive growth in most of the locales coincided with the age of the superhighway. The creation of these primary transportation routes with huge federal subsidies encouraged the outward sprawl of these cities as residential subdivisions, regional shopping malls, industrial parks, and office centers clustered around the off-ramps of the interstate legs and perimeters. These superhighways have solidified the regional leadership of such metropolises as Atlanta, Dallas, and Phoenix by routing more people and products through these cities. But they have had the simultaneous effect of hastening the relative decline of the central business districts.

Urban redevelopment programs also arrived at an opportune time for cities such as Atlanta, Tampa, New Orleans, and Oklahoma City, which wanted desperately to build impressive downtowns, civic centers, stadiums, and universities that would signify their rising national importance. In Fort Worth, Dallas, and San Diego conservative civic leaders were troubled enough by their antihandout principles to drag their feet in the race for federal funding. Other Sunbelt leaders also distrusted these programs at first, fearing the strings that Washington attached to them. Most, however, soon came to welcome and seek them as effective means for enhancing business opportunities in the hearts of their communities.

Other federal programs stand out as important stimulants in particular examples. Without federal assistance, for example, Atlanta could not have built its impressive rapid rail transit system. The establishment of the Johnson Space Flight Center south of Houston and the location of the Federal Aviation Administration's training center in Oklahoma City illustrate how federal spending can boost local economies and images. Federal regional offices are especially important to Atlanta and Albuquerque. Without Social Security and other government retirement programs, the booms in Miami, Tampa–St. Petersburg, and Phoenix would probably have been smaller. In short, through a combination of deliberate redistributive policy, political clout, and plain happenstance, the Sunbelt owes much of its rise to money from Washington.

A third reason for the Sunbelt explosion is that amorphous but very real asset known as "a good business climate." State and local governments in the Sunbelt, especially in the South, have been willing, indeed anxious, to pass legislation that is designed to cut the costs and improve the efficiency of doing business. For example, South Carolina has constructed highways to serve new industrial sites; Texas has hamstrung efforts to limit the influx of cheap Mexican workers; California has established the nation's most elaborate system of junior colleges, including many with industrial training programs. The states and many localities have offered tax concessions to businesses seeking new locations. Some have used public financing to erect facilities that industry could lease on favorable terms. Although most studies have shown that such incentives are seldom the crucial factor in business site location, they are symptomatic of generally cooperative and supportive governments. Sunbelt states, with the partial exception of California, usually promise a bare minimum of governmental interference with the conduct of business, and some even offer to help cut through federal red tape. Sometimes states waive their already minimal environmental protection rules in order to attract industry. Area technical schools often offer start-up training tailored to the needs of new firms.

The Sunbelt's lower rate of unionization appeals to cost-conscious executives. Given the individualistic cultural heritage of much of the region, unionization rates might be low even without legal discouragement, but all of the states of the region except New Mexico, Oklahoma, and California have right-to-work laws. In recent years, the national rate of unionization has hovered at just under 30 percent of the nonagricultural work force, but in many Sunbelt states it is less than half that. . . .

For the most part, studies reveal that the Sunbelt's growth has been due to the creation of new jobs rather than the pirating of firms directly from the Frostbelt. The results, however, are essentially the same. The Northeast and Midwest lose jobs and the Sunbelt gains. Firm closings are about equal in the two belts, but the birth of new companies and branch operations is much more frequent in the Sunbelt.

A combination of state and local agencies and nongovernmental organizations carries out the task of spreading the good word about the Sunbelt to the nation's business leaders. At first the old families of New Orleans and the "geranium" forces in San Diego moved cautiously, but everywhere else the growth ethic, personified in the Chambers of Commerce, predominated. The Atlanta chamber's Forward Atlanta campaign of the 1960s was so effective that dozens of other cities sent observers to copy the Gate City's methods. In Dallas the Chamber of Commerce shares credit with the even more elite Citizens Council for cementing Big D's regional hegemony over merchandising and manufacturing. The Phoenix chamber sold Motorola on the desert city's assets of transportation, education, business climate, and warm weather. Few boosters could match the efforts of the Oklahoma City Chamber of Commerce, which not only instigated and carried out a major industrial and commercial development program, but also guided city hall through the nation's most ambitious municipal annexation program and a huge downtown redevelopment project.

When talking with industrial executives, Sunbelt boosters have been able to stress not only the superiority of their business climates but also the fourth major factor in the growth of the Sunbelt: the region's quality of life. . . . For the more serious-minded potential migrant, the Sunbelt cities now offer a wide variety of educational, cultural, and entertainment facilities that rival those of the North. Over the last three decades state governments have either established or greatly expanded universities in [at least] twelve metropolitan areas [of the Sunbelt]. Symphonies, legitimate theaters, and even opera companies abound. At the end of World War II, big-league sports were confined to the Frostbelt; but by the 1970s local boosters had brought major franchises in baseball, football, and/or basketball to ten Sunbelt towns beginning with the Dodgers celebrated trek to Los Angeles. These activities complement the Sunbelt's two preexisting specialties: stock car racing in the Southeast and college football everywhere.

Life in the Sunbelt can be not only more pleasant but also just about as remunerative. Between 1970 and 1979, every Sunbelt state increased its per capita income more rapidly than the national average. According to one Bureau of Labor Statistics economist, the South, which had the country's lowest per capita income . . . had reached parity in *real* income by 1975. Actual income still lagged, but considering the lower cost of living in the region, the statistically average southerner had reached a standard of living comparable to that of the east of the nation. Areas of prosperity like the Florida peninsula, most of Texas, and metro Atlanta help the southern figures. Problems persist and poverty lingers in many Sunbelt spots, but the strides in income and other quality-of-life indexes have been immense. . . .

Recent detractors have insisted that the quality of life is worsening in the Sunbelt at a rate commensurate with the in-migration of millions of newcomers. More people mean more crime, and violent crime certainly does pose a serious actual and image problem for Miami, New Orleans, Houston, and Atlanta. Air pollution, long the scourge of Los Angeles, now afflicts Houston, New Orleans, Phoenix, and even Oklahoma City. . . . Higher energy costs are making air conditioning more and more expensive, and refrigerated air . . . was instrumental in making Sunbelt life bearable for many transplanted northerners. Severe water shortages threaten the western half of the belt. Ironically, the great gains made by the Sunbelt have actually reduced some of its attractiveness to business. . . .

What have been the political consequences of the historic rise of the Sunbelt? . . . During the late 1940s, both political and economic power in the [Sunbelt] cities . . . rested substantially in the hands of cliques of central city-oriented businessmen. They effectively dominated or circumvented the politicians in city hall and were generally unthreatened by the politically impotent minority groups within the city. Government officials in outlying areas were sometimes troublesome, but suburbanization in the Sunbelt had not advanced to the point that these people could seriously challenge the existing political order. The elites did not always get their way, but they were undoubtedly the driving force in community decision making. In the archetypical city of Dallas, the chief executive officers of the main firms formed the Citizens Council, which planned and carried out an agenda for the entire populace. In Houston it was the 8-F Crowd; in Oklahoma City it was the Chamber of Commerce; in Atlanta it was the group that Floyd Hunter dubbed "the power structure." In New Orleans and Tampa the business elites had to contend with entrenched political machines, but they managed to reach accommodations that acquiesced in the machines' control of patronage in exchange for an agreement that the machines would not disrupt business activities.

In some cities this old guard got too complacent with politics as usual, and young entrepreneurs and professionals in the old-fashioned good-government tradition organized to get politics back on track. The reformers, however, did not question the assumption that downtown business interests should set the agenda for the metropolis. They merely sought honest and efficient politics to carry it out. On the crucial subject of economic growth, they often proved to be "more royal than the king." Their cries for industrial development were often those of men on the make rather than those who had it made. The goal of such groups as the Phoenix Charter Government Committee . . . , the San Antonio Good Government League, and Oklahoma City's Association for Responsible Government was not to challenge rule by business clique but to improve the policy-making process by broadening the elite circle to include themselves.

Whereas these businessmen-reformer-politician alliances did not fundamentally change power-structure rule, real and effective challenges did emerge in most of these twelve metropolitan areas. In none of these metropolises do the downtown commercial-banking professional elites retain the preeminent position they once occupied, although they remain much more powerful in some communities than in others. The two main causes of this political transformation have been the fragmentation of the metropolitan areas into dozens of autonomous governmental units and the rising influence of minority and neighborhood politics. In these ways the Sunbelt cities are becoming more like their many Frostbelt counterparts, which have long faced ethnic politics and suburban strangulation.

The first of these serious challenges—suburban political influence—occurs when the central city is unable to capture peripheral growth within its corporate limits. Sometimes preexisting governments such as counties or formerly rural towns assert authority. In other instances, suburbanites create new governmental units to serve their needs. This fragmentation effectively prevents one group of central city leaders from controlling the destiny of the entire metropolis. The presence of a host of governments (municipalities, counties, special districts, metropolitan councils of governments, and similar agencies) diffuses power throughout the metropolitan areas. Sometimes the cost of government is increased, and always public planning is complicated and public responsibility is obscured. The visions of the downtown promoters are no longer those of the organic city.

As a rule, however, Sunbelt cities have not been as plagued by the multiplicity of governmental units as have the cities of the Northeast. With some exceptions, notably Atlanta and Miami, these central cities tend to contain a relatively high percentage of total SNSA population. In Houston, San Antonio, Albuquerque, and Phoenix, annexation has been so successful that the core cities actually have larger populations than the outlying areas. In Oklahoma City, San Diego, and New Orleans the principal municipalities approach half of the metropolitan total. From the viewpoint of central city power forces, annexation best solves the problems of suburbanization because it increases the city's tax base by including fringe construction within the city's boundaries and because it truncates potential political opposition that often flows from suburban autonomy. When annexation has failed for legal or political reasons, some Sunbelt cities have worked out fairly effective intergovernmental arrangements capable of handling many common problems. Miami and Dade County have a unique sharing arrangement. The Lakewood Plan allows Los Angeles County to influence its municipalities through the sale of service packages on a contract basis. The predecessor agency to the present Atlanta Regional Commission was the nation's first publicly supported, areawide planning agency. Even when such cooperative arrangements move toward solving important service-delivery and planning problems, they reflect a sharing of power that was once virtually unknown to the elites of many Sunbelt cities.

The second serious assault on old-line business leadership has come mainly from within the central cities themselves. Minority politics and neighborhood power are fairly new to the Sunbelt, although aspects of these struggles have their roots in the nineteenth century. Prior to World War II, the electorates of these cities were ethnically homogeneous even if their populations were not. In fact, blacks and/or Hispanics have long constituted significant segments of the populations of [most] cities except Oklahoma City. Generally speaking, the larger the size of the minority population the hardest the dominant whites worked to keep it excluded. Georgia and Texas utilized the white primary to prevent blacks from casting ballots in the Democratic primaries, the only races that really mattered in the solid South. Direct and indirect, legal and illegal pressures kept black and Mexican-American voters away from the polls. Many cities diluted minority voting strength through at-large elections in which votes from the segregated neighborhoods were overwhelmed in the citywide totals that actually chose the mayors and councils. The end of such restrictions has affected politics in all the Sunbelt cities and has literally reshaped it in some. The court-ordered end of the white primary in the late 1940s was the beginning. Early civil-rights legislation helped some more. But the significant changes came with the Voting Rights Act of 1965 and its 1975 amendments that protected Spanish-speaking voters. Sometimes under political pressure and other times under legal compulsion, the Sunbelt cities have ended or limited at-large voting, so minority candidates now often win election to city councils and other governing boards. . . .

Not all neighborhood politics are ethnic or racial in nature, City residents, often in alliance with planning professionals, have worked to preserve in-town communities from highways, high rises, and high-density office and commercial development. Fear of such encroachment led neighborhood groups in San Diego to resist a series of redevelopment ideas. In Atlanta they stopped construction on two major limited-access highways even after right-of-way acquisition had begun. In New Orleans they blocked a river-front expressway. Controlled-growth advocates with neighborhood bases in Albuquerque elected a one-term mayor. Neighborhoods of all races and ethnic groups have often functioned as veto groups for the grand ideas of the downtown elite.

Taken as a whole, these two big challenges have caused varying degrees of change in metropolitan politics. Three broad categories of impact are evident. In Atlanta, Miami, New Orleans, and San Antonio, suburbs or minorities (or combinations thereof) have been relatively effective in challenging the business elite for political control of the metropolitan destiny. The dichotomy between economic and political power in these places means that decision making must be shared. In the second group—Los Angeles, Houston, Tampa, Dallas, San Diego, and Albuquerque—challengers have arisen and have won some significant victories and concessions, but the forces of neighborhood and fringe have not yet upset the power establishments. The movement for change had the least impact in Oklahoma City, Fort Worth, and Phoenix. In these areas, downtown Chamber of Commerce leaders still call most of the shots. Once in a while suburban officials and minority group spokesmen will fire telling blasts, but the elite's armor remains intact.

In the long run, the newer cities of the Sunbelt will age and will probably come more to resemble their older northern counterparts in many aspects of growth and politics. But during the period from 1945 to 1981, the historical development of the Sunbelt cities has been significantly different from that of the sluggish metropolitan areas of most of the Frostbelt. Sunbelt cities have served as the spearheads of a significant transformation of American regionalism. Fred Hofheinz, former mayor of Houston, stated it best: "People have been saying for years that the South and Southwest are frontiers of the new industrial America, where people can still reach the American dream. This is the new Detroit, the new New York. This is where the action is."

James W. Rouse: Dedicating Funds and Know-How from Marketplace Projects to Rebuild Slums

James W. Rouse stands firmly on uneven ground, each foot in a different world. By directing profits from urban marketplace developments to help house the poor, he is giving commercial development social purpose and charity a new twist. He is also sparking civic revival.

"James W. Rouse: Dedicating Funds and Know-How From Marketplace Projects to Rebuild Slums," *Engineering News Record* (February 14, 1985), 52–60. Published by McGraw-Hill Book Co.

"A full life is not achieved through one's material well-being but by dealing with the whole of life wherever one is," says Rouse. "Circumstances have placed me in the life of the city. I see so many things that ought to be better."

Charity Rouse-style means The Enterprise Foundation, formed in 1981 with a sweeping purpose—to help eliminate slums. At first, Enterprise is raising funds like any charity. By the 1990s, if all goes well, it will be sustained by the profits of its subsidiary, The Enterprise Development Co., which specializes in festive marketplaces.

"Jim Rouse has a clear vision of what he's doing. He's a link between for-profit and nonprofit worlds," says one associate. "From the poor to the highest corporate officials, his tone and manner are always the same. It's a phenomenal gift. With it, he challenges others to follow."

Rouse has been putting his gift to work for most of his 70 years. Born on Maryland's Eastern Shore and orphaned as a teenager, he took off for Baltimore to seek his fortune. During the Depression, he worked parking cars while going to law school at night. His avocation was that of urban planner. Soon, he formed a mortgage banking company that he built into the giant retail developer, The Rouse Co., Columbia, Md. Through the Rouse Co., he began honing his skills for innovative developments. Capitalizing on the growing importance of the car and the suburbs, he built shopping centers. He also built the first privately developed covered "shopping mall," coining the phrase.

Malls, however successful, weren't enough for Rouse. He had dreams of creating the perfect new town, a planned, integrated community where people could have the benefits of both the city and the countryside. In 1967, Rouse opened Columbia, a town between Baltimore and Washington, D.C., that today has a population of 60,000.

In the '50s, as chairman of a presidential task force, he coined the phrase "urban renewal." When it became apparent that cities needed something more, he forged ahead in Boston, despite great resistance from banks, as developer of the Faneuil Hall–Quincy Market restoration. This was the first so-called festival marketplace, a modern-day city market selling produce, meat, fish, specialty foods and goods, and clothing. "A place with life, color, vitality," says Rouse, "that people seek without purpose. A place for all kinds of people. A reaction to segregated subdivided suburbs."

Success

Faneuil Hall caught on. Soon thereafter, The Rouse Co. opened up a similar marketplace in Baltimore and then in New York City. The marketplaces have acted as catalysts for other development: office buildings, condominiums, stores, restaurants and more.

"Jim Rouse is a visionary," says John N. Graham, director of Toledo public affairs for Owens-Illinois, a Toledo, Ohio, firm spurring that city's downtown revival. Toledo now has Portside along the Maumee River, the second major Enterprise marketplace. "Rouse has long been on the leading edge of urban revitalization," adds Graham.

Rouse is working his urban wizardry solely for Enterprise these days, as chairman and CEO. Last spring he cut his last ties with the Rouse Co. A multimillionaire, he works about 12 hours a day without salary.

"Rouse is good at getting the business sector to think in social terms and the social sector in business terms," says an associate. The retail developments, because they are in under-utilized nonresidential areas, can mean gentrification without displacement. Eventual profits will help rebuild poor neighborhoods, not eliminate them. In crippled business districts, where rats long reigned over empty lots and abandoned buildings, there is life. In neighborhoods nearby, where people are living in squalor, there is hope.

"It's especially rewarding to know that our hard work creates opportunities for the poor—that we're not just making other people rich," says a development company architect.

It's a Herculean task. Challenged rather than troubled by its proportions, Rouse and his colleagues march on with great spirit, pulling the less-intrepid behind. "He's not a magic man," says K. Aubrey Gorman, president of the development company, "but he sure is a genius. He really can do anything he wants to do."

Rouse can't do it alone, however, Many are crucial to his crusade, especially his wife of 10 years, a founding trustee of the foundation and its secretary-treasurer. "If it weren't for Patty, there wouldn't be an Enterprise Foundation," he says.

Patricia T. Rouse, as a commissioner of the Norfolk, Va, redevelopment and housing authority from 1970 to '75, gained experience in housing and redevelopment. Patricia is, among other things, a liaison between Rouse and the foundation's field staff. They, in turn, are intermediaries between the foundation and what it calls its network—the nonprofit neighborhood groups that actually produce housing for low-income residents. In two startup years, 1,240 units were produced. The foundation plans to double that number this year.

In addition to working with the groups, the foundation—with a staff of 17 and a list of trustees that sounds like *Who's Who in America*—raises funds. It offers the group technical assistance, loans and grants, and invested $1 million in the development company, which is expected to become profitable in a couple of years. So far, the foundation has raised almost $17 million, including $1 million from Rouse.

Some firms, especially those with development and construction expertise, donate employees and pay their salaries. Two Philadelphia developers have submitted a proposal to the city for a market-rate-rent apartment complex that would give 10 to 15% of its profits to Enterprise, with the understanding that Enterprise make an equivalent investment in Philadelphia neighborhoods.

Models

Rouse has built Enterprise on two successful models. The model for the development company is The Rouse Co. The model for the foundation's groups is Jubilee Housing, Inc., Washington, D.C.

The foundation has resolved to be only a tool for the neighborhood groups. They actually build, own and manage their own housing. The groups teach the residents themselves to run the buildings, with an eye on eventual ownership. "You've got to find a way to give people a sense of participation and ownership in their housing, pride and satisfaction" in themselves and their future, says Rouse.

Ideally, the group is a grass-roots operation, with strong leadership and a solid reputation, a history of city and local institutional support and an appetite for problems that seem insurmountable. "We're more concerned that a group work towards meeting the criteria than with the reality of meeting them," says Edward L. Quinn, president of the foundation.

Dallas, Denver, Cleveland, Chicago, Boston, Baltimore and Philadelphia are just a few of the cities involved. So far there are 27 member groups in 15 cities. Five new cities are being added shortly. The foundation hopes to have 80 groups in 50 cities by the end of 1987. It also plans to put its program into effect in one city, citywide, beginning this year.

The field staff is responsible for finding the groups, gaining their trust and guiding them toward appropriate financial, design, and construction assistance in building housing inexpensively. "We ask a group: 'What do you want to do this year and how can we help?'" says Janet E. Raffel, foundation vice president in charge of field staff.

The staff can call upon a roster of inside and outside consultants made available by the foundation. "We teach groups the language of development, not the substance," says Peter C. Werwath, a staff consultant on construction. "They have to learn the substance themselves."

An example is 12 units of scattered-site housing rebuilt by Jubilee West in Oakland, Calif. "They had the promise of subsidies, a number of sites, but were afraid to move without knowing if they were moving into disaster," says Werwath. "We taught them financial feasibility, how to make presentations and helped them run the numbers."

A Detroit group, Church of the Messiah Housing Corp., rehabilitated a 12-unit building and "latched onto an empty 50-unit building," says Werwath. "It was a quantum leap for them." The foundation helped them look at code issues, costs and design. The result is a plan to turn the building into 36 units at a cost of about $25,000 per unit.

Because groups become part of Enterprise, as opposed to receiving funds for a specific project only, "they come to us with their problems and let it all hang out in a way they don't to other foundations," says Raffel. This can mean grappling with social and psychological problems that have no direct connection to housing production—drug addiction and hardcore unemployment, for example. Enterprise is therefore taking a holistic approach to the problem of the poor—housing first and then other needs such as job placement, health care and family counseling.

Groups also have the problem of many landlords—vandalism, nonpayment of rent, occasional eviction. "The groups that do the best are those that have conquered the tension between wanting to do social good and wanting to do business," says Werwath.

Alice Lipscomb, president of the Hawthorne Community Council, one of two Philadelphia groups in the network, says the groups that do the best are the ones that "solve their own problems. The experts don't have the solutions—the people do." Lipscomb, who has several developments under her belt, says she needs money, not assistance or loans.

For other less-experienced groups, the need goes beyond money. "Most of the groups don't know anything about housing," says field staff member Patricia A. Canavan. "Most get into it because they are appalled by the conditions."

The foundation has decided to cut through the thicket of problems by attacking costs first. Cost-cutters include encouraging recycling of materials and fixtures, helping form grass-roots contracting firms, using volunteer labor and trying to get code variances for use of less-expensive materials like plastic pipe. Cash-prize competitions encourage groups to find ways to build for less.

Rouse believes the cost of rehabilitating housing in most cities can be slashed by 20 to 40%. Groups that have accomplished this, such as the Cleveland Housing Network, are encouraged to advise others. An important role in the foundation is that of liaison between groups. A monthly newsletter and annual conference help groups communicate.

One of the ways the foundation hopes to provide inexpensive new units is through modular, factory-built housing. "We can produce a safe house, with unnecessary frills and amenities stripped out, for under $25,000," says Rouse. The foundation has developed such houses with a Baltimore manufacturer. Rouse has approached the city for free land for two-bedroom row houses. Maryland's Howard County, where Columbia is located, has already offered four lots for a two-bedroom detached house and the foundation is working on a similar plan with its Chicago group, Bethel New Life, Inc., and a manufacturer.

No Frills, No Appreciation

The foundation has been criticized for its no-frills approach. Critics say that building what they believe is substandard housing is not helping much.

Rouse doesn't buy the criticism: "There are limited funds available to do the job—I'm very satisfied with the strategy." He says it's better to provide five houses at $20,000 each than two at $50,000 each. "Middle-class standards for housing are fake," he adds.

The foundation defines the poor as a family of four with an income of $9,000 or less. Most units developed by the groups have monthly rents of about $250. This figure can be hundreds of dollars below market rate.

Cushing Dolbeare, a housing consultant in Washington, D.C., and a trustee of the foundation, says: "The foundation doesn't reach the poorest of the poor. What happens to a family of four with an income of $5,000 that can only afford $125 each month for rent?"

Dolbeare says government subsidies are necessary. In 1980 there were about 6 million renter households with incomes under $5,000 and only 2.7 million units renting for $125 per month or less, she says. In 1970, there were 8.4 million such households and 15 million units.

Rouse cautions that the foundation is not meant to replace government support, but to make the best use of it combined with resources of the private sector and the poor. Foundation President Quinn agrees: "We went too far in trying to do everything with money, ignoring the people. Now, we say it's going to be the people pulling themselves up by their bootstraps. The answer is somewhere in between."

Those who believe in government initiative are on the outside looking in. "The basic policy position of [the Reagan] administration is that the federal government has no responsibility to provide the production of new units of housing for the poor," says one congressional aide.

Some of the slack has been picked up by cities and states, but not much. "The situation is pretty dismal," says John A. Gallery, a partner in Urban Partners, Philadelphia, consultant for difficult-to-finance projects. "And there doesn't appear to be much sentiment for it getting better."

Rouse, not easily discouraged, says, "As programs have ceased, new initiatives are generated."

Financing Initiative

One initiative is Enterprise Social Investment Corp. "ESIC is really looking for replicable systems of low-cost financing that it can put into effect for the network groups," says F. Barton Harvey III, the foundation's financial consultant and a former investment banker.

One method is syndication, which involves attracting a for-profit limited partner to a low-income housing development partnership that includes a non-profit neighborhood group by offering the limited partner the nonprofit's tax benefits.

Syndication is complicated. "The paper work alone is deadly," says Harvey. Groups hesitate if it means giving up control and for-profit investors hesitate because few groups have credit records. That's why ESIC acts as a partner, to make sure everyone lives up to the agreement, says Harvey. At the end of the term of agreement, "ownership can revert to the nonprofit, either through sale or donation," he explains. Harvey estimates that 30% of a project can be financed this way. The approach is threatened, however, by the federal tax plan.

Benevolent lending could fill the gap. Here, a firm or a person is asked for a loan with an interest rate up to 6%. The money from the different lenders is deposited in a federally insured bank account and used as needed. "It's really a charitable event," says Rouse, "but you get your money back." The giving is in the reduced interest rate.

Innovative financing, with below-market-rate interest on mortgages is necessary for development company projects, too. "The festival marketplace needs quality that causes it to cost $250 to $300 per sq ft of leased area to build. That's very high," says Robert F. Barton, Jr., development company vice president-finance. "Traditional financing would make rents too high."

Partnerships

The answer, says Enterprise, is public-private partnership. Cities interested in downtown revivals have an interest in the marketplaces. They can use taxing powers, federal grants, industrial revenue bonds or a combination of measures to help. They can also make necessary public improvements.

At Portside in Toledo, funds were raised by the city, Owens-Illinois and the

Toledo Trust Co. The result was a $14.5 million mortgage for Enterprise at about 4% interest and nominal rent for the land. The city also gets 50% of the profits. (The city spent $7 million on public improvements.)

"The Toledo undertaking is high in risk," says George P. Barker, senior vice president-development for Enterprise Development Co. "The area was in a steady period of decline."

Because this is true of most Enterprise projects, the development company has strict criteria for locating, designing and operating its marketplaces. "Our concern for detail is outlandish," says Morton Hoppenfeld, vice president of planning and design. "We emphasize those aspects of the environment that are viscerally perceptible: sound, sight, smell, touch."

Delight

Shops are small, closely spaced and spill over with goods. Flowers and plants are real. "It's the delight that generates the people," says Rouse. "It's a reaction to high-tech, cellophane-wrapped impersonal influences of today."

Merchants really feel the risk. "It's not an easy undertaking, but when it all comes together, it's a great thing," says one merchant at The Waterside in Norfolk, Enterprise's first marketplace.

Gorman says one of the lessons of The Waterside is that "our sink-or-swim technique with new merchants wasn't going to work. They need care and feeding, training and counseling."

Marketplaces, like tourist attractions rely on many visitors and high sales volume to be profitable. The rent alone can be double that at a conventional shopping center. Sales are usually double, too, at about $300 per sq ft per year. . . .

The total Enterprise effort . . . is firmly grounded and carefully structured. But even Rouse admits there's room for improvement, in the hiring of more minorities, for example. And though some criticize the foundation's methods, few question its intentions. Says Lipscomb of the Hawthorne Community Council: "They are the only national foundation that really cares about the needs of the poor. They're the only game in town."

Jack Kemp and the Promise of Enterprise Zones

CLAY OGLESBEE

Jack Kemp kicked off a recent tour of inner cities with a visit to Atlanta. Standing with Representative John Lewis (D., Ga.) and Mayor Andrew Young, the new secretary of housing and urban development said he hoped his firsthand look at urban centers would "help find answers to the problems of homelessness and urban economic development."

Imagining him striding purposefully past a couple of poor homes in Atlanta, I found myself wondering, "Has Kemp really changed from his conservative House days?" Eight years ago four of us from the South Austin Coalition Com-

---

"The Kemp Plan for Rebuilding the City" by Clay Oglesbee, pp. 340–341. Copyright 1989 Christian Century Foundation. Reprinted by permission from the April 5, 1989 issue of *The Christian Century*.

munity Council on Chicago's west side stood in Kemp's congressional anteroom dripping from the rain, uncertain of our welcome. We wanted to hear more about Kemp's urban enterprise zones—areas where tax and regulatory relief would invite new businesses. At the time it seemed the only hope (albeit dim) coming from Washington for inner cities. We had no appointment. We hoped to catch Kemp in his office and press him to explain the zones further. Would they really create jobs for our neighborhood?

Impressive people came and went. A handsome man (perhaps Kemp, for all we knew) passed through the office and smiled inquiringly at us. Eventually we left a note for Kemp telling him we needed businesses and jobs in south Austin. If his zones would reopen the closed factories and employ the jobless, we wanted Kemp to call us with the details.

The return call never came. Maybe it will now that Kemp is walking the streets and looking into the homes and examining the needs of the inner cities.

In struggling communities like south Austin, the urban enterprise zone is an idea whose time won't go away. First proposed in 1977 by British geographer Peter Hasel, enterprise-zone legislation was defined as a package of incentives designed to attract business to designated areas of economic distress. By 1979 American models were being developed that included suspending minimum-wage laws, phasing out rent controls, and simplifying building codes and zoning laws. In 1980 Kemp, as a supply-side congressman in New York, helped to make the zones the centerpiece of Ronald Reagan's new federalism. As untried and inconclusive as the British experience then was, the enterprise zone was nevertheless the sole domestic initiative to emerge from Reagan's first presidential campaign. Its merit was its apparent applicability to inner-city job-hungry "poverty pockets" and its consistency with the entrepreneurial, tax-incentive orientation of the Reagan administration.

During the succeeding eight years several versions of the enterprise-zone plan were introduced in Congress, but none became national policy. The measure stirred bipartisan interest (Walter Mondale endorsed the idea during the 1984 presidential election), but serious questions about the zones' workability surfaced repeatedly and resulted in what *Newsweek* called "Kemp's long-running effort to pound the square peg of conservative economics into the round hole of liberal social causes."

With his recent appointment, Kemp seems to have the opportunity to make enterprise zones, as well as his ideas for the homeless and for low-income housing tenants, a reality. He calls his plans a "new war on poverty." He even says things that sound strange coming from one of the new federalism's architects: "You cannot balance the budget on the backs of the poor. . . . [We must] empower the poor." Arthur Himmelman, a senior fellow with the Hubert H. Humphrey Institute of Public Affairs, remarks, "If we can get Kemp and Bush to keep building on the language . . . I'm almost afraid to say it, but I'm hopeful again."

Initial objections to urban enterprise zones have not been answered, however, and experience with such zones created by state legislatures has tended to confirm people's misgivings. A primary concern, voiced by Marc Bendick, Jr., an economist with the Urban Institute writing in *Congressional Digest*, is that the zones are "based on erroneous assumptions about how urban areas are revitalized, how businesses create jobs, and how government can most usefully aid business. . . . [Tax incentives] generally are not the most cost-effective way for government to provide assistance to workers and firms in distress areas."

Bendick and others have argued that the tax incentives provided in enterprise zones are generally unavailable to unincorporated small businesses and nonprofit corporations, and are nonrefundable for companies that have no short-term profits—a feature that works against new and small firms. Enterprise-zone legislation introduced during the Reagan years also included a Targeted Jobs Tax Credit, but it proved useful to only a few firms in the inner cities, and it seemed such credits might only help firms hire people who would have found employment anyway.

A 1984 study of enterprise zones in Minnesota, sponsored by the Hubert H. Humphrey Institute of Public Affairs, cautioned that "tax credits alone do not determine business locations . . . [and that] this [zone] program involves the risks of granting subsidies to firms which are not in need or do not generate new jobs at livable wages." James Janus, one of the researchers, commented that the enterprise zones tend to overlook the importance of a range of social services: "The current proposals don't deal with child care, health care, public services—all the things that are going to matter to inner-city employees." Also, spokespersons for safety and union concerns have questioned the effects that deregulation within enterprise zones would have upon the occupational safety and rights of employees.

In spite of the doubts, the zones offer hope, and people from a broad range of religious and political persuasions long to see them adapted in order to create jobs and stability in city neighborhoods. AFL-CIO leaders have conditionally endorsed such targeted assistance: first they want to see working-capital grants, seed money, business loans and grants for public improvement available and work safety and workers' rights protected. Himmelman also endorses the enterprise-zone concept if it can be "community-based rather than business-based alone. I would advise Jack Kemp to keep looking at the nonprofit community-development corporations. They exist all over the country, unrecognized by federal officials. The zones won't work without community-wide involvement."

Kemp's proposals for the sale of public housing to tenants and for aid to the homeless are also going to need revamping if they are to be effective in low-income communities. Three years ago Peter Dreier, director of public housing for the Boston Redevelopment Authority, called Kemp's proposal to "privatize" public-housing units "unworkable." The concept is again based on policies in Britain, where 70 percent of public-housing units have at least one wage earner; in the U.S. most tenants in public housing are "too poor to purchase" or maintain such units, Dreier says, and cannot afford the payments. Dreier's alternative is to encourage and subsidize resident-owned, limited-equity cooperatives. He agrees with Kemp that "all should have opportunity to own," but he asks for a more realistic assessment of the capacities of low-income people. Ronald Pasquariello, senior fellow at the Churches' Center for Theology and Public Policy in Washington, D.C., concurs: "Kemp's ideas will work only if cities build a strong organization around it, and only if you sell to a tenant who is part of a cooperative." . . .

Kemp's acknowledgment that homelessness is pervasive and should become a top concern of the Bush administration offers some hope to the homeless and their advocates. Ed Loring, a cofounder of the Open Door Community, an Atlanta

Christian residential community for the homeless, was skeptical about the promises but open: "I'm not much on Washington's efforts unless housing for the poor is integrated into the larger fabric of society, so that we all can share a destiny with the poor."

Kemp's language has encouraged many of us with his priorities for HUD—employment, home ownership, revitalized inner cities, and care for the homeless. As he tours U.S. cities, many will tell him from hard experience and not from ideological biases that his dreams are good ones, but that they won't work unless they are shaped by the realities of poverty and inner-city neighborhoods. Many tools are needed to rebuild the city, and tax incentives alone will not do the job. If he will listen, adapt and lead, Jack Kemp may do some good for the poor. The people in Chicago's south Austin community, in Atlanta's Cabbagetown, and in a hundred other struggling neighborhoods around the country would still be glad to hear from the HUD secretary.

✖ F U R T H E R   R E A D I N G

Carl Abbott, *The New Urban America: Growth and Politics in Sunbelt Cities* (1981)

———, *Urban America in the Modern Age, 1920 to the Present* (1987)

Richard M. Bernard, *Snowbelt Cities: Metropolitan Politics in the Northeast and Midwest Since World War II* (1990)

M. Christine Boyer, *Dreaming the Rational City: The Myth of American City Planning* (1983)

Blaine Brownell and David Goldfield, eds., *The City in Southern History* (1977)

William W. Cutler III and Howard Gilette, Jr., eds., *The Divided Metropolis: Social and Spatial Dimensions of Philadelphia* (1980)

Bernard J. Friedman and Marshall Kaplan, *The Politics of Neglect: Urban Aid from Model Cities to Revenue Sharing* (1975)

Joel Garreau, *Edge City: Life on the New Frontier* (1991)

Mark I. Gelfand, *A Nation of Cities: The Federal Government and Urban America, 1933–1965* (1975)

David Goldfield, *Cottonfields and Skyscrapers: Southern City and Region, 1607–1980* (1982)

William Gorham and Nathan Glazer, *The Urban Predicament* (1976)

Kenneth T. Jackson, *The Crabgrass Frontier* (1985)

Jean Lowe, *Cities in a Race with Time* (1967)

Bradford Luckingham, *The Urban Southwest: A Profile History of Albuquerque, El Paso, Phoenix, and Tucson* (1982)

Alan Lupo, Frank Colcord, and Edmund Fowler, *Rites of Way: The Politics of Transportation in Boston and the U.S. City* (1971)

John H. Mollenkopf, *The Contested City* (1983)

Gerald Nash, *The American West in the Twentieth Century: A Short History of an Urban Oasis* (1973)

Arthur Solomon, *The Prospective City* (1979)

Jon C. Teaford, *City and Suburbs: Political Fragmentation of Metropolitan America, 1850–1970* (1979)

———, *The Twentieth-Century American City: Problems, Promise and Reality* (1986)

Alfred J. Watkins and David C. Perry, eds., *The Rise of the Sunbelt Cities* (1977)

James Q. Wilson, ed., *The Metropolitan Enigma* (1968)

C H A P T E R
14

Race and Poverty in
the Postindustrial City

✖

*From the colonial period onward, social complexity has given cities their excitement,
their problems, and their challenges. In recent decades, the racial and ethnic diversity of American cities has intensified. The results sometimes have been explosive as
people of different beliefs and prejudices have rubbed up against each other and as
the dilemmas of a postindustrial society have weighed heavily upon those least
equipped in education, skills, and financial resources to adjust. The exodus of middle-
class (mostly white and young) residents and jobs (usually the best-paying) to the
suburbs has left behind the poorest people, mostly people of color and the elderly,
plus abandoned inner-city businesses and factories. These conditions, when coupled
with plagues of drug addiction, crime, and violence, have created a seemingly unsolv-
able urban crisis that threatens the entire nation's welfare. The outbursts of rioting
in scores of cities in the 1960s, beginning with the uprising in Harlem in 1964 and
ending with the Detroit riot of 1967, along with the frightening revival of mass street
violence in Los Angeles in 1992, have underscored for all Americans the poverty,
frustration, and failed values of human dignity that fester in decaying neighborhoods.*

*What are the dimensions of the urban crisis? Some scholars have highlighted ra-
cial factors, especially the continuing segregation that has blocked people of color
from access to the advantages and facilities that modern society has bestowed upon
whites. Others blame the crisis on enduring poverty and the creation of a permanent
underclass, black and white, who are victims of the postindustrial economy.*

*Yet in comparison with city dwellers in past eras of American history, urban res-
idents today have better health, transportation, lighting, police and fire protection,
fiscal management, pollution control, and entertainment facilities than their ances-
tors ever had. The questions for the future are these: Is time running out, and can
Americans use whatever time they have to build on past improvements before the crisis deepens so much that it destroys the tradition of ingenuity, confidence, and tolera-
tion that has characterized the American urban past?*

✖ D O C U M E N T S

Johnnie Tillmon, the author of the first document, grew up in Arkansas and moved to Los Angeles. She was the first chairwoman of the National Welfare Rights Organization. Her statement addresses the problems of low-income women who had to meet unreasonable requirements in order to receive public aid, and it accents the pervasiveness of poverty among all races of women. The article also returns to a theme of the feminization of poverty, raised in Chapter 3; and it ties the concerns of welfare women to women's liberation while at the same time revealing the divisions between middle-class and low-income women. The second document presents a cogent statement of sociologist William Julius Wilson's identification of an urban "underclass," which he first described in his controversial book *The Truly Disadvantaged: The Inner City, the Underclass and Public Policy* (1987). Wilson and co-author Loic Waquant argue that individual-level explanations of the causes of poverty need to be replaced by structural explanations. The third document, written by a newspaper reporter, paints a somewhat positive picture of results of the Indian Relocation Act, which attempted to attract Native Americans off reservations and into cities. Written with some of the patronizing biases toward Native Americans that are typical of the 1950s, the article automatically assumes that women would have the hardest time adjusting to modern urban life. The final two documents pertain to mass urban violence at two points in time. First, a statement by a self-proclaimed participant in the 1967 Detroit riots combines adolescent street bravado with intense feelings of rage at racial exploitation that fueled the violence of the riots. Second, a newspaper feature story describes the disparate characteristics of fatalities of the uprising in Los Angeles in April 1992, following the verdict essentially exonerating four police officers who had been videotaped beating Rodney King, a black man arrested for a traffic violation. The victims, all killed by police, varied in their ethnicity, background, and motives.

Johnnie Tillmon on Welfare as a Women's Issue, 1972

I'm a woman. I'm a black woman. I'm a poor woman. I'm a fat woman. I'm a middle-aged woman. And I'm on welfare.

In this country, if you're any one of those things—poor, black, fat, female, middle-aged, on welfare—you count less as a human being. If you're all those things, you don't count at all. Except as a statistic.

I am a statistic.

I am 45 years old. I have raised six children.

I grew up in Arkansas, and I worked there for fifteen years in a laundry, making about $20 or $30 a week, picking cotton on the side for carfare. I moved to California in 1959 and worked in a laundry there for nearly four years. In 1963 I got too sick to work anymore. Friends helped me to go on welfare.

They didn't call it welfare. They called it A.F.D.C.—Aid to Families with Dependent Children. Each month I got $363 for my kids and me. I pay $128 a

"Welfare Is a Women's Issue," from Johnnie Tillmon, *Liberation News Service*, no. 415 (February 26, 1972).

month rent; $30 for utilities, which include gas, electricity, and water; $120 for food and nonedible household essentials; $50 for school lunches for the three children in junior and senior high school who are not eligible for reduced-cost meal programs.

There are millions of statistics like me. Some on welfare. Some not. And some, really poor, who don't even know they're entitled to welfare. Not all of them are black. Not at all. In fact, the majority—about two-thirds—of all the poor families in the country are white.

Welfare's like a traffic accident. It can happen to anybody, but especially it happens to women.

And that is why welfare is a women's issue. For a lot of middle-class women in this country, Women's Liberation is a matter of concern. For women on welfare it's a matter of survival.

Forty-four percent of all poor families are headed by women. That's bad enough. But the *families* on A.F.D.C. aren't really families. Because 99 percent of them are headed by women. That means there is no man around. In half the states there really can't be men around because A.F.D.C. says if there is an "able-bodied" man around, then you can't be on welfare. If the kids are going to eat, and the man can't get a job, then he's got to go. So his kids can eat.

The truth is that A.F.D.C. is like a supersexist marriage. You trade in a man for *the* man. But you can't divorce him if he treats you bad. He can divorce you, of course, cut you off anytime he wants. But in that case, *he* keeps the kids, not you.

The man runs everything. In ordinary marriage, sex is supposed to be for your husband. On A.F.D.C., you're not supposed to have any sex at all. You give up control of your own body. It's a condition of aid. You may even have to agree to get your tubes tied so you can never have more children just to avoid being off welfare.

The man, the welfare system, controls your money. He tells you what to buy, what not to buy, where to buy it, and how much things cost. If things—rent, for instance—really cost more than he says they do, it's just too bad for you.

There are other welfare programs, other kinds of people on welfare—the blind, the disabled, the aged. (Many of them are women too, especially the aged.) Those others make up just over a third of all the welfare caseloads. We A.F.D.C. are two-thirds.

But when the politicians talk about the "welfare cancer eating at our vitals," they're not talking about the aged, blind, and disabled. Nobody minds them. They're the "deserving poor." Politicians are talking about A.F.D.C. Politicians are talking about us—the women who head up 99 percent of the A.F.D.C. families—and our kids. We're the "cancer," the "undeserving poor." Mothers and children.

In this country we believe in something called the "work ethic." That means that your work is what gives you human worth. But the work ethic itself is a double standard. It applies to men and to women on welfare. It doesn't apply to all women. If you're a society lady from Scarsdale and you spend all your time sitting on your prosperity paring your nails, well, that's okay.

The truth is a job doesn't necessarily mean an adequate income. A woman with three kids—not twelve kids, mind you, just three kids—that woman earning the full federal minimum wage of $2.00 an hour, is still stuck in poverty. She is below the Government's own official poverty line. There are some ten million jobs that now pay less than the minimum wage, and if you're a woman, you've got the best chance of getting one.

The President keeps repeating the "dignity of work" idea. What dignity? Wages are the measure of dignity that society puts on a job. Wages and nothing else. There is no dignity in starvation. Nobody denies, least of all poor women, that there is dignity and satisfaction in being able to support your kids through honest labor.

We wish we could do it.

The problem is that our country's economic policies deny the dignity and satisfaction of self-sufficiency to millions of people—the millions who suffer everyday in underpaid dirty jobs—and still don't have enough to survive.

People still believe that old lie that A.F.D.C. mothers keep on having kids just to get a bigger welfare check. On the average, another baby means another $35 a month—barely enough for food and clothing. Having babies for profit is a lie that only men could make up, and only men could believe. Men, who never have to bear the babies or have to raise them and maybe send them to war.

There are a lot of other lies that male society tells about welfare mothers; that A.F.D.C. mothers are immoral, that A.F.D.C. mothers are lazy, misuse their welfare checks, spend it all on booze and are stupid and incompetent.

If people are willing to believe these lies, it's partly because they're just special versions of the lies that society tells about all women. . . .

On TV, a woman learns that human worth means beauty and that beauty means being thin, white, young and rich.

She learns that her body is really disgusting the way it is, and that she needs all kinds of expensive cosmetics to cover it up.

She learns that a "real woman" spends her time worrying about how her bathroom bowl smells; that being important means being middle class, having two cars, a house in the suburbs, and a minidress under your maxicoat. In other words, an A.F.D.C. mother learns that being a "real woman" means being all the things she isn't and having all the things she can't have.

Either it breaks you, and you start hating yourself, or you break it.

There's one good thing about welfare. It kills your illusions about yourself, and about where this society is really at. It's laid out for you straight. You have to learn to fight, to be aggressive, or you just don't make it. If you can survive being on welfare, you can survive anything. It gives you a kind of freedom, a sense of your own power and togetherness with other women.

Maybe it is we poor welfare women who will really liberate women in this country. We've already started on our welfare plan.

Along with other welfare recipients, we have organized together so we can have some voice. Our group is called the National Welfare Rights Organization (N.W.R.O.). We put together our own welfare plan, called Guaranteed Adequate Income (G.A.I.), which would eliminate sexism from welfare.

There would be no "categories"—men, women, children, single, married, kids, no kids—just poor people who need aid. You'd get paid according to need and family size only—$6,500 for a family of four (which is the Department of

Labor's estimate of what's adequate), and that would be upped as the cost of living goes up.

If I were president, I would solve this so-called welfare crisis in a minute and go a long way toward liberating every woman. I'd just issue a proclamation that "women's" work is *real* work.

In other words, I'd start paying women a living wage for doing the work we are already doing—child-raising and house-keeping. And the welfare crisis would be over, just like that. Housewives would be getting wages, too—a legally determined percentage of their husband's salary—instead of having to ask for and account for money they've already earned.

For me, Women's Liberation is simple. No woman in this country can feel dignified, no woman can be liberated, until all women get off their knees. That's what N.W.R.O. is all about—women standing together, on their feet.

William Julius Wilson Considers Racial and Class Exclusion in the Inner City, 1989

After a long eclipse, the ghetto has made a stunning comeback into the collective consciousness of America. Not since the riots of the hot summers of 1966–68 have the black poor received so much attention in academic, activist, and policymaking quarters alike. Persistent and rising poverty, especially among children, mounting social disruption, the continuing degradation of public housing and public schools, concern over the eroding tax base of cities plagued by large ghettos and by the dilemma of gentrification, the disillusion of liberals over welfare have all combined to put the black inner-city poor back in the spotlight. Owing in large part to the pervasive and ascendant influence of conservative ideology in the United States, however, recent discussions of the plight of ghetto blacks have typically been cast in individualistic and moralistic terms. The poor are presented as a mere aggregation of personal cases, each with its own logic and self-contained causes. Severed from the struggles and structural changes in the society, economy, and polity that in fact determine them, inner-city dislocations are then portrayed as a self-imposed, self-sustaining phenomenon. This vision of poverty has found perhaps its most vivid expression in the lurid descriptions of ghetto residents that have flourished in the pages of popular magazines and on televised programs devoted to the emerging underclass. Descriptions and explanations of the current predicament of inner-city blacks put the emphasis on individual attributes and the alleged grip of the so-called culture of poverty.

This article, in sharp contrast, draws attention to the specific features of the proximate social structure in which ghetto residents evolve and strive, against formidable odds, to survive and, whenever they can, escape its poverty and degradation. We provide this different perspective by profiling blacks who live in Chicago's inner city, contrasting the situation of those who dwell in low-poverty areas with residents of the city's ghetto neighborhoods. Beyond its sociographic focus, the central argument running through this article is that the interrelated set

From J. D. Wacquant and William Julius Wilson, "The Cost of Racial and Class Exclusion in the Inner City," *Annals of the American Academy of Political and Social Science* 501 (Jan. 1989), pp. 8–23. Copyright © 1989 Sage Publications, Inc. Reprinted by permission of the publisher.

of phenomena captured by the term "underclass" is primarily social-structural and that the ghetto is experiencing a "crisis" not because a "welfare ethos" has mysteriously taken over its residents but because joblessness and economic exclusion, having reached dramatic proportions, have triggered a process of hyperghettoization. Indeed, the urban black poor of today differ both from their counterparts of earlier years and from the white poor in that they are becoming increasingly concentrated in dilapidated territorial enclaves that epitomize acute social and economic marginalization. In Chicago, for instance, the proportion of all black poor residing in extreme-poverty areas—that is, census tracts with a population at least 40 percent of which comprises poor persons—shot up from 24 percent to 47 percent between 1970 and 1980. By this date, fully 38 percent of all poor blacks in the 10 largest American cities lived in extreme-poverty tracts, contrasted with 22 percent a decade before, and with only 6 percent of poor non-Hispanic whites.

This growing social and spatial concentration of poverty creates a formidable and unprecedented set of obstacles for ghetto blacks. As we shall see, the social structure of today's inner city has been radically altered by the mass exodus of jobs and working families and by the rapid deterioration of housing, schools, businesses, recreational facilities, and other community organizations, further exacerbated by government policies of industrial and urban laissez-faire that have channeled a disproportionate share of federal, state, and municipal resources to the more affluent. The economic and social buffer provided by a stable black working class and a visable, if small, black middle class that cushioned the impact of downswings in the economy and tied ghetto residents to the world of work has all but disappeared. Moreover, the social networks of parents, friends, and associates, as well as the nexus of local institutions, have seen their resources for economic stability progressively depleted. In sum, today's ghetto residents face a closed opportunity structure.

The purpose of this article is to begin to highlight this specifically sociological dimension of the changing reality of ghetto poverty by focusing on Chicago's inner city. Using data from a multistage random sample of black residents of Chicago's poor communities, we show that ghetto dwellers do face specific obstacles owing to the characteristics of the social structure they compose. We begin by way of background, by sketching the accelerating degradation of Chicago's inner city, relating the cumulation of social dislocation visited upon its South and West sides to changes in the city's economy over the last thirty years.

Deindustrialization and Hyperghettoization

Social conditions in the ghettos of Northern metropolises have never been enviable, but today they are scaling new heights in deprivation, oppression, and hardship. The situation of Chicago's black inner city is emblematic of the social changes that have sown despair and exclusion in these communities. [A]n unprecedented tangle of social woes is now gripping the black communities of the city's South Side and West Side. In the past decade alone, these racial enclaves have experienced rapid increases in the number and percentage of poor families, extensive out-migration of working- and middle-class households, stagnation—if not real regression—of income, and record levels of unemployment. As of the last census, over two-thirds of all families living in these areas were headed by women; about half of the population had to rely on public aid, for most adults were out of a job and only a tiny fraction of them had completed college.

The single largest force behind this increasing social and economic marginalization of large numbers of inner-city blacks has been a set of mutually reinforcing spatial and industrial changes in the country's urban political economy that have converged to undermine the material foundations of the traditional ghetto. Among these structural shifts are the decentralization of industrial plants, which commenced at the time of World War I but accelerated sharply after 1950, and the flight of manufacturing jobs abroad, to the Sunbelt states, or to the suburbs and exurbs at a time when blacks were continuing to migrate en masse to Rustbelt central cities; the general deconcentration of metropolitan economies and the turn toward service industries and occupations, promoted by the growing separation of banks and industry; and the emergence of post-Taylorist, so-called flexible forms of organizations and generalized corporate attacks on unions—expressed by, among other things, wage cutbacks and the spread of two-tier wage systems and labor contracting—which has intensified job competition and triggered an explosion of low-pay, part-time work. This means that even mild forms of racial discrimination—mild by historical standards—have a bigger impact on those at the bottom of the American class order. In the labor-surplus environment of the 1970s, the weakness of unions and the retrenchment of civil rights enforcement aggravated the structuring of unskilled labor markets along racial lines, marking large numbers of inner-city blacks with the stamp of economic redundancy.

In 1954, Chicago was still near the height of its industrial power. Over 10,000 manufacturing establishments operated within the city limits, employing a total of 616,000, including nearly half a million production workers. By 1982, the number of plants had been cut by half, providing a mere 277,000 jobs for fewer than 162,000 blue-collar employees—a loss of 63 percent, in sharp contrast with the overall growth of manufacturing employment in the country, which added almost 1 million production jobs in the quarter century starting in 1958. This crumbling of the city's industrial base was accompanied by substantial cuts in trade employment, with over 120,000 jobs lost in retail and wholesale from 1963 to 1982. The mild growth of services—which created an additional 57,000 jobs during the same period, excluding health, financial, and social services—came nowhere near to compensating for the collapse of Chicago's low-skilled employment pool. Because, traditionally, blacks have relied heavily on manufacturing and blue-collar employment for economic sustenance, the upshot of these structural economic changes for the inhabitants of the inner city has been a steep and accelerating rise in labor market exclusion. In the 1950s, ghetto blacks had roughly the same rate of employment as the average Chicagoan, with some 6 adults in 10 working. . . . While this ratio has not changed citywide over the ensuing three decades, nowadays most residents of the Black Belt cannot find gainful employment and must resort to welfare, to participation in the second economy, or to illegal activities in order to survive. . . .

As the metropolitan economy moved away from smokestack industries and expanded outside of Chicago, emptying the Black Belt of most of its manufacturing jobs and employed residents, the gap between the ghetto and the rest of the city, not to mention its suburbs, widened dramatically. By 1980, median family income on the South and West sides had dropped to around one-third and one-half of the city average, respectively, compared with two-thirds and near parity thirty years earlier. Meanwhile, some of the city's white bourgeois neighborhoods and upper-class suburbs had reached over twice the citywide figure. Thus in 1980, half of the families of Oakland had to make do with less than $5500 a year, while half of the families of Highland Park incurred incomes in excess of $43,000. . . .

Fundamental changes in the organization of America's advanced economy have thus unleashed irresistible centrifugal pressures that have broken down the previous structure of the ghetto and set off a process of hyperghettoization. By this, we mean that the ghetto has lost much of its organizational strength—the "pulpit and the press," for instance, have virtually collapsed as collective agencies—as it has become increasingly marginal economically; its activities are no longer structured around an internal and relatively autonomous social space that duplicates the institutional structure of the larger society and provides basic minimal resources for social mobility, if only within a truncated black class structure. And the social ills that have long been associated with segregated poverty—violent crime, drugs, housing deterioration, family disruption, commercial blight, and educational failure—have reached qualitatively different proportions and have become articulated into a new configuration that endows each with a more deadly impact than before.

If the "organized" or institutional ghetto of forty years ago . . . imposed an enormous cost on blacks collectively, the "disorganized" ghetto, or hyperghetto, of today carries an even larger price. For, now, not only are ghetto residents, as before, dependent on the will and decisions of outside forces that rule the field of power—the mostly white dominant class, corporations, realtors, politicians, and welfare agencies—they have no control over and are forced to rely on services and institutions that are massively inferior to those of the wider society. Today's ghetto inhabitants comprise almost exclusively the most marginal and oppressed sections of the black community. Having lost the economic underpinnings and much of the fine texture of organizations and patterned activities that allowed previous generations of urban blacks to sustain family, community, and collectivity even in the face of continued economic hardship and unflinching racial subordination, the inner-city now presents a picture of radical class and racial exclusion. It is to a sociographic assessment of the latter that we now turn.

The Cost of Living in the Ghetto

Let us contrast the social structure of ghetto neighborhoods with that of low-poverty black areas of the city of Chicago. For purposes of this comparison, we have classified as low-poverty neighborhoods all those tracts with rates of poverty—as measured by the number of persons below the official poverty line—between 20 and 30 percent as of the 1980 census. Given that the overall poverty rate among black families in the city is about one-third, these low-poverty areas can be considered as roughly representative of the average non-ghetto, non-middle-class, black neighborhood of Chicago. In point of fact, nearly all—97 percent—of the respondents in this category reside outside traditional ghetto areas. Extreme-poverty neighborhoods comprise tracts with at least 40 percent of their residents in poverty in 1980. These tracts make up the historic heart of Chicago's black ghetto; over 82 percent of the respondents in this category inhabit the West and South sides of the City, in areas most of which have been all black for half a century and more, and an additional 13 percent live in immediately adjacent tracts. Thus when we counterpose extreme-poverty areas with low-poverty areas, we are in effect comparing ghetto neighborhoods with other black areas, most of which are moderately poor, that are not part of Chicago's traditional Black Belt. Even though this comparison involves a truncated spectrum of types of neighborhoods, the contrasts it reveals between low-poverty and ghetto tracts are quite pronounced.

It should be noted that this distinction between low-poverty and ghetto neighborhoods is not merely analytical but captures differences that are clearly perceived by social agents themselves. First, the folk category of ghetto does, in Chicago, refer to the South Side and West Side, not just to any black area of the city; mundane usages of the term entail a social-historical and spatial referent rather than simply a racial dimension. Furthermore, blacks who live in extreme-poverty areas have a noticeably more negative opinion of their neighborhood. Only 16 percent rate it as a "good" to "very good" place to live in, compared to 41 percent among inhabitants of low-poverty tracts; almost 1 in 4 find their neighborhood "bad or very bad" compared to fewer than 1 in 10 among the latter. In short, the contrast between ghetto and non-ghetto poor areas is one that is socially meaningful to their residents.

The Black Class Structure in and out of the Ghetto. The first major difference between low- and extreme-poverty areas has to do with their class structure. A sizable majority of blacks in low-poverty tracts are gainfully employed; two-thirds hold jobs, including 11 percent with middle-class occupations and 55 percent with working-class jobs, while one-third do not work. These proportions are exactly opposite in the ghetto, where fully 61 percent of adult residents do not work, one-third have working-class jobs and a mere 6 percent enjoy middle-class status. For those who reside in the urban core, then, being without a job is by far the most likely occurrence, while being employed is the exception. . . .

These data are hardly surprising. They stand as a brutal reminder that joblessness and poverty are two sides of the same coin. The poorer the neighborhood, the more prevalent joblessness and the lower the class recruitment of its residents. But these results also reveal that the degree of economic exclusion observed in ghetto neighborhoods during the period of sluggish economic growth of the late 1970s is still very much with us nearly a decade later, in the midst of the most rapid expansion in recent American economic history.

As we would expect, there is a close association between class and educational credentials. Virtually every member of the middle class has at least graduated from high school; nearly two-thirds of working-class blacks have also completed secondary education; but less than half—44 percent—of the jobless have a high school diploma or more. Looked at from another angle, 15 percent of our educated respondents—that is, high school graduates or better—have made it into the salaried middle class, half have become white-collar or blue-collar wage earners, and 36 percent are without a job. By comparison, those without a high school education are distributed as follows: 1.6 percent in the middle class, 37.9 percent in the working class, and a substantial majority of 60.5 percent in the jobless category. In other words, a high school degree is a *condition sine qua non* for blacks for entering the world of work, let alone that of the middle class. Not finishing secondary education is synonymous with economic redundancy.

Ghetto residents are, on the whole, less educated than the inhabitants of other black neighborhoods. This results in part from their lower class composition but also from the much more modest academic background of the jobless: fewer than 4 in 10 jobless persons on the city's South Side and West Side have graduated from high school, compared to nearly 6 in 10 in low-poverty areas. It should be pointed out that education is one of the few areas in which women do not fare worse than men: females are as likely to hold a high school diploma as males in the ghetto—50 percent—and more likely to do so in low-poverty areas—69 percent versus 62 percent.

Moreover, ghetto residents have lower-class origins, if one judges from the economic assets of their family of orientation. Fewer than 4 ghetto dwellers in 10 come from a family that owned its home and 6 in 10 have parents who owned nothing, that is, no home, business, or land. In low-poverty areas, 55 percent of the inhabitants are from a home-owning family while only 40 percent had no assets at all a generation ago. Women, both in and out of the ghetto, are least likely to come from a family with a home or any other asset—46 percent and 37 percent, respectively. This difference in class origins is also captured by differential rates of welfare receipt during childhood; the proportion of respondents whose parents were on public aid at some time when they were growing up is 30 percent in low-poverty tracts and 41 percent in the ghetto. Women in extreme-poverty areas are by far the most likely to come from a family with a welfare record.

Class, Gender, and Welfare Trajectories in Low- and Extreme-Poverty Areas. If they are more likely to have been raised in a household that drew public assistance in the past, ghetto dwellers are also much more likely to have been or to be currently on welfare themselves. Differences in class, gender, and neighborhood cumulate at each juncture of the welfare trajectory to produce much higher levels of welfare attachments among the ghetto population.

In low-poverty areas, only one resident in four are currently on aid while almost half have never personally received assistance. In the ghetto, by contrast, over half the residents are current welfare recipients, and only one in five have never been on aid. . . .

None of the middle-class respondents who live in low-poverty tracts were on welfare at the time they were interviewed, and only one in five had ever been on aid in their lives. Among working-class residents, a mere 7 percent were on welfare and just over one-half had never had any welfare experience. This same relationship between class and welfare receipt is found among residents of extreme-poverty tracts, but with significantly higher rates of welfare receipt at all class levels: there, 12 percent of working-class residents are presently on aid and 39 percent received welfare before; even a few middle-class blacks—9 percent—are drawing public assistance and only one-third of them have never received any aid, instead of three-quarters in low-poverty tracts. But it is among the jobless that the difference between low- and extreme-poverty areas is the largest: fully 86 percent of those in ghetto tracts are currently on welfare and only 7 percent have never had recourse to public aid, compared with 62 percent and 20 percent, respectively, among those who live outside the ghetto. . . .

The high incidence and persistence of joblessness and welfare in ghetto neighborhoods, reflecting the paucity of viable options for stable employment, take a heavy toll on those who are on aid by significantly depressing their expectations of finding a route to economic self-sufficiency. While a slim majority of welfare recipients living in low-poverty tracts expect to be self-supportive within a year and only a small minority anticipate receiving aid for longer than five years, in ghetto neighborhoods, by contrast, fewer than 1 in 3 public-aid recipients expect to be welfare-free within a year and fully 1 in 5 anticipate needing assistance for more than five years. This difference of expectations increases among the jobless of both genders. For instance, unemployed women in the ghetto are twice as likely as unemployed women in low-poverty areas to think that they will remain on aid for more than five years and half as likely to anticipate getting off the rolls within a year.

Thus if the likelihood of being on welfare increases sharply as one crosses the line between the employed and the jobless, it remains that, at each level of the class structure, welfare receipt is notably more frequent in extreme-poverty neighborhoods, especially among the unemployed, and among women. . . .

Differences in Economic and Financial Capital.   A quick survey of the economic and financial assets of the residents of Chicago's poor black neighborhoods reveals the appalling degree of economic hardship, insecurity, and deprivation that they must confront day in and day out. The picture in low-poverty areas is grim; that in the ghetto is one of near-total destitution.

In 1986, the median family income for blacks nationally was pegged at $18,000, compared to $31,000 for white families. Black households in Chicago's low-poverty areas have roughly equivalent incomes, with 52 percent declaring over $20,000 annually. Those living in Chicago's ghetto, by contrast, command but a fraction of this figure: half of all ghetto respondents live in households that dispose of less than $7500 annually, twice the rate among residents of low-poverty neighborhoods. Women assign their households to much lower income brackets in both areas, with fewer than 1 in 3 in low-poverty areas enjoying more than $25,000 annually. Even those who work report smaller incomes in the ghetto: the proportion of working-class and middle-class households falling under the $7500 mark on the South and West sides—12.5 percent and 6.5 percent, respectively—is double that of other black neighborhoods, while fully one-half of jobless respondents in extreme-poverty tracts do not reach the $5000 line. It is not surprising that ghetto dwellers also less frequently report an improvement of the financial situation of their household, with women again in the least envi-able position. This reflects sharp class differences: 42 percent of our middle-class respondents and 36 percent of working-class blacks register a financial ameliora-tion as against 13 percent of the jobless.

Due to meager and irregular income, those financial and banking services that most members of the larger society take for granted are, to put it mildly, not of obvious access to the black poor. Barely one-third of the residents of low-poverty areas maintain a personal checking account; only one in nine manage to do so in the ghetto, where nearly three of every four persons report no financial assets whatsoever from a possible list of six and only 8 percent have at least three of those assets. Here, again, class and neighborhood lines are sharply drawn: in low-poverty areas, 10 percent of the jobless and 48 percent of working-class blacks have a personal checking account compared to 3 percent and 37 percent, respectively, in the ghetto; the proportion for members of the middle class is sim-ilar—63 percent—in both areas.

The American dream of owning one's home remains well out of reach for a large majority of our black respondents, especially those in the ghetto, where barely 1 person in 10 belong to a home-owning household, compared to over 4 in 10 in low-poverty areas, a difference that is just as pronounced within each gen-der. The considerably more modest dream of owning an automobile is likewise one that has yet to materialize for ghetto residents, of which only one-third live in households with a car that runs. Again, this is due to a cumulation of sharp class and neighborhood differences: 79 percent of middle-class respondents and 62 percent of working-class blacks have an automobile in their household, con-trasted with merely 28 percent of the jobless. But in ghetto tracts, only 18 percent of the jobless have domestic access to a car—34 percent for men and 13 percent for women.

The social consequences of such a paucity of income and assets as suffered by ghetto blacks cannot be overemphasized. For just as the lack of financial re-sources or possession of a home represents a critical handicap when one can only find low-paying and casual employment or when one loses one's job, in that it literally forces one to go on the welfare rolls, not owning a car severely curtails one's chances of competing for available jobs that are not located nearby or that are not readily accessible by public transportation.

Social Capital and Poverty Concentration.   Among the resources that individ-uals can draw upon to implement strategies of social mobility are those poten-tially provided by their lovers, kin, and friends and by the contacts they develop within the formal associations to which they belong—in sum, the resources they have access to by virtue of being socially integrated into solidary groups, net-works, or organizations . . . . Our data indicate that not only do residents of ex-treme-poverty areas have fewer social ties but also that they tend to have ties of lesser social worth, as measured by the social position of their partners, parents, siblings, and best friends, for instance. In short, they possess lower volumes of social capital.

Living in the ghetto means being more socially isolated: nearly half of the residents of extreme-poverty tracts have no current partner—defined here as a person they are married to, live with, or are dating steadily—and one in five admit to having no one who would qualify as a best friend, compared to 32 percent and 12 percent, respectively, in low-poverty areas. It also means that intact marriages are less frequent. Jobless men are much less likely than working males to have current partners in both types of neighborhoods: 62 percent in low-poverty neighborhoods and 44 percent in extreme-poverty areas. Black women have a slightly better chance of having a partner if they live in a low-poverty area, and the partner is also more likely to have completed high school and to work steadily; for ghetto residence further affects the labor-market standing of the latter. The partners of women living in extreme-poverty areas are less stably employed than those of female respondents from low-poverty neighborhoods: 62 percent in extreme-poverty areas work regularly as compared to 84 percent in low-poverty areas.

Friends often play a crucial role in life in that they provide emotional and material support, help construct one's identity, and often open up opportunities that one would not have without them—particularly in the area of jobs. We have seen that ghetto residents are more likely than other black Chicagoans to have no close friend. If they have a best friend, furthermore, he or she is less likely to work, less educated, and twice as likely to be on aid. Because friendships tend to develop primarily within genders and women have much higher rates of economic exclusion, female respondents are much more likely than men to have a best friend who does not work and who receives welfare assistance. Both of these characteristics, in turn, tend to be more prevalent among ghetto females.

Such differences in social capital are also evidenced by different rates and patterns of organizational participation. While being part of a formal organization, such as a block club or a community organization, a political party, a school-related association, or a sports, fraternal, or other social group, is a rare occurrence as a rule—with the notable exception of middle-class blacks, two-thirds of whom belong to at least one such group—it is more common for ghetto residents—64 percent, versus 50 percent in low-poverty tracts—especially females—64 percent, versus 46 percent in low-poverty areas—to belong to no organization. As for church membership, the small minority who profess to be, in Weber's felicitous expression, "religiously unmusical" is twice as large in the ghetto as outside: 12 percent versus 5 percent. For those with a religion, ghetto residence tends to depress church attendance slightly—29 percent of ghetto inhabitants attend service at least once a week compared to 37 percent of respondents from low-poverty tracts—even though women tend to attend more regularly than men in both types of areas. Finally, black women who inhabit the ghetto are also slightly less likely to know most of their neighbors than their counterparts from low-poverty areas. All in all, then, poverty concentration has the effect of devaluing the social capital of those who live in its midst.

Conclusion: The Social Structuring of Ghetto Poverty

The extraordinary levels of economic hardship plaguing Chicago's inner city in the 1970s have not abated, and the ghetto seems to have gone unaffected by the economic boom of the past five years. If anything, conditions have continued to worsen. This points to the asymmetric causality between the economy and ghetto poverty and to the urgent need to study the social and political structures that mediate their relationship. The significant differences we have uncovered between low-poverty and extreme-poverty areas in Chicago are essentially a reflection of their different class mix and of the prevalence of economic exclusion in the ghetto.

Our conclusion, then, is that social analysts must pay more attention to the extreme levels of economic deprivation and social marginalization as uncovered in this article before they further entertain and spread so-called theories about the potency of a ghetto culture of poverty that has yet to receive rigorous empirical elaboration. Those who have been pushing moral-cultural or individualistic-behaviorate explanations of the social dislocations that have swept through the inner city in recent years have created a fictitious normative divide between urban blacks that, no matter its reality—which has yet to be ascertained—cannot but pale when compared to the objective structural cleavage that separates ghetto residents from the larger society and to the collective material constraints that bear on them. It is the cumulative structural entrapment and forcible socioeconomic marginalization resulting from the historically evolving interplay of class, racial, and gender domination, together with sea changes in the organization of American capitalism and failed urban and social policies, not a "welfare ethos," that explains the plight of today's ghetto blacks. Thus, if the concept of underclass is used, it must be a structural concept; it must denote a new sociospatial patterning of class and racial domination, recognizable by the unprecedented concentration of the most socially excluded and economically marginal members of the dominated racial and economic group. It should not be used as a label to designate a new breed of individuals molded freely by a mythical and all-powerful culture of poverty.

A Contemporary Look at Indian Relocation to the Cities, 1956

What happens when an American Indian brings his family to Los Angeles under the Untied States Indian Bureau's relocation program?

His name, let's say, is Tony Big-Bear. His wife's name is Martha. They have five children, ranging from a strapping teenage lad to a cute papoose.

Tony speaks English. Martha has never before been off the reservation, and speaks a dozen words in English at the very most. Young Manuel, although 16, has just been to school two years. But Mary, Beatrice, and Arbuthnot have been to school as much as any white child. As for the baby, what difference does it make yet?

It wasn't hard for the Big-Bears to move. They had a good old stove. They had a set of real china teacups that belonged to Martha's mother. They had a Model A Ford.

They gave these treasures to Martha's sister and her husband, who could use

From K. Hendrich, "U. S. Helps Indians Move," *The Christian Science Monitor,* March 6, 1956. Reprinted by permission from The Christian Science Monitor. © 1956 The Christian Science Publishing Society. All Rights Reserved them. And Tony, always generous, turned over his extra cash on hand to his brother-in-law "to fix up the car." They needed government help to reach Los Angeles, and were entitled to it under Congressional provision.

Following the mimeographed instructions given them when they left the reservation, they walked the length of impressive Los Angeles Union Station, toting their neat bundles, toward the streetcar.

Tony had ridden on busses, [*sic*] so he knew how to pay the fare. This was all new to Martha. She never said a word and scarcely raised her eyes. But Manuel, Mary, Beatrice, Arbuthnot, and the baby saw everything.

It was four in the afternoon when they reached the Indian Bureau field office. They got a warm welcome. The white people on the staff had, most of them, worked with Indians a good deal. The Indian people, and the Big-Bears saw at once that there were several, were the sort who obviously made service a real specialty.

To make a long story short, the first thing was talking carefully with Tony about money. The office drew him a $50 check from the government funds provided him, and explained how he could go about next morning opening a bank account. The next step, since it was late in the day and everybody felt a little travel-weary, was to take the Big-Bears to a nearby hotel that was modest, certainly, but convenient.

Getting Tony a job was the least of the challenges. Tony had some ideas about wanting to be a commercial artist, but he settled for a job in an aircraft plant at good wages. The Indian Bureau placement officer didn't have much trouble persuading Tony that he should take this first, and look into the art field after he's become familiar with Los Angeles.

Tony went after the job himself. The Indian bureau gave him a letter of introduction to the personnel officer at the plant, but put it up to Tony to find his own way out there and make his own application.

For a reservation Indian, used to a communal society, this was hard—but Tony did it and he found the personnel officer was glad to see him. Indian workers have earned for themselves an excellent reputation in Los Angeles.

Then the family had to have a more permanent place to live. The field officer helped Tony find an apartment—a "slum dwelling," some people might call the place, but it was more adequate than anything Martha was used to.

And the officer knew the Big-Bears would be finding a better place by themselves soon—as soon, anyway, as they knew their way around and could make $60 a month rent stretch to something better.

It was so with Tony's family, anyway. In months they had a first-class house near his work. They were buying furniture. Martha was going to night school. The children, of course, had fitted in perfectly from the moment they landed.

It could have turned out otherwise. It has with some other Indian families. Plants have closed down. Welfare agencies have had to step in. The Indian Center has helped with groceries, clothes. The going has been tough more than once.

And some "Marthas" just haven't been able to adjust. Loneliness, the remembrance of reservation customs, strange speech—these things have sent some families home with the help of Traveler's Aid and public assistance.

But many a Martha, after this has happened, has finally said to her husband,

"Let's try again." So they did. This time, they tried on their own. And the second try worked.

The Testimony of a Detroit Sniper, 1967

A teenage Negro who identified himself as one of the elusive Detroit snipers says "the war" will not be over until "they kill all of us."

But, he insisted yesterday, his activities were not organized.

"When the thing broke out me and my main man were out there helping. We threw some cocktails. But after a while we got tired of that so we decided to go home and get our pieces," he explained.

"Get One or Two"

"We had them ——— cops so scared that first night they were shooting at one another. I know I got one or two of them, but I don't think I killed them. I wish I had, the dirty ———."

The young man explained that he went and got his "piece" after he and his buddy had looted a liquor store.

"We drank a little. And after a while—boom, just like that we decided to do some shootin'."

Did he realize he could be killed?

"I'm not crazy—I'm not crazy to be killed. I'm just gettin' even for what they did to us. Really. That's where it's at."

"Man, they killed Malcolm X just like that. So I'm gonna take a few of them with me. They may get me later on, but somebody else will take my place—just like that."

He explained that he avoided the area patrolled by the airborne troops because of the intensity with which they returned fire.

"They got a lot of soul brothers in their outfit too and I'm not trying to waste my own kind. I am after them honkies . . ." he said.

Mother Died

His mother had died years ago leaving him and his sister in a dilapidated apartment, he said.

"Man, that place was so bad that I hated to come home at night. My sister became a hustler for a guy I grew up with." He said he had heard that she had been shot Wednesday night while looting a store.

"That makes me mad. Why they have to shoot somebody for takin' something out of a store during a riot? These white mothers are something else," he said angrily as he rubbed his long, powerful fingers together.

He said he wished he had a better weapon than the U.S. M—1 automatic carbine because it lacked range and fire power. Thus he could not fire more than one or two rounds at most before National Guardsmen laid down a heavy barrage.

"But I know I got two of them. I saw them mothers fall.

"Testimony of a Sniper, Detroit, 1967," from an article written by Ray Rogers in the *New York Post,* July 29, 1967.

"One was a honky-tonk cop with a big belly and he couldn't run too fast. And when I hit him he hollered and hit the pavement.

"And them stupid mothers fired all over the place except the place where I was—I was laying among some bricks in a burnt-out store. It was beautiful, baby, so beautiful I almost cried with joy."

He said he never carried the carbine with him and he hid it in a different place after each time he used it.

He laughed and said:

"Twice they had their hands on me and searched me but they let me go. That's why I say that the war ain't over until they put all of us in jail or kill us. . . . I mean all of us soul brothers. But they can't do that because there's too many of us."

Suddenly he began talking about his early life.

"I went to school just like you did. I believed in all that oakie-doak and then I woke up one day and said later for that stuff because that stuff would just mess up my mind, just mess up my mind. I hustled and did a little bit of everything to stay alive.

"I got a couple of kids by some sister on the other side of town but I never see them. What can I say to them?"

He said that he and his buddy paid his 10-year-old cousin to watch for National Guard patrols while they were staked out on roofs. They communicated with him by a toy walkie-talkie.

"It was funny for a while because all they could do was lay there and holler at one another. Man, it was beautiful. We controlled the scene.

"We were just like guerrillas—real ones."

Portrait of Men Killed by Police in the Los Angeles Uprising, 1992

The deadliest sector of Los Angeles on the first night of rioting was the heart of Watts, four miles from the now infamous intersection of Florence and Normandie avenues where people were beaten on live TV.

Far from the cameras, as shops blazed on the perimeter of the Nickerson Gardens housing project, police fired 88 rounds in firefights with snipers.

When the smoke had cleared, longtime Watts residents DeAndre Harrison, Anthony J. Taylor, and Dennis R. Jackson were dead, killed by LAPD bullets. Police said the three were part of roving bands shooting at officers, but friends and relatives have questioned the official accounts. . . .

During five days of unrest, 10 young men died at the hands of law officers across the Los Angeles Basin, from Compton to Pasadena.

All were shot by officers who said they were under attack. In one case, the victim was allegedly holding a shotgun. In another, the weapon turned out to be a plastic toy. A third victim, allegedly armed with a beer bottle, was shot during a struggle with a police officer. A 15-year-old was shot below the shoulder blade as he tried to flee over a fence with several alleged looters.

From "Faces of Death: 10 Men Slain by Officers in Riots" by Paul Feldman, *Los Angeles Times,* May 24, 1992, p. A1–A24. Copyright 1992, *Los Angeles Times.* Reprinted by permission.

One man killed by a ricocheting police bullet was just a bystander.

Guns were recovered in two of the 10 fatal shootings. In another instance, officials said a driver threatened the lives of National Guard troops by driving his car wildly toward their barricades. . . .

The percentage of officer-involved deaths—10 out of nearly 60—was lower than in the 1965 Watts riots in which 23 of 34 deaths came from law enforcement fire. . . .

Few victims had expressed strong views about the Rodney G. King verdict that precipitated the violence, according to friends and relatives.

Six of the dead were black, three were Central American immigrants and one was of Mexican ancestry.

All were single males ranging in age from 15 to 38 who were unemployed high school dropouts. Several had criminal records.

Besides grieving parents and friends, the victims left behind 20 children, with four on the way.

What follows are sketches of their lives and deaths.

Wednesday

Less than four hours after truck driver Reginald O. Denny and others were attacked at Florence and Normandie, four LAPD officers in a patrol car said they came under intense fire from looters outside a Korean-American-owned store at Central Avenue and 112th Street.

The officers returned fire, then roared off to await reinforcements. One of seven rounds they fired had hit a heavyset, shirtless gunman.

When they returned, the victim and his weapon had vanished. But LAPD officials later learned that 17-year-old DeAndre Harrison had died of a gunshot wound at the hospital, and ballistics tests showed that he had been struck by a 9-millimeter bullet fired by officer John Alviani.

Harrison was angry over the verdict in the King beating case, relatives said, and had helped loot clothing stores earlier in the night.

But whether he was the shirtless suspect who shot at police is another question.

About 10:30 p.m., there was a soft knock on the door of an apartment Harrison's girlfriend shared with her mother, Myra Collins. It was Harrison, Collins said later, and he was wearing a blood-drenched T-shirt with a small bullet hole in the chest. . . .

After Collins and a friend drove Harrison to the hospital . . . , emergency room staffers tore off the T-shirt, Collins said. . . .

"I don't know what DeAndre was doing," Collins said. "I don't know if he was an angel or a devil. But he did have on a white T-shirt." . . .

Harrison died on the same floor of Martin Luther King Jr./Drew Medical Center as his father, Claudell, did 12 years ago. His father was shot by an unknown gunman. . . .

As a youngster, Harrison dreamed of becoming a football star and won a trophy for playing in the Sheriff's Department youth league. By his early teens, however, he had quit school and begun hanging out with the Bounty Hunters street gang. He fathered three children with three women, one now pregnant with his twins.

As Harrison was driven to the hospital, chaos reigned in the neighborhood around the cinder-block compound of Nickerson Gardens.

"It was anarchy, total anarchy," said Lt. Michael Hillman of the LAPD's Metro Division. . . . "You had people running in the streets, looting, shooting at firefighters, shooting at police. Total chaos."

But nearby, Dennis (Bull) Jackson and Anthony (Romeo) Taylor were doing what they usually did on warm spring nights, according to friends—hanging out in the parking lot near Jackson's apartment, drinking beer. This time, they said, the pair got their liquor for free. . . .

About 11:10 p.m., nearby gunfire caused a dozen or more men in the parking lot to scatter. When the shots stopped, Jackson and Taylor were dead.

[A witness] said officers across the streets had fired on the parking lot because a man, wearing a hood and waving a handgun, had bounded through the area firing at other officers down the block. . . .

According to the LAPD, about 30 Metro Division officers had arrived at Nickerson Gardens shortly after 11 p.m. to cover three Fire Department units sent to fight blazes at Central Avenue businesses. For the next few hours, police engaged in sporadic firefights with three groups of snipers.

Some officers worked their way south along Alvaro Street, taking cover between houses. . . .

Reaching a position across from the parking lot, Officers John Puis and James L. Moody saw a man at the corner of an adjoining building fire a rifle at two officers down the block. . . . Puis fired several rounds from his AR-15 assault rifle.

Although Jackson and Taylor were shot at 11:10 p.m., according to police, officers pinned down by gunfire were unable to recover their bodies and pronounce them dead for more than an hour. They were forced to use a six-ton armored personnel carrier to re-enter the area.

Ballistics tests concluded that Jackson and Taylor were struck once by high-powered 223 caliber bullets fired by Puis, 44, one of two LAPD officers involved in a controversial scuffle with a black woman employee outside the Parker Center jail. The outcome of an internal investigation has not been disclosed.

Jackson, according to a preliminary coroner's account, was shot in the back, and his body was found inside his front door. A bullet passed through Taylor's head and neck, the coroner said, and his body was found outside the building. No weapons were recovered.

Officers said they do not know whether Taylor had been shooting. But they believe that Jackson, based on his clothing, was the gunman firing from the corner of the building.

Jackson lived in the building with his girlfriend, his mother and one of his three children. Taylor, who left six children, lived on the streets. Both were unemployed and had criminal records. Jackson was arrested twice on burglary charges and once served time for setting a fire. Taylor served time for selling cocaine and stealing meat. . . .

Thursday

When Gloria Andrew was sent home before noon from the school where she worked, the streets of Compton were jammed with looters.

"Brian, don't go out there," she recalls warning her son.

Brian Andrew, a happy-go-lucky man who worked odd jobs in construction, agreed to stay home. But 30 minutes later, he left and never returned. . . .

Andrew was seen running from a nearby shoe shop with other looters, police said, and was carrying a pair of shoes and a large bottle of beer.

Andrew had dropped the shoes and was waving the bottle when Detective Stone Jackson, a 21-year veteran, caught up with him in an alley and shot him once in the face as they grappled, police said. . . .

Andrew, the father of two 14-year-old girls, had minor run-ins with the police, his mother said, and had served six months in the California Youth Authority on an assault conviction.

But she said it was "inconceivable" that he would strike an armed officer. "He wasn't that type of person."

By midafternoon, arson had broken out across Los Angeles. Mark Garcia, 15, was one of those attracted by the flames.

Mark lived with his mother and an 18-year-old brother in a converted garage a few blocks southwest of the Forum.

The gangly youth had stayed out of trouble, even if he did run with some gangbangers, his mother said. Moody and quiet, he liked to draw and wanted to be an architect or a police officer.

Friends said he was drawn by curiosity to the looting and fires in a mini-mall at Hawthorne Boulevard and 101st Street but did not participate.

An initial Sheriff's Department report alleged that Mark was one of four jewelry shop looters who fled in a black Ford Tempo and engaged in a shootout with Deputies Wayne Beckley and Jeffrey Moore.

The suspected looters bailed out of their car a few blocks away. Deputies caught up with them at a nearby parking lot and returned fire, killing Mark.

The boy turned out to be unarmed. . . .

Two witnesses deny that the deputies gave a warning to Mark and said none of the youths was shooting. . . .

Franklin Benavidez never said goodby.

Until 5 p.m., the 27-year-old Salvadoran immigrant had been at home with his mate, Maria, and their 3-year-old son, Franklin, Jr., in their cluttered ground-floor apartment in Baldwin Village.

The couple's TV was broken. But a glance out their living room window told them everything they needed to know. People streamed by, arms loaded with loot. Smoke filled the air. And they got several phone calls from Franklin's sister Rosa, who was concerned about them because she was watching the rioting on TV in her home near Carson City, Nev.

Maria was washing dishes about 5 p.m. when there was a knock on the door. She assumed that her husband had stepped outside with a friend. . . . But she would not see him that night. Or the next day. Or ever again.

On Saturday, Maria went to the LAPD's Southwest Division station to inquire about her husband. An officer at the counter wrote down the coroner's phone number and told her to call.

Franklin Benavidez was shot, police said, after fleeing from a gas station that he tried to rob at Western and Vernon avenues. Benavidez pointed a shotgun at officers after being ordered to drop it, they said. . . .

Benavidez, who moved to the United States in 1985, was born in El Salvador and had served in the Salvadoran Army. In Los Angeles, he repaired cars and delivered telephone books. . . .

Sunday

Through much of their stay in Los Angeles, National Guard troops patrolled the streets of Los Angeles without bloodshed.

The exception came Sunday night when Marvin A. Rivas, who had served 10 years in the military of El Salvador, was shot to death after allegedly trying to drive his beat-up Datsun twice through barricades at Pico Boulevard and Vermont.

Los Angeles police said Rivas, who went by several aliases, failed to stop the first time even though a soldier pointed his rifle at the windshield. "He sped off and they let him go," Lt. Hall said.

Five minutes later, Rivas returned and stopped momentarily when a soldier pointed his rifle at him again, Hall said. "Then he accelerated. . . . The guardsmen stepped back [to avoid being hit] and started shooting. . . . Two other guardsmen also fired.

Rivas was struck three times by bullets from the M-16 rifles, authorities said.

Rivas, who left behind a child in El Salvador and a pregnant girlfriend in the Pico-Union district, came to Los Angeles three years ago to try to find work, relatives said.

The relatives were vague about how he made a living. However, Koreatown merchants said he peddled rock cocaine outside their businesses.

One merchant, who spoke on condition of anonymity, said he also saw Rivas using a sledgehammer to break into stores on the second day of the riots. . . .

Some family members speculated that Rivas may have been drunk. Others wondered whether the National Guard had killed him unjustly.

But they said it was difficult to obtain information. Contacting law enforcement authorities for answers, they said, could lead to their deportation. . . .

✖ *E S S A Y S*

The opening essay is by Susan S. Fainstein of the Department of Urban Studies at Rutgers University and Norman I. Fainstein, Dean of Arts and Sciences at Bernard Baruch University of City University of New York. It analyzes various interpretations of the condition of urban blacks in the current era and addresses issues facing urban policymakers. The authors argue that race is the most important factor in the development of urban policy. Their ideas can be related to historical factors presented by the essay by Bauman et al. in Chapter 13 and to the arguments by Wacquant and Wilson excerpted above. The second essay, by historian Donald L. Fixico of Western Michigan University, provides a unique perspective on Indians and urbanization in the modern era. It offers a cogent descriptive analysis of government policy and Indian reactions, linking both to issues of life in the city. The third essay, by Robert M. Fogelson of the Urban Studies and Planning Department of the Massachusetts Institute of Technology, surveys the riots of U.S. cities in the mid-1960s and interprets their causes. Readers should consider whether or not Fogelson's explanations apply to the Los Angeles uprising of 1992.

The Racial Dimension in Urban Political Economy

SUSAN S. FAINSTEIN and NORMAN I. FAINSTEIN

The reorganization of the world economy in recent years has established new patterns of urban development. Scholars have responded with an outpouring of research tracing the relationship between economic processes, spatial forms, and the political choices available to local governments. They have emphasized the increased integration of the world economy, ruthless competition at various territorial levels for capital resources and markets, the transformation from manufacturing to service-based production, the impact of a new occupational structure on income inequality, and the dominance of an ideology prizing economic development over social welfare.

Disagreements among political economists center on the relative importance of the various economic transformations occurring simultaneously, on the universality of new patterns that are evident in a few of our dominant cities, and, most significantly, on the autonomy of local and even national governments in affecting economics. But regardless of their views on these matters, participants in the debate about urban restructuring focus on the interaction between economic processes and social organization. To the extent that political economists examine social groups as actors and mediating forces, they define the relevant groups by those interests that arise directly out of economic processes—for example, the owners of capital, real estate developers, the professional-managerial class, redundant workers, gentrifiers, displaced households, in-migrants. We remain convinced, however, that social groups defined by race, rather than by purely economic factors, continue to define the character of American urban development. Within this country the racial dimension is crucial for understanding the condition of cities, the politics of locality, and, not least, the situation of the black Americans who compose our most urbanized population.

Black Containment and Urban Development

Until fairly recently, the general economic trajectories of cities appeared closely tied to the proportion of their population that was black. Cities like San Francisco, Minneapolis, and Boston, where manufacturing economies were successfully converted to service-based economies during the 1970s, had relatively small black populations, but metropolises that were heavily black continued to founder.

From "The Racial Dimension in Urban Political Economy" by Susan S. Fainstein and Norman I. Fainstein, *Urban Affairs Quarterly* 25 (December 1989), pp. 187–99. Copyright © 1989 Sage Publications, Inc. Reprinted by permission of the publisher.

During the 1980s, however, cities with substantial black populations, including Baltimore, Chicago, Atlanta, and New York, showed strong economic growth led by their service sectors. Even the most down-and-out, heavily black localities of the industrial Midwest, like Cleveland and St. Louis, began to evidence signs of improvement; still this loosening of the bond between racial and economic disadvantage did not point to the declining significance of race for the American urban political economy, but to the fact that in a majority of political jurisdictions, blacks had been isolated sufficiently to become irrelevant to aggregate growth.

The containment of blacks has involved both spatial and political dimensions. Residential segregation by race remains the most powerful mechanism for social sorting in housing markets. A large majority of suburban middle- and upper-income white households in metropolitan areas are able to segregate themselves from blacks and thereby protect their tax bases from the service demands of lower-income households. However, better-off black households, excluded from white suburbs, do not find themselves in economically homogeneous, relatively affluent black suburbs. Their suburbs usually are either economically declining satellite cities or suburban jurisdictions adjacent to central-city ghettos. In both instances, they are like central-city black districts, mixed in income and lifestyles, defined much more by race than by class. Since race overwhelms income as a determinant of where blacks live, high-income whites can isolate themselves from poor people much more easily than can upper-income blacks.

The demobilization of black political activism by the mid-1970s was both a cause and an effect of the shift in the agenda of urban politics from social justice to economic restructuring and development. As a result, the political capacity of blacks to command governmental resources was reduced substantially. Blacks were effectively contained in their fiscal demands, just as they were isolated residentially. Both forms of social control meant that the mere existence of a large black population was far less an impediment to central-city business investment than had been the case in the 1960s and early 1970s.

Blacks have, to be sure, made important gains in American electoral politics over the last two decades. In 1970 there were 48 black mayors; by 1987 the number had grown to 303. Black mayors have led big cities like Newark, Washington, Atlanta, Cleveland, Detroit, Chicago, New Orleans, and Los Angeles. Yet racial containment has not been seriously threatened by the great expansion in the number of black elected officials. . . . Blacks win city hall on the strength of an electoral coalition that cannot be converted into a government coalition. In order to maintain legitimacy, black regimes collaborate with white business. Black regimes produce more government jobs and contracts for blacks, but they are unable to redirect government programs and policies. Although they do not scare off business, neither do they shape development in ways different than white administrations do.

The Economic Situation of Blacks

The great bulk of the research on race indicates that the disproportionate poverty, housing segregation, and job disadvantage suffered by blacks cannot be explained simply by economic determinants. Yet theories of urban economic and spatial restructuring usually subsume race within class-conflict or human capital frameworks in which race as an independent force is downplayed. On the left, racial segregation is shown to offer opportunities for super profits in real estate markets and to allow greater exploitation of disadvantaged labor and the creation of a reserve army.

These ways by which some capitalists take advantage of racial divisions, however, are insufficient to explain their extreme persistence. Capital also loses when its sunk investment is threatened by crime and unsavory neighborhood conditions; major employers are disadvantaged by an unreliable and poorly educated labor force. Whereas there is a clear and identifiable effort by business to obtain tax benefits and other concessions from government, similar actions to maintain racial discrimination are not so evident, even if capitalists are more than willing to make use of racial barriers where they exist. Although racism can prove functional for some segments of capital and may be reinforced by capitalist practice, it is not a clear-cut objective of capitalists. Most of the advantages that racism produces for them, such as a divided working class and a low-cost labor pool, can be obtained in other ways. In fact, the migration of firms to Sunbelt and nonmetropolitan areas without large black populations indicates that many corporate decision makers regard a low-income black mass to be more of a liability than an asset. Social structuration by race therefore cannot be reduced simply to capitalist dynamics and class inequality.

Neither can racial differences be explained within the more mainstream analysis of human capital theory. Here, the argument goes, blacks are disadvantaged by the poverty and low education that are products of past rather than present discrimination. Economic restructuring, it is claimed, eliminates low-skill jobs. Consequently, blacks suffer from a job-skills mismatch exacerbated by a geographical mismatch that keeps unskilled blacks locked in the central city, although jobs have moved to outlying areas.

The evidence to support these assertions is at best weak. First of all, let us consider the shift to a service-centered economy. Blacks who lost jobs in the unionized manufacturing firms of the Midwest, most notably in the automobile industry, certainly were hurt badly by economic restructuring. But the black population as a whole probably has not been differentially harmed by the shift from manufacturing to service production in the Untied States. To begin with, it has never been especially dependent on employment in manufacturing industries. In 1979, for example, 13.1% of employed blacks worked for firms that produced durable goods, compared with 13.9% of whites. By contrast, 35.2% of blacks were employed in service industries in that same year (with only 2.9% working in private households), whereas 28.0% of whites were similarly employed. Service industries have been expanding rapidly, not just at the professional-technical upper end, but at the low-skill bottom as well, where black employment is concentrated. The problem for blacks is that these service jobs pay low wages. Moreover, many blacks hold newly created manufacturing jobs in nonunionized firms, for which they also receive low wages relative to the wage structure in the American economy during the 1950s and 1960s. Blaming black economic problems mainly on the shift to service employment obscures the structural and political forces that effectively have lowered the economic return of the jobs held not only by a majority of blacks, but by many white workers as well.

Second, as we discussed, severe and continuing residential segregation has had important negative effects on black class structure—particularly by inhibiting the spatial mobility of economically successful black households. But human capital theorists exaggerated the importance of spatial disjuncture between employment opportunities and housing as an explanation of black income distribution. It is true that job growth has been more rapid in suburbs than in central cities, and that black populations remain concentrated in central cities, but except for a relatively few places, most workers get to their jobs by automobile and commute along paths that crisis-cross metropolitan areas. The key to employment accessibility, therefore, is in holding a job that is sufficiently remunerative to support automobile ownership, not in living where the job is located.

Until recently, the gap between years of schooling for whites and blacks has steadily narrowed, so that blacks should have acquired most of the crucial human capital necessary to achieving wage parity with white workers. Here, gender differences have been very important. For black men, the economic returns of education have eroded in value and have been insufficient to close the wage gap with whites. Black women, in contrast, actually earn more than white women with comparable years of schooling. But *all* women have low wages compared to equally educated men, and consequently schooling has had only limited payoff to black women who are successfully employed at "women's" jobs. It is not, therefore, so much a mismatch between jobs and skills that hurts blacks as it is the structure of employment opportunities available to black workers. In the face of an increasingly unequal wage structure, black men have been unable to compete with white men for higher-wage "men's work." Black women have been very successful at competing with white women for lower-wage "women's work." But since black families depend heavily on the wages of female wage earners, this group has slumped in the overall distribution of family income.

A convincing explanation of black economic disadvantage would emphasize the interplay between general political-economic processes and specifically racial structures in determining the condition of black Americans. Arguments concerning the declining significance of race for black people were presented most forcefully during the 1970s. Evidence to support this viewpoint was the increasing affluence of the black middle class, which seemed to show that racial status did not inhibit economic progress for those blacks with higher educational attainment. Data on the 1980s, however, indicate that relative differences between black and white income have remained stable despite increases in black educational attainment and that the growth of the black middle class has stalled.

Here are just some of the distressing facts on income. The ratio of black to white median family income *declined* from 61% in 1970 to 57% in 1986. . . . The percentage of black families with incomes less than $10,000 and the percentage of those with incomes over $50,000 *both* increased between 1970 and 1986. But inequality grew for whites as well. In fact, economic restructuring under the Reagan presidency in general made the rich richer and the poor poorer. . . .

Has there been a rising black bourgeoisie? Black middle- and upper-income families (those above $35,000 in constant dollars) did expand as a proportion of the black population, from 15.7% in 1970 to 21.2% in 1986. Most of this gain was in the 1970s, and all along, the white growth was greater. Consider another comparison. Between 1978 and 1986 the number of upper-income black families (those earning $50,000 or more in constant dollars) increased by 1.1%. Nonetheless, the composition of upper-income families became whiter in those years. So, although the black middle class has grown larger, the rate of expansion has never exceeded the rate for the white middle class. Moreover, if wealth and not just income is taken into account, the black middle class not only remains small compared to that of the white middle class, it is insecure as well. For example, high-income black families earning more than $48,000 in 1984 owned only 46% of the assets owned by comparable white families; at lower income levels, the gap in wealth was much larger.

Discussion of the causes of the black underclass—so-called because it does not participate in the economy even as cheap labor—has become the most controversial arena for analysis of the relationship between economic processes and racial outcomes. Much of the debate has involved a rather sterile argument between conservatives, who emphasized cultural factors, and liberals, who stressed economic structures. Although the conservatives have not recanted, the liberals . . . seem recently to have adopted a formulation that implicitly accepts the interplay of cultural and structural elements. No matter what its political slant, however, research on the black underclass still has not confronted the glaring assumption in its own subtext—that the underclass is somehow outside the regular black class structure.

In contrast, we believe the evidence shows that the term *underclass* is applied to a stratum of the black population affected by precisely the same racial and economic forces that disadvantage all blacks. Members of the underclass become a visible social problem because of their reaction to these forces. In the nineteenth century the counterpart was called *the undeserving poor*. Narrowly focused research on the underclass diverts attention not only from the larger group of "deserving" black poor who work at low-wage jobs, but also from the depressed economic situation of most blacks.

We have argued so far that the economic growth of central cities has been *less* affected by race in recent years than a couple of decades ago, and that the economic progress experienced by blacks in the 1960s and 1970s has at best come to a halt. Therefore, our central issue is not the well-being of cities, but the well-being of the black population of cities. Since economic growth in the current political situation has been insufficient to benefit blacks, we are led to ask what might change the political situation. Before addressing that question, however, we should recall the government policies that resulted from the shift to the right since 1980, because they have determined in large part just who would win and lose from economic change.

The Politics of Inequality

During the Reagan years the national government contributed greatly to an upward redistribution of power and income within the class structure. Although Reagan was thwarted by Congress in his efforts to curtail the Social Security and Medicare programs, his administration nonetheless managed to redefine the basic contours of American domestic policy. First, the administration devolved greater responsibility to the state governments for programs targeted narrowly to the poor, most notably Aid to Families with Dependent Children (AFDC). Many state government officials responded by increasing revenue commitments, but, even so, benefit levels in constant dollars declined during the 1980s, causing an absolute reduction in the standard of living of the nonworking poor. About half of AFDC recipients were black, mainly children. The national government also terminated all new public housing construction for the poor. Here the states did little until homelessness reached crisis proportions, and then their efforts were insignificant compared to federally funded low-income housing construction in the 1960s and 1970s.

Second, the administration claimed that resources should not be wasted on those with incomes above its so-called safety net—in other words, on the working poor (about one-third of black families). It was in this policy arena that the administration managed its greatest successes, slashing expenditures for moderate-income housing, employment and training, public education, college scholarships, and work-study programs. Equally important, the national government failed to raise the minimum wage of $3.35/hr after 1980, so that its real value declined from 43% of average earnings in 1981 to 34% in 1986.

Third, the Reagan administration directly shifted power and resources toward big business and the upper classes. Most obvious was its attack against labor unions. The firing of striking air-traffic controllers during the early days of 1981 was only the first volley in a trench war that curtailed the protection of labor under the National Labor Relations Act and thereby reduced the ability of unions to organize new industries. Slightly less obvious was the reduction of progressivity in the federal tax structure. Put most simply, this involved shifting the tax burden from corporate to individual income and from a progressive personal income tax to a regressive social security tax. The final element fell into place when personal income tax rates were flattened to the enormous benefit of the richest households.

Together, these governmental actions and nonactions substantially magnified the tendencies toward greater inequality already inherent in capitalist-led economic restructuring. In the face of a much more hierarchical society, and hampered by the withdrawal of social expenditure programs from which they had disproportionately benefited, black Americans fell back. Their difficulties were compounded by diminishing federal efforts to end racial discrimination in labor and housing markets. Regardless of how effective such programs had been previously, the administration's vocal stance against them signaled to thousands of economic and political actors—from large employers, to real estate brokers, lending institutions, and local governments—that systems of racial exclusion and channeling could be maintained and even strengthened.

We do not lack models of social policy. To the contrary, the macroeconomic policies, targeted community development, and affirmative action programs that constituted the War on Poverty were all working in the technical sense of shifting political and economic resources to black Americans. The reaction to this outcome made the War on Poverty a political failure. That failure was, however, redefined by the conservative victors, who declared that governmental intervention was itself the major cause of poverty.

Recognizing this lesson from the 1960s, liberals, whether black or white, now see policy proposals first and foremost as elements in a political strategy. For this reason, policy discussions center about a series of political choices and trade-offs along the dimensions that define a strategy. These include the following:

1. Targeting programs to those most in need and therefore politically weakest versus spreading benefits among a much larger population, in the hope that political support will be stronger, even if program costs are greater;
2. Basing eligibility on race and thereby having a legally meaningful but politically objectionable social category versus using class-based criteria in a juridical system that rejects class categories;
3. Investing in black ghettos and thereby accepting and reproducing racial segregation versus trying to effect spatial integration, at the cost of strong white resistance and with the possibility of total failure; and
4. Advancing programs that facilitate social mobility, thus drawing on American commitment to equality of opportunity but possibly increasing inequality among blacks versus aiming to reduce economic inequality overall and becoming vulnerable to charges of undermining efficiency and economic growth.

Whatever the choices made on these and other dimensions, a program to benefit blacks must be advanced in a context of declining black political capacity. Although blacks have been incorporated into urban political systems, white sympathy for the black cause as well as race-based organization and activism have waned. In addition, very high Latin and Asian immigration is reducing black Americans to the status of just one more minority group and is widening ethnic cleavages within the lower classes. Equally important, the apparent economic success of at least some immigrants lends credence to the view that America is the land of opportunity for those who work hard, even if their origins are non-European.

These political realities point toward a strategy that soft-pedals race and emphasizes class as the basis for solidarity. Jesse Jackson is pursuing such a program with his Rainbow Coalition. But, as our diagnosis of black economic disadvantage makes clear, universalistic programs alone are insufficient to address the employment and housing problems of blacks. [William Julius] Wilson [in *The Truly Disadvantaged,* 1987] comes to just this conclusion; his "program also would include targeted strategies—both means-tested and race-specific." However, he identifies the political uncertainty inherent in even this best strategy for blacks:

> To the extent that the universal programs draw support from a wider population, the less visible targeted programs would be indirectly supported and protected. To repeat, the hidden agenda for liberal policymakers is to enhance the chances in life for the ghetto underclass by emphasizing programs to which the more advantaged of all class and racial backgrounds can positively relate.

Unfortunately, the prospects are not good for keeping a racial agenda hidden. More likely, even programs weakly targeted toward blacks will be identified by opponents as a disguised form of black empowerment. Thus pragmatism and opportunism seem the order of the day. Programs that improve the opportunity structure for blacks, whether universalistic or targeted, need be seized; a more coherent strategy awaits the next liberal tide in the United States.

The Urban Relocation of Native Americans

DONALD L. FIXICO

The experiences of Native Americans during the war years had a two-fold effect on federal-Indian relations in the postwar period. The courageous performance of Native American men abroad and native women in the war industries at home impressed federal officials, convincing them that Indians possessed an aptitude for working side by side with other Americans. Barton Greenwood, acting commissioner of Indian affairs, estimated that 50 percent of the returning veterans had sufficient experience in working with other Americans away from the reservation to compete with them for jobs.

Unfortunately, returning Indian veterans increased the burden on the reservations' already limited economic resources. High unemployment and widespread poverty pervaded Indian country. In response, the government proposed relocating unemployed Indians or those who returned from the war to urban areas where they could find jobs. Greenwood advised that these people be moved as far as possible from their original communities to prevent them from returning easily to their homelands. Theoretically, this strategy would be conducive to successful Indian adaptation to urban living. Federal officials believed that once the new urban migrants had adjusted to living in the cities there would be no need for reservations. Until then, Indians continued to live on reservations under submarginal conditions.

The severe blizzard of 1947–48 worsened the already poor economy for Indian communities, especially for the populous Navajos in Arizona and New Mexico, who suffered extreme destitution. To help alleviate their suffering, the government supplied emergency aid, but the deplorable conditions on the reservation continued. This impelled the federal government to take one more step in establishing a job placement program, which laid the foundation for the relocation program. The Bureau of Indian Affairs began to resettle employable Indians from the Navajo Reservation in urban areas. The Interior Department soon established additional placement officers in Denver, Salt Lake City, and Los Angeles. . . . Although the program began with the Navajos, the government soon began to extend relocation services to all tribes.

In a conference with area directors in January 1951, Commissioner of Indian Affairs Dillon S. Myer had urged funding for the relocation program to begin the recruitment of Indians for urban placement. He had hoped to be able to expand the program quickly by intensifying and broadening recruitment efforts. Critics alleged that relocation had swept Indians off the reservations, scattered them throughout cities, and then they were abandoned by the Bureau. The commissioner denied that the Bureau of Indian Affairs had forced Native Americans to

From *Termination and Relocation: Federal Indian Policy, 1945–1960* by Donald L. Fixico, pp. 134–57. Copyright © 1986 University of New Mexico Press. Reprinted by permission of the publisher.

relocate. Myer insistently advocated relocation as a policy congruent with his philosophy of termination—the view that Native Americans should be encouraged to live without federal supervision like other Americans. Moving Indians to urban areas to work and to live would, he believed, escalate their standard of living. Although Myer enthusiastically supported relocation during his three years at the helm of the Bureau, the program failed to gain momentum during his administration.

Even though the applicants procedure for relocation was amazingly simple and open to young and old alike, Native Americans initially hesitated to volunteer for the new program. However, curiosity about city life eventually induced many people to apply for relocation. . . .

After an initial request for relocation had been filed with a BIA [Bureau of Indian Affairs] official at an agency or an area office, the paperwork began. After completing a review of the applicant's job skills and employment records, the official usually contacted the relocation office in the city of the applicant's choice. With clothes and personal items packed, the applicant customarily boarded a bus or train to the designated city, where he or she would be met by a relocation worker. Upon arrival, the newcomer received a check to be spent under the supervision of the relocation officer. Next, the officer usually accompanied the new urbanite to a nearby store to purchase toiletries, cookware, groceries, bedding, clothes, and an alarm clock to insure punctual arrival at work. . . .

Relocation officers assisted the new migrants in locating places to shop for groceries, and informed them about nearby churches of their denomination. After the relocatee and his or her family were settled, the relocation worker and neighborhood clergyman visited on a regular basis. Normally, the BIA paid the relocatee's first month's rent, including clothing and groceries, and the expenses incurred while traveling to and from work. After the first month the relocatees were on their own, although Bureau workers remained available for counseling and assistance in job placement; BIA officials would keep tabs on the progress of relocatees for the next nine years.

Young adults, especially men, were the most common applicants for relocation. Frequently, they left families behind until they found jobs and housing, and then sent for their families. . . . The first relocatees arrived in Chicago in early February 1952. In all, relocation workers processed 442 Native Americans for employment in Los Angeles, Denver, and Chicago during that year. With the Bureau expanding the Navajo placement offices in Salt Lake City, Denver, and Los Angeles to service all Native Americans, a new generation of urban Indians came into being. . . .

By the end of 1953, BIA relocation offices had placed 2,600 Indians in permanent jobs. Financial assistance during that year enabled 650 workers to move their families to the nearby communities where they worked, but Bureau officers experienced problems in locating enough jobs for relocatees. They relied primarily on public employment agencies, which too often placed relocatees in seasonal railroad and agricultural work, the lowest paying and least secure type of employment. Because of this, the program received criticism, and suggestions were made to try to find more meaningful jobs. . . .

To help process the increasing number of relocatees, the Bureau opened an office in Oakland in 1954; another office opened in San Francisco a year later, and in 1956 offices were established in San Jose and St. Louis. Soon, additional offices were operating in Dallas, Cleveland, Oklahoma City, and Tulsa. The rising number of applicants prompted the government to quickly expand the relocation program. By late 1954 approximately 6,200 Native Americans of an estimated 245,000 reservation population had resettled in large cities. . . .

BIA publicity portrayed relocation as a "New Deal" for Native Americans, one that offered them a chance to improve their economic status. Indian Bureau officials encouraged Indians to relocate, although ostensibly on a voluntary basis. Throughout the reservations, BIA workers circulated brochures and pamphlets suggesting that a better life awaited Indians in urban areas. Pictures of executives dressed in white shirts, wearing ties, and sitting behind business desks insinuated that similar occupational positions could be obtained by Indians. Photos of a white frame house with shutters enticed the women. The scene suggested that Indians could provide their families with similar homes in suburban America.

Unfortunately, the hard realities of urban life soon destroyed Indian hopes for a successful livelihood and dashed their many dreams. For those who left the reservation and traveled a long distance for the first time, the relocation experience was a threatening cultural shock. Once off a bus and alone in a strange, large city, relocatees encountered a foreign and threatening new world that often proved to be traumatic. Relocatees knew little about such modern gadgets as stoplights, clocks, elevators, telephones, and other everyday objects that Americans took for granted. . . . Newly relocated Indians who had not yet mastered the English language experienced even more difficulty and many were embarrassed to ask for assistance. . . .

Toward the end of 1955, the Muskogee area office in Oklahoma reported a decline in people volunteering for relocation from its area. Fear of big-city life inhibited many Native Americans, making them feel lost, insecure, and inferior to the majority population of urban white Americans. Compared to other, more aggressive urban minorities—blacks, Mexicans, and Puerto Ricans—the uneducated, traditional Indians were isolated and at the bottom of the social order. . . .

Despite the radical socioeconomic problems facing them, the number of applicants for relocation began increasing on the whole. In the 1956 fiscal year, BIA workers processed 5,316 relocatees through four offices—Chicago, Denver, Los Angeles, and San Francisco. Of this number, 732 were single men, 373 were single women, and 424 had families. Relocation officers noted a growing interest in relocation among Indians, and a backlog of applications existed at almost all Indian agencies. . . .

Congress passed Public Law 959 during the first week in August 1956, providing improved vocational training for adult Indians. Shortly afterward, vocational training became a part of the relocation program and offered three types of general services. First, on-the-job training provided a twenty-four month, apprentice-type training for Indian employees. Work in factories on or near reservations trained individuals for jobs and gave them valuable vocational experience. Young Indians, especially, obtained such experience and were trained in rudimentary skills that would increase their chances for employment in urban areas.

Second, the adult vocational training program, designed for Indian adults who usually had families, provided training in specific occupational areas—carpentry, plumbing, and other related manual job skills. Program officers based enrollment selection on the past employment and school records of applicants. The program specified that applicants be between eighteen and thirty-five years of age, but older applicants were accepted if they took full advantage of the training and had a reasonable prospect of being employed in their specialty.

The third branch of the relocation program provided employment only. The direct employment subprogram provided job information and employment for Native Americans near reservations. Hence, industries were urged to locate nearby. Otherwise, program workers negotiated with employers in urban areas to hire relocatees, and the unemployed were placed where jobs were available. . . .

To encourage Native Americans to seek vocational training and employment, the Bureau of Indian Affairs negotiated contracts with business firms to build plants near reservations. Bulova Watch Company built a jewel-bearing plant near the Tuttle Mountain Reservation at Rolla, Northa Dakota, the first company to locate near a reservation and to hire exclusively Indian employees. On the last day in December 1956, the company threatened to close the installation, provoking sharp reactions. Native American leaders, as well as public officials and Indian interest organizations, urged congressmen and the BIA to retain the plant. Closing the facility would threaten the progress of the Tuttle Mountain Indians and the relocation program. Bureau officials believed if all 150 Indian employees at Bulova lost their jobs other Native Americans would question the practicality and advisability of urban relocation or of receiving employment or vocational training through the relocation program. The BIA was also concerned that other industries would be reluctant to accept government subsidies for locating near reservations. . . .

Vocational training and employment assistance for Native Americans were two primary objectives of the relocation program. The availability of employment in cities naturally led to relocation in urban areas. Hence, the need for employment became the basis for relocation. Relocation did not merely mean removing Indians from reservations to cities, but involved preparing them for placement through vocational training and moving them to areas with high employment opportunities. Public Law 959 emphasized employment for Indians, which became the main service provided by the relocation program and led to changing the name of the "relocation program" to "employment assistance." More importantly, "relocation" had become associated with the negative image of dragging Indians from reservations and abandoning them in cities. The BIA hoped the name change would improve the program's image. . . .

Federal funding increased in correlation with the rising number of applicants until the high cost caused disagreement among federal officials. Some congressmen supported the relocation program, while others advocated the development of tribal economic resources, a less expensive route. . . .

Skeptical congressmen questioned the high overhead costs. People, especially those unfamiliar with Indian affairs, wanted clarification of the goals and objectives of the relocation program, fearing that the program was getting out of control. Terminationists who wanted to get the government out of the "Indian business" complained about the expanding and ever-increasing cost of the Bureau of Indian Affairs.

A report entitled "The Program of Relocation Services," dated 28 October 1957, reiterated the purpose of relocation. The prime directive was to assist Native Americans who wanted independence from the federal government and were eager to find their place in the free-enterprise system. The Indian citizenry, the report claimed, would eventually become a component of the urban community scene. . . .

Indian veterans of World War II and the Korean War had a much better chance of succeeding in relocation than reservation Indians who had never left their rural communities. Previous experience with the outside world, plus the possession of knowledge of white American norms and values, accounted for this advantage. For the majority of relocatees, however, urbanization presented a difficult social and psychological adjustment to an alien environment. In early December 1957, a relocation specialist emphasized such problems in a memo to the area director of the Phoenix area office: "Relocation is not easy. It calls for real stamina and vigor—adaptability and strength of character." He added that the Papago Indians possessed these characteristics, for since 1952, 566 Papagos had successfully relocated to urban areas. Among the Navajos, Tribal Chairman Paul Jones admitted that the relocation program was helpful in removing the surplus population on the reservation that the land could not support. Frequently, tribes worked to rid their reservations of undesirable members through relocation. Shiftless, unmotivated members burdened families, friends, reservation resources, and relocation offered them an opportunity to leave. . . .

Unfortunately, many potential relocatees did not anticipate the difficulties that they might encounter in the cities. Louis Cioffi, a missionary, wrote to President Eisenhower: "Under the program, as you know, Indians are urged away from their reservations, given jobs, which soon come to an end. As you may not know, many have returned to the reservation, discouraged and worse off than before. Successful relocation achieved by the government has been very small indeed." One Indian in Southern California called relocation an "extermination program," and said that Eisenhower believed "the Indians would be integrated by taking all the youngsters off the reservation, the old would die off, and young would be integrated, and the land would become free for public domain, and all the people could grab it."

Conversely, the government reported optimistically that the majority of Indian relocatees were acclimating to urban conditions successfully, and the number returning to reservations was actually minuscule. The Bureau of Indian Affairs maintained that between 1953 and 1957 only three out of ten relocatees returned to their home communities. The BIA claimed that one-half of those 30 percent who returned home did so within the first three months, and that 71.4 percent remained in their urban environment. Critics charged that the percentage of returnees was 75 percent. Such differences in statistics helped to fuel the controversy over the relocation program. In fact, both sides probably manipulated figures to favor or disfavor the "return rate."

Another problem area arose when vocational training programs encountered a significant dropout rate in various occupational areas. In the nurse's aide program the rate was 21 percent; for sawmill workers 50 percent; for manufacturers of Indian artifacts 54 percent; and for furniture workers about 62 percent. Specialized occupations, such as diamond processing, wig-making, and the production of women's fashion items, had the highest dropout rates, due to the monotony of the work. Most likely, a disinterest in the work and its long-range impracticality accounted for the high dropout rate in wig-making and the production of women's fashion items. Often the relocatees were persuaded to enroll in a number of widely ranging courses merely to prove that Indians were being trained in diverse occupations.

Monotony and disinterest were not the only reasons why Indians dropped out of vocational training programs. Frequently relocatees were placed in seasonal jobs, like agricultural work, and in other jobs that lacked employee security. For these reasons relocatees became suspicious of government officials who ostensibly would find jobs for them. Unfortunately, low wages accompanied these insecure jobs, forcing Indians to gravitate toward poor housing areas in the cities. In Los Angeles, Indian families were placed in slum dwellings and in rundown motor courts. As more families moved to these areas, Indian ghettos developed. Frustration and discouragement compounded homesickness, prompting many to leave the cities. . . .

As Americans were undergoing an overall economic adjustment to urbanization, dependency on land for a livelihood became less important. The nation's economy now rested on mechanization, which began to replace labor and enabled industrialization in urban areas to develop at a rapid pace. While industries thrived, increasing technology demanded more qualified workers. Schools, colleges, and universities supplied the training for a work force that became increasingly specialized. The relocation program offered Native Americans the opportunity to share in this development.

One of the chief objectives of the relocation program was the desegregation of the reservation Indian population. Federal officials hoped that relocation would assimilate Indians into urban neighborhoods of the dominant society. Instead, Indian ghettos soon resulted. Chicago's Uptown neighborhood is indicative of the Indians' substandard economic living conditions. Bell and Bell Gardens in Los Angeles are other examples. Such areas fostered feelings of isolation, loneliness, and estrangement for Native Americans. Many resorted to alcohol to escape the competitive and social coldness of highly individualized urbanization. Marital and delinquency problems became acute; broken marriages, school dropouts, and increases in crime were so rampant that discouraged relocatees became severely depressed and sometimes committed suicide. Tragically, a people who traditionally cherished life were now broken in spirit. Many would not return home to reservations because of self-pride; they did not want to admit failure, even though relatives beckoned them to return. . . .

A remedy for Indian estrangement in the cities was the establishment of Indian centers. For instance, St. Augustine's Indian Center and the American Indian Center, both in Chicago's Uptown neighborhood, continue to provide counseling, temporary shelter, and other assistance to urban Indians. Similar centers in other cities offer the same services as well as opportunities for socialization among traditional Native Americans, who are a communal people. Interestingly, mutual tribal concerns and interactions dissolved many barriers between tribal groups who had never before associated with each other. Increasingly, Indian Americans in urban areas have identified themselves as Indians rather than by tribal designations.

Such socialization saved the relocated Indians. In essence, the communal tradition of Indians on reservations was imitated in urban areas. Powwows, dances, Indian bowling teams, Indian softball teams, and other related activities have intensified the survival of Indians as an identifiable ethnic group in the large cities.

Those people who remained on reservations during the relocation years of the 1950s experienced considerable economic difficulty. Even though their living conditions have improved since 1945, they often paid a high price for staying in their reservation homelands. In particular, relocation perhaps resulted in less efficient leadership among reservation tribes during the 1950s. Unfortunately, those tribal members possessing the best qualifications, and who could probably have provided a more effective leadership, were apt to relocate; and after relocating, they rarely returned to the reservation to help their tribes.

Ironically, at the same time, the majority of Indians who moved to urban areas suffered socially, economically, and psychologically. In many cases, urban Indians have traded rural poverty on reservations for urban slums. Their survival in urban areas, however, yielded hope and a brighter future for their offspring. Indian youths growing up in an urban environment often become teachers, lawyers, doctors, and other professionals. It is an unfortunate fact that success in the white world is costing them the heritage of their native culture. Today, Indians continue to experience difficulties in substituting traditional values for those of a modern world—materialism and competition.

An Explanation for Ghetto Violence

ROBERT M. FOGELSON

On July 16, 1964, two weeks after Congress passed President Lyndon B. Johnson's civil rights bill, a white policeman shot and killed a black youngster in New York City. Two days later, following a rally protesting police brutality, a crowd marched through Harlem and demonstrated before the 28th precinct headquarters. The police tried to disperse the demonstrators but succeeded only in arousing them, and that evening the first full-scale riots in two decades erupted in Harlem. From July 18 to July 20 blacks not only defied and attacked the police, but also assaulted white passers-by and looted and burned neighborhood stores. Moderate black leaders, including such national figures as James Farmer and Bayard Rustin, pleaded with the rioters to return to their homes, but to little avail. In the meantime the police department ordered all available personnel into Harlem to quell the rioting, and on July 21 order was restored. By then, however, the riots had spread to Bedford-Stuyvesant, the vast black ghetto in Brooklyn. And not until July 23—with one dead, over one hundred injured, nearly five hundred

From "Violence as Protest," in *Violence as Protest: A Study of Riots and Ghettos* by Robert M. Fogelson, 1971, pp. 1–26. Reprinted by permission of the author.

arrested, hundreds of buildings damaged, and millions of dollars of property destroyed—were both communities under control.

A day later riots broke out in Rochester after the police arrested a black teen-ager outside a neighborhood dance. A crowd tried to free the prisoner, stoned the chief of police, and then rampaged through the ghetto, looting and burning, for two days. The rioting in this normally peaceful city was so widespread that Governor Nelson Rockefeller mobilized a thousand National Guardsmen. Except for relatively minor disturbances in Jersey City the following weekend and in Elizabeth and Paterson, New Jersey, and Dixmoor, Illinois, a week later, the next month passed without serious incident. Then on August 28, when it seemed as if the worst were over, riots erupted in Philadelphia after two patrolmen arrested a black woman for blocking traffic at a busy intersection. Intoxicated and apparently angry at her husband, she resisted; and they dragged her out of the car. A crowd quickly gathered; it shouted abuse at the policemen, tossed stones and bricks at their reinforcements, and looted and burned nearby stores. Despite the efforts of the Philadelphia police and the appeals of moderate black leaders, the rioting continued for two more nights and finally subsided on August 31. Leaving two dead, over three hundred injured, and another three hundred arrested, the Philadelphia riots climaxed the nation's most turbulent summer in twenty years.

Except for unreconstructed southerners and northern reactionaries who found reason for their racism that summer, most whites, and especially white liberals, were appalled and perplexed by the riots. Appalled because the conservatives were exploiting the rioting to discredit the civil rights movement and to bolster Barry Goldwater's presidential candidacy, and perplexed because the blacks had probably made more progress in the two decades preceding the riots than at any time since emancipation. The reasons for this progress—the Supreme Court's decisions outlawing segregation, the nation's sustained postwar economic boom, and the black migration from the rural South to the urban North—need not be considered at this point. Suffice it to say, most blacks shared in the nation's wealth and influenced its decisions more in the 1960s than ever before. And though these advances were long overdue and imperfectly realized, at no other time (and in no other administration) was there so strong a commitment to eradicate racial subordination and segregation.

Most whites were also bewildered because blacks were disavowing the principles and tactics of nonviolent protest applied so successfully in the South in the late 1950s and early 1960s. For blacks, after all, civil rights were battles to be won and not gifts to be taken. And to win them they had produced skillful, inspired leadership, maintained rigorous discipline and boundless patience, and abided by strict nonviolence. By 1964, largely as a result of these efforts, most whites were convinced that subordination and segregation were wrong. Hence they found it hard to believe that, as the 1964 riots revealed, many blacks were unhappy with the pace of progress, black leadership, discipline, and patience were at the breaking point, and nonviolence was only one form of social protest. By themselves, however, the 1964 riots showed no clear pattern. And though Attorney General Robert Kennedy and others were aware of incidents in Cleveland, New York, and other cities which had foreshadowed the 1964 riots, it was still conceivable as late as mid-1965 that these disorders were just one summer's deviation from the mainstream of the civil rights movement.

The Los Angeles riots of August 1965, which devastated the Pacific coast's largest black ghetto, proved that this was not the case. These riots closely resembled the 1964 riots. In Los Angeles, as in Rochester, an ordinary arrest triggered the rioting; there, too, the rioters looted and burned stores and assaulted policemen and passers-by, the moderate black leaders failed to restrain the rioters, and the local police and National Guard eventually quelled the rioting. The Los Angeles riots were, however, the country's worst racial disorder since the East St. Louis massacre of 1917. By the time order was restored, thirty-four were dead, over a thousand injured, nearly four thousand arrested, hundreds of buildings damaged, and tens of millions of dollars of property destroyed. Nothwithstanding other disturbances in Chicago and San Diego, the summer of 1965 was less tumultuous than the summer of 1964. But so vast, so awesome, so devastating, and so widely reported were the Los Angeles riots—for a full week they received front-page coverage nationally and internationally—that henceforth there could be no doubt that a distinct pattern of summer violence was emerging in the black ghettos.

For this reason various governmental authorities took precautionary measures to head off rioting in 1966. The Justice Department instructed its Assistant United States Attorneys to report on conditions in a score of inflammable communities, and the Vice-President's Task Force on Youth Opportunity authorized its field representatives to investigate potential trouble-spots. Meanwhile, city officials devised emergency programs to employ and entertain black youths and otherwise keep them off the streets, and local and state police departments, aided by the F.B.I., prepared riot-control plans. But these measures were not designed to alleviate ghetto conditions, only to prevent severe disorders; and so it was with mounting apprehension that local and federal officials awaited the summer. They did not have to wait long. Rioting erupted in Los Angeles, Chicago, and Cleveland in June, and, to list only a few of more than two dozen other places, in Omaha, Dayton, San Francisco, and Atlanta in July and August. It battered cities previously stricken and cities hitherto spared, cities believed to be tense and cities thought to be quiet. None of these riots matched the Los Angeles riots in magnitude or intensity, but taken together they marked the summer of 1966 as the most violent yet.

By June 1967 other riots had erupted in Nashville, Cleveland, and Boston, and most Americans, white and black, expected another turbulent summer. Stokely Carmichael and Martin Luther King, Jr., charging that the federal authorities had done little to alleviate ghetto conditions, predicted more riots. So did Senator Robert F. Kennedy of New York State, Mayor John V. Lindsay of New York City, Mayor Samuel W. Yorty of Los Angeles, and other national and local figures of various political persuasions. Yet the riots which erupted that summer in Cincinnati, Buffalo, Newark, Detroit, and Milwaukee, to list only a few of the scores of stricken cities, far exceeded their worst expectations. Indeed, the Detroit riots, which left forty-three dead, over a thousand injured, over seven thousand arrested, and at least fifty million dollars of property destroyed, were the worst riots since the New York City draft riots a century ago. By the end of the summer city officials, federal administrators, editors, politicians, and state and national commissions were all trying to explain why. Yet wherever criticism was directed and however blame was apportioned, one conclusion was clear: the Los Angeles, Newark, and Detroit riots had assumed a place in the history of American race relations no less important, if not more so, than the East St. Louis, Chicago, and Washington riots a generation ago.

This was made even clearer in April 1968 when the assassination of Martin Luther King, Jr., triggered major riots in Washington, Baltimore, and Chicago and minor riots in more than a hundred other cities. These riots, which closely resembled the previous riots, had a tremendous impact. For a full week the nation, which was already numbed by the assassination, reeled under the rioting; and not until National Guardsmen (and, in Washington, federal soldiers) were summoned was order restored in urban America. The summer of 1968 was relatively peaceful, and so was the summer of 1969; but what future summers hold remains to be seen, and in any event the country has not yet worn off the shock of six years of rioting. Even now there is no agreement among whites and blacks or liberals and conservatives about where responsibility for the riots lies; nor is there agreement among the individuals in these groups. There is, however, substantial agreement that the 1960s riots confronted America with the greatest threat to public order since the dreadful industrial disputes of the late nineteenth and early twentieth centuries. And for this reason, if for no other, a scholarly attempt to interpret these riots is very much in order.

Some observers, including journalists who have written full-length accounts of the Harlem, Bedford-Stuyvesant, and Los Angeles disorders, have implied that the 1960s riots were the latest in a long series of American race riots. There is indeed a tradition of interracial rioting in the United States. To mention only a few examples, race riots erupted in Cincinnati and Philadelphia during the antebellum period and in New York City and Detroit during the Civil War. They broke out immediately after the war in New Orleans and Memphis and around the turn of the century in Wilmington, North Carolina, New York City, Atlanta, Georgia, and Springfield, Illinois. They reached one peak around World War I in East St. Louis, Washington, and Chicago and another during World War II in Detroit and Los Angeles, only to subside later in the 1940s. At a quick glance, moreover, the race riots resemble the 1960s riots: blacks played a prominent role in both types of disorders; so did excitement, rumor, violence, death, and destruction. Nevertheless, a closer examination of the race riots, and especially the 1917, 1919, and 1943 riots, reveals that the 1960s riots were not extensions of this tradition.

Unlike the recent riots, which were as a rule precipitated by routine police actions, the earlier riots were in the main triggered by black challenges to the racial status quo. The outbreak of the Chicago riots of 1919 was a case in point. At a time of tension generated by black migration and white racism a black youth swam from a beach set aside by tacit understanding for blacks to a nearby beach reserved for whites. At the same time several blacks who had been forced to leave this beach earlier in the day returned determined to stay. Whites and blacks started brawling and throwing stones. The black swimmer, rocks falling around him, remained in the water, clinging to a railroad tie; but when a white youth swam toward him, he abandoned the tie, took a few strokes, and then drowned. The police made no arrests, infuriating the blacks, who retaliated by mobbing a patrolman. When gangs of whites counterattacked that evening, the worst interracial riots in the city's history were under way. Hence rioting was precipitated in Chicago in 1919 by the blacks' refusal to accept, and the whites' determination to maintain, segregated recreational facilities and not by routine police actions.

By contrast with the black rioters, who looted and burned stores and only incidentally assaulted passers-by, the white rioters vented their hostility for the most part against people, not property. The violence of the East St. Louis riots of 1917 was characteristic. Angered by the employment of black immigrants as strikebreakers, white mobs attacked blacks in downtown East St. Louis. The rioters dragged their victims out of streetcars, stoning, clubbing, kicking, and afterwards shooting and lynching them. They also burned houses and, with a deliberation which shocked reporters, shot black residents as they fled the flames. They killed them as they begged for mercy and even refused to allow them to brush away flies as they lay dying. The blacks, disarmed by the police and the militia after an earlier riot and defenseless in their wooden shanties, offered little resistance. And by the time the East St. Louis massacre was over the rioters had murdered at least thirty-nine blacks, wounded hundreds more, and, in pursuit of their victims, damaged hundreds of buildings and destroyed about a million dollars of property.

The government authorities, and especially the local police, did not attempt to restore law and order in the race riots with the firmness they exhibited in the 1960s riots. This was certainly true in their response to the Washington riots of 1919. When several hundred sailors (and a few civilians), out to avenge an alleged insult to a mate's wife, rampaged through southwest Washington attacking blacks, the district and military police arrested only two whites (and eight blacks). And when the sailors, joined by soldiers, resumed their assaults the next evening, the police with a handful of reinforcements provided scant protection for the terrified blacks. Law enforcement in the capital broke down not just because the police were outnumbered but also because the policemen as individuals sympathized with the rioters. Not until the police lost control and the blacks armed themselves did the District Commissioners request the cooperation of the military authorities and restore order. Hence the whites rioted in Washington in 1919 with an impunity which was in marked contrast to the danger faced by the blacks a generation later.

Lastly, few responsible white leaders labored so valiantly, if vainly, to prevent the riots and restrain the rioters in 1971, 1919, and 1943 as the moderate black leaders (or at any rate the so-called black leaders) did in the 1960s. This was clearly the case in Detroit in 1943. A host of fascist spokesmen, including Father Charles E. Coughlin and the Reverend Gerald L. K. Smith, and racist organizations, including the Ku Klux Klan and the Black Legion, had long fomented racial animosity there. And though Detroit's civic leaders did not support these agitators, they did not forthrightly oppose them or otherwise deal with the community's racial problems. Once the rioting was under way, Detroit's elected leaders responded ambivalently. Not that they sanctioned the violence; on the contrary, they deplored it, though always from a distance. But they so feared for their political futures and their city's reputation that they did not call for the National Guard until the rioting threatened the whole community and not just the black residents. Whether Detroit's white leaders could have intervened more effectively in 1943 than Los Angeles' black leaders did in 1965 is a moot question because with the exception of a few courageous ministers they did not try.

The distinctive character of the race riots emerges from these brief descriptions. The riots were interracial, violent, reactionary, and ultimately unsuccessful attempts to maintain the racial status quo at times of rapid social change. They were interracial because whites, first- and second-generation European immigrants in Chicago and uprooted southerners in Detroit, were the aggressors, and blacks, newcomers themselves, the victims. They were violent because the whites did not know how to achieve their goals—how to force the blacks to leave East St. Louis and how to keep them in their place in Washington—through legitimate means. They were reactionary because the whites hoped to deprive the blacks of freedom of movement, equal access to public accommodations, and other rights which inhere in Americans whatever their color. And however effective in the short run, they were unsuccessful in the long run. And not simply because the means and ends were at odds with American ideology but also because the economic, social, and political changes underlying the migration of southern blacks and the militancy of northern blacks were too powerful.

The differences between the race riots and the 1960s riots are so marked that it is only necessary now to note a few reasons why the tradition of interracial rioting has waned since World War II. First, the racial status quo has changed so much that the issues which precipitated the race riots are no longer at stake; also, the tremendous expansion of white suburbs and black ghettos has insulated the protagonists from one another. Second, many children of the first- and second-generation immigrants who rioted in 1917, 1919, and 1943 are now middle-class Americans who do not have to rely on violence to uphold their racial privileges. Third, the governmental authorities, and especially the local police, are so determined to maintain public order that except in the rural South few groups, white or black, can riot with impunity anymore. And fourth, again except in the deep South, white leaders are so committed to orderly social change they cannot sanction rioting even on behalf of causes to which they are otherwise sympathetic.

These changes can be exaggerated. The American tradition of interracial violence is waning; but, as intermittent rioting—primarily, though not exclusively, in the South—in the 1950s and 1960s revealed, it is not yet moribund. On several occasions mobs of middle-class whites have forcibly resisted the movement of middle-class blacks into residential suburbs of Philadelphia, Chicago, and other northern metropolises. And gangs of working-class whites, themselves bypassed in the suburban exodus, have violently protested the influx of working-class blacks into East New York and other ethnic communities. Nevertheless, the authorities have restored order so swiftly and thoroughly in these disorders that few people have been injured and few buildings damaged. By such measurements as actual outbreaks, lives lost, arrests booked, and property destroyed, these disturbances are much less serious than the riots under consideration here. There are of course no assurances that whites will restrain themselves in the suburbs or that blacks will confine their violence to the ghettos in the future. But until then inter-racial rioting must be considered a vestige of a waning American tradition.

Other observers, including left-wing radicals and, more recently, black militants, have insisted that the riots, far from being traditional race riots, were incipient colonial rebellions. By this they mean two things. First, that the riots were mani-festations of a world-wide struggle against colonialism, the determined attempt of colored peoples everywhere to overthrow their white masters. The situation of black people in the United States, the radicals assume, is essentially the same as the situation of colored people in Africa and Asia; the blacks are a colonial peo-ple, the whites a colonial oppressor, and the ghettos colonies. Second, that the riots were expressions of a widespread struggle against capitalism, the proletariat's historic effort to regain its manhood, dignity, and freedom through socialism. The blacks resorted to violence, the radicals presume, because they have no hope whatever to achieve meaningful equality under the existing eco-nomic and political system. This interpretation is certainly as much a vision as a definition. But it deserves careful consideration, particularly for its implication that the riots are political actions (and revolutionary ones at that).

There are, as the radicals argue, similarities between the 1960s riots and co-lonial uprisings. In Chicago, Cleveland, and Los Angeles as well as in Nigeria, Uganda, and Nyasaland somewhat earlier, colored people resorted to violence in order to force social change. Afro-Americans and Africans alike rioted in protest against genuine grievances and treated the customary restraints on rioting with indifference and even outright contempt. There are also similarities between the racial problem and the colonial situation. In both cases white people have subor-dinated and segregated colored people and then justified their exploitation and victimization on the grounds of innate racial inferiority. What is more, many blacks who have recently overcome the long-standing antipathy toward their color, ignorance of their origins, and shame about their race have responded by identifying closely with the world's colored people. Their racial pride enhanced by the emergence of independent African nations after World War II, these blacks are now convinced that their future in the United States is inextricably linked with the destiny of colored people everywhere.

There are, however, profound differences between the 1960s riots and colo-nial uprisings. The differences between the recent rioting and terrorist activity against the British in Kenya, guerrilla warfare against the French in Madagascar, and abortive invasions of Portuguese Angola are obvious. Less obvious but no less noteworthy are the differences between the 1960s riots and the colonial up-risings in Nigeria, Uganda, Nyasaland, and other places which took the form of riotous protests. The 1960s riots were spontaneous and unorganized, opposed by the moderate black leaders, confined almost entirely to the ghettos, and quelled with vigor but not without restraint by the authorities. The colonial uprisings, by contrast, developed out of nonviolent demonstrations against colonial exploita-tion; the African leaders led the demonstrations and then directed the uprisings. The rioters rampaged outside the native districts, attacking government buildings as well as private holdings; and the authorities, relying largely on the military, responded relentlessly and ruthlessly. Hence the 1960s riots were more restrained than the colonial uprisings, a pattern which suggests that the stakes were higher and the frustrations deeper in Africa than in America.

The differences between the 1960s riots and the colonial struggle reflect the differences between the racial problem and the colonial situation. The blacks have greater opportunities to enter the middle class and exert political power than colonial people do. But, by the same token, the blacks are much more limited than colonial people in their ultimate aspirations; a minority, they can belong to the nation but cannot take it over. Also, for all their prejudice, white Americans, and especially their leaders, have a more ambivalent attitude towards colored people than European colonialists do. They subordinate and segregate blacks unevenly, as much by omission as by commission, and often against their own law and ideology. Lastly, the ghetto is not a colony—unless by a colony is meant nothing more than a dependent neighborhood, a definition which would include most parts of the modern metropolis. The ghetto is exploited, but not so much by the whole society as by fragments of it, and not so much to oppress its inhabitants as to avoid them. These differences do not mean that the racial problem is less serious than the colonial situation, only that it is very different.

There are also, as the radicals claim, analogies between the 1960s riots and socialist struggles. Although the blacks have traditionally based their pleas for social justice on the sanctity of the law and consistently honored the commitment to orderly social change, they are still the nearest group to an American proletariat nowadays. By rioting for six summers now they have not only broken the law and ignored this commitment, but, by looting and burning stores, disobeying the police, and attacking patrolmen, they have also destroyed private property and challenged public authority. There are also many black militants who have lost all hope of achieving meaningful equality under the existing system—and not only the members of the Revolutionary Action Movement and other fringe groups. Before his assassination Malcolm X (whose ideas on these and other matters were in flux at the time) concluded that racism and capitalism were so intertwined that the one could not be abolished without eliminating the other. And, more recently, Eldridge Cleaver (and, by implication, the members of the Black Panthers) insisted that the blacks cannot expect social justice under the prevailing economic and politicial conditions.

The analogies between the 1960s riots and the socialist struggle do not withstand careful scrutiny, however. No doubt the rioters rejected a long-standing strategy by resorting to violence. But there is no necessary connection between violence and socialism, certainly not in the United States; the race riots of 1917, 1919, and 1943 are all cases in point. Accordingly the test of the analogy lies, if anywhere, in the purposes of the riots, that is, were they directed against private property and public authority? It would appear that they were not. The blacks looted to acquire goods enjoyed by most Americans and burned to even the score with white merchants; they did not attempt to undermine property rights in general. They assaulted patrolmen to express specific grievances against the local police and not, as the blacks' attitude toward the National Guard indicated, overall disaffection with public authority. Perhaps even more pertinent, the rioting was confined to the ghettos; the rioters did not destroy private property else-where, nor did they attack schools, hospitals, or other government buildings. If anything, these patterns reveal that the violence was directed against the system's abuses and not the system itself.

Hence the 1960s riots were attempts to alert America, not overturn it, to de-nounce its practices, not renounce its principles. They were not insurrections, and not because blacks lacked the numbers, power, and leaders but rather because they wanted a change in norms not in values. These conclusions are consistent with the most recent surveys of black opinion and with the ideology of all but a small (though increasing) fraction of the black nationalist organizations. The Black Muslims, the largest of these groups, have no fundamental disagreement with capitalist America, only with white America; their utopia is strict, separate, and black, but otherwise quite familiar. And most Black Power advocates are more concerned with procedures than substance; that they insist on self-determi-nation is clear enough, but whether for capitalism, socialism, or something else is not. Indeed, even Malcolm X's tremendous appeal rested as much on his elo-quence, courage, and blunt defiance of white society as on any particular ideol-ogy, anti-colonialist or anti-capitalist. For the great majority of blacks, the Amer-ican dream, tarnished though it has been for centuries, is still the ultimate aspiration.

To argue that the 1960s riots were not colonial rebellions is not to imply what future riots will be like. The situation is anything but promising. Black moderates are convinced, and rightly so, that current federal, state, and city programs will not materially improve the ghettos. Black extremists are prepared to intensify their opposition to the system; and rumors about terrorism and guerrilla warfare are spreading through many cities. The riots have greatly stirred the black com-munity too; so has the realization that rioting is a sure way to attract attention. Hence it is impossible to say what the future holds. But there is no certainty that the United States will not experience organized and premeditated violence, and not only inside the black ghettos. Nor is there any certainty that blacks will not direct their hostility against the system itself instead of its abuses. In other words, the 1960s riots, revolutionary in their means, may develop into colonial rebel-lions, revolutionary in their ends. For the time being, however, it can safely be concluded that these riots were not colonial rebellions.

Still other observers, including the mayors (or acting mayors) of New York, Los Angeles, and many other cities, have insisted that the riots were meaningless outbursts and not rebellions, colonial or otherwise. They have, in effect, denied that the riots were political expressions, no matter how broadly defined. For these officials this interpretation is highly reassuring; it precludes attempts to blame them for the rioting and also relieves pressures to alleviate longstanding problems in the ghettos. Most of these officials are sincere in their convictions; and so are most of their constituents, who also consider the riots meaningless outbursts. Nevertheless, this interpretation is untenable, and for reasons other than the obvi-ous one that no social phenomenon is meaningless; and a brief analysis of these reasons should help clarify the meaning of the riots.

The conception of the riots as meaningless outbursts is intimately related to the absence of a *tradition* of violent protest in America. Not that the United States has been a peaceful country. Quite the contrary: for three and a half centuries Americans have resorted to violence in order to reach goals otherwise unattainable. The whites who assaulted blacks in Washington and Chicago in 1919 were a case in point. So, to list only a few notorious examples, were the Protestants who attacked Catholics in Boston in 1834, the vigilantes who lynched lawbreakers in San Francisco in 1856, and the citizens who massacred the "Wobblies" in Centralia, Washington, in 1919. Indeed, it is hardly an exaggeration to say that the native white majority has rioted in some way and at some time against nearly every minority group in America. And yet most Americans regard rioting not only as illegitimate but, even more significant, as aberrant. From their perspective, which reflects a boundless confidence in orderly social change, riots, no matter how frequently they erupt, are necessarily unique and wholly unrelated.

Under ordinary circumstances the absence of a tradition of violent protest makes it difficult for Americans to perceive the riots as anything but meaningless outbursts. And circumstances today are far from ordinary. The demand for public order and the opposition to rioting and violence are now greater than ever in the United States. This situation, as Allan Silver has perceptively pointed out, reflects not only the spreading consensus that disorder does irreparable and intolerable damage to modern political and economic mechanisms. It also reflects the growing awareness of the spatial interdependence of American cities, the realization that the outbreak of rioting in one neighborhood threatens the security of all the others. It reflects, too, the increasing confidence in the ability of the governmental authorities, and especially the police, to maintain public order in the face of any challenge. And the demand for public order, which has intensified the middle classes' fear of the lower and working classes (and, above all, lower- and working-class blacks), has made it even harder for most Americans to regard the riots as anything but meaningless outbursts (or left-wing conspiracies).

The absence of a tradition of violent protest makes it just as hard for lower- and working-class blacks to express the meaning of the riots. Except in Harlem and Boston, where the rioting erupted after organized demonstrations against police brutality and welfare abuses respectively, nowhere did the rioters prepare a formal statement of grievances. And whatever the meaning of "Burn, Baby, Burn!" the slogan of the Los Angeles riots, surely no one can argue that it is readily understood. Moreover, the racial problem, complex enough to begin with, is obscured because the nation is committed in principle to equality and, save in the rural South, white attitudes toward black people are marked as much by indifference as by hostility. For these reasons it was no mean task for blacks to explain the rioting. What is more, this situation was aggravated because almost without exception the moderate black leaders disapproved of the riots. No one spoke for the rioters as Martin Luther King, Jr., and the Montgomery Improvement Association spoke for the Montgomery bus boycotters. Whatever the meaning of the riots, then, it has to be sought in the rioting itself, and even sympathetic observers might well have trouble finding it there.

The meaning is there, but only if the riots are viewed as violent protests. That they are violent is obvious. But it is not so obvious that they, like the Montgomery bus boycott and other civil rights demonstrations, are also protests, because most Americans regard a violent protest as a contradiction in terms. There is, however, a long, if declining, *history* of violent protest in western society, a history exemplified by the pre-industrial urban mob in eighteenth-century Europe. The mob, which was composed mainly of common people, as opposed to the riffraff, communicated popular dissatisfaction to the authorities; it protested by rioting and otherwise resorting to violence and not by adopting radical ideologies. It also expected a response, and a favorable one, too, from the authorities. To list only a few examples from London: the mob rioting against the Excise Bill in 1733, the employment of Irish labor in 1736, the expulsion of John Wilkes in 1768, and the Catholic Emancipation Bill in 1780. These riots were articulate not so much because the elites understood them as because, in view of the mob's potential for disorder, the violence was restrained and selective.

Ignoring profound differences in grievances and responses, it is fair to say that the 1960s riots were articulate protests in the same sense. On the basis of the available statistical data, it is evident that the black rioters were not primarily the unemployed, ill-educated, uprooted, and criminal. They were rather a substantial and representative minority of the young adults which was widely supported in the ghettos. Also, far from rejecting the prevailing ideology, the rioters demanded that all citizens honor it; they insisted on changes in practices not principles. They made it extremely clear that most blacks do not want to overthrow American society, but simply to belong to it as equals. Moreover, the rioters indicated to reporters during the riots and to interviewers afterwards that they expected the rioting to improve their position by arousing white concern. They could not know then (and indeed they may not know now) that though some whites are more concerned many are more intransigent. Put bluntly, the blacks delivered a protest, but most whites did not receive it.

Also, viewed from a distance, the riots seem unrestrained and indiscriminate, which is what observers probably mean by meaningless; the mob is overwhelming, the confusion complete. But at closer observation, where individuals are visible and patterns discernible, the opposite appears to be true. Although the rioters vented their rage on patrolmen and passers-by and showed little remorse after the attacks, they killed only a handful of the thousands of whites caught in the rioting and even released unharmed several reporters similarly trapped. This restraint was repeated too often to be considered exceptional. Again, though the rioters damaged hundreds of buildings, destroyed millions of dollars of property, and devastated whole sections of the ghettos, they burned mainly stores that charged excessive prices or sold inferior goods (or did both) and left homes, schools, and churches unharmed. This selectivity was noted by more than one witness, too. Indeed, restraint and selectivity were among the most crucial features of the riots. And it is in these features that the meaning of the disorders is to be found.

Now not all the rioters were restrained and selective. A few, especially the handful of snipers, intended to provoke confrontation, not to arouse concern. Nor were the rioters restrained and selective all the time. The looters did not always choose the merchandise with care, and the arsonists did not always pick the buildings with precision. Nonetheless, most of the rioters were restrained and selective most of the time. What is more, the overwhelming majority of blacks viewed the riots as protests. According to a nation-wide survey conducted for the Kerner Commission, 86 per cent of black men and 84 per cent of black women considered the riots at least in part protests against unfair conditions. And in many cases the rioters' actions confirm these conclusions. During the Harlem riots they surrounded white reporters and instead of beating them told them to write the full story; and after the Los Angeles riots they boasted that they had finally brought the south-central ghetto to the attention of the authorities. All things considered, it is fair to conclude that the riots were protests and, like the civil rights demonstrations of the previous decade, articulate protests too.

It now remains to discuss what the blacks were protesting against and why they were protesting violently. To this end it is instructive to consider the 1960s riots in connection with two earlier disorders which were their direct precursors, namely, the Harlem riots of 1935 and 1943. Given the circumstances, no two riots should have had less in common. The Great Depression was in its fifth year in the spring of 1935; it economic and political repercussions were evident everywhere, and nowhere more so than in Harlem. Fully half the residents were unemployed and on relief; many were standing in long soup lines, and a few were actually starving. Meanwhile, various left-wing groups—so vividly described by Ralph Ellison in *The Invisible Man* —were busily planning for a socialist or communist takeover. How different everything was in the summer of 1943 when World War II was reaching its peak and most Americans, black and white, were mobilized. The nation's economy, stimulated by wartime production, was enjoying full employment and even facing manpower shortages. And the country's radicals were silent because of the emotional demands of wartime patriotism and the Nazi invasion of Soviet Russia. These circumstances notwithstanding, the Harlem riots of 1935 and 1943 had a great deal in common.

Contemporaries were hard pressed to explain what it was, however. Most of them, including Mayor Fiorello La Guardia, black author Claude McKay, and the New York *Times,* realized that the Harlem riots were not, strictly speaking, race riots. Quite correctly and not without pride, they cited the absence of interracial violence in 1935 and again in 1943, the year of the Detroit race riots. If they did not blame the Communists, they claimed that though there was no justification for the Harlem riots there were grounds for the blacks' complaints, particularly the suffering of ordinary blacks during the depression and the attacks on black soldiers during the war. Nevertheless, they did not define the Harlem riots more precisely. Rather, they seconded La Guardia's statements that the riots were criminal and thoughtless acts by hoodlums and other irresponsible people who were a minute fraction of New York's overwhelmingly law-abiding black community. La Guardia, who was at his best quelling the rioting and at his worst analyzing it, exhibited the traditional American misconception of violent protest. But he did not have the benefit of the perspective provided by the 1960s riots, a perspective which highlights the common and distinctive features of the Harlem riots.

The Harlem riots, like the 1960s riots, were spontaneous, unorganized, and precipitated by police actions. The 1935 riots began in a Harlem department store when a youth was caught shoplifting and forcibly subdued by the employees. He was then taken to a back room and after a while set free by the police. The shoppers believed that the police were beating the boy, however, and their fears were confirmed by the arrival of an ambulance called by an employee bitten in the scuffle. A crowd quickly gathered and—when, by a remarkable coincidence, the brother-in-law of another employee parked his hearse nearby—concluded that the police had killed the youth. Nothing the police said or did could persuade the blacks otherwise, and the rumor swiftly spread throughout Harlem, setting off the 1935 riots. The 1943 riots, which erupted in a more credible but basically similar way, started in a Harlem hotel when a white patrolman attempted to arrest a bois- terous black woman for disorderly conduct. A black soldier intervened, grabbing the patrolman's nightstick and striking him with it, and then turned to leave. The patrolman ordered him to halt and, when he refused, shot him in the shoulder. A crowd soon formed in front of the hospital to which the soldier was taken and, though the wound was not serious, the word that a white policeman had killed a black soldier rapidly passed through the ghetto, triggering the 1943 riots.

Once the rioting was under way, the Harlem rioters directed most of their aggression against property rather than people. Several thousand strong in 1935, the rioters first threw bricks and bottles at the department store windows and the policemen patrolling nearby. Later they roamed the streets, attacking white passers-by and looting and burning neighborhood stores, especially white-owned stores. By the next morning one was dead, over one hundred injured, another one hundred arrested, and several hundred buildings damaged. The violence was worse in 1943, but the pattern was much the same. Once again the rioters, num- bering many thousands, assaulted white passers-by, overturned parked automo- biles, and tossed bricks and bottles at policemen. They also looted and burned food and liquor shops, haberdasheries, pawn and jewelry shops, and, again, mainly white-owned shops. By the following day six were dead, over five hun- dred injured, more than one hundred jailed, and a few million dollars of property destroyed. Like the New York riots of 1964, the Harlem riots of 1935 and 1943 were so completely confined to the ghetto that life was normal for whites and blacks elsewhere in the city.

The official response was about as vigorous in the Harlem riots as in the 1960s riots, too. Early in the 1935 riots Police Commissioner Lewis J. Valentine sent policemen organized in special squadrons and armed with special guns to reinforce the mounted and foot patrolmen and radio-car crews at the department store. And later on, while the police, fully armed and often firing, struggled with the rioters, Mayor La Guardia prepared and distributed a circular calling on law- abiding blacks to cooperate with the authorities. This response, however vigor- ous, was dwarfed by the response to the 1943 riots. The police department's af- ternoon shift was kept on duty, freeing the night shift for riot control; and by morning fully five thousand policemen, supported by military police and regular troops, were patrolling Harlem. Another five thousand New York State Guards and fifteen hundred black volunteers were standing by. In the meantime La Guar- dia closed streets and diverted traffic around Harlem, concentrated subway pa- trolmen on the Harlem lines, issued a declaration denouncing the rioting, and, accompanied by two well-known moderate black leaders, toured the ghetto ap- pealing for restraint. By dint of the police department's tactics and the Mayor's virtuoso performance, order was restored the following day.

The moderate blacks disapproved of the Harlem riots almost, but not quite, as strongly as they disapproved of the 1960s riots. Few attempted to restrain the rioters in 1935; more grasped the opportunity to denounce racial discrimination.

This reaction was not surprising: rioting lasted only one night, discrimination had gone on for several centuries. What was surprising was that none of these leaders, no matter how firmly committed to civil rights, sanctioned the rioting. The moderate black leaders reacted far more forcefully in 1943. A few accompanied La Guardia on his tour of the ghetto, others advised him about riot-control strategies, and still others manned voluntary patrols. Even more impressive, many broadcast from sound trucks, denying the rumor that the white policeman had killed the black youth and urging the rioters to clear the streets. And as the rioting was more violent and the nation more united in 1943 than in 1935, even the leaders who used the occasion to condemn racial segregation did so circumspectly. Nonetheless, these efforts (and the riots themselves) highlighted the inability of the moderate black leaders to channel rank-and-file discontent into legitimate channels and when necessary to restrain the rioters.

Even this short discussion of the Harlem riots and the 1960s riots reveals their striking similarities and essential characteristics. These riots were spontaneous and unorganized, triggered by police actions, and distinguished by looting and burning of neighborhood stores and assaults on patrolmen and white passersby. In all of them, the governmental authorities responded vigorously to increase the risks in participating, and, save in 1935, the moderate black leaders labored valiantly, if vainly, to restrain the rioters. Hence the essence of the Harlem riots and the 1960s riots is an intense resentment of the police, an intolerable accumulation of grievances, the ineffectiveness of the customary restraints on rioting, and the weakness of moderate black leadership. It is against police malpractice and other grievances, especially economic deprivation, consumer exploitation, and racial discrimination, that the blacks were protesting; and it is because of the ineffectiveness of the customary restraints on rioting and the weakness of moderate black leadership that they were protesting violently. Needless to say, these conditions are among the fundamental features of life in the black ghetto.

Accordingly it is not surprising that these riots first erupted in Harlem rather than in Chicago or the other sites of the twentieth-century race riots. Harlem was the first black ghetto. Developed as a middle-class community around the turn of the century, it was promptly caught in a severe real estate crash; and instead of being quickly settled by whites, it was slowly filled by blacks. Rioting did not break out there during the turbulent postwar years, however. Rather than fight the black influx, as the working-class first- and second-generation European immigrants did in Chicago, the middle-class native Americans in New York quietly moved elsewhere, leaving a black Harlem in their wake. It was during the 1910s and the 1920s, fully a generation before the massive migration from the South after World War II transformed urban America, that Harlem emerged as the nation's first black ghetto. It was in these decades that as the headquarters of the black renaissance it fascinated white Americans in their misguided quest for the exotic and the primitive. And it was in these decades that the conditions developed which led the blacks in Harlem to protest, and to protest violently, in 1935 and 1943.

What emerges from this deliberately circuitous approach is a rather straightforward interpretation: the 1960s riots were articulate protests against genuine grievances in the black ghettos. The riots were protests because they were attempts to call the attention of white society to the black's widespread dissatisfaction with racial subordination and segregation. The riots were also articulate because they were restrained, selective, and, no less important, directed at the sources of the blacks' most immediate and profound grievances. What is more, the grievances are genuine because by the standards of the greater society the conditions of black life, physically, economically, educationally, socially, and otherwise, are deplorable. And nowhere in urban America are these conditions—economic deprivation, consumer exploitation, inferior education, racial discrimination, and so forth—more deplorable than in the black ghettos. Having offered this interpretation, which I intend to document in more detail later on, I would like to conclude by considering two closely related questions: namely, why did the 1960s riots erupt when they did and where they did?

The timing of the riots is baffling. The blacks' grievances were not developments of the 1960s, nor, for that matter, were the burdens of subordination and segregation. If anything, these grievances were probably less serious and these burdens less severe then than at any time in American history. Since World War II large numbers of blacks moved into highly skilled and well-paying jobs and gained positions of political influence. At the same time a large majority of whites grew fairly reluctant to measure a man strictly by the color of his skin. To add to this, a battery of Supreme Court decisions made it much harder for Americans, individuals and authorities alike, to practice racial discrimination. Thus, for all the inequities and prejudices remaining, most blacks were probably better off in the 1960s than in any decade in the recent past. And yet it was in the 1960s—not in the 1940s when the armed forces were segregated, nor in the 1950s when a civil rights act was an occasion—that blacks rioted.

At the heart of this paradox was the unprecedented rise in the black's expectations. This rise began with the great migration north in the 1910s and 1920s, gathered momentum during World War II, and accelerated during the late 1950s and early 1960s. It accelerated not only because the nation as a whole enjoyed remarkable prosperity but also because some blacks fully shared in it and a few attained standards long reserved for whites only. It accelerated, too, because civil rights programs made progress, white attitudes about race changed for the better, and, even more important, black pride flourished as it has not since the Garvey Movement of the 1920s. The results were momentous. Blacks were more conscious of their deprivations—indeed, deprivation had a whole new meaning for them; they were dissatisfied with conditions that their fathers and grandfathers would have found tolerable (or at any rate inevitable). The blacks were also less concerned about social constraints, more militant and aggressive, at the least impatient and, when frustrated time and again, dangerously desperate. This rise in expectations was self-perpetuating, too; each new gain generated a new goal, and by the 1960s the blacks would settle for nothing less than a complete equality.

What rendered these expectations so explosive in the 1960s were the dreadful conditions of ghetto life. And not only in Harlem. Although the working-class, first- and second-generation European immigrants in Chicago, Detroit, and other cities resisted the black influx in 1919 and 1943, they eventually conceded the issue. Like the middle-class native Americans in New York, they or their children fled before the massive black migration after World War II, leaving behind them the swelling black ghettos. By the 1960s these ghettos were a full generation old, about as old as Harlem was in the 1930s and 1940s; and, in view of the blacks' expectations, conditions there, no matter how much improved, were intolerable. What is more, the blacks realized that these conditions could be readily remedied. Nor, by virtue of their color, could they easily escape to the suburbs like white immigrants before them. A state of permanent subordination and segregation loomed as a distinct possibility. And thus, as ghetto life intensified the group's grievances and undermined the society's restraints, the blacks rioted to protest their plight.

The location of the 1960s riots is baffling, too. With a few exceptions—notably the Atlanta (1966), Nashville (1966), Tampa (1967), and Miami (1968) riots—they have occurred less in the South, where by any objective consideration the blacks have more reason for rioting, than in the North. This paradox cannot be resolved by the explanation (which is true so far as it goes) that the riots are urban phenomena and that the South is the least urbanized region in the nation. Atlanta, Nashville, Tampa, and Miami are not the only southern cities, and among the others Birmingham, Charleston, Little Rock, New Orleans, and Jackson have thus far been spared rioting. Again, with a few exceptions the riots have occurred almost everywhere in the North, a pattern which is particularly perplexing for most Americans. It is one thing for blacks to riot in New York, Chicago, Philadelphia, Cleveland, Detroit, and Los Angeles, the nation's largest metropolitan centers. Of them Americans expect almost anything, especially in the sweltering summer months. But it is another thing for blacks to riot in Rochester, Dayton, Omaha, and Lansing, and many other normally peaceful, presumably content medium-sized cities. From them Americans expect an occasional scandal, but nothing as serious as full-scale rioting.

There are explanations for these paradoxes, however. The South has suffered fewer riots than the North not simply because southern blacks have lower expectations than northern blacks and southern policemen fewer inhibitions than northern policemen. The South, which has about as many blacks as the North, has far fewer ghettos. Blacks have traditionally been more heavily concentrated in northern cities than in southern cities, where the differences between white and black were so well defined that there was little reason for rigorous residential segregation. Only recently, as the racial status quo has been vigorously challenged in the South, have southern whites, like northern whites before them, retreated to segregated suburbs and left black ghettos behind. Where this has happened, as in Atlanta and Miami, southern blacks, like northern blacks, are most resentful of their grievances and less concerned about society's restraints, more conscious of their strength and less reluctant to test it. This pattern now prevails only in Atlanta and a handful of other southern cities; but the same nation-wide forces transforming the North are emerging in the South, and so the probability of further rioting there may well increase in the future.

This explanation applies to the North as well as to the South. Small cities as well as large metropolises have been devastated by riots largely because northern blacks are everywhere confined to ghettos. And for all the differences between Harlem and Chicago's West Side, Rochester's seventh ward and Cleveland's

Hough district, Boston's Roxbury and Brooklyn's Bedford-Stuyvesant, and south-central Los Angeles and all the others, life varies little from one ghetto to the next. In each there are an intense resentment of the police, high unemployment rates, exploitative mercantile practices, excessive levels of violence, widespread residential segregation, and, among other things, ineffective moderate leadership. And in the end the blacks' grievances are no more tolerable in Omaha, Dayton, Lansing, and Rochester than in Chicago, Philadelphia, Newark, and Cleveland. All of which is perhaps another way of saying that the blacks' frustration, resentment, and aggression are a function not of the size of the white communities but of the conditions in the black ghettos.

The interpretation of the 1960s riots as articulate protests against genuine grievances in the black ghettos helps explain why the riots erupted when and where they did. But it does not help explain why they erupted first in Philadelphia, Los Angeles, and Cleveland, later in Buffalo, Newark, and Detroit, and only recently in Washington and Baltimore. A few offhand explanations have been offered, but an extended examination of these explanations is beyond the scope of this introduction; and it would probably not be worth while anyway. For there is no convincing evidence that the blacks' conditions are materially worse in Philadelphia, Los Angeles, and Cleveland than in Buffalo, Newark, and Detroit, or Washington and Baltimore. Indeed, it is probably only a coincidence that the riots erupted in some cities before others (and not at all in still others, such as Oakland, whose turn will doubtless come). And if the interpretation of the 1960s riots offered here is correct, it indicates why they have broken out in nearly every American metropolis except some in the deep South, where the black ghettos are little developed, and others in the Pacific Northwest, where the black population is extremely small.

✖ *FURTHER   READING*

Edward C. Banfield, *The Unheavenly City: The Nature and Future of Our Urban Crisis* (1968)

Robert Fishman, *Bourgeois Utopias: The Rise and Fall of Suburbia* (1987)

Kenneth Fox, *Metropolitan America: Urban Life and Urban Policy in the United States, 1940–1980* (1986)

Dolores Hayden, *Redesigning the American Dream: The Future of Housing, Work, and Family Life* (1984)

Jane Jacobs, *The Death and Life of Great American Cities* (1963)

Michael B. Katz, *In the Shadow of the Poorhouse: A Social History of Welfare in America* (1986)

Ira Katznelson, *City Trenches: Urban Politics and the Patterning of Class in the United States* (1981)

Robert Lake, *The New Suburbanites: Race and Housing* (1981)

Hubert G. Locke, *The Detroit Riot of 1967* (1969)

Doug McAdams, *Political Process and the Development of Black Insurgence, 1930–1970* (1982)

Randall M. Miller and George E. Pozzetta, eds., *Shades of the Sunbelt: Essays on Ethnicity, Race, and the Urban South* (1988)

James T. Patterson, *America's Response to Poverty, 1900–1980* (1981)

Paul E. Peterson, ed., *The New Urban Reality* (1985)

Frances Fox Piven and Richard A. Cloward, *Poor People's Movements: Why They Succeed and How They Fail* (1979)

———, *Regulating the Poor: Functions of Public Welfare* (1971)

Lee Rainwater, *Behind Ghetto Walls: Black Families in a Federal Slum* (1970)

Report of the National Advisory Commission on Civil Disorders (1968)

David O. Sears and John B. McConahay, *The Politics of Violence: The New Urban Blacks and the Watts Riot* (1973)

Clarence Stone et al., *Urban Policy and Politics in a Bureaucratic Age,* 2d ed. (1986)

James W. Sullivan, *Race Riot: New York, 1964* (1964)

Gerald Suttles, *The Social Order of the Slum: Ethnicity and Territory in the Inner City* (1968)

Walter I. Trattner, *From Poor Law to Welfare State: A History of Social Welfare in America* (1979)

Ann Withorn, *Serving the People: Social Services and Social Change* (1984)